PRACTICAL BANKRUPTCY LAW FOR PARALEGALS

SECOND EDITION

PRACTICAL BANKRUPTCY LAW FOR PARALEGALS

SECOND EDITION

PAMELA K. WEBSTER

Partner, Buchalter, Nemer, Fields & Younger
Los Angeles, California

WEST PUBLISHING COMPANY
St. Paul   New York   Los Angeles   San Francisco

Production Credits

Copyediting   Nancy Porter

Composition   Parkwood Composition

West's Commitment to the Environment

In 1906, West Publishing Company began recycling materials left over from the production of books. This began a tradition of efficient and responsible use of resources. Today, 100% of our legal bound volumes are printed on acid-free, recycled paper consisting of 50% new paper pulp and 50% paper that has undergone a de-inking process. We also use vegetable-based inks to print all of our books. West recycles nearly 27,700,000 pounds of scrap paper annually—the equivalent of 229,300 trees. Since the 1960s, West has devised ways to capture and recycle waste inks, solvents, oils, and vapors created in the printing process. We also recycle plastics of all kinds, wood, glass, corrugated cardboard, and batteries, and have eliminated the use of polystyrene book packaging. We at West are proud of the longevity and the scope of our commitment to the environment.

West pocket parts and advance sheets are printed on recyclable paper and can be collected and recycled with newspapers. Staples do not have to be removed. Bound volumes can be recycled after removing the cover.

Production, Prepress, Printing and Binding by West Publishing Company.

 PRINTED ON 10% POST CONSUMER RECYCLED PAPER   ∞

British Library Cataloguing-in-Publication Data. A catalogue record for this book is available from the British Library.

Library of Congress Cataloging-in-Publication Data

Webster, Pamela Kohlman.
    Practical bankruptcy law for paralegals / Pamela Webster. — 2nd
ed.
        p. cm.
    Rev. ed. of: Bankruptcy law for paralegals. © 1991.
    Includes index.
    ISBN 0-314-06664-0 (hard : alk. paper)
    1. Bankruptcy—United States.   I. Webster, Pamela Kohlman.
    Bankruptcy law for paralegals. II. Title.
    KF1524.W35   1996
346.73'078—dc20   95-44757
[347.30678]   CIP

To Chip, Meghan and Caitlin

☐ CONTENTS IN BRIEF

☐ CONTENTS

□ PREFACE

Bankruptcy is big business in America. Bankruptcy debtors come from every strata of society from unemployed factory workers and improvident credit card holders to celebrities such as Kim Bassinger. Huge multi-national corporations such as Johns-Mansville, Texaco, and Olympia & York as well as thousands of small businesses have sought protection in the bankruptcy courts from their creditors. High-profile bankruptcies such as Pan Am Airlines and Macy's Department stores are constantly in the news. The number of bankruptcy cases filed in the last ten years has staggered the bankruptcy courts and often threatens to overwhelm them.

Responding to the deluge of bankruptcy cases, law firms added new bankruptcy lawyers to their insolvency departments and experienced attorneys formed small "boutique" firms specializing in bankruptcy law. Overnight, bankruptcy law became popular in the nation's law schools.

The phenomenal growth in bankruptcy practice has not been without its tensions. Bankruptcy practice is highly procedural and involves an enormous amount of paperwork for which there are not always enough trained personnel. Many bankruptcy lawyers have far more cases than they can comfortably handle. Further, attorneys' fees in bankruptcy cases are reviewed by the court. Bankruptcy judges today are critical of bills submitted by attorneys for services that can be provided competently by nonlawyers at lower hourly rates. Thus, bankruptcy has become an area of law practice where the need for trained legal assistants is critical. Paralegal use is vital in bankruptcy practice to ensure that the myriad administrative and procedural tasks crucial to the success of a case are completed in a timely and competent manner and at reasonable rates.

Bankruptcy is a difficult practice to master on the job. It is a convoluted system of federal substantive and procedural law in which the provisions interrelate to form what is commonly referred to as "the big picture," a view of the case that is not always perceived by bankruptcy practitioners as a case winds its way through bankruptcy court. Hence, a course on the fundamentals of bankruptcy law is a critical first step to the successful practice of bankruptcy law.

This textbook follows a five-level approach to teaching bankruptcy law and procedure for legal assistants. First, the student is provided with an overview of the substantive law of bankruptcy. Second, students are provided with some insights as to why the substantive law provides as it does. Third, the book discusses the written and unwritten rules of procedure that guide and often control how the substantive law of bankruptcy is implemented. Fourth, the student is guided through the procedural labyrinth of bankruptcy practice with timeliness, checklists, and analysis aids. Fifth, the student is given hands-on experience in performing bankruptcy tasks that are common in actual practice.

Following the end of each chapter, students are given questions to answer and research or drafting projects are recommended to reinforce the text discussions. Some of the exercises are quite simple, others are fairly difficult. Most ask for the application of a statute or procedural rule. Some require the student to contemplate the policy behind a bankruptcy law. Examples of pleadings and other forms are provided in many chapters. Since aspects of bankruptcy practice and procedure differ from court to court, the forms should not be used by the practicing legal

assistant without first verifying that they meet the formal requirements of local practice. Further, the forms are not always complete for a particular procedure. In many cases, they need to be accompanied by supporting affidavits or declarations and briefs or memoranda of law.

Students tend to come to a course on bankruptcy practice with different levels of knowledge and experience of the subject, and the needs of all of the students must be reasonably met. Hence, this book covers all the basic, underlying concepts of bankruptcy law and the procedural rules governing bankruptcy cases. Yet it is more than merely an introductory text. Each topic is fully developed to the extent necessary for effective use by a beginning legal assistant, yet the discussions are of sufficient sophistication to keep the attention of an experienced one. This text also includes treatment of tasks that are typically performed by experienced legal assistants and can be used in practice as a continuing reference source.

☐ CHANGES TO THIS EDITION

Not only is the second edition of *Bankruptcy Law for Paralegals* an updated version of the original text, it is also more student and instructor friendly. In revising the text, comments were sought from instructors who have used the text and practicing lawyers and paralegals who appreciate what a student needs to know in order to succeed. These comments were incorporated into the new edition. In addition, chapters were combined and reorganized for an even, streamlined presentation. More graphics, including timeliness, checklists, charts, and sample forms were added.

Some of the other more significant changes are:

☐ The text was modified to reflect the many changes to the Bankruptcy Code, the Bankruptcy Rules, and the Official Forms since the first edition was prepared.

☐ Coverage of the Bankruptcy Code was expanded and reorganized into four new chapters (Chapters 8, 9, 10 and 11) to present the most vital topics in an easier to understand format.

☐ Key terms appear in bold and are defined in the margins, listed at the end of the chapters, and defined in the glossary at the end of the text.

☐ Special attention was given to the role of independent legal assistants and the special bankruptcy rules that impact their business.

☐ The full text of the Bankruptcy Code and the Bankruptcy Rules are found in the Appendices for the student's ease in reference.

Supplementary Support

Instructor's Manual with Test Bank, prepared by the text author, contains lecture outlines, answers to assignments, and suggested test questions.

Instructor's Manual with Test Bank on Disk The complete Instructor's Manual is available on disk for your convenience in testing and organizing.

West's Bankruptcy Practice System Software (Educational version) is an easy-to-use program that readily creates the documents necessary to complete the most common bankruptcy filings.

Strategies and Tips for Paralegal Educators by Anita Tebbe of Johnson County Community College, provides teaching strategies specifically designed for the paraleal educator. It concentrates on how to teach and is organized in three parts of paralegal education: the Who—students and teachers, the What—goals and objectives; and the How—methods of instruction, evaluation, and other aspects of teaching. One copy of this pamphlet is available to qualified adopters.

WESTLAW West's on-line computerized legal research system, offers students "hands-on" experience with a system commonly used in law offices. Qualified adopters can receive 10 free hours of WESTLAW. WESTLAW can be accessed with Macintosh and IBM PCs and compatibles. A modem is required.*

Paralegal Video Library: Qualified adopters can select and exchange videos for use in a number of paralegal courses.*

☐ **"The Drama of the Law II: Paralegal Issues" Videotape.** This series of five separate dramatizations is intended to stimulate classroom discussion about various issues and problems faced by paralegals on the job today. Each dramatization is approximately five to seven minutes. Topics include intake interview, human error, strategic information, client confidentiality, and unauthorized practice. The scripts were written by John Osborne, author of *The Paper Chase* and are professionally produced.

☐ **"I Never Said I Was a Lawyer" Paralegal Ethics Videotape** uses a variety of scenarios to inspire discussion and give students experience dealing with ethical dilemmas. Topics explored include the unauthorized practice of law, identification of paralegals as non-lawyers, waiver of client's rights through breaches of confidentiality, and lack of attorney supervision. "Situation analysis," how to evaluate an ethical situation and decide on the proper course of action, is also covered. The tape was created by the Colorado Bar Association Committee on Legal Assistants but is non-state specific and will be useful in all paralegal programs.

☐ **"The Making of a Case" Videotape** is narrated by Richard Dysart, star of *L.A. Law*. In this introduction to law library materials and legal research, a case followed from the court system to the law library shelf. This gives a better understanding of what case law is, why it is important, and how cases are published.

☐ **"West's Legal Research" Videotapes** teach the basis and rationale for legal research. The three types of legal research tools—Primary Tools, Secondary Tools, and Finding Tools—are covered. Topics like case law reporters, digests, computer assistance, statutes, special searches, and CD-ROM libraries are included. The nine segments are contained on two tapes.

☐ ACKNOWLEDGMENTS

To acknowledge everyone who contributed to this book I would like to mention everyone who helped me to become a bankruptcy lawyer. Outside of my family, that assemblage would certainly include my law school professors John D. Ayer, Frederick Hart, and Theodore Graham not only for their traditional teachings but

*Please ask your West representative about qualifications for these supplements.

for their colorful war stories, which imparted reality to study. I need to thank Stephen F. Biegenzahn, my first practice mentor, for convincing me that bankruptcy law and I were a fit. I also need to thank all the past and present insolvency lawyers of Buchalter, Nemer, Fields & Younger for establishing, without doubt, that bankruptcy practice is at least as much fun as it is rewarding. For encouraging my involvement in legal assistant education, I thank Patricia R. Wheeler and Michele C. Gowen as well as Marcia Todhunter DeRosa, who gave me the opportunity to teach my first paralegal class.

With respect to the content of the book, thanks go to Dawn Coda Dugas, Marc Beilinson, Richard Levin, and Susan McIntyre, for their very generous contributions in the materials on legal research, creditors' committees, taxes, and the role of the legal assistant, respectively. Special thanks to Richard Kohlman Hughey and Rose Peck for their assistance.

Thanks also to Elizabeth Hannan, Patricia Bryant, Paul O'Neill, and Carrie Kish of West Publishing Company.

Finally, thank you to the following reviewers for their contributions to this book:

Reviewers of the First Edition
Bernard Helldorfer
St. Johns University

Jack Williams
Southeastern Paralegal Institute

Edmond Goldberg
Villa Julie College

Phil Davenport
Atlantic Community College

Sharrie Hildebrandt
William Rainey Harper College

Charles Nadler
Kirkwood Community College

Jacqueline Varma
Southern Methodist University

Reviewers of the Second Edition
Paula D. Emmons
Watterson College Pacific

M. Alan Lawson
Mt. San Antonio College

Robert Loomis
Spokane Community College

Allen White
The American Institute

Brenda Bland White
Central Carolina Community College

Sam Whitten
Lamson Junior College

CHAPTER 1

INTRODUCTION

☐ AN OVERVIEW OF BANKRUPTCY

Although bankruptcy is widespread, few people know much about it. Even lawyers perceive bankruptcy practice as hypertechnical and confusing. While there are a few special rules and some very important deadlines, bankruptcy law is primarily an application of basic notions of fairness and common sense.

Simply stated, **bankruptcy** is a legal system that allows someone who owes money to settle his or her debts with creditors. There are several different ways this can happen: reorganization, liquidation, receivership, or an assignment for the benefit of creditors. These are all forms of bankruptcy, available in either state or federal courts. The types of bankruptcy discussed in this textbook are **liquidations** and **reorganizations** under federal law. In a liquidation, all of the debtor's property is turned over to a trustee who sells it and distributes the proceeds to the creditors. In a reorganization, the debtor attempts to reorganize its business and reach a mutually acceptable agreement with its creditors for the payment of the debts.

Federal statutes are found in the **United States Code,** which is a compilation of all of the laws of Congress organized by topics and divided into fifty different titles. Bankruptcy law is found in Title 11 of the United States Code; it is called the **Bankruptcy Code,** and is reprinted in Appendix A. There are also a few sections in Title 18 (Crimes) that define bankruptcy crimes and in Title 28 (Federal Courts) that regulate procedural matters.

Bankruptcy courts are specialized courts that hear bankruptcy cases. To start a bankruptcy case, a debtor, who may be an individual or a business entity such as a partnership or a corporation, files a **petition** with the bankruptcy court. The filing of the petition with the bankruptcy court commences the bankruptcy case

Bankruptcy
An organized system for creditor payment from a debtor's nonexempt assets.

Liquidation
A form of bankruptcy in which the debtor's nonexempt property is sold or otherwise disposed of and the proceeds are distributed to creditors.

Reorganization
A form of bankruptcy in which the debtor's business is preserved and its creditors are paid from the business' earnings.

United States Code
A compilation of the laws enacted by Congress and organized into fifty titles.

1

Bankruptcy Code
The bankruptcy law enacted by Congress that became effective on October 1, 1978, as it has been subsequently amended, and that is found in Title 11 of the United States Code.

Bankruptcy Courts
The branch of the federal judicial system that presides over bankruptcy cases and proceedings. Bankruptcy Courts are units of the district court.

Petition
The paper filed with the bankruptcy court that commences a bankruptcy case.

Petitioner
Another name for the debtor in a voluntary case.

Trustee
A person appointed to administer the bankruptcy estate. The nature and extent of a trustee's duties differs among Chapters 7, 11, 12, and 13 of the Bankruptcy Code.

Exempt Property
The property that a debtor is allowed to keep and not make subject to creditors' claims.

in the same way that a complaint filed in a state court commences a lawsuit. If the petition is in proper form, the clerk of the bankruptcy court will accept it and assign it a docket number that must appear on all other court papers that are filed in the case. A bankruptcy case is not an adversarial proceeding, however, and there are no plaintiffs or defendants. The case is not titled in the name of the debtor versus the creditors. The debtor is known as the **petitioner,** and the case is titled merely "In re" or "In the matter of" followed by the petitioner's name.

The Bankruptcy Code is divided into chapters. Chapter 7 of the Bankruptcy Code contains the laws for a liquidation type of bankruptcy. This type of bankruptcy is sometimes referred to as "a Chapter 7 case." It provides the kind of remedy most people think of when they hear the word **bankruptcy.**

In a Chapter 7 liquidation, all of the debtor's property is turned over to the **trustee,** who is a neutral third party appointed by the court to sell the property. The trustee will not, however, sell all of the debtor's property. Congress has decided that debtors should keep some of their property so that they can live in a decent fashion. The property debtors may keep is called **exempt property.** Exempt property includes such things as household goods and clothes, usually a car, and sometimes a house. All other property is sold by the trustee and the proceeds are divided among the creditors. The creditors are rarely paid in full. Creditors typically receive only a small percentage of their claims but may not collect the balance from the debtor. Upon the conclusion of a Chapter 7 case, the debtor obtains a discharge of the unpaid debts so he or she can make a fresh start.

The other type of relief provided by the Bankruptcy Code is a reorganization. In this type of bankruptcy, the creditors are prevented from enforcing their claims against the petitioner while its business or financial affairs are reorganized in the hope that it will eventually be able to pay its debts. The creditors do not always receive full payment of their claims in a reorganization, but they generally recover more of their debt than they would if the petitioner had filed a Chapter 7 bankruptcy.

There are four different types of reorganizations in the Bankruptcy Code, each of which has its own chapter. Chapter 11, which is the best known, is used primarily by businesses, but it may also be used by individuals. Chapter 13 is only for individuals who have a regular source of income and relatively low levels of debt. Chapter 12 is for farmers who may not qualify for Chapter 13 because his or her income is not regular enough or the amount of debt is too high. Finally, Chapter 9 allows for the reorganization of municipalities such as cities, towns, and special districts. Falling revenues, unwise investments, or large personal injury judgments sometimes force these governmental entities into bankruptcy just as they might affect businesses and individuals.

Although the four types of reorganization in the Bankruptcy Code are different in many respects, there are many similarities among them. For example, the debtor may keep all of its property while it tries to reorganize. While the reorganization takes place the petitioner will, however, be under much greater scrutiny from the bankruptcy court and the creditors. In order to get out of bankruptcy, the petitioner will need to pay creditors more of their claims than the creditors would be paid in a liquidation.

☐ THE HISTORY OF BANKRUPTCY

Bankruptcy itself is not a recent phenomenon. Since one person began borrowing goods from another, there has been a need for debt relief. Societies have usually

provided for such debt relief. Indeed, in the time of the Old Testament, debts were discharged in the Jubilee year. Debts were not always simply forgiven, however; sometimes terrible punishment was exacted of the debtor before any relief was available. For example, in ancient Greece and Rome, a bankrupt debtor would be sold into slavery or imprisoned. Harsh as this remedy was, it was better than the alternatives in other societies, which were mutilation and death. Later, Rome developed a more humane system called *cessio bonorum*, which was a procedure not unlike modern bankruptcy: the debtor ceded all of his or her assets for distribution to creditors. Imprisonment for nonpayment of debt returned in the Dark Ages, however.

The word **bankruptcy** is said to be derived from the Italian phrase *banca rotta* or "broken bench." In fourteenth century Italy, the merchants lined the streets and plazas with their work benches when they performed their crafts. A merchant unable to pay his debts lost his trading place and his bench was smashed by his creditors as a sign to all that the craftsman had become insolvent.

In England the emphasis also was on punishment. From the thirteenth century, when the first English bankruptcy statute was passed, to beyond the time of Dickens, debt relief was accompanied by confinement in the poor house or a debtor's prison, or by transportation and involuntary servitude. Many areas of Australia and the original colonies of America were settled by debtors forced out of England.

These cruel bankruptcy systems hardly allowed for the rehabilitation of the debtor and almost certainly prevented the creditors from being paid.

Bankruptcy Law in the United States

Introduction   Prior to the adoption of the Constitution, several states had bankruptcy laws that were similar to those in Britain and France, with punishment rather than rehabilitation of the debtor as a goal. The Constitution gave Congress the power to write the bankruptcy laws for the United States, but congressional attempts to enact bankruptcy legislation were sporadic and ineffective for over a hundred years after the ratification of the Constitution.

The first American bankruptcy statute was the Bankruptcy Act of 1800, but it was not very comprehensive. It dealt almost exclusively with merchants and bankers who were forced into bankruptcy by their creditors. Its aim was to protect creditors rather than to provide any sort of relief for debtors. The law created the office of a commissioner to exercise power over a debtor's estate. The commissioner is the predecessor to the bankruptcy trustee and the bankruptcy judge today. The statute was repealed by Congress in 1803.

Another short-lived bankruptcy statute was passed by Congress in 1841. This legislation gave the district courts exclusive jurisdiction over bankruptcy matters. It also gave the district courts the right to appoint a person called an assignee who had power over the debtor and the right to sell the debtor's property to pay creditors. This law was repealed in 1843, but it was followed in 1867 by an act that gave the district court the power to appoint "registrars" to assist it in the administration of the bankruptcy estate. This act was repealed in 1878.

The Bankruptcy Act of 1898   Finally, Congress passed the **Bankruptcy Act of 1898.** It is usually referred to as the "Bankruptcy Act" or simply the "Act." Many provisions of today's Bankruptcy Code are carried over from the Bankruptcy Act. The Bankruptcy Act allowed for two methods to start a bankruptcy case:

1. **Voluntarily** in which the debtor begins the bankruptcy case and

Bankruptcy Act
The bankruptcy law enacted by Congress in 1898 that was substantially amended in 1938 and repealed in 1978.

2. Involuntarily in which the creditors commence the proceedings and force the debtor to come into the bankruptcy court.

The Bankruptcy Act also created a comprehensive system for liquidations and reorganizations regardless whether the bankruptcy case was begun voluntarily or involuntarily. Although the Act was extensively modified in 1938 by the Chandler Act, it continued in existence as the controlling bankruptcy law until 1978, when it was replaced by the Bankruptcy Code.

The Bankruptcy Act called for a bankruptcy referee and a bankruptcy trustee. The trustee was responsible for liquidating or reorganizing debtors.

The bankruptcy referee served a dual function under the Act. The bankruptcy referee was given a number of administrative functions that involved the referee in many aspects of the day–to–day operation of the debtor's business until its liquidation or reorganization. At the same time, the referee served as an impartial dispute resolver of those matters impacting the estate. This dual role led to charges of conflict of interest. Further, as the number of bankruptcy filings increased, the burden of administration on the referees became greater and greater.

There were also other problems with the Act. Despite its amendments, the language of the Act was archaic and its provisions were poorly organized. Time exacted its toll; some of the Act became dated because of growth in the economy, and the courts had to interpret and reinterpret other parts frequently to make the Act work efficiently.

The Bankruptcy Reform Act of 1978   In response to growing criticism of the Bankruptcy Act, the Senate Committee on the Judiciary began holding hearings on bankruptcy reform legislation in 1968. In 1970, Congress established a commission made up of practitioners, judges, academicians, and legislators to study and recommend changes in the Act. The commission issued its report in 1973 and proposed new legislation to implement its recommendations, which included a proposal separating the judicial and administrative functions of bankruptcy proceedings and establishing the bankruptcy court. The proposed new legislation was introduced in the same year. Additional legislation was introduced in 1975; it had been proposed by the National Bankruptcy Conference, an organization also made up of prominent persons in the bankruptcy field. Lengthy hearings in the House and Senate were held on both pieces of legislation through the mid-1970s, and what finally emerged from all the congressional wrangling on bankruptcy laws was a compromise that became the Bankruptcy Reform Act of 1978.

The Bankruptcy Reform Act of 1978, usually referred to as the Bankruptcy Code, was more than just a revision of the Bankruptcy Act of 1898. It enacted a total change in the administration of bankruptcy cases. The bankruptcy courts were given expansive jurisdictional powers to determine any dispute involving the debtor as well as authorize acts of the trustee or the debtor.

Automatic Stay
The injunction that becomes effective upon the filing of a bankruptcy petition (whether voluntarily or involuntarily) and that prevents virtually all actions by creditors to collect their claims, enforce their liens, or exercise control over the debtor's property.

Although the Code preserved many of the bankruptcy protections that arose under the Act, sometimes they were to be applied differently under the Code. For example, under the Act there was no **automatic stay** protecting the debtor from enforcement of the creditor's claims. Originally, if the trustee needed to bar creditors from enforcing their claims against the estate, an injunction had to be obtained from the court. The Bankruptcy Code not only provides for such a stay, it is automatic. The instant a bankruptcy petition is filed, all of the debtor's creditors are enjoined from further enforcement of their claims or attempts to take the debtor's property.

Shortly after it was enacted, the Bankruptcy Code's grant of sweeping jurisdiction to the bankruptcy court was criticized. Some of the criticism was based on the Constitution's systems of checks and balances of power between the executive, judicial, and legislative branches of government. Under this system, federal district court judges were given the power to invalidate congressional and presidential acts but they were protected from retaliation by lifetime appointments to the bench and a prohibition against having their salaries reduced. Bankruptcy court judges were given power in bankruptcy cases comparable to that of district court judges, but they were appointed to fourteen-year terms and they could have their salaries reduced by congressional action. This problem could only be resolved by cutting back on the power of the bankruptcy court or by granting bankruptcy judges the same privileges as those bestowed on judges of the federal district courts. Neither solution was popular.

Northern Pipeline v. Marathon Oil It did not take long for a Constitutional challenge to the Bankruptcy Code to reach the Supreme Court of the United States. In mid-1982, in the case of *Northern Pipeline Construction Company v. Marathon Oil Company*, the Court ruled that it was unconstitutional for bankruptcy judges to have such broad powers. In an unusual step, however, the Court delayed the effect of its ruling to give Congress a chance to cure the constitutional defects. Because of intense lobbying on each side of the issue, Congress could not decide whether the bankruptcy court's power should be limited or whether the bankruptcy court judges should be given lifetime appointments. In 1983, the Supreme Court lost patience with Congress and refused to delay the effective date of its decision any further. Many had predicted that chaos in the bankruptcy system would result. But the courts of appeals responded to the emergency by passing resolutions in each of their circuits that established a system that allowed the bankruptcy courts to continue operating.

The emergency system divided all bankruptcy matters into two categories.

1. Core matters were matters that exist only in bankruptcy, such as approving reorganization plans.

2. Related matters were matters that could have been decided in other courts but had come under the jurisdiction of the bankruptcy courts because one of the parties had filed a bankruptcy petition. An example of a related matter is a breach of contract claim. Ordinarily, such a claim would be settled in a state or federal trial court; however, if the debtor was in bankruptcy, the claim would have to be tried in the bankruptcy court.

Core Matters
Those matters directly tied to a bankruptcy case and arising under the Bankruptcy Code.

Related Matters
Disputes that would have existed between parties even if one of them was not in a bankruptcy case.

Under the emergency system, the bankruptcy court could hear and determine all core matters. For a related matter, the bankruptcy court could make a binding ruling only if the parties consented. Otherwise, the bankruptcy court would just issue a proposed ruling and send it to the district court where a final determination could be made. While this system was not perfect, it allowed bankruptcy cases to be administered until Congress tried to resolve the conflicting positions over how much judicial power the bankruptcy courts should have.

The 1984 Amendments Finally, in 1984, Congress passed certain amendments to the Bankruptcy Code contained in the Bankruptcy Amendments and Federal Judgeship Act, which are together usually referred to as "BAFJA" or the "1984 Amendments." In the 1984 Amendments, Congress tried to cure the constitutional problem in the Bankruptcy Code by reducing the power of the bankruptcy

court rather than giving its judges a lifetime tenure. The amendments established a system similar to that put into place by the courts of appeals in 1983, though far more complicated. It is discussed at some length in Chapter 6 of this book.

While Congress was trying to solve the constitutional dilemma of the Bankruptcy Code, a number of special interest groups took advantage of the delay and lobbied for other changes in the law. As a result, the 1984 Amendments also made a number of substantive changes in the Bankruptcy Code. Among other things, the Amendments improved the treatment of real property landlords and institutions who lend money to consumers, made certain prebankruptcy transfers more difficult to unwind, and changed the way that collective bargaining agreements between a debtor and a union were treated in bankruptcy.

The 1986 Amendments   Two years after the 1984 Amendments, Congress passed the Bankruptcy Judges, United States Trustees, and Family Farmer Bankruptcy Act of 1986, which is commonly referred to as the "1986 Amendments." This act authorized the appointment of fifty-two new bankruptcy judges in an effort to reduce the pressure on an overburdened bankruptcy court, which had seen a dramatic increase in filings of bankruptcy petitions since the adoption of the Bankruptcy Code. The 1986 Amendments also made a number of changes in the Bankruptcy Code, including the creation of Chapter 12 that provided reorganizations for family farmers. The most significant amendment, however, was one that institutionalized the office of the **United States trustee** and made it a permanent part of the federal bankruptcy system.

The United States Trustee   During the drafting of the Bankruptcy Act of 1978, Congress sought a way of eliminating the conflict that plagued the referee system and removing bankruptcy court judges from the day-to-day administration of bankruptcy cases. The result of this congressional study was Chapter 15 of the Bankruptcy Code. It established the office of the United States trustee as a five-year experimental program operated by the Department of Justice. Chapter 15 gave nonjudicial governmental personnel the responsibility of overseeing and coordinating many of the administrative functions that had been performed by the bankruptcy court. The program was established in eighteen districts including some of the largest and most active and in some of the smaller and less active districts.

The responsibilities of the United States trustee differ in each type of bankruptcy case. In the large reorganizations, the United States trustee monitors the progress of the entire case by supervising the debtor, ensuring that taxes are paid and that appropriate financial reports are filed, organizing a committee of creditors to oversee the debtor's reorganization efforts, and reviewing reorganization plans to ensure that they meet the requirements of the Bankruptcy Code. The only thing that the United States trustee cannot do is to propose a plan of reorganization. In wage earner and family farmer reorganization cases, the United States trustee appoints and oversees the standing trustees. In liquidation proceedings, the United States trustee appoints the bankruptcy trustees and reviews their work. The United States trustee also works with law enforcement officials in the detection and prosecution of white-collar crimes related to bankruptcy such as embezzlement, fraud, and concealment of assets.

The main office of the United States trustee is in Washington, D.C. and is headed by the United States trustee appointed by the President. Each office of the United States trustee is staffed by the United States trustee for that district and one or more assistant United States trustees along with attorneys, analysts, and

paralegal specialists. The attorneys will represent the United States trustee in court on any matter in which the trustee wishes to be heard. The analysts, who usually have financial backgrounds, are primarily responsible for monitoring a company's performance in a reorganization case. Paralegal specialists assist the attorneys and analysts in performing their duties, and they may also be given primary responsibility for monitoring smaller reorganization cases.

With the adoption of the 1986 Amendments, discussed above, the office of the United States trustee was established on a permanent nationwide basis. The judicial districts were organized into twenty-one regions, each of which is to be administered by a separate United States trustee appointed by the United States attorney for a five-year term. The expenses of the United States trustee system are funded by fees added to the costs of filing bankruptcy petitions and quarterly fees for Chapter 11 reorganization cases that vary according to the amount of money disbursed by the debtor in a particular fiscal quarter.

The 1994 Amendments In October of 1994, Congress made the most sweeping changes to the Bankruptcy Code yet in the Bankruptcy Reform Act of 1994. The 1994 Amendments made changes in bankruptcy administration, commercial bankruptcy issues, the treatment of consumer debtors and their creditors, and the eligibility of governmental entities to file a bankruptcy case. These amendments are discussed later in this book in connection with the substantive provisions amended. The 1994 Amendments also have provisions to reduce the number of fraudulent bankruptcy filings by making criminal the improper activities of "bankruptcy petition preparers." That part of the amendment will be investigated in Chapter 3—the Role of the Legal Assistant in Bankruptcy Practice.

Finally, the 1994 Amendments establish the National Bankruptcy Review Commission. The purpose of the Commission is to study issues and problems related to the Bankruptcy Code. The Commission is composed of nine members. Three are appointed by the President, one by the President *pro temporare* of the Senate, one each by the minority leader of the Senate and the House of Representatives and two by the Chief Justice of the Supreme Court. Distinguished academicians, practitioners, and former legislators or their aides have been appointed.

Additional Amendments Congress has frequently proposed additional amendments to the Bankruptcy Code. For example, in 1988, Congress changed the treatment of license agreements for intellectual property, medical benefits for retirees, and eligibility to file a Chapter 9 case. Undoubtedly, further changes will be made to the substantive provisions of the Bankruptcy Code once the Commission has completed its work. Paperback copies of the Bankruptcy Code are published each year by several legal publishers. The lawyer and the paralegal should have the current edition because each session of Congress usually makes changes to the Bankruptcy Code.

☐ SUMMARY

Bankruptcy is the system of laws that allows a person who owes money to settle those debts with the creditors. There are two methods of settling debts: liquidation and reorganization. In a liquidation a debtor must deliver all of its property other than what it needs to make a fresh start to a bankruptcy trustee, who will sell the property and deliver the sale proceeds to creditors. In a reorganization, the debtor will keep all of its assets and make payments to creditors over time.

The Constitution of the United States gives Congress the power to make bankruptcy laws, which it has done in a series of bills beginning in 1800. The current bankruptcy law is found in the Bankruptcy Code, which is title 11 of the United States Code. It is frequently amended, including extensive changes in 1994. The Bankruptcy Code includes Chapter 7, which provides for a liquidation, and Chapters 9, 11, 12, and 13, which provide for reorganizations of different types of entities.

Specialized federal courts, called bankruptcy courts, preside over bankruptcy judges. The primary parties will be the debtor, the creditors, a bankruptcy trustee if one has been appointed, and the United States trustee.

☐ KEY TERMS

Automatic Stay	Core Matters	Related Matters
Bankruptcy	Exempt Property	Reorganization
Bankruptcy Act	Liquidation	Trustee
Bankruptcy Code	Petition	United States Code
Bankruptcy Courts	Petitioner	

THE BANKRUPTCY CODE AND THE BANKRUPTCY RULES

☐ SUMMARY OF THE BANKRUPTCY CODE

The Format

The Bankruptcy Code applies to all bankruptcy cases commenced on or after October 1, 1979, the date on which it became effective. The few cases that were pending on that date and that have not been completed are governed by the Bankruptcy Act. It is usually easy to determine whether a particular case is governed by the Bankruptcy Code or the Bankruptcy Act. Chapter designations in Bankruptcy Code cases use Arabic numbers (for example, "Chapter 11"). In cases governed by the Bankruptcy Act, Roman numerals are used (for example, "Chapter XIII").

The Bankruptcy Code is divided into Chapters 1, 3, 5, 7, 9, 11, 12, and 13. All of the chapter designations are odd numbers except for Chapter 12. Each chapter (except Chapter 1) is divided into subchapters which are indicated by Roman numerals. Each subchapter (and Chapter 1) is broken into sections. The first one or two digits of a section number indicate the chapter in which the section appears. For example, Section 701 is in Chapter 7 and Section 1104 is in Chapter 11.

Chapters 1, 3, and 5 contain general provisions and are used in all liquidation and reorganization cases. For example, Section 362 applies in Chapter 7, 11, 12, and 13 cases. These general chapters are followed by the one liquidation chapter (Chapter 7) and the four reorganization chapters (Chapters 9, 11, 12, and 13).

Prior to 1986, there was a Chapter 15 devoted to the office of the United States trustee. Chapter 15 modified other provisions of the Bankruptcy Code in the districts involved in the pilot project. For example, in a pilot district such as Colorado, instead of referring to Section 1104 of the Bankruptcy Code, one would refer to Section 151104. Since the office of the United States trustee became established

nationally and permanently in 1986, the provisions of Chapter 15 were folded into the other chapters in the 1986 Amendments and Chapter 15 was deleted.

The General Provisions—Chapter 1

Chapter 1 is broadly entitled General Provisions and contains nine sections. Chapter 1, like Chapters 3 and 5, applies in every bankruptcy case whether it is a liquidation or a reorganization case. The sections of this chapter are very important in understanding how a bankruptcy case works, since they are the foundation upon which the other chapters are built. A few of these sections are briefly discussed here.

Section 101 contains most of the definitions of words and phrases used throughout the Bankruptcy Code. Some of the definitions merely articulate the popular understanding of a term, but other definitions of apparently common terms are very cleverly written. For example, in Section 101 there is an important distinction in the definition of "entity" and the definition of "person." When Congress wanted governmental units to be included within the scope of a provision, it used **entity,** which was defined to include them. When Congress wanted to exclude government units from the scope of a provision, it used the term **person.** An example of this is found in Section 1102(b)(1) which concerns who may sit on a creditors' committee in a Chapter 11 case.

Other definitions found in Section 101 are important in order to understand the language of the substantive sections of the Code. For example, the word **claim** is broadly defined to include virtually every possible type of right of payment or right to a remedy. The automatic stay that comes into effect on the commencement of a bankruptcy case applies to any act to collect, assess, or recover a claim. By defining claim broadly, Congress made the scope of the automatic stay very broad.

Section 102 contains special rules of construction for interpreting the Bankruptcy Code. Of these, the explanation of the phrase "after notice and a hearing," which is repeated frequently throughout the Bankruptcy Code, is the most significant. It provides that " 'after notice and a hearing,' or a similar phrase—

(A) means after such notice as is appropriate in the particular circumstances, and such opportunity for a hearing as is appropriate in the particular circumstances; but

(B) authorizes an act without an actual hearing if such notice is given properly and if—

(i) such a hearing is not requested timely by a party in interest; or

(ii) there is insufficient time for a hearing to be commenced before such act must be done, and the court authorizes such act[.]"

So, this phrase is not interpreted literally. "After notice and a hearing" may mean very limited notice and no hearing at all; it all depends on the circumstances. For example, Section 363 of the Bankruptcy Code allows a trustee to sell the debtor's property "after notice and a hearing." In many instances the trustee will simply send a notice to the creditors that certain property of the debtor will be sold; and if no creditor objects, the court is deemed to have approved the sale although no hearing was actually conducted. This rule of construction allows for the flexibility needed to administer a bankruptcy case effectively and results in substantial savings of time and money by reducing the amount of time the debtor, the trustee, the creditors, and all of their lawyers spend in court.

Entity
A person, estate, trust, governmental unit, and the United States trustee.

Person
An individual, partnership or corporation, but not a governmental unit unless it is acting as a receiver or liquidating agent of a person.

Claim
A right to payment from the debtor, whether or not such right is liquidated contingent, disputed, or secured.

Another important provision of Chapter 1 is Section 109, which establishes the preliminary criteria to file a bankruptcy case and the eligibility for each particular chapter. Section 109 will be examined in detail in Chapter 7. For now it is only important to realize that bankruptcy relief is not available to all who want it.

Case Administration—Chapter 3

Chapter 3, entitled Case Administration, has a wealth of information in its thirty-four sections, including how bankruptcy cases are commenced and how they are administered. Chapter 3 is divided into four subchapters: Commencement of a Case, Officers, Administration, and Administrative Powers.

Commencement of a Case—Sections 301–307   The first subchapter of Chapter 3 covers how bankruptcy cases are commenced (by filing a petition), including cases filed by a husband and a wife, the only two individuals who may file a case together. The subject of an involuntary bankruptcy is also covered. An involuntary bankruptcy is one in which the creditors file a petition with the bankruptcy court and compel the debtor to submit to the bankruptcy proceeding against his or her wishes. This subchapter also covers **abstention** by a bankruptcy court. Abstention is the power of the bankruptcy court to reject a case if the creditors and the debtor would be better served by such a refusal. For example, the bankruptcy court may abstain by dismissing a bankruptcy case that was commenced by the debtor after a receiver had been appointed over the debtor's property by a state court. Finally, Section 307 allows the United States trustee, the arm of the Justice Department charged with supervising bankruptcy case administration, to be heard on any issue arising in a bankruptcy case.

Abstention
The refusal of a court to hear and rule with respect to a particular case or proceeding despite the fact that it has jurisdiction to do so.

Officers—Sections 321–331   The second subchapter covers the employment and compensation of "officers of the bankruptcy case." Officers of the bankruptcy case are the trustee and other professional persons, such as attorneys and accountants, employed at the expense of the bankruptcy estate. The qualifications of those eligible to serve as a bankruptcy trustee and the amount of the trustee's compensation are also covered. The subchapter establishes the qualifications of attorneys and other professionals who represent debtors, trustees, or creditors' committees, and addresses the subject of their compensation. The employment and compensation of the officers of the bankruptcy case are discussed in Chapter 9 of this book.

Administration—Sections 341–350   The subchapter entitled Administration contains ten miscellaneous sections covering a bankruptcy case from its early days to its closing. For the most part these sections are unrelated, but they are very important. They require the debtor to attend a meeting of creditors soon after the case is filed and to answer any questions the creditors may have. This meeting, commonly known as the first meeting of creditors or the Section 341(a) meeting, allows creditors to question the debtor under oath without incurring the expense of a deposition. How these meetings are conducted varies greatly not only by the size and complexity of the debtor's finances and assets but also with the preferences of the trustee or other person conducting the examination. Other provisions of the subchapter on administration set out guidelines that the trustee must follow in investing funds of the debtor's estate, cover certain tax considerations, and deal with the effects of conversion of a case from one chapter to another and dismissal of the bankruptcy case.

Administrative Powers—Sections 361–366   The six sections in the subchapter on administrative powers are the provisions central to a bankruptcy case. Section 361 lists some examples of "adequate protection," a phrase that is used throughout the Bankruptcy Code. For example, it is the consideration a secured creditor or lessor is entitled to for the trustee's or debtor's use of property in which the secured creditor or the lessor has an interest. Section 362 is the automatic stay, the injunction that comes into effect when a case is commenced and which stops creditor action. It delineates which acts are stayed, which are not stayed, and how a creditor can obtain relief from its operation. This is perhaps the most important section of the Bankruptcy Code to debtors and creditors and is the reason most bankruptcy cases are started. Chapter 4 of this book discusses the automatic stay. Section 363 explains the debtor's or the trustee's rights to use, sell, or lease property of the bankruptcy estate. Section 364 lists the conditions that must be met if the debtor or the trustee want to borrow money after the bankruptcy case has been commenced. Section 365 discusses the effect the bankruptcy will have on contracts and leases to which the debtor is a party. Section 365 is also very important and for that reason it is also examined in depth in Chapter 4 of this book. Finally, Section 366 provides the terms and conditions under which a utility service may discontinue service to the debtor.

Creditors, the Debtor, and the Estate—Chapter 5

Chapter 5 contains thirty-four sections of the Bankruptcy Code divided into three subchapters. They cover such things as how the creditors will get paid and from what source the payments will be made; they specify what exempt property the debtor may keep after the bankruptcy and what debts the debtor will have to pay despite the bankruptcy.

Proof of Claim
The form a creditor who has a claim against the debtor must file in order to receive a distribution in a bankruptcy case.

Subchapter I—Sections 501–510   This subchapter is entitled Creditors and Claims, and it covers the filing of a creditor's **proof of claim.** A proof of claim is the form filed by a creditor with the bankruptcy court that states the nature and the amount of the debt owed by the debtor to the creditor. The subchapter also covers how claims incurred after the bankruptcy case began are treated, how a secured creditor's claim is determined, and the order in which claims are to be paid.

Exemptions
Those interests in property that a debtor is allowed to keep and not make subject to creditors' claims.

Subchapter II—Sections 521–525   This subchapter lists the debtor's duties in a bankruptcy case. Principally, the debtor must cooperate with the trustee and file a detailed list of assets and debts. The subchapter also lists some of the benefits to which the debtor is entitled, prohibits discrimination against a debtor by governmental entities and private employers, and enumerates the debtor's **exemptions,** or property that the debtor may keep after the bankruptcy. Also listed in the subchapter are the debtor's **nondischargeable claims,** which are those claims that may be enforced against the debtor after the bankruptcy case.

Nondischargeable Claims
Claims that will be enforceable against the debtor despite the discharge.

Subchapter III—Sections 541–559   This subchapter is simply titled the Estate. A bankruptcy estate is an artificial entity that springs into existence on the filing of a bankruptcy petition. It owns all of the debtor's property and is subject to all of the debtor's debts. It is used to conceptually distinguish between the prebankruptcy debtor and the postbankruptcy debtor. The common theme of Subchapter III is to enlarge the estate as much as possible by defining property of the debtor very broadly. Thus, these sections provide ways to bring property of the estate that is in the control of the debtor or third parties into the hands of the trustee. They also give the trustee certain powers, called avoiding powers, that allow the trustee

to cancel a transfer of the estate property made before or after the commencement of the bankruptcy case and place it in the possession and control of the trustee. The trustee is given the power to cancel transfers that were fraudulent and to recover preferences, which are certain arrangements by which some creditors are treated better than others. Finally, the subchapter deals with **setoff** and **abandonment.** Setoff concerns the ability of a creditor who also owes money to the debtor to apply the debts against each other. Abandonment is the ability of the trustee to decline to administer all or some of the property of the estate.

Setoff
The application of a debt owed to a person against a debt owed from that same person.

Abandonment
The release by the bankruptcy trustee or debtor in possession of the estate's rights in property.

Liquidation—Chapter 7

The remainder of the Bankruptcy Code's chapters provide for specific types of bankruptcy relief. Chapter 7 of the Bankruptcy Code is the only one of these chapters that concerns liquidation, sometimes called a straight bankruptcy. It is the simplest form of debt relief and is available for all types of debtors, whether individuals, partnerships, or corporations. Only railroads, insurance companies, governments, and financial institutions such as banks may not be Chapter 7 debtors.

When a bankruptcy petition is filed, an estate is created that consists of all the debtor's property. A Chapter 7 case then proceeds on two tracks. The first track is the administration of the estate: the collection, liquidation, and distribution to creditors of whatever property is available. The second track is the rehabilitation of the debtor: the debtor will be relieved of the burden of the estate's debts and left with sufficient assets so that a fresh start can be made. Exhibit 2.1 briefly graphs these two tracks.

Administration of the Estate   Under Section 701, an interim bankruptcy trustee is appointed by the United States trustee or by the bankruptcy court's administrative personnel. The interim trustee will usually be an individual but may be a company. In virtually every jurisdiction there is a panel of persons who have applied for and have been selected for appointments as interim trustees.

Generally, trustees have experience in bankruptcy matters and familiarity with selling property. Trustees are often lawyers; but they may be accountants, financial consultants, auctioneers, or other professionals. If the debtor was involved in a particularly complex industry or if the case is of such magnitude that it would be difficult for a panel trustee to administer the estate, the United States trustee or bankruptcy court personnel may select a trustee from the particular industry or other specialist to head the liquidation effort. In addition, if no member of the panel is willing to serve as the trustee, the United States trustee may serve but rarely does.

The interim bankruptcy trustee serves until the meeting of creditors. At that time creditors who are not affiliated with the debtor and who hold at least twenty percent of the claims may elect a different trustee. If there is no election, which is almost always the case, or if the creditors' candidate does not receive a majority of the votes, the interim bankruptcy trustee becomes the trustee for the remainder of the bankruptcy case.

The trustee's duties are listed in Section 704 of the Bankruptcy Code. They include:

☐ Collecting the property of the estate and reducing it to money.
☐ Investigating the financial affairs of the debtor.
☐ Examining the claims filed by creditors and objecting to improper claims if a purpose would be served.

■ EXHIBIT 2.1
The Two Tracks of a Chapter
7 Case

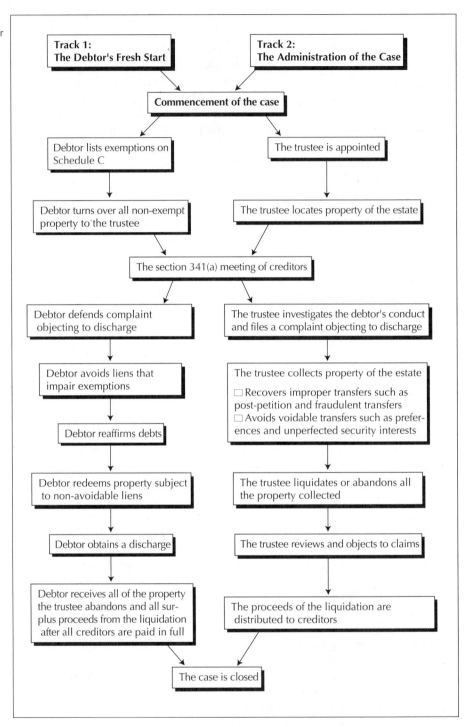

**Track 1:
The Debtor's Fresh Start**

**Track 2:
The Administration of the Case**

Commencement of the case

Debtor lists exemptions on
Schedule C

The trustee is appointed

Debtor turns over all non-exempt
property to the trustee

The trustee locates property of the estate

The section 341(a) meeting of creditors

Debtor defends complaint
objecting to discharge

The trustee investigates the debtor's conduct
and files a complaint objecting to discharge

Debtor avoids liens that
impair exemptions

The trustee collects property of the estate

☐ Recovers improper transfers such as
post-petition and fraudulent transfers
☐ Avoids voidable transfers such as preferences and unperfected security interests

Debtor reaffirms debts

Debtor redeems property subject
to non-avoidable liens

The trustee liquidates or abandons all
the property collected

Debtor obtains a discharge

The trustee reviews and objects to claims

Debtor receives all of the property
the trustee abandons and all surplus proceeds from the liquidation
after all creditors are paid in full

The proceeds of the liquidation are
distributed to creditors

The case is closed

☐ Opposing the discharge of the debtor if advisable.

☐ Furnishing information concerning the estate and its administration requested by creditors.

☐ Making a final report and filing with the court a final account of the administration of the estate.

The trustee is compensated by receiving an allowance set by the court. This amount is usually a percentage of the funds that have been disbursed to creditors. The percentages are set out in Section 326.

In administering the estate, the trustee will rely on the general provision sections of Chapter 3 and 5. For example, the trustee will look to Chapter 5 to determine what property is part of the estate and must be administered. The trustee will attempt to increase the size of the estate by recovering preferences, fraudulent conveyances, and improper postbankruptcy transfers. Once the estate has been made as large as possible, the trustee will use the provisions in Chapter 3 to sell the assets for cash. Any property that cannot bring cash to the estate will be abandoned.

Although Chapter 7 involves the sale of a debtor's assets, the court may allow the trustee to operate the debtor's business for a limited period of time if doing so helps the sale of the business. If the debtor was a manufacturing facility in the middle of processing orders when it filed its bankruptcy petition, for example, the business could be continued for a sufficient time to allow worthless raw materials to be processed into valuable finished goods.

When all the assets have been sold, the trustee will be ready to distribute the funds on hand to creditors pursuant to the provisions of Sections 507 and 726 of the Bankruptcy Code. Section 726 establishes a six-tier priority distribution system under which each tier is required to be paid in full before any person on a lower tier receives anything. On the first tier are those creditors who claim a priority, or a right to be paid first, under Section 507 of the Bankruptcy Code. Section 507 in turn has nine tiers of priority claims that are entitled to preferential treatment. They include administrative expenses, such as trustee's and attorneys' fees and costs; wages earned within ninety days before the bankruptcy case was commenced; claims for contributions to employee benefit plans; deposits paid for customer goods not delivered or provided; and certain types of taxes.

If the Section 507 priority claims are paid in full, a distribution is made to the second tier of claims listed in Section 726 for unsecured creditors who timely filed claims against the estate. Late filing creditors are paid next, followed by claims that are for fines, penalties, and punitive damages. If there are still funds left to be distributed, interest is paid to creditors. In the unlikely event that a balance remains, the funds are paid to the debtor. Exhibit 2.2 ranks the various priorities creditors enjoy and the order in which the funds are disbursed.

Once the distribution is made, the trustee will close the estate and the case will be over.

The Fresh Start   While the trustee is administering the estate, the debtor should be cooperating with the trustee in collecting and liquidating assets. The debtor will also be acting to preserve the **exemptions**—those assets Congress has decided a debtor needs in order to make a fresh start. Although all of the debtor's property comes into the bankruptcy estate, the debtor is allowed to keep the property listed in Section 522. Exempt property includes some equity in a house, a car, household goods and furnishings, pension funds, and certain miscellaneous other assets. Exceptions are discussed in Chapter 8.

In most bankruptcy cases there are no assets for the trustee to administer, other than those the debtor may claim as exempt. As a result, the trustee will have nothing to liquidate and no funds with which to make a distribution to creditors. These cases are usually called **no-asset cases.**

No Asset Case
A bankruptcy case in which there are no assets to sell by the trustee. As a result, creditors do not receive a distribution.

■ EXHIBIT 2.2
Priorities in Distribution

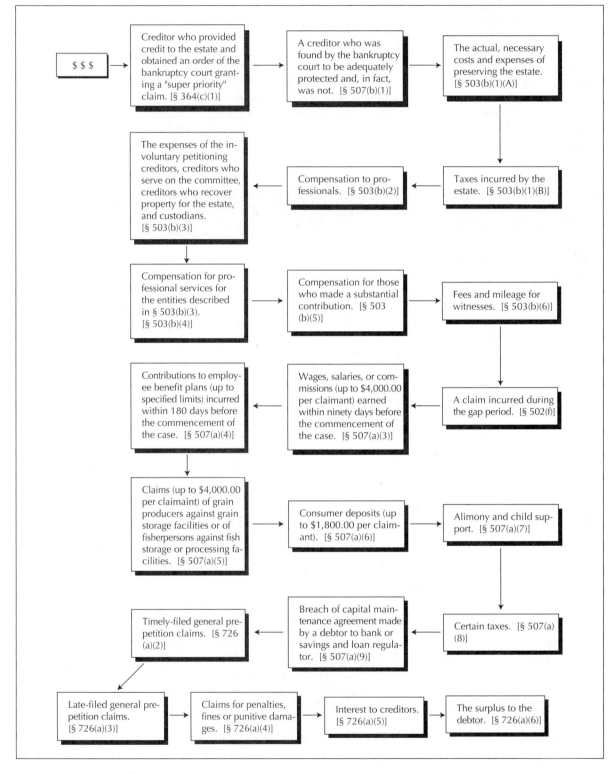

As a payment for giving up all non-exempt property to the trustee, the individual debtor will receive a **discharge** or complete forgiveness of most debts. The creditors will never be able to enforce those obligations against the debtor. There is certainly nothing that prevents the debtor from voluntarily repaying creditors, but he or she cannot be compelled to do so. Corporations do not receive a discharge, but since the corporation will no longer have any assets after commencing a bankruptcy case (exemptions are only available for individuals), the effect is the same.

For public policy reasons, there are a few types of debts that are not discharged and will be enforceable against the debtor even after the Chapter 7 bankruptcy case is over. These debts are generally referred to as **nondischargeable claims** and are listed in Section 523 of the Bankruptcy Code. They include:

Discharge
The release given to an individual debtor of the difference between the amount of creditor's unsecured claims and the assets distributed to creditors in a bankruptcy case.

- ☐ Certain taxes and debts incurred to pay those taxes.
- ☐ Money, property, or service obtained through fraud.
- ☐ Luxury goods or credit card cash advances obtained within sixty days prior to bankruptcy.
- ☐ Debts not disclosed during the bankruptcy case.
- ☐ Alimony and child support.
- ☐ Claims for willful and malicious injury.
- ☐ Certain fines, penalties, and forfeitures.
- ☐ Student loans.
- ☐ Claims for damages caused by a drunk driver.
- ☐ Debts not discharged in the debtor's previous bankruptcy case.
- ☐ Fraud or defalcation to a depository institution.
- ☐ Reckless or malicious failure to fulfill a capital maintenance agreement.
- ☐ Condominium association dues.

A more extensive discussion of nondischargeable claims is found in Chapter 8.

Pursuant to Section 727 of the Bankruptcy Code, in certain limited circumstances, all of the individual's debtor's claims will be nondischargeable. Those situations nearly always involve the debtor's bad conduct and include:

- ☐ The debtor defrauded creditors or the trustee by transferring or destroying property.
- ☐ Without justification, the debtor transferred or destroyed books and records.
- ☐ The debtor knowingly and fraudulently committed perjury, presented a false claim, tried to obtain an advantage by doing or agreeing to do something (or not do something), or withheld books and records.
- ☐ The debtor failed to satisfactorily explain a loss of assets.
- ☐ The debtor refused to obey an order of the court or improperly invoked the privilege against self-incrimination.
- ☐ The debtor received a discharge in a bankruptcy case commenced within the last six years.

There will be a lengthier discussion of the discharge and the acts that can defeat it in Chapter 8.

Stockbrokers and Commodity Brokers   Subchapter III of Chapter 7 has a number of very specialized sections concerning liquidations of the assets of stockbrokers and their spouses. Similarly, Subchapter IV contains provisions for commodity broker

liquidations. Since the possibility of widespread investor loss would be a problem in a stockbroker or commodity broker Chapter 7 case, Congress enacted special provisions concerning subordination of insider claims, recovery of voidable transfers and distributions. The provisions for stockbrokers can be found in Subchapter III of Chapter 7; the provisions for commodity brokers can be found in Subchapter IV.

Reorganization—Chapter 11

Chapter 11 was designed to help business debtors reorganize and continue operations. The benefits flow not only to creditors, who should receive more than they would if the business closed down, but also to the economy that is served by preserving competition and jobs. Chapter 11 cases are usually filed by partnerships and corporations. Individuals can also file a Chapter 11 case. However, individuals are usually better off under Chapter 13, which is less expensive, time consuming, and cumbersome. Because they are heavily regulated by other laws, certain types of individuals and businesses, such as stockbrokers, insurance companies, and banks cannot be Chapter 11 debtors. There are also special provisions for railroad reorganizations under Chapter 11.

Administration of the Case   A Chapter 11 case may be commenced voluntarily by the debtor, or involuntarily by one or more creditors against the debtor. The progress of a typical Chapter 11 case is illustrated in Exhibit 2.3.

Plan of Reorganization
A document filed in a reorganization case that divides the claims of creditors into classes and provides for their payment or other treatment.

The goal of a Chapter 11 case is to have the bankruptcy court approve a **plan of reorganization** that is either voted in by the creditors or found by the court to be in their best interests.

While the plan of reorganization is being developed, the debtor remains in possession and control of the business and its assets and is responsible for administering the estate. For that reason a Chapter 11 debtor is called the **debtor in possession,** or *DIP.* The debtor will be a debtor in possession unless the bankruptcy court appoints a Chapter 11 trustee, which usually occurs only when the debtor has been guilty of incompetence, gross mismanagement, or some other type of bad act.

Debtor in Possession
A debtor in a case under Chapters 9 and 13, and a debtor in a case under Chapters 11 and 12 in which no trustee has been appointed.

The duties of a Chapter 11 trustee are set out in Section 1106 of the Bankruptcy Code. They are similar to those of a Chapter 7 trustee except that, because there will be an effort to reorganize the debtor's business, the Chapter 11 trustee is not required to liquidate the estate's assets.

The duties of the debtor in possession are set out in Section 1107. Generally, the debtor in possession has all of the rights and powers of a trustee and performs most of the functions of a trustee. For example, the debtor in possession may avoid fraudulent conveyances, sell estate property, and reject contracts made by the debtor. Like a trustee, however, the debtor in possession must be accountable for all property received and otherwise act properly.

To ensure that the debtor in possession is behaving properly, it will be required to submit regular reports to the court or the United States trustee showing all receipts and expenditures and whether the estate is losing money. The debtor in possession will also have to pay a fee ranging from $150 to $3,000 each quarter to pay for the United States trustee's monitoring and oversight.

Ordinary Course of Business
Transactions made by a business in its day to day operations.

Since the goal of a Chapter 11 case is the reorganization of the debtor's business, no specific court order is required for the debtor in possession to continue operations. As long as such actions are in the **ordinary course of business,** the debtor in possession may use, sell, or lease estate property without prior approval of the

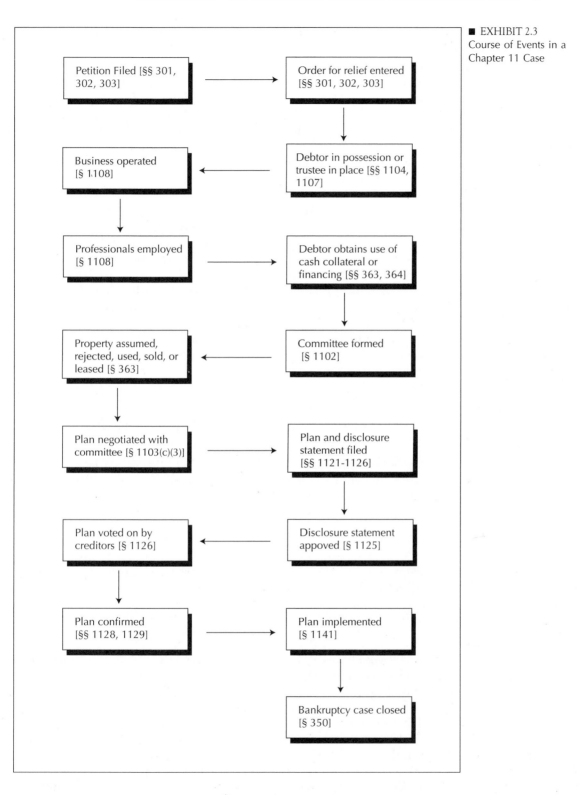

■ EXHIBIT 2.3
Course of Events in a
Chapter 11 Case

bankruptcy court. What constitutes the ordinary course of business is not specifically discussed in the Bankruptcy Code. Because of the many different types of businesses that exist, it is virtually impossible to fashion a definition of "ordinary course of business" that would apply in all cases. Generally, the things a business did as part of its day-to-day operations before bankruptcy would be considered as within the ordinary course of business. For example, a grocery store chain buying produce from vendors and selling it to customers would be acting in the ordinary course of business, and no court order would be required to continue that operation. If the grocery store chain wanted to sell one of its stores to another company, however, that would be out of the ordinary course of business; permission would have to be sought from the bankruptcy court for that sale.

Congress envisioned a Chapter 11 plan of reorganization as a cooperative effort between the debtor and the creditors. To facilitate their negotiations, the Bankruptcy Code provides for the appointment of a committee of creditors. The **creditors' committee** ordinarily consists of the seven largest unsecured creditors and is selected by the United States trustee.

Creditors' Committee
A committee comprised of two or more of the debtor's creditors, appointed in a Chapter 9 or 11 case by the United States trustee.

In larger cases, more than one creditors' committee will be appointed. If the debtor is a corporation, a committee may be appointed to represent the interests of the shareholders. If the debtor is a limited partnership, there may be a committee of limited partners. These last two types of committees are usually referred to as **equity committees.** Equity committees and creditors' committees have the same functions and duties.

Equity Committee
A committee of equity security holders (e.g., stock holders, warrant holders, general or limited partnership interests) appointed in a Chapter 11 case by the United States trustee.

The duties and functions of the committee are listed in Section 1103 of the Bankruptcy Code. They include:

☐ Consulting with the debtor in possession concerning the administration of the case.

☐ Investigating any matter relevant to the case or the plan of reorganization.

☐ Participating in the process of plan formulation and confirmation.

☐ Performing any other service that is in the best interest of those the committee represents.

The committee is entitled to appear before the bankruptcy court and be heard on any issue in a Chapter 11 case. Judges are often interested in the opinion of the creditors committee on any given topic. To assist it in performing its duties and functions, the committee also has the right to employ professionals such as attorneys, accountants, and investment bankers. Fees for these professionals will, as for the professionals employed by the debtor in possession, be paid by the estate.

The Plan of Reorganization   The goal in a Chapter 11 case is the confirmation by the court of a plan of reorganization. The debtor may propose a plan of reorganization at any time during the case. During the first 120 days of the case, only the debtor in possession may propose a plan; this is called the period of **plan exclusivity.** The 120-day period can be extended if the court finds that there is a good reason to do so. Once the exclusivity period has expired, any party in interest, other than the United States trustee, may propose a plan of reorganization.

Plan Exclusivity
The fact that for a period of time only the debtor may propose a plan of reorganization.

A plan of reorganization divides creditors and equity interest holders into classes and provides a method of treating each class. Unless they consent to a different treatment, each senior class must be paid in full before any junior class can receive a payment under the plan. For example, a simple plan for a corporation would have four classes of creditors as follows:

1. Class 1—Priority creditors.
2. Class 2—Secured creditors.
3. Class 3—All nonpriority unsecured creditors.
4. Class 4—Shareholders.

The plan could provide that Class 1 creditors would be paid in full on the effective date of the plan. Class 2 creditors would retain their liens in the debtor's property and receive the monthly installment payments called for in their contracts with the debtor. Class 3 creditors would receive quarterly payments from the debtor's profits over the next five years and all of the debtor's stock, which should equal sixty percent of their claims. Since Class 3 creditors will not be paid in full, Class 4 creditors will receive nothing under the plan.

This example is a very simple, traditional reorganization plan. Most plans either provide for the liquidation of all the debtor's assets and a distribution to creditors or they are a variation on this plan. What the plan actually provides for depends on the debtor's financial situation, the negotiations with the creditors, and the creativity and ingenuity of the **plan proponent.** No two plans are exactly alike, but they must have certain common elements. These include:

Plan Proponent
The entity that proposes a plan of reorganization.

☐ The plan must put into classes the various types of claims and interests. The claims in each class must be substantially similar to each other.

☐ The plan must identify those classes of creditors that are not impaired under the plan. To be impaired means that the creditors' legal, contractual, or equitable rights are altered. An unsecured creditor is impaired if it will not be paid in full. A secured creditor is impaired if it will not be paid on time, will not be paid in full, or will be receiving substitute collateral under the plan.

☐ The plan must state how impaired classes are treated.

☐ The plan must treat each member of a class the same.

☐ The plan must specifically state how the reorganization will happen.

☐ The plan must disclose who will be operating the debtor in the future.

The plan of reorganization may also contain any other provision provided it does not conflict with any of the mandatory provisions. The Bankruptcy Code suggests some optional provisions:

☐ The plan may impair the rights of secured and unsecured creditors and equity interest holders.

☐ The plan may provide for the assumption or rejection of executory contracts and leases.

☐ The plan may provide for the settlement of one or more claims against the estate.

☐ The plan may provide for the sale of all or substantially all of the property of the estate.

Disclosure Statement
The document containing adequate information that is distributed with a Chapter 11 plan of reorganization.

The plan of reorganization must be accompanied by a written **disclosure statement** explaining the plan that has been approved by the court. Its purpose is to provide the information creditors need to intelligently decide whether to vote for or against the plan. The court will approve the disclosure statement only if it contains **adequate information,** which is defined in Section 1125 of the Code as:

Adequate Information
Information in sufficient detail that would enable to hypothetical reasonable investor to make an informed decision whether to vote for or against a plan of reorganization.

information of a kind, and in sufficient detail, as far as is reasonably practicable in light of the nature and history of the debtor and the condition of the debtor's

books and records, that would enable a hypothetical reasonable investor typical of holders of claims or interests of the relevant class to make an informed judgment about the plan.

The disclosure statement is usually filed with the plan. The court then holds a hearing to determine whether the disclosure statement contains adequate information. If it does, the court sets a date for a hearing to confirm the plan. The plan proponent then mails the plan, the disclosure statement, and a **ballot** to creditors and equity interest holders. Creditors who are impaired under the plan may vote for or against the plan by marking their ballots and returning them to the plan proponent as instructed in the disclosure statement.

At a hearing set by the court, the plan will not be confirmed unless each class of creditors or security holders impaired by the plan has voted to accept it or unless it is **crammed down,** a procedure discussed next. To be accepted, creditors who vote yes must hold at least two-thirds in amount and one-half in number of the claims of those who voted. For example, if there are ten creditors in an impaired class who vote, at least five must vote for the plan. If each creditor's claim is $10.00, at least seven creditors must vote for the plan to reach the necessary two-thirds in amount.

If one or more classes votes to reject the plan, the plan may still be confirmed if it can be crammed down. In order to have a cram down, the court must find that the plan does not unfairly discriminate and is fair and equitable as to the classes who have rejected it. In other words, the nonconsenting class must be paid in full before any junior class receives anything. For a class of secured creditors to be crammed down, the secured creditors must receive roughly the economic benefit of their bargain. For example, a secured creditor who is paid in full but not on time can be crammed down if it receives interest to compensate for the delay in the payment.

A plan that has been accepted by all of the impaired classes will not always be confirmed. The Bankruptcy Code provides that a plan cannot be confirmed unless the court specifically finds that the following terms have all been met:

□ The plan complies with Chapter 11 of the Bankruptcy Code.

□ The plan proponent has complied with the provisions of Chapter 11 of the Bankruptcy Code.

□ The plan has been proposed in good faith and not by any means forbidden by law.

□ All payments made or promised for services and costs in connection with the bankruptcy case or the plan have been disclosed.

□ The identities of postconfirmation officers and directors have been disclosed.

□ Any necessary regulatory approval has been obtained.

□ Unless all creditors and equity security holders agree otherwise, the plan provides more to those parties than they would receive in a Chapter 7 bankruptcy case.

□ Unless they agree to a different treatment, the priority classes are paid in full on the effective date of the plan.

□ At least one class has accepted the plan.

□ The plan can be carried out and will not likely fail thereafter.

If the plan is confirmed, it binds the debtor and all parties to it whether they voted in favor of it or not. Any debts that are not paid or are not paid in full by

Ballot

The document submitted by holders of impaired claims or interests accepting or rejecting a Chapter 11 plan of reorganization.

Cram Down

The approval of a plan of reorganization over the objection or negative votes of creditors.

the plan are no longer enforceable. Unless the plan provides otherwise, the debtor is no longer subject to the scrutiny of the bankruptcy court or the United States trustee; the debtor is charged only with living up to the terms of the plan.

The bankruptcy case is closed when the plan has been fully performed.

Small Chapter 11 Cases   As even this brief discussion illustrates, there are a number of time consuming, expensive steps that must be taken in order to successfully complete a Chapter 11 case. Many small companies that would benefit from a reorganization cannot afford costly legal proceedings and their financial affairs are not so complicated that all of the plan procedures are necessary.

In response to these issues, some of the bankruptcy judges in the less busy districts began to implement abbreviated Chapter 11 procedures for the smaller cases on their docket. These procedures eliminated or combined hearings and notices and required plans to be proposed shortly after the petition was filed.

As the 1994 Amendments worked their way through Congress, there was considerable pressure to nationalize these procedures or ones like them in order to reduce the financial burden on debtors in possession and the pressure on the court system. At one stage, Congress even considered enacting a Chapter 10 that would allow small corporate cases to be treated like Chapter 13 consumer reorganizations.

Ultimately, rather than enact an entirely new chapter, Congress changed various sections of Chapter 11 to permit an expedited and less expensive procedure for reorganizing a small business. A small business is defined in Section 101(51)(C) as a person engaged in commercial or business activities (other than solely real estate), with debts of $2,000,000 or less. The changes include: not having a creditors' committee; shortening the exclusivity period to 100 days; requiring a plan to be filed within 160 days; and combining the hearing on the disclosure statement and the plan.

Individual Reorganizations—Chapter 13

Chapter 13 of the Bankruptcy Code was given the title of Adjustment of Debts of an Individual with Regular Income. It is more familiarly known as **wage earner reorganizations.** Chapter 13 provides individual debtors and sole proprietors with relief similar to that given to corporations under Chapter 11, with the same goal of achieving a plan to satisfy the claims of the creditors. Chapter 13 is a less expensive and cumbersome vehicle, however. It is also less time consuming: in many cases, Chapter 13 plans can be confirmed in only a few months. (A time line for Chapter 13 cases is found in Exhibit 2.4.)

Administration   Only individuals are allowed to file Chapter 13 petitions, but not all individuals qualify. An individual must have a **regular income** and noncontingent, liquidated debts in certain amounts to qualify. The limit on unsecured debts is $250,000, and the limit on secured debts is $750,000. If a debtor had an $800,000 mortgage on a home (secured debt) or was a judgment debtor for $350,000 (unsecured debt), relief would have to be sought under Chapter 7 or Chapter 11. The same debt limits apply to a husband and wife filing jointly under Chapter 13.

Although Chapter 13 is called the wage earner reorganization, the Bankruptcy Code requires only that the debtor have a regular income. Gainful employment is not a prerequisite. Thus, debtors who are on welfare or receive some other form of public assistance, or those living on retirement or investment incomes also may

Wage Earner Reorganization
Chapter 13 cases so designated under the misconception that only employed persons qualify for relief. The statute requires only a regular income that may come from a variety of sources.

Regular Income
A source of income that is fairly stable whether earnings, pension or other retirement benefits, public assistance benefits, or dividends.

■ EXHIBIT 2.4
Chapter 13 Timeline

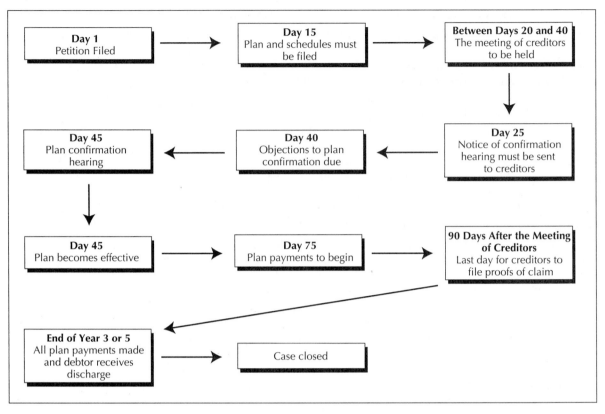

qualify. For a husband and wife filing jointly, only one spouse must have a regular income.

Chapter 13 debtors are also debtors in possession with many of the same rights and duties as Chapter 11 debtors. For example, subject to certain Bankruptcy Code provisions, a Chapter 13 debtor may reject contracts or leases; use, sell, or lease property; and operate a business. Anything out of the ordinary course, such as selling or refinancing real property, requires court approval. Like Chapter 7 debtors, Chapter 13 debtors are entitled to claim some assets as exempt, although exemptions are less important because a trustee under Chapter 13 does not administer the debtor's property.

Chapter 13 trustees conduct the first meeting of creditors, examine the debtor's plan of reorganization to ensure compliance with Chapter 13, collect payments from the debtor, and make disbursements to the creditors under the plan. The trustees do not take possession of the debtor's property or control any of the debtor's assets.

Chapter 13 trustees may come from the same panel as the Chapter 7 trustees; however, in most districts only one or two trustees (called standing trustees) are appointed to serve in all Chapter 13 cases. Only one or two trustees are needed in Chapter 13 cases because their duties are less involved than in Chapter 7 cases.

The Plan Under Chapter 13, only the debtor may propose a plan of reorganization. The creditors and the trustee may not do so. There is no mandatory form

for a Chapter 13 plan although most districts have forms that are in wide use. No disclosure statement must be filed or approved. Unlike Chapter 11 plans, which can be very complicated, Chapter 13 plans typically are only a few pages long.

Chapter 13 specifies certain common provisions for a plan of reorganization:

☐ The plan must submit to the trustee enough of the debtor's regular income so that the payments called for under the plan can be made.

☐ The plan must provide that priority claims such as the trustee's fee, certain wages, taxes, and consumer deposit claims are paid in full.

☐ The plan must provide for equal treatment of claims in the same class.

☐ The plan must provide that secured creditors receive an amount at least equal to the value of their collateral.

☐ The plan must provide that unsecured creditors receive at least as much as they would have received if the debtor had filed a Chapter 7 case instead.

The Chapter 13 plan may also contain the following optional provisions:

☐ The plan may divide claims into several different classes so long as the claims in each class are substantially similar.

☐ The plan may provide a different treatment for each class.

☐ The plan may modify the rights of secured creditors by extending the due date of the last payment or paying less than the full amount owed if the collateral is not worth the amount owed. The one exception is that a Chapter 13 plan may not modify the claim of the mortgage holder on the debtor's home. All the payments required by the original contract must be paid, although any amount in default when the case began may be paid off in time as part of the plan.

☐ The plan may provide that all creditors be paid concurrently regardless of priority. Priority or secured creditors need not be paid in full first.

☐ The plan may provide for the payment of postpetition claims, such as debts the debtor incurred for medical services after the case was filed. All postpetition claims must be paid in full.

Payments to the trustee under the plan may be stretched out for three years. If there is a good reason, the payment plan can be extended to five years. Regardless of the debtor's circumstances, a plan longer than five years cannot be approved.

Once the debtor has proposed a plan of reorganization, the court will hold a confirmation hearing. Unlike under Chapter 11, creditors are not entitled to vote for or against a Chapter 13 plan. They may file objections, but if the plan meets the requirements of Section 1325, it will be confirmed. The creditors do, however, have some leverage. If the plan does not provide full payment for the creditors, they can force the debtor to commit all **disposable income** for payments under the plan merely by filing an objection.

The confirmation hearing is usually held about forty-five days after the petition is filed. At the hearing, the court determines the following:

☐ Does the plan comply with the Bankruptcy Code? (Are the mandatory provisions present?)

☐ Has the debtor paid all fees and charges? This will usually just be the Chapter 13 filing fee.

☐ Has the plan been proposed in good faith and not by any means forbidden by law? Generally, the debtor must have proposed a plan that provides meaningful payments to creditors if at all possible, and performance of the plan must

Disposable Income
Debtor's income not necessary for payment of reasonable expenses for debtor and dependents. If debtor is engaged in business, income not needed for payment of expenses necessary for continuation, preservation and operation of business.

not violate state or federal law. For example, the debtor cannot have a plan confirmed that provides that the payments to creditors will be made from the earnings of the debtor's toxic material disposal service unless the debtor has the proper licenses.

When the debtor has fully performed the plan of reorganization, a discharge of all debts not paid in full will be granted. Unlike Chapter 7, Chapter 13 provides for a discharge of claims based on fraud or the failure to adequately explain loss of assets. In fact, the only types of claims that are not discharged in a Chapter 13 case are obligations for alimony and child support, damages from drunk driving, student loans, and criminal restitution. Even the debtor who is unable to complete the plan of reorganization may obtain a discharge if the court finds that the failure to make the payments was due to circumstances for which the debtor should not be held accountable, that unsecured creditors have already received at least as much as they would have received in a Chapter 7 case, and that a modification of the plan is not practical.

As is true under Chapter 11, once all the plan payments have been made, the case will be closed.

The Family Farmer—Chapter 12

Congress devised Chapter 12 of the Bankruptcy Code in 1986 as emergency debt relief for American farmers. Chapter 12 of the Bankruptcy Code has what is called a sunset provision, giving an ending date originally of October 1, 1993. Already once extended by Congress, Chapter 12's provisions will automatically terminate on October 1, 1998 unless further extended.

Family Farmer
An individual receiving more than fifty percent of income, and incurring debts not exceeding $1,500,000 from farming. Or a corporation or partnership where the majority of stock is held by one family and more than eighty percent of the corporation's assets relate to farming, and debts, arising from farming, do not exceed $1,500,000.

Chapter 12 of the Bankruptcy Code is a combination of the most favorable parts of Chapters 11 and 13, granting far greater protection to **family farmers** than to other debtors. Chapter 12 is like Chapter 11 because it gives debtors in possession considerable powers to restructure their debts; and it is like Chapter 13 because relief under it is relatively fast and inexpensive. Because Chapter 12 incorporates by reference many of the provisions of Chapters 11 and 13, it is relatively short.

Family Farmer with Regular Income
A family farmer whose annual income is sufficiently stable and regular to allow it to make payments under a Chapter 12 plan.

Administration   To qualify for Chapter 12 relief, the debtor, who can be an individual, partnership, joint venture, or corporation, must be a **family farmer with regular income.** A family farmer with a regular income must meet certain criteria, as follows. When it passed Chapter 12, Congress considered that these criteria covered most farming operations.

☐ The debtor must have no more than $1,500,000 of secured and unsecured debt. If the debt load exceeds that amount, relief must be sought under Chapter 7 or Chapter 11.

☐ At least eighty percent of the debt must have been incurred from farming operations.

☐ The debtor must have earned at least fifty percent of the previous year's taxable income from farming.

☐ If the debtor is a corporation, at least fifty percent of the outstanding stock must be held by family members engaged in farming. The stock cannot be publicly traded. In addition, at least eighty percent of the corporation's assets must be farm related.

There are a number of benefits of Chapter 12 relief over a Chapter 11 case. They include:

☐ Chapter 12 is cheaper. Currently, the filing fee is only $200 compared to $800 to $1,000 in a Chapter 11 case. In addition, Chapter 12 debtors do not have to pay quarterly fees to the United States trustee's office.

☐ Payments to secured creditors during the administration of the case may be substantially less in Chapter 12 than in Chapter 11. For example, under Chapter 11 the debtor may be required to make sizable payments to the secured creditors to prevent them from obtaining relief from the stay. Under Chapter 12, however, payments to secured creditors need not exceed the reasonable rental value of the collateral. If there is a glut of available farm land in the area, those payments may be minimal.

☐ In Chapter 11, property cannot be sold free of a creditor's valid lien unless the creditor consents or will be paid in full from the sale. Chapter 12 debtors do not need the permission of creditors before selling unnecessary farmland and farm equipment even though the proceeds will be insufficient to pay the secured creditors in full. The sale will, however, require bankruptcy court approval if it is made out of the ordinary course of business.

An individual Chapter 12 debtor will receive a discharge at the end of the case but this discharge is not as expansive as the one granted to Chapter 13 debtors. In fact, it is very close to the discharge given in Chapter 7 because it also excepts from the discharge the types of claims mentioned in Section 523(a). Like Chapter 13, however, Chapter 12 has a provision that grants a discharge to an individual debtor in certain circumstances even if all of the plan payments have not been made.

A trustee is appointed in all Chapter 12 cases. This trustee is similar to a Chapter 13 trustee who monitors payments under a plan, but the trustee in a Chapter 12 case may have greater duties. The Chapter 12 trustee can appear at any hearing concerning sale of estate property and plan confirmation. The court can also order the Chapter 12 trustee to investigate and report on the conduct and financial condition of the debtor and make a determination as to whether the farming operations should continue. Unlike the debtor in Chapter 13, the family farmer in Chapter 12 may be removed for fraud, dishonesty, incompetence, or gross mismanagement, in which case the Chapter 12 trustee may take over responsibility for operating the farm.

The Plan   Confirmation of a plan in a Chapter 12 case is designed to be every bit as quick as it is in Chapter 13. A plan must be filed within ninety days unless the time is extended upon a showing of substantial justification.

A Chapter 12 plan may be filed only by the debtor. The plan must require the submission of all or a portion of future earnings or other future income to the trustee. It must classify claims and provide for priority creditors to be paid in full. In addition, it must provide for all payments to be made within three years, unless the court approves an extension to five years. As under Chapter 13, all the debtor's disposable income must be used to make payments if a creditor objects to the plan. Unlike Chapter 13, Chapter 12 allows the debtor to modify a residential mortgage.

Chapter 12 plans are not voted on by creditors, and they will be confirmed if they meet the requirements of Section 1225. The hearing on confirmation must be concluded not later than forty-five days after the plan is filed. Once all plan payments are made, the Chapter 12 case is closed.

Municipality Reorganizations—Chapter 9

Municipality
A political subdivision, public agency, or instrumentality of a state.

Chapter 9 provides a means for the adjustment of the debts of certain entities known as **municipalities,** which are political subdivisions, public agencies, or instrumentalities of the states. Generally, Chapter 9 operates similarly to Chapter 11 and many provisions of Chapter 11 are incorporated by reference into Chapter 9. Historically, very few Chapter 9 cases have been filed and those that were filed were small. In late 1994, Orange County, California, and an investment fund it operated filed Chapter 9 petitions, which were the largest cases filed since Chapter 9 was enacted in 1978.

Although Chapter 9 is based on Chapter 11, and the ultimate goal of a Chapter 9 is the confirmation of a plan of reorganization, there are some very meaningful differences that tend to give the municiple debtor much more power than other debtors in possession. For example, because it would be improper for the judicial branch of the federal government to replace elected officials, there is no concept of a trustee in Chapter 9 cases. The court may not interfere with any of the municipality's political or governmental powers, or any of its property or revenues. Also, only the municipality may file a plan. Creditors are given the ability to vote to accept or reject the plan, but the only possible remedy if the debtor cannot confirm its plan is dismissal of the case.

Because so few Chapter 9 cases have been filed, it will not be discussed in this book.

☐ THE RULES GOVERNING BANKRUPTCY PRACTICE AND PROCEDURE

Federal Rules of Bankruptcy Procedure

The Bankruptcy Code establishes the substantive rights, duties, and remedies of debtors, creditors, and trustees. It is the Federal Rules of Bankruptcy Procedure (the "Bankruptcy Rules"), however, that establish the procedures on how the rights are exercised, how the duties are fulfilled, and how the remedies are obtained.

Bankruptcy Rules
The rules of practice and procedure governing bankruptcy cases and proceedings drafted by the Judicial Conference of the United States and adopted by the Supreme Court.

The **Bankruptcy Rules** were formulated by the Supreme Court in 1983 to complement the Bankruptcy Code; they are intended to apply in all bankruptcy cases commenced under the Bankruptcy Code. The Rules are divided into parts by subject matter, and each part applies to all the chapters of the Bankruptcy Code. There are over 200 rules divided into nine parts as shown in Exhibit 2.5.

Each Bankruptcy Rule is assigned a four-digit number, the first digit of which provide a key to the part in which the rule resides. For example, Rule 6006, which concerns the assumption or rejection of contracts, is in Part VI. Rule 9013, which covers the form and service of motions, is in Part IX.

It would not be particularly helpful to discuss a Bankruptcy Rule without at the same time discussing the section of the Bankruptcy Code the rule was intended to implement. Therefore, we review each Bankruptcy Rule at the same time as examining the Bankruptcy Code provision to which it relates.

Federal Rules of Civil Procedure

Adversary Proceeding
A type of action that must be commenced by the filing of a complaint.

Part VII of the Bankruptcy Rules concerns adversary proceedings in the bankruptcy court. In bankruptcy practice, **adversary proceeding** is another term for litigation. (See Chapter 6 of this book.) Many of the adversary proceedings in the bank-

Part	Subject
I	Commencement of case; proceedings related to petition and order for relief
II	Officers and administration; notices; meetings; examinations; elections; attorneys; and accountants
III	Claims and distribution to creditors and equity interest holders; plans
IV	The debtor: duties and benefits
V	Bankruptcy courts and clerks
VI	Collection and liquidation of the estate
VII	Adversary proceedings
VIII	Appeals to district court or bankruptcy appellate panel
IX	General provisions

ruptcy court are similar to—if not identical to—nonbankruptcy litigation that is conducted in U.S. district courts and to which the Federal Rules of Civil Procedure apply. Therefore, in large part, Part VII of the Bankruptcy Rules merely incorporates provisions of the Federal Rules of Civil Procedure and applies them to adversary proceedings in bankruptcy court.

Each rule in Part VII of the Bankruptcy Rules is numbered in a way that makes it easy to determine which federal rule has been incorporated in the rule. The key is in the last two digits of the Bankruptcy Rule. The last two digits of the number of a Bankruptcy Rule in Part VII correspond to the number of the Federal Rule of Civil Procedure it incorporates. Thus, Bankruptcy Rule 7003 incorporates Rule 3 of the Federal Rules of Civil Procedure. Furthermore, the incorporation is usually complete. For example, Bankruptcy Rule 7020, entitled Permissive Joinder of Parties, states in full: "Rule 20 F.R.Civ.P. applies in adversary proceedings." This statement means that the full text of Rule 20 of the Federal Rules of Civil Procedure is used to determine the procedures for the permissive joinder of parties in adversary proceedings conducted before the bankruptcy court. Some of the more common rules of the Federal Rules of Civil Procedure incorporated fully by reference into the Bankruptcy Rules are those relating to third-party practice (Bankruptcy Rule 7015), class actions (Bankruptcy Rule 7023), and discovery (Bankruptcy Rules 7026 through 7037).

Not all of the provisions of the Federal Rules of Civil Procedure apply to adversary proceedings in bankruptcy court. In some instances there have been substantial modifications or revisions to accommodate the special nature of bankruptcy proceedings. For example, Bankruptcy Rule 7003 specifically incorporates most of the provisions of Rule 3 of the Federal Rules of Civil Procedure that apply to the service of a summons and a complaint. Some other parts of Rule 3 are not adopted, however, and Bankruptcy Rule 7003 also sets forth additional methods for serving process in adversary proceedings. Bankruptcy Rule 7012 reflects a similar partial incorporation of provisions from its corresponding Federal Rule of Civil Procedure (Rule 12) that apply to defenses and objections. Provisions governing the time for filing a response to a complaint differ from the federal rule, however, and are specifically provided for in Bankruptcy Rule 7003.

Also, many of the Federal Rules of Appellate Practice have been incorporated in Part VIII of the Bankruptcy Rules, which concerns appeals from bankruptcy court orders. (See Chapter 6 of this book.)

Local Rules

Practice before the bankruptcy court is also governed by local rules that each district has developed to address particular issues or problems left uncovered in the Bankruptcy Rules. Local rules for bankruptcy practice are allowed by Bankruptcy Rule 9029, which states that each district may make whatever rules are needed to govern local practice and procedure. The only limitation is that the local rules cannot be inconsistent with the Bankruptcy Rules.

Local rules often deal with topics such as motion practice, pretrial stipulations and orders, related cases, and the like. Some districts have lengthy local rules while others do not. Copies of the local rules are usually available through the local legal press or from the clerk of the bankruptcy court. Local rules are also reprinted at the end of some bankruptcy court reporting services and bankruptcy treatises, but these versions are not always kept up to date. Historically, the numbering of local rules was left up to each district. The Judicial Conference of the United States has now asked that each district renumber its rules in the format of the Bankruptcy Rules; many districts have already done so.

The authors of local rules are usually local district judges; having written the rules, they are therefore likely to be very particular about compliance. As a consequence, it is crucial that a legal assistant be familiar with all the applicable local rules.

General Orders

Closely related to local rules are general orders. General orders are those issued by one or more of the judges in a particular district concerning specific procedures or other issues impacting cases or appearances before the court. Unfortunately, the distribution of general orders often is not as extensive as it is for local rules, and a good practice is to examine the clerk's bulletin board on a regular basis or ask the clerk whether any new general orders have been made.

In addition to general orders, each bankruptcy judge probably has at least one procedure, idiosyncrasy, or pet peeve that must be observed. These practices may be the most important ones to know from a practical standpoint and are often learned only by trial and error. A good relationship with the court clerk usually helps to avoid transgressing the personal policies of the judge.

Official Forms

To facilitate the processing of paperwork in the bankruptcy administration, twenty-one official forms have been developed by the Judicial Conference of the United States. Copies of these official forms are usually published in books and pamphlets containing the text of the Bankruptcy Rules. Some of the official forms are designed for the use of the court clerk. Others are important forms for practitioners; these include petitions, schedules of assets and liabilities, statements of financial affairs, proofs of claim, and ballots for voting on a plan. The more frequently used forms are available on computer software, ready to be completed.

In addition, the Director of the Administrative Office of the United States Court has created other forms that are used in conjunction with the Official Forms. These forms are for the use of the courts and the clerk. The Director's Forms, which are not widely published, are available from the clerk's office or from some software services.

Use of official forms and supplemental forms is obligatory in bankruptcy practice. The rule of substantial compliance applies, however, and Bankruptcy Rule 9009 specifically allows one to alter or combine the forms to fit particular situations.

□ BANKRUPTCY CRIMES

The Bankruptcy Code offers debtors relief from creditor actions and a fresh start. It does not allow debtors to act without any regard for the rights of others or of the government. In fact, an individual debtor may lose the right to a discharge under Section 727 of the Bankruptcy Code if he or she commits certain bad acts in connection with a bankruptcy case. Also, Section 362(b)(1) excludes from the scope of the automatic stay criminal actions against the debtor.

In addition to state or other federal laws that may punish a company or an individual for illegal acts, Congress has enacted several criminal laws that specifically apply to bankruptcy cases. They are codified in five sections of Title 18 of the United States Code.

Section 152 of Title 18 makes it a crime punishable by a fine of not more than $5,000 or imprisonment of not more than five years, or both, to knowingly and fraudulently perform one of the following acts in connection with a bankruptcy.

□ Conceal property of the estate from anyone charged with the control or custody of property, such as a trustee, or from creditors.

□ Make a false oath or account in or in relation to a bankruptcy case.

□ Present a false declaration, certificate, verification, or statement under penalty of perjury in or in relation to a bankruptcy case.

□ Present or use a false proof of claim.

□ Receive a material amount of property from a debtor after the commencement of a bankruptcy case with the intent to defeat the provisions of the Bankruptcy Code.

□ Give, offer, receive, or attempt to obtain money or property, remuneration, compensation, reward, or advantage for acting or forbearing to act in a bankruptcy case.

□ Transfer or conceal any property before but in contemplation of the commencement of a bankruptcy case with the intent to defeat the provisions of the Bankruptcy Code.

□ Either before or in contemplation of the commencement of a bankruptcy case, conceal, destroy, mutilate, falsify, or make a false entry in any recorded information, including books and records, relating to the financial affairs of a debtor.

□ Withhold from any person entitled to possession recorded information, including books and records, relating to the property or financial affairs of a debtor.

Section 153 makes it a crime punishable by a fine of up to $5,000 or imprisonment for up to five years or both, for a trustee, custodian, marshal, attorney, or other officer of the court, to knowingly and fraudulently appropriate for personal use, embezzle, spend, or transfer any property or secrete or destroy any document belonging to the estate.

Under Section 154, if a trustee, custodian, marshal, or other officer of the court knowingly purchases, directly or indirectly, any property of the estate in which it

is involved, or refuses to permit a reasonable opportunity for the inspection of documents and accounts relating to the affairs of the estate when directed by the court to do so, he or she is subject to forfeiture of office and a fine of up to $500.

Section 155 makes it a crime for any party in interest, or any attorney for a party in interest, to knowingly and fraudulently enter into an agreement with another party in interest or its attorney for the purpose of fixing the fees or other compensation to be paid for services performed in a bankruptcy case or other insolvency proceeding supervised by a federal court. The punishment is a fine of not more than $5,000 and imprisonment of not more than one year, or both.

Section 156 provides for a fine or imprisonment of up to one year, or both, of a **bankruptcy petition preparer** who knowingly attempts to disregard the requirement of the Bankruptcy Code or the Bankruptcy Rules. This section was added with the 1994 Amendments. The subject of bankruptcy petition preparers will be discussed in the next chapter.

Section 157, also added with the 1994 Amendments, provides for a fine or imprisonment of up to five years, or both, for a person who devises or tries to devise a fraudulent scheme and in the course of that scheme files a bankruptcy petition or other document in a bankruptcy case or makes a false statement or promise before or after the commencement of a bankruptcy case.

Prosecution of bankruptcy crimes is handled by the United States attorney. Investigation assistance is provided by the United States trustee, the Internal Revenue Service, the Federal Bureau of Investigation, and the United States marshal.

☐ SUMMARY

The Bankruptcy Code is divided into odd numbered chapters, except for Chapter 12. All chapters are further divided into sections. The first one or two digits of a section will tell you in which chapter it is found.

Chapters 1, 3, and 5 contain sections applicable in all bankruptcy cases. Chapter 1 has a number of general provisions including the definitions that are used throughout the Bankruptcy Code. Chapter 3 controls how a case is commenced and administered. Chapter 5 concerns how creditors are paid, what property the debtor may keep, and what claims are enforceable after bankruptcy.

Bankruptcy liquidations are the subject of Chapter 7. In a liquidation, the debtor must deliver all valuable non-exempt property to the bankruptcy trustee. The bankruptcy trustee will sell the property turned over by the debtor and distribute the proceeds to creditors in the order provided in the Bankruptcy Case. The debtor will be discharged from most of the unpaid debts except for those that Congress has decided should always be repaid. In addition, the debtor could lose the discharge if he or she commits serious wrongdoing.

Chapter 9 is devoted to reorganizations of municipal entities such as counties, cities, and special districts. Very few Chapter 9 cases have been filed.

Chapter 11 primarily concerns reorganization of businesses, but it can be used by individuals. In a Chapter 11 case there is not a bankruptcy trustee unless the debtor has committed a wrongdoing. The goal of a Chapter 11 case is to confirm a plan of reorganization that provides for a greater payment to creditors than they would receive in a Chapter 7 case. Creditors vote on the plan and the bankruptcy court will confirm it if a super-majority of creditors vote yes and the plan otherwise meets the requirements of the Bankruptcy Code.

Chapter 12 and Chapter 13 are small scale reorganizations. Chapter 12 is for farmers and Chapter 13 is for individuals. Each chapter has debt limit and other

qualifications for debtors. The goal in these cases is also a plan of reorganization, but a much less complicated one than is found in a Chapter 11 case. Creditors will not vote on the plan but the bankruptcy court must ensure that the plan complies with the Bankruptcy Code.

The Federal Rules of Bankruptcy Procedure implement the provisions of the Bankruptcy Code. There are over 200 rules divided into nine parts.

The Judicial Conference of the United States and the Director of the Administrative Office of the United States Courts have developed forms for the more common papers filed in a bankruptcy case. Parties are required to use these forms or ones that substantially resemble them.

☐ KEY TERMS

Abandonment	Disclosure Statement	Nondischargeable Claims
Abstention	Disposable Income	Ordinary Course of Business
Adequate Information	Entity	Person
Adversary Proceeding	Equity Committee	Plan Exclusivity
Ballot	Exemptions	Plan of Reorganization
Bankruptcy Rules	Family Farmer	Plan Proponent
Claim	Family Farmer with Regular	Proof of Claim
Cram Down	Income	Regular Income
Creditors' Committee	Municipality	Setoff
Debtor in Possession	No Asset Case	Wage Earner Reorganization
Discharge		

☐ IMPROVE YOUR UNDERSTANDING

1. Make a brief outline of Chapters 1, 3, and 5. Then, without looking at the Bankruptcy Code, determine in what chapter and, if applicable, which subchapter answers to the following questions would likely be found.

a. What is the deadline for bringing an avoiding power action?

b. Who may file a claim on behalf of a creditor?

c. What is the definition of an indenture?

d. Need a debtor's transaction with his or her attorneys be disclosed?

e. What happens if the trustee dies?

f. May the debtor enter into a new lease for its business premises?

g. When used in the Bankruptcy Code, is the phrase "may not" prohibitive or permissive?

h. Can the trustee obtain a loan secured by the estate's property?

i. How many creditors does it take to file an involuntary bankruptcy case?

2. Consult the Bankruptcy Code to see if your answers to Question 1 are correct.

3. Find the section of Bankruptcy Code concerning the following topics:

a. How the trustee sells stock belonging to the estate.

b. The authority of the trustee to operate the debtor's business.

c. The grounds for dismissal of a Chapter 7 case.

d. The definition of commodity options dealer.

e. The role of a creditor's committee in a Chapter 7 case.

f. The taxable year of the Chapter 7 debtor.

4. Answer the following questions *true* or *false*:

a. Chapter 7 requires liquidation.

b. The interim trustee will always serve for the duration of the case.

c. Claims for fines, penalties and punitive damages are paid before payment is made to creditors who file late claims.

d. Alimony and child support claims are nondischargeable.

e. Trustees must be admitted to practice law in

the district in which the bankruptcy court sits.

f. Trustees are required to object to claims.

g. The trustee does not need to sell all non-exempt property of the estate.

h. The debtor is only entitled to keep his or her house to make a fresh start.

i. The priorities in distribution in a Chapter 7 case are set out in Section 727.

j. The debtor's refusal to obey an order of the court is a ground to deny discharge.

k. The debtor's invocation of the Fifth Amendment privilege against self-incrimination will prevent the discharge.

5. Match the following topics to the correct section:

Disclosure statements	1112
Appointment of a Chapter 11 trustee	1127
Conversion of a Chapter 11 case	1104
Modification of a Chapter 11 plan	1101
Exclusivity period	1121
Distributions under a plan	1109
Right to be heard	1143
Definition of substantial consummation	1125
Collective bargaining agreements	1113

6. Answer the following questions about Chapter 11:

a. How long does the exclusivity period last? Can it be extended?

b. What duties of a trustee are not required of the debtor in possession?

c. Is there any deadline by which a plan of reorganization must be filed?

d. What is the role of a creditors' committee in a Chapter 11 case? Does it make any difference if a trustee has been appointed?

e. Why would a debtor in possession consent to the appointment of a Chapter 11 trustee?

f. Section 1123(b)(4) expressly allows a plan to provide for the liquidation of all the debtor's assets. Why would a debtor choose to liquidate in a Chapter 11 case rather than in a Chapter 7 case?

7. Answer the following questions about Chapter 13:

a. Are individuals living on Social Security payments eligible for Chapter 13 relief?

b. May a partnership of two individuals file a Chapter 13 petition?

c. What are the debt limits for individuals who want to commence a Chapter 13 case?

d. What are the limits on a Chapter 13 trustee's compensation?

e. May the Chapter 13 trustee propose a plan?

f. Is there a mandatory number of classes of creditors that a Chapter 13 plan must have?

g. May a Chapter 13 plan stretch out the payments to the Internal Revenue Service or must the IRS be paid first?

h. May a Chapter 13 plan modify the rights of a creditor whose claim is secured by the debtor's houseboat?

i. The debtor owes his mother $100 but does not want her to know about the bankruptcy case or receive payments from the Chapter 13 trustee. If the mother's claim is discovered, can the plan be confirmed?

j. Is there a minimum number of months or years for the payments to creditors under a Chapter 13 plan? Is there a maximum?

k. After filing a Chapter 13 petition, the debtor negligently ran over his neighbor's toe. If he acknowledges liability, can he provide for the payment of his neighbor's claim against him in his Chapter 13 plan?

l. Under what circumstances will a Chapter 13 debtor receive a discharge even if all the terms of the plan of reorganization have not been complied with?

m. Compare Section 1325 to Section 1129. What are the similarities? What are the differences?

8. Answer the following questions about Chapter 12:

a. Is the $1,500,000 maximum debt limit for Chapter 12 eligibility limited to noncontingent and liquidated claims?

b. Does a dairy operator qualify as a family farmer?

c. Does a farmer need a family to be a Chapter 12 family farmer?

d. Must the Chapter 12 trustee be a farmer?

e. What are the differences between Section 1225 and Section 1325?

f. Can the Chapter 12 trustee propose a plan?

g. Can the Chapter 12 trustee file a motion to remove the debtor in possession? If so, on what grounds?

h. Does Section 361 apply in Chapter 12 cases?

i. Is a debt arising from embezzlement dischargeable in a Chapter 12 case?

j. What are the factors to be considered in de-

termining the reasonable rent to be paid to a secured creditor as adequate protection?

9. What is the subject of each of the following?

   a. Bankruptcy Rule 1014

   b. Bankruptcy Rule 3007

   c. Bankruptcy Rule 7024

   d. Bankruptcy Rule 8006

   e. Bankruptcy Rule 9019

   f. Federal Rule of Civil Procedure 4

   g. Federal Rule of Appellate Procedure 8

   h. Official Form 8

   i. Official Form 18

10. List three subjects covered by local rules or general orders of the district where you work.

11. Assume Ford Motor Company files a bankruptcy petition and a trustee is appointed. May the trustee purchase a new Ford Motor automobile without violating Title 18?

12. Just before filing a bankruptcy petition, the debtor accidentally sets fire to all his or her books and records. Has a crime been committed?

THE ROLE OF THE LEGAL ASSISTANT IN BANKRUPTCY PRACTICE

Legal assistants may participate in virtually every aspect of a bankruptcy case. Their participation is limited only by the capability and eagerness of the legal assistant, and by the willingness of the attorney to delegate. This chapter explores the use of legal assistants in many common areas of bankruptcy practice.

The legal assistant's role in bankruptcy cases is very broad for a number of reasons. First, bankruptcy practice involves a great deal of form work. Courts require certain standardized forms. Practitioners use other widely published forms to convey information to the court. Law school training is rarely required to complete these forms properly; they usually can be filled out by a paralegal under an attorney's supervision.

Second, bankruptcy cases move through the courts rapidly and clients need attorneys who can get things done quickly. Without paralegals, a busy lawyer could not satisfy the client's needs or the court's timetable.

Third, the use of legal assistants enables lawyers to more effectively engage in those activities that only lawyers may perform in bankruptcy court, such as making court appearances.

Fourth, use of paralegals lowers the cost of legal services for clients and for the bankruptcy estate because the billing rate for paralegals is approximately one-half of the rate for attorneys. Lower fees also help a law firm remain competitive. Further, paralegal use is mandatory in many courts where the judges refuse to approve fees for lawyers who perform services that could have been delegated to paralegals.

Community Legal Services

Community legal service agencies or legal aid offices are active in representing low income individuals who have financial problems and who may need to file a bank-

ruptcy case. Legal assistants in those offices are often given the responsibility for preparing and managing consumer bankruptcy cases. In a Chapter 7 case, the legal assistant may attend, if not conduct, the initial client interview and thereafter may maintain client contact to obtain all the information necessary to prepare and file a petition, the schedules, and all of the other forms necessary. After the petition has been filed with the court, the legal assistant may be responsible for advising the client of the date, time, and place of the first meeting of creditors; preparing the client to answer questions that may be asked at the meeting; attending the first meeting of creditors; drafting reaffirmation agreements; avoiding liens; solving problems such as utility cut offs, garnishments, repossessions, and foreclosures; and monitoring the case until its end.

In addition to the services just described, the legal assistant helping represent a debtor in a Chapter 13 bankruptcy case may draft a plan of reorganization. The legal assistant may also monitor plan payments, respond to the questions of the client or the creditors, and follow the progress of the case to discharge and closing.

Debtors in consumer bankruptcy cases are very anxious about their financial situations. Legal assistants provide a valuable service by being available to answer debtors' questions, and serve as debtors' guides through the often difficult and stressful experience of a bankruptcy case. Often an understanding and supportive tone from a person who quickly returns a phone call is all that is required to reduce a debtor's anxiety.

A paralegal involved in debtor representation will also have to field many calls from creditors. Some merely need the case number, the amount in which their claim is scheduled, the date and time of the first meeting of creditors, or other information the paralegal can readily provide. Regrettably, in other instances creditors will be extremely angry about the bankruptcy case, will blame the debtor's attorneys and their staff as much as the debtor, and will express that anger to anyone who answers the phone. Although the temptation will be great, responding in kind to an angry call from a creditor will not diffuse the situation. If the creditor or the creditor's lawyer is determined to be rude, the only response is to terminate the call as quickly and politely as possible.

Legal Departments of Corporations, Banking and Lending Institutions, and Government Agencies

The bankruptcy legal assistant working with the legal staff of private corporations, public agencies, and lending institutions may be responsible for such tasks as preparing and filing proofs of claims on behalf of the employer, providing documents to support claims, and protecting the employer's interests with respect to unpaid taxes and unexpired leases. The legal assistant also may be required to research dischargeability issues, to review bankruptcy notices and pleadings received, and to obtain periodic updates on the progress of the case toward final resolution. In many private companies and public agencies, paralegals have responsibility for drafting various motions that may be used in bankruptcy cases, such as a motion to compel the rejection or assumption of an unexpired lease or a motion to lift the automatic stay.

Law Firms

Most legal assistants active in bankruptcy matters are employed by law firms. Many law firms concentrate on a particular type of representation—creditors, debtors, committees or trustees. Other law firm clients may include creditors, debtors, com-

mittees and trustees in different cases. Legal assistants employed by law firms with a diverse clientele must be versatile and knowledgeable in all areas of bankruptcy practice.

Representing Creditors

Many law firms represent creditors in bankruptcy cases. These clients might be suppliers of goods and services, public utilities, property owners, banks and other secured creditors, or other interested parties. Paralegals working in these firms have responsibilities similar to those of legal assistants employed by in-house legal departments of private corporations and public agencies. In addition, the law firm paralegal duties will include keeping the client informed of events in the course of the bankruptcy case. In a firm that has an active creditor practice, a paralegal may be responsible for drafting all relief from stay motions and objections to plans and preparing the attorney for trial.

Representing Debtors

Legal assistants working in firms that represent debtors in bankruptcy perform many of the consumer debtor services discussed in this chapter. They also help lawyers commence bankruptcy cases by attending initial meetings with clients, by gathering and reviewing information from the client and the client's representatives, and by preparing drafts of the petition and related documents.

The role of legal assistants in representing debtors depends largely on the size and complexity of the cases in which they are involved. Usually, their functions include establishing filing systems for complex cases, responding to routine questions from creditors and other interested parties, preparing applications for fees of attorneys and other professionals who provide services to the bankruptcy estates, helping with the sale of assets, managing the claims objection process, and assisting counsel in adversary proceedings commenced by or against the estates.

After the commencement of a Chapter 11 case, the legal assistant may also establish time frames and responsibilities for filing financial reports, hiring accountants and other professionals, assuming or rejecting leases, collecting accounts receivable, preparing liquidation analyses for the reorganization plan and disclosure statement, preparing pleadings to fix cut-off dates for filing proofs of claim, analyzing claims, filing objections to claims, settling disputed claims, and preparing for the distribution of money and assets to creditors.

Representing Committees

Some law firms regularly represent creditors' or equity holders' committees in Chapter 11 cases. Legal assistants in these firms may help their employers gather and analyze information about the debtor's secured and unsecured debt and they may review monthly financial reports filed by the debtor to chart its financial condition.

A legal assistant in one of these firms may also serve as the secretary to the creditors' committee. In this capacity, the legal assistant arranges for and attends meetings of the committee, participates in conference calls, takes notes at meetings, prepares and distributes minutes of meetings, and generally keeps the members apprised of developments in the case. The legal assistant also tracks developments in the case for the committee by following and summarizing motions filed and orders entered in the bankruptcy court.

Paralegals in firms that represent committees also perform services respecting adversary proceedings by preparing reports on specific issues, researching points of law, assisting the examination and analysis of the debtor's records, and by preparing liquidation analyses. The paralegal may also participate in the solicitation of ballots accepting or rejecting a plan of reorganization by organizing mailings, recording results, and filing returned ballots with the court.

Finally, legal assistants in firms representing committees help prepare applications to obtain fees for the firm and secure reimbursement of expenses incurred by the members of the committee in attending meetings.

Representing Trustees

Legal assistants who work in law firms that represent bankruptcy trustees prepare applications and orders for retaining professionals such as appraisers, auctioneers, and accountants. They also prepare the papers that are used to secure payment for the services provided by these individuals. Legal assistants in trustee counsel firms also assist in document production and control in contested matters or adversary proceedings, analyze and prepare objections to claims, prepare applications and orders fixing the final dates for filing administrative claims, and assist in bankruptcy litigation. They also assist their firms in executing on judgments to collect accounts receivable and to recover on preferences and other voidable transfers. Finally, they prepare pleadings and other documents necessary for the sale of assets.

Independent Legal Assistants

It is increasingly common for legal assistants to establish their own firms, providing their services on a contract basis to other legal service providers and, in some instances directly to consumers of legal services. Indeed, many states are examining the merits of licensing paralegals and allowing them to perform certain types of legal services without attorney supervision. Qualified paralegals can deliver high quality, low cost legal services to people of low to moderate means whose legal needs are not too complicated.

For the most part, bankruptcy is no different than any other area of law in which independent legal assistants can play a valuable role in the market. One of the types of legal services being considered which legal assistants could be licensed to perform is consumer bankruptcy relief. There is however, a statutory regulation unique to bankruptcy practice that needs to be considered.

Many districts are experiencing waves of repetitive and abusive filings by individual debtors for the sole purpose of imposing and reimposing the automatic stay in order to stop a foreclosure or an eviction. Most commonly, the debtor intends to do only the minimum amount necessary in order to commence the case and nothing more. For example, the debtor will commence the case by filing only a petition but will never follow up by filing the schedules or a plan. For this reason, the cases are frequently referred to as **face sheet filings.**

Debtors in face sheet filing cases state that they are acting without a lawyer, which is often referred to by the latin phrase **in propria persona,** shortened to "pro per." While it is true that they are not represented by counsel, these debtors did not stumble accidently into bankruptcy court. In most instances they were assisted by an independent legal assistant who helped the debtor prepare the petition and other documents necessary to start the bankruptcy case but nothing

Face sheet filings
The commencement of a bankruptcy case by filing only the minimal amount of papers required, usually just the petition.

In propria persona
A latin term used to describe a person acting without an attorney. Usually shortened to "pro per."

else. These legal assistants, known as bankruptcy petition preparers or more derisively, bankruptcy mills, often solicit clients by contacting people whose names appear on lists of eviction or foreclosure proceedings or by blanketing distressed economic areas with flyers claiming an ability to bring debt relief.

The primary problem with bankruptcy petition preparers is that they usually help commence cases for people who have already filed one or more bankruptcy case and are ineligible to refile, or who have no intention of completing the bankruptcy case but only want the advantage of delay. These cases clog the court and defraud creditors. At the same time, most bankruptcy petition preparers also defraud the debtor. They charge many times more than the value of the limited services they provide. Moreover, sometimes debtors in face sheet filing cases will appear in court and claim to be completely ignorant of the commencement of the case. They testify that they responded to a flyer offering eviction defense services, signed some papers they did not read, and have found themselves in bankruptcy unwillingly.

In the 1994 Amendments, Congress tried to stem the flood of abusive filings by prohibiting some of the conduct frequently attributed to bankruptcy petition preparers. To do this the 1994 Amendments added a new Section 110 to the Bankruptcy Code. Section 110 defines a bankruptcy petition preparer to be a person, other than an attorney or an employee of an attorney, who prepares a petition or other document to be filed by a debtor in a bankruptcy case for money. Section 110 requires bankruptcy petition preparers to:

☐ Sign the documents they prepare;

☐ Print the name, address and Social Security Number of the responsible individual on all documents they prepare;

☐ Give the debtor copies of all documents at the time they are signed;

☐ Not sign any documents on behalf of the debtor;

☐ Not use the word "legal" or any similar term in any advertisements, or advertise under any category that includes the word "legal" or similar term;

☐ Not collect the court fees in connection with filing the petition; and

☐ Within ten days after the filing of a petition, file a declaration under penalty of perjury disclosing any fee received from the debtor within the last year.

If the bankruptcy petition preparer fails to do what is required by Section 110, it can be fined $500 for each failure. In addition, the court can disallow any fee that is in excess of the value of the services provided. That, however, is not the limit of a bankruptcy petition preparer's liability.

If a bankruptcy case is dismissed because of the negligence or intentional disregard of the Bankruptcy Rules by a bankruptcy petition preparer, if the bankruptcy petition preparer violates Section 110, or if the bankruptcy petition preparer commits any fraudulent, unfair, or deceptive act, the court can order the bankruptcy petition preparer to pay to the debtor the debtor's actual damages, the greater of $2,000 or twice the amount the debtor paid to the bankruptcy petition preparer, and attorneys' fees. If a trustee or creditor brings the bankruptcy petition preparer's conduct to the attention of the court, the bankruptcy petition preparer must also pay the trustee or creditor $1,000 in addition to its attorneys' fees.

Section 110 also provides for injunctive relief in addition to damages. Upon the request of the debtor, trustee, creditor or the United States trustee, the court can enjoin future violations of Section 110 if it finds:

☐ The bankruptcy petition preparer violated Section 110, misrepresented his or her experience or education as a bankruptcy petition preparer, or engaged in any other fraudulent, unfair, or deceptive conduct; and

☐ Injunctive relief is appropriate to prevent the recurrence of such conduct.

In the appropriate cases, the court can even enjoin the bankruptcy petition preparer from ever acting as a bankruptcy petition preparer in the future.

☐ ETHICS IN BANKRUPTCY PRACTICE

Conflicts are common in bankruptcy cases because they involve so many different parties, each of whom may have competing interests in the debtor's estate. The rules of ethics governing resolution of conflict issues for lawyers are equally applicable to legal assistants.

Some of these ethical considerations are found in the Bankruptcy Code and the Bankruptcy Rules. For example, the Bankruptcy Code prohibits fee splitting among attorneys, trustees, and other professionals. This rule does not prevent an attorney from hiring paralegals as employees of a law firm and including compensation for their professional services in an application for approval of fees from the bankruptcy court. This rule does prevent a bankruptcy attorney from associating a freelance paralegal to work in a bankruptcy case and applying for fees to cover the services of the attorney and the paralegal. A legal assistant who is not an employee of an attorney or a law firm and who performs services in the bankruptcy case must be employed pursuant to a bankruptcy court order and must file a separate fee application.

Ex parte meetings and communications with the bankruptcy court by parties in interest or their attorneys concerning matters affecting a particular case or proceeding are forbidden by the Bankruptcy Rules. For example, it would be improper to call a bankruptcy judge for the purpose of discussing a pending matter without the participation of adverse parties. It is important to be aware of this rule because legal assistants frequently process pleadings through the clerk's office and act as liaisons between the court and the attorney.

Ex parte
A latin term used to describe an act done without notice to other parties.

The more common ethical problems paralegals face arise not from contact with the courts or attorneys but with debtor clients. Because the legal assistant may have so much interaction with the client, and because the attorney may seem intimidating to the client, the legal assistant is often more likely than the attorney to be asked about improper activities. Although there are some grey areas in the application of ethics to bankruptcy practice, there are some absolutes:

1. No information should be knowingly omitted from the schedules that must be filed with the court. For various reasons, clients sometimes say that they do not want a particular debt disclosed. The paralegal must, however, ensure that all assets and debts are properly disclosed.

2. No false information of any kind should be submitted to the court or given to other parties. More often than not lies in papers filed with the court are discovered and the ramifications are much more severe than they would be if the correct information was provided initially.

3. Documents should not be backdated. A legal assistant should never aid a client in trying to show that an asset was transferred earlier in time than it actually was.

4. Documents should never be modified to disguise or change their original provisions unless all parties to the document agree. A client may say that the document does not express the parties true intent and should be changed before the bankruptcy filing so that there are no problems later. Changing a document in this manner will almost always lead to greater problems.

5. Documents should be fully completed before they are signed by a client. Never leave blanks that will be filled in later. If the information in such blanks is ever challenged, the client will almost always blame the person who filled in the blanks.

6. Unless approved by the attorney as part of prebankruptcy planning, the debtor's property should not be transferred to another person on the eve of the bankruptcy filing. Even if it is transferred, it should be disclosed in the proper space in the schedules.

7. Any confidential information about the bankruptcy case must remain confidential unless the client allows the information to be shared. Telling any person other than the debtor's attorney information the client provided in confidence violates the attorney–client evidence privilege.

8. Do not become personally involved with the client.

9. Do not hold money or other assets for a client so that they cannot be found by creditors.

10. Insure the client understands what he or she is signing. Make it a practice to give them copies of all documents signed.

When in doubt on a particular issue, consult the attorney. Even then, if the attorney asks the legal assistant to perform an act that the legal assistant believes is inappropriate, he or she should take all reasonable steps to avoid acting improperly.

☐ SUMMARY

Legal assistants are particularly valuable in bankruptcy practice. Bankruptcy knowledgeable legal assistants are employed by community legal service agencies, in-house at corporations, banks and government agencies, as well as law firms. Independent legal assistants are increasingly common. Legal assistants are active in debtor, creditor, committee, and trustee representation.

In addition to general ethical considerations, special rules govern the use and practice of legal assistants in bankruptcy law. Section 110 of the Bankruptcy Code has detailed rules concerning bankruptcy petition preparers not employed by an attorney.

☐ KEY TERMS

Ex parte	Face sheet filings	In propria persona

☐ IMPROVE YOUR UNDERSTANDING

Review the list of legal assistant functions below. For each function note whether it would be part of a job description of a legal assistant employed by a law firm representing creditors, committees, or debtors.

1. Attend initial client interview.

2. Prepare list of twenty largest unsecured creditors.

3. Prepare corporate resolution authorizing filing of Chapter 11 case.

4. Maintain calendar of important dates.

5. Review plan of reorganization for structure, classification of claims, and discrepancies.

6. Monitor documents produced by client.

7. Monitor payments to creditors.

8. Prepare order allowing or disallowing claims.

9. Prepare proof of claim.

10. Prepare request for special notice.

11. Draft notices and other routine pleadings.

12. Review clerk's docket.

13. Review advance sheets and report on new significant decisions.

THE BUILDING
BLOCKS OF
BANKRUPTCY

There are many important topics in bankruptcy, all of which will be explored in later chapters. Two topics, the automatic stay and executory contracts, are so important to an understanding of virtually all other bankruptcy topics that they are examined separately in this chapter. In addition, a bankruptcy legal assistant will need an understanding of the law of secured transactions. An introduction to that law is provided in this chapter.

☐ AUTOMATIC STAY

In General

Automatic Stay
The injunction that becomes effective upon the filing of a bankruptcy petition (whether voluntarily or involuntarily) and that prevents virtually all actions by creditors to collect their claims, enforce their liens, or exercise control over the debtor's property.

The most important benefit a debtor has in a bankruptcy case is the **automatic stay.** The automatic stay is an injunction that prevents anyone from doing anything to interfere with the debtor or the debtor's property. This includes repossessions, litigation, foreclosures, or even demand letters. In a reorganization case, the automatic stay gives the debtor some time to reorganize its business, unburdened by the demands of creditors. In a liquidation case, the automatic stay keeps the creditors at bay while the debtor's assets are liquidated. The automatic stay also reduces the cost of the liquidation or reorganization since the debtor or the trustee will not be compelled to defend litigation in many different locations.

The automatic stay also helps creditors. It prevents a race to the courthouse by stopping all further efforts to collect claims from the debtor. This enables creditors to be treated as equally as is possible.

Automatic Stay Provisions

The Bankruptcy Code lists specific acts that are automatically stayed by the filing of a bankruptcy case; it also lists acts that are not stayed. These are described briefly in the following sections.

Acts That Are Stayed   Section 362(a) lists eight separate acts of creditors that are prohibited. Some of these prohibited acts would be against the debtor, some against the property of the debtor, and some against the property of the estate which is not always the same as property of the debtor. For example, exempt property is property of the debtor but not property of the estate. The prohibitions in Section 362(a) of the Bankruptcy Code, appear in the following order:

1. The commencement or continuation of legal proceedings of virtually any kind against the debtor.
2. Any attempt to collect existing judgments against the debtor or the estate's property.
3. Any act to obtain possession or control of property of the estate.
4. Any act to create, perfect, or enforce liens against property of the estate.
5. Any act to impose or enforce liens on the debtor's property that secure a prebankruptcy claim.
6. Any attempt to collect debts against the debtor created before the filing of the petition.
7. The setoff of any prebankruptcy debts due to the debtor against claims due from the debtor.
8. Proceedings in the United States tax court concerning the debtor.

The eight prohibitions overlap, and more than one provision may apply to a particular act. For example several provisions of Section 362(a) prevent the debtor from being sued on an old debt. It would be prohibited by provisions 1 and 6 listed above. An attempt to repossess the debtor's car would be precluded by provisions 3 and 4 if the car was not exempt and provision 6 if it was.

Acts That Are Not Stayed   The automatic stay provisions of the Bankruptcy Code do not prevent all creditor activities. In fact, Section 362(b) of the Bankruptcy Code lists eighteen specific acts that are not stayed by the filing of a bankruptcy case. The six most common exceptions to the automatic stay found in Section 362(b) are:

1. Commencing or continuing criminal proceedings against the debtor.
2. Establishing the right to or collecting alimony, maintenance, or support from property that is not part of the bankruptcy estate.
3. Actions by governmental units to enforce police or regulatory powers, such as environmental controls, consumer safety regulations, and antifraud measures.
4. Tax audits.
5. Issuing tax deficiency notices to the debtor by a governmental unit.
6. Eviction of the debtor from commercial real property under a terminated lease.

Effective Period of the Stay   The automatic stay becomes effective the very instant a bankruptcy petition is filed, regardless of whether the petition is a voluntary

petition filed by the debtor or an involuntary petition filed by the creditors. The moment the stay is in place it is binding on all creditors, even those who have no knowledge of the commencement of the bankruptcy case.

When the automatic stay stops depends on whether the stay is applied to the debtor, the debtor's property, or property of the estate. The stay may be gone as against the debtor yet remain in effect against property of the estate. Each element must be analyzed separately. For example, a stay against property of the estate terminates automatically when the property is no longer property of the estate. If the trustee abandons the property, it is no longer property of the estate and secured creditors may enforce their liens—provided they can do so without violating the stay against the debtor, which is not terminated by the abandonment. Exhibit 4.1 demonstrates how each element should be viewed separately.

The stay terminates against property of the debtor when the bankruptcy case is closed or dismissed. It terminates against the debtor upon the granting or denying of a discharge. Hence, in a Chapter 7 case, the stay terminates against the property and the debtor if and when the trustee abandons all the property and the debtor obtains a discharge.

Secured creditors seldom are content to wait until a case is closed before enforcing their liens against the debtor's property. Typically, secured creditors want the automatic stay lifted as quickly as possible, which can sometimes be accomplished. Section 362(d) of the Bankruptcy Code authorizes the court, on the motion of an interested party and following a hearing, to grant relief from the automatic stay for good cause, such as a lack of adequate protection of the creditor's interest in the property. A creditor may also obtain relief from the automatic stay with respect to an act against property if the debtor does not have equity in such property and if the property is not necessary to an effective reorganization. Typically, creditors seek relief from automatic stays on both grounds. In the 1994 Amendments, Congress made it easier for secured creditors to obtain relief from stay in cases involving real estate. These changes are discussed in Chapter 12 of this book.

Motions to lift the automatic stay provide the most common type of litigation in bankruptcy court. The practice and procedures involved in such motions are covered in Bankruptcy Code Sections 362(d)–(e) and Chapter 12 of this textbook.

Scope of the Stay   The automatic stay is exclusively for the benefit of the debtor, the debtor's property, and property of the estate. The protection of the automatic stay does not extend to others. If a creditor lends money to two persons and only one of them declares bankruptcy, the creditor may pursue the other party to enforce the debt. Similarly, when a corporate debtor files for bankruptcy protection, the automatic stay does not prohibit the creditors from pursuing any legitimate claims against the corporation's officers and directors. If a partnership files a bankruptcy petition, a creditor can still sue the partners.

There are exceptions to these provisions. In Chapter 13 cases, the automatic stay prevents creditors from enforcing debts not only against the debtor but also against others who may be liable for the debts. Examples are cosigners and guarantors. On a case-by-case basis, the court may also expand the automatic stay to prohibit acts by creditors that are not specifically covered by the automatic stay.

Violation of the Stay   Generally, acts done in violation of an automatic stay are void and of no effect. For example, if a secured creditor forecloses on a parcel of real property after the commencement of a bankruptcy case, the foreclosure is invalid and the debtor still owns the property. If a car is repossessed in violation

■ EXHIBIT 4.1
Is the Automatic Stay in Effect?

	Bankruptcy Petition Filed	Trustee Abandons Property of the Estate	Debtor Exempts Property	Court Gives Bank the Right to Foreclose on Property of the Estate	Debtor Obtains a Discharge	Debtor is Denied a Discharge	Case Closed
Acts Against the Debtor or the Debtor's Property	Yes. The automatic stay will go into effect the instant the case is filed.	Yes. If property is abandoned by the trustee, it becomes property of the debtor.	Yes. Exempt property ceases to be property of the estate and becomes property of the debtor.	Yes. The automatic stay protecting the debtor will still be in place. The creditor can foreclose on the property but still cannot sue the debtor.	No. Once the debtor has been discharged, he or she no longer has the benefit of the automatic stay. Note though that if a debt has been discharged it is no longer enforceable against the debtor.	No. If the debtor is denied a discharge, the automatic stay protecting the debtor and his or her property is no longer in effect.	No. The dismissal or closure of a bankruptcy case ends the automatic stay. Whether or not debts can be pursued depends on whether the debtor received a discharge.
Acts Against Property of the Estate	Yes. The automatic stay will go into effect the instant the case is filed.	No. Once property of the estate is abandoned, it is no longer property of the estate and the automatic stay will not prevent creditor actions.	No. Once property is exempt, it is no longer property of the estate.	No. The automatic stay is gone.	Yes. The debtor's discharge will not lift the automatic stay that protects property of the estate.	Yes. Again, the debtor's discharge does not impact whether property of the estate is effected.	No. Once a case is closed or dismissed, there no longer is property of the estate.

of the automatic stay, the repossession is invalid and the car must be returned to the debtor. Some courts say that acts in violation of the automatic stay are merely voidable rather than void. In these jurisdictions the debtor must take some action to undo the effect of a creditor's violation of the automatic stay.

Not every act done in technical violation of an automatic stay is void or voidable. The Bankruptcy Code provides that a transfer of real property in violation of the automatic stay cannot be avoided if it was made to a good faith purchaser who did not know of the bankruptcy case and who paid a fair price, unless, before the transfer, notice of the bankruptcy petition was recorded in the county where the property is located. If less than a fair price was paid for the property, the purchaser may be compelled to return the property, but it will retain a lien on the property for the value given.

A creditor who willfully violates the automatic stay may be liable for damages to any individual injured by the violation. Creditors who commit innocent violations of the automatic stay are unlikely to be compelled to pay damages.

☐ EXECUTORY CONTRACTS AND UNEXPIRED LEASES

In General

In addition to the automatic stay, Congress provided another tool for the protection of creditors in liquidation cases and for the revitalization of business enterprises in reorganization cases. It is the power to avoid performance under **executory contracts** and **unexpired leases.** This authority is found in Section 365 of the Bankruptcy Code, which provides that the trustee will not be bound by an executory contract or lease of the debtor unless it is expressly adopted by the trustee. The other party to the contract or lease may have a claim for damages for breach of the agreement, but the estate will not be forced to perform. A debtor in possession in a reorganization case has the same power to avoid performing under executory contracts and unexpired leases.

The scope of Section 365 includes leases of real and personal property whose terms have not expired and contracts that are executory. An executory contract is not defined in the Bankruptcy Code but is commonly thought of as one in which there is sufficient performance remaining on each side so that if there was a breach by one party it would excuse the other party from performing. This definition of an executory contract was first suggested by Professor Vern Countryman, and it is known as the Countryman test. The following are some examples of what are and what are not executory contracts:

☐ A supply contract is an executory contract. An example of a supply contract would be an agreement by a manufacturer to sell to a builder the concrete it requires each month for a set price. If the selling party fails to deliver the concrete, the buyer is excused from paying.

☐ A management contract is an executory contract. A management contract is an agreement by the owner of property to pay another person or firm to manage the property on the owner's behalf. If the owner failed to pay for the service, the manager would not have to perform further management services. Conversely, if the manager stopped caring for the property, the owner would be relieved of the obligation to make further payments under the contract.

☐ A promissory note is not an executory contract. A promissory note is evidence of an agreement to repay money already lent. The lender fully performs

Executory Contract
An agreement between two parties in which sufficient performance remains on each side such that failure of one party to perform will excuse performance by the other.

Unexpired Lease
A lease whose term has not been reached prior to its rejection or assumption.

by lending the money and there is nothing that could relieve the maker from paying.

The power to avoid an executory contract or unexpired lease need not be used by the trustee or the debtor in possession. Whether one exercises the option to avoid depends on the circumstances of the particular case. For example, assume the debtor was in the business of buying tomatoes and processing them into tomato sauce. The trustee is operating the debtor's business. If the current market price of the same type of tomatoes that the debtor has agreed to purchase under a supply contract is lower than the contract price, the trustee would want to avoid the contract and purchase tomatoes on the market at the lower price. On the other hand, if the market price for tomatoes is more than the contract price, the trustee would insist on performance of the supply contract by the other party. In the lease context, the debtor may have a long term lease for warehouse space that was entered into when lease rates were low. The trustee will want to keep that lease. If the lease was entered into when rents were high, the trustee will want to dispose of the lease and the obligation to pay the high rents.

If the trustee or the debtor in possession does not want to be bound by an executory contract or an unexpired lease because it is uneconomical or otherwise burdensome, the contract or lease must be rejected. If the trustee or the debtor in possession wants to be bound by an executory contract or an unexpired lease, the contract or lease must be assumed. The timing and procedural rules for assumption and rejection are very different.

Rejection

The mere fact that a contract is executory or that the term of a lease has not expired does not alone justify rejection of the agreement. The trustee or the debtor in possession is required to exercise good judgment and there must be a legitimate reason for rejecting the contract or the lease. This is not a difficult test to meet; it is met by proof that the trustee can obtain a better deal elsewhere or that rejection will save the estate money. Application of the test, however, will prevent the trustee or the debtor in possession from rejecting a lease or contract for the purpose of entering into a new, more expensive agreement with an affiliated person.

The **rejection** of an executory contract or an unexpired lease is treated like any other breach of the agreement except that the party entitled to the debtor's performance cannot obtain a court order requiring the debtor to perform as would be true outside of bankruptcy. In order to preserve its damage claim, the other party to the contract or lease must file a proof of claim with the estate. The claim will be treated as if it arose before the commencement of the case and be paid with all the other pre-bankruptcy claims.

Rejection
The means for the estate to rid itself of any ongoing obligations under an executory contract or unexpired lease of the debtor.

Assumption

Good judgment is also required for an **assumption;** in fact, the rules for an assumption are much more stringent than they are for rejection. For example, although any lease or executory contract can be rejected, some types of executory contracts can never be assumed unless the other party consents. The following are some examples:

Assumption
The means for the estate to bind itself to an executory contract or unexpired lease of the debtor.

☐ Contracts to perform personal services, such as painting a portrait or making a record.

□ Contracts to loan money.

□ Contracts to issue the debtor's stocks or bonds.

These contracts cannot be assumed because of their type. Their inability to be assumed is not caused by the terms of the contract. Some contracts and leases try to prevent an assumption by specifically providing that the agreement terminates on the debtor's insolvency, by the commencement of a bankruptcy case, or on the appointment of a trustee. These provisions are called **ipso facto clauses.** Generally they are not enforceable and will not prevent a trustee or debtor in possession from assuming a contract where there is good reason for doing so.

If a contract is assumable and the trustee or the debtor in possession wishes to assume it, certain conditions must be fulfilled before the court will allow the contract or lease to be assumed. Those conditions are:

□ All pre-bankruptcy monetary defaults (other than those created by *ipso facto* clauses) must be cured or adequate assurance given that the defaults will be cured promptly.

□ The other party to the contract or lease must be compensated for any loss incurred by the debtor's breach or must be given adequate assurance that compensation will be paid.

□ The other party must be provided with adequate assurance that the contract or lease will be fully performed in the future.

There are also special requirements for the assumption of a lease of part of a shopping center. They are as follows:

□ The funds generated from the operation of the store must be sufficient to pay the rent.

□ If the lease calls for all or a part of the rent to be based on a percentage of the store's receipts, these receipts will not substantially decline in the future.

□ Assumption will not breach any condition of a master lease applicable to all tenants in the shopping center.

□ Assumption will not substantially disrupt any tenant mix or balance in the shopping center.

Assignment

If a lease or a contract has value, the trustee or the debtor in possession may find it advantageous to sell or assign rights under the contract or lease to a third party. A lease or contract has value when the property or service to be provided is worth more than the trustee or debtor in possession is obligated to pay under the terms of the agreement. For example, the estate may be entitled to receive under a contract computer equipment it no longer needs. The equipment may have a market value of $10,000 but the contract price is only $8,000. The trustee could sell the estate's rights under the contract to a third party for $1,000, and the third party could obtain the equipment by paying the vendor $8,000. The estate earns $1,000, the buyer saves $1,000 and the vendor has received the benefit of its bargain.

In order to be able to assign a valuable contract or lease, the trustee or debtor in possession must first assume it by complying with the assumption requirements listed earlier. The assumption and the assignment are commonly done at the same time with adequate assurance of future performance given by the third party. Like

Ipso Facto Clauses
A provision in a contract or lease that provides that the contract or lease is breached or terminated if one of the parties become insolvent or the subject of a bankruptcy case.

ipso facto clauses, any restriction on assignment in the contract or lease is not enforceable.

Once a contract or lease has been assumed and assigned, the estate has no further liability under it. If there is a breach, no claim can be asserted against the estate.

Timing

The deadline for assuming or rejecting an executory contract or unexpired lease depends on the chapter in which the case is pending; for leases, a distinction is also made based on whether the lease is for personal property or real property. In a Chapter 7 case, the trustee must assume an executory contract or an unexpired lease within sixty days of the entry of the order for relief or the agreement is deemed rejected and cannot be revived. In a voluntary case, the order for relief is entered on the same date as the petition is filed; in an involuntary case, it is sometime later.

In a Chapter 11, 12, or 13 case, a lease for nonresidential real property must be assumed within sixty days of the entry of the order for relief or it too will be deemed rejected. The sixty-day period for assumption may be extended by the court, however. For all other contracts and leases, the trustee or the debtor in possession may reserve the decision to assume or reject the agreement until confirmation of a reorganization plan. The other party to the contract or the lessor may ask the court to shorten that deadline, however, and the court may in fact order an earlier assumption of the agreement. The creditor's options are discussed in greater detail in Chapter 12 of this textbook.

Special Situations

In order to avoid prejudice to the nondebtor party and as a result of special interest lobbying, Congress has created four exceptions to the general rules for the treatment of executory contracts. These exceptions apply if the debtor is a seller of real property, a licensor of a right to intellectual property, has entered into a collective bargaining agreement, or puts at risk the medical, accident, or death benefits of retired employees. A discussion of each of these special situations follows.

Debtor as Seller of Real Property or Landlord   There are special rules for contracts in which the debtor is the seller of real property and for leases in which the debtor is the landlord. Mindful of the detriment that could be suffered by the other parties to those contracts and leases by their rejection, Congress gave them greater protection than other parties.

If the debtor is a landlord and rejects the lease, the tenant may treat the lease as terminated and move out. Alternatively, the tenant can remain in possession for the term of the lease and any renewal. If the tenant remains in possession, any damages suffered on account of the rejection may be offset against the rent that is owing; but the right to sue the debtor for damages is lost, as is the right to enforce a provision in the lease for special services. For example, if the lease obligated the landlord to provide guard services, the tenant who remains in possession may have to make other arrangements for security of the leased premises. It can, however, reduce the rent by the amount it is reasonably required to spend for replacement guards.

If the debtor entered into a contract to sell real property before filing bank-ruptcy, and the buyer took possession of the property, the buyer may treat the contract as terminated, give up possession, and file a claim for damages upon the rejection of the agreement by the trustee or the debtor in possession. The buyer will also have a lien on the property to secure repayment of any money already paid in performance of the contract. The buyer may also elect to remain in pos-session of the property, enforce the contract, and setoff any damages against the remaining money due under the agreement. By such election, however, the pur-chaser waives any claim for damages against the estate. Once the buyer has made all payments due under the contract, the trustee or the debtor in possession must deliver appropriate documents transferring title of the property to the buyer.

There is also a special provision for a buyer of property from the debtor who has not taken possession at the time the bankruptcy case is filed and thus has no right to be in possession after the contract is rejected. That purchaser will have a lien of the property as security for recovery of any payments made as well as a claim for damages.

License Agreements   Special provisions are also made for cases in which the debtor is the licensor of a right to intellectual property, such as computer software, pat-ents, and copyrighted material. Congress was concerned that a licensee who had built a business around the intellectual right would be ruined by the licensor's subsequent bankruptcy and the trustee's rejection of the agreement in order to force a more advantageous contract or license with third party. Hence, the Bank-ruptcy Code provides that if the trustee or debtor in possession rejects an executory contract under which the debtor is a licensor of a right to intellectual property, the licensee has an election to treat the contract as terminated or to continue performance of the contract for the duration of the agreement and any extension. If the licensee elects to retain his or her rights under the contract, all royalty payments must be paid and the licensee is deemed to waive any right of setoff and any claim for damages arising from performance of the contract.

Collective Bargaining Agreements   Special requirements also apply to the assumption or rejection of a collective bargaining agreement that was entered into by the debtor before filing for bankruptcy under Chapter 11. The danger Congress sought to address was the likelihood that a person or firm would seek protection under the bankruptcy laws in order to be in a position to reject a union contract, pay lower wages, and offer fewer benefits for the employees. Thus, the Bankruptcy Code requires that the debtor and an agent of the collective bargaining unit attempt to work out an acceptable modification of the agreement. If this cannot be done, the debtor may seek an order authorizing the rejection of the collective bargaining agreement. In order to prevail, however, the debtor must show that the balance of the equities clearly favors the rejection. This is a substantially higher standard than is imposed for the rejection of other contracts.

Retirement Benefits   Congress had similar concerns for retirees who receive medical and other benefits from their former employers who might decide to seek Chapter 11 protection in order to reduce or eliminate those benefits. The Bankruptcy Code provides that the trustee or debtor in possession may not modify the health, ac-cident, or death benefits of retired employees under any program established before the bankruptcy case was commenced in the absence of consent to do so by an authorized representative of the retirees. The court may allow a modification of

benefits over the objection of a representative of the retirees but only if the court first finds that:

1. the trustee has made a modification proposal to the retirees that meets certain criteria;

2. the authorized representative of the retirees has refused to accept the proposal without good cause; and

3. the modification is necessary to permit the reorganization of the debtor and assure that all of the creditors, the debtor, and all of the affected parties are treated equitably.

Procedures

The procedures for obtaining court approval of an assumption or a rejection of an executory contract or an unexpired lease are set forth in Bankruptcy Rule 6006. The court is required to hold a hearing on a motion by the trustee or the debtor in possession and the creditors must have received notice of the hearing. Court approval is not required for a contract or lease that has been deemed rejected by operation of law because no assumption had been made within the first sixty days and no extension of time was sought or obtained.

There are also some limitations on the amount of a claim for damages that the nondebtor party may assert. If the claimant is the owner of leased property, the claim is limited to the amount that was due at the filing of the case plus future rent for one year or fifteen percent of the remaining rent due under the lease for a term not to exceed three years. If the claimant was employed by the debtor under a contract of employment, the amount of the claim is limited to the wages or salary due at the time of the filing of the petition plus wages and salary for one year after termination.

☐ OTHER SUBSTANTIVE LAW IMPORTANT IN BANKRUPTCY PRACTICE

Although the Bankruptcy Code is very comprehensive, sometimes it incorporates or refers to other federal or state law. To know how a bankruptcy case functions, it is important to have a basic understanding of a few other bodies of law. This chapter examines the two most significant: the **Uniform Commercial Code,** which governs the sale of personal property and its use as collateral, and general real estate law, including the various forms of ownership and financing mechanisms. This chapter is not an exhaustive discussion of either of these two important areas of the law, but is designed to give the legal assistant an understanding of the issues that might arise in a bankruptcy case.

☐ THE UNIFORM COMMERCIAL CODE

In General

As methods of communication and transportation improved in the United States, business transactions began to cross state lines more frequently. A uniform set of rules to conduct interstate business was needed. The Uniform Commercial Code, usually referred to as the UCC, was created as the set of rules of law to govern **commercial transactions** in all the States. Commercial transactions can include

Uniform Commercial Code
The law enacted in every state that governs commercial transactions.

Commercial Transaction
A phrase used to designate dealings of persons engaged in business.

virtually any aspect of business, in part because the definition of commerce is very broad.

The American Law Institute and the National Conference of Commissioners on State Laws prepared the UCC in 1949 and it has been modified continually ever since. Unlike the Bankruptcy Code, a federal law enacted by Congress that applies throughout the United States, the UCC is just a proposed law for the various states to enact if their legislatures so choose. Each state is free to adopt the UCC in whole or in part or with any variations the legislature finds appropriate. Despite the fact that it need not be enacted, the UCC is now in force in every state.

There are ten articles (in some states called divisions) in the UCC, as follows:

Article	Title
1	General Provisions
2	Sales
2A	Leases
3	Commercial Paper
4	Bank Deposits and Collections
5	Letters of Credit
6	Bulk Sales
7	Warehouse Receipts, Bills of Lading, and Other Documents of Title
8	Investment Securities
9	Secured Transactions

Each article has a number of sections. Like the Bankruptcy Code, the first digit of the section number indicates which article it is in. For example, Section 2101 is in Article 2, Section 9301 is in Article 9, and so on. Issues in virtually every article of the UCC may arise. The articles that have the most significance in a bankruptcy case are Sales and Secured Transactions.

Article 2—Sales

Goods
All things that are movable or are fixtures, but not money, documents, instruments, accounts, chattel paper, general intangibles or minerals or the like before extraction.

A sale for Article 2 purposes is simply a transaction by which a seller transfers ownership of goods to a buyer for a price. **Goods** are defined as all things that are movable; money and securities are excluded. Article 2 describes the obligations of the seller and the obligations of the buyer and the remedies available to each if either one breaches, or if both of them breach those obligations. It specifically allows the parties to alter those obligations and remedies set in Article 2 by agreement.

Article 2 is important in a bankruptcy case especially when the buyer becomes the debtor. It is crucial in order to understand whether a seller has a right to be paid, whether title for the goods has passed to the buyer, or whether the seller has a right to reclaim the goods if title has already passed. It is also needed to measure damages in order to analyze whether to assume or reject a contract for the sale of goods.

Article 2 also includes a list of contracts that are not enforceable either because they were unacceptably unfair at the time they were made; were not in writing when the law required them to be; or were based on fraud, duress, or mistake. This

is important for bankruptcy purposes because under Section 502, any claim that is unenforceable can be disallowed in the bankruptcy case.

Obligations Under a Contract   Article 2 sets forth the various obligations of a seller and of a buyer to a contract. To fully perform its side of a contract, the seller must transfer ownership and deliver the goods. In the absence of an agreement between a buyer and a seller as to how the seller will perform its obligations, delivery is to be made at the seller's place of business, within a reasonable time after the contract is made, and the offering of the goods is to be made in a single lot rather than in pieces.

A buyer's obligations are to accept the goods when they are tendered by the seller and to pay the agreed upon price. If the parties fail to specify in their contract how the buyer accepts or pays, Article 2 will fill in the missing terms. Generally, the buyer can accept by signifying that it is accepting, by using the goods, or by failing to reject. A buyer's obligation to pay is usually performed by paying the price as the parties have agreed. If they do no specify when payment is due, it is to be made when the goods are delivered.

Title   Title is the legal recognition of who owns and is responsible for the goods. Under Article 2, the parties may determine by agreement when title to the goods will pass from the seller to the buyer. Obviously, the seller will not want title to pass until the buyer has paid for the goods. The buyer will want title to pass as quickly as possible. Absent an agreement that provides otherwise, the UCC provides that title passes when the seller completes its delivery obligations. When title passes is very important for bankruptcy purposes because this determines whether the seller or the buyer has the right to sell the goods to pay creditors. For a seller, whether title has passed will determine if the seller can take back the goods or the seller will be an unsecured creditor in the buyer's bankruptcy case.

Breaches   Article 2 details how a contract for the sale of the goods is breached and describes the aggrieved party's remedies for the breach. A seller can breach by not making any tender of the goods at all, by making a bad tender by delivering to the wrong place, or by delivering the wrong goods. A buyer breaches by refusing to accept goods properly tendered or by refusing to pay for the goods.

If the seller fails to make any tender at all, the buyer has two remedies. First, the buyer can force the seller to perform by obtaining a court order requiring the seller to deliver the goods. This remedy is usually only available if the goods are unique or there is some other reason why the buyer will not be satisfied by a money judgment. Second, the buyer may seek damages. The amount of damages the buyer will be entitled to is the difference between the regular price of the goods and the price the buyer agreed to pay. The buyer will be entitled to these damages if it does not buy new goods. If the buyer actually buys replacement goods, the amount of damages will be the difference between what was paid for the replacement goods and the contract price. The new purchase must be in good faith and without unreasonable delay or upon unreasonable terms. In addition to these damages, the buyer will also be entitled to **incidental damages,** such as the cost of traveling in order to buy the replacement goods, and **consequential damages.** Consequential damages include any loss caused by the breach that the seller knew of and that was not remedied by buying new goods. If, for instance, the buyer was going to use the goods as a component to a part it was selling, and would be

Incidental Damages
Damages incurred in connection with the principal damages.

Consequential Damages
Damages that do not flow directly and immediately from the wrongful act of the party but only from the consequences or results of such act.

financially penalized by its buyer if it did not deliver the part on time, the breaching component seller could be liable for the amount of the financial penalty as a consequential damage.

If the seller breaches by making a bad tender, the buyer can accept the goods despite the nonconformity or reject them. If the buyer rejects the goods, its remedies are the same as though no tender was made at all. However, the seller may have the right to cure the defect if the time for performance has not expired. If the buyer rejects but has possession of the goods, it must hold the goods for a reasonable period of time to permit the seller to remove them. If the seller does not, the buyer must either store the goods, ship them back to the seller, or sell them on the seller's behalf.

Even if the buyer accepts nonconforming goods it is still entitled to damages but it must give notice to the seller of the breach within a reasonable period of time after the breach is discovered. If the notice is not given, the buyer is barred from all remedies. If a proper notice is given, the buyer may be able to collect damages for breach of warranty, measured as the difference between the value of the goods without the defects and the value of the goods delivered. If the breach involved how the tender was made, such as the delivery was late, the buyer is entitled to recover damages caused by that breach.

If the buyer wrongfully refuses to accept goods properly tendered, the seller can sue for damages, measured by the contract price minus the market price. Alternatively, the seller can sell the goods to a third party and sue for the difference between the contract price and the resale price. If the goods are not salable in the seller's ordinary course of business, the seller can sue for the entire contract price. In all cases, the seller is also entitled to its incidental damages, including expenses incurred because of the breach.

If the buyer accepts the goods but then breaches by failing to pay the purchase price, the seller's remedy is to sue to collect the purchase price. However, if after the goods are accepted by the buyer the seller discovers the buyer's insolvency, the seller may reclaim the goods if the buyer still has them and if a demand is made within ten to twenty days after the receipt of the goods. As you will learn, reclamation right are preserved, indeed made stronger, if the buyer files a bankruptcy case (see Chapter 12 of this book).

Article 9—Secured Transaction

The other most significant article of the UCC for bankruptcy purposes is Article 9. It concerns **secured transactions** involving **personal property** such as goods, bank accounts and almost any other property that is not real estate. A secured transaction under Article 9 involves a relationship between the debtor and a creditor in which the debtor has given or the creditor has obtained by operation of law an interest in all or some of the debtor's assets to secure repayment of a debt. The assets subject to the interest, which is called a **security interest** or a lien, are labeled **collateral.** The creditor is called the **secured party.** A diagram of a secured transaction is provided in Exhibit 4.2.

There are three purposes of a security interest. The first is to make the debt more easily collectible if the debtor will not or cannot pay when the debt is due. The second purpose is to give the secured party a position superior to that of the other creditors of the debtor who might attempt to take the collateral to satisfy their debts. The third purpose is to protect the secured party's rights in the collateral if it is sold by the debtor.

Secured Transactions
A phrase used to describe dealings involving the granting or taking of a security interest.

Personal Property
Property that consists of temporary or moveable things.

Security Interest
A lien created by an agreement.

Collateral
Property subject to a security interest.

Secured Party
A lender, seller or other person in whose favor there is a security interest.

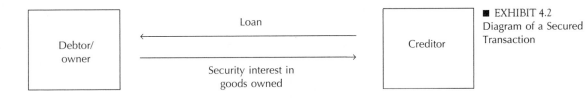

■ EXHIBIT 4.2
Diagram of a Secured
Transaction

A brief discussion of how a consensual security interest is created follows. Article 9 does not discuss how nonconsensual security interests, which usually arise by operation of law, such as warehouse liens, are created; but it does control the rights of the secured parties as against creditors holding those sorts of liens.

Article 9 is frequently applied in bankruptcy cases. One of the most common issues is a bankruptcy trustee's ability to defeat a secured party's rights in collateral. A bankruptcy trustee becomes cloaked with all the rights of certain hypothetical persons. If one of these hypothetical persons would prevail over a secured creditor, so will the trustee. If the trustee prevails, the collateral can be sold and the proceeds distributed to all creditors—not just the secured party. This is a very powerful tool for the trustee; the following discussion is key to understanding just how powerful.

Creation of a Security Interest   A security interest can be created in two ways. The first is by a **security agreement.** A security agreement must be in writing, contain a description of the collateral, state that the debtor is granting a security interest in the collateral to the creditor, and must be signed by the debtor. The second method of creating a security interest is by the creditor taking possession of the debtor's property with the intent that the possession is to secure a debt. If the secured party has possession of the collateral, an oral agreement will be sufficient to create the security interest.

A security interest is effective when it has **attached.** In order to have the security interest attach, there must be the written or oral agreement, value must have been given by the secured party, and the debtor must have rights in the collateral. Even though there may be a signed security agreement between the debtor and the creditor, the security interest is not valid until the secured party has loaned money to the debtor or given other value. Even if there is a signed security agreement and the secured party has made the loan, there is no security interest until the debtor owns the collateral. For example, suppose the debtor wants to buy a washing machine. The debtor borrows money from a finance company and agrees to grant the finance company a security interest in the washing machine. The debtor then orders the washing machine. At that point there is an agreement and the creditor has given value. However, if title has not passed from the seller of the washing machine to the debtor, the secured creditor will not have a security interest in the washing machine because the debtor does not have rights in the collateral. Until all three elements of attachment have occurred, the finance company has no greater rights against the debtor or any of its property than does any other creditor.

Types of Collateral   There are three types of collateral: *goods*, **rights evidenced by a writing,** and **intangibles.** Familiarity with these types of collateral is very important in order to understand who wins when a secured party is competing against third parties who also claim an interest in the collateral.

Security Agreement
An agreement that creates or provides for a security interest.

Attachment
Making a security interest enforceable. Unless explicit agreement postpones the time of attachment, it occurs when: (a) secured party pursuant to agreement possesses collateral, or debtor has signed a security agreement describing collateral; (b) value has been given; (c) debtor has rights in the collateral.

Rights Evidenced by a Writing
Instruments, documents of title, and chattel paper.

Intangibles
Assets that are owned by an going business such as goodwill, trade marks, copyrights, franchises and the like.

Fixtures
Goods that are so related to a particular parcel of real estate that an interest in them arises under real estate law.

The definition of goods was provided earlier in the discussion of Article 2, which concerns the sale of goods. To review, goods include **fixtures** and everything that is movable. A fixture is a good that becomes so related to a particular parcel of real estate that an interest in it arises under real estate law. A heating system installed in a building is an example of a fixture.

Goods can be further broken down into four groups according to how the debtor uses them primarily. The four groups are

1. *consumer goods*—those goods used primarily for personal, family or household purposes;

2. *inventory*—goods sold, leased, or furnished; raw materials to be processed; and materials consumed in a business;

3. *farm products*—crops, livestock, or supplies used or produced in farming operations and products of crops or livestock in their unmanufactured states; and

4. *equipment*—goods used primarily in a business and that are not inventory, farm products, or consumer goods.

If a particular good does not fit in any of the other categories, it is usually labeled as equipment. How a debtor primarily uses a particular good determines the good's category. For example, to a farmer, a tractor is equipment; to a dealer in tractors, a tractor is inventory.

The second category of collateral includes those rights that a person may have that are reduced to a written form. These rights are transferred by transferring the writing. The UCC breaks these rights into three types: *instruments, documents of title,* and *chattel paper.* Instruments include promissory notes, stocks and bonds, and any other piece of paper evidencing a right to the payment of money that is, in the ordinary course of business, transferred by delivery of the paper. Documents of title are bills of lading, warehouse receipts, delivery orders, and the like. Unlike instruments, which usually represent obligations to pay money, documents of title represent ownership in goods. If you had goods stored in a warehouse and obtained a warehouse receipt, you could transfer ownership of the goods by transferring the warehouse receipt. Chattel paper means a writing evidencing both a monetary obligation and a security interest in or a lease of goods. Chattel paper would include security agreements and personal property leases.

The last category of collateral is intangibles. Many intangibles are evidenced by writings but the writings have no significance on their own. Under the UCC, there are two types of intangibles: accounts and general intangibles. Accounts are payments due for goods sold or leased or for services performed that are not evidenced by an instrument or chattel paper. A debtor's receivables are usually accounts. The accounts may be evidenced by invoices but the invoices have no significance other than to show the debt in written form. If the invoice was destroyed, the debt would still be collectible. General intangible is a catchall term for collateral that does not fit into any other category. Examples of general intangibles include copyrights and trademarks.

Purchase Money Security Interest
A security interest to the extent that it is taken or retained by the seller of the collateral to secure all or part of its price, or taken by a person who gives value in order to enable the debtor to acquire the collateral if such value is in fact so used.

Purchase Money Security Interests   In many instances, the UCC gives preferential treatment to holders of **purchase money security interests.** A security interest is purchase money to the extent that it is taken or retained by the seller of the collateral to secure all or a part of its price, or taken by a person who gives the money to the debtor to enable the debtor to acquire the collateral. For example, if the debtor bought a washing machine from a dealer who agreed to accept payments over time

secured by a lien on the washing machine, the dealer would have a purchase money security interest. If the debtor borrowed the money from a finance company and took that money to the dealer and bought the washing machine for cash, the finance company's lien would be a purchase money security interest.

Secured Party versus Debtor   Remember that secured transactions involve the giving or taking of a lien in a person's property to secure repayment of a debt. If a debtor defaults in repaying its debt to the secured party, the secured party has an immediate right to possession of the collateral if it does not already have possession. Outside of bankruptcy, if possession can be accomplished peacefully, then the secured creditor can simply take the collateral. If the secured creditor cannot obtain the collateral without breaking into the debtor's premises or if the debtor resists the creditor's efforts, a court order must be obtained.

Once the secured creditor has obtained the collateral, one of three things will happen.

1. The debtor will take the property back by paying what is owed.
2. The secured party will keep the collateral.
3. The secured party will sell the collateral.

If the secured creditor wishes to keep the collateral, it must give notice of its intention to do so to the debtor and to any other known secured parties. Each of those persons will have thirty days to object. If there is an objection, the secured party must sell the collateral. If there is no objection, the secured party may keep the collateral. If it does, it will be in full satisfaction of the debt.

The secured party's other alternative is to sell the collateral and use the proceeds to satisfy all or a part of the debtor's obligation. The sale may be private (to a particular buyer) or public, such as by auction. In either case, the sale must be conducted reasonably. For example, the secured party could not take highly technical scientific equipment and try to sell it at a garage sale. However, although there must be a reasonable attempt to obtain a fair price, the fact that a better price could have been obtained does not necessarily mean that the sale was not reasonable.

Unless the collateral is perishable, a notice that the secured creditor intends to sell the collateral must be given to the debtor and to all known secured parties within a reasonable time before the sale. What is considered a reasonable time varies from state to state and may be as little as five days.

If the sale of the collateral does not produce enough money to pay the secured party in full, the secured party may bring an action to collect the balance due which is called the deficiency. If the sale was not conducted by the secured creditor in a reasonable manner, it may have lost its right to collect the deficiency. If the sale produces excess proceeds, those funds belong to the debtor.

Secured Party versus Third Parties   Even though a secured party may have better rights than the debtor to the collateral, it will not necessarily have better rights than others such as other secured creditors, purchasers, or bankruptcy trustees. In order to obtain the best possible rights against these other parties, the secured party must "perfect" its security interest. **Perfection** is similar to recording a mortgage or deed of trust in real property law and the purpose is the same: to put the world on notice of the security interest.

There are two methods of perfection. The first is by taking possession of the collateral. Obviously, if a creditor has possession of the collateral, the world is on

Perfection
The steps necessary under the Uniform Commercial Code or other law to make a lien effective against a third party and a bankruptcy trustee.

notice that the creditor has rights in the collateral. Perfection by possession is the only way to perfect a security interest in instruments. Perfection by possession will not work for intangibles since there is nothing to take possession of. Perfection by possession is also not feasible if the debtor needs the collateral to operate its business. For example, if the collateral is a printing press, if the secured creditor takes possession of the press, the debtor cannot then use the press to make books that could be sold to repay the secured creditor.

The second method of perfection is to file a **financing statement** with either a state or county official. A financing statement is a simple form that contains the name of the debtor and the secured party, describes the collateral, and is signed by the debtor and the secured party. A sample financing statement for a transaction in which a finance company took a security interest in only particular goods is shown in Exhibit 4.3. In most states financing statements are filed with the secretary of state. A security interest in fixtures is usually perfected by filing a document similar to a financing statement in the local real property records.

The secretary of state or the county recorder will keep a list of all financing statements that have been filed with respect to a particular debtor. The list, usually referred to as a search or a UCC search, can be obtained upon request. In that way, the world and, more particularly those who might care, are on notice of a creditor's security interest.

In one limited situation the UCC provides that there is a permanent automatic perfection as soon as the security interest attaches and neither possession nor a financing statement is required. That situation is a purchase money security interest in consumer goods.

Usually, perfection takes place immediately upon the occurrence of all of the events that are needed for perfection. When the security interest is purchase money, if the creditor perfects within a period of time set by each state, usually ten or twenty days after the time the debtor came into possession of the collateral, the date of perfection will then be the date of the debtor's possession.

Priority Problems   A dispute in which two or more creditors claim rights in the same property and at least one of those creditors is a secured party under Article 9 is called a priority problem or dispute. In determining who wins in a priority dispute, the general rule is that the first-in-time (that is, the first to obtain the security interest or lien) is the first-in-right. In other words, the first to obtain the lien has the first claim to the collateral. There are, however, many, many exceptions to this rule. Some possible priority problems are presented here.

1. *Secured Party versus General Creditors without Security Interests.* A general creditor is a creditor who does not have a lien on any of the debtor's property. A secured party will prevail against a general creditor, whether or not the secured party has perfected its security interest. However, since many general creditors become judicial lien creditors, perfection should not be ignored.

2. *Secured Party versus Judicial Lien Creditors.* A judicial lien creditor is a general creditor who obtained a judgment against the debtor and completed the act (usually called a **levy**) the state law requires in order to obtain a lien on particular collateral. The levy can consist of having the sheriff take possession of the property or it can be simply filing a notice. Once the levy is made, the creditor has a lien and becomes a judicial lien creditor. In determining who wins as between the secured party and the judicial lien creditor, the first-in-

Financing Statement
The document typically filed with the secretary of state that contains the name of the debtor, the name of the secured creditor, and a description of the collateral and that is used to perfect a secured interest for most types of collateral.

Levy
The physical or constructive seizure of property in order to enforce a judgment.

■ EXHIBIT 4.3
Uniform Commercial Code—Financing Statement—Form UCC–1

INSTRUCTIONS:

1. PLEASE TYPE this form. Fold only along perforation for mailing.

2. Remove Secured Party and Debtor copies and send other 3 copies with interleaved carbon paper to the filing officer. Enclose filing fee.

3. If the space provided for any item(s) on the form is inadequate the item(s) should be continued on additional sheets, preferably 5" × 8" or 8" × 10". Only one copy of such additional sheets need be presented to the filing officer with a set of three copies of the financing statement. Long schedules of collateral, indentures, etc., may be on any size paper that is convenient for the secured party. Indicate the number of additional sheets attached.

4. If collateral is crops or goods which are or are to become fixtures, describe generally the real estate and give name of record owner.

5. When a copy of the security agreement is used as a financing statement, it is requested that it be accompanied by a completed but unsigned set of these forms, without extra fee.

6. At the time of original filing, filing officer should return third copy as acknowledgment. At a later time, secured party may date and sign Termination Legend and use third copy as a Termination Statement.

This FINANCING STATEMENT is presented to a filing officer for filing pursuant to the Uniform Commercial Code:	3. Maturity date (if any):
1. Debtor(s) (Last Name First) and address(es) Videos by Joe, Inc. 18 Hollywood Drive Hollywood, CA 90001 2. Secured Party(ies) and address(es) B & G Finance Company 456 Harass Drive Princeton, N.J. 08890	For Filing Officer (Date, Time, Number and Filing Office)
4. This financing statement covers the following types (or items) of property: Five (5) Sony Model 111N Video Cameras and accessories.	5. Assignee(s) of Secured Party and Address(es)

This statement is filed without the debtor's signature to perfect a security interest in collateral.   (check ☒ if so)

☐ already subject to a security interest in another jurisdiction when it was brought into this state.

☐ which is proceeds of the original collateral described above in which a security interest was perfected:

Check ☒ if covered: ☒ Proceeds of Collateral are also covered.   ☐ Products of Collateral are also covered. No. of additional sheets presented:

Filed with: California Secretary of State

Videos by Joe, Inc.   B & G Finance Company

By: _____   By: _____
      Signature(s) of Debtor(s)   Signature(s) of Debtor(s)

(1) Filing Officer Copy—Alphabetical

STANDARD FORM—FORM UCC-1.

time, first-in-right rule applies. If the judicial lien creditor levies before the secured party perfects its security interest, then the judicial lien creditor wins. If the secured party perfects before the levy, the secured party prevails. Under the Bankruptcy Code, the trustee is given the status of a hypothetical lien creditor. As a result, a trustee will prevail over any unperfected secured creditor.

3. *Secured Party versus Other Secured Parties.* When there are two or more creditors holding security interests in the same collateral, the first to perfect will prevail. If none of the security interests is perfected, the winner will be the first to have attached. There is an exception for purchase money security interests in inventory. If a creditor has such an interest and it perfects before it turns over possession of the inventory to the debtor and if the creditor gives a notice to the other secured creditor of its interest, it will prevail over the other secured party—even if that other party perfected first.

4. *Secured Party versus Transferees.* If there is a conflict between the secured party and buyer of the collateral, the general rule of first-in-time, first-in-right usually applies. A buyer who gives value and takes delivery without actual knowledge of the security interest will win over an unperfected security interest because the buyer did not and could not have known of the secured creditor. The secured creditor could have protected itself simply by perfecting its security interest. On the other hand, if the purchaser takes delivery after the security interest is perfected, the secured party prevails. The purchaser could have ordered a search and discovered the security interest. There are a number of exceptions.

a. If the secured party gives the debtor permission to sell the collateral, the buyer will take the collateral free of any perfected security interest. If, for instance, the debtor is an appliance dealer, and the secured party who has a lien on the dealer's inventory knows that the dealer is selling washing machines, the buyer can have the washing machine free of the security interest because the secured party implicitly consented to the sale.

b. A consumer buyer always takes title free and clear of all unfiled security interests even if the secured party was not required to file in order to perfect such as a purchase money security interest in consumer goods. So, a purchase money secured creditor with a lien in consumer goods does not have to file in order to win against another secured creditor but it will need to file to win against a buyer.

c. A *buyer in the ordinary course of business*, who is a buyer in good faith who buys goods from a person in the business of selling goods of that kind and without knowledge that the sale to it is in violation of the security interests of others, takes title free of all security interests created by the seller even though they are filed or otherwise perfected and even though the buyer had knowledge of the security interest. Thus, under this exception, even if the washing machine dealer had granted a security interest in inventory to a finance company, the washing machine could be bought from the dealer free of the claims of the finance company, unless the buyer knew that the finance company had forbidden the dealer from selling any of the collateral.

Other Applicable UCC Provisions

Articles 2 and 9 of the UCC are the most common UCC Articles a legal assistant will encounter in a bankruptcy case. They are not, however, the only ones. Two

other articles that the legal assistant should be familiar with are Article 2A and Article 6. A short discussion of each of these articles follows.

Article 2A—Leases   In 1986, the National Conference created Article 2A to deal with **leases** of personal property. The term lease means any transfer of the right to possession and use of goods for a period of time in exchange for some consideration. A lease is formed when there is a writing signed by the parties that indicates an intent to enter into a lease, states a term, and identifies the leased goods. Under certain circumstances, such as goods specially manufactured or obtained for the lessee, goods accepted by the lessee, or the admissions of the party, a written lease will not be necessary. Like Article 2, if the parties to a lease have left out important terms, Article 2A will fill those terms in. Also like Article 2, Article 2A addresses such things as how a lease is accepted or rejected, what constitutes a breach by the lessee or the lessor, and each side's remedies.

In a bankruptcy case it is very important to know the difference between a lease and a security interest because the rights of a secured creditor are very different from the rights of a lessor. Article 2A establishes some rules to help determine the difference in cases where a document may be called a lease but the provisions are similar to those of a security agreement.

Because it is relatively new, Article 2A has not been adopted by all of the states. States that have adopted Article 2A may number it Article 10.

Article 6—Bulk Sales   The bulk sales law set forth in Article 6 of the UCC is based on long existing state law that was designed to protect creditors from a situation in which a debtor sold all or a substantial part of its assets and then absconded with the sale proceeds. Bulk sales law places the responsibility on the buyer to notify all of the seller's creditors that there will be a sale of the debtor's property and gives them the opportunity to file a claim into an escrow. The sale proceeds will be put into the escrow and the claims paid. If the seller does not make a good faith and reasonable effort to comply with the notice and escrow requirements, it could be liable for the full amount of the creditors' claim even though it had already paid the buyer what the goods are worth.

Bulk sale law will not apply to every transaction. In many states it does not apply if the seller is a restaurant or the sale is for anything other than equipment and inventory. It may not apply if the sale is for less than $10,000 or more than $5,000,000.

Bulk sales law does not apply to a sale by a bankruptcy debtor or trustee. But, many bankruptcy cases are filed because of bulk sales law. If creditors receive notice of a bulk sale they may file an involuntary bankruptcy case to stop it from closing. A buyer may ask the seller to file a bankruptcy case because it is easier to sell under Section 363 of the Bankruptcy Code than it is to comply with bulk sale law. The seller may decide to sell its assets in a bankruptcy case rather than under Article 6 if the claims submitted by creditors into the escrow are greater than anticipated. Finally, a bankruptcy trustee may seek to assert claims against the buyer who failed to comply with bulk sales law.

☐ REAL ESTATE OWNERSHIP AND FINANCING

In many bankruptcy cases, the most valuable asset is the debtor's interest in a parcel of real estate. In some cases, it will be the only asset. Accordingly, it is very important in most bankruptcy cases to know the nature of a debtor's interest in

real property and to understand what interests others may have in that same real property. Unfortunately, there is no uniform law on real property interests or financing such as the UCC. However, there are a number of general rules.

Real Property Interests

There are many types of interests (sometimes called estates) in real property. The same parcel of real property may have interests held in it by many different people. These interests are distinguished by their extent and duration. Exhibit 4.4 summarizes the types of interests. Determining the nature and scope of a real property interest is very important in bankruptcy cases because that interest, whatever it is, will be property of the estate.

Fee simple absolute is the greatest interest. An owner of land in fee simple absolute, sometimes referred to as just a *fee interest*, has the right to the surface of the land and to everything above or below it for an endless period of time. The

Fee Simple Absolute
An estate in property held by a person and his or her heirs and assigns forever and without limitation.

■ EXHIBIT 4.4
Common Types of Interests in Real Property

Rights in Land
Fee Simple Absolute: the right to the surface and to everything permanently situated beneath or above it. Example: "I convey this land to you."
Fee Simple Defeasible: has a special limitation causing the estate to expire automatically upon the occurrence of a stated event. Example: "I convey this land to you in fee simple unless liquor is sold on the premises."
Life Estates: The life tenant has the same right of possession as an owner in fee simple, may make reasonable use of the land, and may receive profits from the land but only for so long as he or she lives. Example: "I convey this land to my husband for so long as he is alive."

Rights in the Land of Another
Easement: An interest in the land of another that entitles the owner of the easement to a limited use or enjoyment of the other's land. Example: "The owners of the adjacent parcel may cross my land to get to the highway".
License: A permission or authority to do an act on land of another. Example: "XYZ company may harvest timber from my land."
Covenants Running With the Land: A promise respecting the use of land. Example: "I will give my neighbors a right of first refusal if my land is ever sold."
Equitable Servitudes: Like a covenant but one that cannot be remedied by money damages. Example: "I will not erect a building on my land so high that it blocks the view from your land."
Leases
   Estate for Years: The estate is for a definite period. Example: "I lease this land to you for three years."
   Estate at Will: The tenancy has no fixed term and is terminable at the will of either party. Example: "I lease this land to you for so long as you pay rent."
   Estate From Period to Period: The tenancy continues for successive period of the same length, unless sooner terminated by notice at the end of one period. Example: "I lease this land to you for one year periods, which will continue unless I give you notice or you give me notice at the end of any year of termination of the lease."
   Estate at Sufferance: The tenant goes into possession lawfully but holds over after the expiration of the lease.

Ownership By Several Persons
Joint Tenancy: A joint interest is one owned by two or more persons in equal shares with the right of survivorship. If one tenant dies, the other tenants take the dead tenant's share.
Tenancy by Entireties: A joint tenancy held by a husband and wife.
Tenancy in Common: A cotenancy without the right of survivorship. The parties can leave to their heirs their interests in the land.

fee owner has the right to dispose of the real property in whole or in part, to possess it, to lease it, and to otherwise use it for any reasonable purpose. It is possible that one person might own a fee interest in everything below the ground and another to own the surface and everything above. It is also possible for one person to own the surface and another to own all the buildings on the surface.

There are also interests for a limited number of years. One such interest is a **life estate,** which is ownership so long as a person is alive. An interest that carries the right to possession and some use for a period of time is a **leasehold estate.** It does not give the holder the right to dispose of the property.

Real property ownership interests, especially fee interests, are transferred through documents known as **deeds.** To be valid, deeds must be in writing and must contain the seller or the grantor's signature, words of transfer, and a description of the property and the interest transferred. There are a number of different types of deeds. A **grant deed** is the most common. Under a grant deed, the owner of a real property interest transfers that interest to another giving a warranty in the deed that it owns the interest being transferred. Another common type of deed is a **quitclaim deed.** Under a quitclaim deed, the owner transfers its interest to another without giving any warranty as to what is being transferred.

Deeds are filed with the county recorder or other official who keeps track of the transfers of a particular parcel of property. Through those records it is possible to trace all the deeds from the initial recorded owner to the present. This is known as the **chain of title.** Sometimes leases will also be recorded and will appear of record in the chain of title.

Real Estate Financing

Ever since real estate interests have been recognized, there have been various methods of using those interests to secure repayment of debts or to finance the purchase of property. In most states, the document used when real property is the security is a **mortgage.** It is very similar to a security agreement. If the debtor defaults, the lender takes the property described in the mortgage (called a foreclosure). Although foreclosure usually takes much longer, the process is akin to what a personal property secured creditor follows under the UCC.

Some states use a **deed of trust** rather than a mortgage. In a deed of trust the owner of the property, called the trustor, deeds the property to a third person known as the trustee who holds the property for the benefit of the lender who is the beneficiary of the deed of trust. If the trustor (debtor) defaults on its obligations to the beneficiary (lender), the beneficiary can instruct the trustee to foreclose and hold a sale of the property.

Mortgages and deeds of trust are more alike than they are different and both must be recorded to be valid as against third parties. If the mortgage or deed of trust is unrecorded, a buyer of real property without knowledge of the security interest will take title to the property free of it. The general rule of first-in-time, first-in-right will also apply to other secured creditors. The bankruptcy trustee has the status of a purchaser of real property. By using this status or that of a hypothetical lien creditor, the trustee will take the bankruptcy estate's interest in the property free and clear of unrecorded mortgages or deeds of trust.

The mechanics of **foreclosures** and sales by or on behalf of lenders are controlled by state law and vary considerably from state to state. There are two basic types. The first is a **judicial foreclosure** in which a court issues a decree of foreclosure. The sheriff will then sell the property at an auction. The second, and

Life Estate
An estate whose duration is limited to the life of the person or of some other person.

Leasehold
An estate in real property held under a lease; an estate for a fixed term.

Deed
A document conveying an interest in real property other than a leasehold estate.

Chain of Title
A list of successive transfers of real property arranged consecutively, from the government or original source of title down to the present holder.

Mortgage
An agreement that creates or provides for a security interest in real property.

Deed of Trust
A document used in many states that takes the place of a mortgage and by which legal title is placed in a trustee to secure repayment of a loan or performance of an obligation.

Foreclosure
The enforcement of a security interest, mortgage or deed of trust in which the secured creditor takes the collateral in partial or full satisfaction of the debt.

Judicial Foreclosure
An action to obtain a court order requiring the sheriff to hold an auction sale of collateral.

more common in many jurisdictions (especially those that use deeds of trust), is a public auction conducted by the mortgagor or the trustee. These sales do not require an order of the court. Private sales similar to the type authorized by the UCC for personal property are not allowed although the debtor can give the lender a quitclaim deed.

All foreclosure sales, regardless of type, have a notice period that requires the lender or the trustee to inform the owner of the real property that there is a default in the underlying obligation and that a foreclosure sale will be conducted on or after a certain date. The owner will then be given an opportunity to cure the default or satisfy the obligation and prevent the foreclosure. The owner could also attend the sale and repurchase the property. In some states, even if the property is sold to a third party, the former owner is given an additional period of time to pay off the obligation and take back the property. This is called the debtor's **right of redemption.**

In most states, the mechanics of a foreclosure must be strictly adhered to in terms of timing, extent, and form of notice. If a foreclosure or a sale is improper, the owner may be entitled to damages, to declare the sale a nullity or, if the sale has not yet taken place, to obtain a court order preventing the sale from being conducted.

If there is a sale of real property collateral, the foreclosing lender will receive the proceeds less any prior secured claims and the costs of the sale. If those proceeds are less than the unpaid balance of the secured debt, the lender will suffer a deficiency. In a number of states, if a lender forecloses on its real property collateral, it is not entitled to collect the deficiency. The purpose of such **antideficiency laws** is to deter underbidding at foreclosure sales. There are many variations on the antideficiency rules and few states have the same rules.

In addition to having the right to foreclose, many mortgages and deeds of trust also grant a lender an **assignment of rents** from the underlying property that serves as collateral for the obligation. This assignment can be a very significant right for the lender to exercise pending a foreclosure sale of an apartment house or office building, especially in the states in which there is a long period of time between the date the lender declares a default and the date the foreclosure sale can take place. If the lender is able to exercise its assignment of rents provision, it will be able to obtain the rent receipts and ultimately will have the property too. In those jurisdictions that have enacted an antideficiency statute, the rents collected before the foreclosure sale may make a difference between the lender being paid in full and suffering a deficiency.

Finally, there is a real property financing tool that is common in some jurisdictions, especially in the sale of single family residences by private parties. It is known as a **land sale contract.** In a land sale contract, the seller will retain ownership of the property until all the payments are made by the buyer. Once the purchase price is paid in full, the seller will give the buyer a grant deed. Usually the buyer will take possession while the installments are being made, will be responsible for the payment of taxes, and may make improvements.

The remedies available upon breach of a land sale contract will depend on which of the parties breaches. An aggrieved seller can regain possession but may have to return to the buyer all amounts in excess of actual damages. An aggrieved buyer can usually obtain specific performance and obtain title or can be awarded damages. Land sale contracts frequently are the subject of bankruptcy court decisions because the seller or the buyer may become a debtor and want to be rid of

Right of Redemption
The right to free property from a foreclosure or other judicial sale or recover the title that passed in a foreclosure by paying what is due.

Antideficiency Laws
Legislation that prevents a secured creditor from recovering its deficiency (the difference between what is owed and what is received in the liquidation of its collateral) from the debtor.

Assignment of Rents
An agreement between a lender and a borrower that provides that the rental proceeds from property will be paid to the lender.

Land Sale Contract
An agreement whereby the seller of real property retains title to the property until the full purchase price is paid by the buyer.

the obligations required under the contract. These issues were discussed earlier in this chapter in connection with their treatment as executory contracts.

☐ SUMMARY

The automatic stay is the most important protection a bankruptcy debtor has. It prevents virtually all creditor actions against the debtor and its property. The automatic stay becomes effective the instant a bankruptcy case is commenced and lasts against the debtor until he or she receives a discharge. It lasts against the debtor's property until it is no longer property of the estate. Creditors may be entitled to relief from the automatic stay if they can make certain showings. If they violate the stay without first obtaining relief, they may be liable for damages.

Executory contracts and unexpired leases receive special treatment in the Bankruptcy Code. Executory contracts are ones in which meaningful performance remains on the part of each party to the contract. The Bankruptcy Code allows a debtor or a trustee to reject the contract or lease, which eliminates the need for the debtor to perform under the contract. Alternatively, the debtor or the trustee may assume the contract and agree to be bound by it. An assumed contract or lease can also be assigned to a third party even if the contract or lease prohibits assignment. Real property leases must be assumed or rejected within sixty days unless the court grants an extension of that sixty day period. In a Chapter 7 case, all executory contracts or unexpired leases must be assumed or assigned within sixty days after the case is commenced.

Many questions of law that arise in a bankruptcy case can only be answered by reference to state law. The two most important state law areas are the provisions of the Uniform Commercial Code and a state's real estate ownership and financing laws. The UCC governs commercial transactions in every state, although there are some variations among the states. The most widely used portions of the UCC are Article 2, which concerns the sales of goods, and Article 9, which concerns secured transactions. Also very important for a bankruptcy legal assistant to know are Articles 2A (leases) and Article 6 (bulk sale law).

There are a number of different types of real estate ownership, from fee simple absolute to a leasehold estate. An interest in real estate other than a lease is conveyed by use of a deed. A security interest in real estate will be reflected either in a mortgage or a deed to trust.

☐ KEY TERMS

Antideficiency Laws	Financing Statement	Perfection
Assignment of Rents	Fixtures	Personal Property
Assumption	Foreclosure	Purchase Money Security Interest
Attachment	Goods	Rejection
Automatic Stay	Incidental Damages	Right of Redemption
Chain of Title	Intangibles	Rights Evidenced by a Writing
Collateral	Ipso Facto Clauses	Secured Party
Commercial Transaction	Judicial Foreclosure	Secured Transactions
Consequential Damages	Land Sale Contract	Security Agreement
Deed	Leasehold	Security Interest
Deed of Trust	Levy	Unexpired Lease
Executory Contract	Life Estate	Uniform Commercial Code
Fee Simple Absolute	Mortgage	

☐ IMPROVE YOUR UNDERSTANDING

For Exercises 1 through 11, determine whether the acts described are prohibited by the automatic stay.

1. The commencement of a suit against the guarantor when the primary obligor is a debtor.

2. An action by the Environmental Protection Agency to stop the debtor from polluting a nearby lake.

3. The filing of a financing statement to perfect a security interest in the debtor's assets.

4. A demand letter sent to the debtor by an unsecured prepetition creditor.

5. A statement sent to the debtor by an unsecured prepetition creditor.

6. The repossession of the debtor's automobile.

7. A writ of attachment hearing seeking a lien on the debtor's exempt assets for a claim that arose after the petition had been filed.

8. An unlawful detainer action commenced by a landlord on a lease that terminated five days before the petition was filed.

9. The repossession of a Chapter 7 debtor's automobile after the trustee has abandoned all assets and the debtor has received a discharge.

10. The garnishment of the debtor's checking account by the Internal Revenue Service for unpaid payroll taxes.

11. The issuance of a fine against the debtor by the Environmental Protection Agency as a result of pollution caused by seepage from the debtor's underground storage.

Before answering Exercises 12 through 14, review Section 362 of the Bankruptcy Code.

12. For each of the acts described in Exercises 1 through 11 that you determined was prohibited by the automatic stay, state the subsection of the Bankruptcy Code that justifies your answer.

13. For any acts described in Exercises 1 through 11 that you determined were not stayed, state why they were not stayed.

14. If you felt that additional information was needed to accurately determine whether an act would be prohibited, identify the information that was needed.

Matters relating to the assumption and rejection of executory contracts and unexpired leases are controlled by Section 365 of the Bankruptcy Code. For Exercises 15 through 20, determine which subsection of the Code—365(a), 365(b)(3), 365(d)(4), 365(e)(1), 365(h), or 365(k)—relates to the statement given.

15. An unexpired lease of nonresidential real property must be assumed within sixty days after the case is commenced or it will be deemed to have been rejected.

16. Assignment of a lease terminates the estate's liability for assumption or rejection.

17. Court approval is required for assumption or rejection.

18. A provision in a lease that purports to terminate it upon the appointment of a trustee is not enforceable.

19. The special provisions for shopping center leases.

20. The special provisions if the debtor is a seller of time-share interests.

21. Give two examples of contracts that would be executory under the Countryman test. Give two examples of contracts that would not be executory under the Countryman test.

22. The debtor entered into a fifty-year lease for a warehouse at a rent of $1,000 per month. At the beginning of year ten, the debtor was in default for four months' rent. If the debtor filed a Chapter 7 case on January 1 of year ten, when must the trustee assume or reject the lease? If the decision is to assume the lease, what must the trustee do? If the trustee uses the property for one month and then rejects the lease, what claims will the landlord have?

23. List all the ways in which a seller of goods can breach.

24. List all the ways in which a buyer of goods can breach.

25. With a classmate, negotiate a contract for the purchase and sale of a year's supply of strings to be used in the manufacture of a professional model of yo-yos. One person should assume the role of the buyer and the other, the seller. The price of three cents per string has already been agreed on and the buyer estimates it needs at least 10,000 strings per year with the need evenly spread over the year. All other terms remain to be negotiated.

26. After you have negotiated the contract pursuant to Exercise 25, discuss the rights of the buyer if the seller does not ship or if the strings delivered

are too long. Discuss the rights of the seller if the buyer does not accept a proper tender of the strings.

27. Does a seller who refuses to perform a contract because the debtor has commenced a bankruptcy case violate the automatic stay? If the seller commences a bankruptcy case, does a buyer who refuses to pay violate the automatic stay?

28. Construct a chart showing the three types of collateral, including the four categories of goods, and how a security interest is perfected for each type and category.

29. How is a security interest created? What are the steps required for it to attach? What are the steps required for it to be perfected?

30. What must a security agreement contain that is lacking in a financing statement?

31. Determine who prevails in the following situations:

    a. A bankruptcy trustee against a secured party with an unperfected security interest.

    b. A debtor in possession against a secured party with an unperfected security interest.

    c. A bankruptcy trustee against a secured party with a security interest in equipment who perfected by taking possession of the equipment before the commencement of the case.

    d. A bankruptcy trustee against a creditor with a security interest in promissory notes who perfected before the commencement of the case by filing a financing statement with the secretary of state.

    e. A bankruptcy trustee against a seller of washing machines who allows its customers to pay for their purchases over time in exchange for a security interest in the washing machines and who does not file a financing statement.

32. Has your state enacted Article 2A? If so, briefly summarize sections 2A–401, 2A–501, 2A–508, 2A-509, and 2A–523.

33. Myra Rosenthal needs expensive new video equipment for her business. The manufacturer has that equipment available. Can you think of reasons why Myra would rather buy or would rather lease the equipment? Can you think of different reasons why the manufacturer would rather sell or would rather lease the equipment to Myra?

34. If Myra is in bankruptcy, is the manufacturer better off if it leased the equipment to Myra or better off if it sold the equipment and took back a purchase money security interest?

35. What sales are exempted from your state's version of Article 6 of the UCC?

36. In what ways is a mortgage similar to a security agreement? In what ways is it dissimilar?

37. Why is there no system for determining personal property ownership as there is for real property?

38. What is the form and timing of the notice required to conduct a real property foreclosure sale in the state in which you live?

CHAPTER 5

BANKRUPTCY LEGAL RESEARCH AND WRITING

Most legal assistants clamor for the opportunity to do a legal research and writing assignment. Often lawyers are hesitant to give legal assistants these projects. Why? An explanation may be that lawyers, particularly more recent graduates, have generally spent a semester or a year in a special class or workshop designed to teach them legal research and writing. Legal assistants, however, may not have had the luxury of that training. Yet legal research and writing can be mastered and added to the legal assistant's repertoire of skills. In their most basic form, legal research and writing are merely answering a question and writing down the answer.

Of course, it is not that simple. The first step, finding the answer, may require looking at a variety of specialized sources. Those specialized sources for bankruptcy law and procedure are the focus of this chapter. The second step, expressing the answer, can take many forms (a letter, a memorandum, a pleading, or a brief). The answer is usually not a simple yes or no. Learning how to describe an answer that is neither black nor white, but shades of gray and applying the facts of a client's case to determine whether the gray is lighter or darker is the essence of legal analysis. This analysis is at the heart of all well-written letters, memoranda (usually referred to simply as memos), and briefs. It is beyond the scope of this textbook to discuss legal writing in depth, but we can review the basics.

A hypothetical situation will be used to examine bankruptcy legal research. The example may be familiar. An attorney, looking frazzled and obviously short on time, enters the legal assistant's office and sits down on the edge of the desk. The attorney relays the story of the client, a debtor in a Chapter 7 bankruptcy case. Thirty days before she filed the bankruptcy petition, the debtor charged $2,500 on her credit card to purchase that year's models of twelve inch fashion

dolls. Now six months later, the credit card company has filed a lawsuit in the bankruptcy court claiming that the $2,500 debt cannot be discharged in the debtor's bankruptcy case. New to these issues, the attorney wonders whether the debt is dischargeable.

The attorney asks the legal assistant two research questions:

1. Is this type of debt dischargeable?
2. Was the credit card company's lawsuit filed on time?

The legal assistant may not be sure of the answer to either question but agrees to do the research.

☐ LEGAL RESEARCH

This discussion first presents an overview of the various books the legal assistant might consult to answer the questions posed. It then examines the various approaches that might be used to answer the questions.

Sources

Statutes and Rules   The starting point for an answer to most substantive bankruptcy law questions is the Bankruptcy Code itself. Answers to procedural questions are often found in the Bankruptcy Rules or in the local rules adopted by the courts of each district.

The legal assistant can find the Bankruptcy Code in the multivolumed, hardbound set of the *United States Code Annotated*, published by West Publishing Company, or in the *United States Code Service*, published by Bancroft-Whitney Company. Each set takes up several shelves in the library. The Bankruptcy Code is found in Title 11 of each service.

As discussed earlier in this book, Congress frequently changes the Bankruptcy Code. Rather than republishing all of the Title 11 volumes each year, publishers update the books by the use of **pocket parts,** which are attached to the inside back cover. It is a cardinal rule of legal research to check the pocket part for an amendment to the statute; without that step, the statute cannot be relied upon.

The *United States Code Annotated* volumes are quite lengthy because each Code section is followed by short summaries of cases that interpret the section. The case summaries are a useful research tool; they are discussed in depth later in this chapter. A more succinct version to use is a single-volume softbound edition of the Bankruptcy Code. A number of companies publish such a version each year.

The Bankruptcy Rules can be found either at the end of the *United States Code Annotated* or, more commonly, in a desktop softbound version that is a companion to the Bankruptcy Code softbound volume. The local rules are available from the clerk of the bankruptcy court (often on diskette) or from a local legal publisher.

Legislative History   Legal research would certainly be easier if all questions were answered in the Bankruptcy Code. Unfortunately, it is impossible for any written law to be so precise. As a result, an important key to legal research is to look at other sources to determine how the Bankruptcy Code should be interpreted and applied to a given set of circumstances.

One source is the record of the passage through Congress of the Bankruptcy Code and its amendments. This record contains the written and oral statements

Pocket Parts
The method of updating bound compilations of decisions, statutes or digests that consist of periodically issued paperback editions that are usually attached to the inside back cover of a bound volume.

made by various members of Congress and its committees when they were considering the law. The congressional record for the Bankruptcy Code also contains committee recommendations, results of studies, testimonies by academicians and practitioners, and discarded versions of the bill that eventually became the Bankruptcy Code. Needless to say, the opinions and statements made in the record sometimes conflict. Because of this conflict, the legislative history of a particular statute is not binding upon a court, but it will be considered if the law itself is ambiguous.

Congressional legislative history is found in the *United States Code Congressional and Administrative News*, which is a multivolume set. Another source for this information is Volumes 2 and 3 of the appendix to the treatise *Collier on Bankruptcy*.Unfortunately, the material is voluminous and relatively unindexed; there are, however, helpful references at the end of each section of the *United States Code Annotated*. If the research must be done quickly, a useful source is the softbound desktop volume of the Bankruptcy Code. Most editions include excerpts from the legislative history after each Bankruptcy Code section.

Case Law   Congress could not have foreseen every possible factual situation that could arise under the Bankruptcy Code. As a consequence, bankruptcy courts must apply the law to the facts before them. To do this, they usually look to the decisions of other courts for guidance. Decisions made by higher courts in the same circuit as the bankruptcy court making the decision must be followed. The higher court's ruling is called **precedent,** and the notion that the lower court must follow it is called **stare decisis.** Exhibit 5.1 presents an abbreviated version of the hierarchy of the federal court system.

United States Supreme Court decisions must be followed by all other federal courts. United States court of appeals decisions must be followed by all of the district courts, the Bankruptcy Appellate Panel, and the bankruptcy courts *in that circuit.* For example, a Ninth Circuit Court of Appeals decision is binding upon all lower courts in Arizona, which is in the Ninth Circuit. The same Ninth Circuit decision is not binding on any of the other courts of appeals or on any lower court within other circuits. In other words, the bankruptcy courts in New York, which is in the Second Circuit, are not bound by Ninth Circuit decisions. Bankruptcy

Precedent

A case or decision considered as authority for an identical or similar case or question of law arising later.

Stare Decisis

The policy of courts to abide by or adhere to precedent.

■ EXHIBIT 5.1
The Bankruptcy Court Within the Federal Court System

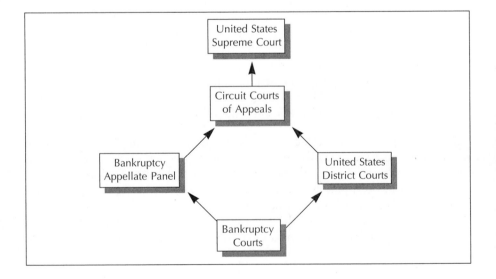

court decisions are not binding upon any other bankruptcy court. This does not mean that the decision of another court is not important. The bankruptcy court in Tennessee may find a Maine bankruptcy court's decision to be well-reasoned and may choose to follow it. Likewise, the Hawaiian bankruptcy court, which is in the Ninth Circuit, may find persuasive and follow a nonbinding decision rendered by the bankruptcy court in Texas, which is located in the Fifth Circuit.

In short, while it is important and helpful to find and review all the significant cases that address a given research topic, it is absolutely necessary to find and advise the court of all binding precedent in its circuit and district.

The next question is how to find precedental case law. Unlike other areas of law, no one legal publisher is the official reporter for bankruptcy court decisions. Instead, several publishers report decisions concerning bankruptcy issues regardless of which court issued the decision. Supreme Court and bankruptcy court decisions are contained in the same volume. Exhibit 5.2 presents a list of the more widely used bankruptcy case reporters, arranged by the type of issuing court.

Reporters of bankruptcy court and Bankruptcy Appellate Panel decisions also contain decisions of higher federal courts when a bankruptcy law issue is involved. But, not all district court cases involving bankruptcy law are published in the *Federal Supplement.*

Each publisher has a different method of indexing the cases in its system, yet each method involves the use of **headnotes.** Headnotes are very brief summaries (drafted by the publisher, not by the court) of the issues of law decided in the case. The printed version of the case usually presents a summary of the case or the headnotes after the title of the case and before the actual opinion. The case usually has as many headnotes as it has issues or points of law. The section in this chapter on research approach discusses how to use each publisher's system of headnotes and indexing.

Headnotes
Summaries of points of law made in a judicial opinion. They generally precede the text of the opinion.

Secondary Sources   Secondary sources are a catchall category of books, articles, outlines, treatises, and other materials that contain general explanations of the law and how it has been applied. These sources are particularly useful when the researcher is unfamiliar with the Bankruptcy Code section and needs a broad overview to help guide the research.

There are many excellent secondary sources that can be used in bankruptcy practice. Most bankruptcy libraries will contain at least one single or multi-volume

■ EXHIBIT 5.2
Bankruptcy Case Reporters

Court Issuing Decision	Where to Find the Decision	Publisher
U.S. Supreme Court	*U.S. Reports*	Government Printing Office
	Lawyers Edition, 2d	Bancroft-Whitney
	Supreme Court Reporter	West
Court of appeals	*Federal Reporter*	West
District courts	*Federal Supplement*	West
The above courts, bankruptcy courts, and Bankruptcy Appellate Panels	*Bankruptcy Court Decisions*	L.R.P. Publications (formerly C.R.R.)
	Bankruptcy Law Reporter	Commerce Clearing House
	Bankruptcy Reporter	West
	Collier Bankruptcy Cases	Matthew Bender

treatise of the law, usually arranged by Bankruptcy Code section. In addition, there are a number of law reviews dedicated to bankruptcy law such as *The American Bankruptcy Journal,* the *Bankruptcy Developments Journal,* the *Journal of Bankruptcy Law and Practice,* and the *California Bankruptcy Journal.* Each of these has insightful articles concerning various bankruptcy issues.

Secondary sources are not binding. They are not pronouncements from courts and they are sometimes merely statements of the author's opinion. However, if a definitive and binding decision does not exist, it is quite acceptable to quote from secondary sources. The bankruptcy judge may find the logic or reasoning attractive and it may help to explain an otherwise difficult concept.

The Approach

There are two general approaches to research. Which one you use depends upon whether you are unfamiliar with the topic to be researched, have been asked to research a particular Bankruptcy Code section, or know that the answer will turn on the interpretation of that section. We use the hypothetical given earlier to demonstrate each approach. Exhibit 5.3 may help you visualize the necessary steps for each of the two approaches.

Finding the Law by Topic   When little or nothing is known about a subject, it is best to start by consulting secondary sources for a general understanding. For example, if the legal assistant does not know the general discharge concepts, it would be wise to consult a treatise for a general explanation of how and why a debtor is discharged from debt.

Having learned through secondary sources that there are certain categories of debts that will not be discharged in a Chapter 7 case, the legal assistant will be ready to address the question of whether this particular debt can be discharged

■ EXHIBIT 5.3
Approaches to Legal
Research

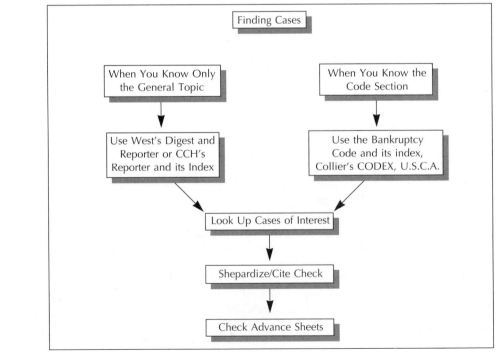

under the facts given. The first step is to determine whether a particular Bankruptcy Code section is on point. The easiest way to make this determination is to turn to the Bankruptcy Code index. The index shows that Section 523 lists the exceptions to discharge.

Finding Section 523 does not conclude the research. The section states only that consumer debts for "luxury goods and services" owed to a single creditor, aggregating more than $1,000, and incurred within sixty days before the order for relief (the date the voluntary petition was filed) are presumed to be nondischargeable. Section 523 (a)(2)(C) does not say whether collectibles are luxury goods. Because a Bankruptcy Code section that applies has been found, it would be appropriate at this point to branch into the second approach of finding the law—by indexes based on a Code section. But, for discussion purposes, the topic approach will be explored a little further.

Sometimes bankruptcy research cannot be accomplished very well or efficiently by use of a Bankruptcy Code section. The research assignment may involve the interrelation of a number of sections or an issue may not be specifically addressed in the Bankruptcy Code. In those situations, it is more efficient to research by topic.

Although there are many sources that publish cases, the West or Commerce Clearing House (CCH) Reporters are best organized for using a topic approach. Of the two, West is the more commonly used.

The West system for locating cases is divided into two parts. The cases are printed in hardbound volumes called West's *Bankruptcy Reporter*. The cases are indexed by topic in West's *Bankruptcy Digest*, which accompanies the *Bankruptcy Reporter*. The two sets of books are usually found side-by-side in the library.

The *Digest* is used to locate cases. The editors of West Publishing Company divide every area of the law into topics and narrow categories called key numbers. Each key number represents one category or issue in the area. Bankruptcy law has been divided into over one thousand key numbers.

Each case is assigned as many key numbers as there are issues in the case. The key numbers appear at the beginning of the case, after the title, and are cross-referenced in the *Digest* by topic. Once the correct topic and key number are identified, it is easy to turn to the *Digest* for the list of all cases that address that key number topic.

In the front of each volume of the *Digest* is an outline that lists the key numbers numerically. The outline should be reviewed for relevant words and phrases in the index. For example, the first word that may come to mind in researching the hypothetical is *discharge*. If you consult the outline, a part which is reprinted in Exhibit 5.4, you will see key number 3353 (15) which should lead to all the cases that discuss this subject matter.

After the *Digest* outline, the next stop is the *Digest* itself. Key number 3353 is in Volume 17 of the Digest. A page from the *Digest* is reproduced here in Exhibit 5.5. Under the relevant key number there are short summaries of all the cases that contain the key number. All relevant cases in the topic area can be previewed by reading these summaries; only the most relevant need be read in their entirety in the *Bankruptcy Reporter* volumes.

In 1988, West reassigned all of the bankruptcy key numbers. A conversion chart is located in the front of the more recent *Digest* volumes. You will need to use the conversion chart if you find a useful topic entry in a pre-1988 opinion.

Key number 3353(15) contains many headnotes, most of which address the issue. The initials preceding the headnote indicate the place of origin of the case and the level of the court (for example, C.A. is the court of appeals, D.C. is the

■ EXHIBIT 5.4
West's Bankruptcy Digest Outline

---

17 Bkrptcy D—25

BANKRUPTCY

X. DISCHARGE.—Continued.

    (C). DEBTS AND LIABILITIES DISCHARGED.—Continued.

        1. IN GENERAL.—Continued.

            ⟸3353. Debts for goods, services, or credit obtained by fraud, etc.—Continued.

                (14). Reliance; time element.

                (14.5). Reasonableness.

                (14.10). —— Creditor's duty to investigate; sufficiency of investigation.

                (14.15). —— Loss or prejudice.

                (14.20). —— Partial reliance.

                (14.25). —— Particular cases.

                (14.30). —— Banks, cases involving.

                (15). Luxury goods.

            3354. Torts and crimes.

            3355. —— Wilful or malicious injury.

                (1). In general.

                (1.10). Wilful, deliberate, or intentional injury.

                (1.15). Recklessness or negligence.

                (1.20). Knowledge; knowing disregard.

                (1.25). Malice; malicious injury.

                (1.30). Spite, hatred, or ill will.

                (1.35). Just cause or excuse.

                (2). Particular injuries; fraud.

                (3). —— Trover and conversion.

                (4). —— Disposition of or injury to collateral.

                (5). —— Drunk or reckless driving; vehicular homicide.

            3356. —— Larceny or embezzlement.

            3357. —— Fraud or defalcation in fiduciary capacity.

                (1). In general.

                (2). Fiduciaries and fiduciary capacity.

                (3). —— Trustees.

                (4). Defalcation.

                (5). Fraud.

            3358. —— Fines, penalties, and forfeitures; punitive damages.

            3359. —— Probation and conditions; restitution.

            3360. Costs and fees.

            3361. Debts not scheduled or listed.

            3362. Post-petition debts or liabilities.

        2. DETERMINATION OF DISCHARGEABILITY.

            ⟸3381. In general.

            3382. Time for proceedings.

            3383. —— Extension of time.

            3384. Pleading.

            3385. Parties, standing.

            3386. Evidence.

            3387. Hearing and determination; default.

            3388. —— Award on determination of non-dischargeability.

■ EXHIBIT 5.5
West's Bankruptcy Digest

17 Bkrptcy D—537

BANKRUPTCY   ☜3353(15)

For collateral, non-bankruptcy questions, see other West Digests

Bkrtcy.D.Utah 1984. Debtor's offhand remarks about campaign debts which he did not expect to be required to pay did not require bank to investigate whether those debts had been reduced to judgment against debtor prior to giving loan to debtor.

In re Harmer, 61 B.R. 1.

Bank acted reasonably within meaning of provision of Bankruptcy Code governing nondischargeability of debt based upon materially false financial statement in writing, where bank followed its normal business practice of not only procuring debtor's signature on loan application, but also met with debtor and interviewed him, discussing his financial statement and asking for updated version. Bankr.Code, 11 U.S.C.A. § 523(a)(2)(B).

In re Harmer, 61 B.R. 1.

Bkrtcy.Vt. 1983. In order to sustain a claim of nondischargeability, it must be established that debtor made a materially false representation, that representation was made with intent to defraud, and that the bank relied on false misrepresentation; burden of proving each of these elements is upon the party seeking to come within statutory exception to discharge, and this must be proven by clear and convincing evidence. Bankr.Code, 11 U.S.C.A. §§ 523, 523(a)(2).

In re Griffis, 29 B.R. 110.

Bkrtcy.Vt. 1981. Where consolidated loan was made at request of bank's management, debtor was called into bank by loan consultant and was handed both application for loan which was made out by representative of bank and promissory note, there was no attempt by bank's agent to explain necessity of signing accurate statement of then outstanding debts of debtor, and only purpose of consolidation loan was to convert number of delinquent loans into one which was current, there was no intent to deceive on part of debtor and bank could not reasonably have relied on statement which it prepared and was signed by debtor; thus, consolidation loan was not subject to provisions of bankruptcy statute which makes debt nondischargeable on account of false financial statement. Bankr.Act, § 17(a)(2), 11 U.S.C.A. § 35(a)(2); Bankr.Code, 11 U.S.C.A. § 523(a)(2)(B)(i–iv).

In re Bacon, 13 B.R. 559.

Bkrtcy.E.D.Va. 1987. Fact that debtor estimated his annual income in loan application did not render bank's reliance on financial statement unreasonable, for purpose of determining whether debt was dischargeable, where bank took reasonable steps to determine accuracy of estimate and was entitled to rely on information supplied by debtor and third party. Bankr.Code, 11 U.S.C.A. § 523(a)(2)(B)(iii).

In re Dishaw, 78 B.R. 120.

Bkrtcy.Va. 1981. Bank which made its own title search of property and failed to discover existence of deed of trust did not rely on affidavit of seller which did not mention the deed of trust and thus could not avoid discharge of the debtor's debt on the theory that he had acted fraudulently.

In re Hallman, 12 B.R. 502.

Bkrtcy.Wis. 1984. Debtor's debt to bank was not excepted from discharge on basis of debtor's false representations that he had authority to pledge several diamonds as additional security because bank's reliance on the representation was unreasonable and the loan did not remain unpaid as proximate result of debtor's representations. Bankr.Code, 11 U.S.C.A. § 523(a)(2)(A).

Matter of Eaton, 41 B.R. 800.

* Bkrtcy.Tenn. 1979. Bank could not be deemed to have reasonably and justifiably relied on financial statement so as to obtain relief from discharge of its debt on grounds of falsity of the statement, though statement listed certain real estate as being owned by bankrupt when in fact it was owned with his wife as tenants by the entirety, since bank president's actual knowledge that title to the property had been vested in bankrupt and his wife a year and a half earlier was sufficient to put him on inquiry to determine whether there had been the change in title that bankrupt's financial statement indicated. Bankr.Act, § 17(a)(2), 11 U.S.C.A. § 35(a)(2).

In re Yeiser, 2 B.R. 98.

☜3353(15). **Luxury goods.**

Bkrtcy.S.D.Fla. 1988. In order to obtain order denying dischargeability of debt, as having been obtained by false financial statement, creditor must prove by clear and convincing evidence that statement: is "materially false"; that it "reasonably relied" upon statement; in "extension, renewal of refinancing of credit"; and that debtor "caused [the statement] to be made or published with intent to deceive." Bankr.Code, 11 U.S.C.A. § 523(a)(2)(B).

In re Figueredo, 84 B.R. 856.

Bkrtcy.La. 1984. Debtor's use of credit card to go on "spending spree" involving largely luxury, nonnecessary items at time when he was unemployed, hopelessly insolvent, and had discussed bankruptcy with his attorney demonstrated debtor's fraudulent intent sufficient to render resulting debt, including contractually agreed upon interest, attorney fees, and expenses, nondischargeable in bankruptcy. Bankr.Code, 11 U.S.C.A. § 523(a)(2)(A).

In re Kramer, 38 B.R. 80.

Bkrtcy.Minn. 1984. Debt representing credit card purchases of two oriental throw rugs was nondischargeable under Bankruptcy

* denotes cases governed by laws preceding Bankruptcy Code

district court). This is important for *stare decisis* purposes. The end of the headnote provides a cite to the name of the case, the case reporter volume, and the page on which the case may be found. The reporter abbreviations are explained in the front of the *Digest*. The most common abbreviations are B.R. for West's *Bankruptcy Reporter* and F.2d for West's *Federal Reporter*, second edition. Also, *Id.* is used as a shorthand way to refer to the case cited immediately previous, without having to repeat the long formal citation.

Once you have located the appropriate key number, there are two ways of proceeding. The first is to locate and read the actual cases. The second is to simply write down the cites and move on to another *Digest*, looking for more cases under the same or the updated key number.

It is imperative that the text of any case cited be read in full. The headnotes are not authority; they are merely summaries written by editors who have read the case and attempted to pick out what they thought were the important points. The headnotes can be incomplete.

Once all of the relevant cases have been located, they must be checked to be sure they are up to date. This must be done prior to drafting a memo or other paper to be sure that the cases relied upon are not on appeal or, worse yet, overruled. This process of updating, called **Shepardizing** after the publications used, is discussed later in this chapter.

Shepardizing
Determining the subsequent history of a case by use of *Shepard's Citations*.

Finding the Law by a Code Section   Starting with the Bankruptcy Code itself can be a shortcut for bankruptcy research. If there is a Bankruptcy Code section on point, the research can focus on the cases that interpret that section.

Under the hypothetical, the best word to look for in the index is *discharge* which leads to Bankruptcy Code Section 523. As mentioned, this section dictates that certain types of debts, including those for luxury goods and services, can be excepted from the debtor's discharge. The section gives an answer of sorts to the research question, but it is an incomplete answer.

Although the topic approach just explained could be used, there is another method. A Matthew Bender publication, *Collier Bankruptcy Cases* categorizes cases by the Bankruptcy Code section they interpret. Instead of a *Digest* or key number system, Collier's has a single volume at the end of the bound volumes of cases called the *Codex*. A list of cases that interpret Section 523 appears under Section 523 in the *Codex*. The *Codex* is quite specific, and cites to cases that interpret subparts of subsections of the bankruptcy Code. *Bankruptcy Code Decisions* published by L.R.P. Publications are indexed in the same manner, but each index only covers certain volumes.

Although this method is very useful when there is a known Bankruptcy Code section on point, it is not as useful when the task involves integrating a number of different sections or is topical, and not Bankruptcy Code specific. To be completely thorough, time permitting, it is wise to use both the topic approach and the statute approach. One service may often refer to cases that, for some reason, the other has decided not to report.

A similar statute-specific approach can be used in connection with the *United States Code Annotated* and *United States Code Service*. Although these services cite to every federal code section from criminal law to civil procedure, there are several volumes devoted solely to Title 11. Like the *Codex*, these volumes are arranged numerically by Code section and the headnotes are arranged under each section. Again, the pocket part in the back of each volume must always be checked because it contains the most recent cases.

Updating Case Law   Once a case on point has been located and will be relied upon in the written analysis, it must be updated to ensure that it is still good law and has not been reconsidered, reversed, or modified. The case also needs to be updated to determine if a higher court affirmed the decision (thereby adding weight to the authority.)

This procedure of updating is referred to by some as **cite checking,** that is, checking to see that the cite in a brief or memo is still good law. Complete cite checking also includes a review of the case cited to be sure it stands for the principal for which it is cited. Frequently, page or volume numbers are mistranscribed: it is only through the cite checking process that such errors are caught.

Shepard's Citations, a publication of McGraw-Hill, makes updating fairly easy. Its abbreviations are sometimes confusing, but there is a table of abbreviations in the front few pages of every volume.

All of the services that report cases containing bankruptcy issues are listed in various *Shepard's Citations*. The bound volumes are divided into sections based upon the name of the reporter: there is a special section for *U.S. Supreme Court Reports*, one for West's *Fed.2d* series, one for Collier's *Bankruptcy Cases*, one for West's Bankruptcy Reporter, and another for CCH *Bankruptcy Law Reports*, to name a few. The softbound volumes of Shepard's, which contain the more recent citations, follow the same format.

The first step in checking a cite is to determine the reporting service and volume in which the case to be checked is found. By way of example, one of the cases located during the dischargeability research was *In re Orecchio* found in Volume 109 of West's *Bankruptcy Reporter* beginning at page 285. In Shepard's *Bankruptcy Citations* (1993) in the West's Bankruptcy Reporter section is a page like that shown in Exhibit 5.6. The volume number is listed at the top of the column and is then followed by a series of numbers and letters. The numbers that are in bold and preceded and followed by dashes indicate the first page on which the case may be found in that volume.

Page 285 for Volume 109 is not listed. This could mean that the wrong page is being looked at or that the volume and page number were incorrectly copied. It could also mean that the case is so new that there has been no subsequent history and no other reporting service has thought that the case was significant enough to report it. When this occurs, Shepard's is simply blank.

As with any cite checking, the most recent volumes must always be checked. What was good law when the 1993 edition of Shepard's was published may have since been overruled. Exhibit 5.7 shows the pocket supplement that followed the 1993 bound volume. The *Orecchio* case is reported in this volume. The cite is to one from the Eleventh Circuit decided subsequent to the *Ocecchio* case that refers to or mentions *Ocecchio*.

Shepard's often gives editorial help by preceding the citation with a letter reference. A small *r*, *o*, or *c* is crucial since those symbols are used to indicate that the subsequent case reversed, overruled, or criticized the case being shepardized. Other common symbols are *e* for explained, *d* for distinguished, and *f* for followed.

A similarly useful aspect of Shepard's is that when it cites to cases reported in West's publications, it also cites to the headnotes, where appropriate. As you've seen, in West's *Reporters*, the actual opinion in each case is preceded by a summary of the case and a list of the key numbers found in the case. West's assigns each headnote and paragraph in the opinion numbers corresponding to the key numbers. Therefore, if you are interested in only one legal point in a thirty-page opinion, you can then turn immediately to that paragraph and point of law rather than

Cite Checking
The process of reviewing legal writing to ensure that all cases have not been reversed or modified, are correctly cited, and that all quotations are accurate.

■ EXHIBIT 5.6
Shepard's Bankruptcy Citations (1993)

BANKRUPTCY REPORTER (WEST)

Vol. 109

Cir. 5	—243—	—283—	132BRW¹	Nebr	—442—	—524—	21BCD1153
134BRW212	a114BRW473	Cir. 7	[1006	457NW²801	(19BCD1952)	Cir. 7	22BCD608
Cir. 6	142BRW162	914F2d³106	Cir. 8		(23CBC2d	f114BRW612	
118BRW524	BLD¶74660	20BCD1700	927F2d³417	—382—	[354)	f20BCD867	—600—
26CBC2d87		BLD¶73622	Cir. 9	Cir. 8		fBLD¶73405	(BLD¶
	—245—	23CBC2d	f954F2d572	130BRW299	—445—	f23CBC2d533	[73210)
—197—	Cir. 9	[1161	954F2d574		(20BCD184)		r121BRW140
s92BRW172	f116BRW⁴224		21BCD751	—384—		—527—	r21BCD162
s102BRW71	Cir. 10	—291—	f22BCD846	a131BRW137	—455—	s872F2d496	rBLD¶73729
s117BRW231	122BRW¹441	Cir. 6	22BCD847	Cir. 9	(20BCD33)	s684FS319	
Cir. 5	122BRW²441	140BRW458	BLD¶73991	123BRW878	s75BRW580	26COA295§8	—605—
d914F2d⁵736	122BRW³441	140BRW³459	fBLD¶74539	21BCD553			s936F2d640
d914F2d¹²736			BLD¶74539		—467—	—534—	s602FS511
113BRW⁵257	—250—	—294—	24CBC2d	—392—	(19BCD1937)	Case 1	s603FS370
	Cir. 6	(19BCD1882)	[1532	a940F2d558	85NwL941	Cir. 3	s629FS860
—202—	125BRW¹179	Cir. 4	25CBC2d¹			c141BRW¹87	s709FS70
m22BCD1055	136BRW696	d128BRW²		—397—	—478—	Cir. 9	s747FS194
mBLD¶74471	Cir. 10	[959	f26CBC2d652	(22CBC2d	s116BRW854	c116BRW¹	N Y
s960F2d1277	129BRW¹252		26CBC2d655	[271)		[226	cc121NYA1D
s26CBC2d990	25CBC2d320	—297—	N M	Cir. 4	—481—		[923
Cir. DC		(21CBC2d	824P2d358	127BRW⁸365	(20BCD11)	—534—	cc504NYS2d
131BRW¹762	—255—	[1431)		Cir. 8	e125BRW¹	Case 2	[646
Cir. 2	(20BCD181)		—341—	120BRW²529	[365	Cir. 2	Cir. 2
125BRW⁹77	Cir. 6	—301—	(19BCD1940)	Cir. 10		130BRW¹401	d113BRW⁴
Cir. 7	115BRW¹584	Cir. 2	(22CBC2d	f136BRW873	—484—	cBLD¶74690	[851
137BRW292	20BCD1035	e142BRW³50	[468)		a127BRW62		d113BRW⁵
22BCD160	23CBC2d274	Cir. 6	Cir. 9	—403—	s108BRW799	—541—	[851
BLD¶74262		115BRW603	124BRW²804	(22CBC2d	Cir. 2	Cir. 10	d20BCD797
	—260—	115BRW³604	124BRW⁴804	[246)	121BRW¹139	138BRW971	dBLD¶73392
—210—	Cir. 6		c124BRW⁴	Cir. 5	Cir. 4	138BRW³973	d22CBC2d
Cir. 2	d142BRW⁷	—308—	[805	d128BRW155	f141BRW106		[1733
117BRW¹784	[814	s90BRW344	c21BCD703		26COA773§	—548—	
117BRW⁵786	142BRW⁸814	Cir. 3	c24CBC2d	—405—	[14	cc61BRW349	—609—
Cir. 5	dBLD¶74790	d124BRW182	[1901	(19BCD1879)		Cir. 9	cc77BRW433
125BRW⁵167				(22CBC2d1)	—489—	cc75BRW92	Cir. 2
f127BRW⁵793	—264—	—315—	—347—	a126BRW822	Cir. 2		118BRW²236
24CBC2d	(BLD¶	Cir. DC	(19BCD1899)		121BRW139	—550—	119BRW²233
[2120	[73242)	d910F2d¹963	Cir. 2	—410—	Cir. 10	Cir. 4	121BRW¹441
	s99BRW768		140BRW838	(19BCD1851)	121BRW75	139BRW²379	139BRW²796
—214—	Cir. DC	—321—	Cir. 6	(BLD¶	121BRW²277	BLD¶74614	Cir. 3
Cir. 5	f118BRW¹154	Cir. 1	f139BRW³832	[73240)	Cir. 11		138BRW¹445
e134BRW852	Cir. 3	f126BRW⁹417	Cir. 7	(22CBC2d	f142BRW¹518	—557—	
	f135BRW¹501	Cir. 2	112BRW960	[412)		Cir. 8	—613—
—216—	f122BRW¹493	132BRW⁵7	20BCD598		—492—	121BRW³574	D924F2d480
Cir. 1	127BRW16	Cir. 5	22BCD1555	—412—	Cir. 11	24CBC2d	s826F2d1177
968F2d²⁵1361	Cir. 6	130BRW494	85NwL929	Cir. 5	127BRW²493	[1038	s87BRW779
Cir. 5	f131BRW¹814	142BRW⁹784		135BRW³815	e132BRW²		922F2d989
120BRW80	Cir. 8	Cir. 6	—352—	e139BRW²	[466	—562—	922F2d⁸995
Cir. 7	130BRW¹532	118BRW554	(BLD¶	[819		(BLD¶	120BRW657
133BRW¹5	f130BRW¹533	Cir. 7	[73195)	Cir. 10	—494—	[73236)	120BRW657
[220	Cir. 11	967F2d1154	Cir. 3	120BRW³576	Cir. 1	26COA773§9	[658
Cir. 8	f142BRW¹532	f117BRW⁹345	d126BRW¹39	20BCD1982	f113BRW¹112		124BRW⁹642
126BRW583	21BCD1132	c132BRW⁹	dBLD¶73903		120BRW¹5	—569—	129BRW¹0
21BCD861	f21BCD1651	[726		—421—	f125BRW¹68	s103BRW379	[843
BLD¶74697	f22BCD248	133BRW⁹624	—362—	Cir. 6	Cir. 5		136BRW²926
26COA773§9	f22BCD811	Cir. 9	(19BCD1980)	115BRW¹95	134BRW217	—570—	Cir. 5
	BLD¶73992	129BRW⁹635	(22CBC2d		134BRW¹219	(22CBC2d	134BRW⁸205
—229—		Cir. 11	[1316)	—424—	Cir. 9	[374)	Cir. 6
(20BCD109)	—273—	125BRW⁹854	Cir. 8	123BRW¹564	134BRW10	Cir. 2	142BRW⁹184
Cir. 3	Cir. 6	21BCD1648	112BRW⁴973	Cir. 6	f21BCD828	128BRW⁴331	142BRW185
127BRW¹350	133BRW³881	fBLD¶73433	Cir. 10	123BRW¹564	22BCD404		21BCD180
105ARF568n	133BRW¹882	BLD¶74752	123BRW909	—434—	d22BCD434	—575—	BLD¶73747
105ARF579n	140BRW³457	23CBC2d818	20BCD610	s109BRW441	fBLD¶73893	Case 2	BLD¶74030
	140BRW⁴457			Cir. 8	26CBC2d108	Cir. 1	
—238—	140BRW³888	—335—	—368—	f924F2d²787	26CBC2d109	142BRW¹585	—626—
Cir. 9		Cir. 3	Cir. 6	924F2d³791		d142BRW³	s129BRW375
119BRW³775	—278—	141BRW²54	130BRW254	947F2d⁴866	—497—	[586	s25CBC2d237
24CBC2d436	Cir. 6	141BRW³54	Cir. 8		s135BRW912	Cir. 2	Cir. 3
	113BRW398	c141BRW55	120BRW⁵526	—441—		133BRW19	137BRW175
—241—	140BRW⁴699	Cir. 7	Cir. 11	s109BRW434	—506—	133BRW³22	Cir. 7
Cir. 7	140BRW³702	e118BRW²	140BRW⁶587		(22CBC2d13)	Cir. 3	129BRW²
130BRW285		[650	22BCD1625			119BRW469	[1009
21BCD1624		119BRW²644	22BCD1626			Cir. 8	f134BRW281
25CBC2d519		c125BRW972	BLD¶74670			132BRW³615	
101ARF554n		125BRW976	Minn			Cir. 10	
		c125BRW980	485NW²706			126BRW³103	
						136BRW⁴873	*Continued*

■ EXHIBIT 5.7
Shepard's Supplement

BANKRUPTCY REPORTER (WEST)

Vol. 108

—815—
Cir. 1
f151BRW636
Cir. 10
160BRW670
Okla
871P2d425

—823—
Cir. 8
144BRW[1]850
145BRW[1]298

—826—
Cir. 5
164BRW545
169BRW626
Cir. 11
157BRW909
29CBC2d856

—838—
Cir. 11
123BRW[8]121
d162BRW[8]
[920
164BRW793

—854—
s148BRW702
s160BRW404
Cir. 1
147BRW298
153BRW383
164BRW209
164BRW215
Cir. 4
148BRW446
Cir. 9
166BRW923
24BCD231
25BCD995
BLD¶75930
N M
114NM160
836P2d79

—901—
Case 2
Cir. 2
148BRW[21]
[200
28CBC2d63

—951—
Cir. 2
f165BRW367
Cir. 8
153BRW293
153BRW[4]295
24BCD243
24BCD244
28CBC2d
[1179

—956—
Cir. 3
d148BRW[59]
111ALRF457n

—962—
Cir. 2
e131BRW[8]
[930
162BRW[1]434
25BCD124

30CBC2d889
c30CBC2d890

—971—
Cir. DC
148BRW682
Cir. 2
166BRW[1]566
Cir. 3
f141BRW[4]883
144BRW[4]263
e146BRW644
155BRW101
160BRW769
161BRW135
161BRW[1]140
163BRW[5]56
163BRW[6]60
163BRW760
165BRW[12]
[567
165BRW[4]570
165BRW[5]571
165BRW[5]575
169BRW[7]109
169BRW[18]
[112
Cir. 6
152BRW502
7F3d131
Cir. 9
166BRW433
Cir. 10
168BRW758
Cir. 11
144BRW[18]
[940
160BRW223
163BRW[1]399
168BRW440
e23BCD47
23BCD211
23BCD212
f23BCD213
24BCD611
24BCD1239
24BCD1405
24BCD1562
25BCD1179
BLD¶74986
BLD¶75443
BLD¶75467
BLD¶75901
BLD¶75993
BLD¶75994
q27CBC2d241
27CBC2d568
e27CBC2d
[1371
29CBC2d
[1587
30CBC2d826
44StnL95

—998—
Cir. 3
164BRW[11]
[902
Cir. 5
148BRW[4]270
148BRW[1]271
f148BRW[10]
[271

—1007—
Cir. 9
157BRW[1]895
24BCD1066
29CBC2d882

—1009—
Cir. 11
164BRW[1]674
164BRW1007
25BCD637
BLD¶74927

Vol. 109

—1—
Cir. 7
f142BRW[1]284
153BRW[1]542
f23BCD149
f27CBC2d711

—14—
Cir. 1
f149BRW243
f156BRW7
163BRW[1]915
Cir. 3
146BRW944
c23BCD82
23BCD1429
BLD¶75097

—18—
Cir. 2
145BRW[22]
[753
164BRW[22]
[819
Cir. 8
168BRW[1]966

—36—
Cir. 1
150BRW[5]289
156BRW359
24BCD121
Cir. 5
151BRW[4]392
Cir. 6
989F2d[1]213
147BRW19
Cir. 7
144BRW[1]82
c171BRW[2]60
24BCD121
BLD¶75022
BLD¶75169
BLD¶75388
28CBC2d
[1122
110ALRF179n

—51—
Cir. 2
840FS991
Cir. 9
154BRW313
Cir. 10
q146BRW35
c27CBC2d124
27CBC2d125
78VaL477

—64—
Cir. 7
c985F2d321
cBLD¶75282

—74—
Cir. 3
160BRW[7]746
Cir. 8
796FS1242
24BCD1483
30CBC2d181

—96—
Cir. 9
147BRW243

—101—
Cir. 2
165BRW366
Cir. 3
145BRW486
27CBC2d
[1302

—107—
Cir. 4
164BRW248

—113—
Cir. 3
155BRW[13]
[925
Cir. 7
166BRW[11]
166BRW[4]652
BLD¶75907
28CBC2d419

—127—
Cir. 3
148BRW781
f148BRW[2]782
d148BRW[3]
[782
169BRW[1]562
25BCD1431

—136—
Cir. 3
151BRW352
155BRW682

—140—
Cir. 3
22F3d1238
f145BRW[3]498
Cir. 10
148BRW587
f23BCD806
25BCD784
fBLD¶74965
BLD¶75828

—149—
Cir. 10
167BRW[6]980
167BRW[7]980

—157—
Cir. 1
c146BRW899
c27CBC2d
[1348

—167—
Cir. 11
169BRW[3]
[1022
BLD¶76006
14ALR527n

—179—
Cir. 2
166BRW[4]815
f166BRW816
Cir. 9
d150BRW242
Cir. 11
160BRW248
dBLD¶75200
BLD¶76083
29CBC2d
[1374

—182—
Cir. 7
170BRW379
Cir. 8
156BRW633
BLD¶75394
29CBC2d764

—195—
Cir. 8
145BRW[3]295
Cir. 11
f166BRW983
e23BCD1276
25BCD579
f25BCD969
fBLD¶75896

—197—
Cir. 7
d3F3d[12]1048
dBLD¶75398

—210—
Cir. 2
149BRW59
Cir. 3
156BRW939
23BCD1355
BLD¶75393

—216—
Cir. 2
169BRW839
Cir. 5
f154BRW912
Cir. 6
153BRW482
Cir. 10
990F2d559
990F2d[20]571
Cir. 11
f146BRW306
e154BRW
[1021
169BRW[2]233
f23BCD924
f24BCD483
e24BCD580
e24BCD581
25BCD1374
BLD¶75218
BLD¶75220
BLD¶75995
28CBC2d
[1001
1992WLR
[1002

—229—
Cir. 6
155BRW461

—243—
27CBC2d317

—245—
999F2d[3]613
Cir. 11
f150BRW[1]806
150BRW[2]807

—250—
Cir. 6
e147BRW[2]
[413
147BRW[1]414
162BRW[1]750
166BRW[3]321
eBLD¶75001
BLD¶75883

—255—
Cir. DC
170BRW7
Cir. 5
164BRW942
Cir. 7
e148BRW530
Cir. 11

—260—
Cir. 2
d27CBC2d352

—264—
Cir. 3
f135BRW[1]501
146BRW530
148BRW[1]231
148BRW240
Cir. 5
164BRW940
166BRW866
Cir. 7
c145BRW[1]
[604
f148BRW[1]310
f148BRW[2]313
152BRW528
c23BCD853
23BCD854
23BCD1159
25BCD578
cBLD¶74966
BLD¶74966
27CBC2d
[1284

—285—
Cir. 11
154BRW768

—291—
Cir. 6
158BRW952

—297—
Cir. 6
158BRW[1]975
24BCD1179

—301—
e27CBC2d410

—321—
Cir. 2
167BRW19
23BCD299
BLD¶75838
27CBC2d747

—335—
Cir. 1
152BRW[2]13
Cir. 6
990F2d[2]910
Cir. 7
f149BRW[3]520
c149BRW522
150BRW426
156BRW[2]
[1005
d156BRW
[1011
167BRW[1]524
167BRW[2]525
Cir. 11
144BRW[3]936
147BRW[3]
[1019
q23BCD65
23BCD688
f23BCD1391
c23BCD1393
25BCD1049
BLD¶74936
fBLD¶75105
cBLD¶75105
BLD¶75438
dBLD¶75438
25BCD2d421
q27CBC2d422
27CBC2d
[1242
28CBC2d[2]289
28CBC2d
[1007
29CBC2d646
d29CBC2d653
La
635So2d714
N M
113NM218

—341—
Cir. 11
j30CBC2d466

—347—
Cir. 8
e160BRW352
c24BCD1332
e30CBC2d27

—352—
Cir. 1
164BRW[1]405
BLD¶75736

—368—
Cir. 2
163BRW[4]696
Cir. 7
150BRW40
Ga
212GaA456
442SE267

—384—
Cir. 8
149BRW937

—390—
Cir. 5
157BRW991

—397—
Cir. 3
19F3d843
Cir. 4
153BRW[6]719
Cir. 8
148BRW[8]562
Cir. 9
171BRW[4]111
25BCD613
25BCD1499
BLD¶75768
30CBC2d
[1274

—412—
Cir. 3
150BRW[2]353
115ALRF621n

—434—
s977F2d1318

—441—
s977F2d1318
114ALRF385n

—455—
Cir. 2
161BRW566
Cir. 3
f160BRW770
25BCD51
BLD¶75664

—481—
Cir. 7
147BRW[1]472
Cir. 9
f167BRW[2]586

—484—
Cir. 11
154BRW594
f154BRW[2]596
154BRW780
d154BRW786
161BRW[1]740
f24BCD144
f24BCD145
d24BCD148
30CBC2d510

—489—
Cir. 11

Continued

reading the entire opinion. Shepard's refers to this paragraph numbering system by use of a small, raised number preceding the page number. Referring to Exhibit 5.6 for a case distinguishing the first headnote of the case found at 109 B.R. 352, Shepard's points to 126 *BRW* at page 39, which discusses only the issue in that headnote.

To properly shepardize, all recent paperback versions of Shepard's must be reviewed. Yet, even the most recent Shepard's are sometimes several months old. To be absolutely sure that the case is still valid, the legal assistant must also check the advance sheets. Almost every case reporting service publishes a list and short summary, or advance sheet, of the most recent cases on a weekly or biweekly basis.

Researching the Procedural Question If there is a legal basis for the action a client wants to take, the question of procedure or how the action is implemented must be addressed. This important determination is often left to the paralegal. If the procedure is incorrect or incomplete, the result may range from the papers being "bounced" at the court filing window to complete loss of the client's cause of action.

As is true for legal analysis, a good starting point for procedural analysis is the Bankruptcy Code. Many relevant statutes will give clues as to appropriate procedure. For example, the statute in the hypothetical, Section 523, states in subsection (c)(1) that the debtor will receive the discharge for the debts listed in Section 523 (a)(2), which includes the luxury goods exception, unless "on request of the creditor to whom such debt is owed, and after notice and a hearing, the court determines such debt to be excused from discharge [.]". The procedural requirements are vague as to timing but they can be interpreted by using the Bankruptcy Rules.

The Bankruptcy Rules, like the Bankruptcy Code, are indexed at the back of the volume. The index lists Discharge: determination of dischargeability, and in this case points to Rule 4007 (c) for the time for filing a complaint in a Chapter 7 case.

Here, the Bankruptcy Rules do not give the complete procedural answer. They do not state, for example, exactly how the complaint is filed. These matters are instead addressed by local rules.

☐ LEGAL WRITING

The answer to a research question may take a variety of written forms: a letter to the client, a memo to the lawyer, a brief or memorandum of points and authorities. Although each has a different format and a different tone, the essence of good legal writing is the same.

General Rules of Legal Writing

Plain English As a group, lawyers seem to be unable to write plain English. They use six words when one will do and unnecessarily use old, arcane phrases. Their writings are generally wordy, unclear, pompous, and dull. Historically, this could be excused as the result of English law and practice being transplanted to the United States. Now there is no valid excuse.

A legal assistant should not fall into the trap of writing like a lawyer because he or she is writing for a lawyer. Even lawyers who are bad writers recognize and

appreciate clarity in style and substance. Clarity in substance will be addressed below. The following rules will help develop clarity in style:

1. *Do not use outdated legal jargon.* Wheretofores, heretofores, hereinafters, witnesseth, the party of the first part, and the like have no place in good legal writing. Use definitions rather than "said".

2. *Use familiar words.* There is no reason to write "utilize" if "use" will do fine.

3. *Write short sentences.* The rule of thumb is that no sentence should have more than twenty-five words, but that may be too many for most writing. Try to have each sentence convey only one thought.

4. *Use the active voice.* When you use the active voice, the subject of your sentence acts. If you use the passive voice, the subject of your sentence is acted upon. An example of the active voice is "The debtor filed the bankruptcy case." An example of the passive voice is "The bankruptcy case was filed by the debtor."

Compare these two paragraphs:

It was ordered, adjudged and decreed on December 1, 1995 by the United States Bankruptcy Court for the Eastern District of Tennessee that the lease of the real property located on Beale Street, to which theretofore a restaurant had been operated by the debtor, could be abandoned by the trustee. Thereafter, said lease was abandoned by said trustee and the debtor's tenancy terminated by its vacation of the property.

The debtor leased and operated a restaurant on Beale Street (the "Lease"). On December 1, 1995 the Bankruptcy Court for the Eastern District of Tennessee ordered the trustee to abandon the Lease. The trustee abandoned the Lease and the debtor moved out.

Organized Writing   When approaching a legal writing project the first task, regardless of the type of document to be produced, is to outline its contents. The importance of outlining cannot be overstated; not only does it help the reader follow the argument or points of information, it also serves as a checklist so that issues and arguments are not omitted.

Outlining is simple. No particular format is needed. It may be that ultimately two outlines will be made: the first listing all the points to be mentioned, in no particular order; and the second, a more refined outline, listing the points in logical sequence with subheadings where appropriate.

Once the outline is done, it is time to write. Whether it is dictated, handwritten, typed, or input in a computer, the strategy is the same: first, state the question or issue raised; second, state the law; third, and this is the most difficult part, analogize or draw comparisons between the actual facts and the case law that led to the conclusion; and fourth, draw a conclusion. Law students use the mnemonic devise of IRAC to remember this writing form: *Issue, Rule, Analysis, and Conclusion.* If the analysis section is long, the writer may want to add a short summary of the conclusion right after the Rule section for the benefit of the reader.

The third step draws comparisons between the actual case and those facts found in the cited cases. The task is to highlight similarities in the facts and the circumstances. Any case that is controlling and decides the issue must be brought to the court's attention, regardless of the harm it may do to the desired conclusion. Failure to do so is an ethical violation in most states. It is however, acceptable to distinguish the facts or advocate that the case not be followed.

■ EXHIBIT 5.8
A Sample Memo Answering the Procedural Question Posed Using the IRAC Method

---

TO: BANKRUPT C. LAWYER
FROM: L. C. O'PERA
DATE: April 15, 1995
RE: Timing of Dischargeability Complaint

I.   Issue

On October 1, 1995, Samuel Pearstein filed a Chapter 7 petition. The meeting of creditors under Section 341(a) of the Bankruptcy Code was first scheduled for November 1, 1995 but, due to the debtor's illness, was continued to February 1, 1996. On that date it was held and concluded. First City Bank received notice of the first date set for the meeting of creditors.

On March 1, 1996, First City Bank filed a complaint against the debtor under Section 523(a)(2) claiming that the debt due to it was nondischargeable (the "Complaint").

Was the Complaint filed timely?

II.   Rule

Federal Rule of Bankruptcy Procedure 4007(c) provides that all complaints seeking to determine the dischargeability of any debt must be filed not later than sixty days following the *first* date set for the meeting of creditors. The court may extend the sixty day deadline, but only upon the motion of a party in interest made before the sixty days has expired.

III.   Analysis

The first date set for the meeting of creditors was November 1, 1995. Any complaint to determine dischargeability should have been filed by approximately January 1, 1995.

The fact that the meeting of creditors was not actually held until February 1, 1996 is irrelevant. In *Kelly v. Gordon (In re Gordon)*, 988 F.2d 1000 (9th Cir. 1993), the meeting of creditors was set for March 9, 1990 but not held until March 30, 1990. The creditor filed the dischargeability complaint on May 10, 1990, two days late. The Ninth Circuit rejected the creditors' argument that the sixty days begins to run from the date the meeting takes place rather than the date for which it is first scheduled. The Court stated:

> "The rule makes the deadline 60 days after the 'first date *set*' for the meeting, not the date the hearing is actually held. '[H]eld pursuant to § 341(a)' simply describes the type of meeting being scheduled."

IV.   Conclusion

First City Bank did not file the Complaint until 120 days after the first date set for the meeting of creditors. Since it did not seek an extension of the time period, it untimely filed the Complaint.

If the suggested organization—issue, citation to the law, comparison and contrast (analysis) and conclusion—is followed and applied to each point in the outline, the result should be a well written and easy to follow piece of legal writing.

Citation Format

Bluebook
The common name for *A Uniform System of Citation,* the standard most often used for proper citation format.

Sometimes a particular jurisdiction requires a special format for citation to cases, statutes, and other authorities. In the absence of any rule, the system of citation provided in *A Uniform System of Citation*, published and distributed by the Harvard Law Review Association on behalf of four prestigious law reviews, can be followed. This is commonly referred to as **bluebook** citation form, due to the color of recent editions of the book's cover.

■ EXHIBIT 5.9
The Most Commonly Used Bankruptcy Sources

Source	Citation	Additional Information
Statute		
Bankruptcy Reform Act of 1978	11 U.S.C. § 101 *et seq.* (1994)	
	11 U.S.C. § 506(c) (1994)	
	28 U.S.C. § 157(a)(2) (1994)	
Bankruptcy Reform Act of 1898	11 U.S.C. § 101 *et seq.* (repealed 1978)	
Legislative History	S.Rep. No. 989, 95th Cong., 2d Sess. 104 (1977)	If possible, give a parallel citation to the pertinent edition of the *United States Code Congressional and Administrative News.* For example, S.Rep. No. 989, 95th Cong., 2d Sess. 104, *reprinted in 1977 U.S. Code Cong.Ad.News* 9260.
	H.R.Rep. No. 595, 95th Cong., 2d Sess. 390 (1977)	
Rules of Procedure	Fed. R. Bankr. P. 9016	
	Fed.R. Civ.P. 41(a)	
Cases		
United States Supreme Court	*Cryts v. French (In re Cox Cotton Co.),* 460 U.S 1072 (1984)	Note that civil actions, such as adversary proceedings, that are brought in bankruptcy court are cited with the name of the bankruptcy case appended parenthetically.
Court of Appeals	*Sulmeyer v. Pacific Suzuki (In re Grand Chevrolet, Inc.)* 25 F.3d 728 (9th Cir. 1994)	
District Court	*In re Battle,* 457 F.Supp. 719 (E.D.Pa.1978)	
Bankruptcy Court and Bankruptcy Appellate Panel Cases		
Bankruptcy Reporter (West):	*Moneymaker v. Bank of America (In re Benning),* 2 B.R. 256 (Bankr.E.D.Ca.1980); or	
	In re Herskowitz, 166 B.R. 764 (Bankr. 9th Cir. 1994)	
Bankruptcy Law Reporter (CCH):	*In re Iacovoni,* Bankr. L. Rep. (CCH) ¶ 67444 (Bankr.D.Utah 1980)	
Collier Bankruptcy Cases (Matthew Bender):	*Smith v. Brown (In re Green),* 1 Collier Bank. Cas.2d (MB) 378 (Bankr.M.D.GA.1985)	
Bankruptcy Court Decision (LRP)	*In re Iacovoni,* 5 Bankr.Ct.Dec. (LRP) 1270 (Bankr.D. Utah 1980)	
Treatises, Loose Leaf Services, Books, and Pamphlets	2 L. King, *Collier on Bankruptcy,* § 101.09 (15th ed. 1983)	
	McQueen & Crestol, *Federal Tax Aspects of Bankruptcy,* § 5.03 (1984)	
Periodicals		
Articles	Vix, *Protecting Shopping Centers under the Bankruptcy Code,* 1984 Ann.Surv.Bankr.L. 15.	
	Brown, *U.S. Recognition of Foreign Bankruptcies,* 18 Am.Bankr.L.J. 416 (1980)	
Student Written Materials	Note, *Collective Bargaining Agreements and Bildisco,* 45 U.Chi.L. Rev. 255 (1984)	
	Comment, *Arbitration Agreements and the New Bankruptcy Act,* 77 Mich.L.Rev. 363 (1979)	

The *Uniform System of Citation* is not well indexed but it is comprehensive. It lists citation form for cases, articles, statutes, legislative history, treatises, and almost every other imaginable source. It does not, however, list in one place all citations for the most commonly used bankruptcy sources. For ease of reference, these citations are compiled in Exhibit 5.9.

Table of Contents and Authorities

A local rule may require that all motions or briefs over a certain length be accompanied by a table of contents and authorities. It is generally a good idea to include the table of contents, regardless of whether it is required, since it gives the reader a quick preview of the arguments.

Sample tables of contents and authorities follow as Exhibits 5.10 and 5.11. There is no special format unless one is required by a local rule.

■ EXHIBIT 5.10
Sample Table of Contents

■ EXHIBIT 5.11
Sample Table of Authorities

TABLE OF AUTHORITIES

CASES   **Page(s)**

Air America, Inc. v. Hatton Bros., Inc.,
   570 F.Supp. 747 (S.D.Fla.1983) 23, 25

Andre Matenciot, Inc. v. David & Dash, Inc.,
   422 F.Supp. 1199 (S.D.N.Y.1976) 26

Chapman v. Pacific Tel. & Tel. Co.,
   613 F.2d 193 (9th Cir.1979) 24

Donovan v. Mazzola
   716 F.2d 1226 (9th Cir.1983) *cert. denied* 464 U.S. 1040 (1984) 24

Gramling v. Food Machinery and Chemical Corp.
   151 F.Supp. 853, 856 (W.D.S.C.1957) 16

In re Bel Air Associates
   706 F.2d 301 (10th Cir.1983) 19, 21

In re Exennium, Inc.,
   715 F.2d 1401 (9th Cir.1983) 18–19

In re Gustafson,
   650 F.2d 1017 (9th Cir.1981) 23

In re Kings Inn Ltd.,
   37 B.R. 239 (Bankr. 9th Cir.1984) 18

In re Petro,
   18 B.R. 566 (Bankr.E.D.Pa.1982) 24

In re Robert's Farms, Inc.,
   652 F.2d 793 (9th Cir.1981) 20, 22

In re Royal Properties, Inc.,
   621 F.2d 984 (9th Cir.1980) 21

Lowe v. Willacy
   239 F.2d 179 (9th Cir.1956) 14

Maness v. Meyers,
   419 U.S. 449 (1975) 24

Matter of DePoy,
   29 B.R. 471 (Bankr.N.D.Ind.1983) 26

Oliver v. Mercy Medical Center, Inc.,
   695 F.2d 379 (9th Cir.1982) 14

Parker v. United States,
   126 F.2d 370 (1st Cir.1942) 25

Shuffler v. Heritage Bank,
   720 F.2d 1141 (9th Cir.1983) 23, 26

United States Consol. Seeded Raisin Co. v. Chaddock & Co.
   173 F. 577 (9th Cir.1909) *cert. denied,* 215 U.S. 591 (1910) 16

United States v. Stine,
   646 F.2d 839 (3rd Cir.1981) 24

Vertex Distributing, Inc. v. Falcon Foam Plastics, Inc.,
   689 F.2d 885 (9th Cir.1959) 15, 23

OTHER AUTHORITY   **Page(s)**

11 U.S.C. § 363(m) 18–22
28 U.S.C. § 151 11
28 U.S.C. § 157 11
28 U.S.C. § 1291 12
Federal Rule of Appellate Procedure 3 12
Federal Rule of Appellate Procedure 4 12
Federal Rule of Appellate Procedure 31 13
Federal Rule of Appellate Procedure 37 15,28
Federal Rule of Appellate Procedure 38 13,15
Federal Rule of Appellate Procedure 39 15
Federal Rule of Bankruptcy Procedure 8005 18–20
Ninth Circuit Local Rule 13 .... 13, 29, 31
Ninth Circuit Local Rule 14 15
Ninth Circuit Local Rule 19 13
Ninth Circuit Local Rule 32 15

☐ SUMMARY

A bankruptcy legal researcher looks to statutes, procedural rules, legislative history, case law and secondary sources for information. There are two approaches to bankruptcy research: by topic or by Bankruptcy Code section. To research using the topic method, start with a general discussion in a secondary source and then find an appropriate headnote in West's *Bankruptcy Digest*. Case summaries are arranged by headnote in the *Digest*. To research using the Bankruptcy Code, use the index to find a relevant Bankruptcy Code section. The *Codex* or the *United States Code Annotated* or *United States Code Service* can then be used to find cases concerning a Code section. Always update the cases researched using *Shepard's Citations*.

A written report of the research conducted should follow IRAC: issue, rule, analysis, and conclusion. Legal writing should be in plain English. Avoid outdated legal jargon. Use short sentences, the active voice and familiar words.

☐ KEY TERMS

Bluebook	Pocket Parts	Shepardizing
Cite Checking	Precedent	Stare Decisis
Headnotes		

☐ IMPROVE YOUR UNDERSTANDING

Correct this citation:

In re Granada, Inc. (Billings v. Zions First National Bank), 110 Bankr. 548 (D.Utah Bankr.1990).

☐ RESEARCH PROJECT

1. The partner in charge of the firm's bankruptcy practice wants to know if the phrase "reasonable compensation" in Section 330(a)(1) of the Bankruptcy Code includes paying interest. Map out a research strategy and perform the research. Write a short memorandum detailing the research steps you took.

2. Using only the research and hypothetical facts provided to you in this textbook, draft a memo answering the question of whether the debt incurred for the dolls is dischargeable.

CHAPTER 6

BANKRUPTCY LITIGATION AND APPEALS

One of the purposes of bankruptcy is to resolve all of the disputes between the debtor and its creditors in one place—the bankruptcy court. As a result, bankruptcy practice necessarily includes some litigation. The litigation may involve special bankruptcy issues such as relief from the automatic stay. It may involve state law causes of action such as breach of contract. As shown in this chapter, litigation in the bankruptcy courts is not—or at least should not be—very different from practice in the district courts. An understanding of federal civil procedure and the local rules of practice will almost always suffice.

Since legal assistants cannot practice law, they may not appear at trials or hearings on behalf of clients. There are, however, many tasks related to litigation in which their assistance is very helpful. Legal assistants may prepare drafts of pleadings, organize documents and other evidence, summarize deposition transcripts, attend the hearings, and take notes. During the tense and often frantic moments of trial, a well prepared legal assistant can help assure that everything moves like clockwork.

Legal assistants can also facilitate bankruptcy litigation by being on cordial terms with court personnel (the courtroom and calendar clerks especially) and by having a thorough understanding of the court system and the functions of the various departments. There will be situations in which the ability to convince a clerk to enter a judgment on the docket immediately will be as important as obtaining the judgment.

To familiarize the legal assistant with the process, the following discussion covers the types of litigation that may be held in bankruptcy courts, and how that

litigation is started, conducted, and terminated. A short discussion of bankruptcy appellate practice is also included.

☐ JURISDICTION

In General

Jurisdiction

The power of a court to preside over and decide a dispute between people or property.

Jurisdiction is the power of a court to preside over a dispute. Title 28 of the United States Code, not Title 11, governs matters of bankruptcy court jurisdiction and related issues. Under 28 U.S.C. § 1334(b), the district courts have jurisdiction over all civil proceedings arising under the Bankruptcy Code and arising in or related to a case under the Bankruptcy Code. Proceedings are the lawsuits or other procedures within the bankruptcy case that resolve the disputes between the creditors, the trustee, and the debtor.

So that the district courts will not have to hear all bankruptcy related disputes, Section 157(a) of Title 28 provides that the district court may refer any or all proceedings in a bankruptcy case to the bankruptcy judges sitting in the district. A blanket reference of all proceedings has been made in every district. At least initially, all litigation involving the debtor or the estate will proceed in the bankruptcy court.

Core and Noncore Proceedings

Even though Section 157(a) provides that the bankruptcy court may preside over all proceedings, it does not mean that the bankruptcy judge will make the final determination of a dispute. Section 157(b)(1) of Title 28 only allows bankruptcy judges to hear, determine, and enter a final order in **core proceedings.** Core proceedings are those matters involving rights or duties created by bankruptcy law. Some examples are objections to claims or exemptions, the request by a trustee for authority to obtain credit, suits to compel turnover of property of the estate or to recover preferences, motions concerning the automatic stay, and determinations as to the dischargeability of a particular debt.

Core Proceeding

Those matters directly concerning the bankruptcy case and arising under the Bankruptcy Code.

Section 157(b)(2) provides a noninclusive list of core proceedings. This list, shown in Exhibit 6.1, covers general and specific matters.

Related Proceeding

Those matters concerning a bankruptcy case only because one of the parties to the dispute is a debtor in a bankruptcy case.

A noncore, or **related proceeding,** is everything that is not a core proceeding. Usually these are lawsuits pending in the bankruptcy court only because one of the parties commenced a bankruptcy case. If there was no bankruptcy case, the litigation probably would still have been commenced but in a different court. Under Section 157(c) of Title 28, noncore proceedings may be heard by a bankruptcy judge, but unless all parties consent to the bankruptcy judge entering the order, the judge can only propose findings of fact and conclusions of law. The district court then enters the order or judgment after reviewing any of the bankruptcy judge's findings or conclusions objected to by the losing side.

Withdrawal of Reference

Even though an action is core under Section 157(a), the bankruptcy court may not be the one to hear and finally decide the dispute. Section 157(d) provides that the district court can always withdraw the reference to the bankruptcy court. Section 157(d) also provides that if the lawsuit involves both bankruptcy law and

General Core Proceedings
1. Matters concerning the administration of the estate.
2. Counterclaims by the estate against creditors who filed proofs of claim.
3. Any other proceeding affecting the liquidation of the estate's assets or creditor claims (other than personal injury or wrongful death claims).

Specific Core Proceedings
4. Objections to claims.
5. Objections to a debtor's claimed exemptions.
6. Estimation of claims (other than personal injury or wrongful death claims).
7. Motions for the debtor or trustee to obtain credit.
8. Turnover disputes.
9. Preference disputes.
10. Motions concerning the automatic stay.
11. Fraudulent conveyance actions.
12. Discharge and dischargeability disputes.
13. Questions of the validity, extent or priority of liens.
14. Confirmation of plans.
15. Motions approving the use, sale, or lease of property.

other federal law, such as questions involving federal securities or pension law, the district court must withdraw the reference if a party makes an appropriate motion in a timely manner.

Abstention

Abstention is a court's ability to avoid hearing a matter that it otherwise has the power to hear. There are two types of abstention that are important in bankruptcy practice. The first type of abstention is described in Section 305 of the Bankruptcy Code; it allows the bankruptcy court to abstain from—to refuse to get involved with—the entire case. If the court abstains, it is as if the bankruptcy case was never commenced. Usually a bankruptcy court will abstain under Section 305 if there is a state or district court receivership proceeding pending and the receiver is doing everything that a bankruptcy trustee would otherwise do. The bankruptcy court will abstain because there simply is no need for a bankruptcy case.

The second type of abstention is much more limited but more widely used. It has two statutory sources. First, Section 1334(c)(1) of Title 28 states that the bankruptcy and district courts *may* abstain from hearing a proceeding in the interest of justice, comity for state courts (in deference to them), or out of respect for state law. Under this section, a bankruptcy court could send two parties to state court to have it decide a particular dispute, but still keep the rest of the bankruptcy case alive. Second, Section 1334(c)(2) provides that the courts *must* abstain if a timely motion is made and the proceeding is based on a state law claim, federal court jurisdiction is otherwise unavailable, and the action is commenced and can be timely adjudicated in a state court. For example, if before

Abstention
The refusal of a court to preside over a bankruptcy case or proceeding despite the fact that it has jurisdiction to do so.

bankruptcy the debtor had brought a lawsuit for breach of contract in the state courts, the defendant may be able to force the bankruptcy court to abstain. If the bankruptcy court abstains, the matter will be sent back to the state court for a ruling.

☐ VENUE

Venue

Where, either geographically or among different types of courts, a case or proceeding is or may be pending.

As mentioned, jurisdiction is the power of a federal court to hear a particular matter. **Venue** is the determination of which court is the correct one to hear the matter. Assuming jurisdiction is available, Section 1409 provides that proceedings must usually be commenced in the district in which the bankruptcy case is pending. There are a few exceptions listed in 28 U.S.C. § 1409(b)–(e), including:

☐ An action to recover a money judgment or property worth less than $1,000 or a consumer debt of less than $5,000 is proper only in the district in which the defendant resides.

☐ A claim arising from the postpetition operation of the debtor's business is properly brought only where it would have been had no bankruptcy case been commenced unless the nondebtor party sues, in which case it can also be brought in the district in which the bankruptcy case is pending.

If a proceeding is commenced in the wrong venue, there is no provision that allows the proceeding to remain there even if all parties agree. Technically, the case must be dismissed so that it can be refiled in the proper district.

Even if venue over a particular proceeding is appropriate where the case is commenced, it may not always stay there. Section 1412 of Title 28 allows a court to transfer a proceeding to another district in the interest of justice or for the convenience of the parties. Such changes are usually the result of a creditor making a motion for a change of venue.

☐ REMOVAL

Removal

The transfer of an adversary proceeding from the court in which it was commenced to a different type of court.

Remand

The return of a removed proceeding to the court in which it was originally commenced.

Section 1452 of Title 28 concerns **removal** of claims related to bankruptcy cases. Removal allows a party to transfer litigation from a state court to the district court where the bankruptcy case is pending, if the district court has jurisdiction. If state court litigation is pending when the case is commenced, the debtor or another party can remove it to the district court and it automatically will be referred to the bankruptcy court. Pursuant to Section 1452(b), the court may **remand** it (send it back) on any equitable ground.

Bankruptcy Rule 9027 gives the mechanics for removing a proceeding. It is very detailed and the procedure should be followed carefully. Generally, a notice for removal must be filed in the district court. If the lawsuit to be removed is pending at the time of the commencement of the bankruptcy case, the notice must be filed ninety days after the order for relief, thirty days after the automatic stay is lifted if the claim or cause of action has been stayed, or thirty days after appointment of a Chapter 11 trustee. If the action is not pending at the time the bankruptcy case is commenced, the removing party has only thirty days to act. After the application is filed, there are a number of requirements imposed on the party seeking to remove.

☐ TYPE OF PROCEEDING

In General

Separate and distinct from the question of whether an action is a core or a noncore proceeding is the determination of whether it is an **adversary proceeding,** a **contested matter,** or another type of judicial proceeding in the bankruptcy court. That determination will govern the type of pleadings used as well as the procedure and rules to be followed.

Adversary proceedings are governed by the 7000 series of the Bankruptcy Rules, which largely adopt the Federal Rules of Civil Procedure (commonly abbreviated as Fed.R.Civ.P.). Adversary proceedings are described in Bankruptcy Rule 7001 and outlined in Exhibit 6.2.

An adversary proceeding is commenced by the filing of a complaint. The procedure is almost identical to litigation in other federal courts.

All controversies that are not specifically listed in Rule 7001 as adversary proceedings are contested matters. They are commenced by a motion. Rule 9014 governs the procedure for contested matters, which are discussed later in this chapter. The most common contested matters in bankruptcy practice are actions for relief from the automatic stay and motions seeking authority to sell property of the estate.

Finally, the general rule that a complaint commences an adversary proceeding and a motion commences a contested matter is not always true. The following is a list of a very few types of contested matters in which the Bankruptcy Rules require that an application, objection, or other type of paper be filed.

Type of Proceeding	Type of Pleading	Bankruptcy Rule Number
Opposition to a claim	Objection	3007
Compensation or reimbursement	Application	2016
Opposition to a disclosure statement	Objection	3017(a)
Opposition to a notice of intent to sale, or lease estate property	Objection and request for hearing	6004(b)

A number of the Bankruptcy Rules and certain Bankruptcy Code sections make reference to a request for action by the court. The use of the term request does not prescribe a particular form of procedure. Rule 9013 states that a "request for an order, except when an application is authorized, shall be by written motion."

Adversary Proceedings

As mentioned, pursuant to Bankruptcy Rule 7003, adversary proceedings are commenced by the filing of a complaint. There are a few minimum requirements for a complaint: it must identify the parties, establish jurisdiction, and state a cause of action.

The Complaint   The first important party to be identified in the complaint will be the plaintiff, the person starting the lawsuit. Bankruptcy Rule 7017 allows "a party

Adversary Proceeding
Litigation in the bankruptcy court that is commenced by the filing of a complaint.

Contested Matter
An action in the bankruptcy court seeking relief that is commenced by the filing of a motion.

1. Recover money or property other than a proceeding to:
   a. Compel the debtor to deliver property to the trustee;
   b. Compel the trustee to abandon or otherwise dispose of property;
   c. Recover money from the debtor's attorneys; or
   d. Require a custodian to give an accounting.
2. Determine the validity, priority, or extent of a lien or other interest in property other than an action by a debtor to avoid a lien on exempt property.
3. Obtain the approval for the sale of both the interest of the estate and of a co-owner in property.
4. Object to or revoke a discharge.
5. Revoke an order of confirmation of a Chapter 11 plan.
6. Determine the dischargeability of a debt.
7. Obtain an injunction or other equitable relief.
8. Subordinate any claim or interest unless the subordination is provided for in a plan.
9. Obtain a declaratory judgment with respect to any matter listed in 1–8.
10. Determine a claim or cause of action that has been removed.

Any action not found on this list is a contested matter.

authorized by statute" to sue without joining the party for whose benefit the action is brought. Bankruptcy Code Section 323 allows a trustee to bring an action on behalf of the creditors of the estate without joining the creditors or the debtor as a party. This allows the trustee to file a complaint on behalf of all creditors.

Pursuant to Bankruptcy Rule 7019, a person must be made a defendant to an adversary proceeding if in its absence complete relief cannot be granted, or if it has a significant interest in the subject of the action. These people are known as indispensible parties.

Federal courts are courts of limited jurisdiction and have no power to hear a particular action unless Congress allows them to do so. Pursuant to Bankruptcy Rule 7008(a), a complaint must contain a short and plain statement of the grounds on which the court's jurisdiction depends so the court can determine whether it has the power to entertain the suit. Bankruptcy Rule 7008(a) also requires the jurisdictional allegation to contain a reference to the name, number, and chapter of the bankruptcy case to which the adversary proceeding relates, the district and division where the case is pending, a statement of whether the proceeding is core or noncore and, if noncore, whether the pleader consents to the entry of a final order or judgment by the bankruptcy judge. A sample of an allegation that complies with this requirement in a preference action is shown in Exhibit 6.3.

Jurisdiction and Venue

1. This Court has jurisdiction over this action pursuant to 28 U.S.C. §§ 157 and 1334(a) and the Order of the Chief Judge of the United States District Court, Western District of California, referring bankruptcy cases and proceedings, entered on July 20, 1984. This adversary proceeding is a core matter pursuant to 28 U.S.C. § 157(b)(2)(F) and Plaintiff consents to the entry of a final order or judgment by the Bankruptcy Court.

2. Venue properly resides in the United States Bankruptcy Court for the Western District of California pursuant to 28 U.S.C. § 1409 in that this adversary proceeding is related to *In re Videos by Joe, Inc.*, Bk. No. 95-00001-JF, pending as a Chapter 11 case in the United States Bankruptcy Court for the Western District of California.

The rules for pleading the cause of action in an adversary proceeding are set forth in Bankruptcy Rules 7008, 7009, and 7010. Generally, every pleading must contain a caption; allegations must be made in numbered paragraphs; and each claim founded upon a separate transaction or occurrence must be stated in a separate count if it would clarify the facts. Exhibits and earlier statements in a pleading may be incorporated by reference.

A complaint may have one or more claims for relief (sometimes also called causes of action). For example, a complaint filed by a debtor against the same person could seek to recover a preference, determine the dischargeability of a debt and determine the priority of a lien. Typically, the complaint will set out these three different types of relief in separate claims. The complaint should set out each and every element of the claim for relief in addition to the important facts. For example, if a complaint is filed to recover a preferential payment under Section 547, each of the elements of a preferential transfer provided in Section 547(b) should be listed.

Complaints are filed with the bankruptcy court along with the prescribed filing fee. In many districts, along with the complaint and the filing fee, the plaintiff must also file a cover sheet, which sets forth the parties, the attorneys, and the nature of the cause of action. The local rules of each district should be consulted for more particulars on these additional requirements.

Bankruptcy Rule 7004 sets forth the rules regarding service of the **summons** and the complaint. The clerk will issue the summons. It will give the date the response must be filed and the date of the trial or pretrial conference if one is preset by the court. The summons must be served with the complaint on the defendant.

Service of the summons and the complaint may be made by personal service, or may be made by first class mail anywhere in the United States. Service by first class mail is not usually allowed in other courts and is one of the benefits of litigating in the bankruptcy court. Service must be made within ten days after issuance of the summons or the summons will no longer be good and a new one will be needed. If service is not made within 120 days after the complaint is filed, it will have to be refiled. Once the complaint and the summons have been served, the person who served the papers must make a proof of service to the court. Usually this will be done by tendering an affidavit as provided in Bankruptcy Rule 7004(a).

The Response   To oppose the claims for relief made in a complaint, the defendant must file an **answer** or some other form of response. Under Bankruptcy Rule 7008, the answer must state in short and plain terms the defenses to each claim and must either admit or deny the plaintiff's allegations. If the defendant has no knowledge or information regarding the truth of the allegation, it should so state; this will be deemed the same as a denial. If only part of a paragraph is to be denied, the defendant must specify what part is admitted and deny the remainder. Any allegation that is not denied will be deemed admitted.

In addition to merely responding yes or no to the plaintiff's allegations, the defendant may plead other matters known as **affirmative defenses.** Fed.R.Civ.P. 7008(c) lists the defenses that constitute affirmative defenses. Under Bankruptcy Rule 7012, certain defenses are waived if not pled prior to or included in the answer, including:

1. lack of jurisdiction over the defendant;
2. improper venue; and
3. insufficiency of service.

Summons
A document issued by the clerk of the court when a complaint is filed that informs the defendant when it must answer or otherwise respond to the complaint.

Answer
The pleading filed by a defendant that admits or denies the allegations in a complaint and asserts any affirmative defenses.

Affirmative Defenses
Procedural or substantive claims that a defendant may use to defeat the claims made by the plaintiff in a complaint.

Bankruptcy Rule 7012 also requires the defendant to admit or deny the allegation that the proceeding is core or noncore. If the defendant responds that it is noncore, it must say whether it consents to the bankruptcy judge entering the final order or judgment.

The defendant must serve the answer within thirty days after issuance of the summons, unless a different time has been set by the court. If the United States or one of its officers or agencies is a defendant, their answer must be filed within thirty-five days.

Bankruptcy Rule 7012 details certain motions that may be filed by the defendant instead of an answer. If the complaint is too vague or ambiguous, a party may move for a more definite statement before answering. A party may also move to strike any allegation that is redundant, immaterial, impertinent, or scandalous. In addition, a party may move to dismiss a complaint for any of the following deficiencies:

1. lack of subject matter jurisdiction;
2. lack of jurisdiction over the defendant;
3. improper venue;
4. insufficiency of service of the complaint;
5. failure to state a claim upon which relief can be granted; or
6. failure to join an indispensable party.

A motion to dismiss for failure to state a claim upon which relief can be granted is a very common motion made to delay the filing of an answer. Usually the motion asserts that the plaintiff failed to make an important allegation against the defendant. For example, if the lawsuit is based on a preference, the plaintiff may have failed to allege or give the supporting facts to establish that the defendant was a creditor of the debtor at the time the preferential transfer was made. Most of the time the court will allow the plaintiff to cure any defect by amending the complaint. Then the defendant will have an opportunity to file an answer to the amended complaint or file another motion to dismiss if the defect was not cured or the amended complaint has a new problem.

Most of the bases for dismissal listed above must be made before an answer is filed or will be waived. An objection based on lack of subject matter jurisdiction can be made at any time, even at trial.

Pretrial Procedures   Bankruptcy Rule 7016, which incorporates Fed.R.Civ.P. 16, provides for extensive pretrial procedures so that the court and the parties will focus early on the issues and disputes. Not only does a pretrial procedure force the parties to not put off trial preparation until the last minute, but it often facilitates settlement discussions. The pretrial procedure is discretionary with the court. Usually each district and often each judge will have their own pretrial rules; these rules might vary with the type of proceeding.

Discovery   Rule 7026 contains the general provisions regarding discovery. It fully incorporates Fed.R.Civ.P. 26, which was changed on December 1, 1993 to add very controversial sections concerning mandatory disclosure requirements of counsel. Generally, it requires each side to disclose to the other the names and addresses of witnesses, all documents, and computations of damages without the other side asking for any of the information. Many people claim that these disclosure requirements undermine the adversarial nature of the United States justice system. As a

result of the controversy, the Judicial Conference has allowed districts not to adopt the new provisions.

There are other provisions of the Bankruptcy Rules concerning discovery, all of which largely copy the Federal Rules of Civil Procedure. Depositions are covered in Rules 7027 through 7032. Interrogatories are the subject of Rule 7033 and provisions concerning the production of documents are found in Rule 7034. Rules 7035 and 7036 provide for physical and mental examinations and requests for admissions. The subject of failure to make or cooperate in discovery and sanctions is found in Rule 7037.

The Bankruptcy Rules also provide a method of fact finding not available under the Federal Rules of Civil Procedure. Under Bankruptcy Rule 2004, the court may order the examination of any person upon motion of a party in interest. Ordinarily, a Bankruptcy Rule 2004 examination is just like a deposition; however, an adversary proceeding need not be pending. In fact, many courts will not allow a party to an adversary proceeding to examine pursuant to Bankruptcy Rule 2004 and will require adherence to the discovery rules.

A Rule 2004 examination can cover the acts, conduct, liabilities, and financial condition of the debtor, and any other matter that may affect the administration of the debtor's estate or the right to a discharge. If the debtor is operating a business, the examination may cover the operation of the business. In a Chapter 12, 13, or 11 case, the examiner may also inquire into matters relevant to a plan of reorganization. A sample motion seeking a Bankruptcy Rule 2004 examination is set forth in Exhibit 6.4.

A Bankruptcy Rule 2004 examination can also involve the production of documentary evidence. The attendance of a person or the production of documents can be compelled by the issuance of a subpoena by the court.

Default Judgments/Dismissals   A default judgment may be entered when a party has failed to answer or otherwise defend an action. Default judgments are governed by Bankruptcy Rule 7055. Generally, the plaintiff will file a request for the entry of default and lodge an appropriate judgment.

Dismissal is governed by Bankruptcy Rule 7041. A dismissal may be voluntary or involuntary. Except for an action objecting to a discharge, the plaintiff can dismiss an adversary proceeding by merely filing a notice of dismissal anytime prior to the defendant's answer or summary judgment motion. An action may also be dismissed by stipulation signed by all parties who have appeared.

If an adversary proceeding cannot be dismissed as discussed in the previous paragraph, or if it is an action objecting to a discharge, the party that wants the dismissal must make a motion. The proceeding can only be dismissed by order of the court and upon such terms and conditions as the court deems proper.

In addition to a motion to dismiss based on those defenses set out in Bankruptcy Rule 7012, a defendant may move for dismissal for failure of the plaintiff to prosecute, or comply with the rules or an order of the court.

Trials   Trials in bankruptcy court are no different from trials in the district courts. The same rules of evidence and procedure apply. The one exception is the right to a trial by jury, which in bankruptcy court is somewhat confused. Section 1411 of Title 28 states that nothing in the Bankruptcy Code affects any right to trial by jury that an individual otherwise has for personal injury or wrongful death tort claims. However, 28 U.S.C. § 1334(c)(2) requires federal court abstention from these matters if brought by the bankruptcy estate. Claims against the estate are

■ EXHIBIT 6.4
Sample Pleadings

GEORGE G. SNOW
SNOW & WEST
Four Wheel Drive
Los Angeles, California 90017

Attorneys for First City Bank

UNITED STATES BANKRUPTCY COURT
WESTERN DISTRICT OF CALIFORNIA

In re	)	Case No. 95-00001-JF
	)	
VIDEOS BY JOE, INC.	)	Chapter 11
	)	
Debtor.	)	
	)	
Debtor's Address:	)	MOTION FOR ORDER AUTHORIZING EXAMI-
18 Hollywood Drive	)	NATION PURSUANT TO FED.R.BANKR.P.
Los Angeles, CA 90001	)	2004(a); REQUEST FOR PRODUCTION OF DOC-
	)	UMENTS PURSUANT TO FED.R.BANKR.P. 9016
Employer's Tax Id. No. 99-999899	)	
	)	
	)	

TO THE HONORABLE JUSTIN CLAY, UNITED STATES BANKRUPTCY JUDGE:

First City Bank (the "Bank"), through its attorneys, in support of its Motion for Order Authorizing Examination Pursuant to Fed.R.Bankr.P. 2004(a); Request for Production of Documents Pursuant to Fed.R.Bankr.P. 9016, respectfully represents that:

1. The Bank is a creditor in the above-captioned bankruptcy case and is therefore a party in interest within the meaning of 11 U.S.C. § 1109.

2. In connection with this case, it is essential that the Bank undertake certain discovery.

3. Under Fed.R.Bankr.P. 2004, the Bankruptcy Court may order the examination of any person, and compel the production of documentary evidence in the matter provided in Fed.R.Bankr.P. 9016.

4. The Bank requests that Joe Businessman, the President of debtor, be compelled to: (a) appear and testify at the office of the attorney for the Bank on November 15, 1995, at 10:00 A.M. to be examined with respect to the acts, conduct, and property of debtor and matters which may affect the administration of this case; and (b) to produce for copying and inspection at the same time and place those documents more particularly described in Exhibit 1 attached hereto.

WHEREFORE, the Bank requests that the Court enter its order compelling the appearance and document production requested in this Motion, and grant such other and further relief as the Court shall deem just and proper.

Dated: October 15, 1995

SNOW & WEST

_____

GEORGE G. SNOW
Attorneys for First City Bank

not subject to mandatory abstention but are noncore proceedings that may be tried in district court.

Further, Section 1480 of Title 28 provides that the right to a jury trial is not affected by the Bankruptcy Code. Yet, the fact that the right to jury trial is not affected does not mean that the parties are entitled to one. The legislative history indicates that Congress intended to repeal Section 1480 when the 1984 Amendments were passed. By oversight or otherwise, it was not repealed.

Because of the confusion, former Bankruptcy Rule 9015 concerning jury trials was deleted in 1987. The comments to the Rule indicate that when and if there is a judicial decision determining whether bankruptcy judges can conduct jury trials, local rules should be used until a new Bankruptcy Rule can be adopted. In 1989 the United States Supreme Court ruled that parties are entitled to jury trials in types of litigation frequently conducted by bankruptcy judges, but the Court did not say whether a bankruptcy judge could preside over a jury trial. The lower courts are split on the issue.

Judgments, Findings, and Conclusions Bankruptcy Rules 7052 and 7054 concern findings of fact, conclusions of law, and judgments. Bankruptcy Rules 9026 and 9027 cover new trials, amendments of judgments, and relief from judgments.

Contested Matters

Actions that are not specifically described in Bankruptcy Rule 7001 are not adversary proceedings. They are contested matters and are governed by certain rules in the 9000 series of the Bankruptcy Rules. Contested matters are far more common than adversary proceedings but are far less discussed in the Bankruptcy Rules.

Unless the Bankruptcy Rules provide otherwise, relief in contested matters must be requested by motion. The motion must be in writing unless made orally during a hearing and must state with particularity its grounds and the order sought. Unless the court directs otherwise, service must be made in the manner directed by Bankruptcy Rule 7004 and upon those whom Bankruptcy Rule 2002 specifies.

In the 1994 Amendments, Congress added Section 342(c), which states that all notices of hearings in contested matters must contain the name, address and taxpayer identification number of the debtor. However, if this information is not put on the notice there appears to be no negative result. Section 342(c) specifically states that the failure to follow it will not invalidate the legal effect of the notice.

In March of 1995, the Judicial Conference amended Official Forms 16A and 16C to insert the debtor's address below its name on the caption in order to comply with Section 342(c). Official Forms 16B and 16D do not have this additional information. To be safe, the legal assistant may want to use only the Official Form 16A and 16C versions and make the Debtor's address and tax identification or social security number part of every pleading in the case. All Sample Pleadings in this textbook will do so.

Bankruptcy Rule 9014 provides that no response is required to a contested matter unless the court orders otherwise. In almost all jurisdictions, there are local rules that govern motion practice. Many local rules require a response or at least notice that the party intends to oppose the motion.

Bankruptcy Rule 9014 also requires that reasonable notice and opportunity for a hearing must be afforded the person against whom relief is sought. Local rules

of practice usually establish the notice period and any procedures for shortening that time.

Finally, Bankruptcy Rule 9014 provides that many of the rules governing adversary proceedings, including the discovery rules, also apply for contested matters. It also allows the court to direct that other Bankruptcy Rules apply in contested matters.

☐ APPEALS

Appeals from orders issued in adversary proceedings and contested matters in bankruptcy cases are not substantially different than appeals from other courts. Under Section 158 of Title 28, an appeal from a final order of a bankruptcy judge is to the district court. A bankruptcy court order can also be appealed to the Bankruptcy Appellate Panel (often called the BAP) if one has been established in a particular district and if all parties consent.

The Bankruptcy Appellate Panel is comprised of bankruptcy judges from districts within one or more circuits. The district judges in a circuit must authorize the referrals of appeals to the BAP. Three judges form the panel that will hear a particular appeal. No judge from the district in which the appeal originated may sit on the panel for that appeal.

In noncore proceedings, unless the parties consent to allow the bankruptcy court to do it, the final order is entered by the district court. These appeals are governed by the Federal Rules of Appellate Procedure in the same manner as all other district court judgments and orders. An appeal from the affirmance or reversal by the district court or the BAP is to the court of appeals and proceeds under the Federal Rules of Appellate Procedure.

The mechanics of taking an appeal are governed by the 8000 series of the Bankruptcy Rules and are summarized in Exhibit 6.5. Rule 8001 concerns how an appeal is taken as a matter of right and when leave of the court is required. Generally, appeals are commenced by the filing of a very short and simple notice of appeal. Official Form No. 17 is a sample notice of appeal.

A notice of appeal is filed with the bankruptcy court and it must be filed within ten days after the entry of the judgment or order. If it is not timely filed, the appellate court will have no jurisdiction and will be forced to dismiss the appeal. If the party who wants to appeal needs more time, it can seek an order extending the time to appeal, but that order must be entered before the expiration of the initial ten-day period. Any extension cannot be for more than an additional twenty days.

If the order or judgment appealed from allows the prevailing party to do something that is the subject of the appeal, such as sell property, foreclosure on collateral, or the like, the appealing party will need to obtain a stay of the effectiveness of the order or judgment on appeal. If the appealing party does not do so, the appeal may be moot because it is too late for the appellate court to reverse. Stays pending appeal are governed by Bankruptcy Rule 8005 and are usually made to the bankruptcy court. If made to the district court or the Bankruptcy Appellate Panel, the moving party must show why the relief was not obtained from the bankruptcy judge.

Briefs and the appendix are governed by Bankruptcy Rules 8009 and 8010. The appellant's brief usually will be due fifteen days after the entry of the appeal of the docket, which is done after the record is complete. The appellee's brief is due fifteen days after the brief of the appellant. The appellant may then file a reply brief within ten days. No further briefs are usually allowed.

■ EXHIBIT 6.5
Procedures and Deadlines for Appeals

Timing	Action	Bankruptcy Rule Number	Deadline
Day 1	Notice of appeal filed with bankruptcy court	8001, 8002, 8004	Within 10 days of entry of bankruptcy order
Day 1 or sooner	Order a copy of the docket to use to designate the record.		
Day 10	Designation of items to be included in the record and statement of issues presented.	8006	Within 10 days of notice of appeal
Day 10	Notice of transcript	8007(a)	Within 10 days of notice of appeal
Day 30 or sooner	Reporter files transcript, record is complete. Bankruptcy clerk submits to appellate clerk either the record or a certificate of record.	8007(a)	Approximately 30 days after notice of appeal
	Appellate clerk gives notice to all parties that the record or the certificate has been filed. That date is the date the appeal is considered "entered on appellate docket" for purposes of Bankruptcy Rule 8009.		
Approximately day 45	Appellant must file opening brief. Fifty-page limit. Copies of all statutes, rules, and regulations cited must be appended to the brief or supplied to the court in pamphlet form.	8009 (a)(1)	15 days after appeal docketed
	Appellant to file appendix to brief if appeal is to Bankruptcy Appellate Panel.	8009(b)	With opening brief
Approximately day 60	Appellee must file brief. Fifty-page limit. Copies of all statutes, rules, and regulations cited must be appended to the brief or supplied to the court in pamphlet form.	8009(a)(2)	15 days after service of appellant's brief
	Appellee may file an appendix of any material required to be included but omitted by appellant.	8009(b)	15 days after service of appellant's brief
Approximately day 70	Appellant may file reply brief. Twenty-page limit.	8009(a)(3)	10 days after service of appellee's brief
Anytime thereafter	Court sets matter for oral argument.	8012	

☐ SUMMARY

The bankruptcy court derives from the district court jurisdiction to make final rulings in all core proceedings and to make proposed rulings in all related or non-core proceedings in a bankruptcy case. The proceedings can be commenced in the bankruptcy court or removed to it. The bankruptcy court's jurisdiction can be withdrawn by the district court or the bankruptcy court can abstain from ruling in a particular case or proceeding.

There are two main types of proceedings in a bankruptcy case: adversary proceedings and contested matters. The Bankruptcy Rules determine which type is involved. Adversary proceedings are commenced by the filing of a complaint. They are managed much the same as other federal court litigation. Contested matters are commenced by the filing of a motion.

An appeal from a bankruptcy court order can be made to the district court or, in some jurisdictions, to a bankruptcy appellate panel.

☐ KEY TERMS

Abstention	Contested Matter	Remand
Adversary Proceeding	Core Proceeding	Removal
Affirmative Defenses	Jurisdiction	Summons
Answer	Related Proceeding	Venue

☐ IMPROVE YOUR UNDERSTANDING

1. Compare Exhibit 6.1 and Exhibit 6.2. To the extent it can be determined by reference only to those tables, which adversary proceedings are core matters and which are not?

2. Who determines whether a matter is core or noncore?

3. If a matter is noncore, under what circumstances can a bankruptcy judge enter the final order or judgment?

4. If a matter is core, under what circumstances would the bankruptcy judge not enter the final order or judgment?

5. Why do you think Section 305 is in Title 11 but Section 1334(c) is in Title 28?

6. What is the primary difference between 28 U.S.C. § 1408 and 28 U.S.C. § 1409?

7. What is the last date for a defendant to plead lack of subject matter jurisdiction? When is the last date for a defendant to plead lack of personal jurisdiction?

8. If the defendant has answered, how can an action be dismissed?

9. List three fact situations in which the losing party would want to obtain a stay pending appeal.

☐ RESEARCH PROJECT

1. Locate a reported decision discussing a motion made pursuant to 28 U.S.C. § 1412. What factors did the court consider in determining whether to change venue?

2. Is there a local rule in your jurisdiction for pretrial meetings or status conferences?

3. What do the local rules in your jurisdiction provide with respect to motion practice?

☐ DRAFTING PROJECT

1. Review Bankruptcy Rule 9027. Prepare a chart listing the steps required to remove a lawsuit from the state court to the bankruptcy court and the deadlines for performing those steps.

CHAPTER 7

BEGINNING A BANKRUPTCY CASE

Later sections of this book examine each of a Chapter 7, 11, 12, and 13 case in detail. Very different rules apply to each chapter. At the beginning, however, all bankruptcy cases are subject to the same rules and forms. They are begun with identical petitions and identical schedules of assets and liabilities need to be filed. So, before examining each type of case separately, we examine the elements common to the beginning of a liquidation and reorganization bankruptcy case.

☐ CONSIDERING WHETHER A BANKRUPTCY CASE MAY OR SHOULD BE FILED

Limitations on Filing a Bankruptcy Case

Bankruptcy law provides debtors with extraordinary abilities that do not otherwise exist, including the ability to compel a creditor to accept less than the full amount owed, to assign contracts not otherwise assignable, and to extend the term of a promissory note. Yet, for a number of reasons, Congress did not want these valuable protections to be available to everyone. As you may recall from Chapter 1, Section 109(a) of the Bankruptcy Code provides that only a person that resides or has a place of business or property in the United States can be a debtor. Person is defined in Section 101(41) to include individuals, partnerships, and corporations—but not governmental units. When governmental units are meant to be included within the scope of a particular section, the Bankruptcy Code uses the word entity, which is defined more broadly in Section 101(15).

In an effort to stem the tide of abusive bankruptcy cases, Congress has determined that there are other persons who, although technically qualified to be debt-

ors under Section 109(a), should not enjoy the protections the Bankruptcy Code has to offer. As Section 109(g) states, an individual or a family farmer cannot file a bankruptcy case if he or she was a debtor in a case that had been pending within the previous 180 days and that was dismissed by the court either because of the debtor's willful failure to abide by the court's orders, or to appear before the court in proper prosecution of the case, or if the debtor voluntarily dismissed the case after a creditor moved for relief from the automatic stay.

Section 109(g), which was added with the 1986 Amendments, requires the court to interpret what constitutes willful failure. The section also has serious problems of enforcement. The court's clerk is unlikely to know whether the debtor was a debtor in a case pending within the previous six months. Even if that fact is known, the clerk is not qualified to determine whether the debtor willfully failed to adhere to a court order. As a result, the petition commencing the second bankruptcy case will be accepted and, at least until a creditor or the United States trustee is able to file a motion to have the case dismissed, the debtor will be able to take advantage of the automatic stay and the other protections of the bankruptcy system.

In addition to the enforcement problems of Section 109(g), it applies only to individuals and family farmers. No similar help is given to creditors from multiple corporate or partnership bankruptcy cases. However, creditors are certainly not without their remedies since they may move to dismiss the second case, claiming it was filed in bad faith as discussed in later chapters of this book.

Choosing the Right Chapter

Assuming eligibility to be a debtor under Sections 109(a) and 109(g), the debtor must decide the chapter of the Bankruptcy Code under which to file. That decision has two inquiries:

1. In which chapters is the debtor eligible?
2. What chapter will best assist in achieving the debtor's goals?

Determining the answer to the first question is simply a matter of applying the statute. The second question involves many different considerations.

■ EXHIBIT 7.1
Ineligible Debtors

Type of Debtor	Chapters For Which Debtor Is Ineligible
Railroads	All except 11
Insurance companies	All
Banks, savings & loans, and credit unions	All
Stockbrokers or commodity brokers who are not individuals	All except 7
Stockbrokers or commodity brokers who are individuals and who qualify for Chapter 13 relief.	All except 7 and 13
All entities other than individuals who have less than $250,000 of liquidated, noncontingent, unsecured debts, $750,000 of noncontingent, liquidated secured debts, and a regular income.	Chapter 13
All entities other than "family farmers who have regular annual income" as defined in Section 101(19)	Chapter 12
All entities other than municipalities authorized by the state to be debtors, who are insolvent, and who desire to effect a plan to adjust their debts.	Chapter 9

Eligibility   Not all persons can file under every chapter. Section 109 provides that the following persons are ineligible for the chapter indicated.

In short, virtually any entity can be a Chapter 7 debtor but only a select number qualify for relief under Chapters 9, 12, or 13. Certain entities, such as banks and insurance companies, can never be debtors. Those entities are heavily regulated by other laws of Congress or by the laws of each state that contain special insolvency proceedings for those types of entities.

Appropriateness   Once one determines under which chapters the debtor *may* file, there remains the decision of under which chapter the debtor *should* file. Between Chapter 7, on the one hand, and Chapters 11, 12, or 13 on the other, the question should be simple: does the debtor want to reorganize and pay creditors over a period of time or does the debtor simply want to deliver all nonexempt property to the trustee and allow it to be liquidated? For consumer debtors who may be eligible for Chapter 7 and Chapter 13 relief, the answer may be a function of how much they know about the two. The question also becomes more complicated when the issue is between Chapter 11 and Chapter 13 or between Chapter 7 and Chapter 11 when the debtor wants to liquidate but wants to control the liquidation.

When Congress was considering the 1984 Amendments, it was informed that in a large percentage of the no-asset Chapter 7 cases a debtor could have confirmed a Chapter 13 plan and paid creditors at least a portion of their claims. Congress saw no benefit to the economy in allowing people who could pay at least something to not pay. Yet a person cannot be forced into a Chapter 13 case; that might compel debtors to work to pay off debts, which is prohibited by the Thirteenth Amendment to the Constitution. As a result, the 1984 Amendments included a number of provisions to encourage individuals filing Chapter 7 cases to file Chapter 13 cases instead. This encouragement primarily takes the form of debtor education because Congress believed that most debtors would like to pay their debts and would prefer Chapter 13 if they knew more about it.

One encouragement provision is Section 342(b). It requires the clerk of the court to give written notice to an individual with primarily consumer debts of all the chapters under which that debtor is eligible to file. To comply, the clerk's office will usually insist that when the petition is filed, it is accompanied by Director's Form B 201, which briefly explains Chapters 7, 11, 12, and 13. The form must be signed by the debtor under a statement that the debtor has read the notice.

Another attempt to encourage debtors to file under Chapter 13 is Official Form 1, which is the bankruptcy petition. All individual Chapter 7 debtors who have primarily consumer debts must sign a statement that: they are aware that they may proceed under Chapters 7, 11, 12, or 13 of the Bankruptcy Code; they understand the relief available under each Chapter; and they choose to proceed under Chapter 7. In addition, Exhibit B to Official Form 1 requires a consumer debtor's lawyer to sign a declaration stating that the debtor has been informed of the right to proceed under Chapters 7 or 13 and that the relief available under each chapter has been explained to the debtor.

The 1994 Amendments added yet another consumer education provision regarding alternatives to a Chapter 7 case. New Section 341(d) provides that, prior to the conclusion of the Section 341(a) meeting of creditors, the trustee must examine each Chapter 7 debtor (not just those with primarily consumer debts) to ensure that he or she is aware of: (1) the potential consequences of seeking a discharge, including the effects on credit history; (2) the debtor's ability to file a

petition under Chapters 11, 12, or 13; (3) the effect of receiving a discharge of debts; and (4) the effect of reaffirming a debt.

Practitioners may devise a form for clients that details the criteria for filing a Chapter 13 case (which is the most common alternative to a consumer debtor's Chapter 7 case) and has a list or chart of the differences and relative merits of the two. Preparation of that document and providing it to the clients would be an appropriate task for the legal assistant. The list or chart should include a brief discussion of the following points:

1. The eligibility criteria for Chapter 13 relief as set out in Section 109(e).

2. Debts that are nondischargeable under Chapter 7 may be dischargeable under Chapter 13 (as discussed in Chapter 8 of this text).

3. There can be no denial of discharge in Chapter 13 as there can be in Chapter 7 cases.

4. A Chapter 13 discharge, unlike a Chapter 7 discharge, can be obtained more than once every six years.

5. The automatic stay also protects some friends and relatives in Chapter 13 cases.

6. Chapter 13 enables a debtor to stretch out payments to secured creditors; there is no such ability in Chapter 7.

7. Control and use of nonexempt property remains with the debtor in Chapter 13; it must be turned over to the trustee in Chapter 7.

8. Redemption of property can be accomplished through installments in Chapter 13 but only in a lump sum payment in Chapter 7.

9. A Chapter 13 case can be dismissed automatically. A Chapter 7 dismissal requires a hearing before the court.

10. The discharge in Chapter 13 is delayed until plan payments have been made.

11. There is continued supervision in Chapter 13 cases. There is an immediate fresh start in Chapter 7 cases.

12. A Chapter 13 plan will be confirmed only if it meets certain requirements. One such requirement is that, if there is an objection, all disposable income must be used to make plan payments.

The selection of the appropriate chapter for a debtor will not be made by the legal assistant. Instead, the legal assistant may give valuable assistance in the education of consumer debtor clients of their right to proceed under either Chapter 7 or Chapter 13 of the Bankruptcy Code.

Substantial Abuse

Substantial Abuse
A Chapter 7 bankruptcy case of a debtor with primarily consumer debts that offends notions of the proper use of bankruptcy. Typically used to refer to a case in which the debtor could fund a Chapter 13 plan.

In the 1984 Amendments, in partial response to creditors' complaints of abusive and multiple filings, Congress enacted Section 707(b), which provides that after notice and a hearing, the court may dismiss a consumer's Chapter 7 case if it finds that it is a **substantial abuse** for the debtor to be allowed to be in Chapter 7. A substantial abuse case may involve a debtor who files a Chapter 7 case on the eve of signing a large contract so that the contract proceeds become unavailable for creditors. Another example may be a debtor with a $50,000 annual salary and $1,000 per month of disposable income who has only $10,000 in debts.

Section 707(b) reflects a number of congressional compromises. Although Congress considered the creditors' complaints that individuals were taking unfair ad-

vantage of Chapter 7's discharge, the legislators also heeded warnings that it would be unwise to allow a flood of motions brought by creditors claiming that a consumer's bankruptcy case should be dismissed as a substantial abuse under Section 707(b). At the time the section was enacted Congress' compromise was that only the court could raise the substantial abuse issue.

Section 707(b) as enacted was an effort to stem a very real problem; nevertheless it had many difficulties. For example, how is a bankruptcy judge to know which cases are a substantial abuse? The judges are too busy to examine every petition and its supporting papers to try to discern which debtors are abusing the system. In addition, if the court dismisses a case as a substantial abuse and the debtor appeals, who will defend the dismissal? There may not be a creditor willing to pay the cost.

These concerns were remedied by the 1986 Amendments. As it now reads, Section 707(b) allows the United States trustee to move to dismiss a case as a substantial abuse. Creditors still may not make such a motion.

☐ CASE PREPARATION

Client Relationships

Many papers must be prepared and filed by the debtor in a bankruptcy case. These papers require a substantial amount of information from the debtor. To expedite the case and limit costs, it is likely that the legal assistant will gather most of the necessary information. As a result, at the beginning of the case the legal assistant may spend much more time with the debtor than will the attorney.

As commonplace as bankruptcy has become in the United States, it is still an emotional event for individuals and one that is sometimes frustrating and depressing. The debtor may have undergone a serious illness, the loss of employment, or the failure of the family business. The debtor may be worried about losing the home he or she took years to save for. While bankruptcy will give the debtor a fresh start and relief from distressing financial problems, the emotional problems may not be as easily relieved. The legal assistant may frequently have to listen to and comfort the client.

The need to be sympathetic is not limited to bankruptcy cases for individuals. Sometimes the fact that corporations are composed of individuals is overlooked. The stress of a company in trouble falls most heavily on the persons with whom the legal assistant will spend the most time—the accountants and bookkeepers. They spend a considerable amount of their time placating and cajoling creditors. When the bankruptcy case approaches, their burdens will be increased by the reporting requirements of the Bankruptcy Code, the Bankruptcy Rules, and the United States trustee. They will become frustrated and often angry. The legal assistant may well become the inadvertent target of some of this frustration and anger.

While sympathy may help to alleviate the employees' negative feelings, there are other constructive things the legal assistant can do to help. The first is to educate the employees about the bankruptcy system and what the employees can expect over the following months. The second is to inform them how the automatic stay will stop the flood of phone calls that they may experience from angry creditors. Third, if the employees know that once the schedules and statements (the lengthy disclosure documents that we discuss later in this chapter) are filed, their tasks will ease considerably, they may be more cooperative. Finally, and most

importantly, if they know that the legal assistant will help them with all the bankruptcy-related tasks that they do not understand and will answer or find answers to their questions, they may be able to approach their jobs more calmly. It is helpful to call a stressed accountant, bookkeeper, or other client contact at least once a week to see if there are any problems and to let them know that their efforts are appreciated.

File Management

In many law firms, paralegals are not responsible for filing. There are good reasons for this, only one of which is the fact that, since paralegals' time is usually billed to the client, it is unrealistic to expect a client to pay for the firm's filing. Although paralegals may not be responsible for doing the day–to–day filing in all firms, they still may be required to determine which files and subfiles should be created. Because a bankruptcy case has so many facets and counsel for the debtor must be integrally involved with the debtor's business, the files may be voluminous and need careful indexing and organization. There will also be matters that defy the categorizations often used in filing systems.

The particular files that will be created in a case will depend on the size of the case, the nature of the debtor, and the chapter under which the filing is being made. The filing for an individual's Chapter 7 case in which there is no litigation over dischargeability or other issues may be contained in a single folder. The filing for a large Chapter 11 business reorganization may occupy an entire room.

Each law firm has its own filing system for litigation matters and transactional work. Bankruptcy is really both and neither system will be exactly right. The legal assistant must develop some variations or refinements to the traditional filing approaches to accommodate the bankruptcy process. The sample system discussed here, which is set up for a medium-sized Chapter 11 business case, may be helpful.

General Organization   Like a litigation file, there should be folders for correspondence, notes, documents, and pleadings. There should also be a separate folder for single subject matters. The first folder for each type of file should be numbered 1. When it is full, a new folder should be created and numbered 2, and so on.

Whatever the numbering system, a log or index should be kept and continually updated so that a person looking for a particular piece of correspondence can check the index and then go directly to the correct file rather than needing to first search through the folders. If, for example, you were searching for a letter that was written in November of 1995, you could look in the index and see that correspondence file 4 has all correspondence from October to December of 1995. It is also very helpful if, as soon as a folder is full, a sheet is attached to the top indicating that the next folder in order should be consulted for later material.

Pleadings   In a bankruptcy case there will be at least two types of pleadings or papers filed with the court. The first type is pleadings concerning the administration of the estate. The second type is pleadings filed in adversary proceedings in the case. At least one file should be created for the general administrative pleadings; these documents should be placed in the file in chronological order. Separate folders should be created for each adversary proceeding and everything filed with the court in that proceeding should be in the separate pleading file. The pleading files should be numbered 1, 2, 3, and so on as they are filled. Some law firms also put adversary proceeding papers in the general administrative file so that a particular paper can be located in at least two places.

In addition to adversary proceedings, separate pleadings folders may be created for fee applications and their related notices and orders. Even if a particular dispute being waged on paper and before the court is not an adversary matter and the papers would otherwise be filed in the general pleading file, a separate pleading file might be advisable simply for ease in finding a particular paper. For example, if there is a contested motion to appoint a trustee, a separate pleading file for that motion and its response may be appropriate. In addition, because they will be frequently referred to during the pendency of the bankruptcy case, the petition and its supporting documents and the schedules and statements should also be in separate files. At the appropriate time in the case, separate files can be made for the plan of reorganization and the disclosure statement.

Again, a well-maintained log or index will prevent time-wasting rummaging and dog-eared files. It will also help a user know if any files are missing.

Subfiles Listed here in alphabetical order are some suggested subfile topics. Their need and ultimate size will depend on the facts of each case.

Agendas from Meetings	Ballots
Appraisals	Bids
Creditors—Bulletins	Newspaper Releases and Articles
Creditors—Committee	Operating Reports
Creditors—List of	Pension Issues
Creditors—Proofs of Claim	Plan Back-Up
Equity Security Holders—List of	Preference Analysis
Executory Contracts	Priority Claims
Fee Application Back-up	Returned Mail
Financial Statements	Sale Documents
Insurance	SEC Matters
Inventory	Secured Creditor Documents
Leases	Special Notice List
☐ Personal Property	Tax Issues
☐ Real Property	United States Trustee Compliance
Legal Research	Utilities
Mailing Lists—Master	
Mailing Lists—Special Notice	

Gathering Information

A great deal of information will need to be gathered from the debtor prior to commencing the bankruptcy case so that all the court documents can be completed. Since the legal assistant can prepare at least the first draft of those documents and may be the one in the office most familiar with what they require, it is efficient for the legal assistant to gather the information.

The first contact with the client will likely be by telephone. During that call, the legal assistant should try to determine the existence of any conflicts, whether the debtor is qualified to file a bankruptcy case, whether the debtor can afford to hire counsel to help file the bankruptcy case, and whether a bankruptcy case makes the most sense for the debtor. If the indications are that the debtor wants to and should file a bankruptcy case, a more detailed interview should be scheduled.

For consumer cases, the debtor can be told what additional information is needed during the telephone call and can bring it to the first meeting. In other cases, the client can be given a list of the information needed and then return to its business or home to have all the information assembled. Frequently, the debtor's response to being asked to compile information will be to bring in a brown paper bag full of correspondence, records, invoices, and cancelled checks; the legal assistant will have to make sense of the information provided.

Whether the information is to be obtained at the first client meeting or later, the legal assistant should not rely on memory for all that is needed. Two detailed, comprehensive lists of what is needed should be made, one for individual cases and one for business cases. If the individual debtor is in business, the two lists can be combined. As with all other lists made, they should be updated frequently.

A very simple sample list for an individual consumer might resemble the one that follows. Since there are very short time deadlines in cases under Chapters 7, 12, and 13, virtually all the documents need to be received and the questions answered before the case can be commenced.

1. The debtor's full name and all other names used in the last six years.

2. The debtor's social security number.

3. The debtor's current address and all addresses used in the last six years.

4. The debtor's occupation, employer, pay rate, and all other sources of income.

5. Name, relationship, and age of all dependents.

6. Description of all property.

7. Description of all litigation involving the debtor.

8. Description of all property sold or given away in the last year.

9. List of all property lost to theft or to fire, flood, earthquake, or other disaster. All insurance claims, satisfied and unsatisfied, connected with such losses.

10. For federal, state, and city, if applicable, copies of tax returns and whether any tax due was paid or whether any refunds were received in the last two years.

11. All creditors, including the amounts of their claims and any collateral.

12. Details as to any prior bankruptcy cases.

13. All monthly expenses including mortgage or rent payments; utilities, food, clothing; medical, dental, and insurance costs; taxes; car or other transportation payments; dues; recreation; education; and so on.

14. Value of car, household goods, home (if owned), jewelry, tools of the trade, and cash surrender value of life insurance contracts. Any social security, unemployment, or other public benefits; veteran's benefits; disability, illness, or unemployment benefits; alimony or child support; or payments under a pension plan. Any right to receive funds under a crime victim's reparation law; benefits under an insurance policy owned by an individual of whom the debtor was a dependent; payments on account of personal injury, pain and suffering, and loss of future earnings.

15. Description of all the debtor's secured property.

A sample list for a corporation intending to file under Chapter 11 might resemble the following. Those items marked with an asterisk(*) must be received before the case is commenced. The other items can follow shortly thereafter.

*1. The debtor's full name and all tradename and division names.

*2. The state of incorporation.

*3. The number of classes of stock.

*4. For each class of stock, the number of shares authorized and the number of shares issued.

*5. The names of all shareholders and the number of shares each holds.

*6. A list of all corporations in which the debtor holds stock and the percentage of ownership.

*7. The names and addresses of all the debtor's creditors, including all creditors with disputed and contingent claims.

*8. All pending lawsuits involving the debtor.

*9. Identification of the debtor's twenty largest unsecured creditors who are not insiders or governmental units. For each include the name and address, telephone number, name of person familiar with the debt, and the amount owed.

10. A list of all taxing agencies (federal, state, and local) to which the debtor makes payments.

11. A description of all real and personal property leases.

12. A description of all employment agreements, supply or production agreements, pension, profit sharing or health benefit plans, and any other contracts that have not expired.

*13. Copies of the debtor's articles of incorporation and bylaws.

*14. The names of all the debtor's officers and any director or shareholder employed by the debtor.

15. A short (two- or three-page) summary of the history of the debtor, the size and extent of operations, a discussion of product lines and customer bases, and an explanation of current financial problems.

*16. As of a given date, the total dollar amount of assets and liabilities; these should be identified and broken down as secured and unsecured.

☐ CASE COMMENCEMENT

The Checklist

Once all the preliminary information has been gathered, the bankruptcy case will be ready to start. The rules and procedures for starting a voluntary bankruptcy case are generally the same whatever the chapter. There are several critical documents that must be filed to commence the case. If one of them is omitted, the clerk may refuse to accept the other documents and the start of the bankruptcy case could be delayed. That could be a disaster for the debtor, especially if the automatic stay is needed to prevent a foreclosure sale of property.

The days immediately preceding and following the filing of a bankruptcy petition are frequently chaotic. To prevent the chance of a document being inadvertently omitted in this hectic period, a detailed list should be made that includes a description of every document or item that is needed and every task that needs to be done as soon as the case is commenced or shortly thereafter.

The list should include those documents and items required by the Bankruptcy Rules and everything required by the local rules and by the United States trustee.

■ EXHIBIT 7.2
Sample Checklist for Bankruptcy Filing

In re _____ , a _____ [individual, corporation, or partnership]		
Document or Task	**Responsible Person**	**Date Completed**
Prefiling		
1. Filing Fee		
a. Chapter 7 $145.00	_____	_____
b. Chapter 11 $800.00		
c. Chapter 12 $200.00		
d. Chapter 13 $130.00		
2. Administrative Fee		
a. Chapter 7 $30.00		
b. Chapter 13 $30.00		
3. Petition		
Official Form 1	_____	_____
4. Exhibits		
Corporations—A		
Individuals—B	_____	_____
5. Notice to individual consumer debtor		
Director's Form B 201	_____	_____
6. Disclosure of compensation		
Director's Form B 203	_____	_____
7. Corporate resolution and minutes authorizing the bankruptcy case	_____	_____
8. List of twenty largest unsecured creditors (Chapter 11 only)		
Official Form 4	_____	_____
9. List of all creditors (if petition not accompanied by schedules)	_____	_____
10. Master mailing list (Paper or Diskette)	_____	_____
Shortly after Filing		
11. List of equity security holders	_____	_____
12. Statement of intentions (individuals only)		
Official Form 8	_____	_____

The list should be updated every time a new or amended rule or procedure is implemented.

A good idea is to make the list into a checklist. Next to each item could be space for the insertion of the name or initials of the person responsible for preparing the document or doing the task. When the document is ready or the task is done, that person could place his or her initials next to the item. All professionals assigned to coordinate the preparation of documents and completion of tasks should have a copy and one person should keep a master list.

Exhibit 7.2 presents a sample checklist that incorporates many of the items discussed in the balance of this chapter and other portions of this book. The checklist is a good *starting* point. Bear in mind that since it does not reflect any local requirements, it must be supplemented to be complete.

Petition
The paper filed with the bankruptcy court that commences a bankruptcy case.

The Petition and Supporting Documents

Section 301 of the Bankruptcy Code provides that a bankruptcy case is commenced by the filing of a **petition.** Slightly more information is provided in Bank-

■ EXHIBIT 7.2
Sample Checklist for Bankruptcy Filing—*Continued*

In re _____ , a _____ [individual, corporation, or partnership]		
Document or Task	**Responsible Person**	**Date Completed**
13. Schedule of assets and liabilities Official Form 6	_____	_____
a. Schedule A Real Property		
b. Schedule B Personal Property		
c. Schedule C Property Claimed as Exempt		
d. Schedule D Creditors Holding Secured Claims		
e. Schedule E Creditors Holding Unsecured Priority Claims		
f. Schedule F Creditors Holding Unsecured Nonpriority Claims		
g. Schedule G Statement of Executory Contracts		
h. Schedule H Codebtors		
i. Schedule I Current Income of Debtor		
j. Schedule J Current Expenditures of Debtor		
14. Statement of financial affairs Official Form 7	_____	_____
15. Motion for extension to file 13 and 14	_____	_____
16. Schedule meeting with United States trustee	_____	_____
17. Application to employ attorneys for debtor	_____	_____
18. Application to employ accountants for debtor	_____	_____
19. Motion to pay prepetition wages	_____	_____
20. Application to employ insiders	_____	_____
21. Motion to extend time to assume or reject real property leases	_____	_____
22. Notice of removal	_____	_____
23. Record petition in county where real property is located	_____	_____
24. Distribute notice of commencement of case and the automatic stay	_____	_____
25. Letters to employees	_____	_____
26. Letters to vendors	_____	_____

ruptcy Rule 1002, which states that the petition is filed with the bankruptcy court and must conform substantially with Official Form 1.

Official Form 1's size and simplicity hides its importance since the filing of the petition will have a tremendous impact on the debtor's financial affairs. The petition consists of just one, two-sided sheet with two exhibits that are mutually exclusive. If a corporation is the debtor, a short exhibit "A" must be added to the petition. A sample petition for a corporate debtor is presented in Exhibit 7.3. A sample petition for a debtor with consumer debts is presented in Exhibit 7.4.

Official Form 1 consists of a series of boxes, each requesting different information. Preprinted form petitions are widely available. A number of companies market computer software for the creation of petitions and other documents needed in a bankruptcy case.

There are nine parts to the petition: the caption, the venue provisions, information regarding the debtor, statistical and administrative information, the plan statement, related case information, the certification, Exhibit A, and the alternative relief advisement that includes Exhibit B.

■ EXHIBIT 7.3
Sample Pleading For Corporate Debtor—*Continued*

B1
(Rev. 12/94)

United States Bankruptcy Court Western District of California	VOLUNTARY PETITION

IN RE (Name of debtor - If individual, enter Last, First, Middle) Videos By Joe, Inc.	NAME OF JOINT DEBTOR (Spouse) (Last, First, Middle)
ALL OTHER NAMES used by the debtor in the last 6 years (Include married, maiden, and trade names.)	ALL OTHER NAMES used by the joint debtor in the last 6 years (Include married, maiden, and trade names.)
SOC. SEC./TAX I.D. NO. (If more than one, state all.) 99-999899	SOC. SEC./TAX I.D. NO. (If more than one, state all.)
STREET ADDRESS OF DEBTOR (No. and street, city, state, and zip code) 18 Hollywood Drive Los Angeles, California 90001	STREET ADDRESS OF JOINT DEBTOR (No. and street, city, state, and zip code)
COUNTY OF RESIDENCE OR PRINCIPAL PLACE OF BUSINESS LOS ANGELES	COUNTY OF RESIDENCE OR PRINCIPAL PLACE OF BUSINESS
MAILING ADDRESS OF DEBTOR (If different from street address)	MAILING ADDRESS OF JOINT DEBTOR (If different from street address)

LOCATION OF PRINCIPAL ASSETS OF BUSINESS DEBTOR (If different from address listed above)	VENUE (Check one box only)
	[X] Debtor has been domiciled or has had a residence, principal place of business, or principal assets in this District for 180 days immediately preceding the date of this petition or for a longer part of such 180 days than in any other District. [ ] There is a bankruptcy case concerning debtor's affiliate, general partner, or partnership pending in this District.

INFORMATION REGARDING DEBTOR (Check applicable boxes)

TYPE OF DEBTOR (Check one box)
[ ] Individual
[ ] Joint (Husband & Wife)
[ ] Partnership
[ ] Other: _____
[ ] Corporation Publicly Held
[X] Corporation Not Publicly Held
[ ] Municipality

NATURE OF DEBT
[ ] Non-Business/Consumer
[X] Business - Complete A & B below

A. TYPE OF BUSINESS (Check one box)
[ ] Farming
[ ] Professional
[ ] Retail/Wholesale
[ ] Railroad
[ ] Transportation
[ ] Manufacturing/Mining
[ ] Stockbroker
[ ] Commodity Broker
[ ] Construction
[ ] Real Estate
[X] Other Business

B. BRIEFLY DESCRIBE NATURE OF BUSINESS
Video taping services.

CHAPTER OR SECTION OF BANKRUPTCY CODE UNDER WHICH THE PETITION IS FILED (Check one box)
[ ] Chapter 7
[ ] Chapter 9
[X] Chapter 11
[ ] Chapter 12
[ ] Chapter 13
[ ] Sec. 304 - Case Ancillary to Foreign Proceeding

SMALL BUSINESS (Chapter 11 only)
[ ] Debtor is a small business as defined in 11 U.S.C. § 101.
[ ] Debtor is and elects to be considered a small business under 11 U.S.C. § 112(e). (Optional)

FILING FEE (Check one box)
[X] Filing fee attached
[ ] Filing fee to be paid in installments. (Applicable to individuals only.) Must attach signed application for the court's consideration certifying that the debtor is unable to pay fee except in installments. Rule 1006(b); see Official Form No. 3

NAME AND ADDRESS OF LAW FIRM OR ATTORNEY
White Charger Legal Clinic
One Learned Way
Los Angeles, California 90001
Telephone No. (213) 891-0000

NAME(S) OF ATTORNEY(S) DESIGNATED TO REPRESENT THE DEBTOR (Print or Type Names)
Bankrupt C. Lawyer

[ ] Debtor is not represented by an attorney. Telephone No. of Debtor not represented by an attorney: ( )

STATISTICAL/ADMINISTRATIVE INFORMATION (28 U.S.C. § 604)
(Estimates only) (Check applicable boxes)

[X] Debtor estimates that funds will be available for distribution to unsecured creditors.

[ ] Debtor estimates that, after any exempt property is excluded and administrative expenses paid, there will be no funds available for distribution to unsecured creditors.

THIS SPACE FOR COURT USE ONLY

ESTIMATED NUMBER OF CREDITORS

1-15	16-49	50-99	100-199	200-999	1000-over
[X]	[ ]	[ ]	[ ]	[ ]	[ ]

ESTIMATED ASSETS (In thousands of dollars)

Under 50	50-99	100-499	500-999	1000-9999	10,000-99,000	100,000-over
[ ]	[X]	[ ]	[ ]	[ ]	[ ]	[ ]

ESTIMATED LIABILITIES (In thousands of dollars)

Under 50	50-99	100-499	500-999	1000-9999	10,000-99,000	100,000-over
[ ]	[X]	[ ]	[ ]	[ ]	[ ]	[ ]

EST. NO. OF EMPLOYEES - CH 11 & 12 ONLY

0	1-19	20-99	100-999	1000-OVER
[ ]	[X]	[ ]	[ ]	[ ]

EST. NO. OF EQUITY SECURITY HOLDERS - CH 11 & 12 ONLY

0	1-19	20-99	100-999	1000-over
[ ]	[X]	[ ]	[ ]	[ ]

■ EXHIBIT 7.3
Sample Pleading For Corporate Debtor—*Continued*

Name of Debtor   Videos By Joe, Inc.

Case No.   _____
(Court use only)

FILING OF PLAN

For Chapter 9, 11, 12 and 13 cases only. Check appropriate box.

[ ] A copy of the debtor's proposed plan dated _____   [X] Debtor intends to file a plan within the time allowed by statute, rule, or order of
is attached   the court

PRIOR BANKRUPTCY CASE FILED WITHIN LAST 6 YEARS (If more than one, attach additional sheet)

Location Where Filed	Case Number	Date Filed

PENDING BANKRUPTCY CASE FILED BY ANY SPOUSE, PARTNER, OR AFFILIATE OF THIS DEBTOR (If more than one, attach additional sheet.)

Name of Debtor	Case Number	Date
Relationship	District	Judge

REQUEST FOR RELIEF

Debtor is eligible for and requests relief in accordance with the chapter of title 11, United States Code, specified in this petition.

SIGNATURES

x *Bankrupt C. Lawyer*   **ATTORNEY**   October 1, 1995
Signature   Bankrupt C. Lawyer   Date

INDIVIDUAL/JOINT DEBTOR(S)	CORPORATE OR PARTNERSHIP DEBTOR
	I declare under penalty of perjury that the information provided in this petition is true and correct and that I have been authorized to file this petition on behalf of the debtor.
x _____ Signature of Debtor Videos By Joe, Inc. October 1, 1995 Date	x *Joseph Businessman* Signature of Authorized Individual Joseph Businessman Print or Type Name of Authorized Individual
x _____ Signature of Joint Debtor _____ Date	President Title of Individual Authorized by Debtor to File this Petition October 1, 1995 Date If debtor is a coproration filing under chapter 11, Exhbit "A" is attached and made part of this petition.

TO BE COMPLETED BY INDIVIDUAL CHAPTER 7 DEBTOR WITH PRIMARILY CONSUMER DEBTS (See P.L. 98-353 § 322)	CERTIFICATION AND SIGNATURE OF NON-ATTORNEY BANKRUPTCY PETITION PREPARER (See 11 U.S.C. § 110)
I am aware that I may proceed under chapter 7, 11, or 12, or 13 of title 11, United States Code, understand the relief available under each such chapter, and choose to proceed under chapter 7 of such title. If I am represented by an attorney, exhibit "B" has been completed. x _____ _____ Signature of Debtor Date x _____ _____ Signature of Joint Debtor Date	I certify that I am a bankruptcy petition preparer as defined in 11 U.S.C. § 110, that I prepared this document for compensation, and that I have provided the debtor with a copy of this document. _____ Printed or Typed Name of Bankruptcy Petition Preparer _____ Social Security Number _____ Address Tel. No. Names and Social Security numbers of all other individuals who prepared or assisted in preparing this document:
EXHIBIT "B" (To be completed by attorney for individual chapter 7 debtor(s) with primarily consumer debts.) I, the attorney for the debtor(s) named in the foregoing petition, declare that I have informed the debtor(s) that (he, she, or they) may proceed under chapter 7, 11, 12, or 13 of title 11, United States Code, and have explained the relief available under such chapter. x _____ _____ Signature of Attorney Date	If more than one person prepared this document, attach additional signed sheets conforming to the appropriate Official Form for each person. x _____ Signature of Bankruptcy Petition Preparer A bankruptcy petition preparer's failure to comply with the provisions of title 11 and the Federal Rules of Bankruptcy Procedure may result in fines or imprisonment or both. 11 U.S.C. § 110; 18 U.S.C. § 156

■ EXHIBIT 7.3
Sample Pleading For Corporate Debtor—*Continued*

Exhibit "A"

(If a debtor is a corporation filing under chapter 11 of the Code, this Exhibit "A" shall be completed and attached to the petition.)

UNITED STATES BANKRUPTCY COURT
<u>Western</u> DISTRICT OF <u>California</u>

In re <u>Videos by Joe, Inc.</u>   ,   Case No. <u>95-00001-JF</u>
                              Debtor   Chapter <u>11</u>

Exhibit "A" to Voluntary Petition

1. Debtor's employer identification number is <u>   99-999899   </u> .
2. If any of the debtor's securities are registered under section 12 of the Securities and Exchange Act of 1934, the SEC file number is _____ .
3. The following financial data is the latest available information and refers to debtor's condition on <u>   October 1, 1995   </u> .

   a. Total assets   <u>$50,000.00</u>
   b. Total liabilities   <u>$70,000.00</u>

		Approximate number of holders
Fixed, liquidated secured debt	$ _____ 25,000.00	2
Contingent secured debt	$ _____ 0	0
Disputed secured claims	$ _____ 0	0
Unliquidated secured debt	$ _____ 0	0

		Approximate number of holders
Fixed, liquidated unsecured debt	$ _____ 45,000.00	12
Contingent unsecured debt	$ _____ 0	0
Disputed unsecured claims	$ _____ 0	0
Unliquidated unsecured debt	$ _____ 0	0
Number of shares of preferred stock	0	0
Number of shares of common stock	10,000	3

Comments, if any: _____
_____
_____
_____
_____
_____
_____
_____

Continued

■ EXHIBIT 7.3
Sample Pleading For Corporate Debtor—*Continued*

---

4. Brief description of debtor's business: <u>Debtor is in the business of providing video-taping services for social functions and presentations.</u>

5. List the name of any person who directly or indirectly owns, controls, or holds, with power to vote, 20% or more of the voting securities of debtor: <u>Joseph Businessman—40%; Myra Businesswoman—40%; Maximillian Businessboy—20%</u>

6. List the names of all corporations 20% or more of the outstanding voting securities of which are directly or indirectly owned, controlled, or held, with the power to vote, by debtor: <u>None</u>

WRITTEN CONSENT OF THE BOARD OF DIRECTORS OF VIDEOS BY JOE, INC. A CALIFORNIA CORPORATION

We, the undersigned Board of Directors as presently constituted of Videos by Joe, Inc., a duly organized California corporation (the "Corporation"), acting pursuant to the provision of Section 307(b) of the California Corporations Code and Section 18 of Article III of the Corporation's bylaws, hereby consent to, approve and adopt the following resolutions and the actions and proceedings contemplated therein:

WHEREAS, the Corporation has determined that it would be in its best interest to immediately file a voluntary petition (the "Petition") under Chapter 11 of Title 11, United States Code (the "Bankruptcy Code") in the Western District of California.

NOW, THEREFORE, BE IT RESOLVED, that the Corporation hereby authorizes the preparation and filing of the petition and such additional documentation as required by the Bankruptcy Code or otherwise to allow the Corporation to avail itself of the relief available under the Bankruptcy Code; and it is

RESOLVED FURTHER, that the President of the Corporation is authorized, empowered, and directed to execute the petition and any further actions and to execute and deliver all such further instruments and documents in the name and on behalf of the Corporation, and to pay and incur expenses as shall in the President's judgment be necessary or appropriate to carry out the purpose and intent of each and everyone of the resolutions set forth herein; and it is

RESOLVED FINALLY, that the Corporation is authorized to retain the services of White Charger Legal Clinic (the "Firm") as its insolvency counsel and to pay to the Firm the sum of $10,000 prior to the filing of the petition as a retainer with the Firm's compensation to be paid in conformity with the Bankruptcy Code.

DATED: October 1, 1995

_____

Joseph Businessman

_____

Myra Businesswoman

_____

Maximillion Businessman

■ EXHIBIT 7.4
Sample Pleading For Consumer Debtor

B1
(Rev. 12/94)

United States Bankruptcy Court **Western** District of **California**	VOLUNTARY PETITION

IN RE (Name of debtor - If individual, enter Last, First, Middle) **Joseph Consumer**	NAME OF JOINT DEBTOR (Spouse) (Last, First, Middle)
ALL OTHER NAMES used by the debtor in the last 6 years (Include married, maiden, and trade names.)	ALL OTHER NAMES used by the joint debtor in the last 6 years (Include married, maiden, and trade names.)
SOC. SEC./TAX I.D. NO. (If more than one, state all.) **558-15-1402**	SOC. SEC./TAX I.D. NO. (If more than one, state all.)
STREET ADDRESS OF DEBTOR (No. and street, city, state, and zip code) **18 Hollywood Drive** **Los Angeles, California 90001**	STREET ADDRESS OF JOINT DEBTOR (No. and street, city, state, and zip code)
COUNTY OF RESIDENCE OR PRINCIPAL PLACE OF BUSINESS **LOS ANGELES**	COUNTY OF RESIDENCE OR PRINCIPAL PLACE OF BUSINESS
MAILING ADDRESS OF DEBTOR (If different from street address)	MAILING ADDRESS OF JOINT DEBTOR (If different from street address)

LOCATION OF PRINCIPAL ASSETS OF BUSINESS DEBTOR (If different from address listed above)	VENUE (Check one box only)
	[X] Debtor has been domiciled or has had a residence, principal place of business, or principal assets in this District for 180 days immediately preceding the date of this petition or for a longer part of such 180 days than in any other District. [ ] There is a bankruptcy case concerning debtor's affiliate, general partner, or partnership pending in this District.

INFORMATION REGARDING DEBTOR (Check applicable boxes)

TYPE OF DEBTOR (Check one box)		CHAPTER OR SECTION OF BANKRUPTCY CODE UNDER WHICH THE PETITION IS FILED (Check one box)
[X] Individual [ ] Joint (Husband & Wife) [ ] Partnership [ ] Other: _____	[ ] Corporation Publicly Held [ ] Corporation Not Publicly Held [ ] Municipality	[X] Chapter 7 [ ] Chapter 11 [ ] Chapter 13 [ ] Chapter 9 [ ] Chapter 12 [ ] Sec. 304 - Case Ancillary to Foreign Proceeding

SMALL BUSINESS (Chapter 11 only)
[ ] Debtor is a small business as defined in 11 U.S.C. § 101.
[ ] Debtor is and elects to be considered a small business under 11 U.S.C. § 112(e). (Optional)

NATURE OF DEBT
[X] Non-Business/Consumer   [ ] Business - Complete A & B below

FILING FEE (Check one box)
[X] Filing fee attached
[ ] Filing fee to be paid in installments. (Applicable to individuals only.) Must attach signed application for the court's consideration certifying that the debtor is unable to pay fee except in installments. Rule 1006(b); see Official Form No. 3

A. TYPE OF BUSINESS (Check one box)
[ ] Farming   [ ] Transportation   [ ] Commodity Broker
[ ] Professional   [ ] Manufacturing/   [ ] Construction
[ ] Retail/Wholesale [ ] Mining   [ ] Real Estate
[ ] Railroad   [ ] Stockbroker   [ ] Other Business

B. BRIEFLY DESCRIBE NATURE OF BUSINESS

NAME AND ADDRESS OF LAW FIRM OR ATTORNEY
White Charger Legal Clinic
One Learned Way
Los Angeles, California 90001
Telephone No. **(213)891-0000**

NAME(S) OF ATTORNEY(S) DESIGNATED TO REPRESENT THE DEBTOR (Print or Type Names)
Bankrupt C. Lawyer

[ ] Debtor is not represented by an attorney. Telephone No. of Debtor not represented by an attorney: (   )

STATISTICAL/ADMINISTRATIVE INFORMATION (28 U.S.C. § 604) (Estimates only) (Check applicable boxes)	THIS SPACE FOR COURT USE ONLY

[ ] Debtor estimates that funds will be available for distribution to unsecured creditors.
[X] Debtor estimates that, after any exempt property is excluded and administrative expenses paid, there will be no funds available for distribution to unsecured creditors.

ESTIMATED NUMBER OF CREDITORS

1-15	16-49	50-99	100-199	200-999	1000-over
[X]	[ ]	[ ]	[ ]	[ ]	[ ]

ESTIMATED ASSETS (In thousands of dollars)

Under 50	50-99	100-499	500-999	1000-9999	10,000-99,000	100,000-over
[X]	[ ]	[ ]	[ ]	[ ]	[ ]	[ ]

ESTIMATED LIABILITIES (In thousands of dollars)

Under 50	50-99	100-499	500-999	1000-9999	10,000-99,000	100,000-over
[ ]	[X]	[ ]	[ ]	[ ]	[ ]	[ ]

EST. NO. OF EMPLOYEES - CH 11 & 12 ONLY

0	1-19	20-99	100-999	1000-OVER
[ ]	[ ]	[ ]	[ ]	[ ]

EST. NO. OF EQUITY SECURITY HOLDERS - CH 11 & 12 ONLY

0	1-19	20-99	100-999	1000-over
[ ]	[ ]	[ ]	[ ]	[ ]

■ EXHIBIT 7.4
Sample Pleading For Consumer Debtor—*Continued*

Name of Debtor **Joseph Consumer**

Case No. _____

(Court use only)

FILING OF PLAN

For Chapter 9, 11, 12 and 13 cases only. Check appropriate box.

☐ A copy of the debtor's proposed plan dated _____ is attached

☐ Debtor intends to file a plan within the time allowed by statute, rule, or order of the court

PRIOR BANKRUPTCY CASE FILED WITHIN LAST 6 YEARS (If more than one, attach additional sheet)

Location Where Filed	Case Number	Date Filed

PENDING BANKRUPTCY CASE FILED BY ANY SPOUSE, PARTNER, OR AFFILIATE OF THIS DEBTOR (If more than one, attach additional sheet.)

Name of Debtor	Case Number	Date
Relationship	District	Judge

REQUEST FOR RELIEF

Debtor is eligible for and requests relief in accordance with the chapter of title 11, United States Code, specified in this petition.

SIGNATURES

X *Bankrupt C. Lawyer* **ATTORNEY**   October 1, 1995
Signature Bankrupt C. Lawyer   Date

INDIVIDUAL/JOINT DEBTOR(S)	CORPORATE OR PARTNERSHIP DEBTOR
I declare under penalty of perjury that the information provided in this petition is true and correct	I declare under penalty of perjury that the information provided in this petition is true and correct and that I have been authorized to file this petition on behalf of the debtor.
X *Joseph Consumer* Signature of Debtor Joseph Consumer October 1, 1995 Date	X _____ Signature of Authorized Individual _____ Print or Type Name of Authorized Individual
X _____ Signature of Joint Debtor _____ Date	_____ Title of Individual Authorized by Debtor to File this Petition _____ Date If debtor is a coproration filing under chapter 11, Exhbit "A" is attached and made part of this petition.

TO BE COMPLETED BY INDIVIDUAL CHAPTER 7 DEBTOR WITH PRIMARILY CONSUMER DEBTS (See P.L. 98-353 § 322)	CERTIFICATION AND SIGNATURE OF NON-ATTORNEY BANKRUPTCY PETITION PREPARER (See 11 U.S.C. § 110)
I am aware that I may proceed under chapter 7, 11, or 12, or 13 of title 11, United States Code, understand the relief available under each such chapter, and choose to proceed under chapter 7 of such title. If I am represented by an attorney, exhibit "B" has been completed. X *Joseph Consume* October 1, 1995 Signature of Debtor Date Joseph Consumer X _____ _____ Signature of Joint Debtor Date	I certify that I am a bankruptcy petition preparer as defined in 11 U.S.C. § 110, that I prepared this document for compensation, and that I have provided the debtor with a copy of this document. _____ Printed or Typed Name of Bankruptcy Petition Preparer _____ Social Security Number _____ Address Tel. No. Names and Social Security numbers of all other individuals who prepared or assisted in preparing this document:

EXHIBIT "B"	
(To be completed by attorney for individual chapter 7 debtor(s) with primarily consumer debts.) I, the attorney for the debtor(s) named in the foregoing petition, declare that I have informed the debtor(s) that (he, she, or they) may proceed under chapter 7, 11, 12, or 13 of title 11, United States Code, and have explained the relief available under such chapter. X *Bankrupt C. Lawyer* October 1, 1995 Signature of Attorney Date Bankrupt C. Lawyer	If more than one person prepared this document, attach additional signed sheets conforming to the appropriate Official Form for each person. X _____ Signature of Bankruptcy Petition Preparer A bankruptcy petition preparer's failure to comply with the provisions of title 11 and the Federal Rules of Bankruptcy Procedure may result in fines or imprisonment or both. 11 U.S.C. § 110; 18 U.S.C. § 156

The Caption The caption is required to be on all pleadings and other papers filed with the court. Its contents are listed in Bankruptcy Rule 1005. On Official Form 1 it consists of the top eight boxes. The first requirement, located in the upper left hand box, is the name of the court, such as the United States Bankruptcy Court, Middle District of Tennessee. The second part of the caption is the title of the document. In the case of the petition, the title "Voluntary Petition" is found on the upper right hand box.

The third item for the caption is the title of the case. The title of the case will be "In re," or sometimes "In the matter of," followed by all names used by the debtor during the six years before filing the petition. Aliases, fictitious business names, tradenames, maiden names, married names, and the like should be included. They are to be on all papers so that creditors can identify the debtor when they receive notices and orders concerning the bankruptcy case. The title of the case must also include the debtor's social security number if the debtor is an individual or its tax identification number if the debtor is a partnership or corporation. All of the information concerning the title of the case is found in the six boxes directly below the name of the court and the name of the document. If the case is filed by a husband and wife, the information will be given separately with one person identified on the right and the other on the left. Obviously, if only one person is filing, the right side boxes will be left blank.

For every pleading other than the petition, the caption will also include the docket or case number. Every jurisdiction has its own method for numbering cases. The clerk will assign a docket number to the case when the petition is filed. On a petition, the case number will now be inserted in the open space in the lower right area of the front page. Local practice dictates where the case number will appear on other pleadings.

Venue Following the caption are the venue boxes; it is here that the debtor gives its street and mailing address, including the county or parish, and the location of its assets. In the eighth box down on the right side, the debtor must indicate which of two bases exist for the bankruptcy case to be filed in the particular district. The venue conclusion is now done simply by making one of the elections in that box.

Where a bankruptcy petition should be filed is governed by Section 1408 of Title 28 of the United States Code. Under Section 1408, the debtor cannot file the petition anywhere it chooses. Instead, it may only commence the case in one of the following locations:

Domicile
The principal place of residence in which the debtor intends to remain.

☐ where the debtor is domiciled.
☐ where the debtor resides;
☐ where the debtor has its principal place of business; or
☐ where the debtor has its principal assets.

Domicile is where the debtor resides and intends to remain. The debtor's domicile and residence are usually the same location.

Affiliate
An entity that owns twenty percent or more of the debtor's stock, a corporation twenty percent or more of whose stock is owned by the debtor, a person whose business or property is operated by the debtor, or an entity that operates the debtor's business or property.

In addition, as the second option in the venue box indicates, the debtor may file a petition in the district where there is already a pending bankruptcy case concerning the debtor's **affiliate,** which is defined in Section 101(2). If the debtor has moved its domicile, residence, or the location of its principal place of business or principal assets during the 180 days prior to the filing of the petition, venue is proper where the debtor or its business or its assets were for the greater part of the 180 days.

Information Regarding the Debtor   The middle of the first page of Official Form 1 has five boxes that request various information. In the first of these boxes, located on the left side, the debtor will need to indicate whether it is an individual, a husband and wife (joint case), partnership, public corporation, non-public corporation, municipality or "other." Below that the debtor must indicate whether its debt is primarily consumer or business. If the debtor primarily has business debt, it must also indicate in Question A the type of business (such as farming or construction) and in Question B briefly describe the business. Questions A and B are not completed in consumer debtor cases.

The first box of the middle section on the right side requires the debtor to indicate in which chapter the case is filed, and whether the debtor is and wants to be treated as a small business under Section 1121(e). The small business election is discussed in Chapter 11 of this book. Below that, the debtor indicates whether it is paying the filing fee with the petition or whether the debtor wishes to pay the filing fee in installments. Only individuals who have not paid an attorney to represent them may apply to pay the filing fee in installments. The last set of boxes of the middle section ask for the name, address and phone number of the law firm or attorney representing the debtor, and the particular attorney designated to represent the debtor (which may duplicate the information in the previous box). If the debtor is not represented by counsel, the debtor must set forth his or her telephone number in the last box of this section.

Statistical and Administrative Information   The last box on the first page of Official Form 1 asks for certain statistical and administrative information. The information is beneficial to the Administrative Office of the United States Courts that uses it to monitor the size, type, and number of cases each district has pending. There are five types of information asked for in this section. First, the debtor is asked to estimate whether or not there will be funds available to distribute to unsecured creditors. For most consumer debtors there will not be. If an undersecured creditor has a lien on all the business debtor's assets, there will not be funds to distribute either. Second, it asks the debtor to estimate, within the ranges provided, the number of creditors, the value of assets, the amount of liabilities, and for Chapter 11 and 12 cases only, the number of employees and equity security holders. The bankruptcy case will not be impacted if these amounts cannot be estimated, or are estimated inaccurately.

Plan   The next box, found on the top of the second page, is the plan statement. This paragraph should be ignored for Chapter 7 cases. It merely states that a copy of the debtor's plan is attached or the debtor intends to file a plan pursuant to Chapter 9, 11, 12, or 13. It is common for Chapter 12 or 13 plans to be filed along with the petition. It is very rare for a Chapter 9 or 11 plan to accompany the petition.

Related Case Information   The second set of boxes on page 2 of Official Form 1 requires certain information concerning the debtor's prior bankruptcy cases in the last six years and the pending bankruptcy cases of a spouse, partner, or affiliate. This information was formerly required by most local bankruptcy rules.

Certification   Following the debtor's request for relief are signature spaces. The petition must be signed by the attorney for the debtor, if the debtor is represented,

or by the debtor if the debtor is not represented. If a husband and wife are filing a joint case, each must sign the petition. If the debtor is a partnership, all the general partners must sign the petition. Regardless of who signs the petition, Bankruptcy Rule 1008 requires that there be a certification that the statements in the petition are true.

Exhibit A   If the debtor is a corporation, Exhibit A must be completed and attached to the petition as provided in the corporate or partnership debtor certification box. Exhibit A requires the debtor to give the following information:

☐ The debtor's employer identification number (which is also part of the caption).

☐ The debtor's Securities and Exchange Commission file number if any of its securities are registered.

☐ Certain financial information, including the amount of
  - assets;
  - liabilities;
  - secured debt and the number of secured creditors broken down by whether the debt is agreed to or disputed;
  - unsecured debt and the number of holders broken down by whether the debt is agreed to or disputed.

☐ The number of shares of the debtor's preferred and common stock and the number of holders.

☐ A brief description of the debtor's business (which is also on the first page of Official Form 1).

☐ The name of any person who directly or indirectly owns, controls, or holds twenty percent or more of the debtor's stock; and

☐ The name of all corporations the debtor owns, controls, or of which the debtor holds twenty percent or more of the outstanding voting securities.

Some local rules require a resolution or minutes of a meeting of the board of directors authorizing the commencement of the bankruptcy case to be attached to the petition of a corporate debtor. A sample corporate resolution authorizing the filing of a petition is included as a part of Exhibit 7.3.

Consumer Relief Alternatives and Exhibit B   The last two boxes on the left side of page 2 of Official Form 1 encourage individual debtors who have primarily consumer debts to file a reorganization case rather than a Chapter 7 liquidation case. Both boxes should be ignored if the petition is being filed under any chapter other than Chapter 7 or by an individual who does not have primarily consumer debts.

The first box is a statement by the debtor that the debtor is aware that he or she may proceed under Chapter 7, 11, 12, or 13 of the Bankruptcy Code, knows the difference between them, and still chooses to file the petition under Chapter 7. As discussed earlier, in order for debtors to make an intelligent choice, Section 342(b) requires the clerk of the court to give written notice to the debtor of the differences between the chapters. The clerk's office will use a notice similar to Director's Form B 201 which briefly describes the various chapters. If the individual with primarily consumer debts is represented by an attorney, Exhibit B, which is simply the bottom box, must be included in the petition. Exhibit B is merely a one-sentence statement that the debtor's attorney has informed the debtor that

the debtor may proceed under the various chapters and has explained the relief available under each chapter. It must be dated and signed by the attorney.

Bankruptcy Petition Preparers   As discussed in Chapter 3 of this book, Section 110 of the Bankruptcy Code, which was added with the 1994 Amendments, requires bankruptcy petition preparers to sign all documents they prepare, and print their name, address, and the Social Security Number of the responsible individual on all documents they prepare. The last box on the right side of page 2 of Official Form 1 has space for all the information required of bankruptcy petition preparers.

Supporting Documents   The Bankruptcy Rules require that a number of documents and other items be filed with the petition or shortly thereafter. Several of the items, including the schedules and statements, the filing fee, and the master mailing list, are discussed later in this chapter. Other documents include:

☐ *List of all creditors*. Unless the petition is accompanied by the schedule of liabilities described later, Bankruptcy Rule 1007(a)(1) requires that a list containing the name and address of each creditor be filed with the petition. There is no official form for this list. A simple caption page attaching the list will suffice.

☐ *List of all equity security holders*. In Chapter 11 cases of corporations and partnerships, Bankruptcy Rule 1007(a)(3) requires the debtor to file a list of its equity security holders of each class showing the number and kind of interests registered in the name of each holder, and the last known address or place of business of each holder. This list must be filed within fifteen days of the filing of the petition.

☐ *List of the twenty largest unsecured creditors*. In Chapter 11 cases, in addition to the list of all creditors, Bankruptcy Rule 1007(d) requires the debtor to separately file with the petition a list containing the names, addresses, and amount of claims of the twenty largest noninsider unsecured creditors. Official Form 4 has been drafted for use in complying with this rule. Official Form 4 adds certain information to be inserted in the list. This information, including the phone number and the name of the employee or agent of the creditor who has the most knowledge of the claim, is not required by Bankruptcy Rule 1007. The form also asks for the nature of the debt, such as trade debt, bank loan, judgment, and so on. The purpose of the list is to give the United States trustee the names of the persons who should be solicited to serve on the creditors' committee. The description of the nature of the debt will help the trustee select a committee representative of the varying interests in the case.

☐ *Statement of intentions*. If a Chapter 7 debtor is an individual with consumer secured debts, Section 521(2)(A) of the Bankruptcy Code requires that, within thirty days after the filing of the petition or at the meeting of creditors held pursuant to Section 341(a), whichever is earlier, the debtor file a statement of intentions specifying whether the debtor intends to retain or surrender the secured property, whether the property is exempt, and whether the debtor intends to redeem the property or reaffirm the debt secured by the property. The statement of intentions is Official Form 8. All of the options it concerns are discussed later in this book.

☐ *Attorney's statement*. Bankruptcy Rule 2016(b) requires every attorney for a debtor to file a statement of compensation paid or agreed to be paid in connection with the bankruptcy case and the source of that compensation. This

statement must be filed with the court on or before the first date set for the Section 341(a) meeting of creditors. Director's Form B 203 is to be used for this statement. A sample follows in Exhibit 7.5.

□ *Bankruptcy Petition Preparers' Statement.* Section 110 requires every bankruptcy petition preparer to file within ten days of filing the petition a declaration disclosing any compensation received from or on behalf of the debtor within twelve months prior to filing the case and an unpaid fee due. Director's Form B 280 has been developed for this required disclosure.

The number of copies of the petition and the supporting documents that are required to be filed are governed by local rules. The former Bankruptcy Rule on the subject has been deleted.

The Filing Fee

Bankruptcy Rule 1006(a) provides that a filing fee must accompany the petition. The amounts are set in Section 1930 of Title 28. Currently, the amounts are

Chapter 7	$ 145.00
Chapter 9	$ 300.00
Chapter 11	$ 800.00
Chapter 11 (railroad)	$1,000.00
Chapter 12	$ 200.00
Chapter 13	$ 130.00

In addition, in a Chapter 7 or 13 case, the debtor must pay a $30.00 "administrative fee."

If a case is converted to Chapter 11 or 12 from Chapter 7 or 13, the difference in the filing fee must be paid upon the conversion. The clerk will usually not accept the debtor's check for the filing fee.

No matter how poor the debtor may be, it must pay the filing fee and the administrative fee. How much is paid is strictly a function of the chapter of the bankruptcy case. The debtor's wealth or poverty is irrelevant. There is no bankruptcy law or rule equivalent to *in forma pauperis* or other status which allows for the wavier of filing and other fees as exists in other federal and state courts. The reason that has been given is that although access to the civil courts is critical if an individual is to remedy wrongs or defend other actions, access to the bankruptcy court is not as critical. If a debtor wanted to restructure its debts, it could do so by negotiating with creditors and without calling upon the bankruptcy court for assistance. Whether that reasoning makes sense in light of economic and practical reality is of some dispute.

Although there cannot be a waiver of the filing fee or the administrative fee when the petition is filed, in certain circumstances an individual debtor may be able to pay the filing fee and the administrative fee in installments. Bankruptcy Rule 1006(a) states that if an individual debtor cannot afford the fees, the debtor may propose to pay them in up to four installments the last of which must be paid no later than 120 days after the case is commenced. However, the court must first approve the installment payments and no attorney may be paid by the debtor until the entire filing fee is paid. Official Form 3 is the approved form of a combined application for permission to pay the filing fee in installments.

■ EXHIBIT 7.5
Disclosure of Attorney Compensation

UNITED STATES BANKRUPTCY COURT
WESTERN DISTRICT OF CALIFORNIA

In re Videos By Joe, Inc.,   Case No. 95-00001-JF

Debtor.

DISCLOSURE OF COMPENSATION OF ATTORNEY FOR DEBTOR

1. Purusant to 11 U.S.C. § 329(a) and Bankruptcy Rule 2016(b), I certify that I am the attorney for the above debtor(s) and that compensation paid to me within one year before the filing of the petition in bankruptcy, or to be paid to me, for services rendered or to be rendered on behalf of the debtor(s) in contemplation of or in connection with the bankruptcy case is as follows:

For legal services, I have agreed to accept $10,000.00

Prior to the filing of this statement I have received $10,000.00

Balance Due   -0-

2. The source of compensation paid to me was:
   ☒ Debtor   ☐ Other (specify)

3. The source of compensation to be paid to me is:
   ☒ Debtor   ☐ Other (specify)

4. ☒ I have not agreed to share the above-disclosed compensation with any other person unless they are members and associates of my law firm.

   ☐ I have agreed to share the above-disclosed compensation with a person or persons who are not members and associates of my law firm. A copy of the agreement, together with a list of the names of the people sharing the compensation is attached.

5. In return for the above-disclosed fee, I have agreed to render legal service for all aspects of the bankruptcy including:

   a. Analysis of the debtor's financial situation, and rendering advice to the debtor in determining whether to file the petition in bankruptcy;

   b. Preparation and filing of any petition, schedules, statement of affairs and plan which may be required;

   c. Representation of the debtor at the meeting of creditors and confirmation hearing any and adjourned hearing thereof;

   d. Representation of the debtor in adversary proceedings and other contested bankruptcy matters;

   e. [Other provisions as needed].

6. By agreement with the debtor(s), the above-disclosed fee does not include the following services:

Any non-bankruptcy related legal services.

CERTIFICATION

   I certify that the foregoing is a complete statement of any agreement or arrangement for payment to me for representation of the debtor(s) in this bankruptcy proceeding.

October 1, 1995   Bankrupt C. Lawyer
                                                  Signature of Attorney

                                                  White Charger Legal Clinic
                                                  Name of Law Firm

Schedules
The document filed by a debtor that discloses all of its property and debts and other pertinent information.

The Schedules

In General In all cases, the debtor is required to file with the court a detailed schedule of assets, liabilities, and various other types of information as well as a simple budget. This information is designed to give a snapshot of the debtor's financial condition on the date the bankruptcy case was commenced.

Bankruptcy Rules 1007(b) and (c) provide that in a voluntary case, these schedules must be filed with the petition. However, if the petition is accompanied by a list of the names and addresses of the debtor's creditors, the debtor may have an additional fifteen days to file the schedules. Bankruptcy Rule 1007 allows the court to grant an extension of the fifteen-day deadline if the debtor makes a motion; if the debtor gives notice to any committee, trustee, examiner, or other party as the court may direct; and if cause is shown. Preparation of the schedules in even a medium-sized case is a monumental undertaking and extensions are frequently sought and granted. Exhibit 7.6 is a sample motion to obtain an extension of the fifteen-day deadline.

The schedules are found in Official Form 6. Preprinted forms are readily available and are commonly used. In addition, a number of software companies market these forms. Not only is a customized form more pleasing to the eye, but it is easier to make corrections. If preprinted forms are going to be used, it is practical to first write out a rough draft on a copy before having the information typed onto the form itself. Some of the preprinted forms even come with an extra copy for making a draft.

If the preprinted forms are used, it is unlikely that there will be enough room to include all the information required in the space allotted. In those instances, insert "See Attachment Number _____ " or similar language on the schedule and include the information on a separate attachment.

There should never be a blank space in the schedules. If the debtor has no assets or liabilities of the type described in a particular part of the schedules, insert "none" in the space provided.

The number of copies of the schedules that are to be filed with the court is the same as the number of copies of the petition required by the local rules. Since the schedules are papers filed with the court, they will have the same caption as the petition as described in Bankruptcy Rule 1005.

It is important to remember that the schedules should reflect the debtor's financial condition on the date the order for relief was entered in the case. That is the rule no matter when the schedules are ultimately filed. Accordingly, no debts incurred after the order for relief date will be reflected in the schedules. Conversely, any asset disposed of after the commencement of the bankruptcy case will still be listed among the debtor's assets. The one exception is property that is acquired after the petition is filed but is considered property of the estate under Section 541 of the Bankruptcy Code. An example of this type of property is anything inherited within six months after the petition is filed. If such property is acquired after the schedules have been filed, Bankruptcy Rule 1007(h) requires the debtor to file a supplemental schedule listing the new property within ten days after the debtor knows about it.

If mistakes are found after the schedules are filed, the schedules can be amended by following Bankruptcy Rule 1009. The clerk will usually charge a small fee for the filing of an amendment to the schedules even though there is no fee for filing the schedules themselves.

■ EXHIBIT 7.6
Sample Motion For Extension

BANKRUPT C. LAWYER
WHITE CHARGER LEGAL CLINIC
One Learned Way
Los Angeles, California 90001

Attorneys for Debtor

UNITED STATES BANKRUPTCY COURT
WESTERN DISTRICT OF CALIFORNIA

In re)	Case No. 95-00001-JF
)	
VIDEOS BY JOE, INC.,)	Chapter 11
)	
Debtor.)	
)	
Debtor's Address:)	MOTION FOR ORDER GRANTING AN EX-
18 Hollywood Drive)	TENSION OF TIME TO FILE SCHEDULES AND
Los Angeles, California 90001)	STATEMENTS
)	
Employer's Tax Id. No. 99-999899)	
)	

TO THE HONORABLE JUSTIN FAIR, UNITED STATES BANKRUPTCY JUDGE:

   Videos by Joe, Inc. (the "Debtor"), through its attorneys, in support of its Motion for Order Granting an Extension of Time to File Schedules and Statements, respectfully represents as follows:

1. Debtor is the debtor in possession in the above-captioned case having filed a petition for relief under Chapter 11 of Title 11, United States Code, on October 1, 1995.

2. Debtor's petition was accompanied by a list of all Debtor's creditors. Pursuant to Bankruptcy Rule 1007(c), Debtor is allowed fifteen (15) days in which to file its schedules and its statement of financial affairs (collectively, the "Schedules").

3. As evidenced by the declaration of Joseph Businessman filed concurrently, Debtor has approximatley 300 creditors, operates in six states, and has seventeen business premises. The analysis and compilation of the information necessary to complete the Schedules will require more than fifteen days given the size of Debtor's operations, the urgency of other demands created by the filing of the petition, the need to maintain continuity in Debtor's business, and the reduced number of qualified staff to perform and oversee all of the above.

   WHEREFORE, pursuant to Bankruptcy Rule 1007(c), Debtor requests that the Court enter its Order granting Debtor an additional thirty days, up to and including November 15, 1995, within which to file the schedules.

DATED: October 3, 1995

WHITE CHARGER LEGAL CLINIC

_____

BANKRUPT C. LAWYER
Attorneys for Debtor

The schedules consist of the following parts:

Summary of Schedules

Schedule A —Real Property

Schedule B —Personal Property

Schedule C —Property Claimed as Exempt

Schedule D —Creditors Holding Secured Claims

Schedule E —Creditors Holding Unsecured Priority Claims

Schedule F —Creditors Holding Unsecured Nonpriority Claims

Schedule G —Executory Contracts and Unexpired Leases

Schedule H —Codebtors

Schedule I —Current Income of Individual Debtor(s)

Schedule J —Current Expenditures of Individual Debtor(s)

Unsworn Declaration under Penalty of Perjury

Each schedule will be examined separately. Even though the Summary is the first page in the schedule package, it will be completed last.

Schedule A   Schedule A is the list of the debtor's real property. A sample is shown in Exhibit 7.7. Schedule A requires the following information for each parcel of real estate in which the debtor has an interest: its description and location; the nature of the debtor's interest; whether it is owned by the husband, wife, jointly, or as community property; the current market value of the debtor's interest in the property; and the amount of any secured claim.

The property to be listed in Schedule A includes all real property in which the debtor has any legal, equitable, or future interest, including property in which the debtor only holds a partial interest. It will not include leased property.

The description and location should be the street address and a more specific legal description if possible. An attachment will usually be needed for the legal description. If the debtor does not own any real estate interests, "none" should be inserted into Schedule A.

■ EXHIBIT 7.7
Schedule A

In re Joe Consumer, Debtor.				Case No. 95-00002-JF	
			Schedule A—Real Property		
Description and Location of Property	**Nature of Debtor's Interest in Property**	**H W J C**	**Current Market Value of Debtor's Interest in Property, Without Deducting Any Secured Claim or Exemption**	**Amount of Secured Claim**	
Debtor's single family residence: 18 Hollywood Drive Los Angeles, California 90001	Fee simple absolute	C	$240,000.00	$225,000.00	
Total ▶			$240,000.00		

The different types of interests that a debtor may have were discussed in Chapter 4. Whatever interest it is will be set forth in the second column.

If the debtor is married, he or she must state in the third column who owns the property. If the answer is both, the debtor must state whether it is held in joint tenancy or as community property. The differences between those two types of interests in property were also discussed in Chapter 4. If the debtor is not an individual or is not married, this column should be left blank.

The next column asks for the current market value of the debtor's interest in the property. This will sometimes be difficult to set. Market value is a very broad term and could mean the price received by waiting for the highest offer or it could mean setting the property at an auction. The money received at those two types of sales could be very different. The debtor may have a recent appraisal or another good indication of the value of its interest. Alternatively, the debtor can insert the **book value** of the property. Book value is the value of the property on the debtor's books and records. That number is usually the property's cost less depreciation. Book value is not a good indicator of value because it does not take into account property that is appreciating in value rather than depreciating. Often the best that can be done is to insert "unknown" as the current market value. If book value is used, it should be labeled as such. The bottom of the column of Schedule A should be totalled and the sum placed in the Summary.

Book Value
The value of an asset as carried in the owner's books and records. Typically, cost less accumulated depreciation.

The final column in Schedule A is for the amount of any claim secured by this parcel of real property. This information will also be inserted into Schedule D (Secured Claims). By putting in the amount of the secured debt next to the current market value, a reader of Schedule A can make a quick determination if the debtor has any equity in the property available for unsecured creditors.

Schedule B   Schedule B is a list of the debtor's personal property contained on three pages. Schedule B gives 33 categories of personal property. A sample is shown in Exhibit 7.8. Schedule B asks for the following information for each type of personal property: the description and location of the property; whether it is owned by the husband, wife, jointly, or as community property; and the current market value of the debtor's interest.

Most of the categories are very self–explanatory. The legal assistant should understand where each type of personal property is inserted and how it should be described. There are a few nuances involved in completing Schedule B which are shown in Exhibit 7.9.

If the debtor does not have a particular category of personal property, and it is extremely rare for any debtor to have them all, the "None" box should be checked. If all or most of the property is located in one place, it is better to simply state at the beginning of Schedule B that "All the property is located at [list address here] unless otherwise indicated." If the debtor's property is being held by someone else, that person's name and address should be provided in the third column.

The market value of the debtor's interest in each particular category of personal property is also required. For liquid assets such as cash, this is easy. For most other categories it is not. If the debtor knows the market value it can be used. Otherwise it is better to use book value or simply state unknown.

The last page of Schedule B should be totalled and the number inserted into the Summary Page.

Schedule C   The individual debtor uses Schedule C to claim the exemptions that are discussed in Chapter 8 of this book. A sample of Schedule C is shown in that

■ EXHIBIT 7.8
Schedule B

| In re Joe Consumer, Debtor. | | | Case No. 95-00002-JF | |
| Schedule B—Personal Property | | | | |
Type of Property	N O N E	Description and Location of Property	H W J C	Current Market Value of Debtor's Interest in Property, Without Deducting Any Secured Claim or Exemption
		All property is located at 18 Hollywood Drive, Los Angeles, California 9001 unless otherwise indicated		
1. Cash on hand.			C	$250.00
2. Checking, savings or other financial accounts, certificates of deposit, or shares in banks, savings and loan, thrift, building and loan, and homestead associations or credit brokerage houses or cooperatives. * * *		Checking Acct. No. 99 34005 First City Bank Hollywood Branch Los Angeles, California	C	$3,000.00
4. Household goods and furnishings, including audio, video and computer equipment. * * *		Miscellaneous home furniture and supplies. One IBM personal computer with monitor and laser printer	C	$4,500.00
6. Wearing apparel. * * *		Miscellaneous family clothing	C	$500.00
12. Stock and interests in incorporated and unincorporated business. Itemize. * * *		100% ownership of Videos By Joe, Inc., a California corporation	C	0
23. Automobiles, trucks, trailers, and other vehicles and accessories. * * *		1992 Dodge Caravan	C	$5,000.00
33. Other personal property of any kind not already listed. Itemize.	X			
___ continuation sheets attached Total ▶				$13,250.00

chapter. Because nonindividual debtors are not entitled to exemptions, in a case commenced by a corporation or partnership, Schedule C is left blank.

Schedule C requires that the debtor give the following information:

☐ A description of property claimed as exempt, such as a residence, household furnishings, and automobile. This usually will be as described in the statute giving rise to the right for the exemption.

■ EXHIBIT 7.9
Additional Information Concerning Schedule B

Question	Property	Comments
1.	Cash on hand	For nonindividual debtors, this should be petty cash only. Individual debtors will disclose the cash they actually have in their possession. Any amounts in bank accounts should be in question 2.
9.	Interests in insurance policies	Often companies will purchase key-person life insurance for its senior executives. The cash surrender value of those policies or any other life insurance policies in which the debtor has an interest should be listed here by the type of insurance, the owner, the beneficiary, the name and address of the carrier, and the surrender value of the policies.
12.	Stocks and interests in incorporated and unincorporated companies	The debtor's stock holdings by company, number of shares, and if publicly traded, their market value must be itemized. If the debtor is a corporation, any subsidiaries and their value should be listed here. Although this question calls for interests in unincorporated companies, the assets of any sole proprietorship and interests in partnerships would be reflected in other places in the schedules.
13.	Interests in partnerships or joint ventures	For each partnership in which the debtor has an interest, the name and type of partnership (general, limited, joint venture) and the percentage of the debtor's holding should be inserted.
17.	Other liquidated debts owing debtor	This section will include employee advances, judgments obtained in debtor's favor, and the like. This is only undisputed tax refunds.
20.	Contingent and unliquidated claims	These are claims owing to the debtor that either are uncertain to arise or have not been fixed as to amount. An example of a contingent claim is a contract awarded to the debtor to construct a building. Upon satisfaction of the contingency—that is, completion of the building—the claim will arise. An example of an unliquidated claim in the favor of the debtor is a lawsuit that the debtor has brought as a plaintiff where the amount has not been fixed.
23.	Automobiles, trucks, trailers, and other vehicles	All vehicles should be itemized by make, model, and year.
28.	Inventory	Inventory should be itemized by type (such as raw materials, work in progress, or finished goods).

□ The specific law creating the exemption, including the subsection. This will be either a citation to a subsection of Section 522 of the Bankruptcy Code or a state law.

□ The value claimed as exempt.

□ Current market value of the property.

Schedule D   As seen, there were three schedules (A, B, and C) which covered the debtor's assets. There are also three Schedules (D, E, and F) which cover the debtor's liabilities. Schedule D is the list of all secured claims, Schedule E is the list of all priority creditors, and Schedule F is the list of all unsecured, nonpriority creditors.

A secured creditor is one who holds a judgment lien, garnishment, statutory lien, mortgage, deed of trust, or any other type of security interest. Schedule D requests the following information for each secured creditor:

☐ The name and address of the creditor and the account number.

☐ Whether there is a codebtor; i.e. anyone else also liable for the debt (other than the spouse in a joint case).

☐ Whether the debt is owed by the husband, wife, jointly, or as a community debt.

☐ When the claim was incurred, the nature of the lien, a description of the collateral, and the market value of the collateral.

☐ Whether the claim is contingent, unliquidated or disputed.

☐ The amount of the claim.

☐ The unsecured portion, if any.

Exhibit 7.10 shows how Schedule D can be completed for three different types of secured creditors. If practical, list the creditors in alphabetical order. As is true for all of the schedules listing liabilities, if the creditor is represented by an attorney or has involved a collection agent, the name and address of the attorney and the collection agency should also be listed.

As was true for preparing Schedules A and B, the greatest difficulty in preparing Schedule D is stating the market value of the collateral. Again, unknown may be the best choice.

Contingent Claim

A debt for which liability is dependent on a future event that may or may not occur.

Unliquidated Claim

A debt that has not been fixed as to amount.

Disputed Claim

A debt of which the debtor objects to the amount or allowability.

The terms **contingent, unliquidated,** and **disputed** are not defined in the Bankruptcy Code. Generally, a contingent claim is one that is awaiting the occurrence of an event, which may never occur, to make the underlying debt due. For example, if the debtor guaranteed a loan made by the bank to a relative, the liability would arise only if the relative defaulted on repayment of the loan. The debtor's liability under the guaranty would give rise to a contingent claim. An unliquidated claim is one in which the dollar amount due has not been fixed. If the debtor was at fault in an automobile accident and because of ongoing medical treatment the victim's damages have not been finally determined, the liability of the debtor is unliquidated. A disputed claim is just that. The debtor disputes the existence of the creditor's claim or disputes the dollar amount claimed to be owing.

Since the purpose of all of the liability schedules is to give as accurate as possible a statement of the debtor's liabilities, contingent, unliquidated, and disputed claims should be listed regardless of how farfetched the debtor believes the claim to be. Over inclusion is the rule because under inclusion may cause problems in the areas of discharge and binding the provisions of a plan on dissident creditors. It is crucial that if a claim is contingent, unliquidated, or disputed that it be so marked. "Unknown" should be inserted in the column for the amount of the claim if it is contingent or unliquidated or if the entire claim is disputed.

The final column for Schedule D is the unsecured portion of the secured claim. This will be the amount by which the amount of the secured creditor's claim exceeds the value of its collateral. In all of the schedules a creditor's claim need only be inserted once. Even if a secured creditor has an unsecured deficiency claim, it only need be listed in Schedule D instead of placing the secured portion of the claim in Schedule D and the unsecured portion in Schedule F. If the value of the collateral is more than the amount of the claim, the unsecured portion is zero. If either the value of the collateral or the value of the claim is unknown, the unsecured portion of the claim will also be unknown.

■ EXHIBIT 7.10
Schedule D

Creditor's Name and Mailing Address (Including Zip Code)	C O D E B T	H W J C	Date Claim Was Incurred, Nature of Lien, and Description and Market Value of Property Subject to Lien	C O N T	U N L I Q	D I S P	Amount of Claim Without Deducting Value of Collateral	Unsecured Portion If Any
In re Joe Consumer, Debtor.								Case No. 95-00002-JF
Schedule D—Creditors Holding Secured Claims								
ACCOUNT NO. 14357495 ABC CORPORATION 123 "M" Street Los Angeles, CA 90017	C	C	October 30, 1990 Voluntary security interest Lien on all personal property Value: $10,000.00				$6,000.00	
ACCOUNT NO. 59475341 ICM Corporation P.O. Box 1 Denver, CO 80808		H	June 7, 1994 Voluntary security interest Lien on personal computer Value: $1,000.00				$2,000.00	$1,000.00
ACCOUNT NO. None. P. Powers c/o J. Barrister, Esq. 124 Main Street Los Angeles, CA 90001		H	September 15, 1995 Judgment lien Debtor's residence located at 18 Hollywood Drive, Los Angeles, California 90001 Value: $240,000			X	$15,000.00	
			Subtotal ▶				$23,000.00	
			Total ▶				$23,000.00	

Finally, each page of Schedule D should have a subtotal, and the final page a total, of the amount of the secured claims. The total should also be added to the Summary Page.

Schedule E   Schedule E is for unsecured creditors who hold priority claims. As discussed in Chapter 1 of this book, there are eight different types of prepetition debts listed in Section 507(a) of the Bankruptcy Code that Congress has decided to treat better than others. These claims are placed in Schedule E. They should be segregated by type, with each new type starting a new page, and then in alphabetical order per type.

For each priority claim, Schedule E requires:

☐ The name and address of the creditor and the account number.

☐ Whether there is a codebtor (other than the spouse in a joint case).

☐ Whether the debt is owed by the husband, wife, jointly, or as a community debt.

☐ When the claim was incurred and the consideration for the claim.

☐ Whether the claim is contingent, unliquidated or disputed.

☐ The total amount of the claim.

☐ The amount entitled to priority.

As mentioned earlier, in all of the schedules a creditor's claim need only be inserted once. Even if a creditor's claim is only entitled to a priority in payment in part, it only need be listed in Schedule E instead of placing the priority portion of the claim in Schedule E and the nonpriority portion in Schedule F.

The first type of priority claim is for any unpaid claims arising after an involuntary case was filed against a debtor but prior to the entry of the order for relief. These claims are entitled to be paid just after all administrative claims are paid pursuant to Section 507(a)(2). There is no limit on the dollar amount of these types of priority claims.

The second type are priority claims under Section 507(a)(3) of the Bankruptcy Code. Congress has given employees a priority in treatment for unpaid wages, salaries, and commissions, including vacation, severance, and sick-leave pay earned within ninety days before the filing of the petition or the cessation of the debtor's business, whichever happened first. This priority is limited to $4,000 per employee.

To complete Schedule E for these priority claims, insert—either in the space provided or on an attachment—the name and address of each employee with a Section 507(a)(3) claim.

For the consideration column, indicate whether the claim is for wages, salaries, or commissions. Employees are not entitled to this priority for expense reimbursement. If they have such a claim, it should be listed in Schedule F with the unsecured creditors without priority. The time period in which the claim was incurred must also be shown. If the claim is contingent, unliquidated, or disputed, the schedule should so state. An employee's claim may be disputed if, for example, the employee also owes the employer money. The total amount of the claim must be inserted in the next to last column. The final insertion is the amount entitled to priority, not to exceed $4,000. This amount should be the employee's portion of the wages due. Amounts that the debtor must pay in connection with the wages, such as the debtor's portion of payroll taxes, should be included elsewhere.

A sample insert for an employee's wage priority on Schedule E appears in Exhibit 7.11.

The third type of priority is in Section 507(a)(4). It is for unpaid contributions to an employee benefit plan for services performed within 180 days of the filing of the petition or the cessation of the debtor's business, whichever first occurred. The type of plans with which this priority is concerned are such plans as health insurance. These priority claims are limited to the number of the employees covered by the plan multiplied by $4,000, less the aggregate amount listed in Schedule E for priority wage claims, plus the amount paid by the estate on behalf of the same employees to any other employee benefit plan.

The insertions for these priority claims should include the name of the plan, the plan administrator, the time periods involved, and the amount.

The next two possible inclusions for Schedule E relate to the special priorities granted to people in farming and fishing in the 1986 Amendments after the failure of a number of fish and grain storage companies. Section 507(a)(5)(A) gives a priority to persons engaged in the production or raising of grain with unsecured

■ EXHIBIT 7.11
Schedule E Pursuant to Section 507(a)(3)

In re Videos By Joe, Inc., Debtor.								Case No. 95-00001-JF	
Schedule E—Creditors Holding Unsecured Priority Claims									
							Section 507(a)(3)		
							TYPE OF PRIORITY		
Creditor's Name and Mailing Address (Including Zip Code)	**C O D E B T**	**H W J C**	**Date Claim Was Incurred and Consideration for Claim**	**C O N T**	**U N L I Q**	**D I S P**	**Total Amount of Claim**	**Amount Entitled to Priority**
ACCOUNT NO. None Myra Doe 123 Main Street San Francisco, CA 94628			September 1, 1995 through September 30, 1995 Wages				$6,000.00	$4,000.00
Sheet no. 1 of 3 sheets Schedule of Creditors Holding Priority Claims						Subtotal ▶	$6,000.00	
						Total ▶		

claims against a debtor who owns or operates a grain storage facility. Similarly, Section 507(a)(5)(B) gives a priority to claims of United States residents engaged in fishing against a debtor who has acquired fish or fish produce through a sale or conversion and who is engaged in operating a fish produce storage or processing facility. The priority of the claim under both Section 507(a)(5)(A) and (B) is limited to $4,000.

Schedule E may also include claims described in Section 507(a)(6), which are unsecured claims of the individuals arising form the deposit of money in connection with the purchase, lease, or rental of consumer property or the purchase of services that were not delivered or provided. This claim priority is limited to $1,800 per individual. Any claim that does not meet the criteria of Section 507(a)(6), such as deposits made by companies rather than individuals or deposits for nonconsumer goods, should be listed in Schedule F. Two different types of inserts for the deposit priority are shown in Exhibit 7.12.

The next priority provided in Section 507(a) is claims for debts to a spouse, former spouse, or child for alimony to, maintenance for, or support of such spouse or child in connection with a separation agreement, divorce decree or other order or law unless the debt was assigned to another entity. This priority, which was added with the 1994 Amendments, does not have a dollar limit.

The next type of claims for Schedule E is for the unsecured claims of governmental units that are granted a priority under Section 507(a)(8). There are seven types of governmental claims that are afforded this priority. They are primarily taxes, but they also include some penalties and custom duties. These claims are discussed in Chapter 13 of this book. If the debtor is liable for any of these taxes, they should be listed on a separate page of Schedule E, broken down by type of tax (F.I.C.A., personal property tax, and so on) and taxing agency. Claims owing to the United States should be listed first, followed by those owing to any state, and finally those

■ EXHIBIT 7.12
Schedule E Pursuant to 507(a)(6)

In re Videos By Joe, Inc., Debtor.								Case No. 95-00001-JF	
Schedule E—Creditors Holding Unsecured Priority Claims									
							Section 507(a)(6)		
							TYPE OF PRIORITY		
Creditor's Name and Mailing Address (Including Zip Code)	**C O D E B T**	**H W J C**	**Date Claim Was Incurred and Consideration for Claim**	**C O N T**	**U N L I Q**	**D I S P**	**Total Amount of Claim**	**Amount Entitled to Priority**
ACCOUNT NO. None Myra Doe 123 Main Street San Francisco, CA 94126			September 1, 1995 Layaway deposit				$100.00	$100.00
ACCOUNT NO. None Zane Grey 987 "A" Street San Francisco, CA 94567			September 15, 1995 Deposit on custom order.				$2,000.00	$2,000.00
Sheet no. 2 of 3 sheets to Schedule of Creditors Holding Priority Claims						Subtotal ▶	$2,100.00	
						Total ▶		

owing to any other taxing authority such as city, county, or special district. A sample Schedule E for a debtor's tax claims is shown in Exhibit 7.13.

The final type of priority claim properly listed on Schedule E is described in Section 507(a)(9). Added with the 1990 Amendments, it is for claims based on a commitment by the debtor to a federal depository institutions regulatory agency (such as the Federal Deposit Insurance Corporation) to maintain the capital of a bank or savings and loan. This priority applies in only a very few cases.

The only task remaining to complete Schedule E is to subtotal each page, total all pages and insert that number at the bottom of the last page and on the summary page. If the schedule has included claims for which the amount is unknown, it is helpful to put an asterisk next to the total and indicate (at a convenient spot in the schedule) that the total does not include claims that were listed on the schedule with an unknown amount.

Schedule F   Since most of the claims against a debtor will be on account of unsecured debts, Schedule F, Creditors Holding Unsecured Nonpriority Claims, will probably be the largest part of the schedules, even though it requires the least amount of information. In order to complete Schedule F, only the following information need be listed for each claim:

☐ The name and address of the creditor.

☐ Whether there is a codebtor (other than the spouse in a joint case).

■ EXHIBIT 7.13
Schedule E Pursuant to Section 507(a)(8)

In re Videos By Joe, Inc., Debtor.								Case No. 95-00001-JF	
Schedule E—Creditors Holding Unsecured Priority Claims									
							Section 507(a)(8) TYPE OF PRIORITY		
Creditor's Name and Mailing Address (Including Zip Code)	**C O D E B T**	**H W J C**	**Date Claim Was Incurred and Consideration for Claim**	**C O N T**	**U N L I Q**	**D I S P**	**Total Amount of Claim**	**Amount Entitled to Priority**	
ACCOUNT NO. 99-999899 Internal Revenue Service P.O. Box 1 Fresno, CA 94126			Income Taxes due for 1994				$66,000.00	$66,000.00	
ACCOUNT NO. 99-999899 Franchise Tax Board P.O. Box 2 Sacramento, CA 96000			Sales taxes collected June 1, 1995 to September 30, 1995				$13,500.00	$13,500.00	
Sheet no. 3 of 3 sheets to Schedule of Creditors Holding Priority Claims						Subtotal ▶	$79,500.00		
						Total ▶	$87,600.00		

☐ Whether the debt is owed by the husband, wife, jointly, or as a community debt.

☐ The date the claim was incurred, the consideration for the claim and whether the claim is subject to setoff.

☐ Whether the claim is contingent, unliquidated, or disputed.

☐ The amount of the claim.

If there are quite a few claims, rather than having the list prepared on Schedule F, it may be possible to attach the debtor's accounts payable register. This is especially convenient if the debtor has the information on its computer system and the printout can be reformatted to give the information in the manner called for in Schedule F. In addition, it will save a considerable amount of time later if the listings for Schedule F are in alphabetical order. Names of attorneys and collection agencies should be included if known. The total of all Schedule F claims should be filled in at the bottom of the last page of the Schedule and transferred to the Summary Page.

Schedule G Bankruptcy Rules 1007(b) and (c) require the debtor to file a statement of executory contracts and unexpired leases within fifteen days of the commencement of the case. A description of executory contracts and unexpired leases was given in Chapter 4 of this book. Generally, the contents of this statement will include all real and personal property leases including timeshares, employment

contracts, insurance agreements, purchase or supply contracts, pension and medical benefit plans, and collective bargaining agreements to which the debtor was a party.

Schedule G to Official Form 6 is the statement required. For each executory contract and unexpired lease Schedule G requires:

☐ The name and address of the other party to the lease or contract.

☐ A description of the contract or lease including the nature of the debtor's interest (e.g. lessor lessee, agent), whether the lease is for nonresidential real property, and the contract number of any government contract.

By identifying in Schedule G which leases are for nonresidential real property, a trustee can quickly see which leases must be assumed within sixty days or be deemed rejected under Section 365(d) of the Bankruptcy Code.

These parties listed in Schedule G will also have secured or unsecured claims against the debtor if for no other reason than they have contingent claims based on a possible default by the debtor. Hence, all of the parties listed in Schedule G should also appear in Schedules D, E, or F.

Schedule H Schedule H is the schedule of codebtors. This Schedule only requires the name of each codebtor and the name of each creditor that can look to the codebtor. As stated earlier a codebtor is anyone else who is liable on a debt with the debtor, such as a guarantor or cosigner, but does not include a spouse if the case was filed jointly by a husband and a wife. If the case was not filed by both the husband and wife, and the husband and wife live in a community property state, include in Schedule H the nonfiling spouse's name and, all names used in the previous six years.

Schedules I and J Section 521(1) of the Bankruptcy Code requires all debtors to file a statement of current income and expenditures. The statement is also required by Bankruptcy Rule 1007(b). The purpose of this requirement is to determine if the debtor projects that it will lose money in bankruptcy or if it believes it will at least break even on a cash basis. For individual debtors, it will also help determine what the debtor's disposable income is.

Schedule I of Official Form 6 is a statement of current income and Schedule J of Official Form 6 is a statement of current expenditures. Curiously, they are only for individuals to use. For corporate or partnership debtors, a simple sources and uses of cash statement can be attached to a page containing the caption and labeled "Statement of Current Income and Expenditures."

Schedules I and J are simple to use and largely self-explanatory.

Summary Page After Schedules A–J have been completed, the final page of the schedules, the summary page, should be filled in. A sample page is shown in Exhibit 7.14. Next to the left column listing each schedule, indicate with a yes or no answer whether each particular schedule is attached and, if so, the number of pages of each schedule. The number of pages should be totaled at the bottom of the page. The dollar amounts that have been placed at the bottom of each page of Schedules A, B, D, E, F, I, and J are carried to this page and inserted into the appropriate box in the three right columns. If the totals have been annotated in any way (for example, if there were a large number of claims listed as unknown in amount), these legends should also be indicated on the summary page. There

■ EXHIBIT 7.14
Summary of Schedules

In re Videos By Joe, Inc., Debtor.   Case No. 95-00001-JF

Summary of Schedules

Name of Schedule	Attached (Yes/No)	No. of Sheets	Assets	Liabilities	Other
				Amounts Scheduled	
A. Real Property					
B. Personal Property					
C. Property Claimed As Exempt					
D. Creditors Holding Secured Claims					
E. Creditors Holding Unsecured Piority Claims					
F. Creditors Holding Unsecured Nonpriority Claims					
G. Executory Contracts and Unexpired Leases					
H. Codebtors					
I. Current Income of Individual Debtor(s)					
J. Current Expenditures of Individual Debtor(s)					
Total Number of Sheets in ALL Schedules					
Total Assets					
Total Liabilities					

should be no blanks. If the debtor had no entries on a particular schedule, a zero dollar amount should be indicated on the summary page.

Declaration   The schedules should be followed by a declaration that they are true and correct and signed by the debtor or, if the debtor is a partnership or corporation, by an appropriate person. The last page of Official Form 6 gives both forms of this declaration. The total number of pages, which will be the number on the summary page plus one (for the summary page) should be inserted into the applicable declaration. In 1995 this page was amended to add an appropriate certification for a bankruptcy petition preparer as required by Section 110.

The Statement of Financial Affairs

In addition to the schedules, in order to give interested parties a complete picture of the debtor's financial condition on the date the petition was filed, the Bankruptcy Rules require every debtor to file a **statement of financial affairs,** which is

Statement of Financial Affairs
The document filed by a debtor that discloses all information not found in the schedules that a trustee would need to effectively administer the estate.

Official Form 7. The time limits for filing the statement and the number of copies needed are identical to those of the schedules.

Like the schedules, there are preprinted statement forms. They should be compared to the official form before being used to confirm that they are the most current version. If there is insufficient room to respond completely on the form, attachments can be used.

There are twenty-one inquiries in the statement, some of which have multiple parts. Each inquiry must either be answered or the failure to answer explained. If the inquiry is not applicable or if the answer is none, the box or bank next to the question should be checked. There should not be any blanks.

Questions 1–15 of Official Form 7 must be completed by all debtors. Debtors that are or have been in business must also complete questions 16–21. A debtor is "in business" if it is: (a) a corporation, (b) a partnership, or (c) individual that is, or has been within the previous two years, (i) an officer, director, managing executive, or person in control of a corporation, (ii) a general partner, (iii) a sole proprietor, or (iv) self-employed.

Question 1   This question requires the debtor to disclose the gross amount and source of its income derived from its employment, trade, or profession during the current calendar year and the two previous years.

Question 2   This question requires the debtor to disclose the gross amount and source of its income other than that derived from its employment, trade, or profession during the current calendar year and the two previous years. This income may be dividends or other earnings on investments, interest on savings, or rental income.

Question 3   There are two subparts to this question each of which is designed to elicit the information necessary to determine whether the debtor made any preferential transfers prior to the commencement of the bankruptcy case. Subpart (a) asks for a list of all payments made to creditors of more than $600 made within ninety days preceding the filing of the bankruptcy petition. The response is to be given in a four column matrix with the following information:

- ☐ Name and address of creditor.
- ☐ Dates of payment.
- ☐ Amount paid.
- ☐ Amount still owing.

For a business, the answer to this question could require a stack of paper. In those situations, it is reasonable to exclude payments to trade creditors and employees that are made in the ordinary course of business and according to ordinary terms. The response should mention that those transactions are not included and that anyone who desires the additional information may request it from the debtor's attorney.

Subpart (b) of question 3 asks for the same information for payments made to or for the benefit of insiders and expands the payments to any made within one year prior to the commencement of the case. The specific information requested is the same as in subpart (a) but the debtor must also provide the creditor's relationship to the debtor such as officer or relative.

Question 4   Question 4 also has two subparts. Subpart (a) concerns lawsuits in which the debtor was involved at the time or within one year before the commencement of the bankruptcy case even if those lawsuits have been terminated. It does not matter whether the debtor was a plaintiff or a defendant. To answer subpart (a), provide the following information:

1. Caption of the suit and the case number.
2. The nature of the proceeding.
3. Name of the court and its location.
4. The present status of the case or the disposition.

If the debtor has widespread operations, the information needed to complete this part may be difficult to gather. If the debtor does not have in–house counsel monitoring all litigation, as soon as the petition is filed the legal assistant should contact all the law firms the debtor has employed or paid in the previous year and ask for a case status report. The information in those case status reports can then be arranged as part of the response to this inquiry.

Subpart (b) of question 4 requires a description of all property that has been attached, garnished, or seized under any legal or equitable process within the previous year. The needed information is:

☐ The name and address of the person for whose benefit the property was seized.
☐ The date of the seizure.
☐ A description and the value of the property.

Question 5   Question 5 requires the debtor to detail any property that has been repossessed or foreclosed by, or returned to, the secured creditor or seller during the previous year. If there have been any such transfers—whether voluntary or involuntary—the details, including the name and address of the creditor, the date of repossession, foreclosure sale, transfer or return, and a description and value of the property, should be given.

Question 6   Question 6 has two subparts. Subpart (a) requires the debtor to describe any property assigned for the benefit of creditors within 120 days before the commencement of the case by providing the name and address of the assignee, the date of the assignment, and the terms of the assignment or settlement. An **assignment for the benefit of creditors** is a proceeding created by state law. Under this proceeding, the debtor turns over all nonexempt assets to someone called the assignee, who acts very much like a Chapter 7 trustee. The assignee liquidates the assets and distributes the proceeds of the liquidation to creditors. Assignments for the benefit of creditors are no longer common, but they do still occur especially in the fabric and garment industries.

Subpart (b) requires the debtor to list all property that has been in the hands of a custodian, receiver, or other court-appointed official within one year prior to the commencement of the case. For example, as part of its foreclosure proceedings on an apartment house owned and operated by the debtor, a secured creditor may have a receiver installed to collect the rents. If there has been such an appointment, subpart (b) requires the name and address of the custodian or receiver, the name and location of the court, the case title, and the case number in which the

Assignment for the Benefit of Creditor
A nonbankruptcy proceeding that is similar to a Chapter 7 case, in which the debtor turns over all of its nonexempt property to a third party for liquidation and distribution of the proceeds to creditors.

custodian or receiver was appointed, the date of the order, and a description and the value of the property.

Question 7 This question and question 10 are designed to discover whether the debtor made any prepetition fraudulent conveyances. In question 7, the debtor must disclose all gifts and charitable contributions within one year before the commencement of the case other than ordinary and usual gifts to family members aggregating less than $200 per individual family member and charitable contributions of less than $100 per recipient. If there were any such gifts or contributions, question 7 requires the name and address of the person or organization, the relationship to the debtor (if any), the date of the gift or contribution, and a description and value of the gift.

Question 8 Question 8 concerns losses. If the debtor has suffered any losses from fire, theft, other casualty, or from gambling in the year prior to the commencement of the case, it must provide the following information:

- ☐ A description of the property and its value.
- ☐ A description of the circumstances of the loss.
- ☐ Whether the loss was covered in whole or in part by insurance.
- ☐ The date of the loss.

Question 9 Question 9 deals with payments or other transfers to any persons, including attorneys, for debt counseling or bankruptcy services within one year before the commencement of the bankruptcy case. This includes payments to the attorney or bankruptcy petition preparer who drafted and filed the petition. For each such person, the debtor must list the person's name and address, the date of payment, the name of the person making the payment if other than the debtor, and the amount paid or the value of the property transferred.

Question 10 Question 10 is also designed to discover whether the debtor made any prepetition fraudulent conveyances. In question 10, the debtor must disclose any other transfers of its property not disclosed in earlier responses to questions in Official Form 7 that were out of the ordinary course of the debtor's business or financial affairs and were made within the past year. Transfer is broadly defined in Section 101 of the Bankruptcy Code and includes the granting of a security interest or statutory or judicial lien as well as absolute transfers such as a sale. if there were any such transfers, the debtor must list the name and address of the transferee, its relationship to the debtor if any, the date of the transfer, and a description of the property transferred and its value.

Question 11 Question 11 asks the debtor to list all bank and other financial accounts and instruments (such as certificates of deposit) held by or for the benefit of the debtor and that were closed, sold or otherwise transferred within the year before the commencement of the bankruptcy case. For each such event, the debtor must provide the name and address of the financial institution, the type of account, the account number, the balance in the account when it was closed or sold, and the date of the sale or closing.

Question 12 If the debtor has or had within the past year any safe deposit boxes in which it had securities, cash or other valuables, question 12 requires the debtor

to provide the name and address of the bank, the names and addresses of all persons who had access to the box, a description of its contents, and, if the box has been transferred or surrendered, the date the transfer or surrender occurred.

Question 13   Question 13 concerns setoffs, which are the application of a debt owed to the debtor against a debt owed by the debtor. Setoffs have the potential of being preferences. As a result, question 13 asks that any setoffs made by a creditor against a debt or deposit of the debtor within ninety days before the commencement of the bankruptcy case be listed by name and address of creditor, date of setoff, and amount of setoff.

Question 14   When liquidating the property of the estate, the trustee will want to ensure that nothing is sold that does not belong to the estate. To help guard against this, question 14 requires a listing of all property the debtor holds for another person. These may be goods that were sold but not yet delivered, items stored at the debtor's business premises, and the like. To respond to question 14 the debtor must identify the name and address of the owner, a description of the goods and their value, and the location of the goods.

Question 15   If the debtor has moved within the last two years, all former addresses and dates of occupancy should be listed in question 15.

Question 16   Question 16 requires a listing of the nature, location, and name of the debtor's business, including all names used in the last two years. Other information needed is the dates the business commenced and terminated, if it has in fact been terminated.

Question 17   The four subparts of question 17 focus on who has kept the debtor's books and records. The first subpart asks for a list of all bookkeepers and accountants who within the previous six years kept or supervised the keeping of the debtor's books and records. Names, addresses, and pertinent periods of time should be provided for such in-house personnel. Subpart (b) asks for the identity of any persons who audited the books and records or prepared a financial statement during the previous two years. This may be an outside accountant. If no audits have been performed, check none. If there have been audits, the dates of the audits are required. For subpart (c) the current location of the books and records should be indicated. Also, if any portion of the books and records is unavailable, an explanation (such as that they have been destroyed) should be inserted.

The last subpart concerns the debtor's financial statements issued within the previous two years. If any financial statements have been issued in that period, the dates they were issued and the names and addresses of those to whom they were issued must be listed. Typically, the debtor will issue financial statements to secured creditors, Dunn & Bradstreet, trade associations, prospective investors, and others.

Question 18   Question 18 involves inventories. Here the debtor must describe the last two physical counts of its goods including the person who supervised the counts, if any such counts have been performed. Some debtors do not take a physical count of their inventory but rely instead on daily adjustments to a starting balance. This is usually called a perpetual inventory. If the response to the fourth question is based on perpetual inventory reporting, that fact should be disclosed.

Part six concerns the debtor's tax returns and tax refunds. The statement asks for the location of returns for the previous three years, the amount of any refund in the previous two years, and whether the debtor believes it may be entitled to a refund. In each of the three subparts to this question, the debtor should give separate answers for each taxing agency.

Questions 19–21   Finally, Questions 19–21 request certain information from debtors who are partnerships or corporations. Specifically, question 19 inquires as to the name, title, and address of each partner, officer, and director, and each shareholder who holds five percent or more of the issued and outstanding stock. There is no requirement that the addresses be home addresses but if it is a Chapter 7 case, the debtor's business address should not be used since the business likely will be closed.

Question 20 asks for the name and address of any partner, officer or director who withdrew from his or her relationship in the previous year. If there have been any of those events, not only must the person be identified, but the debtor must give the reason for the withdrawal, termination, or disposition if it is known.

Finally, in order to determine whether the insiders have drained the business of capital, question 21 seeks information concerning how much money any insiders have taken out of the business during the previous year. This would include salaries, loans, fees, advances, perquisites, and expense reimbursement paid or given to each of the partners or officers, directors, or shareholders.

The statement is concluded with a verification that is at the end of Official Form 7. It is virtually identical to the verification at the end of the schedules.

The Master Mailing List

Indenture Trustee
A trustee appointed under a mortgage, deed or trust or other document under which there is a debt against or interest in the debtor.

Bankruptcy Code Section 342 and Bankruptcy Rule 2003(f) require the clerk of the bankruptcy court to give notice of the order for relief to all creditors and the **indenture trustee** (typically a financial institution that is the trustee for holders of bonds or notes issued by the debtor). Bankruptcy Rule 2003(f) also requires that the notice be sent to the debtor although, except in an involuntary case, notice to the debtor that it has commenced a bankruptcy case would seem unnecessary. There are other parties who should receive notice of the pendency of a bankruptcy case even though they are not creditors. For example, even if the debtor is current in paying taxes, the taxing agencies should be notified. All regulatory agencies, such as the Securities and Exchange Commission, if the debtor is a corporation, or the Federal Aviation Agency, if the debtor is an airline, should be notified. How is the clerk of the court to provide such notice?

Bankruptcy Rule 1007 requires the debtor to accompany the petition with a list of creditors unless the petition is accompanied by the schedules. The clerk could then make a mailing from the list of creditors or the schedules; however, there are two problems with the clerk doing so. First, as just discussed, a list of creditors would leave out some parties who should get notice. Second, although using the list of creditors may be acceptable in a small case, for the clerk to prepare mailing labels from a creditor list in a large case would be very labor intensive, time consuming, and simply too unreasonable to expect. The solution that has been developed is to require the debtor to submit along with the petition a list of parties who should receive notice. This list must be in a form that the clerk can use to make mailing labels. In many jurisdictions, this list is called the master mailing list and is a matrix of thirty-three squares, with one name and address to be typed into each square. A sample matrix form is shown in Exhibit 7.15. In

■ EXHIBIT 7.15
Sample Matrix for Master Mailing List

ABE'S OFFICE SUPPLY 19640 7th Street Santa Monica, CA 91202	ACE TRUCKING 58 W. Post Road St. Paul, MN 55164	B & O FINANCE COMPANY 456 Harass Drive Princeton, NJ 08890
BEN'S MAINTENANCE 6123 Hollywood Blvd. Hollywood, CA 90027	BIG BANK 4 Wheel Drive Los Angeles, CA 90017	JOSEPH BUSINESSMAN 12462 Highland Street Beverly Hills, CA 90033
CALIFORNIA STATE BOARD OF EQUALIZATION 12 Hill Street Sacramento, CA 95606	GERALD CAMERAMAN 1901 Exposition Blvd. Los Angeles, CA 90044	DIAMOND RADIATOR P.O. Box 70005 Chino, CA 92113
G & P HONEYMOONERS P.O. Box 482 Lake Isabella, CA 90068	GIGGIE, INC. 1643 Ocean Blvd. Miami, FL 06067	GREAT FILM, INC. 84 Steel Plate Drive City of Industry, CA 90002
IMPERIAL PROCESSING 1000 Milan Way Denver, CO 60606	INTERNAL REVENUE SERVICE 300 N. Los Angeles St. Los Angeles, CA 90015	JUNE FILM CO. 1223 Via Beach Blvd. San Diego, CA 90666
BANKRUPT C. LAWYER, ESQ. White Charger Legal Clinic One Learned Way Los Angeles, CA 90001	M & M GAS COMPANY 155 Flower St. West Covina, CA 98002	VIDEOS BY JOE, INC. 1223 Hollywood Blvd. Hollywood, CA 90027

other jurisdictions, local rules may require the debtor to file coded cards, a computer readable tape or diskette in a particular format, or mailing labels of some sort. The local rules of each jurisdiction must be consulted for the precise requirements. Whatever the format, a copy should be kept for the debtor's use in mailing notices.

It is helpful to alphabetize the names of at least the unsecured creditors. It will then be much easier to check later to confirm that these creditors received notice. It is also a good idea to leave the three squares along the top blank. Since the matrix may be placed in a file folder with a two-hole top clip, the holes might destroy some of the entries.

☐ SUMMARY

The first step in beginning a bankruptcy case is determining under which chapters the debtor is eligible. Not all persons can file each type of reorganization and some companies cannot file bankruptcy cases at all. The debtor must also elect the most appropriate chapter among those for which it may be eligible. There is an emphasis to steer consumer debtors toward a Chapter 13 reorganization and away from a Chapter 7 liquidation. If a Chapter 7 case is filed that is a "substantial abuse," the court may dismiss the case.

There is a great amount of information that must be obtained from the debtor before a bankruptcy case is filed and the first few weeks after it is filed. A list of the needed information should be made. Another list of all of the documents that must be prepared should also be made.

The pleading that commences a bankruptcy case is called a petition. It is a two-sided document that asks very basic information about the debtor. If the debtor is a corporation, Exhibit A must be attached to the petition. If the debtor is a consumer, Exhibit B to the petition must be completed. In most cases the following documents must be filed with the petition or within a short time period: a list of all creditors; a list of all equity interest holders, and an attorney's statement. The debtor in a Chapter 11 case must also file a list of the twenty largest unsecured creditors. A Chapter 7 debtor who is an individual with consumer secured debts must file a Statement of Intentions.

Each debtor must file, within fifteen days after the petition, schedules showing various information including its assets and liabilities. These schedules are Official Form 6 and are numbered Schedule A through J. Schedules A and B are for the debtor's real and personal property. Schedule C is the claimed exemptions. Schedules D, E, and F show the debtor's secured, priority, and unsecured nonpriority debts, respectively. Schedule G is a list of the debtor's executory contracts and unexpired leases. Schedule H is a list of the debtor's obligations in which someone else is also liable. Schedule I is information on the debtor's current income and Schedule J is information on the debtor's current expenses.

Each debtor must also file a Statement of Financial Affairs, which is Official Form 7. There are twenty-one questions in the Statement. The first fifteen must be answered by all debtors. The last five need only be answered by debtors engaged in business. The questions require a wide-range of information including details on past income, possible preferential and fraudulent transfers, location of assets and bank accounts, and the identity of debtor's officers and directors.

Local rules also require the debtor to submit a mailing list to be used to send notices to creditors. The form of the list will vary based on local practice.

☐ KEY TERMS

Affiliate	Disputed Claim	Schedules
Assignment	Domicile	Statement of Financial Affairs
Book Value	Indenture Trustee	Substantial Abuse
Contingent Claim	Petition	Unliquidated Claim

☐ IMPROVE YOUR UNDERSTANDING

1. Answer the following questions true or false.

a. Joe Conway, a citizen of the Philippines, now lives in Houston, Texas. Joe owns real estate in Manila and in Houston. Joe is ineligible to file a bankruptcy case in Texas.

b. Joe Conway filed a Chapter 13 bankruptcy case on October 1, 1995. First City Bank, who had a secured lien on Joe's car, immediately filed a motion for relief from the automatic stay. Prior to the hearing on the motion, Joe dismissed the Chapter 13 case. Because the bank's motion was never heard, Joe is eligible to immediately file another Chapter 13 case.

c. Joe Conway filed a Chapter 7 bankruptcy case on October 1, 1995. When his friend told him that the trustee would be asking for the turnover of his extensive stamp collection, he did not attend the first meeting of creditors or file any of the required papers. The trustee successfully moved to dismiss the case. Since it was the trustee—and not Joe—who moved to dismiss, Joe may immediately file another bankruptcy case.

d. Banks may file Chapter 7 cases.

e. Joe Conway owes $800,000 to First City Bank; this loan is secured by a mortgage on his house. He also owes $100,000 to his other creditors, none of whom is secured. Joe is eligible for relief under Chapter 13 of the Bankruptcy Code.

f. Stockbrokers are never eligible for Chapter 11 relief.

g. Orange County, California could not have filed a Chapter 7 case.

h. A Chapter 7 trustee may move to dismiss a case as a substantial abuse.

2. List all the additional documents and portions of the petition that must be included if the debtor is an individual with primarily consumer debts.

3. Joe's Video's Inc., a company with its headquarters at 1643 Ocean Boulevard, Miami, Dade County, Florida 06067, wants to file a Chapter 7 case. It is represented by your employer, Bankrupt C. Lawyer, who instructs you to prepare the petition. Draft as much of the petition as you can. Also draft a letter to the company requesting the additional information you need.

Use the following fact situation in answering Exercises 4 and 5:

Wildcat River Partners, a limited partnership organized under the laws of the state of Texas, has as its sole asset an apartment complex in Detroit, Michigan. Its office is located with its general partner in Los Angeles, California.

4. Could Wildcat River Partners file its bankruptcy case in Texas, Michigan, or California?

5. Sixteen other limited partnerships with the same general partner as Wildcat River Partners have bankruptcy cases pending in Los Angeles. List the benefits and detriments to Wildcat and its creditors in having the case pending in the various possible locations.

6. If a secured creditor's collateral is worth less than the amount owed, could the secured creditor be included on the list of the twenty largest unsecured creditors?

7. Can a partnership pay a filing fee in installments?

8. When must the schedules be filed?

9. If, two weeks after the case was commenced, the debtor inherited $100,000, would the money be disclosed in the schedules? What if the debtor immediately spent it?

10. Give two examples (other than the ones in this book) of contingent claims and unliquidated claims.

11. Brad Stockman is owed the following from his employer, who filed a Chapter 11 petition on October 1, 1995:

Commissions: May 1995	$ 500
Commissions: July, August, and September 1995	$2,500
Wages: March 1995	$2,500
Expense Reimbursement: September 1995	$ 200

In addition, Brad owes his employer for an advance he received at Christmas, 1994, of $1,000.00. Where and in what amounts should Brad and his employer's claims be scheduled in the bankruptcy case of the employer?

12. Is a business owner entitled to a priority claim for prepaid pest control services?

13. If a secured creditor did not perfect its security interest prior to the filing of the bankruptcy petition, should it be included in Schedule D or Schedule F?

14. Where on Schedule B should the following assets be disclosed?

a. Savings bonds.

b. Interests in a mutual fund.

c. Antique gun collection.

d. Computers that are used by the debtor in its business.

e. Computers that are sold by a business.

f. Insurance proceeds for a building that burned down.

g. The value of debtor's franchise rights.

h. A kayak.

☐ DRAFTING PROJECT

1. Prepare a fact sheet that could be given to consumer debtors who are trying to decide between Chapter 7 or Chapter 13. Organize it by benefits of Chapter 7 and benefits of Chapter 13.

2. Prepare a list of information needed to commence a case for a potential debtor, a limited partnership engaged in raising cattle.

3. The debtor informs you that it has litigation pending against it in another state. The debtor is not sure of the status of that litigation. Draft a letter to the attorney representing the debtor in that litigation asking for the information required by question 4(a) of Official Form 7.

CHAPTER 7: THE DEBTOR'S PERSPECTIVE

☐ DISCHARGE

Discharge in General

For most consumers, the primary reason for commencing a Chapter 7 bankruptcy case is to take advantage of the discharge of debts provision of Section 727. Generally speaking, a discharge bars any collection action against the debtor for debts incurred prepetition. Although a theme of bankruptcy law is to fiercely protect the right to a discharge, in certain circumstances the debtor will lose the discharge, all debts will remain enforceable, and the benefits of the Chapter 7 case will vanish. How a debtor could lose the discharge is the subject of this section.

Even if the debtor preserves the right to a discharge, not all of the debtor's debts will vanish. Certain types of obligations are always enforceable despite the completion of a bankruptcy case. For other debts, if the creditor can prove certain things, that creditor's debt will remain enforceable. Those instances are discussed in the next section.

Loss of a Discharge

The discharge is the payoff the debtor receives for turning over all nonexempt assets to the trustee and living up to other duties and responsibilities. By engaging in what can be described as bad acts, the debtor may be denied that payoff and not receive a discharge. Bankruptcy Code Section 727 lists the following bad acts of the debtor that may result in a loss of a discharge:

☐ The debtor transferred, destroyed, or concealed property within one year prepetition or property of the estate postpetition with the intent to defraud a creditor or the trustee.

☐ The debtor unjustifiably concealed, destroyed, falsified, or failed to keep or preserve the books and records necessary to determine the debtor's financial condition or business transactions.

☐ In connection with the bankruptcy case, the debtor knowingly and fraudulently made a false oath; presented a false claim; gave, offered, received, or attempted to obtain money, property or advantage for acting or forebearing to act; or withheld from the trustee books and records related to the debtor's property or financial affairs.

☐ The debtor failed to satisfactorily explain any loss of assets.

☐ The debtor refused to obey an order of the court.

These bad acts are not limited to the debtor's case. They will also prevent the debtor from receiving a discharge if those acts were committed within one year before or after the bankruptcy case of an insider such as a relative or a controlled company. For example, if before the debtor is in bankruptcy but during the bankruptcy case of a corporation in which the debtor is the sole shareholder, the debtor falsely informs the trustee that the corporation has no assets, the debtor may lose the right to a discharge in his or her own bankruptcy case.

Other ways a debtor can be deprived of a discharge that do not relate to the commission of a bad act are also set out in Section 727. The first way is if the debtor is not an individual. As a matter of bankruptcy law, only individuals are entitled to a discharge. As a practical matter, however, if a corporation filed a Chapter 7 petition and the trustee liquidates and distributes all the assets, there is nothing left for creditors to look to for payment of their nondischarged claims. A debtor is also not entitled to a discharge if the debtor received a discharge in a Chapter 7 or Chapter 11 case commenced within six years of the pending case or was the debtor in a Chapter 13 case commenced within six years of the pending case in which the unsecured creditors were not paid in full or did not receive at least seventy percent and that payment was the debtor's best efforts. In other words, a debtor is entitled to a discharge only once every six years.

Procedure

Before a debtor will lose the discharge there must be a court hearing commenced by the trustee, a creditor, or the United States trustee. Among the duties of the trustee listed in Section 704 of the Bankruptcy Code is the duty to oppose the discharge of the debtor if advisable. If a creditor does not want to go to the trouble or expense of bringing a discharge action, the creditor can request that the court order the trustee to determine whether a ground exists for denying the debtor a discharge.

Although Bankruptcy Code Section 727(c)(1) refers to an objection, Bankruptcy Rule 4004 dictates that opposition to a debtor's discharge must be done by the filing of a complaint no later than sixty days after the Section 341(a) meeting of creditors. This is a very important deadline and a creditor should schedule it as soon as the creditor learns of the case. The sixty-day time period may be extended but cause must be shown and the extension must be obtained before the sixty-day period runs. A proceeding commenced by the filing of a complaint objecting to a discharge (see Exhibit 8.1) is governed by Part VII of the Bankruptcy Rules; it is

■ EXHIBIT 8.1
Sample Pleading

GEORGE G. PORTER
PORTER & PORTER
Four Wheel Drive
Los Angeles, California 90017

Attorneys for First City Bank

UNITED STATES BANKRUPTCY COURT
WESTERN DISTRICT OF CALIFORNIA

In re	)	Case No. 95-00003-JF
	)	
JOSEPH BUSINESSMAN,	)	Chapter 7
	)	
Debtor's Address:	)	
18 Hollywood Drive	)	
Los Angeles, California 90001	)	
	)	
Debtor's S.S. No. 559-15-1402	)	
_____	)	
	)	
FIRST CITY BANK,	)	Adv. No. 95-00003-JF
	)	
Plaintiff,	)	COMPLAINT OBJECTING TO
	)	DISCHARGE OF DEBTOR
v.	)	
	)	
JOSEPH BUSINESSMAN,	)	
	)	
Defendant,	)	
_____	)	

First City Bank (the "Bank") complains and alleges as follows:

PARTIES

1. Defendant Joseph Businessman ("Debtor") is the debtor in the above-captioned case having filed a petition for relief under Chapter 7 of Title 11, United States Code (the "Bankruptcy Code") on October 1, 1995.

2. The Bank is the holder of an unsecured claim against Debtor in the amount of $50,000.00.

JURISDICTION AND VENUE

3. This action objecting to Debtor's discharge is an adversary proceeding over which this Court has jurisdiction pursuant to 28 U.S.C. §§ 157 and 1334 and the Order of the Chief Judge of the United States District Court, Western District of California, referring bankruptcy cases and proceedings, entered on July 20, 1984. This adversary proceeding is a core matter pursuant to 28 U.S.C. § 157(b)(2)(J) and the Bank consents to the entry of a final order or judgment by the Bankruptcy Court.

4. Venue over this adversary proceeding properly resides in the United States Bankruptcy Court for the Western District of California pursuant to 28 U.S.C. § 1409(a) in that this adversary proceeding is related to *In re Joseph Businessman*, Case No. 95-00003-JF, pending as a Chapter 7 case in the United States Bankruptcy Court for the Western District of California.

—continued

■ EXHIBIT 8.1
Sample Pleading—*Continued*

FACTUAL ALLEGATIONS

5. Since in or about 1990 until on or about September 1, 1995, Debtor operated a videotape store under the name of Videos by Joe. On or about September 1, 1995 Debtor transferred the assets of Videos by Joe to Videos by Joe, Inc., a newly formed corporation, the President and sole shareholder of which is Maximillion Businessman, Debtor's six-year old son.

6. The transfer described in the immediately proceeding paragraph was for less than reasonably equivalent value.

FIRST CLAIM FOR RELIEF
[11 U.S.C. § 727(a)(2)]

7. The Bank incorporates by this reference the allegations contained in paragraph 5 and 6.

8. The transfer described in paragraph 5 was made with the intent to hinder, delay, or defraud the Bank and constitutes a transfer of Debtor's property within one year before the date of the filing of the petition.

SECOND CLAIM FOR RELIEF
[11 U.S.C. § 727(a)(4)]

9. The Bank incorporates by this reference the allegations contained in paragraphs 5 and 6.

10. Debtor knowingly and fraudulently made a false oath or account in connection with his bankruptcy case by failing to reveal the transfer of property described in paragraph 5 in his Statement of Financial Affairs filed on October 15, 1995.

THIRD CLAIM FOR RELIEF
[11 U.S.C. § 727(a)(3)]

11. The Bank incorporates by this reference the allegations contained in paragraph 5 and 6.

12. Debtor concealed, destroyed, mutilated, falsified, or failed to keep or preserve any recorded information, including books, documents, records, and papers, from which the transfer described in paragraph 5 might be ascertained.

WHEREFORE the Bank requests that the Court enter judgment as follows:

1. That Debtor be denied a discharge;

2. For the Bank's cost incurred in this suit and reasonable attorneys' fees;

3. For such other and further relief to which the Bank may be entitled.

PORTER & PORTER

_____

GEORGE G. PORTER
Attorneys for First City Bank

---

an adversary proceeding. The procedures for adversary proceedings were discussed in Chapter 6 of this book.

Revocation of a Discharge Already Granted

The debtor may have obtained a discharge prior to the commitment of bad acts or before those acts were discovered. Bankruptcy Code Section 727(s) allows a creditor, the trustee, or the United States trustee to seek to revoke a discharge if one of the following occurred:

□ The discharge was obtained through the fraud of the debtor—the creditor or the trustee did not know of the fraud at the time the discharge was granted.

□ The debtor acquired, or became entitled to acquire, property of the estate and knowingly and fraudulently failed to report it or deliver the property to the trustee.

□ The debtor committed one of the bad acts described in the previous section after the discharge was granted.

The request for revocation, which is done by the filing of a complaint, must be brought before the later of one year after the granting of the discharge and the date the case is closed unless the discharge was obtained by fraud, in which case the complaint must be filed within one year after the discharge was granted.

Dismissal of a Discharge Action

Bankruptcy Rule 4005 provides that the burden of proof of an objection to discharge is on the plaintiff (the nondebtor party). Because these types of actions should not be brought lightly, Bankruptcy Rule 7041 provides that a complaint objecting to discharge may not be dismissed on the plaintiff's request alone. There must be notice and it may be dismissed only on terms and conditions that the court deems proper. A condition may be the payment of the debtor's attorneys' fees in defending the complaint.

☐ DISCHARGEABILITY

It is very hard to deprive a debtor of a discharge. There are, however, times when a creditor can achieve the same result or an even better result by just having that creditor's particular claim declared **nondischargeable.** The creditor then will receive a distribution on its claim from the trustee from the proceeds of liquidation of the estate's assets and will be free to pursue the debtor for the balance from new or exempt assets after the bankruptcy case is closed.

There are two types of nondischargeable claims. The first are those claims Congress has determined should always be binding obligations notwithstanding the filing of a bankruptcy case. The second are those claims that also stem from bad acts although the acts are not as bad as the ones listed in Section 727. For the first type, those claims that are always nondischargeable, the creditor need do nothing to preserve its rights. For the claims based on bad acts, the creditor must seek a bankruptcy court judgment declaring the debt nondischargeable. How that declaration is obtained will be discussed shortly.

Nondischargeable Claims
Claims that will be enforceable against the debtor despite the discharge.

Claims that are Always Nondischargeable

Section 523 of the Bankruptcy Code provides that the following types of claims will survive and be binding on a Chapter 7 debtor despite a discharge:

□ Taxes or custom duties recently incurred or with respect to which the debtor made a fraudulent return or willfully attempted to evade or defeat the tax.

□ Unscheduled debts where the creditor did not have actual knowledge of the bankruptcy case in time to file a proof of claim or an action to contest the dischargeability of the debt.

□ Alimony, maintenance, and child support.

☐ Student loans unless the obligation is more than seven years old or it would be an undue hardship on the debtor and the debtor's dependents to exempt the debt from discharge.

☐ Fines, penalties, or forfeitures payable to the government.

☐ Debts arising as a result of the debtor's drunk driving.

☐ Debts that were not discharged in a prior bankruptcy case of the debtor.

☐ Debts for fraud or defalcation to a depository institution (a bank, savings and loan or credit union).

☐ Debts for reckless or malicious failure to fulfill a capital maintenance agreement to a depository institution.

☐ For money borrowed to pay a nondischargeable tax.

☐ For postpetition condominium fees or assessments for a condominium in which the debtor resided or rented to a paying tenant.

The creditor with one of these types of claims need not take any act to preserve the nondischargeable nature of its claim. If the creditor is not completely confident that its claim is of the type listed, it may want to obtain a declaration from the court that the claim fits within the list. In addition, the debtor may want to start an action to declare a particular debt not within the scope of the exempted claims.

Claims that May Be Dischargeable

For public policy reasons Congress also wanted to make claims arising from the debtor's bad acts nondischargeable. As discussed, very bad acts or bad acts directed to creditors as a group will destroy the debtor's right to a discharge. Because those bad acts rest on factual issues, a hearing must be held to resolve any dispute concerning the bad acts. The bad acts that will make a particular claim nondischargeable will also usually be surrounded by factual disputes; as a result, there must be an action commenced to allow the court to resolve the factual disputes. The types of claims that may be nondischargeable arise from the following bad acts:

☐ The debtor obtained money, property, services, or an extension, renewal, or refinancing of credit by fraud.

☐ The debtor used a materially false financial statement with the intent to deceive and upon which the creditor reasonably relied.

☐ The debtor incurred a debt to a single creditor of more than $1000 for "luxury goods or services" within sixty days of the commencement of the bankruptcy case.

☐ The debtor obtained cash advances of more than $1,000 under a consumer credit plan, such as a credit card, on or within sixty days before the commencement of the bankruptcy case.

☐ The debtor committed fraud or defalcation while acting in a fiduciary capacity, or committed embezzlement or larceny.

☐ The debtor willfully and maliciously injured another or the property of another.

☐ The debtor incurred debt in the course of a divorce or separation other than alimony and support (which are always nondischargeable) unless the debtor has no ability to pay the debts and discharging the debt would outweigh any detriment to a spouse, former spouse, or child of the debtor.

Procedures

In order to obtain a court determination of nondischargeability for the types of debts listed earlier, Bankruptcy Rule 4007 provides that a request must be brought by the filing of a complaint within sixty days following the first date set for the Section 341(a) meeting of creditors. (See Exhibit 8.2.) The courts are very strict about the sixty-day time limit and will extend this limit only if the extension is obtained before the end of the sixty-day period. The litigation commenced by the filing of the complaint is governed by Part VII of the Bankruptcy Rules, which concerns adversary proceedings. They are the subject of Chapter 6 of this book.

In order to discourage baseless dischargeability litigation that a debtor may not be able to afford to defend, if a creditor seeks to have a consumer debt allegedly incurred through fraud or certain consumer debts procured on the eve of bankruptcy held nondischargeable, and the creditor loses that lawsuit, under Section 523(d) the court must grant the debtor reimbursement of costs and attorneys' fees from the creditor if the court finds the creditor's position was not substantially justified. The court may make an exception if special circumstances would make such an award unjust.

☐ REAFFIRMATIONS

As discussed, once a debtor has been granted a discharge, unsecured prepetition debts and any deficiency suffered by a secured creditor do not have to be paid. However, Bankruptcy Code Section 524(f) provides that a debtor may voluntarily repay one or more of those debts even if a discharge has already been granted. A debtor may want to repay a debt out of a moral obligation, because a secured creditor may seek relief from the stay and repossess its collateral otherwise, or for many other reasons. Yet a debtor's repayment of a discharged debt is enforceable only when the debtor has officially **reaffirmed** the debt. For example, Joe Consumer may decide to repay a prepetition loan of $10 from his friend Al even though Joe has received his discharge. This does not mean that Al may now automatically go to court and force Joe to pay. Al and Joe must have first fully complied with the steps provided in Bankruptcy Code Sections 524(c) and (d) and Bankruptcy Rule 4008.

Reaffirm
The act of agreeing to remain liable on a claim despite a discharge.

Bankruptcy Code Section 524(c) and Bankruptcy Rule 4008 state that to reaffirm a prepetition debt the debtor and the creditor must enter into a written agreement in which the debtor reaffirms the debt. (See Exhibit 8.3.) The debtor must also make a motion seeking the agreement's approval and file it with the court before receiving a discharge.

If the debtor has been represented by an attorney while negotiating the reaffirmation agreement, the attorney must file a declaration or affidavit stating that the debtor is fully informed of the consequences and legal effect of the reaffirmation, that it is voluntarily done, and that it will not impose an undue hardship on the debtor or his or her dependents. The attorney will want to explain the consequences of the reaffirmation agreement very carefully to the debtor, ensure that the creditor has not coerced the debtor in any way, and inquire whether the debtor's income is sufficient to repay the reaffirmed debt.

If the debtor was not represented by a lawyer during the negotiation of the reaffirmation agreement, the court must find that the agreement does not impose an undue hardship and is in the debtor's best interest before approving it. The court will also inform the debtor at the discharge hearing of the legal consequences of entering into the reaffirmation agreement.

■ EXHIBIT 8.2
Sample Pleading

GEORGE G. PORTER
PORTER & PORTER
Four Wheel Drive
Los Angeles, California 90017

Attorneys for First City Bank

UNITED STATES BANKRUPTCY COURT
WESTERN DISTRICT OF CALIFORNIA

In re	Case No. 95-00003-JF
JOSEPH BUSINESSMAN,	Chapter 7
Debtor's Address: 18 Hollywood Drive Los Angeles, California 90001	
Debtor's S.S. No. 559-15-1402	
FIRST CITY BANK,	Adv. No. 95-00003-JF
Plaintiff,	COMPLAINT TO DETERMINE DISCHARGEABILITY FOR:
v.	
JOSEPH BUSINESSMAN,	1. FALSE PRETENSES, FALSE REPRESENTATIONS, AND ACTUAL FRAUD; AND
Defendants.	2. FALSE STATEMENT RESPECTING FINANCIAL CONDITION

First City Bank (the "Bank") complains and alleges as follows:

PARTIES

1. Defendant Joseph Businessman ("Debtor") is the debtor in the above-captioned case, having filed a petition for relief under Chapter 7 of Title 11, United States Code (the "Bankruptcy Code") on October 1, 1995.

2. The Bank is the holder of a claim against Debtor in the amount of $50,000.00.

JURISDICTION AND VENUE

3. This action to determine the dischargeability of the Bank's claim is an adversary proceeding over which this Court has jurisdiction pursuant to 28 U.S.C. §§ 157 and 1334 and the Order of the Chief Judge of the United States District Court, Western District of California, referring bankruptcy cases and proceedings, entered on July 20, 1984. This adversary proceeding is a core matter pursuant to 28 U.S.C. § 157(b)(2)(I) and the Bank consents to the entry of a final order or judgment by the Bankruptcy Court.

4. Venue over this adversary proceeding properly resides in the United States Bankruptcy Court for the Western District of California pursuant to 28 U.S.C. § 1409(a) in that this adversary proceeding is related to *In re Joseph Businessman*, Case No. 95-00003-JF, pending as a Chapter 7 case in the United States Bankruptcy Court for the Western District of California.

—continued

■ EXHIBIT 8.2
Sample Pleading—*Continued*

FACTUAL ALLEGATIONS

5. On or about September 1, 1994, the Bank and Debtor executed a Security Agreement, a complete and accurate copy of which is attached hereto as Exhibit 1 and incorporated herein by this reference. Under the provisions of the Security Agreement, the Bank lent to Debtor $50,000 (the "Loan").

6. In order to secure repayment of the Loan, Debtor executed three (3) deeds of trust on parcels of real property (the "Property") with the Bank as beneficiary.

7. As of October 1, 1995, Debtor was indebted to the Bank in the sum of $50,000.00 as a result of the Loan. No portion of the Loan has been paid.

FIRST CLAIM FOR RELIEF
[11 U.S.C. § 523(a)(2)(A)]

8. The Bank incorporates by reference the allegations set forth in paragraphs 5 through 7.

9. The Bank made the Loan to Debtor based upon the value of the Property.

10. During 1994, Debtor orally, falsely, and fraudulently overstated to the Bank the value of the Property.

11. Debtor's representations were false and they were then and thereafter known by Debtor to be false. In fact and truth, Debtor did not own the Property as Debtor represented.

12. The Bank believed and relied on Debtor's representations; based upon Debtor's representations, the Bank made the Loan to Debtor.

SECOND CLAIM FOR RELIEF
[11 U.S.C. § 523(a)(2)(B)]

13. The Bank incorporates by reference the allegations set forth in paragraphs 5 through 7.

14. The Loan to Debtor was obtained by use of written statements respecting the Debtor's financial condition (the "Statements") which Debtor delivered to the Bank with the intent to deceive.

15. The Statements were materially false in that Debtor represented to the Bank that the Property was owned by Debtor thereby overstating Debtor's value.

16. Debtor made the Statements for the purpose of inducing the Bank to make the Loan to Debtor.

17. Debtor knew the Statements were false when they were made and made the Statements with the intent to cause reliance by the Bank and to induce the Bank to make the Loan.

18. The Bank was unaware of the falsity of the information provided by Debtor, believed and relied on the Statements, and was thereby induced to make the Loan to Debtor. The Bank's reliance on the Statements was justified due to Debtor's superior knowledge of the Property. If not for the Statements by Debtor, the Bank would not have made the Loan.

WHEREFORE, the Bank requests that the Court enter judgment as follows:

1. That the Court determine that the Bank's claim in the amount of $50,000.00 is nondischargeable;

2. That the Bank have judgment against Debtor for the sum of $50,000.00, together with interest as provided for in the Security Agreement;

3. For the Bank's costs including reasonable attorney's fees incurred in this suit; and

4. For such other and further relief to which the Bank may be entitled.

PORTER & PORTER

GEORGE G. PORTER
Attorneys for First City Bank

■ EXHIBIT 8.3
Sample Pleading

BANKRUPT C. LAWYER
WHITE CHARGER LEGAL CLINIC
One Learned Way
Los Angeles, California 90001

Attorneys for Debtor

UNITED STATES BANKRUPTCY COURT
WESTERN DISTRICT OF CALIFORNIA

In re)	Case No. 95-00002-JF
)	
JOSEPH CONSUMER,)	Chapter 7
)	
Debtor's Address:)	
18 Hollywood Drive)	MOTION FOR APPROVAL OF
Los Angeles, California 90001)	REAFFIRMATION AGREEMENT;
)	DECLARATION OF BANKRUPT C.
Debtor's S.S. No. 524-47-7448)	LAWYER IN SUPPORT THEREOF
)	

TO THE HONORABLE JUSTIN FAIR, UNITED STATES BANKRUPTCY JUDGE:

Joseph Consumer ("Debtor"), through his attorney, in support of this Motion for Approval of Reaffirmation Agreement, respectfully represents as follow:

1. Debtor and B & B Stereo Company, a creditor of Debtor ("Creditor"), have entered into a Reaffirmation Agreement, a complete and accurate copy of which is attached to this Motion (the "Agreement").

2. The Agreement does not impose any undue hardship on Debtor or the dependents of Debtor and is in the best interest of Debtor.

WHEREFORE, Debtor requests that the Court enter its Order approving the Agreement.

DATED: November 15, 1995

WHITE CHARGER LEGAL CLINIC

_____

BANKRUPT C. LAWYER
Attorneys for Debtor

Reaffirmation Agreement

This Agreement is entered into by and between Joseph Consumer ("Debtor") and B & B Stereo Company ("Creditor") as of November 15, 1995), and is based on the following facts:

1. On or about February 1, 1995, Debtor made, executed and delivered his written Promissory Note to Creditor in the original principal sum of $5,000 (the "Note").

2. Payment of the Note was guaranteed by Flora Consumer.

3. On October 1, 1995 Debtor filed a voluntary petition under Chapter 7 of Title 11, United States Code [11 U.S.C. § 101 et seq.]

4. At the time Debtor commenced his bankruptcy case, there remained the sum of $4,000 due and owing under the Note.

—*continued*

In consideration of Debtor's obligations under the Note and in order to induce Creditor to forbear from any legal action on the guarantee of the Note, it is mutually agreed, subject to Court approval of this Reaffirmation Agreement, that:

1. Debtor hereby unconditionally promises to pay Creditor the remaining principal amount of the Note plus any accrued interest and other charges properly payable under the Note by paying the sum of $100.00 per month to Creditor commencing on January 1, 1996 and continuing on the first day of every month thereafter until the Note and all other obligations of Debtor to Creditor are paid in full.

2. Debtor hereby agrees that, except as modified by this Reaffirmation Agreement, the Note and the guarantee shall remain in full force and effect; provided, however, so long as Debtor performs pursuant to the preceding paragraph, Creditor shall take no action to enforce the guarantee.

3. Debtor and Creditor hereby acknowledge and understand that this Reaffirmation Agreement will become enforceable against Debtor at the time of his discharge hearing if he is granted a discharge at that time.

4. DEBTOR UNDERSTANDS AND ACKNOWLEDGES THAT THIS REAFFIRMATION AGREEMENT IS NOT REQUIRED BY THE BANKRUPTCY CODE, NONBANKRUPTCY LAW, OR UNDER ANY AGREEMENT NOT IN ACCORDANCE WITH SECTION 524 (C) OF THE BANKRUPTCY CODE.

5. DEBTOR AND CREDITOR ACKNOWLEDGE THAT DEBTOR MAY CANCEL AND RESCIND THIS REAFFIRMATION AGREEMENT AT ANY TIME UP TO SIXTY (60) DAYS AFTER THIS REAFFIRMATION AGREEMENT IS FILED WITH THE COURT OR THE GRANTING OF ANY DISCHARGE, WHICHEVER IS LATER.

6. DEBTOR UNDERSTANDS AND ACKNOWLEDGES THAT IF HE DOES NOT CANCEL OR RESCIND THIS REAFFIRMATION AGREEMENT BEFORE THE END OF THE ABOVE-REFERENCED PERIODS, HE WILL BE BOUND BY THIS REAFFIRMATION AGREEMENT AND THE TERMS AND CONDITIONS OF THE NOTE.

7. Any cancellation or rescission of this Agreement by Debtor as set forth in paragraphs 5 and 6 hereinabove, shall be in writing and delivered to Creditor at 100 Highhanded Drive, Los Angeles, California 90001.

DATED: November 15, 1995

_____

JOSEPH CONSUMER

DATED: November 15, 1995

B & B STEREO COMPANY

_____

Harlan Band
Credit Manager

Declaration of Bankrupt C. Lawyer

I, Bankrupt C. Lawyer, declare as follows:

1. I am an attorney licensed by the state of California and admitted to practice before the United States Bankruptcy Court for the Western District of California.

2. I am the attorney for Joseph Consumer, the above-captioned debtor ("Debtor"). I submit the Declaration in support of Debtor's Motion for Approval of Reaffirmation Agreement and the words defined in the Motion are used in this Declaration with the same meaning.

3. I represented Debtor during the course of negotiating the Agreement with Creditor.

—*continued*

■ EXHIBIT 8.3
Sample Pleading—*Continued*

4. I have fully advised Debtor of the legal effect and the consequences of the Agreement and of any default of his under the Agreement.

5. To the best of my knowledge, information, and belief, the Agreement represents a fully informed and voluntary agreement by Debtor.

6. After due inquiry, and to the best of my knowledge, information, and belief, the Agreement does not impose an undue hardship on Debtor or a dependent of Debtor.

I declare under penalty of perjury that the foregoing is true and correct, is of my own personal knowledge, and if called as a witness I could and would testify competently.

Executed on November 15, 1995 at Los Angeles, California.

_____

BANKRUPT C. LAWYER

Even if the debtor successfully performs all the steps necessary to reaffirm and the agreement is approved by the court, the debtor may rescind the agreement at any time within sixty days of the discharge or the filing of the reaffirmation agreement whichever was earlier. The Bankruptcy Code requires the reaffirmation agreement to contain a "clear and conspicuous" statement to this effect. "Clear" means stated in plain, easily understandable language. "Conspicuous" means capital or bold letters, underlining, or the like. To rescind, the debtor merely gives notice to the creditor.

As a practical matter, creditors with a large volume of consumer customers will frequently send debtors a reaffirmation agreement upon receiving notice of the bankruptcy case. The creditor may have developed a form agreement and motion with blanks for the pertinent information. Director's Form B 240, which is a combination reaffirmation agreement, attorney's and debtor's declaration, motion for approval of the agreement and order is available. It does not contain the "clear and conspicuous" notices, which must be added.

☐ EXEMPTIONS

Exemption
Those interests in property that a debtor is allowed to keep and not make subject to creditors' claims.

As mentioned earlier, one of the purposes of bankruptcy is to allow an individual debtor a fresh start, a chance to put financial problems in the past. Congress and the state governments have always determined that in order to make that fresh start, an individual debtor needs to retain certain ordinary possessions. Weighing between what was fair for a debtor to keep and what would be unfair to creditors, the legislatures developed a list of **exemptions:** categories and limits on assets a debtor will be able to retain despite being in bankruptcy. The congressionally-created exemptions are listed in Section 522(d) of the Bankruptcy Code and are highlighted in Exhibit 8.4.

Congress created the exemptions listed in Exhibit 8.4 by balancing the different interests of creditors and debtors. They reflect nationwide values. Yet the purpose behind a particular exemption may not be served if the amount allowed for an exemption is too low in a particular state. For example, the federal homestead exemption is designed to ensure that the debtor has a place to live. A $15,000

■ EXHIBIT 8.4
Exemptions under Bankruptcy Code Section 522(d)

Exemption	Explanation
Homestead	Up to $15,000 of value in real or personal property (such as a mobile home) that the debtor or a dependent uses as a residence or intends to use as a burial plot.
Car	One motor vehicle up to $2,400 in value.
Personal effects	$400 per item up to $8,000 in total of household furnishings, households goods, clothes, animals, books, crops, and musical instruments for the personal, family, or household use of the debtor or a dependent.
Jewelry	Up to $1,000 in jewelry held primarily for the personal, family, or household use of the debtor or a dependent.
General exemption	$800 in any item plus up to $7,500 of any unused portion of the residence exemption in any property. If the debtor rents, the exemption will be $8,300 in any asset or group of assets. This is frequently referred to as the grubstake exemption.
Tools of the trade	Up to $1,500 in implements, professional books, or tools of the trade of the debtor or a dependent.
Life insurance	An unmatured life insurance contract owned by the debtor.
Loan value of life insurance contract	Up to $8,000 in any accrued dividend, interest under, or loan value of any unmatured life insurance contract if the insured is the debtor or an individual on whom the debtor is dependent.
Health aids	Professionally prescribed health aids for the debtor or a dependent.
Benefits akin to earnings	Social Security, unemployment, public assistance, veteran's benefits, disability, or illness benefits; alimony and support to extent necessary; payments on account of disability, death, age, or length or service to the extent necessary for support.
Compensation for losses	Reparation awards to crime victims; wrongful death awards for an individual to whom the debtor was a dependent to the extent necessary for support; insurance payments for an individual to whom the debtor is a dependent to the extent necessary for support; up to $15,000 for personal bodily injury, other than pain and suffering, and actual pecuniary loss awarded to debtor or an individual on whom debtor is a dependent; and payment for loss of future earnings to the extent necessary for support.

exemption of the debtor's interest in a residence may be more than sufficient to allow a debtor who is residing in an area where land is inexpensive. A $15,000 exemption for a resident of New York City, where property values and replacement costs are very high, probably will not allow the debtor to retain the residence or purchase replacement housing. Along these same lines, some state legislatures might find it important that a debtor have twenty acres of land, regardless of whether the debtor's interest is worth $5,000 or $500,000.

So that each state might reflect what is necessary for a fresh start in that state, in Section 522(b) Congress provided that a debtor could use either state-law-created exemptions or the congressionally-created exemptions unless the state had specifically provided that a debtor could not use the federal exemptions. In other words, each state could decree that a debtor filing in its state could use only the state-created exemptions. This section was commonly referred to as the **opting out** provision and has been invoked by the majority of the states.

If a husband and wife file a joint case, they are each entitled to claim a set of exemptions but they must each choose the same set. In a state that has not opted out, one spouse cannot elect the state law exemptions while the other elects those provided in Section 522. They must both elect either the federal or the state exemptions. If they cannot agree, they will be deemed to have elected the federal exemptions.

Opting Out
An option granted to the states allowing them to require their residents to use the state statutory exemptions rather than those in the Bankruptcy Code.

The procedure for claiming exemptions is relatively simple. The debtor merely lists the property on Schedule C of Official Form 6. Also listed will be the statutory basis for the exemption and the value of the exempt property. A sample Schedule C is shown in Exhibit 8.5. Schedule C, like all of the schedules, must be filed no later than fifteen days after the case is commenced and can be amended later if necessary. The debtor may want to amend to include an omitted item or exclude an asset later returned to a secured creditor in order to take advantage of the exemption for a different item.

If no objection is filed to the exemptions, they are allowed. A creditor or the Chapter 7 trustee might object; for an example, see Exhibit 8.6. The property may be worth substantially more than what the debtor claimed or the amount exempted from a pension plan may be more than is necessary for the debtor's support. If a creditor or the trustee wishes to oppose a claimed exemption, Bankruptcy Rule 4003 provides that an objection must be filed no later than thirty days after the first meeting of creditors held pursuant to Section 341(a) or after the filing of any amendment to Schedule C. How the hearing will be scheduled differs from jurisdiction to jurisdiction. In some, the objecting party must call the court and obtain a date first. In others, the court will set the hearing after review of the objection. No matter how the hearing is set, the objecting party will have the burden of proving that the exemption was not properly claimed.

■ EXHIBIT 8.5
Schedule C

In re Joe Consumer, Debtor.   Case No. 95-00002-JF

SCHEDULE C—PROPERTY CLAIMED AS EXEMPT

Debtor elects the exemptions to which debtor is entitled under:
(Check one box)

☒ 11 U.S.C. § 522(b)(1): Exemptions provided in 11 U.S.C. § 522(d). Note: These exemptions are available only in certain states.

☐ 11 U.S.C. § 522(b)(2): Exemptions available under applicable nonbankruptcy federal laws, state or local law where the debtor's domicile has been located for the 180 days immediately preceding the filing of the petition, or for a longer portion of the 180-day period than in any other place, and the debtor's interest as a tenant by the entirety or joint tenant to the extent of the interest is exempt from process under applicable nonbankruptcy law.

Description of Property	Specify Law Providing Each Exemption	Value of Claimed Exemption	Current Market Value of Property Without Deducting Exemption
Debtor's Residence: 18 Hollywood Drive Los Angeles, CA 90001	11 U.S.C. § 522(d)(1)	$15,000	$240,000
1992 Dodge Caravan	11 U.S.C. § 522(d)(2) and (5)	$3,000	$5,000
Household goods and furnishings, including audio, video and computer equipment	11 U.S.C. § 522(d)(3)	$4,500	$4,500 (No one item more than $400 in value)
Gold ring with one carat diamond inset	11 U.S.C. § 522(d)(4) and (5)	$1,200	$1,200

■ EXHIBIT 8.6
Sample Pleading

MILDRED PIERCE
700 Flower Street
Los Angeles, California 90001

Trustee

UNITED STATES BANKRUPTCY COURT
WESTERN DISTRICT OF CALIFORNIA

In re	Case No 95-00003-JF
JOSEPH BUSINESSMAN and MYRA BUSINESSWOMAN,	Chapter 7
Debtor's Address: 18 Hollywood Drive Los Angeles, California 90001	OBJECTION TO CLAIM OF EXEMPTIONS AND REQUEST FOR HEARING
Debtors' S.S. No. 559-15-1402 and 743-47-8459	

Mildred Pierce, the duly appointed, qualified, and acting Chapter 7 trustee in the above-captioned case (the "Trustee"), pursuant to Section 522(1) of the Bankruptcy Code and Bankruptcy Rule 4003(b), objects to the debtors' claim of exemptions and in support of this objection states as follows:

1. Debtors have claimed as exempt pursuant to Bankruptcy Code Section 522(d)(6), an antique blackboard eraser collection (the "Collection").

2. The Collection is not implements, professional books, or tools of the trade for either of the debtors or any of their dependents.

3. The Trustee requests that the Court set a hearing on this objection and notify the Trustee and the debtors as to the date and time of the hearing.

DATED: November 15, 1995

MILDRED PIERCE
Trustee

Even if a particular exemption is allowed, the property may still be sold by the trustee. Usually what is protected is not the property itself but a dollar amount of the debtor's interest. For example, if the debtor owns property used as a residence that has a fair market value of $100,000 and was subject to a mortgage in favor of a bank with a balance owing of $60,000, the debtor's interest in the property is the amount of the equity, or $40,000. If the debtor chose the federal exemptions, all that is exempt is $15,000 of the $40,000. The Chapter 7 trustee could sell the residence for $100,000, pay the bank $60,000, pay the debtor $15,000, and distribute $25,000 to the debtor's creditors. The debtor could use the $15,000 as a down payment on a new house for the fresh start. As a practical matter, unless the house is worth at least ten percent more than the secured debt and the amount

of the debtor's exemption, the trustee will not bother to sell it since the broker's fees and other costs of the sale could easily deplete the funds available to the unsecured creditors.

☐ LIEN AVOIDANCE

Because of the public policy of allowing a debtor to keep certain ordinary property for a fresh start, Bankruptcy Code Section 522(e) provides that a prepetition waiver of those exemptions in favor of an unsecured creditor is not enforceable. Similarly, in certain circumstances, the Bankruptcy Code allows a debtor to avoid a lien of a secured creditor on the debtor's exempt property so that the debtor will be able to keep the property for a fresh start.

Bankruptcy Code Section 522(f) allows two types of liens to be avoided if they impair an exemption; these liens are:

1. A judicial lien other than one that secures payment of alimony, maintenance or support.

2. A nonpossessory, nonpurchase money security interest in the types of assets exempt under:

☐ Sections 522(d)(3) and (4)—household furnishings, household goods, wearing apparel, appliances, books, animals, crops, musical instruments, and jewelry held primarily for the personal, family or household use of the debtor or the debtor's dependent;

☐ Section 522(d)(5)—implements, professional books, or tools of the trade of the debtor or the debtor's dependent; and

☐ Section 522(d)(9)—professionally described health aids of the debtor or the debtor's dependents.

Judicial Lien
A lien obtained by judgment, levy or other legal or equitable process or proceeding.

A **judicial lien** is defined in Section 101(36) as a lien obtained by judgment, levy, sequestration, or other legal or equitable process or proceeding. It does not include statutory liens such as tax liens or material or service liens created by any nonbankruptcy statute. A judicial lien other than one that secures payment of alimony, maintenance or support is avoidable on every type of property or interest that the debtor may claim as exempt. The avoidance of a nonpossessory, nonpurchase money security interest on the other hand, is limited to those liens on types of property specified. Thus, an impairing consensual lien given on the debtor's residence, even though nonpossessory and nonpurchase money, could not be avoided using Section 522(f) because the homestead is not one of the covered exemptions. A consensual lien on all of the debtor's household goods could be avoided unless the lien was created to secure repayment of the money borrowed to purchase those same household goods.

A lien can be avoided only to the extent it impairs an exemption. If a $5,000 judgment lien attached to the debtor's jewelry that has a value of $7,000, the lien cannot be avoided because the exemption is only $1,000 and there is $2,000 available after satisfaction of the judgment lien. If the judgment was in the amount of $5,000 and the jewelry is worth $5,000, only $1,000 of the judgment lien could be avoided because that is the extent it impairs the exemption.

Section 522(d)(3) was added in the 1994 Amendments. It provides that in those cases where the debtor may or is required to take state exemptions (as opposed to the federal exemptions in Section 522(d)), and state law either: (1) provides an exemption of unlimited amount or (2) prohibits avoidance of con-

sensual liens on property otherwise eligible to be claimed as exempt, then the debtor may not use Section 522(f) to avoid a nonpossessory, nonpurchase money security interest in implements, tools of the trade, farm animals or crops to the extent the value of those assets exceeds $5,000.

Also, the 1994 Amendments provide that if there are two liens on the same piece of property, one of them can be avoided to the extent that when their amounts are added together the exemption is impaired. For example, if a car is worth $5,000 and subject to two liens each in the amount of $2,000, $1,600 of one lien can be avoided because the $4,000 amount of the two liens impairs the debtor's $2,400 exemption.

There is no stated time limit, other than when the case is closed, to seek to avoid a lien. Bankruptcy Rule 4003(d) states that a proceeding by the debtor to avoid a lien under Section 522(f) is initiated by the filing of a motion in accordance with Bankruptcy Rule 9014, which governs contested matters generally. (See Exhibit 8.7.) Because lien avoidance motions are frequently brought and rarely contested, even jurisdictions that require hearings on all motions will commonly provide that all the debtor must do is file and serve the motion. If no objection is made by the secured creditor, the court will enter an order avoiding the lien.

Section 522(f) was new with the enactment of the Bankruptcy Code in 1978. Many companies in the business of lending to consumers in return for security interests in the types of goods described in Section 522(d)(3) complained that it violated due process of law in violation of the Fifth Amendment to the United States Constitution. The courts have generally agreed; as a result, any lien created before the enactment of the Bankruptcy Code (November 6, 1978) cannot be avoided under Section 522(f).

☐ REDEMPTIONS

The Bankruptcy Code provides another mechanism for protecting a consumer debtor's exemptions in addition to lien avoidance. It is called **redemption.** Redemption allows the debtor to extinguish a security interest in certain property by paying the creditor only what the property is worth rather than the full amount due. Typically, a debtor will want to redeem when the property is worth less than what is owed, but avoidance under Section 522(f) is not available because the secured creditor has a purchase money security interest.

Redemption
The payment to a secured party of the value of its collateral in exchange for the release of the security interest.

Section 722 of the Bankruptcy Code governs redemption and it provides that an individual debtor may redeem tangible personal property intended primarily for personal, family, or household use from a lien securing a dischargeable consumer debt, if such property is exempt or has been abandoned by the trustee. In other words, to redeem, each of the following facts must exist:

☐ The debtor is an individual.

☐ A creditor has a lien on tangible personal property.

☐ The property is intended to be used primarily for personal, family, or household use.

☐ The property has either been declared as exempt or abandoned by the Chapter 7 trustee.

☐ The creditor's claim is a dischargeable consumer debt.

If any one of these elements is missing, the debtor will not be able to use Section 722 and must reaffirm the entire debt in order to keep the property. If all

■ EXHIBIT 8.7
Sample Pleading

BANKRUPT C. LAWYER
WHITE CHARGER LEGAL CLINIC
One Learned Way
Los Angeles, California 90001

Attorneys for Debtor

UNITED STATES BANKRUPTCY COURT
WESTERN DISTRICT OF CALIFORNIA

In re)	Case No. 95-00002-JF
)	
JOSEPH CONSUMER,)	Chapter 7
)	
Debtors's Address:)	
18 Hollywood Drive)	MOTION FOR ORDER AVOIDING
Los Angeles, California 90001)	LIEN ON EXEMPT PROPERTY;
)	DECLARATION OF JOSEPH
Debtor's S.S. No. 524-47-7448)	CONSUMER IN SUPPORT THEREOF
_____)	

TO THE HONORABLE JUSTIN FAIR, UNITED STATES BANKRUPTCY JUDGE:

Joseph Consumer ("Debtor"), through his attorneys, in support of his Motion for Order Avoiding Lien on Exempt Property, respectfully represents as follows:

1. On January 1, 1994, Debtor borrowed $500.00 (the "Loan") from Consumer Finance Company ("CFC").

2. In order to secure repayment of the Loan, Debtor granted to CFC a security interest in all debtor's household goods (the "Lien").

3. The Lien is nonpossessory, nonpurchase money and impairs the exemption to which Debtor is entitled and has claimed under Sections 522(b) and (d)(3) of the Bankruptcy Code.

4. The Lien is avoidable pursuant to Section 522(f) of the Bankruptcy Code.

WHEREFORE, Debtor requests that the Court enter its Order avoiding the Lien and granting such other and further relief to which Debtor may be entitled.

DATED: November 15, 1995

WHITE CHARGER LEGAL CLINIC

_____

BANKRUPT C. LAWYER
Attorneys for Debtor

Declaration of Joseph Consumer

I, Joseph Consumer, declare as follows:

1. I am the debtor in the above captioned case ("Debtor"). I submit this Declaration in support of my Motion for Order Avoiding Lien on Exempt Property, and the words defined in the Motion are used in this Declaration with the same meaning.

—continued

■ EXHIBIT 8.7
Sample Pleading

---

2. On January 1, 1994 I borrowed the Loan from CFC and granted the Lien to CFC. As of the date I commenced my Chapter 7 bankruptcy case, I owed CFC $400.00.

3. I have claimed as exempt all my household furnishings. No individual item exceeds $400.00 in value and the aggregate value of all my household furnishings does not exceed $8,000.00.

I declare under penalty of perjury that the foregoing is true and correct, is of my own personal knowledge, and if called as a witness I could and would testify competently.

Executed on November 15, 1995 at Los Angeles, California.

                                              JOSEPH CONSUMER

---

the elements exist, the debtor must pay the creditor the allowed secured claim, which Section 506(a) of the Bankruptcy Code defines as the value of the creditor's interest in the estate's interest in the property. The difference between the creditor's claim and the amount paid to redeem will be an unsecured claim and discharged. If the creditor is owed $50 but the collateral is only worth $35, the creditor has an allowed secured claim of $35 and an unsecured claim of $15. If the creditor is owed $50 and the collateral is worth $60, the allowed secured claim is $50. Although the Bankruptcy Code is silent on the point, most courts have required debtors who wish to redeem to make a lump sum payment to the creditor. Installment payments usually will not be allowed.

Bankruptcy Rule 6008 implements Section 722 and provides that redemption is accomplished by the filing of a motion (see Exhibit 8.8) and having a hearing on such notice as the court may direct. At a minimum, the debtor would want to ensure that the secured creditor receives notice so that any objection can be made. Notice should also be sent to the Chapter 7 trustee.

For several reasons, redemption is not a remedy frequently used by debtors. First, there are only limited circumstances where it is available. Second, few debtors have the money to redeem or the credit worthiness to borrow in order to redeem.

☐ CONVERTING OR DISMISSING THE CASE

Changing Chapters

Regardless of how much thought went into the decision of under which chapter the debtor should file, during the pendency of the case the question may arise among the debtor and the creditors as to whether the case should have been originally filed under a different chapter or whether the case should proceed in the future under a different chapter. In most instances the case can proceed in a different chapter. The act of changing the chapter under which a case is pending is called **conversion.** The rules governing conversion vary from chapter to chapter.

The one general rule is that a case cannot be converted to a chapter if the debtor was ineligible to begin in that chapter. For example, a debtor with $500,000 in unsecured debts could not convert a Chapter 11 case to a case under Chapter

Conversion
The act of changing the chapter of the Bankruptcy Code in which a bankruptcy case is pending.

■ EXHIBIT 8.8
Sample Pleading

BANKRUPT C. LAWYER
WHITE CHARGER LEGAL CLINIC
One Learned Way
Los Angeles, California 90001

Attorneys for Debtor

UNITED STATES BANKRUPTCY COURT
WESTERN DISTRICT OF CALIFORNIA

In re	)	Case No. 95-00002-JF
	)	
JOSEPH CONSUMER,	)	Chapter 7
	)	
Debtor's Address:	)	
18 Hollywood Drive	)	MOTION FOR ORDER
Los Angeles, California 90001	)	AUTHORIZING REDEMPTION;
	)	DECLARATION OF JOSEPH
Debtor's S.S. No. 524-47-7448	)	CONSUMER IN SUPPORT THEREOF
	)	

TO THE HONORABLE JUSTIN FAIR, UNITED STATES BANKRUPTCY JUDGE:

Joseph Consumer ("Debtor"), through his attorneys, in support of this Motion for Order Authorizing Redemption, respectfully represents as follows:

1. On January 1, 1994, Debtor purchased a Sony Video Camera Model 111N (the "Camera") from B & B Stereo Company ("Creditor"). As part of the same transaction, Creditor retained a security interest in the Camera and duly perfected its security interest by filing a financing statement with the Secretary of State for the State of California.

2. Debtor purchased the Camera primarily for personal use.

3. Debtor has claimed the Camera as exempt pursuant to 11 U.S.C. § 522(d)(5).

4. At the time he commenced his Chapter 7 bankruptcy case, Debtor owed Creditor $100.00 on account of his purchase of the Camera.

5. The fair market value of the Camera is $50.00.

6. Debtor is ready, willing, and able to pay Creditor $50.00 in order to redeem the Camera from Creditor's lien.

WHEREFORE, Debtor requests that the Court enter its Order authorizing Debtor to redeem the Camera from Creditor's lien upon the payment to Creditor of $50.00 and granting such other and further relief to which Debtor may be entitled.

DATED: November 15, 1995

WHITE CHARGER LEGAL CLINIC

_____

BANKRUPT C. LAWYER
Attorney for Debtor

Declaration of Joseph Consumer

I, Joseph Consumer, declare as follows:

—continued

1. I am the debtor in the above-captioned case. I submit this Declaration in support of my Motion for Order Authorizing Redemption, and the words defined in the Motion are used in this Declaration with the same meaning.

2. On January 1, 1994, I purchased the Camera from B & B and granted B & B a security interest in the Camera.

3. I filed a Chapter 7 bankruptcy case on October 1, 1995 and have claimed the Camera as exempt.

4. I owe B & B $100.00 for the Camera.

5. I asked Al Garza, the manager of B & B, what the fair market value of the Camera was and he told me $50.00.

I declare under penalty of perjury that the foregoing is true and correct, is of my own personal knowledge, and if called as a witness I could and would testify competently.

Executed on November 15, 1995 at Los Angeles, California.

JOSEPH CONSUMER

13 because the debtor does not meet the eligibility requirements for Chapter 13 set out in Section 109 of the Bankruptcy Code. Similarly, a stockbroker could not convert a Chapter 7 case to a case under Chapter 11 because stockbrokers are ineligible for Chapter 11 relief.

To further the congressional goal of encouraging debtors to reorganize rather than liquidate, Section 706(a) of the Bankruptcy Code provides that the debtor may convert a Chapter 7 case to a case under Chapter 11, 12, or 13 at any time as a matter of right. No hearing or court approval is required. All the debtor must do is file the appropriate motion. Although no order is required, it is wise to prepare and lodge one and provide it to creditors so that they will not be confused as to the chapter under which the case is proceeding.

An exception to the debtor's absolute right to convert to a reorganization case is if the case was previously converted to Chapter 7 from a different chapter. If the debtor commenced the case in Chapter 11 and then converted or had it converted to Chapter 7, it cannot as a matter of right convert it back to Chapter 11. In those situations, court approval after a hearing on notice of creditors must be obtained.

The debtor is not the only one who is entitled to convert a Chapter 7 case. Section 706(b) states that at the request of a party in interest, which could include the Chapter 7 trustee, and after notice and a hearing, the court may convert a Chapter 7 case to a case under Chapter 11. Section 706(c) contains a flat prohibition against a conversion from Chapter 7 to Chapter 12 or 13. Since Chapter 12 cases frequently involve individuals and Chapter 13 cases always do, and the cases usually provide for a payment to creditors out of future earnings, for the court to require the debtor to be in Chapter 12 or 13 would likely violate the Thirteenth Amendment of the United States Constitution's prohibition against slavery.

The procedure for the nondebtor to convert a Chapter 7 case to Chapter 11 is to file a motion as provided in Bankruptcy Rule 9014. Twenty days' notice to creditors is required by Bankruptcy Rule 2002(a).

Dismissing a Bankruptcy Case

An alternative to converting a bankruptcy case is to dismiss it. The Chapter 7 debtor may want the case dismissed because it no longer has any need for the protections bankruptcy affords or may have thought that bankruptcy could accomplish more than it does.

Although converting from a Chapter 7 case is granted to debtors as a matter of right, dismissing a case is not as easy. Section 707(a) allows the court to dismiss a Chapter 7 case only after notice and a hearing and only for cause. Court approval is necessary regardless of whether it is the debtor, the trustee, or the creditors making the motion. Section 707(a) gives examples of cause for dismissal including unreasonable prejudicial delay, nonpayment of fees and costs required to be paid, and the failure to file the statement of intentions. Like the other sections of the Bankruptcy Code that attempt to explain cause, the list in Section 707(a) is not exhaustive. A common ground for dismissal is that the debtor is now in a position to pay all of its creditors in full.

The procedure for dismissing a Chapter 7 case is governed by Bankruptcy Rule 1017(a). The effect of the dismissal of a bankruptcy case is set out in Section 349 of the Bankruptcy Code. Section 349(b) provides that unless the court orders otherwise, dismissal reinstates any proceeding or custodianship superseded by the bankruptcy filing and any avoided transfer or lien. It also vacates any order concerning turnover, liability of a transferee of an avoided transfer, and setoff. Property of the estate will be revested in the entity in which such property was vested immediately before the commencement of the bankruptcy case.

Unless the debtor is prohibited from filing a new bankruptcy case for 180 days under Section 109(f), upon dismissal the debtor may refile a new bankruptcy case and obtain a discharge in the new case unless the court finds cause to order otherwise.

☐ SUMMARY

For most debtors who are individuals, the primary reason for filing a Chapter 7 case is to obtain a discharge. A discharge releases the debtor from his or her obligation to pay unsecured debts. In certain circumstances the debtor can lose the right to a discharge. Those circumstances almost always involve fraud or other serious wrongdoing by the debtor to creditors generally. An example is the hiding of assets from the trustee. The creditor or the trustee must file a complaint to prevent the debtor from obtaining a discharge.

There are also some types of debt that are nondischargeable; they can be enforced against the debtor even after the discharge is granted. These types of debts include student loans, taxes, alimony and child support, and debts incurred by fraud or the use of a false financial statement. Some debts are automatically dischargeable, others will be discharged unless the creditor commences an adversary proceeding and prevails.

Even though a debt may be discharged, the debtor can agree to pay it. For that agreement to be enforceable, the debtor must reaffirm the debt by having the reaffirmation agreement properly approved by the bankruptcy court.

The Bankruptcy Code does not require an individual debtor to turn over all of his or her assets to the trustee. The property the debtor may keep is called exempt property. Exempt property includes some equity in a residence, a car, personal effects, and tools needed by the debtor in his or her trade. In some states a debtor

may use either the exemptions provided in the Bankruptcy Code or in the state's statutes. In other states, the debtor may only use the exemptions provided by state law. Exemptions are claimed by listing them in Schedule C.

If the debtor is entitled to an exemption but the property is subject to a lien, the debtor may be able to avoid the lien to the extent it impairs the exemption. Lien avoidance is only available for certain types of property and against only certain types of liens.

If the debtor cannot avoid a lien, he or she may be able to redeem the property from the lien by paying the creditor the lesser of the value of the property or the amount of the creditor's claim. This is beneficial to the debtor if the creditor is owed much more than the property is worth.

A Chapter 7 debtor has the right to convert its case to a reorganization chapter at any time unless it was previously in a reorganization chapter. An individual's Chapter 7 case cannot be converted to a reorganization chapter against his or her will but a corporation's or partnership's case can. A Chapter 7 case can be dismissed only after notice to parties in interest and upon the bankruptcy court's order.

☐ KEY TERMS

Conversion	Nondischargeable Claims	Reaffirm
Exemption	Opting Out	Redemption
Judicial Lien		

☐ IMPROVE YOUR UNDERSTANDING

1. Read Bankruptcy Code Sections 727 and 523. Then, for each of the factual situations presented in exercises a. through j., indicate if there are grounds sufficient to hold a claim nondischargeable, deny a discharge, both, or neither. If not enough information is provided, list the additional facts needed.

   a. Shortly before filing his bankruptcy case, the debtor told a creditor that he would pay him soon.

   b. The bankruptcy court ordered the debtor to turn over to a secured creditor all the rents from an apartment building the debtor owned. The debtor did not do so.

   c. The debtor hired an arsonist who set fire to the business premises of debtor's corporation, destroying all the books and records.

   d. The debtor transferred his home to his mother. She had made the down payment, all subsequent payments, and had always thought the home was hers.

   e. The debtor's obligations include monthly child support of $500.00.

   f. The debtor under-reported the number of employees he had and thereby paid less in payroll taxes than was actually required. When the under-reporting was discovered, the taxing agency imposed a penalty of one hundred percent (100%).

   g. The debtor gave a creditor a false financial statement after the creditor had lent money to the debtor.

   h. The debtor gave the bank a financial statement that showed that the debtor owned 100 shares in a corporation with a value of $100 per share. The bank knew that the corporation was insolvent and the shares valueless but it lent the debtor the money anyway.

   i. The debtor owes $10,000 for student loans. After graduation, the debtor is stricken by a disease from which he is not expected to recover.

   j. The debtor is arrested and convicted of drunk driving. As part of his sentence he is ordered to pay a fine of $500.00.

2. The debtor has income of $25,000 per year. A creditor who holds what she believes to be a nondischargeable claim for $50,000 believes that the debtor failed to disclose $1,000,000 in assets to the

trustee. The debtor has $5,000,000 worth of debts. What should the creditor do?

3. Read Bankruptcy Code Sections 524(c), (d), (e), and (f) and Bankruptcy Rule 4008. Then answer Exercises a. through f. based upon the following factual situation:

Joe Consumer bought a video camera from B & B Stereo Company; it was to be paid for over time. Joe's mother Flora, a pensioner on a limited salary, guaranteed to B & B that if Joe did not pay she would. Joe filed a Chapter 7 petition when he still owed B & B $100. His discharge hearing is set for December 1. Joe does not want B & B pursuing Flora for the $100.

a. If Joe receives a discharge, will Flora's obligation also be discharged?

b. Joe decides to reaffirm his debt to B & B. To be enforceable by B & B, when is the last day the reaffirmation agreement must be filed?

c. What else must Joe file with the reaffirmation agreement?

d. If Joe is represented by a lawyer during the course of negotiating the reaffirmation agreement, what must the lawyer file and what must it contain?

e. If Joe is not represented by a lawyer, what types of questions will the judge ask Joe at the hearing on the reaffirmation agreement?

f. Joe filed the reaffirmation agreement on November 15. Flora filed her own Chapter 7 bankruptcy case on December 15, and received a discharge on her guaranty obligation to B & B. Since the threat of B & B pursuing Flora was the only reason Joe reaffirmed, he has decided to rescind. When is the last day Joe may do so?

4. List three reasons other than to prevent enforcement of a guaranty why a debtor might want to reaffirm a debt.

5. Do your local rules have any provisions concerning reaffirmations?

6. Read Section 522(f) carefully. Then, for each of the following fact patterns, determine whether the lien can be avoided under Section 522(f) and, if so, whether the basis is Section 522(f)(1) or 522(f)(2).

a. The applicable state law creates a lien on all assets in favor of unpaid seed suppliers to farmers. Joe, a farmer, claims as exempt his tractor, which is worth $700.

b. Joe owns a set of antique dueling pistols worth $2,000, which he has claimed as exempt. Consumer Finance Company ("CFC") lent Joe $6,000 so that he could build a swimming pool and took a security interest in all of his assets of every description.

c. Assume the same facts as Exercise b., except that CFC was an unsecured creditor who obtained a judgment against Joe and levied on all of his personal property.

d. The applicable state law creates a lien in favor of an unpaid car mechanic and allows the mechanic to retain the car until paid. Joe's car is being held by Bill's Service Station because Joe cannot pay Bill the $1,000 he owes for repairs to the car. Joe files a Chapter 7 bankruptcy case and claims the automobile as exempt.

7. For each of the fact patterns given in Exercise 7, decide whether redemption is available to the debtor; if so, whether the debtor should redeem.

a. In order to capture the first steps his child took, Joe Consumer purchased a video camera from B & B Stereo Company on an installment plan with B & B retaining a security interest in the camera. At the time Joe commenced his Chapter 7 case, he owed B & B $100 and the camera was worth $50. Joe used part of his general exemption under Section 522(d)(5) to exempt the camera.

b. Same fact pattern as Exercise 7.a., but Joe purchased the camera for his business of videotaping weddings.

c. Same fact pattern as Exercise 7.b., but the camera was purchased by the Chapter 7 debtor, Videos by Joe, Inc.

d. Same fact pattern as Exercise 7.a., but the camera is worth $150.

e. A month after Joe purchased a video camera, he borrowed $100 from Consumer Finance Company ("CFC") and granted CFC a security interest in the camera. Joe still owes CFC $100 and the camera, claimed as exempt under Section 522(d)(5), is worth $50.

f. Joe borrowed $500 from his mother Flora and gave her a lien on his as-yet uncollected judgment of $400 for bodily injury against a motorist who rear-ended him. Joe claimed the judgment as exempt under Section 522(d)(11)(D).

8. Same fact pattern as Exercise 7.a. B & B objects to Joe's motion for redemption claiming the camera is worth $200. What are two ways Joe can prove the camera's value?

9. Bankruptcy Rule 6008 provides that a trustee may bring a motion seeking redemption. Can you think of a set of facts that would compel a trustee to bring such a motion?

☐ RESEARCH PROJECTS

1. Has the state in which you work opted out?

2. Are there any local rules in your jurisdiction governing lien avoidance procedure?

3. Cite one case for each of the following holdings:

   a. A debtor may reopen a case to avoid a lien under Section 522(f).

   b. Section 522(f) is applicable in Chapter 13 cases.

   c. Section 522(f) is inapplicable in Chapter 13 cases.

   d. A lien on an automobile cannot be avoided under Section 522(f)(2).

4. Locate two reported decisions in which the courts have held that redemption under Section 722 must be made in a lump sum payment and not on an installment basis.

☐ DRAFTING PROJECTS

1. Draft a complaint, based on facts you create, objecting to a discharge based on Section 727(a)(4) or Section 727(a)(9) of the Bankruptcy Code.

2. Draft a complaint, based on facts you create, to determine whether a debt is nondischargeable based on Section 523(a)(4) or Section 523(a)(6) of the Bankruptcy Code.

3. When B & B sold the stereo to Joe they retained a security interest in the stereo to secure payment of the note. Revise the sample Reaffirmation Agreement (included as part of Exhibit 8.3) to provide for this new fact.

4. B & B had filed a complaint to determine dischargeability of Joe's debt under Bankruptcy Code Section 523(a)(2)(B). The Reaffirmation Agreement (included as part of Exhibit 8.3) moots that action and it should be dismissed. Revise the sample Reaffirmation Agreement to provide for this new fact.

5. Use the following set of facts to draft a Schedule C maximizing the exemptions. Assume there are no state created exemptions.

Joe Businessman and his wife Myra, a schoolteacher, are the shareholders of Videos by Joe, Inc. All three are Chapter 7 debtors and Joe and Myra filed a joint case. Joe owns free and clear a 1978 Ford Pinto that is worth $1,000. Myra drives a 1987 BMW 318i that is worth $8,000 but on which she still owes $6,000. Myra and Joe jointly own a house with an equity of $21,500. Their other personal property is modest although they do own a piano with a value of $600, Myra's engagement ring is worth $1,000, and Myra's prized blackboard eraser collection is worth $1,000. Joe owns one video camera and their company owns two, each worth $700. The value of the stock of Videos by Joe, Inc. is $2,000.

6. Prepare a table comparing the exemptions provided in Section 522(d) of the Bankruptcy Code with the exemptions enacted by your state.

CHAPTER 7: THE TRUSTEE'S PERSPECTIVE

The previous chapter examined Chapter 7 from the debtor's perspective. That perspective is only half of the story. While the debtor is busy obtaining a discharge, claiming exemptions, avoiding liens, and redeeming collateral, the nonexempt assets of the estate will be sold or otherwise liquidated and creditor claims will be paid. Those later tasks will be performed by the trustee rather than the debtor. This chapter will focus on the role of the trustee.

☐ COLLECTING THE ESTATE

Section 541 of the Bankruptcy Code provides that the commencement of a bankruptcy case creates an estate that consists of all the debtor's legal and equitable interests as of the date the petition is filed. The interests become property of the estate wherever they are located and by whomever they are held. The estate will also include property recovered by the trustee on account of fraudulent conveyances, unenforceable statutory liens, preferences, authorized postpetition transfers, and improper setoffs. As the following chart shows, in a Chapter 7 case, the trustee has the duty of assembling all of the property of the estate, liquidating it, and then distributing the proceeds to creditors.

Locating Property of the Estate

It is very important for the trustee to identify, locate, and obtain all of the property of the estate in order to maximize the distributions to creditors. Usually the trustee will make an initial identification as to what constitutes property of the estate by reviewing the schedule of assets and reviewing the statement of financial affairs.

Duties of the Chapter 7 Trustee

☐ Take into Possession and Control Property of the Estate
- ■ Identify Property
- ■ Locate Property
- ■ Possess and Control Property
  - ■ Lock Up What Debtor Possesses
  - ■ Obtain Turnover of Debtor's Property in Third Party's Hands
  - ■ Notify Post Office, Banks, and Taxing Agencies
- ■ Safeguard Property

☐ Account for All Property Received

☐ Liquidate Property
- ■ Personal Property
- ■ Real Property
- ■ Claims for Relief
  - ■ Preferences
  - ■ Fraudulent Conveyances
- ■ Abandon Property of No or Minimum Value

☐ Ensure Performance With Debtor's Statement of Intentions

☐ Furnish Information to Parties in Interest

☐ Investigate Debtor's Financial Affairs

☐ Examine and Object to Proofs of Claims

☐ Oppose Debtor's Discharge

☐ File Final Report and Account

■ EXHIBIT 9.1
Duties of the Chapter 7
Trustee

The trustee will also question the debtor at the meeting of creditors held pursuant to Section 341(a) or earlier about the existence and location of other assets.

In a larger case, if the debtor is uncooperative or if the trustee suspects that the debtor may have hidden assets, the trustee will examine the debtor's books and records to see if there are missing assets. The trustee may also question the debtor's employees about property held by third parties or transfers made prepetition. A search in the debtor's name of the county recorder's office or the Department of Motor Vehicles may also yield information about unscheduled assets. Creditors, who have an interest in making the estate as large as possible, will sometimes come forward to advise the trustee about the location of assets.

Once the trustee identifies property of the estate, it still must be located and obtained. Movable property may be very difficult to locate and, even once located, the holder may not be willing to give it to the trustee.

The trustee should obtain the debtor's mail that was delivered after the case commenced. The post office should be notified to divert all future mail to the trustee. Similarly, all bank accounts in the name of the debtor should be discovered as soon as possible and closed. Any funds in those accounts should be transferred to new accounts the trustee will open. All taxing agencies should be notified to send any refunds due to the trustee.

The trustee should try to discover if any of the debtor's property is in the hands of a third party, whether because it is on consignment, leased, or for some other reason. If the arrangement is profitable or if it saves storage fees, the trustee may elect to keep the property where it is for the time being. If the trustee would like

Turnover
The act of delivering possession or control of property of the estate to the trustee.

to sell the property, the trustee should make immediate demand for its possession. If the third party refuses, the trustee will have to bring a **turnover** action, which is discussed later in this chapter.

Safeguarding Business Assets

In an ideal Chapter 7 business bankruptcy case, the debtor would wind the business down as best it could before filing; deliver all customer orders; turn all raw inventory and work in process to finished goods; pay all employees before termination; deliver the books, records, and keys to its attorney; and notify all creditors that it would be filing a Chapter 7 case. Unfortunately, the ideal is rarely seen. More commonly the trustee will be appointed in an estate where customers are clamoring for their goods, the employees are confused and bitter, the principals are disinterested, and no one is quite sure where the keys are.

The first task the trustee and the trustee's agents will want to undertake is to make some order out of the chaos. Perhaps the trustee or the trustee's administrator will try to meet with the former owners to obtain their ideas on the best way to maximize the value of the assets. The trustee might discover that it makes good business sense for the operations to continue for a short period of time so that raw material inventory can be converted to finished goods, which can then be shipped to customers to create valuable accounts receivable. Bankruptcy Code Section 721 allows the trustee to operate the debtor's business for a limited period if it is in the best interest of the estate, consistent with the orderly liquidation of the assets, and if the court approves. The trustee might hire a few employees in the areas of production, sales, and accounting to help run the operations for this short period of time.

Whether the business is operated or not, the trustee will want to ensure that the debtor's assets are protected so that they can be liquidated for their maximum value. What this preservation will mean varies from case to case. For real property it may mean that needed repairs are made to the roof. For equipment, it may mean hiring someone to service it on a regular basis so that it does not become dysfunctional. For assets that are easily portable, the trustee may need to have the locks on the debtor's business premises changed and arrange for guard service. The books and records will be very valuable for the administration of the estate since they will be needed to collect accounts receivable and object to proofs of claim. It is usually better that all books and records be put in storage or kept at the trustee's office. If the debtor's books and records are on computer tape or disk, copies should be made to protect them from loss of power or damage.

If the debtor's insurance has lapsed, the trustee should obtain coverage for all real and personal property to safeguard against loss and damage. If the debtor's insurance policies are still in effect, the trustee should maintain them and have his or her name added as an insured.

The trustee must also pay immediate attention to the debtor's leased business premises. The trustee should discover as quickly as possible whether there is any value in the lease. The lease may be valuable if the rent payments are less than the current market rate. If so, someone may be willing to pay the trustee to take an assignment of the lease. If the lease is not valuable, the trustee must evaluate whether it makes sense to stay in the premises while liquidating or whether the assets should be moved to a different location and stored at a lesser cost. For every month the trustee remains in the leased premises an administrative expense that could be very substantial is incurred.

Turnover

Once the trustee has located all estate property, the property must be collected so that it can be sold. The debtor has a duty to deliver all nonexempt property of the estate to the trustee upon the trustee's appointment. Sometimes property of the estate may be in the hands of the debtor or third parties who will not voluntarily turn it over. In those circumstances, the Bankruptcy Code gives the trustee several weapons to use to recover the property.

Under Section 542   The first of these weapons is Section 542. It provides (with some exceptions) that someone in possession, custody, or control of property of the estate must account for and deliver such property or its value to the trustee. If there is someone who owes a debt to the estate, Section 542 also requires that the debt be paid to the trustee unless and only to the extent that the person may have a right to offset claims it has against the debt. In addition, subject to any applicable privilege, an attorney, accountant, or other person who holds books and records relating to the debtor's property or financial affairs must turn the information over to the trustee. If the professional does not do so voluntarily, the trustee is authorized (under Section 542) to compel turnover in the bankruptcy court. The trustee may want also to include a cause of action for conversion (theft) under applicable state law. An action to compel turnover against anyone but the debtor is listed in Bankruptcy Rule 7001 as an adversary proceeding that is commenced by the filing of a complaint. (See Exhibit 9.2) An action to compel the debtor's turnover is commenced by the filing of a motion.

The exceptions to Section 542 are:

☐ If the property is of inconsequential value or benefit to the estate, it need not be turned over.

☐ If an entity does not have actual notice or knowledge of the commencement of the case, it may transfer property of the estate or pay a debt owing to the debtor in good faith to an entity other than the trustee.

☐ A life insurance company may transfer property of the estate it holds to itself to pay the premium on a life insurance contract that is property of the estate.

☐ If a custodian is in control of property of the estate it need not be turned over under Section 542. Instead, Section 543 will apply. Section 543 is discussed next.

Under Section 543   The rules for turnover by a custodian are set forth in Section 543. A custodian is defined in Section 101(11) as a **receiver** or trustee appointed in a nonbankruptcy case, an **assignee for the benefit of creditors,** or a trustee, receiver, or agent appointed by contract or applicable law. Section 543(a) states that if a custodian has knowledge of the commencement of the case, the custodian may not make any disbursements or take any action with respect to property of the estate in his or her control unless the expenditures or actions are necessary to preserve the property.

Section 543(b) requires the custodian to deliver the property of the estate in his or her control to the trustee when the custodian has knowledge of the case. The custodian must also file an accounting of his or her administration. Bankruptcy Rule 6002 requires that the accounting be filed promptly. Upon the filing of the accounting and after an examination has been made into the custodian's administration, the bankruptcy court will determine the propriety of the custodian's actions, including all the disbursements. The examination may be initiated on

Receiver
A person usually appointed by a state court whose duties are similar to those of a bankruptcy trustee.

Assignee for the Benefit of Creditors
The person who acts like a bankruptcy trustee in an assignment for the benefit of creditors.

■ EXHIBIT 9.2
Sample Pleading

MILDRED PIERCE
700 Flower Street
Los Angeles, California 90001

Trustee

UNITED STATES BANKRUPTCY COURT
WESTERN DISTRICT OF CALIFORNIA

In re)	Case No. 95-00001-JF
)	
VIDEOS BY JOE, INC.,)	Chapter 7
)	
Debtor.)	
)	
Debtor's Address:)	
18 Hollywood Drive)	
Los Angeles, California 90001)	
)	
Debtor's Tax Id. No. 99-999899)	
)	
_____)	
)	Adv. No. 95-00002-JF
MILDRED PIERCE, Trustee)	COMPLAINT FOR TURNOVER OF
)	PROPERTY OF THE ESTATE
Plaintiff,)	
)	
v.)	
)	
SUZANNE'S WEDDING)	
PHOTOGRAPHY,)	
)	
Defendant,)	
)	
_____)	

Mildred Pierce (the "Trustee") complains and alleges as follows:

THE PARTIES

1. The Trustee is the duly appointed, qualified, and acting Chapter 7 trustee in the above-captioned case.

2. The Trustee is informed that Suzanne's Wedding Photography ("Defendant") is a Delaware corporation authorized to and operating its business in the state of California.

JURISDICTION AND VENUE

3. This action for the turnover of property of the estate is an adversary proceeding over which this court has jurisdiction pursuant to 28 U.S.C. §§ 157 and 1334 and the Order of the Chief Judge of the United States District Court, Western District of California, referring bankruptcy cases and proceedings, entered on July 20, 1984. This adversary proceeding is a core matter pursuant to 28 U.S.C. § 157(b)(2)(E) and the Trustee consents to the entry of a final order or judgment by the Bankruptcy Court.

4. Venue over this adversary proceeding properly resides in the Western District of California pursuant to 28 U.S.C. § 1409(a) in that this adversary proceeding is related to *In re Videos by Joe, Inc.*, Case No. 95-00001-JF pending as a Chapter 7 case in the United States Bankruptcy Court for the Western District of California.

—continued

■ EXHIBIT 9.2
Sample Pleading—*Continued*

FACTUAL ALLEGATIONS AND CLAIM FOR RELIEF

5. Among the assets of the estate are five (5) Sony Model 111N Video Cameras and related equipment (the "Cameras"). The Cameras are property that the Trustee may use, sell, or lease pursuant to 11 U.S.C. § 363(b).

6. The Cameras are in the possession and under the control of Defendant.

7. Despite demand, Defendant has refused to turn over the Cameras to the Trustee.

8. The Cameras have a fair market value of $5,000.00.

WHEREFORE, the Trustee requests that the Court enter judgment against Defendant ordering it to surrender and deliver possession of the Cameras to the Trustee or, in the alternative, in the amount of $5,000.00 together with costs of suit, and for such other and further relief as the Court deems just and proper.

_____

MILDRED PIERCE
Trustee

---

motion of the custodian for approval of the accounting, on motion (or objection to the accounting) by the trustee or other party in interest, or even at the court's own initiative. At the hearing the court can protect all entities with whom the custodian became indebted (presumably by authorizing the trustee to pay them or otherwise allow their claim) and may set compensation for the custodian. The court can also surcharge the custodian for any improper or excessive disbursement unless it had been made pursuant to law or approved by a court.

Under certain circumstances it makes sense for the custodian to remain in control of the property of the estate. Perhaps the state court appointed a receiver over a large construction project that the debtor was mismanaging. The receiver has specialized knowledge in the area and since having been appointed, has become very familiar with the project. The debtor subsequently files the Chapter 7 petition because the custodian refuses to employ an affiliate. There is a serious question in those circumstances whether the creditors are better served by the appointment of a trustee or whether the receiver should stay. Section 543(d) allows the court to excuse turnover by a custodian if the interests of the creditors and the equity security holders would be better served. Such an order would be obtained by filing a motion. If it is important that the custodian's administration not be disturbed because it is effective or if the property should not be turned over to an untrustworthy debtor in possession, the motion may need to be made on an emergency basis immediately after the filing of the petition.

Finally, under Section 543(d)(2), if the custodian is an assignee for the benefit of creditors and was appointed or took possession more than 120 days before the filing of the petition, the court must let the assignee remain in possession or control of the property unless fraud or injustice would result.

Improper Postpetition Transactions

Sometimes unscrupulous debtors abscond with or sell property of the estate after the bankruptcy case is commenced. In addition, creditors sometimes violate the automatic stay and foreclose on their collateral without a bankruptcy court order

Postpetition Transfers
A transfer made after the commencement of a bankruptcy case that may be avoidable.

allowing them to do so. Finally, in an involuntary case, the debtor may make some unwise transfers before the order for relief and the appointment of the trustee.

The trustee is not helpless in face of these acts that deplete the estate and reduce the distribution to the other creditors. In addition to the remedies given to the trustee in the Bankruptcy Code sections concerning violation of the automatic stay, turnover, preferences, and fraudulent conveyances, Section 549 allows the trustee to avoid a transfer of property of the estate made after the commencement of the case that was not authorized by the Bankruptcy Code or by the bankruptcy court. Section 549 also allows the trustee to recover postpetition transfers if their only authorization was Section 303(f), which allows a debtor in an involuntary case to continue to use or dispose of property pending the entry of an order for relief as if no involuntary case had been commenced.

The trustee may also recover postpetition transfers that were only authorized under Section 542(c). Section 542(c) protects someone who owed money to the debtor and who paid the debt to other than the trustee because it did not have notice or knowledge of the bankruptcy case. The transferor will still be protected because Section 549 is directed at avoiding the transfer and recovering the property from the transferee.

There are some exceptions to the recovery of postpetition transfers. Section 549(b) provides that in an involuntary case the trustee cannot avoid a transfer to the extent of any value, including services but excluding satisfaction or securing of a prepetition debt, given in exchange for the transfer. Section (c) prohibits the avoidance of a transfer of real property to a good faith purchaser without knowledge of the commencement of the case and who paid fair value unless a copy of the petition was recorded with the county recorder before the transfer of the real property is recorded.

Section 549 gives the trustee the cause of action to avoid a postpetition transfer. That is really only half a remedy if there has been a physical transfer of the property because the trustee must also either recover the property or the property's value so that the estate can be made whole. This second half of the remedy is given in Section 550, which provides that if a transfer is avoided under Section 549, or a number of other sections discussed later, the trustee is also entitled to recover the property or, if the court so orders, its value. (See Exhibit 9.3.) An action under Section 549 should always be coupled with an action under Section 550 and perhaps a claim for state law conversion as well as damages for violation of the automatic stay.

An action to avoid a postpetition transfer and recover the property or its value is an adversary proceeding, is commenced by the filing of a complaint, and is governed by the procedures in the 7000 series of the Bankruptcy Rules. Section 549(d) states that the action must be brought within the earlier of two years after the transfer or the time the bankruptcy case is closed or dismissed. Pursuant to Bankruptcy Rule 6001, to prevail, the trustee need merely show that there was a transfer. The party who asserts the validity of any postpetition transfer under Section 549 has the burden of proof in establishing that the transfer was valid.

Preferences

In General   To ensure a fair distribution to all unsecured creditors, Section 547 of the Bankruptcy Code authorizes the trustee to avoid many transfers that were made within ninety days of the filing of the bankruptcy case, if those transfers benefit one or more creditors at the expense of others. The transfers that may be avoided are called **preferences.**

Preferences
A transfer of the debtor's property to a creditor in satisfaction of an existing debt made during the ninety days (or one year if the transfer was made to an insider) before the bankruptcy case was commenced and which enable the creditor to receive more than other creditors.

■ EXHIBIT 9.3
Sample Pleading

MILDRED PIERCE
700 Flower Street
Los Angeles, California 90001

Trustee

UNITED STATES BANKRUPTCY COURT
WESTERN DISTRICT OF CALIFORNIA

In re)	Case No. 95-00001-JF
)	
VIDEOS BY JOE, INC.)	Chapter 7
)	
Debtor.)	
)	
Debtor's Address:)	
18 Hollywood Drive)	
Los Angeles, California 90001)	
)	
Debtor's Tax Id. No. 99-999899)	
)	
_____)	
)	
MILDRED PIERCE,)	Adv. No. 95-00003-JF
)	
Plaintiff,)	COMPLAINT TO:
)	
v.)	(1) AVOID POSTPETITION
)	TRANSFER; AND
PERFECT PROCESSING, INC.,)	
)	(2) RECOVER PROPERTY OR ITS
Defendant,)	VALUE
)	
_____)	

Mildred Pierce (the "Trustee") complains and alleges as follows:

PARTIES

1. The Trustee is the duly appointed, qualified, and acting Chapter 7 trustee in the above-captioned case.

2. The Trustee is informed that Perfect Processing, Inc. ("Defendant") is a corporation organized and doing business in the state of California.

JURISDICTION AND VENUE

3. This action to avoid a postpetition transfer and recover property or the value thereof is an adversary proceeding over which this Court has jurisdiction pursuant to 28 U.S.C. §§ 157 and 1334 and the Order of the Chief Judge of the United States District Court, Western District of California, referring bankruptcy cases and proceedings, entered on July 20, 1984. This adversary proceeding is a core matter pursuant to 28 U.S.C. § 157(b)(28)(D) and the Trustee consents to the entry of a final order or judgment by the Bankruptcy Court.

4. Venue over this adversary proceeding properly resides in the Western District of California pursuant to 28 U.S.C. § 1409(a) in that this adversary proceeding is related to *In re Videos by Joe, Inc.*, Case No. 95-00001-JF pending as a Chapter 7 case in the United States Bankruptcy Court for the Western District of California.

—continued

FACTUAL ALLEGATIONS

5. Prior to the commencement of Debtor's bankruptcy case, Defendant was a creditor of Debtor with a claim in the amount of $5,000.00 (the "Claim").

6. On October 1, 1995, Debtor filed a petition for relief under Chapter 7 of Title 11, United States Code.

7. At the time of the commencement of Debtor's bankruptcy case, it had in its deposit account at First City Bank in excess of $10,000 (the "Account").

8. On October 2, 1995 Debtor's president withdrew the sum of $5,000.00 from the Account and paid such sums to Defendant in satisfaction of the Claim (the "Transfer").

FIRST CLAIM FOR RELIEF
[11 U.S.C. § 549]

9. The Trustee incorporates by this reference the allegations contained in paragraphs 5 through 8 above.

10. The Transfer was made after the commencement of Debtor's bankruptcy case and was not authorized by the Court or by Title 11 of the United States Code.

11. The Trustee is entitled to avoid the Transfer pursuant to 11 U.S.C. § 549.

SECOND CLAIM FOR RELIEF
[11 U.S.C. § 550]

12. The Trustee incorporates by this reference the allegations contained in paragraph 5 through 8 and 10 through 11 above.

13. The trustee is entitled to recover the Transfer from Defendant pursuant to the provisions of 11 U.S.C. § 550.

WHEREFORE, the Trustee requests that the Court enter judgment against Defendant as follows:

1. On the First Claim for Relief, that the Court avoid the Transfer.

2. On the Second Claim for Relief, that the Trustee have judgment against Defendant in the amount of $5,000.00 plus interest thereon as provided by law;

3. On all Claims for Relief, for the Trustee's reasonable attorney's fees and costs incurred in this action; and

4. For such other and further relief as the Court may deem just and proper.

_____

MILDRED PIERCE
Trustee

Section 547(a) establishes six elements of a preferential transfer, all of which must be present. If even one out of the six is absent, the transfer cannot be recovered by the trustee. The six elements are:

1. A **transfer** of property of the debtor must be made.

2. This transfer must be to or for the benefit of a creditor.

3. It must be on account of an **antecedent debt** owed by the debtor.

4. It must be made while the debtor was **insolvent.**

5. It must be made within ninety days before the date of the filing of the petition or within one year of the filing if the transferee was an insider.

6. It must have enabled the transferee to receive more than it would have received in a Chapter 7 case had the transfer not been made.

Transfer is broadly defined in Section 101(54) and encompasses virtually every conceivable mode, voluntary or involuntary, of disposing of an interest in property. A typical preferential transfer is the payment of money but it also could be the granting of a security interest, the attachment of a judgment lien, or the levy of a garnishment order.

The transfer must be of the debtor's property. If a third party pays a creditor, there is no preference because there is no transfer of the debtor's property. If the third party gives the money to the debtor who then pays the creditor, there may be a preference.

Usually, the element of "to or for the benefit of a creditor" is easily met. Most transfers are simply payments made by the debtor to its suppliers of goods or services.

A payment to a creditor is not a preference unless it is for or on account of an antecedent debt owed by the debtor. An antecedent debt merely means one that previously existed. Under this element, a prepayment or a payment at the same time as the delivery of goods or services would not be on account of an antecedent debt and would not be a preference. Also, as mentioned earlier, the transfer must be to or for the benefit of a creditor. If the debtor prepaid for goods, the supplier would not be a creditor.

Section 547 requires the debtor to be insolvent at the time the transfer was made for it to be preferential. Insolvent is defined in Section 101(32) to mean that the value of the debtor's assets is less than the debtor's liabilities. This is sometimes called **balance sheet insolvency.** Although a debtor need not be insolvent to file a petition, most bankruptcy debtors are. In order to prevent lengthy and needless hearings on the issue, pursuant to Section 547(f), the debtor is presumed to have been insolvent on and during the ninety days immediately preceding the date of the filing of the petition. Insolvency is only presumed and the creditor may attempt to rebut the presumption; in such cases, insolvency will need to be proved by the trustee.

In most cases, a preference must have been made during the ninety days preceding the filing of the petition. When the transfer is to an **insider,** a term defined in Section 101(31), the preference period is one year. If the trustee is trying to recover a preferential transfer to an insider made more than ninety days before the case was filed, there is no presumption of insolvency; the trustee will have to prove it.

Section 547(e)(2) governs when a transfer is deemed made. It is usually the date the transfer takes effect between the parties. If the transfer was a payment in cash, it is the date the cash was turned over. A payment by check is made when the check clears. If the transfer involves the perfection of a security interest, the transfer is made when the interest is perfected. But if the interest is perfected within ten days after the transfer took effect between the parties, it relates back to the date the transfer took effect.

The transfer must improve the return to the creditor. It will not be preferential unless it enables the creditor to receive more than it would have received in a hypothetical Chapter 7 case had the transfer not been made. If all creditors are being paid in full or if the transferee is a secured or priority creditor, there can be no preference since the transferee is not being treated better. For example, suppose the debtor's total debts were $100,000 and within ninety days before the petition it paid a creditor it owed $10,000 in full leaving only $90,000 in debt. If the trustee was able to accumulate only $50,000, the creditor recovered a preference because it was paid in full while other creditors were not. If the trustee had $90,000

Balance Sheet Insolvency
When the amount of liabilities on an entities' balance sheet exceeds the value of the assets on the balance sheet.

Insider
For individual debtors, a relative, partnership in which the debtor is the general partner, or corporation in which the debtor is an officer, director or otherwise in control. For partnership debtors, a general partner or its relative or person in control. For corporate debtors, a director, officer, or person in control, or a relative of an insider.

to distribute to the remaining creditors, there would be no preference because all creditors will be paid in full.

Exceptions A common theme running through the Bankruptcy Code is to lay down a general rule and then make a number of exceptions. Section 547 is a prime example of this theme. Section 547(b) lists the elements of a preference. Section 547(c) identifies eight types of transfers that, although they meet all of the preference requirements, nevertheless may not be avoided by the trustee. The exceptions are:

1. A contemporaneous exchange for new value.

2. A payment made and received in the ordinary course of business.

3. A security interest given to a lender whose loan enabled the debtor to obtain the collateral and which was perfected within twenty days.

4. Transfers where the transferee subsequently gave new value to the debtor.

5. A transfer to an account receivable or inventory financier who did not improve in position during the preference period.

6. Any statutory lien that cannot be successfully attacked under Section 545.

7. Transfers to a former spouse or child for alimony, maintenance, or support under a separation agreement, divorce decree or other court order unless the debt was assigned to someone else or is not actually in the nature of alimony, maintenance, or support.

8. A transfer by a consumer debtor that does not exceed $600.

The reason for these exceptions is that the creditor did something good for the debtor by, for example, selling it more goods, dealing with it in the ordinary course, or otherwise increasing the value of the estate. This conduct should be encouraged. If the transfers the creditor did receive had to be paid back, it would discourage creditors from dealing with companies in financial trouble. Next, the four most common exceptions are examined in a bit more detail.

Substantially Contemporaneous Exchange for New Value

A preference defense that destroys the creditor's liability if the antecedent debt was intentionally created at or about the same time as the otherwise preferential transfer was made.

For a successful contemporaneous exchange defense, the transfer must have been intended by the parties as a **substantially contemporaneous exchange for new value** and it must have been in fact a substantially contemporaneous exchange. Section 547(a)(2) defines new value to mean new money, goods, or services. It does not include the substitution of a new obligation for an old obligation. If there was an existing unsecured debt between the parties, rewriting the note and securing it with collateral would not save the transfer from preference attack as a substantially contemporaneous exchange for new value. What constitutes "substantially" in this context depends on the facts of the transaction. Obviously, if the debtor gave money to a creditor and received the money's worth in goods or services at the same time, there would have been a contemporaneous exchange for new value.

The most commonly used preference exception is for ordinary trade transactions. Prior to 1984, any payment made more than forty-five days after it was first due was preferential. In the 1984 Amendments Congress did away with this hard-and-fast rule in favor of one that is more flexible. Now, to fit within this exception the debt must have been incurred in the ordinary course of the debtor's business, the payment must have been made in the ordinary course of the debtor and the creditor's business, and the payment must have been made according to ordinary business terms. What is ordinary between the debtor and the creditor will need to be examined for every preference. It may be that a creditor gives only very short

credit terms and requires all invoices to be paid within ten days. Any payment made on the eleventh day could be a recoverable preference. If the creditor gives longer credit terms, that payment may not be recoverable. It will also be important in some instances to know what was ordinary in a particular industry. For example, if in the automobile parts industry payments to suppliers are usually due in twenty days but a particular supplier gives forty day terms, those payments may not be considered ordinary in the industry. As a result, even though the debtor paid the supplier timely pursuant to their agreement, it still might be preferential.

Enabling loans, which are almost identical to purchase money loans, are also exempted from preference attack. A lien will be protected if it is given in exchange for the money to acquire particular property. The money must have been actually used by the debtor to acquire the property and the security interest must be perfected on or before twenty days after the debtor receives possession of the property.

Enabling Loans
A loan made for the purpose of paying the purchase price of property.

To encourage creditors who do business with insolvent entities, Congress shielded from preference attack transfers to the extent that, after the transfer, the creditor gave new value to the debtor. The transfer of the new value must have been unsecured and not paid for by the debtor unless the payment can be recovered as a preference. For example, if the creditor sold goods to the debtor and received a preferential payment for them, the preference will not have to be paid back if the creditor later delivered more goods to the debtor.

Procedure to Analyze Preferences   An analysis of the debtor's records to determine what transfers may be preferential could be the task of the legal assistant. For most preferences, when the forty-five day rule was in effect it was a simple matter of comparing dates on checks to dates on invoices. Now that the standard is more flexible, the legal assistant must do a much more thorough analysis of the payment history between the creditor and the debtor to see if the payment was in the ordinary course of business. Exhibit 9.4 may be helpful in analyzing the payment history to determine whether a transfer is potentially recoverable because it was outside the ordinary course of business and whether there are any new value defenses.

Procedure to Recover Preferences   Typically, the trustee will first send demand letters to those who have received preferences requesting that the preferences be repaid. Not only does this lessen litigation costs to the estate, most courts will allow the estate to collect interest from the transferee from the date of the demand. A sample demand letter is given as Exhibit 9.5.

An action to set aside a preference should be joined with an action under Section 550 to recover the transferred property or its value. Such an action is an adversary proceeding and, under Bankruptcy Rule 7001, commenced by the filing of a complaint. (See Exhibit 9.6.)

If the bankruptcy case was commenced prior to the effective date of the 1994 Amendments (October 22, 1994), under Section 546(a) of the Bankruptcy Code the trustee will have two years after his or her appointment to sue to set aside the preference unless the case is closed or dismissed before those two years are up. In a case commenced after the effective date of the 1994 Amendments, the trustee will have two years after the case was commenced (which in a Chapter 7 case may be a few days before the appointment unless the case is closed or dismissed earlier).

At trial on the preference lawsuit, the trustee has the burden of proving all of the elements of the transfer under Section 547(b) except insolvency which will

■ EXHIBIT 9.4
Analysis of Potential Preferential Transfers

Invoice Date	Invoice Number	Date Due*	Amount		Check Date	Check Number	Check Amount

*There may be two or more dates an invoice is due. The creditor may allow a discount of a certain percentage if the invoice is promptly paid. This discount is usually reflected by the shorthand "2/10, n/30", which translates to a two percent discount if the invoice is paid in ten days with the full amount ("net") amount due in thirty days. For preference purposes, the net date is the appropriate date to use.

be presumed although the presumption is rebuttable. The preference recipient has the burden of proving that one more of the exceptions applies.

Finally, a creditor who is forced to repay a preference to the estate will have a general unsecured claim for the amount repaid and will be entitled to share in the proceeds of the estate.

Statutory Liens

Statutory Liens
A lien arising under a state or federal statute solely due to specified circumstances or conditions.

Secret Liens
A lien, usually created by statute, the existence of which cannot be discovered through a search of the applicable public records.

Statutory liens are defined in Section 101(53) of the Bankruptcy Code to be liens created by a state or federal law concerning very specific circumstances or conditions or a lien arising on the nonpayment of rent because of a provision in a statute or in a lease. Some statutory liens are referred to as **secret liens** because they will not appear of record in the county recorder's or the secretary of state's office. A creditor trying to locate any evidence of the lien could not find it. An example of a statutory lien would be if state law provided that if an electrician did work on a house and was not paid for those services, without further act, the electrician would have a lien on the house. Statutory liens do not include security interests consensually granted. They also do not include liens arising from the enforcement of a judgment even though those liens may be provided for by a statute.

■ EXHIBIT 9.5
Sample Pleading

Mildred Pierce, Trustee
700 Flower Street
Los Angeles, California, 90001

December 1, 1995

Perfect Processing, Inc.
444 Main Street
San Francisco, CA 94041

Re: In re Videos by Joe, Inc.,
Case No. 95-00001-JF

Dear Sir or Madam:

The undersigned is the duly appointed, qualified, and acting Chapter 7 trustee in the above-referenced bankruptcy case that was commenced on October 1, 1995.

The debtor's records reflect that on or about September 1, 1995, you received a payment of $1,000.00 from the debtor on account of a preexisting debt that was overdue for payment. It is my opinion that this transfer constitutes an avoidable preference which I am entitled to avoid and recover pursuant to Sections 547 and 550 of the Bankruptcy Code.

I would like to resolve this matter without the need for litigation. Therefore, I request that you immediately send me the sum of $1,000.00. Alternatively, if you are of the opinion that the payment was not a preference, kindly immediately provide me with whatever information you have to support your assertion.

Very truly yours,

Mildred Pierce,
Trustee

Section 545 of the Bankruptcy Code states that the trustee may avoid a statutory lien to the extent that the lien becomes effective at the following times:

☐ At the commencement of the bankruptcy case or other insolvency proceeding.

☐ When a custodian is appointed.

☐ When the debtor becomes insolvent or fails to meet a particular financial standard.

☐ When another party levies on the debtor's property.

A statutory lien is also avoidable if a good faith purchaser of the property could buy the property free and clear of the lien. In addition, all liens for rent are avoidable.

Like postpetition transfers, statutory liens are avoided by the filing of a complaint and commencing of an adversary proceeding. Such a complaint is presented in Exhibit 9.7. The claim for relief to avoid the lien should be coupled with a claim under Section 550 of the Bankruptcy Code to recover the property transferred or its value.

The limitation period for bringing an action to avoid a statutory lien is in Section 546. As was true for preferences, if the bankruptcy case was commenced

MILDRED PIERCE
700 Flower Street
Los Angeles, California 90001

Trustee

UNITED STATES BANKRUPTCY COURT
WESTERN DISTRICT OF CALIFORNIA

In re	)	Case No. 95-00001-JF
	)	
VIDEOS BY JOE, INC.	)	Chapter 7
	)	
Debtor.	)	
	)	
Debtor's Address:	)	
18 Hollywood Drive	)	
Los Angeles, California 90001	)	
	)	
Debtor's Tax Id. No. 99-999899	)	
	)	
_____	)	
	)	Adv. No. 95-00004-JF
MILDRED PIERCE, TRUSTEE,	)	COMPLAINT:
	)	
Plaintiff,	)	(1) TO AVOID PREFERENTIAL
	)	TRANSFER; AND
v.	)	
	)	(2) TO RECOVER PROPERTY OR
PERFECT PROCESSING, INC.,	)	THE VALUE THEREOF
	)	
Defendant.	)	
	)	
_____	)	

Mildred Pierce (the "Trustee") complains and alleges as follows:

PARTIES

1. The Trustee is the duly appointed, qualified, and acting Chapter 7 trustee in the above-captioned bankruptcy case.

2. The Trustee is informed that Perfect Processing Inc. (the "Defendant"), is a California corporation organized and authorized to do business in the state of California.

JURISDICTION AND VENUE

3. This Court has jurisdiction over this action pursuant to 28 U.S.C. §§ 157 and 1334(a) and the Order of the Chief Judge of the United States District Court, Western District of California, referring bankruptcy cases and proceedings, entered on July 20, 1984. This adversary proceeding is a core matter pursuant to 28 U.S.C. § 157(b)(2)(F) and the Trustee consents to the entry of a final order or judgment by the Bankruptcy Court.

4. Venue properly resides in the United States Bankruptcy Court for the Western District of California pursuant to 28 U.S.C. § 1409 in that this adversary proceeding is related to *In re Videos by Joe, Inc.*, Case No. 95-00001-JF pending as a Chapter 7 case in the United States Bankruptcy Court for the Western District of California.

—continued

■ EXHIBIT 9.6
Sample Pleading—*Continued*

FACTUAL ALLEGATIONS

5. At all times relevant herein Defendant was a creditor of Debtor within the meaning of 11 U.S.C. § 547.

6. Debtor filed a petition for relief under Chapter 7 of Title 11 United States Code on October 1, 1995 (the "Petition").

7. Defendant received a transfer of monies from debtor in the amount of $5,000.00 (the "Transfer"):

(a) for or on account of antecedent debt;

(b) within ninety (90) days before the date of the filing of the Petition; and

(c) which enabled Defendant to receive more than Defendant would receive if:

(i) The case were a case under Chapter 7 of Title 11 of the United States Code;

(ii) the transfer had not been made; and

(iii) Defendant received payment of its debts to the extent provided by the provisions of Title 11 of the United States Code.

FIRST CLAIM FOR RELIEF
[11 U.S.C. § 547]

8. The Trustee hereby incorporates by reference the allegations contained in paragraphs 5 through 7 above.

9. The Trustee is entitled to avoid the Transfer pursuant to the provision of 11 U.S.C. § 547(b).

SECOND CLAIM FOR RELIEF
[11 U.S.C. § 550]

10. The Trustee hereby incorporates by reference the allegations contained in paragraphs 5 through 7, and 9 above.

11. The Trustee is entitled to recover the Transfer from Defendant pursuant to the provisions of 11 U.S.C. § 550.

WHEREFORE, the Trustee requests the Court enter judgment against Defendant as follows:

1. On the First Claim for Relief, that the Court avoid the Transfer.

2. On the Second Claim for Relief, that the Trustee have judgment against Defendant in the amount of $5,000.00 plus interest thereon from the date of demand;

3. On all Claims for Relief, for the Trustee's reasonable attorneys' fees and costs incurred in this action; and

4. For such other and further relief as the Court may deem just and proper.

MILDRED PIERCE
Trustee

---

prior to the effective date of the 1994 Amendments, the trustee will have two years after his or her appointment, or the time the case is closed or dismissed if that occurs first, to sue to set aside the statutory lien. In a case commenced after the effective date of the 1994 Amendments, the trustee will have two years after the case was commenced or until the case is closed or dismissed.

Fraudulent Transfers or Obligations

Under state law creditors are sometimes allowed to undo the debtor's transfers or debts if they were fraudulently made or incurred. A transfer or debt may be fraud-

Fraudulent Conveyances
The transfer of the debtor's property with an actual intent to defraud creditors or for less than reasonably equivalent value while the debtor was insolvent or became insolvent as a result.

■ EXHIBIT 9.7
Sample Pleading

MILDRED PIERCE
700 Flower Street
Los Angeles, California, 90001

Trustee

UNITED STATES BANKRUPTCY COURT
WESTERN DISTRICT OF CALIFORNIA

In re)	Case No. 95-00001-JF
)	
VIDEOS BY JOE, INC.,)	Chapter 7
)	
Debtor.)	
)	
Debtor's Address:)	
18 Hollywood Drive)	
Los Angeles, California 90001)	
)	
Debtor's Tax Id. No. 99-999899)	
)	
————————————————————)	
)	Adv. No. 95-00005-JF
MILDRED PIERCE, TRUSTEE,)	COMPLAINT TO:
)	
Plaintiff,)	(1) AVOID STATUTORY LIEN; AND
)	
v.)	(2) RECOVER PROPERTY OR ITS
)	VALUE
LLOYD PROPERTIES,)	
)	
Defendant.)	
)	
————————————————————)	

Mildred Pierce (the "Trustee") complains and alleges as follows:

THE PARTIES

1. The Trustee is the duly appointed, qualified, and acting Chapter 7 trustee in the above-captioned case.

2. The Trustee is informed that Lloyd Properties ("Landlord") is a corporation organized and doing business under the laws of the state of California.

JURISDICTION AND VENUE

3. This action to avoid a statutory lien and recover property or its value is an adversary proceeding over which this Court has jurisdiction pursuant to 28 U.S.C. §§ 157 and 1334 and the Order of the Chief Judge of the United States District Court, Western District of California, referring bankruptcy cases and proceedings, entered on July 20, 1984. This adversary proceeding is a core matter pursuant to 28 U.S.C. § 157(b)(2)(E) and the Trustee consents to the entry of a final order or judgment by the Bankruptcy Court.

4. Venue over this adversary proceeding properly resides in the Western District of California pursuant to 28 U.S.C. § 1409(a) in that this adversary proceeding is related to *In re Videos by Joe, Inc.*, Case No. 95-00001-JF pending as a Chapter 7 case in the United States Bankruptcy Court for the Western District of California.

—continued

FACTUAL ALLEGATIONS

5. Debtor leased from Landlord improved real property located at 18 Hollywood Boulevard, Los Angeles, California (the "Premises").

6. At the time of the commencement of Debtor's bankruptcy case, Debtor was indebted to Landlord for the sum of $5,000.00 on account of Debtor's lease of the Premises (the "Debt").

7. At the time of the commencement of the Debtor's bankruptcy case, the Debtor owned five (5) Sony Model 111N Video Cameras which were stored in the Premises (the "Cameras").

8. The Cameras are property of the estate with a value of $5,000.00.

9. Pursuant to the laws of the state of California codified in Civil Code Section 3406.47, a statutory lien in the Cameras is asserted by Landlord to secure repayment of the Debt.

10. Despite demand, Landlord has refused to deliver the Cameras to the Trustee.

FIRST CLAIM FOR RELIEF
[11 U.S.C. § 545]

11. The Trustee incorporates by this reference the allegations contained in paragraphs 5 through 9 above.

12. The Trustee is entitled to avoid the lien asserted by Landlord pursuant to 11 U.S.C. § 545.

SECOND CLAIM FOR RELIEF
[11 U.S.C. § 550]

13. The Trustee incorporates by this reference the allegations contained in paragraphs 5 through 9 and 12 above.

14. The Trustee is entitled to recover the Cameras or their value from Landlord pursuant to 11 U.S.C. § 550.

WHEREFORE, the Trustee requests that this Court enter judgment against Landlord as follows:

1. On the First Claim for Relief, that the Court void the lien on the Cameras asserted by Landlord;

2. On the Second Claim for Relief, that the Trustee have judgment against Landlord in the amount of $5,000.00 plus interest thereon or that Landlord immediately surrender the Cameras to the Trustee;

3. On all Claims for Relief, for the Trustee's reasonable attorneys' fees; and

4. For such other and further relief as the Court deems just and proper.

_____

MILDRED PIERCE
Trustee

---

ulent because it was intentionally made to prevent creditors from being paid, which is actual fraud, or because the debtor received less than the property was worth, which is constructive fraud.

This right of creditors is continued in the Bankruptcy Code but is given to the trustee as a representative of all the creditors. It is yet another way for the trustee to increase the size of the estate (or decrease the amount of claims) and maximize the distribution to creditors. The Bankruptcy Code has two sections that give fraudulent transfer or debt avoidance rights to trustees: Section 544(b) and Section 548.

Section 544(b) permits the trustee to avoid a transfer of property or the incurrence of a debt by the debtor if it is voidable under applicable nonbankruptcy law by an unsecured creditor with an allowable claim. In other words, if the state

or other federal law would allow a creditor to undo a transfer or the incurring of an obligation, the trustee may step into the shoes of that creditor. But there must actually be an unsecured creditor who could otherwise sue. This is rarely a problem since all that is needed is a creditor who was owed money at the time of the transfer or the incurring of the debt. Even if that is not possible because all those creditors were subsequently paid, some state fraudulent conveyance laws grant standing to creditors who became creditors after the transfer.

Section 548 is the Bankruptcy Code's own fraudulent transfer or obligation law. It allows the trustee to recover property that was fraudulently transferred and to disallow obligations that were fraudulently incurred within one year before the filing of the petition. There are two types of transfers or debts that can be set aside under Section 548.

The first type of transfer or obligation avoidable under Section 548 is those in which there was an actual intent to hinder, delay, or defraud an existing or future creditor. An example would be a doctor transferring all personal assets to a professional corporation to prevent judgment creditors from levying on those assets. If the doctor's motivation can be proved, the transfer can be undone as a transfer made with the intent to defraud creditors. It is rare for actual intent to be proved since the transferor is usually unwilling to admit that intent. Sometimes the court will infer actual fraud if the circumstances indicate that there could be no other motivation.

The second type of avoidable transfer or obligation under Section 548 does not require any bad intent. It merely requires that the debtor received less than reasonably equivalent value in exchange for the transfer or obligation and one of the following:

☐ The debtor was insolvent when the transfer was made or the obligation was incurred or became so as a result of the transfer or obligation.

☐ The transfer or obligation left the debtor with an unreasonably small amount of money to run its business or financial transactions.

☐ The debtor intended to incur or believed it would incur debts beyond its ability to pay.

Obviously, proving that reasonably equivalent value did not change hands is very important. Value is defined in Section 548(d)(2) as property or the satisfaction or securing of a debt. It does not include an unperformed promise to furnish support to the debtor or to a relative of the debtor. Thus, if a debtor transferred all of his assets to a nursing home in exchange for the nursing home's pledge to support his mother when she became infirm, no value was given to the debtor and the transaction could be set aside. The Bankruptcy Code is silent as to what exactly constitutes reasonably equivalent value preferring instead to let the court make that determination in each case.

The trustee may use Section 548 only when the transfer was made or the obligation was incurred within the year preceding the commencement of the bankruptcy case. If it took place earlier, only a Section 544(b) action is available.

As is true for other avoiding power actions, a suit to avoid a fraudulent transfer that is not a lien or a fraudulent debt is typically joined with an action to recover the property or its value under Section 550 and is commenced by the filing of a complaint. If the trustee is trying to avoid a lien or a debt under Section 544(b) or 548 it is not necessary to include a claim to recover property or its value. The parties must follow the rules governing adversary proceedings in the 7000 series of the Bankruptcy Rules.

The deadline for bringing a fraudulent conveyance action under either Section 544(a) or Section 548 by the trustee will either be two years after the trustee was appointed (in a case commenced prior to the enactment of the 1994 Amendments) or two years after the case was commenced (in a case commenced after the enactment of the 1994 Amendments). In either event, if the case is closed or dismissed prior to the two year period, that will be the deadline.

Other Avoiding Powers

Suits to avoid preferences, statutory liens, and fraudulent conveyances are not the only tools a trustee has to bring property into the estate. Section 544(a) gives a trustee three other ways to maximize the estate by avoiding transactions. It does so by giving the trustee the status of three different types of creditors. These creditors are hypothetical. Unlike the creditor needed under Section 544(b), the creditors need not actually exist for the trustee to exercise their rights. Section 544(a) is sometimes known as the "strong arm clause" and it brings into play many of the provisions of the Uniform Commercial Code and state real property law discussed in Chapter 4 of this book.

The first status given to the trustee in Section 544(a) is that of a creditor who extended credit to the debtor when the case was commenced and who received at that time a judicial lien on all property. Under this provision, if there are any unperfected secured creditors their security interest will be subordinate to the trustee's hypothetical judicial lien.

The second type of creditor is one who extended credit to the debtor when the case commenced and who obtained at that time an execution that was returned unsatisfied. Some states may provide certain remedies to creditors in those circumstances that are not available to the holder of a judicial lien. If so, the trustee would be able to take advantage of those remedies.

Finally, the trustee is given the status of a buyer of real property from the debtor that purchased the property when the case was commenced. If there is any interest a buyer of real property would take free and clear of under applicable state or federal law, such as an unrecorded mortgage or an easement, the trustee will also take free and clear of that interest. Remember that the trustee's status in these situations is hypothetical. The trustee's actual knowledge is immaterial. If the trustee knows of the mortgage or easement, the trustee may still use the strong arm clause to avoid the interest because a hypothetical buyer could.

If the trustee can take advantage of any of these hypothetical statuses to increase the extent of property of the estate, the correct procedure is to commence an adversary proceeding by filing a complaint. (See Exhibit 9.8). The deadline for bringing an action under the strong arm powers of Section 544(a) is identical to the limitation for preferences, statutory liens, and fraudulent conveyances.

☐ LIQUIDATING THE ESTATE

Abandonment

After all of the property of the estate has been gathered into the trustee's control, the trustee will need to liquidate it to cash. Yet not all property of the estate will have value and sometimes the cost of preserving and selling an asset will be more than the asset is worth. In situations where the property is burdensome or is of inconsequential value to the estate, Bankruptcy Code Section 554(a) authorizes the trustee to abandon the property. **Abandonment** is common when the property

Abandonment
The release by the bankruptcy trustee of the estate's rights in property.

■ EXHIBIT 9.8
Sample Pleading

MILDRED PIERCE
700 Flower Street
Los Angeles, California 90001

Trustee

UNITED STATES BANKRUPTCY COURT
WESTERN DISTRICT OF CALIFORNIA

In re	)	Case No. 95-00001-JF
	)	
VIDEOS BY JOE, INC.,	)	Chapter 7
	)	
Debtor.	)	
	)	
Debtor's Address:	)	
18 Hollywood Drive	)	
Los Angeles, California 90001	)	
	)	
Debtor's Tax Id. No. 99-999899	)	
	)	
_____	)	
	)	
MILDRED PIERCE, TRUSTEE,	)	Adv. No. 95-00006-JF
	)	
Plaintiff,	)	COMPLAINT TO AVOID
	)	UNPERFECTED SECURITY INTEREST
v.	)	
	)	
FIRST CITY BANK,	)	
	)	
Defendant.	)	
	)	
_____	)	

Mildred Pierce (the "Trustee") complains and alleges as follows:

PARTIES

1. The Trustee is the duly appointed, qualified, and acting Chapter 7 trustee in the above-captioned bankruptcy case.

2. The Trustee is informed that First City Bank is a financial institution chartered and doing business in the state of California (the "Bank").

JURISDICTION AND VENUE

3. This Court has jurisdiction over this action to avoid an unperfected security interest pursuant to 28 U.S.C. § 157 and 1334(a) and the Order of the Chief Judge of the United States District Court, Western District of California, referring bankruptcy cases and proceedings, entered on July 20, 1984. This adversary proceeding is a core matter pursuant to 28 U.S.C. § 157(b)(2)(K) and the Trustee consents to the entry of a final order or judgment by the Bankruptcy Court.

4. Venue properly resides in the United States Bankruptcy Court for the Western District of California pursuant to 28 U.S.C. § 1409 in that this adversary proceeding is related to *In re Videos by Joe, Inc.*, Case No. 95-00001-JF pending as a Chapter 7 case in the United States Bankruptcy Court for the Western District of California.

—continued

■ EXHIBIT 9.8
Sample Pleading—*Continued*

FACTUAL ALLEGATIONS AND CLAIM FOR RELIEF

5. Prior to the commencement of Debtor's bankruptcy case, Debtor executed and delivered to the Bank a written security agreement whereby Debtor granted a security interest in all of Debtor's inventory to the Bank (the "Security Interest").

6. The Bank did not perfect the Security Interest.

7. The Trustee is entitled to avoid the Security Interest pursuant to the provisions of 11 U.S.C. § 544(a)(1).

WHEREFORE, the Trustee requests that the Court enter judgment against the Bank as follows:

1. Avoiding the Security Interest;

2. For the Trustee's reasonable attorneys' fees and costs incurred in this action; and

3. For such other and further relief the Court may deem just and proper.

_____

MILDRED PIERCE
Trustee

---

has more liens against it than it is worth or the costs of sale would eat up what little equity there may be.

Abandonment may happen by a bankruptcy court order or through neglect. Section 554(c) provides that if the trustee does not affirmatively abandon property, and it is not otherwise administered during the course of the case, it will be deemed abandoned when the case is closed if it was listed in the debtor's schedule of assets. Nonscheduled property will remain property of the estate and will not be deemed abandoned.

Court authorization for the abandonment of property may be obtained on the trustee's notice or on the motion of a party interest. The procedure for both is found in Bankruptcy Rule 6007. Bankruptcy Rule 6007(a) provides that the trustee must give notice of a proposed abandonment or other disposition of property to all creditors, indenture trustees, and any committees in the case. (See Exhibit 9.9.) They then have fifteen days after the mailing of the notice to file and serve an objection. A party might object if it believes the property has value and should be liquidated for the benefit of the creditors. Alternatively, a party in interest might believe that the property is unsafe and should be dealt with rather than abandoned to a debtor who may not be around. If an objection is made, the trustee or the objecting party must set a hearing and give notice of the hearing to the other party. If no objection is filed and served, no hearing need be held, no order authorizing the abandonment will be required, and there will be no inquiry as to the propriety of the abandonment.

Bankruptcy Rule 6007(b) briefly discusses a motion to compel abandonment. It merely states that a party in interest may file and serve a motion requiring the trustee to abandon property and the court shall set a hearing on notice to such entities as it shall direct. Assuming the motion is granted, the order will compel the trustee to abandon the property. The abandonment is not automatic and the trustee will still have to send out the required notice.

If property is abandoned it is released to whomever is entitled to it. All liens and other interests remain attached to the property. For example, if the trustee

■ EXHIBIT 9.9
Sample Pleading

MILDRED PIERCE
700 Flower Street
Los Angeles, California 90001

Trustee

UNITED STATES BANKRUPTCY COURT
WESTERN DISTRICT OF CALIFORNIA

In re	)	Case No. 95-00001-JF
	)	
VIDEOS BY JOE, INC.,	)	Chapter 7
	)	
Debtor.	)	
	)	
Debtor's Address:	)	NOTICE OF INTENT TO ABANDON
18 Hollywood Drive	)	PROPERTY
Los Angeles, California 90001	)	
	)	
Debtor's Tax Id. No. 99-999899	)	
	)	
	)	
_____	)	

TO THE DEBTOR, CREDITORS, AND OTHER PARTIES IN INTEREST:

NOTICE IS HEREBY GIVEN that pursuant to 11 U.S.C. § 554(a), Mildred Pierce, the duly appointed, qualified, and acting Chapter 7 trustee in the above-captioned estate (the "Trustee"), intends to and will abandon all uncollected accounts receivable of the debtor as burdensome and of inconsequential value to the estate unless, within fifteen (15) days from the date of service of this Notice, a party in interest files a written objection and request for hearing with the Bankruptcy Court and serves a copy of such objection on the Trustee and the United States Trustee. Any objection not timely filed and served may be deemed waived.

DATED: December 1, 1995

_____
MILDRED PIERCE
Trustee

abandoned the debtor's residence, the debtor would be revested with possession and ownership. If the house was subject to a mortgage, the debtor's rights in the house would be still subject to that mortgage and if the mortgagee obtained relief from the automatic stay, it could foreclose.

Sale of Assets

In General As soon as possible, the trustee will begin liquidating property of the estate. The trustee may negotiate a sale for all the assets to one purchaser, may sell the property piecemeal to a number of different buyers, or may hold an auction. If the trustee requires their assistance to complete any of these types of sales, the trustee will seek bankruptcy court authority to employ attorneys, brokers, auctioneers, and other professionals as discussed later in this chapter.

Section 363(b) of the Bankruptcy Code governs sales of property of the estate in and out of the ordinary course of business. Unless the trustee is operating the debtor's business pursuant to a court order, all sales in a Chapter 7 case are out of the ordinary course of business. Section 363(b) authorizes the trustee to sell property of the estate out of the ordinary course of business after notice and a hearing. Bankruptcy Rule 6004(a) is more informative and it dictates that twenty days' notice of a proposed sale must be given to the debtor, all creditors, any committee, and all indenture trustees.

The contents of the notice are described in Bankruptcy Rule 2002(c)(1). The notice must have the time and place of any public sale, the terms and conditions of any private sale, and the time fixed for filing objections. It must also describe the property to be sold although it is sufficient if it does so generally. (See Exhibit 9.10.) If a camera is to be sold, the make and model will suffice without reference to the serial number. A notice of an intended sale of real property need not contain the legal description.

A party in interest may oppose the sale for any legitimate reason including that the purchase price is inadequate. Any objection to the proposed sale must be filed and served not less than five business days before the date set for the proposed action. Bankruptcy Rule 6004(b) states that an objection is governed by Bankruptcy Rule 9014, which means that it is a contested matter. If there is no objection, the court is deemed to have authorized the sale and no separate order is required.

If an objection is made, Bankruptcy Rule 6004(e) provides that the date of the hearing may be set out in the original notice of the intended sale. Yet, since no hearing is required if there is no objection, it would be unusual for the notice to set the hearing on an objection that has not yet been made. The more common method of providing notice of a hearing on the objection is for the objecting party to obtain a date and time from the court and state it on the objection.

If all of the nonexempt property of the estate has a value of less than $2,500, the trustee may merely give a general notice of intent to sell such property without having any offers or auction dates chosen. The notice must still be provided to all creditors. Any objection must be filed and served by a party in interest within fifteen days of the mailing of the notice.

Conduct of the Sales Pursuant to Bankruptcy Rule 6004(f), unless it is impracticable, an itemized statement of the property sold, the name of each purchaser, and the price received must be filed with the clerk of the bankruptcy court. If the property is sold by an auctioneer, the auctioneer must file the statement and furnish a copy to the trustee.

Sales Free and Clear Commonly, property of the estate will be subject to liens or security interests. The trustee may want to sell the property free and clear of those liens and security interests because buyers typically pay a higher price for unencumbered property. Section 363(f) allows the trustee to sell property free and clear only if one of the following is true:

☐ Applicable nonbankruptcy law allows it.

☐ The lien holder consents to a sale free and clear of its interests, which it might do if its lien will attach to the proceeds of the sale. Any such consent should be in writing.

☐ The purchase price is greater than the amount of all the liens.

■ EXHIBIT 9.10
Sample Pleading

MILDRED PIERCE
700 Flower Street
Los Angeles, California 90001

Trustee

UNITED STATES BANKRUPTCY COURT
WESTERN DISTRICT OF CALIFORNIA

In re)	Case No. 95-00001-JF
)	
VIDEOS BY JOE, INC.,)	Chapter 7
)	
Debtor.)	
)	
Debtor's Address:)	NOTICE OF INTENT TO SELL REAL
18 Hollywood Drive)	PROPERTY
Los Angeles, California 90001)	
)	
Debtor's Tax Id. No. 99-999899)	
)	
)	

TO THE DEBTOR, CREDITORS, AND OTHER PARTIES IN INTEREST:

NOTICE IS HEREBY GIVEN that Mildred Pierce, the duly appointed, qualified, and acting trustee in the above-captioned case (the "Trustee") intends to sell to Bountiful Buyer all the estate's right, title, and interest in and to improved real property commonly known as 18 Hollywood Drive, Los Angeles, California (the "Property") on or after January 1, 1996.

NOTICE IS FURTHER GIVEN that the purchase price for the Property is $100,000.00 to be paid at closing in cash or certified funds (the "Purchase Price"). The Trustee has reserved the right to accept offers for the Property received prior to January 1, 1996 in excess of the Purchase Price.

NOTICE IS FINALLY GIVEN that any objection to the sale of the Property for the Purchase Price must be in writing, filed with the Bankruptcy Court, and served on the Trustee and the United States Trustee no later than December 22, 1995. Any objection not timely filed and served may be deemed waived.

DATED: December 1, 1995

_____
MILDRED PIERCE
Trustee

☐ There is a bona fide dispute about the lien. For example, the trustee might allege that the granting of the lien was a preference.

☐ The lien holder could be compelled by law to accept a money satisfaction of its claim.

The procedure to sell free and clear of liens is provided in Bankruptcy Rule 6004(c), which states that a motion must be filed for authority to sell free and clear and it must be served on the parties who have liens or other interests in the property to be sold. As a practical matter, the motion for authority to sell free and clear (see Exhibit 9.11) will be noticed with the intent to sell (see Exhibit 9.10)

■ EXHIBIT 9.11
Sample Pleading

MILDRED PIERCE
700 Flower Street
Los Angeles, California 90001

Trustee

UNITED STATES BANKRUPTCY COURT
WESTERN DISTRICT OF CALIFORNIA

In re	)	Case No. 95-00001-JF
	)	
VIDEOS BY JOE, INC.,	)	Chapter 7
	)	
Debtor.	)	
	)	
Debtor's Address:	)	MOTION TO SELL PROPERTY FREE
18 Hollywood Drive	)	AND CLEAR OF LIENS
Los Angeles, California 90001	)	
	)	
Debtor's Tax Id. No. 99-999899	)	
	)	

TO THE HONORABLE JUSTIN FAIR, UNITED STATES BANKRUPTCY JUDGE:

Mildred Pierce, the duly appointed, qualified, and acting trustee in the above-captioned case (the "Trustee"), for and in support of her Motion to Sell Property Free and Clear of Liens, respectfully represents as follows:

1. Among the assets of the estate is certain improved real property commonly known as 18 Hollywood Drive, Los Angeles, California (the "Property").

2. The Trustee is informed that the Property is subject to the following encumbrances:

(a) A lien in favor of the County of Los Angeles for 1995 real property taxes (the "Tax Lien").

(b) A mortgage in favor of First City Bank securing a promissory note with a remaining principal balance of $80,000.00 (the "First Lien").

(c) A mortgage in favor of B & B Finance Company securing an obligation of $20,000.00 (the "Second Lien").

(d) A judgment lien in favor of Perfect Processing, Inc. securing a judgment in the amount of $5,000.00 (the "Third Lien").

3. The Trustee has negotiated a sale of the Property free and clear of the First Lien, the Second Lien, and the Third Lien, and all other encumbrances other than the Tax Lien, to Bountiful Buyer for a purchase price of $100,000.00 to be paid in cash at closing (the "Sale"). Bountiful Buyer has agreed to purchase the Property subject to the Tax Lien. The Trustee is of the opinion that the sale of the Property to Bountiful Buyer is for terms that are fair and reasonable and the best that may be obtained under the circumstances.

4. The Trustee requests that this Court authorize the sale free and clear of the First Lien, the Second Lien, and the Third Lien pursuant to 11 U.S.C. § 363(f) on the following bases:

(a) The Second Lien is in bona fide dispute in that the Second Lien is not of record and may be avoided by the Trustee pursuant to 11 U.S.C. § 544(a)(3). The Trustee has filed her Complaint to Avoid Lien against B & B Finance Company concurrently with this Motion.

(b) The Third Lien attached within ninety days prior to the filing of the petition that commenced the above-captioned case and meets all the other elements of a preference and may be avoided by the Trustee pursuant to 11 U.S.C. § 547. The Trustee has filed her Complaint to Avoid Preference against Perfect Processing, Inc. concurrently with this Motion.

—continued

■ EXHIBIT 9.11
Sample Pleading—*Continued*

(c) First City Bank has consented to the Sale provided the First Lien attaches to the proceeds of the Sale in the same extent, priority, and validity as it attached to the Property.

WHEREFORE, the Trustee requests that the Court enter its Order authorizing the Sale free and clear of the First Lien, the Second Lien, and the Third Lien with only the First Lien to attach to the proceeds of the Sale.

DATED: December 1, 1995

MILDRED PIERCE
Trustee

---

and served on all creditors. All secured creditors have a right to bid at any auction sale of their collateral pursuant to Section 363(c). They may deduct from the purchase price the amount of their claim and merely pay the balance to the trustee.

Sale of Co-owner's Interest   Often the debtor owns property with another who is not a debtor in a bankruptcy case. The debtor may be a tenant in common or a joint tenant. The trustee can sell just the debtor's interests but there may not be a market for a one-half interest in a piece of property. For that reason, in certain limited circumstances, Section 363(h) of the Bankruptcy Code authorizes the trustee to sell the entire property, including the nondebtor's interest, even if the nondebtor owner objects. The circumstances under which this may occur are as follows:

☐ Partition of the property among the various co-owners is impracticable.

☐ The sale of the debtor's interest alone would yield substantially less than the proceeds due to that interest after a sale of the entire property.

☐ The benefit to the estate outweighs any detriment to the co-owners.

☐ The property is not being used for public utility purposes.

All four of these elements must be shown.

Co-owners are not without their remedies if the trustee seeks to sell their interest in property over their objection. Not only can they dispute that the trustee has met all of the elements of Section 363(h), they also have certain explicit protections. For example, the co-owner has a right of first refusal. If the trustee has negotiated a sale of the property to a third party, the co-owner has a right to buy the property for the same consideration. If the co-owner opts to buy the property itself, it can credit bid in the value of its share and pay to the trustee only the value of the debtor's share. The co-owner will also not have to pay from its share any of the trustee's compensation although it is liable for a share of the sale costs and expenses.

Unlike ordinary sales or sales free and clear of lien interests, authority to sell a co-owner's interest requires the filing of a complaint and the commencement of an adversary proceeding under the 7000 series of the Bankruptcy Rules.

Financing the Liquidation

In General   While performing Section 704 duties, the trustee will incur expenses. There will be costs for appraisers, security, rent, utilities, accountants and attor-

neys, and numerous other items that are necessary to maximize the value of the assets and the return to creditors. If the estate has a lot of cash, the trustee will be able to satisfy the estate's obligations as they are incurred or allowed by the court. Yet, rarely will the trustee initially have enough cash to pay those expenses. To meet the shortfall until property is sold, Section 364(b) allows the trustee to incur unsecured debt and borrow funds out of the ordinary course of business provided there is prior court approval. Despite the fact that they would be entitled to an administrative expense priority for repayment, however, not many creditors are willing to extend credit or otherwise lend money on an unsecured basis to a bankruptcy estate.

Recognizing the problems trustees would have in obtaining unsecured credit, the Bankruptcy Code allows the trustee to use two different methods to attempt to obtain the cash required to finance a liquidation. The first method is the use of a secured creditor's **cash collateral.** The second method allows the trustee to obtain new financing by borrowing funds on a secured or on a super priority unsecured basis.

Cash Collateral   The term cash collateral is used frequently in the Bankruptcy Code. It is defined in Section 363(a) to be "cash, negotiable instruments, documents of title, securities, deposit accounts or other cash equivalents whenever acquired in which the estate and an entity other than the estate have an interest." Cash collateral also includes the proceeds of property subject to a security interest. If a creditor has a lien on the debtor's accounts receivable, the cash or checks that are the proceeds of the accounts are cash collateral. If a creditor has a lien on the debtor's bank account, the contents of that account are cash collateral.

The Bankruptcy Code states that the trustee cannot use cash collateral unless the other party with an interest in the cash collateral consents or unless the court, after notice and a hearing, authorizes its use. If a secured creditor has a lien on the debtor's accounts receivable, as the payments come in, the trustee will not be able to use any of those payments to pay expenses unless the secured creditor first authorizes the cash collateral to be used or until the court gives its authorization. Pending the authorization, the trustee must put the cash collateral in a separate account and must provide an accounting. This prohibition against use applies even if the secured creditor allowed the debtor to use all or a portion of the proceeds before the case was commenced.

If the secured creditor and the trustee come to an agreement allowing the use of cash collateral, the agreement must be reduced to writing. Bankruptcy Rule 4001(d) provides that a notice and a motion for approval of such a written agreement must be served on the debtor and whomever the court directs. A copy of the agreement must accompany the motion. Sample Pleadings involving cash collateral agreements for debtors in possession that can be readily adapted for trustees are found in Chapter 11 of this book.

If any party in interest objects to the agreement between the trustee and the secured creditor, that party must file and serve an objection within fifteen days of the date of the notice. If no objection is filed, the court can approve or disapprove of the agreement without a hearing. If there is an objection or if the court wants to hold a hearing, the hearing will be held. The debtor, the objecting party, those who received the motion, and anyone else the court requires must receive at least five days' notice of the hearing.

If an agreement cannot be reached, the trustee will have to make a motion for authority to use cash collateral. Bankruptcy Rule 4001(b) provides that such a

Cash Collateral
Property of the estate that is cash, negotiable instruments, deposit accounts, and other cash equivalents in which a creditor has an interest.

motion must be served on any creditor that has an interest in the cash collateral, the debtor, and any other person the court may direct. The hearing must be held no earlier than fifteen days after the motion is served. If the trustee has an immediate need for the use of cash collateral, the court can hold a preliminary hearing before the expiration of the fifteen-day period but may authorize the use of only that amount of cash collateral as is necessary to avoid immediate and irreparable harm to the estate pending the hearing on full notice.

At any contested hearing concerning cash collateral use, the trustee will have the burden of showing that he or she should be allowed to use the secured creditor's cash collateral because the creditor is adequately protected or, in other words, that the estate's use of cash collateral will not harm the creditor. Section 361 establishes three nonexclusive means by which adequate protection may be provided, including:

1. periodic payments to the secured creditor to compensate for any cash collateral used;

2. additional collateral; and

3. any other method that gives the creditor the equivalent of the cash collateral used.

Equity Cushion
The excess of the value of property over the claims secured by that property.

For example, the trustee may argue that in consideration for the use of the proceeds of the accounts receivable he or she will grant the secured creditor a lien on all new accounts created. Alternatively, the trustee may argue that the **equity cushion,** the difference between the value of the collateral and the amount of the loan, is so large that it alone is sufficient to provide adequate protection. Whether the facts and the trustee's offer point to adequate protection will be for the court to decide.

Section 364 Financing In some cases the trustee will need more than cash collateral use alone. In such instances the trustee will need to borrow new funds rather than only use cash collateral as it comes in.

As mentioned, the trustee may borrow funds on an unsecured basis in the ordinary course of business without notice, a hearing, or a court order. Section 364(b) also authorizes the trustee to borrow funds on an unsecured basis other than in the ordinary course of business with repayment entitled to an administrative expense priority. The trustee, however, must first obtain an order allowing the loan. Bankruptcy Rule 4001(c) governs the procedure for obtaining an order authorizing borrowing. It is virtually identical to Bankruptcy Rule 4001(b), which concerns motions for orders authorizing the use of cash collateral.

Typically, despite the ability to be repaid as an administrative expense claimant, most lenders will not be willing to make new funds available on this basis because they will share pro rata with all other Chapter 7 administrative claims if there are not enough funds to pay all administrative claims in full. Section 364(c) provides that if the trustee is unable to obtain credit otherwise, he or she may incur debt with priority over all other administrative expenses (which gives the creditor a super priority claim), secured by a lien on property of the estate that is not otherwise subject to a lien, or secured by a junior lien on property that is already subject to a lien. For example, the creditor might agree to lend the trustee $10,000 to pay immediate expenses secured by a second in priority mortgage on the debtor's office building.

In the event that even those protections for a lender are insufficient, the trustee may obtain financing secured by a senior or equal lien on property of the estate

that is already encumbered. In the example just given, the creditor's lien on the office building would be first in priority and the existing mortgage holder will drop down to a second priority position. This is typically referred to as a **priming lien.** It is available only if the trustee can prove that sufficient funds are not otherwise available and the creditor with the former priority lien is adequately protected.

Unlike cash collateral use, financing cannot be compelled by the court. The lender can only make funds available to the trustee voluntarily. As a result, lenders often request substantial protections as the price of their cooperation. Among the terms they may insist on in any agreement for Section 364 financing other than a super priority claim and a lien on all the assets of the estate are:

□ An acknowledgment of the validity, perfection, and enforceability of any prepetition claim and liens.

□ A ruling that the prepetition loans are secured by the liens obtained for the postpetition financing and the postpetition loans are secured by the prepetition liens. This is known as **cross-collateralization.**

□ A prohibition against any equal or senior liens or a surcharge for the costs of administration of the Chapter 7 case.

□ A lifting of the automatic stay to allow the secured creditor to exercise its rights and remedies in the event of default and to setoff all proceeds received against the debt.

□ A provision that the new liens and security interests are perfected without further act.

Bankruptcy Rules 4001(c) and (d) deal with the notice and procedure for obtaining court approval of secured debt financing. The procedure is exactly the same as it is to obtain approval of cash collateral use.

Surcharge The trustee may take advantage of two other sections of the Bankruptcy Code to find the funds needed to pay the estate's expenses. The first is Section 506(c) which states that the trustee may recover from property securing an allowed claim the reasonable, necessary cost of preserving or disposing of such property to the extent of any benefit to the creditor. This ability to recover the expenses from the property is commonly known as **surcharge.**

Section 506(c) is very controversial and the courts seem to be having difficulty in determining what is reasonable and necessary, what constitutes preservation or disposal, and how benefit is measured. Section 506(c) will usually be invoked only if the Chapter 7 estate is insolvent, which means that the trustee incurred more in expenses than he or she received in proceeds from the liquidation of all of the unencumbered assets. In those situations, the secured creditor probably was not paid in full from the sale of its collateral. Predictably, when a secured creditor has suffered a deficiency, it will not want to voluntarily pay over money to the trustee so that administrative creditors can be paid. As a result, surcharge actions are almost always hotly contested.

One example of when surcharge might be allowed would be where the trustee conducted an auction of the debtor's printing press, which was a large piece of machinery occupying a substantial portion of the debtor's premises. The trustee hired the auctioneer, paid for the advertising and, during the period before the auction, paid for rent, guard service, utilities, and a worker to lubricate the press once a day to keep it from becoming unusable. During this time the secured creditor knew of the trustee's efforts and made no effort to obtain relief from the

Priming Lien
A new lien that is made senior in priority to existing liens.

Cross Collateralization
The securing of prepetition claims with assets acquired postpetition or the securing of postpetition claims with prepetition assets.

Surcharge
The payment of administrative expenses from the proceeds of collateral because the expenses benefited the secured party.

automatic stay. Assuming the expenses were reasonable, the court might well allow the surcharge and force the secured creditor to pay the trustee's expenses from the auction proceeds. The trustee's expenses are the same ones the secured creditor would have to pay if it sold its collateral and its benefit is directly related to the trustee's costs. In addition, it could be argued that the secured creditor agreed to pay the expenses since it knew that the trustee was incurring them and it made no effort to obtain the right to conduct its own liquidation.

Another section the trustee may be able to use is Section 552(b) which provides that if the creditor had a prepetition security agreement that granted it a lien in particular collateral and the proceeds of that collateral, the commencement of the bankruptcy case will not interfere with its lien in the proceeds unless the court orders otherwise based on the equities of the case. Using the example just given, the trustee could argue that because it incurred all those expenses that served the interest of the secured creditor, equity dictates that the creditor's lien not extend to the proceeds of the sale to the extent of the trustee's costs.

Surcharge actions under Section 506(c) and actions under Section 552(b) are adversary proceedings controlled by the 7000 series of the Bankruptcy Rules and are commenced by the filing of a complaint (see Exhibit 9.12).

☐ EMPLOYMENT AND COMPENSATION OF PROFESSIONALS

Employment of Professionals

In General   In a large case, or a case involving litigation, it will be difficult for a trustee to perform all the required duties without professional assistance. For this reason, Section 327 of the Bankruptcy Code provides that the trustee may employ attorneys, accountants, appraisers, auctioneers, or other professional persons to represent the trustee or assist in the duties listed in the Bankruptcy Code.

Conflicts of Interest   Whether a professional can accept employment from the trustee is subject to very strict rules in the Bankruptcy Code. Section 327(a) allows a person to be employed only if they "do not hold or represent an interest adverse to the estate, and are disinterested." A "disinterested person" is defined in Section 101(14). It excludes a creditor, an equity interest holder, and an insider. Accordingly, creditors, stockholders, and insiders are disqualified from representing the estate.

Bankruptcy Rule 5002 sets forth further restrictions. It prohibits the employment of a trustee or professional related to the bankruptcy judge approving the employment. It also provides that if the individual is ineligible for appointment, so is the individual's firm, partnership, corporation, and any other form of business association or relationship, and all members, associates, and professional employees thereof. If the case judge's daughter is a lawyer, the daughter and her entire law firm are disqualified from being employed at the expense of the estate. Even if the trustee, examiner, or professional is not a relative of the judge, Bankruptcy Rule 5002(b) prohibits the appointment or employment if the person is or has been so connected with the judge to render the appointment or employment improper. Typically, however, it is the judge who will disqualify himself or herself and have the case reassigned to a judge who is not related or closely connected to the professionals.

MILDRED PIERCE
700 Flower Street
Los Angeles, California 90001

Trustee

UNITED STATES BANKRUPTCY COURT
WESTERN DISTRICT OF CALIFORNIA

In re	)	Case No. 95-00001-JF
	)	
VIDEOS BY JOE, INC.,	)	Chapter 7
	)	
Debtor.	)	
	)	
Debtor's Address:	)	
18 Hollywood Drive	)	
Los Angeles, California 90001	)	
	)	
Debtor's Tax Id. No. 99-999899	)	
	)	
_____	)	
	)	
MILDRED PIERCE, TRUSTEE	)	Adv. No. 95-00007-JF
	)	
Plaintiff,	)	COMPLAINT FOR REIMBURSEMENT
	)	OF EXPENSES OF PRESERVING AND
v.	)	DISPOSING OF COLLATERAL
	)	
FIRST CITY BANK,	)	
	)	
Defendant,	)	
	)	
_____	)	

Mildred Pierce (the "Trustee"), complains and alleges as follows:

PARTIES

1. The Trustee is the duly appointed, qualified, and acting Chapter 7 trustee in the above-captioned case.

2. Defendant First City Bank (the "Bank"), is a creditor of debtor.

JURISDICTION AND VENUE

3. This action seeking reimbursement for the cost of preserving and disposing of collateral is an adversary proceeding over which this Court has jurisdiction pursuant to 28 U.S.C. §§ 157 and 1334 and the Order of the Chief Judge of the United States District Court, Western District of California, referring bankruptcy cases and proceedings, entered on July 20, 1984. This adversary proceeding is a core matter pursuant to 28 U.S.C. § 157(b)(2)(O) and the Trustee consents to the entry of a final order or judgment by the Bankruptcy Court.

4. Venue properly resides in the United States Bankruptcy Court for the Western District of California pursuant to 28 U.S.C. § 1409 in that this adversary proceeding is related to *In re Videos by Joe, Inc.*, Case No. 95-00001-JF pending as a Chapter 7 case in the United States Bankruptcy Court for the Western District of California.

—*continued*

FACTUAL STATEMENT AND CLAIM FOR RELIEF

5. Upon appointment, the Trustee took possession of certain machinery and equipment that was property of the estate (the "Equipment").

6. At the time the Trustee took possession of the Equipment it was located in a warehouse pursuant to a written lease agreement between the debtor and the landlord that had expired by its own terms prior to the commencement of the debtor's bankruptcy case.

7. The Trustee caused the Equipment to be moved to a storage facility where it remained until it was sold by the Trustee for the sum of $5,000.00.

8. In connection with the relocation and sale of the Equipment, the Trustee incurred the following expenses (the "Expenses"):

Moving	$250.00
Rent	$150.00
Advertising	$100.00
Total	$500.00

9. The Trustee determined that the Equipment was subject to a perfected security interest in favor of the Bank to secure an indebtedness of $10,000.00. All proceeds from the sale of the Equipment were turned over to the Bank by the Trustee.

10. Despite demand by the Trustee, the Bank has refused to reimburse the Trustee for the Expenses.

11. The Trustee is entitled to recover the Expenses from the Equipment pursuant to 11 U.S.C. § 506(c).

WHEREFORE, the Trustee requests that the Court enter judgment in favor of the Trustee and against the Bank in the amount of $500.00, for attorney's fees and costs incurred by the Trustee in this action, and for such other and further relief as this Court deems just and proper.

_____

MILDRED PIERCE
Trustee

There are exceptions that reflect the difficulty of finding competent professionals to accept employment in a particular case or the cost savings in employing a professional already knowledgeable about the facts of a particular case. For example, Section 327(c) provides that a professional will not automatically be disqualified for employment simply by virtue of having once been employed by a creditor unless the United States trustee or a creditor expressly objects. If either objects, the court must disapprove the employment if an actual conflict of interest exists.

Similarly, Section 327(e) allows the trustee to employ an attorney that has represented the debtor for a specified special purpose if it is in the best interest of the estate and if the attorney does not represent or hold any interest adverse to the debtor or the estate with respect to the matter on which the attorney is to be employed. This helps solve the problem of litigation pending at the time of the appointment of the trustee. The cause of action now belongs to the estate and the trustee steps into the shoes of the debtor as plaintiff or defendant. Section 327(e) allows the debtor's counsel to continue in the litigation as the trustee's special counsel for that limited purpose.

Requirement of Court Approval   As indicated earlier, all professionals who will be performing services to the trustee and who want to be compensated for those services must have their employment first approved by the court. When approval has not been obtained before the services are performed, it may be possible to obtain an order approving employment retroactively. Most courts disfavor retroactive employment and it should be relied on only as a last resort.

Procedures   Bankruptcy Rule 2014 gives the procedure for obtaining approval of employment. First, there must be an application of the trustee. This is one of the few times in bankruptcy practice that relief is properly sought by application. The application must state the following:

☐ Specific facts showing the necessity for the employment.

☐ The name of the professional to be employed.

☐ The reason for the selection of that professional. A resume or statement of past experience is the best method for meeting this requirement.

☐ The professional services to be performed.

☐ The proposed arrangement for compensation. This would include any retainer and the current hourly rate or the percentage of recovery to be received in a contingent fee arrangement.

☐ All of the professional's connections with the debtor, creditors, any other party in interest, and their attorneys.

If more than one of a particular type of professional is to be employed, the application should detail the need for multiple professionals, the services to be performed by each, and an affirmative statement that there will be no duplication of services.

Generally, a separate application is required for each professional. If the trustee needs counsel in many jurisdictions, it may be possible to prepare and have approved one application for all of these assorted professionals.

Although the Bankruptcy Rules do not require it, it is good practice, and may be required by the United States trustee or local rules, for an employment application to be accompanied by the declaration or affidavit of the person sought to be employed. (See Exhibit 9.13). The declaration or affidavit can put into evidence any connection the professional has with the debtor, creditors, or any other party in interest.

Because of the general disfavor shown to retroactive orders, court approval should be obtained immediately. The United States trustee may require that the application be presented first for its review. Unless there is an objection to the application, it will usually be approved without a hearing.

A well stocked form book should contain an application and accompanying order for employment of attorneys and accountants by the trustee. A form application for employment of an auctioneer and an appraiser should also be prepared. (See Exhibit 9.14.)

Compensation of Professionals

The preceding section discussed employment of professionals by the estate. As it showed, certain hoops must be jumped through before a professional can be employed. There is always the possibility that the employment will not be authorized. But, even if the professional has successfully cleared the employment hurdle, there

■ EXHIBIT 9.13
Sample Pleading

MILDRED PIERCE
700 Flower Street
Los Angeles, California 90001

Trustee

UNITED STATES BANKRUPTCY COURT
WESTERN DISTRICT OF CALIFORNIA

In re)	Case No. 95-00001-JF
)	
VIDEOS BY JOE, INC.,)	Chapter 7
)	
Debtor.)	
)	
Debtor's Address:)	TRUSTEE'S APPLICATION TO
18 Hollywood Drive)	EMPLOY COUNSEL; DECLARATION
Los Angeles, California 90001)	OF IRWIN SULLY IN
)	SUPPORT THEREOF
Debtor's Tax Id. No. 99-999899)	
)	
_____)	

Mildred Pierce, the duly appointed, qualified, and acting Chapter 7 trustee in the above-captioned case (the "Trustee"), in support of this Application to Employ Counsel, respectfully represents that:

1. The petition commencing this case was filed on October 1, 1995. The Trustee was appointed on October 2, 1995, accepted the appointment, and qualified on October 4, 1995.

2. To perform her duties as trustee, the Trustee requires the services of attorneys for the following purposes:

(a) To advise and consult with the trustee regarding questions arising in the case and concerning the rights and remedies of the Trustee with regard to property of the estate, including rights in property which may have been the subject of voidable transfers prior to the filing of debtor's petition, and in regard to any secured, priority, or unsecured creditors of the estate;

(b) To appear in, prosecute, and defend suits and proceedings concerning property of the estate;

(c) To take all necessary steps in other matters involving or connected with the affairs of the estate;

(d) To prepare or assist in preparing necessary applications, answers, orders, reports, and other papers, if any, required to be filed in the case; and

(e) To perform all other legal services for the Trustee that may be necessary and appropriate in the case or to ensure the retention of such special counsel as may be necessary and proper for such services.

3. The Trustee desires to employ the law firm of Sully, Cooper and Rausch (the "Firm") for the purposes set forth in Paragraph 2. The attorneys of the Firm who will appear in the case are duly admitted to practice before this court. The Trustee has selected the Firm because it has considerable experience in matters of this character.

4. Based upon the foregoing, pursuant to the provisions of 11 U.S.C. § 327 and Rule 2014(a) of the Bankruptcy Rules, the Trustee requests this Court's approval of the employment of the Firm.

5. The Firm proposes to charge fees based upon its prevailing hourly guideline rates which currently range between $80 for the most junior associates to $250 for certain of the more senior partners. The Firm intends to apply to this Court in conformity with 11 U.S.C. §§ 330 and 331 for interim compensation and reimbursement for costs advanced.

—continued

■ EXHIBIT 9.13
Sample Pleading—*Continued*

6. At the conclusion of the case the Firm will file an appropriate application seeking allowance of all fees and costs, regardless whether interim compensation has been paid. Upon allowance of such fees and costs the Trustee will pay to the Firm the difference between the amounts allowed and any interim compensation paid.

7. The Firm understands and agrees that the proposed compensation arrangement shall be subject to 11 U.S.C. § 328, which authorizes this Court to allow compensation different from what is provided here if the fee arrangement appears, in retrospect, to have been improvident in light of developments unanticipated at the outset. The Firm understands and agrees that if aggregate interim payments exceed the amount which is ultimately allowed, the Firm will be required to and will promptly repay the difference to the estate.

8. Except as disclosed in the accompanying Declaration of Irwin Sully, the Trustee is informed and believes that the Firm is not connected with debtor, its attorneys, accountants, or creditors. The Trustee is further informed that the Firm represents no other party in interest and that it neither represents nor holds any interest adverse to the estate and that the employment of the Firm would be in the best interest of the estate.

WHEREFORE, the Trustee requests that she be authorized to employ the Firm at the expense of the estate upon the terms set forth above.

DATED: October 10, 1995

_____

MILDRED PIERCE
Trustee

Declaration of Irwin Sully

I, Irwin Sully, declare that:

1. I am an attorney at law duly admitted to practice in the State of California and before the United States Bankruptcy Court for the Western District of California.

2. I am a partner of Sully, Cooper and Rausch, the attorneys whom Mildred Pierce (the "Trustee") wishes to have represent her in the bankruptcy case of Videos by Joe, Inc. (the "Firm").

3. I know of no reason why, if the Firm is appointed as the Trustee's counsel, it cannot fairly and efficiently discharge all duties required of the Firm to be performed in this case.

4. To the best of my knowledge, information, and belief, and except as stated below, the Firm has no connection with debtor, its attorneys, accountants, creditors, or any other party in interest; moreover, the Firm neither represents nor holds any interest adverse to the estate in the matters upon which it is to be engaged. It is possible that the Firm may have represented from time to time one or more creditors of debtor in matters unrelated to this case; however, I am not aware of any conflict which would exist and moreover I warrant that the Firm will not represent any creditor or other party in interest in this case nor will it hereafter represent any person in connection with this case other than the Trustee.

5. No agreement exists in violation of the prohibitions of 11 U.S.C. § 504(a) or Rule 2016(b) of the Bankruptcy Rules for a division or sharing of any fees which may be awarded in this case.

I declare under penalty of perjury that the foregoing is true and correct, is based upon personal knowledge except for those matters stated to be on information and belief, and if called as a witness, I could and would testify competently thereto.

Executed at Los Angeles, California, on October 10, 1995.

_____

IRWIN SULLY

■ EXHIBIT 9.14
Sample Pleading

MILDRED PIERCE
700 Flower Street
Los Angeles, California 90001

Trustee

UNITED STATES BANKRUPTCY COURT
WESTERN DISTRICT OF CALIFORNIA

In re)	Case No. 95-00001-JF
)	
VIDEOS BY JOE, INC.,)	Chapter 7
)	
Debtor.)	
)	
Debtor's Address:)	TRUSTEE'S APPLICATION TO
18 Hollywood Drive)	EMPLOY AUCTIONEERS
Los Angeles, California 90001)	
)	
Debtor's Tax Id. No. 99-999899)	
)	
_____)	

Mildred Pierce, the duly appointed, qualified, and acting Chapter 7 trustee in the above-captioned case (the "Trustee"), in support of her Application to Employ Auctioneers respectfully represents that:

1. Among the assets of the above-captioned estate are eighteen (18) Sony Model 111N Video Cameras (the "Property"). The Trustee has attempted to sell the Property without third party involvement, but is of the considered opinion that a well advertised, well conducted auction sale will generate the highest net return to the estate.

2. Going & Going & Gone, licensed auctioneers (the "Auctioneers"), have agreed, subject to Court approval, to conduct an auction sale of the Property. The terms of the understanding are set forth in a written Auction Agreement, a complete and accurate copy of which is attached hereto (the "Agreement").

3. The Agreement provides, *inter alia*, that Auctioneers will be paid their actual costs, up to a maximum of $500.00, and ten percent (10%) of the gross sales price for the Property. The Auctioneers will file a fee application upon the completion of their services and understand that the Court may modify the compensation arrangement at that time.

4. The compensation to be paid the Auctioneers is competitive with other bids the Trustee received.

5. As indicated in the Declaration of B. B. Going filed concurrently, the Auctioneers have no connection with debtor or its creditors and are a "disinterested party" as the phrase is used in 11 U.S.C. § 327.

WHEREFORE, the Trustee requests that she be authorized to employ the Auctioneers at the expense of the estate on the terms set forth above.

DATE: December 1, 1995.

_____
MILDRED PIERCE
Trustee

is still the risk that it will not be paid for the services performed. Professionals employed at the expense of the estate must apply to the court for approval of their compensation and Section 328(a) provides that the court may allow different (including less) compensation than that which was earlier agreed to and approved by the same court.

More specifically, Section 328(a) states that the court may change the compensation if the terms and conditions approved become improvident in light of developments not capable of being anticipated at the time of the fixing of such terms and conditions. Fortunately for professionals, this section is infrequently invoked since there is little that is not capable of being anticipated at the time the employment is negotiated.

Section 328(c) allows the court to deny compensation and reimbursement of expenses altogether if at any time during the bankruptcy case the professional becomes not disinterested or represents or holds an interest adverse to the estate. If, for example, after an attorney was approved as special litigation counsel to the trustee for the purpose of collecting a fraudulent transfer from XYZ Corporation, the attorney was appointed to XYZ's board of directors, all compensation could be denied.

Finally, Section 330 provides that professionals are entitled only to *reasonable* compensation for actual and necessary services based on the nature, the extent, and the value of such services, the time spent, and the cost of comparable services in nonbankruptcy cases. The subject of professional fees in bankruptcy cases has generated tremendous controversy. Congress expressed outrage by the levels paid in the larger cases and sought in the 1994 Amendments to limit fees. In the past, courts have always had substantial discretion in this area.

One of the things Congress did was extensively modify Section 330 in the 1994 Amendments. Section 330(a)(2) now specifies that the court may, on its own motion or on motion by a party in interest, award compensation less than the amount requested. In determining the reasonable amount of compensation, as required by subsection (a), Section 330(a)(3) states that the court must consider the following relevant factors:

- ☐ the time spent
- ☐ the rates charged
- ☐ whether the services were necessary to the administration of, or beneficial at the time at which the service was rendered toward the completion of the case
- ☐ whether the services were performed within a reasonable amount of time commensurate with the complexity, importance, and nature of the problem, issue or task addressed
- ☐ and whether the compensation is reasonable based on the customary compensation charged by comparably skilled practitioners in nonbankruptcy cases.

Pursuant to Section 330(a)(4), except in the consumer bankruptcy context, no compensation can be awarded for unnecessary duplication or services that were not reasonably likely to benefit the debtor's estate or necessary to the administration of the case. Any compensation paid for the preparation of the fee application must be based on the level and skill reasonably required to prepare the application.

The issue of the reasonableness of compensation and expense reimbursement is brought before the court by the filing of a fee application. Typically, professionals seek court approval for their requested compensation and reimbursement of ex-

Interim Compensation
Postpetition payments made to professionals employed at the expense of the estate prior to the end of the bankruptcy case.

Interim Fee Application
The document filed with the court by which professionals seek interim compensation.

penses at the end of a Chapter 7 case. The Bankruptcy Code does not, however, require that a professional wait to be paid until the end of a case. Section 331 of the Bankruptcy Code states that a professional may apply to the court not more than once every 120 days after the order for relief, or more often if the court permits, for compensation and reimbursement of expenses. This is called **interim compensation** and the applications are **interim fee applications.** Circumstances that would warrant bringing an interim application more often include large, complex cases where the work is very extensive.

Sometimes the court will not allow all of a professional's requested compensation to be paid on an interim application. The court may authorize only seventy-five percent or so to be disbursed with a twenty-five percent holdback to be received at the end of the case. Even if the court authorizes the disbursement of the entire amount, the award is only interim and the court can always reconsider its interim allowance, reduce it, and force the professional to pay back the excess amount.

Whether it is interim or final, an application for compensation and expense reimbursement (see Exhibit 9.15) must contain the information required by Bankruptcy Rule 2016. That rule requires a written application, setting forth:

☐ A detailed statement of the services rendered, the time expended, the expenses incurred, and the amounts requested.

☐ A statement of payments previously received or promised to the applicant for services rendered or to be rendered in any capacity whatsoever in connection with the case.

☐ The source of any compensation paid or promised.

☐ Whether any compensation previously received has been shared.

☐ Whether an agreement or understanding exists between the applicant and any other person for the sharing of compensation received or to be received for services performed in or in connection with the bankruptcy case.

☐ For the particulars of any sharing of compensation or agreement or understanding for the sharing of compensation.

Much of the information required by Rule 2016 will be in all applications, which may be prepared by the legal assistant. With respect to the detailed statement of the services performed and the time spent, the best method is to attach the pertinent time records for the professionals as an exhibit to the application. Since reading the time records will give the court and parties in interest a lot of detail but not the flavor of the case and the professionals' involvement, a narrative in the body of the application highlighting the professionals' services is always well received. It will also supplement time records that are not explicit.

One of the more common objections to a professional's fee application is that the hourly rate charged is too high. It is helpful to include a short biography in the fee application of each professional involved. The biography could include length of practice, educational background, major cases involved in, publications, and other information to justify the hourly rate charged in comparison to other professionals.

Bankruptcy Rule 2002 requires twenty days' notice to all creditors and other parties in interest of any hearing on an application for compensation or reimbursement of expenses totalling in excess of $100.00. Typically, in a case where a number of professionals are employed, such as attorneys and accountants for the debtor in possession and the creditors' committee, the parties will confer before

■ EXHIBIT 9.15
Sample Pleading

IRWIN SULLY
Sully, Cooper and Rausch
633 Hill Lane
Los Angeles, California 90001

Attorneys for the Trustee

UNITED STATES BANKRUPTCY COURT
WESTERN DISTRICT OF CALIFORNIA

In re	)	Case No. 95-00001-JF
	)	
VIDEOS BY JOE, INC.,	)	Chapter 7
	)	
Debtor.	)	
	)	
Debtor's Address:	)	
18 Hollywood Drive	)	APPLICATION FOR APPROVAL OF
Los Angeles, California 90001	)	COMPENSATION AND
	)	REIMBURSEMENT OF EXPENSES
Debtor's Tax Id. No. 99-999899	)	
	)	
_____	)	

TO THE HONORABLE JUSTIN FAIR, UNITED STATES BANKRUPTCY JUDGE

Sully, Cooper and Rausch (the "Firm"), in support of its Application for Approval of Compensation and Reimbursement of Expenses, respectfully represents that:

1. The Firm was retained by Mildred Pierce, the Chapter 7 trustee (the "Trustee") of Video's By Joe, Inc. (the "Debtor") to serve as her bankruptcy counsel in connection with Debtor's bankruptcy case. On October 15, 1995, the Court issued its order authorizing the employment of the Firm by the Trustee.

2. For the period from October 15, 1995 through and including this date, the Firm has provided legal services to the Trustee in connection with Debtor's bankruptcy case. Those services, together with all costs incurred in connection with those services, are particularly described in Exhibit A to the Declaration of Irwin G. Sully which is filed concurrently (the "Declaration"). Exhibit A also identifies the professional who performed the services.

3. A review of Exhibit A indicates the following initials which reflect that time was expended by the following attorney and paralegal:

Initials	Identity
IGS	Irwin G. Sully
JAM	Julius A. Murray

4. Irwin G. Sully is, and at all relevant times has been, a member of the Firm. He graduated from the University of California School of Law at Berkeley (Boalt Hall) in 1970 and has practiced law in the insolvency area for almost twenty-five years. Mr. Sully's billing rate is $200.00 per hour. As set forth in Exhibit A, Mr. Sully performed forty hours of professional services to the Trustee since the Firm was retained. During that time, Mr. Sully's services ensured that the Trustee was fully, fairly, and adequately represented.

5. Julius A. Murray is an insolvency paralegal whose billing rate is $50.00 per hour. Mr. Murray holds a paralegal certificate from the University of Santa Clara Institute for Paralegal Studies and is experienced and capable in bankruptcy procedure, case management, and administrative matters. Mr. Murray also spent forty hours assisting in the representation of the Trustee.

—continued

6. The billing rates set forth in paragraphs 4 and 5 are identical to the rates charged all the Firm's clients for whom the referenced individuals performed services during the same period.

7. Billed at the Firm's ordinary hourly rates, fees total $10,000.00.

8. All of the services for which compensation is requested were performed by the Firm for and on behalf of the Trustee, and not on behalf of the Debtor, any creditor, or any other person.

9. No agreement exists in violation of the prohibitions of 11 U.S.C. § 504(a) or Bankruptcy Rule 2016 for the division or sharing of any fees which may be allowed pursuant to this Application or any future Application.

10. Also attached to the Declaration is a list of all disbursements made by the Firm in connection with its representation of the Trustee. Total costs are $750.00.

11. The firm believes and represents that the services performed have been beneficial to the estate, and that fees of $10,000.00 and costs of $750.00 are fair and reasonable, represent services or costs actually performed or incurred, and were necessary.

12. This Application seeks allowance of a claim for $10,750.00; the Firm also requests at this time authorization for the Trustee to pay the allowed amount. The Trustee has ample funds on hand to pay the balance of the amount allowed.

WHEREFORE, the Firm requests that this Court enter its Order:

1. Approving compensation and reimbursement of expenses for the Firm as follows:

Fees:	$10,000.00
Expense Reimbursement:	$ 750.00
Total:	$10,750.00

2. Authorizing the Trustee to disburse the sum of $10,750.00 to the Firm; and

3. Granting such other and further relief as the Court deems just and proper.

DATED: February 1, 1996

SULLY, COOPER and RAUSCH

_____

IRWIN G. SULLY
Attorneys for the Trustee

the hearing is set and one of the attorneys will prepare and serve the notice of the hearing for all professionals.

☐ DISTRIBUTING THE ESTATE

Objections to Claims

Once the trustee has reduced all of the estate's assets to cash, the next step is to distribute the funds to the creditors in the order of priority. Naturally, before making any distributions, the trustee will need to know the dollar amount of all the allowed claims to ensure that there are sufficient funds to make such a distribution.

The trustee has the duty under Section 704(5) to examine the proofs of claims that have been filed and make objections to improper claims if a purpose would be served. Obviously, if it was a no asset case and there were no funds in the

estate to distribute to unsecured creditors, no purpose would be served by objecting to claims.

If the trustee will have funds to distribute, the first step in determining the amount of allowed claims is to order a **claims register** from the clerk of the court. This will list all the proofs of claims filed and their dollar amount if the creditor specified one. The claims register will also indicate those creditors who asserted that their claim was secured or entitled to a priority of some sort. The clerk will assign each claim a number, usually in the order it was received. The trustee must then compare the claims listed in the register with the debtor's schedules or the debtor's books and records to see if the amounts correspond. If they do not, the trustee will want to examine the proof of claim on file with the court. Alternatively, the trustee can send a form letter to the claimant asking it to send a copy of the proof of claim to the trustee.

Claims Register
A list prepared by the clerk of the bankruptcy court of all proofs of claim filed in the bankruptcy case.

Sometimes the debtor's books and records will be wrong and the proof of claim correct. Other times, the proof of claim will be invalid for a number of reasons, most of which are listed in Section 502(b) of the Bankruptcy Code. The most common reason to object to a claim is that it is a duplicate of another proof of claim. Creditors often file two or more claims in a particular case because they have forgotten that they already filed one or in an abundance of caution to ensure that they receive a distribution.

Other reasons the claim would be invalid in whole or in part are:

□ The claim is unenforceable against the debtor or its property under any agreement or applicable law. For example, the claim could be based on a contract entered into by the debtor under duress.

□ The claim is for interest that was not earned by the creditor as of the date of the filing of the petition.

□ The claim is for taxes against the property and the taxes are more than the property is worth.

□ The claim is made by an insider or the debtor's attorney and the amount of the claim is unreasonable.

□ The claim is for postpetition alimony or child support. These amounts are not dischargeable and the claimant should seek to be paid from the debtor rather than from the estate.

□ The claim is for damages due to the rejection of a lease of real property and the amount claimed is more than the amount due at the commencement of the case and either one year's rent or fifteen percent of the remaining term of the lease as long as it is no more than three years.

□ The claim is for damages due to rejection or an employment agreement and the amount claimed is more than one year's salary plus any actual amounts due.

□ The claim results from a reduction due to late payment of a credit available to the debtor in connection with an employment tax on wages, salaries, or commissions earned from the debtor.

In addition, if the estate has a claim against an entity for turnover; improper postpetition transaction; improper setoff; a voidable lien that impairs an exemption; a fraudulent conveyance, statutory lien, or preference; or if the claimant has a lien that secures payment of a claim for punitive damages or a fine, the court can disallow the claim until the entity or transferee had paid the amount, released the lien, or turned over any property. Finally, if the claim was filed late, it should be objected to as untimely. Creating a table like the one in Exhibit 9.16 may be helpful in reviewing the claims and preparing a large number of objections.

■ EXHIBIT 9.16
Worksheet for Objections to Claims

Claim Number	Claimant	Claim Amount	Wrongly Filed As Priority/ Secured	Duplicate Of Claim #	Late-Date Filed	Estate Has Claim Against Claimant	Other Basis for Objection

Pursuant to Section 502(a), any party in interest has standing to object to claims. The procedure is discussed in Bankruptcy Rule 3007. It requires the objection to be in writing and filed with the court. A copy of the objection with a notice of the hearing must be mailed to the claimant, the debtor, and the trustee at least thirty days prior to the hearing. If in addition to objecting to the claim, the trustee asks for affirmative relief of some sort (such as to recover the preference) the objection process is turned into an adversary proceeding and, as required by Bankruptcy Rule 7001, a complaint must be filed.

There are many different ways of preparing the appropriate pleading for objections to claims. Two different methods are shown in Exhibits 9.17 and 9.18. If there are only a few objections, a separate pleading may be made for each one. If there are many, the trustee may prepare one notice and attach as a schedule a list of all the claims to which objections are being interposed. In some jurisdictions the local rules dictate the form of objections.

Sometimes the trustee will first write letters to the claimants explaining why their claims are invalid. At that point a claimant may simply withdraw its claim by filing a notice of withdrawal as authorized by Bankruptcy Rule 3006. If the trustee has already filed the objection, a complaint has been filed against that creditor, or the creditor has significantly participated in the case, the claimant must obtain court approval of the claim withdrawal.

If a claim is allowed or disallowed, Bankruptcy Rule 3008 specifically authorizes a party in interest to move for reconsideration at any time before the case is closed. Notice and a hearing are required.

Payment of Claims

Once the trustee has reduced all of the estate's assets to cash and objected to all improper claims, the next step is to pay the proceeds to the creditors. Bankruptcy Rule 3009 states that "In Chapter 7 cases, dividends to creditors shall be paid as promptly as practicable." Despite the requirement that dividends to creditors be paid as promptly as practicable, it is the unusual case in which any distributions are made before the case is ready to close. The reasons for this are many. Objections to claims are often among the last tasks done in a case and it may not be until the case is ready to close that the trustee knows the total dollar amount of the claims. Similarly, until the case is ready to close, the trustee will not know the full amount of the administrative liabilities, thereby leaving the amount of the dividend to nonpriority creditors in question. This is not to suggest that interim distributions are never made to creditors. It is possible that the trustee could set aside sufficient reserves for anticipated future administrative expenses and disputed claims that might later be allowed, pay the priority creditors, and make a partial distribution to the general unsecured claimants.

The mechanics of making the payments are set by the Bankruptcy Rules. Bankruptcy Rules 3009 and 6003 require the payments to be made by check. Many financial institutions offer a free service of preparing the distribution check for trustees who have deposits of estate funds at that institution. The trustee need only supply the institution with the name and address of the claimant and the amount of the claim and the bank will figure the exact amount of each check. The checks will then be issued by computer with the name of the trustee, the debtor, the bankruptcy case number, the full amount of the allowed claim, and the percentage distribution that the check reflects stated on the check. The trustee will also receive a register with the check number, claimant, amount of claim, and

■ EXHIBIT 9.17
Sample Pleading

MILDRED PIERCE
700 Flower Street
Los Angeles, California 90001

Trustee

UNITED STATES BANKRUPTCY COURT
WESTERN DISTRICT OF CALIFORNIA

In re   ) Case No. 95-00001-JF
)
VIDEOS BY JOE, INC.,   ) Chapter 7
)
Debtor.   )
)
Debtor's Address:) NOTICE OF HEARING ON
18 Hollywood Drive   ) OBJECTION AND OBJECTION TO
Los Angeles, California 90001   ) CLAIM NUMBER 11
)
Debtor's Tax Id. No. 99-999899   )
)
_____)

TO DIAMOND RADIATOR AND ITS ATTORNEY OF RECORD:

 NOTICE IS HEREBY GIVEN that Mildred Pierce, the duly appointed, qualified, and acting Chapter 7 trustee in the above-captioned case (the "Trustee") hereby objects to claim number 11 in the amount of $3,666.25 filed by Diamond Radiator on November 1, 1995 on the ground that debtor's records reflect that only $1,479.36 is owing.

 NOTICE IS FURTHER GIVEN that a hearing on this Objection will be held on January 1, 1996, at 10:00 A.M., or as soon thereafter as the parties may be heard by the Honorable Justin Fair, United States Bankruptcy Judge, sitting in his courtroom located in the United States Courthouse, 312 North Spring Street, Los Angeles, California.

 NOTICE IS FURTHER GIVEN that if you wish to oppose this Objection, you must file a written response with the Court and serve it upon the Trustee not less than eleven (11) days prior to the hearing on the Objection.

 NOTICE IS FINALLY GIVEN that should you fail to oppose this Objection, the Trustee will request that the Court enter its Order sustaining the Objection.

DATED: December 1, 1995

_____

MILDRED PIERCE
Trustee

amount of distribution listed. This will be important for preparation of the final report and account. If the trustee does not have access to such a service, suitable software for preparing the checks and the register can be used. Alternatively, the checks can be manually prepared but that is a labor intensive and expensive task in a large case.

MILDRED PIERCE
700 Flower Street
Los Angeles, California 90001

Trustee

UNITED STATES BANKRUPTCY COURT
WESTERN DISTRICT OF CALIFORNIA

In re	)	Case No. 95-00001-JF
	)	
VIDEOS BY JOE, INC.,	)	Chapter 7
	)	
Debtor.	)	
	)	
Debtor's Address:	)	NOTICE OF HEARING ON
18 Hollywood Drive	)	OBJECTION AND OBJECTION TO
Los Angeles, California 90001	)	CLAIMS
	)	
Debtor's Tax Id. No. 99-999899	)	
	)	
_____	)	

TO THE CLAIMANTS LISTED IN EXHIBIT 1 ATTACHED HERETO:

NOTICE IS HEREBY GIVEN that Mildred Pierce, the duly appointed, qualified, and acting Chapter 7 trustee appointed in the above-captioned case (the "Trustee") hereby objects to your claim for the reason set forth in Exhibit A to this objection. Hearing on these objections will be held before the Honorable Justin Fair, United States Bankruptcy Judge, sitting in his courtroom located in the United States Courthouse, 312 North Spring Street, Los Angeles, California on January 1, 1996 at 9:00 A.M., or as soon thereafter as the Trustee may be heard.

NOTICE IS FURTHER GIVEN that if you wish to contest the Trustee's objection, you must file and serve upon the Trustee a written response not less than eleven (11) days prior to the date of the hearing on the objection. Any ground for opposition to the relief requested by the Trustee not timely and properly filed and served will be deemed waived.

DATED: December 1, 1995

_____
MILDRED PIERCE
Trustee

Exhibit A

Claim No.	Claimant	Amount of Claim	Reason for Objection
4	Giggie, Inc.	$ 7,000.00	This claim is a duplicate of claim no. 14. This claim should be disallowed in its entirety.
10	Joseph Businessman	$20,000.00	Debtor's records do not reflect that it is indebted to this claimant in any amount. This claim should be disallowed in its entirety.
12	Diamond Radiator	$ 3,666.25	Claimant filed its claim in the amount of $3,666.25. Debtor's records reflect that only $1,479.36 is owing. This claim should be allowed in the amount of $1,479.36 only.

Since most Chapter 7 cases are "no asset" cases in which the creditors do not receive any distribution, it is not surprising that even in many asset cases the dividend to creditors is quite small. In order to reduce the costs as well as the inconvenience of making dividends, Bankruptcy Rule 3010 provides that no dividend can be made to a creditor in an amount less than $5.00 unless authorized by a local rule or approved by the court. If any dividend is not distributed to a creditor because it is too small, the funds are paid into the court.

Dividend checks are mailed to the claimant unless a power of attorney, substantially in the form of Official Form 11A (the general power of attorney form) or Official Form 11B (the special power of attorney form) has been filed. If a power of attorney form has been filed, the dividend check is to be made payable to the creditor and the other person and mailed to the other person. Any power of attorney form received by the trustee should be noted on the claims register or other place where it will be handy when it is time to prepare the distribution checks.

☐ CLOSING THE CASE

Final Report and Account

The document filed by the trustee at the end of a Chapter 7 case that sets out the receipts, distributions, and allowed claims of the estate as well as any other relevant information.

Once an estate is fully administered, the case will be ready to close. How a case is closed is primarily a matter of local practice although the clerks have imposed some standardization. Generally, the trustee will file what is referred to as a **final report and account** concerning all of the estate's activities including what assets were located and what they sold for; what expenses were incurred in the administration of the estate; and the total amount of allowed secured, priority, and general unsecured claims. The final report may also seek authority to pay dividends to creditors and seek the discharge of the trustee. A sample final report is presented as Exhibit 9.19. In some jurisdictions the trustee will be required to give the clerk ninety days' notice of his or her intent to file a final report so that the asset closing section of the clerk's office can perform the tasks it needs to do before the case can be closed.

Several weeks before the trustee is ready to file the final report, the trustee should notify all professionals of his or her intent to file the report. This will put the professionals on notice that they should file their final fee applications so that they can be heard by the court at the same time as the final report. Once the final report is filed, the clerk will prepare a notice of filing final account of trustee, of hearing on application for compensation, and of hearing on abandonment of property by the trustee under Bankruptcy Rule 2002(f). It will summarize much of the information in the final report and the various fee applications filed by the professionals. The notice will be served on the debtor, all creditors, and any indenture trustee if the net proceeds realized by the trustee exceed $1,500.00. Presumably, if the net proceeds do not exceed $1,500.00, no notice need be given.

At the hearing on the final report, the court will either approve or disapprove it, any applications by professionals, and any request for authority to pay dividends. Assuming all requests are approved, the trustee will make a final distribution in the manner discussed in the previous section. Ninety days after the dividend checks are sent, Bankruptcy Code Section 347(a) requires the trustee to stop payment on any check remaining unpaid. The funds that were on deposit to cover those checks must be paid into the court by turning the funds over to the clerk. Bankruptcy Rule 3011 also requires that the trustee file with the clerk a list of all

■ EXHIBIT 9.19
Sample Pleading

MILDRED PIERCE
700 Flower Street
Los Angeles, California 90001

Trustee

UNITED STATES BANKRUPTCY COURT
WESTERN DISTRICT OF CALIFORNIA

In re) VIDEOS BY JOE, INC.,) Debtor.) Debtor's Address:) 18 Hollywood Drive) Los Angeles, California 90001) Debtor's Tax Id. No. 99-999899)	Case No. 95-00001-JF Chapter 7 FINAL REPORT AND ACCOUNT OF CHAPTER 7 TRUSTEE

TO THE HONORABLE JUSTIN FAIR, UNITED STATES BANKRUPTCY JUDGE:

Mildred Pierce, the duly appointed, qualified, and acting trustee in the above-captioned estate (the "Trustee") hereby submits to the Court and to the Office of the United States Trustee this Final Report and Account in accordance with 11 U.S.C. § 704, and respectfully represents that:

1. The petition commencing this case was filed on October 1, 1995. The Trustee was appointed on October 2, 1995, accepted the appointment, and qualified on or about October 4, 1995. The Trustee's bond was set in the amount of $5,000.00.

2. At the meeting of creditors held pursuant to 11 U.S.C. § 341(a) on November 10, 1995, the Trustee examined the debtor with respect to its financial affairs and subsequently investigated matters concerning the administration of the estate.

3. To the extent required by 11 U.S.C. § 704, all claims have been examined and all objections have been determined by the Court. The time for filing claims in this case expired on February 10, 1996.

4. The claims filed in this case can be summarized as follows:

Administrative	$ 3,000.00
Priority	$ 1,000.00
Secured	$ —0—
Unsecured	$48,000.00
Total	$52,000.00

5. To the best of the Trustee's knowledge, all professionals employed by the estate have been notified of the Trustee's intent to file this Final Report and Account.

6. The time for filing applications for compensation has expired.

7. All property of the estate was inventoried, collected and liquidated, abandoned or should be deemed abandoned. The estate is ready to close.

—*continued*

■ EXHIBIT 9.19
Sample Pleading—*Continued*

8. The receipts and disbursements made during the administration of the case are summarized below and detailed in Exhibit 1 to this Final Report and Account:

Receipts	$7,000.00
Disbursements	$1,000.00
Interest	$ 500.00
Balance on hand:	$6,500.00

9. The Trustee respectfully requests the statutory fee be allowed in this case in the sum of $405.00, based upon the total disbursements of $7,500.00. The Trustee also requests the further sum of $95.00 for reimbursement of administrative expenses.

10. As of this date, no dividends have been paid to creditors. After the payment of administrative expenses sought to be allowed, the Trustee will have on hand $4,900.00, which she seeks authorization to pay to those creditors in those amounts listed on Exhibit 2.

11. No agreement exists between the Trustee and any other person for sharing of compensation received or to be received for services rendered in connection with the case.

WHEREFORE, the Trustee requests that the Court enter its Order: (1) allowing, approving and confirming this Final Report and Account; (2) fixing, establishing and directing paid the fees, allowances and expenses of administration incurred herein; (3) authorizing the payment of dividends; (4) discharging the Trustee and exonerating the Trustee's bond; and (5) granting such other and further orders as may be necessary or convenient for any orderly termination of the estate.

DATED: March 30, 1996

_____
MILDRED PIERCE
Trustee

Exhibit 1
RECEIPTS AND DISBURSEMENTS

Receipts:

Sale of Personal Property	$4,000.00
Refunds	
Utilities	$ 50.00
Workers Compensation	$ 50.00
Insurance Premiums	$ 50.00
Collection of Accounts Receivable	$2,850.00
Interest	$ 500.00
TOTAL:	$7,500.00

Disbursements:

Administrative Rent	$ 500.00
Utilities	$ 50.00
Auction Commission/Expenses	$ 200.00
Collection Agency	$ 200.00
Storage	$ 50.00
TOTAL:	$1,000.00

—*continued*

Balance on Hand:	$ 6,500.00
Proposed Trustees' Fees	$ (405.00)
Administrative Expenses	$ (95.00)
Attorneys	$ (750.00)
Accountants	$ (250.00)
Estimated Closing Costs	$ (100.00)
Estimated Balance Available for Creditors:	$ 4,900.00

Exhibit 2
DIVIDEND REGISTER LEDGER

Claim Number	Claimant	Allowed Amount	Amount of Dividend
1	June Film Co.	$ 5,410.71	$ 552.43
2	Imperial Processing	$ 2,417.54	$ 246.83
3	Ace Trucking	$ 990.00	$ 101.08
5	A–D Motor Freight	$ 6,800.00	$ 649.28
6	J. Businessman	$20,000.00	$2,042.00
7	Ben's Maintenance	$ 100.00	$ 10.26
8	United Parcel Svc.	$ 1,611.58	$ 164.54
9	Abe's Office Supply	$ 61.65	$ 6.29
11	Shell Oil	$ 129.16	$ 13.19
12	Diamond Radiator	$ 1,479.36	$ 151.04
13	XYZ Advertising	$ 2,000.00	$ 204.20
14	Giggie, Inc.	$ 7,000.00	$ 714.70

the names and addresses of the persons entitled to a distribution but who did not cash their checks.

Once the final report is approved, the final distribution made, and all unclaimed funds paid into the court, the case is fully administered and it will be closed.

☐ SUMMARY

The trustee's duties in a Chapter 7 case are to collect and liquidate all property of the estate and to distribute the proceeds of the liquidation to creditors. To collect property of the estate, the trustee must first locate and safeguard it. The trustee may need to bring a turnover action to obtain property of the estate in the hands of a third party. The trustee will also try to make the estate as large as possible by recovering any improper postpetition transfers of property of the estate. The trustee may also seek to recover any prepetition transfers of the debtor's property if the transfers acted to prefer one creditor over others, or if the transfers were made fraudulently: either with actual intent to defraud creditors or for too little consideration. The trustee can also avoid various debts and liens that are either improper or give one creditor a benefit over others.

Once the estate is as large as possible, the trustee will reduce the valuable assets to cash. Property that has little value or is burdensome to administer can be aban-

doned. Other assets will be sold. The Bankruptcy Code allows the trustee to sell assets without bankruptcy court approval in the ordinary course of business. All other sales require notice to creditors and, in most circumstances, a court order. Under certain circumstances, a trustee can sell assets free and clear of liens or any co-owner's interests.

If the trustee does not have enough cash to finance the liquidation, he or she may borrow the funds on a secured or unsecured basis with court approval. The trustee may also use a secured creditor's cash collateral with the creditor's consent or with court approval, which will require a finding that the creditor is adequately protected. A trustee may also be able to involuntarily surcharge the secured creditor for the trustee's costs in preserving and protecting collateral.

The trustee is entitled to employ attorneys, accountants, auctioneers, and other professionals to assist in the performance of the trustee's duties. Court approval is required for any such employment and certain procedural and substantive requirements must be met. In addition, the professionals can only be paid by filing fee applications, which must be approved by the court.

After or during the sale or other disposition of property of the estate, the trustee will review the proofs of claims filed by creditors and will object to the claims believed improper. Once all the objectionable claims have been resolved and the estate has been otherwise fully administered, the trustee will prepare a report of the administration of the case, pay creditor claims to the extent possible, and close the case.

☐ KEY TERMS

Abandonment
Assignee for the Benefit of
    Creditors
Balance Sheet Insolvency
Cash Collateral
Claims Register
Cross Collateralization
Enabling Loans

Equity Cushion
Final Report and Account
Fraudulent Conveyances
Insider
Interim Compensation
Interim Fee Application
Postpetition Transfers
Preferences

Priming Lien
Receiver
Secret Liens
Surcharge
Statutory Liens
Substantially Contemporaneous
    Exchange for New Value
Turnover

☐ IMPROVE YOUR UNDERSTANDING

1. Why would Bankruptcy Rule 7001 carve out actions to compel the debtor to deliver property to the trustee from its list of adversary proceedings?

2. One example of a situation in which it might be proper for a custodian to remain in possession of the estate's assets was given. Develop two others.

3. Why does the burden concerning allowing a custodian to stay in place shift when the custodian is an assignee for the benefit of creditors?

4. Postpetition, one of the debtor's customers pays the debtor for goods the debtor delivered prepetition. What are the trustee's remedies if the customer did not know that the debtor had commenced a bank-

ruptcy case? What if the customer did know that a case had been commenced?

For each of the following exercises, determine whether the postpetition transfers are invalid under Section 549.

5. The trustee pays for guard service to protect the debtor's business premises.

6. Before the appointment of the trustee, the debtor pays its attorneys for their services in connection with the filing of the bankruptcy case.

7. Same question as above but the services were performed in contesting an involuntary petition.

8. A secured creditor forecloses on a parcel of real property the day after the petition is filed. The petition was not recorded with the county recorder's office and the secured creditor had no notice or knowledge of the commencement of the case. A third party who knows of the commencement of the bankruptcy case successfully bids for the property at the foreclosure sale and pays fair equivalent value.

9. An involuntary petition is filed against the debtor on June 10. On June 12, the debtor pays its landlord June's rent. The order for relief is entered on June 30.

In the following hypotheticals, first determine whether any of the transfers are preferences. If so, then determine whether any of the exceptions apply. For each hypothetical, assume the petition was filed on October 1, 1995.

10. On January 1, 1995, Big Bank obtained a judgment against the debtor and immediately filed an abstract of judgment with the county recorder. On August 1, 1995, debtor sold a parcel of real property to which Big Bank's judgment lien had attached and paid the judgment.

11. On June 1, 1995, the debtor repaid his mother a loan of $1,000.00 made the year previously. On September 1, 1995, the debtor's mother lent him $500.00.

12. The debtor was very delinquent in his payments to the telephone company. On September 1, 1995, he paid the telephone company $500.00 in order to prevent it from terminating service.

Use the following factual situation in answering Exercises 13 through 15.

The debtor and her brother each own an undivided fifty percent interest in a twelve-unit apartment building. The apartment building is subject to a mortgage in favor of First City Bank securing a note with a remaining principal balance of $50,000.00. There is also a junior mortgage securing an obligation of $5,000.00 held by B & B Finance Company but this mortgage was never recorded. Two weeks before the debtor filed her petition, a previously unsecured creditor levied and obtained a judgment lien against the debtor's interest in the property in the amount of $1,000.00

The debtor's brother has offered to purchase the estate's interest subject only to First City Bank's interest for $5,000.00. The trustee has been informed by a broker that similar properties in the same neighborhood are selling for approximately $75,000.00. Costs of sale would approximate ten percent of the purchase price.

13. What should the trustee do?

14. If the trustee accepts the brother's offer, what steps must be taken and what papers must be prepared?

15. If the trustee decides to try to sell the entire apartment building, what steps must be taken and what papers must be prepared?

16. List the different types of financing by how difficult they are to obtain. Next to each type of financing, indicate the showing the debtor must make in order to get the financing approved.

17. Which Bankruptcy Rule concerns motions to use cash collateral? What does it require if the secured creditor does not consent? What does it require if the secured creditor consents?

18. Can you think of any professionals other than those mentioned who would require bankruptcy court approval before they could be employed by the estate?

19. Through the course of a two-year long case, the trustee's counsel files and has approved a series of interim fee applications. Will counsel have to file a final application covering the services that were the subject of the interim applications?

20. Must the attorney for a Chapter 7 debtor file a fee application?

21. If a petition is filed on December 1, 1995, when is the first date that an interim application can be made?

☐ RESEARCH PROJECTS

1. Locate two cases that discuss the meaning of substantially contemporaneous exchange.

2. Locate a case interpreting the ordinary course of business exception. What factors did the court identify as material in determining whether the payment was in or out of the ordinary course of business?

3. Can you discover any statutory liens for the state in which you reside? Would they be avoidable under Section 545?

4. Obtain a copy of the fraudulent transfer statute of the state in which you reside. Compare it to Section 548 and note the similarities and the differ-

ences. What is the statute of limitations under the state law?

5. Locate a case under Section 548 in which the plaintiff prevailed on a claim for actual fraud. How was it proved?

6. One issue receiving substantial attention in the area of abandonment is whether the trustee can or should abandon real property that poses a health risk because of prepetition hazardous material storage or disposal. Locate and summarize two published decisions on this issue.

7. Locate a Section 506(c) case in which surcharge was granted and another in which it was denied. Compare the factual differences between the two cases.

8. Locate a case where retroactive employment was denied.

9. Locate another case where retroactive employment was approved.

10. Locate a reported decision that used the "lodestar" approach to determining the reasonableness of attorneys' fees. What is the "lodestar" approach?

11. Are there any local rules in your jurisdiction concerning objections to claims?

12. Are there any local rules in your jurisdiction concerning how a case is closed?

☐ DRAFTING PROJECTS

1. Draft a letter to the debtor's bank on behalf of the trustee effectuating the trustee's rights to the debtor's accounts.

2. Draft a letter to the United States Postal Service on behalf of the trustee effectuating the trustee's rights to the debtor's mail.

3. The debtor is in the business of renting videos. It operates in five locations, all of which are leased. Its other assets consist of five cash registers, 19,000 videocassettes, and some cash. Its liabilities consist almost exclusively of membership fees for which creditors will have refund claims. Prepare a list of tasks the Chapter 7 trustee will need to do to safeguard the assets and preserve their value. Think of some ways in which the trustee may be able to increase the distribution to creditors.

4. The debtor manufactures doorknobs. It buys components and assembles and packages the door-

knobs for sale to retailers. It filed its Chapter 7 case suddenly and in the middle of its busiest season. Draft a motion on behalf of the trustee seeking authority to operate the business until all the components have been assembled and shipped to customers. Develop whatever facts are necessary.

5. Draft a complaint under Sections 548(a)(2) and 550 seeking to recover a transfer of a debtor's vacation home to his mother.

6. Draft a motion seeking approval of a Section 364(c) or Section 364(d) financing agreement.

7. Draft a withdrawal of claim notice pursuant to Bankruptcy Rule 3006 containing facts that allow simply a notice to be used.

8. Draft a motion requesting authority to withdraw a claim using facts that require the filing of a motion.

CHAPTERS 12 AND 13: FAMILY FARMER AND INDIVIDUAL REORGANIZATIONS

Chapter 7 cases are the most common type of bankruptcy cases filed in the United States. The second most frequently filed case is a Chapter 13 reorganization for individuals. Chapter 12 is a family farmer counterpart to Chapter 13 and is as common for those persons who meet its eligibility requirements. In most jurisdictions, however, few Chapter 12 petitions are filed.

There are many similarities between Chapters 12 and 13. In fact, Chapter 12, which was enacted eight years after Chapter 13, merely copies many of its provisions. For this reason, and the fact that far more Chapter 13 cases are commenced than are Chapter 12 cases, we will consider them out of order.

☐ CHAPTER 13 SPECIAL ISSUES

Chapter 13 Administration

A Chapter 13 bankruptcy is available generally to individuals with **regular income** and less than $750,000 in secured debt and $250,000 in unsecured debt. Although most Chapter 13 debtors are wage earners, there are some small business Chapter 13 cases in which the debtor is self-employed or runs a small sole proprietorship. In those Chapter 13 cases the business will continue to operate in the ordinary course without trustee or court control. Only transactions out of the ordinary course of business, such as a sale of the business, will require notice and a hearing. In addition, a Chapter 13 business debtor will be required to submit periodic reports concerning the operations of the business to the court or to the Chapter 13 trustee.

In virtually all cases the Chapter 13 trustee serves merely to insure the debtor's compliance with Chapter 13 rules and make disbursements under the plan. The

Family Farmer
A person engaged in farming with relatively low debt levels that primarily arise from farming operations, who relies on farming income. Includes partnerships and corporations if at least half of the ownership interests are held by one family.

Family Farmer with Regular Income
A family farmer whose annual income is sufficiently stable and regular to allow it to make payments under a Chapter 12 plan.

Regular Income
A source of income that is fairly stable whether earnings, pension or other retirement benefits, public assistance benefits, or dividends.

Chapter 13 trustee has the power to compel turnover of property of the estate in a third party's hands and has all the avoiding powers of a Chapter 7 trustee. These powers, however, are rarely exercised except by the debtor. Further, nothing in the Bankruptcy Code authorizes a Chapter 13 trustee or any other person to operate the debtor's business regardless of how badly the debtor may be doing so.

The Chapter 13 Plan

In General   The unique feature of a Chapter 13 case is the plan, which can be proposed only by the debtor, not by any of the creditors. Although it looks like a relatively simple document, it allows for a substantial restructure of an individual debtor's secured and unsecured debt. Unlike Chapter 11 reorganizations, creditors are not given an opportunity to vote to accept or reject the plan. As long as it adheres to the requirements of Chapter 13, the court will confirm it.

Some Chapter 11 cases will drag on for years without a plan being proposed, but a Chapter 13 plan must be filed no later than fifteen days after the petition is filed. Bankruptcy Rule 3015 does allow the fifteen-day period to be extended by the court, but cause must first be shown. If the plan is not timely filed, the court may dismiss the case or convert it to Chapter 7. Usually, the plan is filed with the petition.

There is no official form for a Chapter 13 plan and the only requirement in Bankruptcy Rule 3015 is that it be dated. Preprinted forms are in widespread use. If the legal assistant's work involves many Chapter 13 cases, a personalized form can be developed and placed on the word processor. It might be wise to have the Chapter 13 trustee make comments as to its contents first since the trustee's review of the plan will be the first hurdle to overcome at confirmation.

The number of copies and the persons to whom service of the plan should be made are controlled by the local rules of each district. Even though Bankruptcy Rule 3015 requires only that the creditors receive a summary of the plan's terms, some districts require that the plan itself be served on all creditors.

The Terms of the Plan   Exhibit 10.1 presents a very simple but very common Chapter 13 plan. It provides for the restructure of the debts of an individual who is behind in his house payments and taxes and is proposing to cure the defaults to his mortgage holder, redeem other secured debt, cure all tax obligations over time, and contribute a portion of future earnings to pay all other claims. As you examine the plan and the following discussion of it, you will see how all of these goals are achieved in the plan.

The first part of the plan is its means of implementation or, in other words, how creditors are going to be paid. Section 1332(a) requires debtors to submit to the Chapter 13 trustee enough of their regular income so that the payments called for in the plan can be made. As will be shown, this plan provides that the debtor's monthly mortgage payment of $700 will be made by the trustee. In addition, the debtor will pay $400 of **disposable income** to the trustee each month so that the payments to the other creditors can be made. Thus, in order to implement the plan, the debtor will pay the trustee $1,100 each month for the term of the plan.

The second part of the plan is its duration. Plan payments must be completed within three years. If the debtor can establish good cause, the court can allow the payments to be stretched to up to five years but no longer. The exception to this rule is if the debtor has long-term debt such as car or mortgage payments that

Disposable Income
A debtor's income that is not necessary for the payment of the reasonable living expenses of the debtor and his or her dependents, or if the debtor is engaged in business, the income that is not necessary for the payment of the expenses necessary for the continuation, preservation, and operation of the business.

■ EXHIBIT 10.1
Sample Pleading

BANKRUPT C. LAWYER
White Charger Legal Clinic
One Learned Way
Los Angeles, California 90001

Attorneys for Debtor

UNITED STATES BANKRUPTCY COURT
WESTERN DISTRICT OF CALIFORNIA

In re	)	Case No. 95-00002-JF
	)	
JOSEPH CONSUMER,	)	Chapter 13
	)	
Debtor.	)	
	)	
Debtor's Address:	)	CHAPTER 13 PLAN OF REORGANIZATION
18 Hollywood Drive	)	
Los Angeles, California 90001	)	
	)	
Debtor's S.S. No. 524-47-7448	)	
	)	

Joseph Consumer, the debtor in the above-captioned Chapter 13 case ("Debtor"), hereby proposes this Chapter 13 Plan:

I
Means of Implementing Plan

Debtor will submit future earnings or income of $1,100.00 per month to the Chapter 13 trustee to make the distributions required by this Plan.

II
Term of Plan

Payments under this Plan shall be made over a period of thirty-six (36) months.

III
Classifications and Treatment of Claims

1. Class 1 claims are those entitled to priority in payment under Section 507 of Title 11, United States Code. Class 1 claims will be paid in full, in deferred cash payments with interest, as follows:

	ALLOWED PRIORITY CLAIM	MONTHLY PAYMENT	NUMBER OF PAYMENTS	TOTAL
a. Trustee's charges	$ 500.00	$ 56.00	10	$ 560.00
b. Attorneys' fees	$ 500.00	$ 56.00	10	$ 560.00
c. Internal Revenue Service	$1,000.00	$112.00	10	$1,120.00
d. State of California	$ 200.00	$ 22.40	10	$ 220.40

2. Class 2 consists of the allowed secured claim other than the claim secured solely by an interest in the Debtor's principal residence. It shall be treated as follows:

—continued

■ EXHIBIT 10.1
Sample Pleading—*Continued*

NAME OF CREDITOR	ALLOWED SECURED CLAIM	MONTHLY PAYMENT	NUMBER OF PAYMENTS	TOTAL
B & B Finance Company	$ 500.00	$ 15.00	36	$ 540.00

3. The Class 3 claim is the allowed secured claim secured by the Debtor's principal residence. It is treated as follows:

NAME OF CREDITOR	AMOUNT IN DEFAULT	MONTHLY PAYMENT	NUMBER OF PAYMENTS
First City Bank			
a. Cure of default	$1,400.00	$ 53.00	36
b. Maintenace of payments		$700.00	

4. Class 4 claims are allowed unsecured claims not otherwise referred to in the Plan. Class 4 claims shall be paid pro rata seventy percent (70%) of such claims.

5. Class 5 claims are postpetition claims allowed under Section 1305 of Title 11, United States Code. Postpetition claims allowed under Section 1305 shall be paid in full by Debtor when due.

IV
Liquidation Analysis

As of the effective date of the Plan, Debtor owns property which if a case under Chapter 7 of Title 11, United States Code, were commenced, would be a part of the Section 541 estate and which has a fair market value of $20,000.00 Debtor would also be entitled to exempt property having a value of $20,000.00. Debtor would owe claims entitled to priority under Section 507 in the total amount of $1,200.00 and allowed unsecured claims in the total amount of $13,500.00.

As a result, there would be no funds available for distribution to creditors holding allowed unsecured claims under Chapter 7.

DATED: October 1, 1995

_____

JOSEPH CONSUMER
Debtor

---

have more than three or five years to go. Payments to those creditors must continue after the end of the plan period. In this case, the debtor has proposed a thirty-six month plan. If the proposed plan was to exceed thirty-six months, in the second section the debtor would detail the cause for the extension.

Section 1322(b) of the Bankruptcy Code allows a Chapter 13 debtor to divide the claims of creditors into different classes as long as the claims in each class are substantially similar. Section 1332(b) also allows the debtor to provide a different treatment for each class, but there must be the same treatment for claims in the same class. In the sample plan, the debtor has divided claims into five classes. They are:

Class 1   Priority Claims

Class 2   General Secured Claims

Class 3   Residential Secured Claim

Class 4   Unsecured, Nonpriority Claims

Class 5   Postpetition Claims

Class 1 claims under the plan are those claims entitled to a priority in payment under Section 507(a) of the Bankruptcy Code. They include administrative expenses, such as the Chapter 13 trustee's fee and the fee charged by the debtor's counsel. They also include the claims of the taxing agencies. Section 1322(a) of the Bankruptcy Code provides that all priority claims must be paid in full for the plan to be confirmed. It does not, however, require that the claims be paid upon confirmation or before payments can be made to nonpriority creditors. Under the sample plan, the debtor has provided that all priority claims will be paid in full over a period of ten months. The debtor could have chosen fewer or more months to make these payments, but not more than thirty-six months. The payments are not exactly a simple division of the amount of the claim by the number of months the payments will be made because the debtor has provided that the claimants will receive interest on their claims. Of the payments the debtor sends to the trustee each month $226.40 will be used to pay the Chapter 13 trustee and the other priority creditors. After the debtor makes ten months of payments and the priority claims have been paid in full, the debtor will still pay $1,100 per month, but the trustee will use the $226.40 that was previously paid to the priority creditors to make payments to the other creditors.

Class 2 claims are the allowed secured claims against the debtor that are not secured by the debtor's residence. This could include appliances or furniture purchased on credit terms, an automobile, or other personal property secured loans. Class 2 claims could also include real property owned by the debtor that is not used as a principal residence.

For these types of secured claims, Section 1322(b) states that the debtor may modify the creditor's rights by extending the due date of the last payment or paying it less than the full amount that is owed; however, Section 1322(a) states that the secured creditors must receive no less than the value of their collateral. If the creditor is owed $100 and the collateral is only worth $50, its allowed secured claim is $50. The creditor will have an unsecured claim for the deficiency, which in the example would be $50. The deficiency will share in the amounts paid to unsecured creditors and usually will not be paid in full. This is exactly the same result as redemption (discussed in Chapter 8) except that in a Chapter 7 case the redemption amount must be paid in a lump sum at the time of the redemption. In Chapter 13 cases, the debtor can redeem by making installment payments under the plan.

In the sample plan, there is only one Class 2 claimant. Its allowed secured claim is $500 which the plan proposes to pay in full, and with interest, over thirty-six months. Of the $1,100 the debtor pays under the plan each month, the Chapter 13 trustee will pay $15 to B & B Finance Company. If B & B's total claim was greater than $500, the balance would have been a Class 4 claim.

In a separate class from the other secured creditors is the creditor whose claim is secured by the debtor's home. For these creditors, Section 1322(b) prohibits a modification of rights. If the debtor wants to keep the house, even if it is only worth a fraction of what is owed against it, the full amount due to the creditor must be paid and the debt must be paid according to its terms. If the underlying note is due in one year, the debtor cannot stretch the amount due to two years. The debtor can stretch out repayment of the prepetition arrearages, but it can only do so for the length of the plan or until the note is due, whichever is shorter.

There are, however, two exceptions added by the 1994 Amendments. First, a Chapter 13 debtor may cure a default on a lien secured by the debtor's principal residence up to the time of the sale at foreclosure. Many states also give the debtor

this right. Second, a debtor can now cure defaults within a reasonable time and maintain payments on a residence's mortgage even if the last payment due on the original payment schedule is due before the final payment on the plan. The courts will need to decide what constitutes a reasonable time.

Under the sample plan the debtor has provided that the two monthly payments missed before the case was commenced will be paid with interest over thirty-six months. In addition to the arrearage payment, the regular monthly payment of $700 will also be made. In some jurisdictions the debtor is allowed to make these payments directly rather than making them through the trustee.

Class 4 claims are those of the general unsecured, nonpriority creditors of the estate. Under the plan, they will receive a pro rata share of what is left of the $400 paid by the debtor to the trustee each month that is not needed to make payments to the other creditors. Beginning in the first ten months, the amount available to these creditors will be $85.60. In month eleven, after all the priority creditors are paid in full, the Class 4 creditors will share $332.00. In all, there will be $9,488.00 to be distributed to the unsecured creditors. This will be approximately seventy percent of their claims.

There is no minimum amount or percentage that must be paid to unsecured, nonpriority creditors. However, if the amount is too low in light of the debtor's disposable income, the court may refuse to confirm the plan because the debtor is acting in bad faith. Also, if the creditors will not be paid in full, a creditor can object and force a debtor to contribute all disposable income to the plan.

The final class of creditors under the sample plan is postpetition claims. The debtor will continue to incur various debts after the Chapter 13 case is commenced. Section 1322(b) requires all postpetition claims to be paid in full. These claims can be paid through the Chapter 13 plan or, as is done in the sample plan, by the debtor directly. If postpetition claim payments are to be made by the trustee, the debtor should provide in the first section that, in addition to other amounts required under the plan, the amount paid to the trustee will be increased to whatever is necessary to pay Class 5 claims in full.

Under Section 1322(a) the bankruptcy court cannot confirm a Chapter 13 plan if the unsecured creditors will receive less under the plan than they would receive if the debtor's assets were liquidated under Chapter 7. In order to satisfy the court that the plan payments are greater than anything the creditors would receive if the debtor had filed a Chapter 7 case, many Chapter 13 plans include a liquidation analysis to compare the difference. In the sample plan, the debtor has shown that there would be no distribution to unsecured creditors in a Chapter 7 case because all assets would be exempt. Since the plan provides for a payment of seventy percent on unsecured claims, the debtor has easily met Section 1322(a)'s requirement.

As mentioned, the sample plan is a fairly simple one. There are other provisions that could be added depending on a debtor's needs and wishes. For example, the plan can provide for the rejection or assumption of executory contracts or leases to which the debtor is a party. A plan can also provide for the sale of some of the debtor's assets with the proceeds distributed to creditors.

Plan Confirmation   Once the debtor has proposed a plan and it or a summary have been provided to all creditors, the court will hold a confirmation hearing. Section 1325 of the Bankruptcy Code provides that the plan will be confirmed at that hearing if it meets all the requirements of the Bankruptcy Code, if the debtor has paid all required fees and charges to the court, and if the plan has been proposed

in good faith and not by any means forbidden by law. Creditors are not entitled to vote for or against the plan. Their sole remedy if they do not like the plan is to object to confirmation. They will object if the plan has their claim in the wrong amount. For example, in the sample plan, First City Bank may claim that it is owed $1,500 in arrearages not $1,400. B & B Finance company may assert that its collateral is worth $95 and not $50. Finally, creditors can claim that the plan was proposed in bad faith.

Discharge

In a Chapter 7 case, an individual debtor obtains a discharge of all of its debts except those listed in Section 523(a). To review, the most common nondischargeable debts are:

- ☐ Most taxes.
- ☐ Debts incurred through fraud or false financial statements.
- ☐ Debts incurred on the eve of bankruptcy for luxury goods or services or cash advances.
- ☐ Claims for fraud or defalcation in a fiduciary capacity, embezzlement, or larceny.
- ☐ Alimony and child support.
- ☐ Fines, penalties, or forfeitures payable to the government.
- ☐ Student loans.
- ☐ Claims arising from drunk driving liability.
- ☐ Debts that were not discharged during a prior bankruptcy case.

The Chapter 7 debtor need do nothing other than comply with its obligations under the Bankruptcy Code to be entitled to a discharge. In a Chapter 13 case, a discharge is also available—but it is much more difficult to obtain. Yet once received, it is much broader than the discharge granted to a Chapter 7 debtor.

Under Section 1328(a), if a Chapter 13 debtor fully complies with the terms of the confirmed plan, there will be a discharge of all debts except claims for alimony and child support, claims for drunk driving, student loans, criminal restitution obligations, repayment of reenlistment bonuses, and claims on which payments are due after the plan is completed (such as residential mortgages). All other debts, including those that would not be discharged in a Chapter 7 case (such as fraud claims and claims not discharged in an earlier Chapter 7 case), are forgiven. The discharge will be automatic.

In some circumstances the debtor can obtain a discharge in Chapter 13 even if all payments due under the confirmed plan were not paid. To obtain this discharge, Section 1328(b) requires that the court find that the debtor's failure to complete the payments is due to circumstances for which the debtor should not be held accountable, unsecured creditors have already been paid at least as much as they would have received in a Chapter 7 case, and a modification of the plan is not practicable. This is called a **hardship discharge** and it is more limited than a regular Chapter 13 discharge. It will not discharge those types of debts that would have been nondischargeable in a Chapter 7 case (such as fraud claims). The debtor must make a motion requesting a hardship discharge.

Another difference between a Chapter 13 discharge and a Chapter 7 discharge is the frequency in which they can be granted. A Chapter 7 discharge is available only once every six years. There is no bar in the Bankruptcy Code to receiving a

Hardship Discharge
The discharge granted to a Chapter 12 or 13 debtor who did not complete all plan payments but whose failure to do so was due to circumstances for which the debtor should not justly be held accountable.

Chapter 13 discharge shortly after a Chapter 7 discharge. In fact, some debtors file a Chapter 7 case to discharge most debts and then file a Chapter 13 case to pay the nondischarged debts over time under the plan. These strategies are sometimes referred to as a Chapter 20. Many courts disapprove strongly of the practice.

According to Section 1328(e), once granted, a Chapter 13 discharge may be revoked only if the debtor obtained the discharge through fraud that is discovered after the discharge is granted. The motion requesting that the discharge be revoked must be made no later than one year after the discharge. Even if the fraud is not discovered until the one-year period has run, the discharge will still stand.

Converting, Dismissing and Closing the Case

Changing Chapters As discussed in Chapter 9 of this book, a Chapter 7 case cannot be converted to Chapter 13 against the debtor's will. The reason is that to force the debtor to work to repay creditors violates the Thirteenth Amendment to the U.S. Constitution. For this same reason, a debtor cannot be forced to remain in Chapter 13. The debtor has the absolute right to convert the Chapter 13 case to a Chapter 7 case at any time and for any reason. The procedure is not covered in the Bankruptcy Rules but since it is an absolute right, and the court has no discretion, no notice to creditors or opportunity for a hearing need be given. A simple motion indicating that the debtor desires to convert to Chapter 7 and a corresponding order for clarity in the file is all that is needed.

The rules for converting a Chapter 13 case to a case under Chapter 11 or 12 are very different. That conversion is entirely within the discretion of the court. It can be done at any time before the Chapter 13 plan is confirmed on request of any party in interest, including the debtor, the Chapter 13 trustee, the United States trustee, or a creditor.

Creditors may also want to convert a Chapter 13 case to Chapter 7. The Chapter 13 trustee may also believe that the case should proceed under Chapter 7 instead of Chapter 13. In such cases, upon request of a party in interest and after notice and a hearing, the court may convert the case to Chapter 7 if "cause" is shown and so long as the debtor is not a farmer. Section 1307(c) lists some examples of cause, including:

☐ The debtor's unreasonable and prejudicial delay.

☐ The debtor's nonpayment of fees and charges assessed by the Bankruptcy Code.

☐ The debtor's failure to timely file a plan or the debtor's failure to commence making timely payments under the plan.

☐ The court's denial of plan confirmation or revocation of a previously confirmed plan.

☐ The occurrence of a material default in the terms of a plan or termination of the plan.

To convert a Chapter 13 case to a case under Chapter 7, the party in interest must make a motion alleging the cause. Bankruptcy Rule 1017(a) concerns the notice and opportunity for a hearing that must be provided on such a motion.

Section 348 of the Bankruptcy Code details the effects of conversion of a case from one chapter to another. As discussed in Chapter 8 of this book, Section 348(a) provides that conversion constitutes an order for relief but, unless specifically stated otherwise, does not effect a change in the date of the commencement of the case, the filing of the petition or the first order for relief.

Those items where the date of conversion controls over any earlier date are listed in Section 348(b) and (c). They include the debtor's exclusivity period, the end of debtor's tax year, and the enforceability of any discharge waiver. In addition, the timing requirements of Section 365(d) start anew with the conversion of a case. Dates that had no significance in the prior case, such as the deadline to file a complaint to determine the dischargeability of a debt in the debtor's prior Chapter 13 case, spring in to existence in the converted Chapter 7 case.

To facilitate a smooth transition to a Chapter 7 case and the administration of the Chapter 7 trustee, Bankruptcy Rule 1019 requires that when a Chapter 13 case has been converted to Chapter 7, the following must be done:

☐ If the debtor has not filed the schedules, statements, inventories, or any required list, it must do so.

☐ Within twenty days after entry of the order converting the case, notice of the order must be given to all creditors.

☐ Chapter 13 debtors must turn over to the Chapter 7 trustee all records and property of the estate in their control.

☐ Within thirty days of the conversion, the Chapter 13 debtor must submit to the United States trustee a final report and account.

☐ Within fifteen days of the conversion the debtor must file a schedule of the unpaid debts incurred during the Chapter 13 case.

Dismissing a Chapter 13 Case An alternative to converting a Chapter 13 case is to dismiss it. Creditors may believe the case was filed in bad faith and may want to proceed with their state law collection remedies. The Chapter 13 trustee may not be receiving sufficient cooperation from the debtor and may dismiss the case because it cannot be administered effectively. The debtor may want the case dismissed because it no longer has any need for the protections bankruptcy affords or may have thought that bankruptcy could accomplish more than it does.

Like conversion, and for the same policy reasons, a Chapter 13 debtor can dismiss the bankruptcy case at any time as a matter of right. A sample request for a case to be dismissed is shown in Exhibit 10.2. The only exception is if the case was originally commenced under a different chapter, in which event court authorization is required. Court approval will not be withheld but the requirement for notice and a hearing will allow creditors the opportunity to object to the dismissal and request conversion instead.

Creditors and trustees will frequently add to their request for conversion an alternative request for dismissal (or will add conversion to their motion to dismiss as the alternative remedy). The coupling of these two types of relief is natural since the Bankruptcy Code generally provides that the basis for the relief is the same. In fact Section 1307(c) states that the court may convert or dismiss "whichever is the best interest of the creditors and the estate." The best interest of the debtor is not a consideration. Bankruptcy Rule 1017(a) governs motions seeking the dismissal of Chapter 13 cases.

The effect of the dismissal of a Chapter 13 case is set out in Section 349 of the Bankruptcy Code. Section 349(b) provides that unless the court orders otherwise, dismissal reinstates any proceeding or custodianship superseded by the bankruptcy filing and any avoided transfer or lien. It also vacates any order concerning turnover, liability of a transferee of an avoided transfer, and setoff.

Unless the debtor is prohibited from filing a new bankruptcy case for 180 days under Section 109(f), upon dismissal the debtor may refile a new bankruptcy case

BANKRUPT C. LAWYER
White Charger Legal Clinic
One Learned Way
Los Angeles, California 90001

Attorneys for Debtor

UNITED STATES BANKRUPTCY COURT
WESTERN DISTRICT OF CALIFORNIA

In re)	Case No. 95-00002-JF
)	
JOSEPH CONSUMER,)	Chapter 13
)	
Debtor.)	REQUEST THAT CASE BE
)	DISMISSED AND ORDER THEREON
)	
Debtor's Address:)	
18 Hollywood Drive)	
Los Angeles, California 90001)	
)	
Debtor's S.S. No. 524-47-7448)	
_____)	

Joseph Consumer, the debtor in the above-captioned Chapter 13 case (the "Case"), pursuant to Section 1307 of Title 11 of the United States Code, requests that the Court dismiss the Case.

DATED: October 30, 1995

_____

JOSEPH CONSUMER

WHITE CHARGER LEGAL CLINIC

_____

BANKRUPT C. LAWYER
Attorneys for Debtor

ORDER

IT IS SO ORDERED.

DATED: October 30, 1995

_____

JUSTIN FAIR
United States Bankruptcy Judge

and obtain a discharge in the new case unless the court finds cause to order otherwise.

Closing the Chapter 13 Case   In a Chapter 13 bankruptcy case, the debtor is not required to do anything to close the case. When all the Chapter 13 plan payments have been made, Section 1302(b) requires the Chapter 13 trustee to file with the court and the United States trustee a report that shows all funds received and paid out and a certification that the estate has been fully administered. Under Bankruptcy Rule 5009, if no objection to the report is filed by the United States trustee or a party in interest within thirty days, there will be a presumption that the estate has been fully administered and no order closing the case will be required.

☐ CHAPTER 12 SPECIAL ISSUES

Chapter 12 Administration

To review, a Chapter 12 may be voluntarily commenced by a **family farmer with regular income.** This is a person, which can include an individual and some partnerships and corporations, who:

☐ Is engaged in farming operations.

☐ Has annual income sufficiently stable and regular to fund a Chapter 12 plan.

☐ Has less than $1,500,000 in debts.

☐ Incurred 80 percent or more of its debts in farming operations.

☐ Received 50 percent or more of its gross income in the previous year from farming operations.

☐ If a corporation or a partnership, 80 percent or more of its assets relate to farming operations.

☐ If a corporation, has no publicly traded stock and 50 percent or more of the stock is held by one family.

☐ If a partnership, 50 percent or more of the partnership interests are held by one family.

Upon the filing of the Chapter 12 case, the debtor becomes a debtor in possession. As debtor in possession, the Chapter 12 debtor will remain in control of its farm and will operate it subject to the benefits and restrictions of the Bankruptcy Code. For example, under Section 363, the debtor may use, sell or lease property in the ordinary course of business without notice and a hearing. This would include cultivating and harvesting its crops or raising its livestock.

The trustee in a Chapter 12 case, like a Chapter 13 trustee, usually only serves to disburse plan payments to creditors. Unlike Chapter 13, however, the debtor can be removed as the debtor in possession. In that event, the Chapter 12 trustee's duties will expand to include management and operation of the debtor's farm. Under Section 1204, a debtor can be removed as debtor in possession only upon the request of a party in interest and after notice and a hearing. The grounds for removal are fraud, dishonesty, incompetence, gross mismanagement or similar cause.

The Chapter 12 Plan

In General   Only a debtor may file a Chapter 12 plan even if the debtor has been removed as the debtor in possession. Under Section 1221, the plan must be filed

within ninety days of the filing of the petition. The bankruptcy court can extend that ninety day period, but only if it finds that the extension is needed because of circumstances that are not the debtor's fault. Like Chapter 13, in most cases the Chapter 12 plan is filed with the petition or shortly thereafter.

The Terms of the Plan   Like Chapter 13 plans, most Chapter 12 plans are very similar and relatively simple. Usually they will designate one or more classes of secured claims, one class of unsecured claims, and if the debtor is a partnership or corporation, one class of equity interests. The plan payments to creditors will be funded from the income of the farming operations after the payment of the debtor's operating and living expenses for three or sometimes five years. Priority creditors will be paid in full. Secured creditors will be paid their full allowed claim and unsecured creditors will receive a percentage of this claim depending on the profit projected. Payments will be made by the debtor to the Chapter 12 trustee who will then distribute the funds to the creditors in the manner and amounts provided in the plan. A typical Chapter 12 plan is shown in Exhibit 10.3.

Section 1222 sets forth the mandatory provisions that must be contained in every Chapter 12 plan. It also lists certain permissible provisions that the debtor may opt to include. The mandatory provisions set out in Section 1222(a) are:

☐ The plan must provide for the submission of the debtor's future income to the Chapter 12 trustee as is necessary under the plan.

☐ The plan must provide for the payment in full of all priority claims listed in Section 507, such as taxes and administrative expenses, unless the priority creditor agrees to different treatment.

☐ Each claim within a class must receive the same treatment unless a holder in the class agrees to less favorable treatment.

Section 1222(b) lists the optional provisions of a plan. They include:

☐ The plan may designate various classes of unsecured claims provided the claims in each class are substantially similar and the plan does not discriminate unfairly among the classes. The plan may also create an administrative convenience class consisting of claims that are less than a certain amount. These small claims will usually be paid in full so that very small distributions to these creditors will not have to be paid over time to the creditors.

☐ The rights of holders to secured claims, including home mortgages can be modified. Payment terms can be reduced, stretched out, or otherwise changed provided the secured creditor is paid the full amount of its allowed claim.

☐ Payments to unsecured creditors can be made at the same time as payments are being made to secured creditors.

☐ Executory contracts and unexpired leases can be assumed or rejected.

☐ The plan can provide for a sale of all or most of the debtor's property.

Section 1222(c) provides that under the plan payments to unsecured creditors can be made over three years unless the court approves up to five years. The Chapter 12 trustee will receive all payments under the plan for priority and unsecured claims. The trustee may receive payments for secured claims but Chapter 12 allows those payments to be made directly by the debtor.

Plan Confirmation   The bankruptcy court must finish the Chapter 12 plan confirmation hearing within forty-five days after the plan is filed, unless it finds cause

BANKRUPT C. LAWYER
White Charger Legal Clinic
One Learned Way
Los Angeles, California 90001

Attorneys for Debtor

UNITED STATES BANKRUPTCY COURT
WESTERN DISTRICT OF CALIFORNIA

In re	Case No. 95-00005-JF
JOSEPH FARMER,	Chapter 12
Debtor.	CHAPTER 12 PLAN OF REORGANIZATION
Debtor's Address: 18 Hollywood Drive Los Angeles, California 90001	
Debtor's S.S. No. 524-47-7448	

Joseph Farmer, the debtor in the above-captioned Chapter 12 case ("Debtor"), hereby proposes this Chapter 12 Plan:

I
Means of Implementing Plan

Debtor shall make annual payments to the trustee on October 1st of each year, commencing October 1, 1995, and continuing until October 1, 1998, in the amount of the debtor's excess income for the previous year, but in no event less than $10,000 per year. Excess income shall mean the net income received by Debtor from farming operations during the applicable year less $47,000 which constitutes the debtor's living expenses and $5,000 which the debtor shall retain as a reserve for funding of the next year's crop.

II
Classification and Treatment of Claims

1. Class 1 claims are those entitled to priority in payment under Section 507 of the Bankruptcy Code. The trustee shall receive and retain as the trustee's percentage fee under the Plan an amount equal to five percent (5%) of all payments distributed by the trustee pursuant to the plan from the effective date of the plan to and including October 1, 1998. All other Class 1 claims shall be paid in cash in full out of the funds received and distributed by the trustee.

2. Class 2 consists of the allowed secured claim of Credit Agribusiness Bank ("CAB"). CAB has a lien on debtor's real property securing a debt of $100,000. The debtor values the real property at $60,000 and, accordingly, the secured claim of CAB shall be reduced to $60,000. CAB's allowed secured claim shall bear interest at the existing contract rate of ten percent (10%). CAB's allowed secured claim shall be paid directly by Debtor in 120 equal monthly installments of principal of $500 plus accrued interest, on the first day of each month commencing October 1, 1995, and continuing through October 1, 2005. The balance of CAB's claim in excess of $60,000 shall be a Class 3 claim.

3. Class 3—Allowed Unsecured Claims. These claims shall share *pro rata* in the distributions made by Debtor to the trustee after payment in full by the trustee of the Class 1 claim.

—*continued*

III

Executory Contracts and Unexpired Leases

All executory contracts and unexpired leases not previously rejected are hereby assumed.

IV

Liquidation Analysis

Based upon its projections of farming income during the term of the Plan, Debtor believes that he will distribute to creditors approximately 50 percent of the allowed amount of their claims. Based upon the values of the Debtor's assets and the amount of secured and unsecured claims as set forth in Debtor's schedules, Debtor believes that the return to general unsecured creditors in a Chapter 7 case would be zero because all of Debtor's assets are encumbered by liens or security interests. Accordingly, Debtor believes that the value, as of the effective date of the plan, of property to be distributed under the plan on account of each allowed unsecured claim is not less than the amount that would be paid on such claim if the estate of Debtor were liquidated under Chapter 7 of the Bankruptcy Code.

DATED: October 1, 1995

_____

JOSEPH FARMER

---

to extend that deadline. Bankruptcy Rules 2002(a)(9) and 2002(b) require twenty days notice to the trustee, all creditors and all equity interest holders of the confirmation hearing. Bankruptcy Rule 3015(d) states that a copy of the plan, or a court approved summary of the plan must accompany the notice.

The Bankruptcy Rules do not set a deadline for filing objections to a Chapter 12 plan other than before the plan is confirmed. Because only twenty days notice is provided, a creditor or other objecting party will want to act quickly. A sample objection to a Chapter 12 plan is shown in Exhibit 10.4.

The requirements for confirmation of a Chapter 12 plan are set out in Section 1225. There are five requirements that apply in all Chapter 12 cases and two that sometimes apply. If the plan meets all applicable requirements, it will be confirmed.

The five general requirements are:

☐ The plan complies with Chapter 12 and all other relevant provisions of the Bankruptcy Code.

☐ All required fees and costs have been paid.

☐ The plan was proposed in good faith and not by any means forbidden by law.

☐ Creditors will receive at least as much under the plan as they would under the debtor's Chapter 7 liquidation.

☐ The debtor will be able to make all payments under the plan and to otherwise comply with the plan.

The sixth requirement only applies if the debtor has secured creditors. Unless the secured creditor consents, or unless the debtor returns the creditor's collateral, under Section 1225(a)(5)(B) the plan must satisfy two requirements for each secured creditor. First, the creditor must retain its lien. Second, the creditor must receive under the plan the allowed amount of its claim. The allowed amount is

■ EXHIBIT 10.4
Sample Pleading

WARREN PEASE
Pease, Inyore, & Time
1000 Star Boulevard
Los Angeles, California 90001

Attorneys for Credit Agribusiness Bank

UNITED STATES BANKRUPTCY COURT
WESTERN DISTRICT OF CALIFORNIA

In re	)	Case No. 95-00005-JF
	)	
JOSEPH FARMER,	)	Chapter 12
	)	
Debtor.	)	OBJECTION TO CHAPTER 12 PLAN
	)	
Debtor's Address:	)	
18 Hollywood Drive	)	
Los Angeles, California 90001	)	
	)	
Debtor's S.S. No. 524-47-7448	)	
	)	

Credit Agribusiness Bank ("CAB"), the holder of an unsecured and a secured claim against Joseph Farmer, the above-named debtor ("Debtor"), hereby objects to confirmation of Debtor's Chapter 12 plan for the reasons set forth below:

1. Debtor is not eligible to be a Chapter 12 debtor under Section 109(f) because, on the date of the filing of the petition, Debtor received less than 50 percent of his gross income for the taxable year immediately preceding the taxable year in which the case was filed from a farming operation.

2. Debtor is not eligible to be a Chapter 12 debtor under Section 109(f) because Debtor's annual income is not sufficiently stable and regular to enable Debtor to make payments under a Chapter 12 plan.

3. The plan does not meet the confirmation requirements of Section 1225(a)(1) because it does not comply with the provisions of Chapter 12 and with other applicable provisions of the Bankruptcy Code for the following reasons:

   (A) The plan does not provide for submission of sufficient income to the trustee as is necessary for execution of the plan;

   (B) The plan does not provide for full cash payment of all claims entitled to priority under Section 507; and

   (C) The plan discriminates unfairly by placing the claim of CAB in a separate class from other claims which are substantially similar.

4. The plan does not provide for the submission of all of Debtor's disposable income as that term is defined in Section 1225(b)(2) of the Bankruptcy Code.

DATED: October 15, 1995

PEASE, INYORE, & TIME

_____

WARREN PEASE
Attorneys for Credit Agribusiness Bank

the amount due up to the value of the collateral. If the creditor is due $100 and the collateral is worth $100, the allowed amount of the claim is $100. If the collateral is only worth $50, the allowed amount of the claim is $50.

The debtor is not obligated to pay the creditor all at once. The plan can stretch out the payments to a secured creditor provided the creditor is paid interest. The length of time the payments can be stretched out and the interest rate are not set in the Bankruptcy Code or the Bankruptcy Rules but will depend on the existing contract of other parties, market conditions and the type of collateral. Payments to secured creditors can exceed the three to five year term of the Plan.

The final plan confirmation requirement only applies if the Chapter 12 trustee or an unsecured creditor objects to confirmation. If there is an objection by one of those parties, Section 1225(b)(1) states that the plan can only be confirmed if unsecured creditors are being paid in full or all of the debtor's disposable income is being used to make plan payments. Disposable income is defined in Section 1225(b)(2) as the debtor's income that is not necessary for the maintenance and support of the debtor and his or her dependents or for the continuation, preservation, and operation of the debtor's business.

The provisions of a confirmed plan will bind the debtor and each of the creditors. If the Chapter 12 debtor is a partnership or corporation, confirmation will also bind the partners or shareholders. However, if the debtor does not receive a discharge the plan will have no binding effect.

Discharge

Once all the plan payments have been made, the debtor is entitled to a discharge of all debts provided for in the plan or disallowed. The only exceptions under Section 1228 are those payments that extend beyond the plan, such as long term obligations to secured creditors, and those listed in Section 523(a) that would not be discharged in a Chapter 7 case. The list of claims exempted from discharge under Section 523(a) was set forth in the discussion of a Chapter 13 discharge.

Even if the debtor cannot make all the payments called for in the plan, it can apply for a hardship discharge. The court may grant a family farmer a hardship discharge if:

☐ The debtor's failure to make all plan payments is due to circumstances for which the debtor should not justly be held accountable.

☐ The creditors received as much under the plan as they would have received if the debtor had commenced a Chapter 7 case.

☐ Modification of the plan is not feasible.

The only differences between a typical Chapter 12 discharge and a hardship discharge is that the hardship discharge is not automatic and does not extend to postpetition debts.

Pursuant to Section 1228(d), a discharge can be revoked by the court upon the request of a creditor or other party in interest within one year if the discharge was obtained through fraud and the moving party did not know about it at the time the discharge was granted.

Converting, Dismissing, and Closing the Case

Changing Chapters As is true for debtors under Chapters 11 and 13, a family farmer has an absolute right under Section 1208(a) to convert its Chapter 12 case

to a Chapter 7 case at any time unless the case was previously converted to Chapter 12 from another Chapter.

The court may also convert a case to Chapter 7 upon the request of a party in interest. However, the grounds allowing the court to do so is limited solely to fraud on the debtor's part in connection with the bankruptcy case. Even gross mismanagement, dishonesty and incompetence are not sufficient cause under Section 1208(a) to involuntarily convert a Chapter 12 reorganization to a Chapter 7 liquidation. Accordingly, one of the benefits of filing a Chapter 12 case is that it is very difficult for creditors to force a liquidation against the debtor's wishes. The best the creditors can do is to move to dismiss the case as discussed below. That will still not, however, force a liquidation. Remember that creditors cannot involuntarily commence Chapter 7 cases against farmers.

The effect of the conversion of a Chapter 12 case is the same as it is for a Chapter 13 case discussed earlier in this Chapter.

Dismissing a Chapter 12 Case   The family farmer's right to dismiss a Chapter 12 case is identical to that found in Chapter 13. The right is absolute unless the case has been previously converted from Chapter 7, 11, or 13. As examined in the discussion of conversions earlier in this Chapter, the court's ability to convert a Chapter 12 case against the debtor's will is extremely limited. It can be done only on a finding that the debtor has committed fraud in the bankruptcy case. The ability to dismiss is more expansive. Section 1208(c) provides that on the request of a party in interest, and after notice and a hearing, the court may dismiss a Chapter 12 case for cause including:

☐ Unreasonable delay or gross mismanagement by the debtor that is prejudicial to creditors.

☐ Nonpayment of fees and costs.

☐ Failure to timely file a plan.

☐ Failure to timely make payments required by a confirmed plan.

☐ Denial of confirmation of a plan.

☐ Material default by the debtor with respect to a term of a confirmed plan.

☐ Revocation of an order of confirmation of a plan.

☐ Termination of a confirmed plan by reason of the occurrence of a condition specified in the plan.

☐ Continuing loss to or diminution of the estate and absence of a reasonable likelihood of rehabilitation.

Bankruptcy Rules 1017(a) and (c) also govern the procedural aspects of dismissing Chapter 12 cases. The effect of dismissal is the same as it is for Chapter 13 cases.

Closing the Chapter 12 Case   Upon the completion of all plan payments, the Chapter 12 trustee will file a final report and account as discussed in Bankruptcy Rule 5009. Thirty days later, unless there is an objection, the case will be deemed to be fully administered and closed.

☐ SUMMARY

Chapters 12 and 13 are alike, although each is designed to assist different types of debtors. Chapter 12 is for family farmers (which can include partnerships and

corporations) with stable income. Chapter 13 is only available for individuals with relatively small debts and stable income. Chapter 13 cases are more common.

In a Chapter 13 case, a trustee is appointed but the trustee's duties are limited to administering the distributions to creditors under the plan of reorganization. The Chapter 13 plan is a simple document that divides creditors into classes and proposes a payment schedule to them. A Chapter 13 plan may only be proposed by the debtor. Creditors will not vote on the plan but they can file objections. If the plan meets the requirements of the Bankruptcy Code, it will be confirmed. If a Chapter 13 debtor completes the payment schedule in the plan, he or she will receive a discharge that relieves the debtor of the obligation to pay most unsatisfied debts. Even if all plan payments are not made, in some circumstances the debtor can still receive a discharge. The debtor can dismiss the Chapter 13 case, or convert it to Chapter 7, at any time. Creditors can seek to dismiss or convert a Chapter 7 case in some situations.

In a Chapter 12 case, a trustee like a Chapter 13 trustee is appointed. If the debtor has engaged in serious misconduct, however, the Chapter 12 trustee can be called upon to operate the farm. A Chapter 12 plan is similar to a Chapter 13 plan and the confirmation procedures and results are also similar. The Chapter 12 conversion and dismissal rules are based on the Chapter 13 rules; however, a Chapter 12 case cannot be converted to Chapter 7 without the debtor's consent unless the court finds fraud.

☐ KEY TERMS

Disposable Income
Family Farmer

Family Farmer with Regular Income

Hardship Discharge
Regular Income

☐ IMPROVE YOUR UNDERSTANDING

1. Can a family farmer file a Chapter 13 case?

2. Who may file a Chapter 12 case but not a Chapter 13 case?

3. Compare Sections 1222(a) and 1322(a). What is the difference? Why?

4. Compare Sections 1222(b) and 1322(b). List the differences.

5. Compare Section 1225 and 1325. Are there any meaningful differences?

6. How does a Chapter 12 discharge compare to a Chapter 13 discharge?

7. Under what circumstances would a creditor prefer to have a case converted rather than dismissed?

8. Under what circumstances would a creditor prefer to have a case dismissed rather than converted?

☐ RESEARCH PROJECTS

1. Locate at least one case in which a hardship discharge was sought. What facts did the court consider in granting or denying the discharge?

2. Locate at least one case in which a debtor sought a Chapter 13 discharge after having received a Chapter 7 discharge. Was it granted? Why or why not?

☐ DRAFTING PROJECTS

1. Myra Consumer is trying to decide between filing a Chapter 7 case and starting all over or filing a Chapter 13 case. Given the following facts, outline a possible confirmable Chapter 13 plan for her. Assume that the matter will be handled by a legal aid clinic without charge and that the trustee's fee will be $100. Also assume that it is not necessary to pay interest on any claim or arrearage.

☐ Myra owns and operates a dress shop where she creates custom designs for her clientele. She has a steady group of loyal customers who provide her with a disposable monthly income of $200 when she can work. She charges $100 for her custom designs, half of which is paid when the dress is ordered and the other half when the dress is picked up, usually two or three weeks later.

☐ Myra lives in a small apartment over her shop in a building she rents.

☐ Myra has recently recovered from a lengthy illness. During her illness, she became behind in her orders and, therefore, behind in her rent and other bills.

☐ Presently, Myra has orders and deposits for six designs. She owes her landlord $200, the phone company $30, the electric company $30, a bevy of doctors $1,000, a sales tax agency $50, a fabric and pattern supplier $500, and the store where she bought her industrial-model sewing machine $500. The store has a purchase money security interest in the sewing machine, which is worth $300.

☐ The fabric supplier sued Myra in small claims court and obtained a judgment lien that attached to her sewing machine.

2. Using Sections 109, 1322 and 1325, make a checklist of possible objections to a Chapter 13 plan.

COMPLEX REORGANIZATIONS

In the previous chapter of this book we examined bankruptcy reorganizations for the consumer and small farmer. The other type of bankruptcy reorganization is designed for larger businesses and individuals with substantial debt or entangled financial problems. In this Chapter we consider these larger and more complicated reorganizations controlled by Chapter 11 of the Bankruptcy Code.

☐ THE MANAGEMENT OF A CHAPTER 11 DEBTOR

The Debtor in Possession

In Chapter 11 the debtor ordinarily continues to operate its business throughout the case. For this reason, unless the court appoints a trustee, the debtor is known as the **debtor in possession.** Section 1107 of the Bankruptcy Code gives the debtor in possession all the rights and most of the responsibilities of a trustee. Debtors in possession can sue to recover preferences, sell assets, reject leases, and otherwise use all the tools a trustee has available. The only duties the debtor in possession need not perform are to investigate its own operations and make a report to the court as a trustee must do under Sections 1106(a)(3) and (4) of the Bankruptcy Code. In almost all instances in a Chapter 11 case, whenever the word trustee appears in the Bankruptcy Code in connection with some right or power the trustee may exercise, the words debtor in possession may be substituted.

The Appointment of a Trustee

In General   Although a debtor in possession is usual in Chapter 11, there are some situations in which a trustee should be appointed. Perhaps the debtor's owners

Debtor in Possession
A debtor in a case under Chapter 13, a debtor in a case under Chapter 11 in which no trustee has been appointed, and a debtor in a case under Chapter 12 unless the standing trustee has been directed to take control of the debtor's farming operations.

believe the business can be reorganized but they want to be involved and cannot find anyone to take over. In those situations, the debtor will ask the court to appoint a Chapter 11 trustee. More commonly, a trustee is appointed by the court on a motion by the United States trustee or a creditor and over the objection of the debtor in possession. Chapter 11 trustees are not frequently appointed. They are something of a rarity and a party other than the debtor seeking the appointment of a trustee has a heavy burden to convince the court that one should be inserted into the debtor's affairs.

Grounds for the Appointment of a Trustee   Section 1104 of the Bankruptcy Code authorizes the appointment of a trustee at any time prior to confirmation of a plan. The grounds for such an appointment are cause and the best interests of creditors. Obviously, by using such broad concepts, Congress wanted to give the courts substantial flexibility in determining whether a trustee should be appointed. What constitutes cause and what is in the best interests of creditors will be tested on a case-by-case basis.

Congress has not, however, left the courts without guidance. Examples of cause are set out in Section 1104. They include fraud, dishonesty, gross mismanagement, and similar acts or omissions either before or after the commencement of the bankruptcy case. The mismanagement required is gross mismanagement; simply poor management is not enough. In fact, some mismanagement is usually expected in companies that have been forced to seek the protections of Chapter 11.

The second ground for the appointment of a trustee, the best-interests-of-creditors test, is designed for those situations that fall outside the scope of cause but where there is still the need for a trustee. For example, there may be so much dislike between the debtor in possession and the creditor body that attempts to negotiate a plan have been stymied. Appointing a neutral trustee might move the case along towards confirmation. Alternatively, the debtor in possession may be guilty of only poor mismanagement. Although insufficient to constitute cause, poor mismanagement may be enough for a trustee to be appointed as in the best interests of creditors. Typically, whatever the basis for the appointment of a trustee, the moving party will allege both grounds so that if the court finds insufficient cause, it may still determine that the best interests of creditors compel the appointment of a trustee.

Duties of a Chapter 11 Trustee   A Chapter 11 trustee steps into the shoes of the debtor in possession in running the business, filing reports with the United States trustee or the court, and otherwise attempting to reorganize the debtor. The Chapter 11 trustee is also required to investigate the debtor's acts, conduct, assets, liabilities, and business. The trustee must file a written report of the investigation and make recommendations. Subject to court approval, the trustee is authorized to employ accountants and other professionals under Section 327. One significant difference is that while the debtor in possession management will be paid a salary, the trustee's compensation is limited to a percentage of assets administered.

Procedures   The procedure for the appointment of a trustee is governed by Bankruptcy Rule 9014, which requires the filing of a motion. The trustee will be selected by the United States trustee after consultation with the creditors. If the creditors do not like the trustee selected by the United States trustee they have remedies. The 1994 Amendments provide that on the request of a party in interest made not later than thirty days after the court orders the appointment of a trustee, the

United States trustee must convene a creditor's meeting for the purpose of electing a trustee. The Chapter 11 trustee election will be conducted in the same manner as a Chapter 7 trustee election under Section 702 of the Bankruptcy Code.

Termination of Trusteeship   Once appointed, a trustee usually remains until the case is closed. The trustee will try to have a plan confirmed, or will move to have the case converted to Chapter 7, or will move to have it dismissed if it is not feasible to propose a plan. There are exceptions that allow a trustee's appointment to be terminated before the case is over. Bankruptcy Code Section 1105 expressly states that at any time before plan confirmation, after notice and a hearing, the court may terminate the trustee's appointment and restore the debtor in possession. The court may grant such a motion if the debtor demonstrates that it has cured whatever caused the trustee's appointment or if it is shown that the trustee was wrongfully appointed.

Examiners   In many cases the appointment of a trustee will be very disruptive to the debtor's business and will merely herald the death of the debtor. Courts are mindful of this disruption and to the expense of the trustee. One alternative the courts and the parties can use to avoid a trustee but still give creditors some comfort that the debtor is not engaged in any wrongdoing is the appointment of an **examiner.**

Examiner

A court appointed investigator authorized to delve into the financial and business affairs of a debtor in possession in a Chapter 11 case.

Section 1104(b) authorizes the court to appoint an examiner to conduct whatever investigation of the debtor the court orders. The investigation can include allegations of fraud, dishonesty, incompetence, misconduct, or mismanagement by the debtor's officers. The grounds for the appointment of an examiner are in the interests of the creditors, stockholders, or other interested parties, or if the total unsecured debts exceed $5,000,000, excluding debts for goods, services, taxes, or debts owing to insiders.

The role of the examiner is much different than that of a trustee. The examiner does not replace the debtor in possession or in any way control the business operations. The examiner merely makes the investigation ordered and reports back to the court and all parties in interest on the findings. Based on the examiner's report, the court may then proceed to appoint a trustee. To prevent an examiner from too enthusiastically recommending the appointment of a trustee in a case, Section 321(b) specifically prevents the examiner from serving as the trustee.

Unlike the trustee, the compensation paid to an examiner is not limited to a percentage of the assets administered in the estate but is only limited by what is reasonable and comparable for similar services performed in nonbankruptcy cases.

The Creditors' Committee

Creditors' Committee

A committee comprised of two or more of the debtor's creditors appointed in a Chapter 11 case by the United States trustee for the purpose of representing the creditors' interests in the case.

Formation   As stated earlier, the general rule is that a Chapter 11 debtor will be a debtor in possession and will remain in control of its assets while in bankruptcy. This is not to suggest that it is business as usual. A number of controls prevent the situation from becoming analogous to a fox in the hen house. The first control is the requirement that anything unusual or out of the ordinary course of business first be noticed to creditors and approved by the court. The second is the creation of a **creditors' committee.** A significant role of a creditors' committee is to keep an eye on the debtor in possession and its activities. Another important role is to

facilitate representation of the creditors' interests and their communication with the debtor.

As soon as practical after the commencement of a Chapter 11 case, the United States trustee will appoint a committee of unsecured creditors. Sometimes the creditors who serve on the committee will also be secured creditors but they qualify for appointment on the committee because their collateral is not worth as much as they are owed.

Generally, even if a creditor's claim is disputed by the debtor, the creditor is still eligible to serve on the committee. However, in at least a few cases, creditors who are competitors of the debtor will not be allowed to serve because the committee may be provided with confidential information that could be used against the debtor. Governmental agencies are not usually eligible to serve on the committee.

In most cases the United States trustee will select the members of the committee from the list of the twenty largest creditors that the debtor filed with the petition. The United States trustee will normally select seven of those from the list willing to serve. If fewer than seven are willing to join the committee, the United States trustee will appoint a smaller committee provided it has more than one or two members. A larger committee may also be chosen.

Often the debtor will have made an attempt at reorganization prior to the filing of the bankruptcy petition. There may have been a committee created in that out-of-court workout to negotiate a payment plan with the debtor. Where a committee has been selected prepetition, rather than create a new committee, the United States trustee may have the existing committee continue. The United States trustee has that option if, as required by Section 1102 of the Bankruptcy Code, the prepetition committee was "fairly chosen and is representative of the different kinds of claims to be represented." Bankruptcy Rule 2007 is more specific. It allows an already formed committee to continue if the following criteria are met:

☐ It was selected by a majority in number and amount of unsecured creditors who could and did vote at a meeting in which all unsecured creditors with claims over $1,000 or the 100 largest creditors were invited on at least five days' notice. There must be written minutes of the meeting and the voting results.

☐ All proxies are filed with the court.

☐ The organization of the committee was in all other respects fair and proper.

Usually only one creditors' committee is appointed. If the debtor has a large number of shareholders, there might also be a shareholders' committee formed to represent the equity interests. In large reorganization cases there might also be a need to have more than one creditors' committee. For example, the debtor may have issued a large amount of bonds whose repayment is subordinated to that of the general trade debt. The bondholders' interests are different than those of the debtor's vendors and the subordinated debt may require their own committee to make sure that their interests are adequately considered. Section 1102(a)(2) provides that, on request of a party in interest, the court may order the appointment of additional committees of creditors or equity security holders if necessary to assure their adequate representation. If the motion is granted, the United States trustee will select the new committee's members. The debtor and the existing creditors' committee frequently oppose motions to appoint additional committees because of the added expense.

Once a committee is formed, its size may not remain static. The United States trustee may appoint additional members if the existing members are not as representative as first thought. In addition, the United States trustee may decrease the size of a committee by excusing members who do not participate or attend meetings thereby making it difficult to obtain a quorum or who are later found to have a conflict of interest.

Operation   The powers and duties of a creditors' committee are set out in Section 1103(c) of the Bankruptcy Code. They are to:

☐ Consult with the debtor in possession concerning the administration of the case.

☐ Investigate the acts, conduct, assets, liabilities, and financial condition of the debtor, the operation of the debtor's business, and the desirability of continuing that business, as well as any other matter relevant to the case or the formulation of a plan.

☐ Participate in the formulation of a plan, advise the creditors of the committee's determination as to the plan, and collect and file with the court acceptances or rejections of a plan.

☐ Request the appointment of a trustee or an examiner.

☐ Perform such other services as are in the interest of the creditors.

The committee's role is generally to advise—not to replace—the debtor. For example, the committee is not given an explicit statutory grant of the right to bring suit or to intervene in an adversary proceeding in which the committee is interested. Most courts, however, will allow the committee to do so if the debtor in possession has unjustifiably refused or has abused its discretion in commencing suit.

To assist the committee in the performance of its duties and the exercise of its powers, Section 1103(a) allows it to select and employ one or more attorneys, accountants, or other agents with the employment subject to the approval of the court. The selections must be made at a scheduled meeting of the committee at which a majority of the members are present.

The committee will also likely choose a chairperson to call or otherwise arrange committee meetings and to be the primary representative of the committee. Depending on the committee's size and the complexity of the debtor's operations and case, one or more subcommittees may be formed. The committee may also appoint or employ a secretary to keep minutes and to ensure that all committee members are informed of events in the case between committee meetings. These tasks might fall to the chairperson of the committee or the committee's counsel. Often, coordination of these matters will be the task of the legal assistant to the committee's counsel. Another task that might be delegated to the legal assistant in the larger cases is preparation of bylaws for the committee so that there is no confusion as to procedure and authority. A sample set of bylaws is presented as Exhibit 11.1.

Compensation   Members of a committee will not be compensated by the estate for their time spent while serving on the committee. Committee members are entitled to be reimbursed for their out-of-pocket expenses such as airfare, hotel costs, and parking as an administrative expense when the expenses are incurred in the performance of their duties. It will generally be the responsibility of the legal assistant employed by the committee's counsel to gather all amounts with backup documentation such as receipts from each committee member who has incurred expenses. A motion should then be prepared detailing the amounts sought.

■ EXHIBIT 11.1
Sample Pleading

BYLAWS
OF THE
OFFICIAL COMMITTEE OF CREDITORS
HOLDING UNSECURED CLAIMS

In re Videos by Joe, Inc.

ARTICLE I
NAME

This Committee is the Official Committee of Creditors Holding Unsecured Claims in the Chapter 11 bankruptcy case pertaining to Videos by Joe, Inc., may be referred to as the VBJ Creditors' Committee, and is referred to herein as the "Committee."

ARTICLE II
PURPOSE

The purpose of the Committee is to carry out the functions provided by the Bankruptcy Code.

ARTICLE III
MEMBERSHIP

The membership of the Committee shall consist of those creditors that have been duly appointed by the United States trustee.

ARTICLE IV
OFFICERS

The Officers of the Committee shall be the Chairperson and Vice-Chairperson.

ARTICLE V
DUTIES OF OFFICERS

Section 1. CHAIRPERSON. The Chairperson shall organize the agenda and preside at all meetings of the Committee. The Chairperson may consult with counsel and other professionals to the Committee on all matters, and all such communications may be discussed and reviewed by the Committee at the appropriate Committee meeting. The Chairperson shall have other executive powers, perform such other duties, and be available for such specific assignments as are directed by the Committee.

Section 2. VICE-CHAIRPERSON. The Vice-Chairperson shall perform the duties of the Chairperson when the Chairperson is absent, or as directed by the Chairperson.

Section 3. SECRETARY. The Secretary, although not an officer of the Committee, shall be responsible for arranging meetings of the Committee, recording and distributing minutes of each meeting of the Committee, notifying members of meetings of the Committee, distributing such notices and materials as are directed by the Committee, and for such other matters as are assigned by the Committee. Counsel shall act as secretary to the Committee.

Section 4. TERM. Each officer shall serve until removed, with or without cause, by the vote of a majority of the members of the Committee or until resignation.

ARTICLE VI
SUBCOMMITTEES

If the Committee determines that the work of the Committee would be benefited by the establishment of one or more subcommittees, the Committee may from time to time establish one or more such subcommittee to facilitate and economize the work of the Committee. Subcommittees shall have rights and powers as designated by the Committee.

ARTICLE VII
MEETINGS

Section 1. REGULAR MEETINGS. Regular meetings of the Committee shall be those as established by the vote of the Committee at a duly held meeting of the Committee.

—continued

Section 2. SPECIAL MEETINGS. Special meetings of the Committee may be called by the Chairperson or Vice-Chairperson, as the case may be, on such notice as is appropriate.

Section 3. NOTICE. Notice of a regular meeting of the Committee shall be given orally or by writing, whichever method is appropriate, to each member at least three (3) days prior to the date of such meeting.

Section 4. PARTICIPATION IN MEETINGS BY CONFERENCE TELEPHONE. If and when such procedure is appropriate, members of the Committee and any subcommittee may participate in a meeting through use of a conference telephone or similar communications equipment, as long as all members participating in such meeting can hear one another. In such case, votes may be taken and certified by the Chairperson or by the Secretary. Participation in such a meeting shall constitute presence at such meeting. The notice provisions of Section 3 above shall apply to such meetings.

Section 5. QUORUM. The presence of a majority of the members of the Committee constitutes a quorum of the Committee for the transaction of business.

Section 6. VOTING. All voting shall be oral or by show of hands. No member may vote except by its representative, alternate representative, or by proxy. The Secretary shall record a Committee member's specific vote, if requested. Every act or decision done or made by a majority of the members present (or through proxy) at a duly held meeting shall be regarded as the act of the Committee.

Section 7. PROXY. A member may vote by proxy, whether oral or written, by providing the proxy to any member of the Committee or counsel.

Section 8. DISSEMINATION OF NOTICES, MINUTES, MATERIALS. Notice of Committee meetings, minutes of such meetings, and copies of all reports and other significant written information generated or obtained by the Committee, or prepared for the Committee by its counsel or accountants, shall be provided by the Secretary to all members.

Section 9. PARTICIPATION BY NONMEMBERS. At the invitation of the Committee, or Officers of the Committee, nonmembers may attend all or any portion of Committee meetings.

ARTICLE VIII
EXPENSES

Reasonable expenses of Committee members incurred in connection with Committee and subcommittee business shall be sought to be reimbursed by the Debtor. Reasonable expenses shall include, at a minimum, travel, hotel, and meal expenses for meetings for one representative or alternate representative of each member; telephone calls; and postage or delivery costs incurred on the Committee's behalf.

ARTICLE IX
AMENDMENTS TO BYLAWS

These Bylaws may be amended by a vote of a majority of the members of the Committee.

ARTICLE X
RATIFICATION UPON CHANGE OF COMPOSITION

Notwithstanding any other provision hereof, if the court or United States trustee orders a change in the composition of the voting members of the Committee, these procedures shall continue only upon the affirmative vote of one-half of the members of the Committee at the meeting of the Committee immediately following the effectiveness of any order mandating such change in Committee membership.

ARTICLE XI
NO LIMITATION ON INDEPENDENT ACTION

Nothing herein and no action taken by the Committee shall be construed or interpreted as binding upon each member of the Committee, or as limiting or restricting action taken by each such member, when acting other than as a member of the Committee.

ARTICLE XII
EXECUTIVE SESSION

The Chairperson may, as may be appropriate, call for an executive session during any meeting wherein one or more members of the Committee or other persons are excused from the meeting and not present for all or a portion of such meeting.

☐ ADMINISTERING THE CHAPTER 11 CASE

Joint Administration

The only two entities that may file a bankruptcy petition together, although they may also file separate cases, are a husband and wife. All other entities must file individual bankruptcy petitions and they will have separate bankruptcy cases each identified by its own docket number.

Many Chapter 11 debtors have affiliates or entities that are otherwise closely related that are also debtors. A parent corporation may have one or more of its subsidiaries in bankruptcy. Limited partnerships controlled by a common general partner may all have filed bankruptcy cases. An individual may be in bankruptcy along with his or her wholly owned corporation. The affiliated debtors may be represented by the same attorneys, have cases pending before the same judge and may have the same trustee. Whatever the nature of the affiliation, there will likely be tasks that need to be done in each case. It makes sense for one motion or other action to accomplish the task in all the cases. For example, if two closely related debtors in possession want to extend the time to assume or reject executory contracts, it is much more efficient for only one motion—rather than two separate motions—to be filed to accomplish that goal.

Bankruptcy Rule 1015(b) provides that if two or more petitions are pending in the same bankruptcy court by or against a husband and wife; a partnership and one or more of its general partners; two or more general partners; or a debtor and its affiliate, the court may order **joint administration** of the estates. Joint administration allows a combining of the estates so that a single docket for the matters occurring in the administration will be kept, only one notice to creditors of the different estates need be sent and the other purely administrative matters can be handled together to expedite the cases and make the process less costly. Often joint administration will be referred to as **administrative consolidation.** Either label is correct but they should not be confused with **substantive consolidation,** which is a form of consolidation that actually merges the two or more entities involved into one company. Substantive consolidation is discussed in the next section of this chapter.

It does not make any difference in joint administration whether one case was commenced voluntarily and one was commenced involuntarily. Likewise, although virtually all jointly administered cases are pending in Chapter 11, it does not matter if one is pending under Chapter 7 and one is pending in Chapter 11. This last situation is not common since the purposes of Chapter 11 are very different from Chapter 7 but it may be feasible to administratively consolidate a liquidating Chapter 11 case where a trustee has been appointed and a Chapter 7 case that has the same trustee.

If a trustee has been appointed, Bankruptcy Rule 2009 specifically authorizes one trustee to serve in jointly administered cases unless there is a showing that creditors or equity security holders would be prejudiced by a conflict of interest. Since joint administration does not mean that the estates are merged, if a single trustee is appointed over administratively consolidated estates, there must be separate accounts of all receipts and disbursements.

Under the general procedure outline of Bankruptcy Rule 9014, to obtain an order granting joint administration, a motion is filed. One such motion is presented in Exhibit 11.2.

Joint Administration or Administrative Consolidation
The merger of two or more bankruptcy cases for the limited purpose of making their administration more convenient.

Substantive Consolidation
The merger of two or more entities, at least one of which is a debtor, into a single entity under a plan of reorganization or by motion.

BANKRUPT C. LAWYER
White Charger Legal Clinic
One Learned Way
Los Angeles, California 90001

Attorneys for Debtors

UNITED STATES BANKRUPTCY COURT
WESTERN DISTRICT OF CALIFORNIA

In re	Case No. 95-00001-JF
VIDEOS BY JOE, INC.,	Chapter 11
Debtor.	
Debtor's Address:	
18 Hollywood Drive	
Los Angeles, California 90001	
Debtor's Tax Id. No. 99-999899	
In re	Case No. 95-00006-JF
JOE'S VIDEO, INC.,	MOTION FOR ORDER DIRECTING
	JOINT ADMINISTRATION OF
Debtor.	ESTATES PURSUANT TO
Debtor's Address:	BANKRUPTCY RULE 1015(b)
18 Hollywood Drive	
Los Angeles, California 9001	
Debtor's Tax Id. No. 03-999899	

TO THE HONORABLE JUSTIN FAIR, UNITED STATES BANKRUPTCY JUDGE:

Videos by Joe, Inc. ("VBJ") and Joe's Videos, Inc. ("JVI"; collectively "Debtors"), through their attorneys, in support of their Motion for Order Directing Joint Administration of Estates Pursuant to Bankruptcy Rule 1015(b), respectively represent as follows:

1. Debtors are the debtors in possession in the above-captioned separate Chapter 11 cases. VBJ and JVI both filed their petitions on October 1, 1995.

2. JVI is a wholly-owned subsidiary of VBJ. Debtors are, therefore, affiliates within the meaning of 11 U.S.C. § 101(2) and Federal Rule of Bankruptcy Procedure 1015(b).

3. Debtors believe that unnecessary and expensive duplication can be avoided by jointly administering their cases.

4. Debtors propose that all pleadings relating to one or both of Debtors' Chapter 11 cases contain a consolidated caption in the form of Exhibit 1 to this Motion and that all such pleadings be filed and maintained under Case Number 95-00001-JF. However, each pleading will indicate either that both Debtors are parties to or are affected by the pleading or shall indicate which of Debtors is a party to or is affected by the pleading.

—continued

■ EXHIBIT 11.2
Sample Pleading—*Continued*

5. Nothing contained in this Motion is intended to effect a substantive consolidation of Debtors' respective estates.

WHEREFORE, Debtors request that this Court enter its Order directing the joint administration of the cases of Debtors in the manner set forth in this Motion.

DATED: October 15, 1995

WHITE CHARGER LEGAL CLINIC

_____

BANKRUPT C. LAWYER
Attorneys for Debtors

- -

BANKRUPT C. LAWYER
White Charger Legal Clinic
One Learned Way
Los Angeles, California 90001

Attorneys for Debtors

UNITED STATES BANKRUPTCY COURT
WESTERN DISTRICT OF CALIFORNIA

In re)) VIDEOS BY JOE, INC. and JOE'S VIDEO, INC.,)) Debtors.)) Debtors' Address:) 18 Hollywood Drive) Los Angeles, California 90001)) _____)	Case No. 95-00001-JF Chapter 11 (Joint Administration of Case Nos. 95-00001-JF and 95-00006-JF) THIS PLEADING AFFECTS [BOTH DEBTORS] [ONLY _____]

Exhibit 1

Substantive Consolidation

There are circumstances in which even joint administration of separate debtors will not lead to an effective administration of the estates. An illustration would be two affiliated corporate debtors whose management did not treat them as separate entities, kept only one set of books and commingled funds. The cost to straighten up the intertwined affairs would cost the estate a substantial amount of money otherwise available to creditors. There are other times when continuing to recognize the separateness of the debtors will lead to unfairness in the treatment of creditors. For example, there may be two corporate debtors that were structured so that one debtor had all the assets and the other had all the debt, which division was kept hidden from creditors who relied on the value of the assets in making their credit decision.

In those circumstances the bankruptcy court may go beyond administrative consolidation and order a substantive consolidation of two or more debtors. The effect of substantive consolidation is to treat the debtors as if there always had been only one entity or as if before the bankruptcy cases were commenced the debtors had affected a merger under applicable state law. After substantive consolidation, the cases continue together with a combination of the assets and liabilities of the formerly separate debtors. Again, although substantive consolidation is not limited to Chapter 11 cases, it is more likely to occur in a Chapter 11 case.

The authority for a bankruptcy court to order substantive consolidation is not expressly provided for by statute or rule except through the court's general equity power to enter any order necessary to effectuate the provision of the Bankruptcy Code as provided in Section 105. Substantive consolidation can be accomplished through filing a motion seeking such relief or, in a Chapter 11 case, a joint plan of reorganization can be proposed that calls for substantive consolidation. In either event, the party in interest proposing substantive consolidation must show that there is a necessity for substantive consolidation, or a harm to be avoided, and that the benefits of substantive consolidation outweigh any harm that would be caused to creditors.

Limiting Notice

Bankruptcy Rule 2002 governs the timing and the extent of notice of certain activities in a bankruptcy case. Subpart (a) of Rule 2002 requires that twenty days' notice by mail of the following acts be given to the debtor, the trustee, all creditors, and any indenture trustees:

- ☐ The date and time of the Section 341(a) meeting.
- ☐ A proposed use, sale, or lease of property out of the ordinary course of business.
- ☐ A hearing for approval of a compromise or a settlement.
- ☐ The last date to file claims.
- ☐ In a Chapter 7 or Chapter 11 case, a hearing on conversion or dismissal.
- ☐ The time fixed for acceptance or rejection of a proposed plan modification.
- ☐ Hearings on applications for compensation.

Other Bankruptcy Rules set when and to whom certain other notices must be sent. For many matters these requirements will be established only by local rule.

If the debtor has many creditors, it may be unnecessarily expensive and cumbersome to comply with Bankruptcy Rule 2002(a) and other rules by giving notice of every act to every creditor. Many small creditors may not care every time the debtor or a trustee seeks to sell an asset or obtain approval of a settlement of a dispute concerning an account receivable. This will be especially true in a Chapter 11 case in which there is an active creditors' committee that has hired counsel to assist it in monitoring the debtor's conduct.

Recognizing that complying with Bankruptcy Rule 2002(a) may not be necessary in all cases, Bankruptcy Rule 2002(m) expressly provides that the court may enter orders designating the matters in respect to which, the person to whom, and the form and manner in which notices must be sent. This rule can be used to more effectively and economically administer an estate in two ways.

1. Rule 2002(m) is authority for obtaining an order limiting notice on a particular motion or procedure. For example, the debtor in possession may seek an

order limiting notice of an upcoming hearing on applications for compensation to the twenty largest creditors and to the United States trustee.

2. Rule 2002(m) can be used by the debtor or the trustee to obtain an order limiting notice on most motions, applications, and other procedures early in the case. For example, the debtor in possession could seek an order providing that notice of all future compromise motions, applications for compensation, and other regular administrative matters be noticed only to the creditors' committee's counsel, the United States trustee, and any party in interest who has requested special notice. (See Exhibit 11.3.)

If an order limiting notice has been obtained, and the notices will be sent by the debtor in possession or the trustee, a separate mailing list should be created and maintained by the legal assistant.

Employees

The successful reorganization of most companies will often depend on maintaining or increasing prepetition production levels. In order to achieve that goal, the employees' cooperation will be essential. Because those employees may not understand bankruptcy and reorganizations, and may automatically assume that they are about to be laid off, early communication is needed if the debtor's goodwill with its workers is to be preserved. Management should consider scheduling a meeting with the employees in the first few days after a case is commenced, if not before, to give them an honest report of the causes of the bankruptcy filing, the immediate plans for continued operations, and the long-term prospects. Ideally, such a meeting will calm fears, reassure those financially dependent on the next paycheck and quash the invariably present and usually harmful rumors. If a face-to-face meeting cannot be held or would be impractical, a letter to all employees might be a good substitute if it explains in layperson terms what bankruptcy is all about and what the employees can expect.

If the employees are also creditors because their last paycheck bounced or was never issued, a meeting or a letter is not likely to cool their anger. Trade creditors, although they may be very insistent that they be paid, are familiar with nonpayment and have probably experienced one of their customers filing a bankruptcy case before. Employees do not usually have such experience and generally are not sympathetic to the debtor's financial problems. The ideal is for the debtor to do enough prepetition planning so that employees do not become creditors. If the debtor has enough cash and the luxury of being able to decide when to file the petition, it should wait until the end of a payroll period to file its petition and pay all the employees in cash just before the filing. As a practical matter this is difficult because payday usually follows the end of a payroll period by a week, or it takes time to process the payroll and figure the deductions, or there may be three shifts at the debtor's plant and regardless of when the debtor files there will be employees owed wages. Adding to the problem of preventing employees from becoming creditors is the fact that a debtor in possession should be closing all its checking accounts immediately after the bankruptcy case is commenced. No matter how strongly employees are encouraged to cash their payroll checks immediately upon receipt, there will be unpresented checks when the account is closed leaving those employees as prepetition creditors.

When prepetition planning is not practical, a common solution is to seek, shortly after the case is commenced, court approval to pay outstanding prepetition

■ EXHIBIT 11.3
Sample Pleading

BANKRUPT C. LAWYER
White Charger Legal Clinic
One Learned Way
Los Angeles, California 90001

Attorneys for Debtor

UNITED STATES BANKRUPTCY COURT
WESTERN DISTRICT OF CALIFORNIA

In re)	Case No. 95-00001-JF
)	
VIDEOS BY JOE, INC.,)	Chapter 11
)	
Debtor.)	
)	
Debtor's Address:)	MOTION TO LIMIT EXTENT OF
18 Hollywood Drive)	NOTICE ON CERTAIN
Los Angeles, California 90001)	ADMINISTRATIVE MATTERS
)	
Debtor's Tax Id. No. 99-999899)	
)	
)	

TO THE HONORABLE JUSTIN FAIR, UNITED STATES BANKRUPTCY JUDGE:

Videos by Joe, Inc. ("Debtor"), through its attorneys, in support of its Motion to Limit Extent of Notice on Certain Administrative Matters, respectfully represents as follows:

1. Debtor is the debtor in possession in the above-captioned case having filed a petition for relief under Chapter 11 of Title 11, United States Code, on October 1, 1995.

2. In the course of its Chapter 11 case, Debtor anticipates undertaking the review of numerous outstanding executory contracts relating to its business of providing videotaped depositions, wills, musical productions, and weddings. Debtor further anticipates numerous hearings with respect to assumption and rejection of such contracts, as well as for other relief pertaining to the administration of its bankruptcy case.

3. Pursuant to Bankruptcy Rule 2002(m) and 9007, this Court is authorized to limit the scope of notice required on matters generally, including those relating to the use, sale, or lease of property other than in the ordinary course of business, hearings on approval or compromises or settlements, and similar administrative matters.

4. Debtor's final creditor list will likely exceed 200 creditors. The claims of the majority of these creditors do not exceed $100.00 each. Debtor submits that it would be unduly burdensome to require it to notice each of these parties in interest with respect to matters that can, under the Bankruptcy Rules, be heard on limited notice.

5. Under the circumstances, Debtor proposes that this Court limit notice on motions to assume or reject executory contracts, on motions to authorize the use, sale, or lease of property, for hearings on employment and compensation, on motions to approve compromises and settlements, and on other similar administrative proceedings, to the following persons:

    (a) the United States trustee;

    (b) debtor's twenty largest unsecured creditors;

    (c) the members of Debtor's creditors' committee;

    (d) all secured creditors; and

    (e) parties in interest who have requested special notice.

—continued

■ EXHIBIT 11.3
Sample Pleading—*Continued*

---

6. Debtor believes that notice to the entities referred to above will be representative notice to all major positions in this case. Furthermore, upon analysis of the list of the twenty largest creditors filed by Debtor in this case, all creditors owed more than $100.00 will receive notice. These creditors hold approximately eighty percent (80%) of the dollar amount of claims.

WHEREFORE, Debtor requests that this Court enter its Order limiting notice with respect to administrative matters described in this Motion to the entities listed above.

DATED: October 15, 1995

WHITE CHARGER LEGAL CLINIC

_____

BANKRUPT C. LAWYER
Attorneys for Debtor

---

wages. The debtor may also seek authority to honor vacation and sick leave accrued days and other personnel policies. This relief is almost always granted in a Chapter 11 case. An example of such a motion is shown in Exhibit 11.4.

Finally, as discussed in Chapter 4 of this textbook, there are special issues concerning rejection of executory contracts when a collective bargaining agreement or retiree medical benefits are involved. Generally, before the debtor can reject those executory contracts, a strong showing of need must be made.

Relationships With Suppliers

Just as frequent and honest communication is essential for good continued relations with the employees, it is important to keep the suppliers of the debtor's inventory and needed services informed of the debtor's financial condition and of its intentions. Without an ability to obtain inventory and services, the debtor will not have a business to reorganize. If the debtor has not been keeping current on its obligations in the months preceding the filing of the bankruptcy petition, it may have already begun meeting with representatives of its creditors to obtain a moratorium on debt collection or other forms of cooperation. Discussions should continue during the pendency of the bankruptcy case. In fact, the debtor in possession should consider calling a meeting of its suppliers soon after the case is commenced to discuss its financial condition and business plan. The legal assistant can assist in that meeting by helping to ensure that notice of the meeting is provided to the creditors; that the information the debtor wishes to distribute to the creditors— such as financial information, a list of creditors, and a business plan—is collated and presented in a useful manner; and that sign-up sheets and name tags are made.

If a meeting cannot be held, the debtor's attorney may ask the legal assistant to prepare a letter to suppliers similar to the one presented here as Exhibit 11.5. During the course of the case the legal assistant may be called upon to draft other communications to the creditors to give them status reports on the reorganization effort.

Utilities

Because of the monopolies given by various laws to utilities, such as an electric company, gas supplier, or telephone company, the Bankruptcy Code protects debt-

BANKRUPT C. LAWYER
White Charger Legal Clinic
One Learned Way
Los Angeles, California 90001

Attorneys for Debtor

UNITED STATES BANKRUPTCY COURT
WESTERN DISTRICT OF CALIFORNIA

In re)	Case No. 95-00001-JF
)	
VIDEOS BY JOE, INC.,)	Chapter 11
)	
Debtor.)	
)	
Debtor's Address:)	MOTION FOR ORDER
18 Hollywood Drive)	AUTHORIZING DEBTOR TO PAY
Los Angeles, California 90001)	PREPETITION WAGES AND
)	HONOR OUTSTANDING PAYROLL
Debtor's Tax Id. No. 99-999899)	CHECKS, VACATION DAYS, SICK
)	LEAVE DAYS, AND OTHER
)	PERSONNEL POLICIES
)	

TO THE HONORABLE JUSTIN FAIR, UNITED STATES BANKRUPTCY JUDGE:

Videos by Joe, Inc. ("Debtor"), through its attorneys, in support of its Motion for Order Authorizing Debtor to Pay Prepetition Wages and Honor Outstanding Payroll Checks, Vacation Days, Sick Leave Days, and Other Personnel Policies, respectfully represents as follows:

1. Debtor is the debtor in possession in the above-captioned case having filed a petition for relief under Chapter 11 of Title 11, United States Code (the "Bankruptcy Code"), on Monday, October 1, 1995.

2. It is Debtor's policy to pay its employees by check each Friday for services performed through the previous Saturday. Hence, at the time it filed its petition, all seventeen of Debtor's employees had performed prepetition services for which wages had accrued but were not yet due. In addition, on the Friday before it filed its petition, Debtor issued payroll checks to all of its employees from its general payroll account. Many of those checks were not cashed prior to the filing of the petition.

3. At the time that it filed its petition, Debtor had certain employment and personnel policies including allowing each employee one day of paid vacation and one-half day of paid sick leave for each full month that the employee worked.

4. In order to avoid the risk of resignations and of discontent or loss of morale among its employees, and in view of the priority awarded to wage claims, Debtor requests that it be permitted to take whatever steps are necessary to:

(a) ensure that the uncashed payroll checks of its employees are honored by retaining its present payroll account;

(b) pay accrued payroll through the date Debtor commenced its bankruptcy case; and

(c) continue personnel policies and permit employees to use accrued benefits such as sick leave days and vacation leave even if earned prior to October 1, 1995.

Debtor believes that obtaining such relief will enable it to retain employees and keep their morale high, all of which is vital to the success of Debtor's bankruptcy case.

—continued

■ EXHIBIT 11.4
Sample Pleading—*Continued*

5. The amount to be paid to each employee, whether by honoring prepetition issued payroll checks, paying prepetition accrued wages, or allowing use of accrued vacation and sick leave days, will not exceed $4,000.00. Accordingly, the amounts to be paid would have distribution priority under any plan of reorganization of Debtor. Further, this Motion is not intended to apply to any officer of Debtor and is not intended to be an assumption pursuant to Section 365 of the Bankruptcy Code of any employment contract.

WHEREFORE, Debtor requests that this Court enter its Order authorizing Debtor to retain its present payroll account, to permit uncashed payroll checks drawn on the payroll account to be honored, to pay prepetition wages, and to honor existing employee and personnel policies including vacation day and sick leave commitments to its employees, not to exceed $4,000.00 per individual.

DATED: October 15, 1995

WHITE CHARGER LEGAL CLINIC

_____

BANKRUPT C. LAWYER
Attorneys for Debtor

ors from termination of a utility's services because of unpaid prepetition bills. Section 366(a) of the Bankruptcy Code prevents a utility from altering, refusing, or discontinuing services to, or discriminating against, the trustee or the debtor solely on the basis of the commencement of a bankruptcy case or a debt for prepetition services. If the trustee or the debtor believes that a utility is discriminating or threatening to discontinue services because of unpaid prepetition bills, they may seek an injunction from the bankruptcy court preventing the utility's actions.

Section 366 is not one-sided. It also gives considerable protection to the utilities in exchange for the protection given to trustees and debtors. Section 366(b) provides that utilities may alter, refuse, or discontinue service if the trustee or the debtor does not furnish to the utility "adequate assurance of payment" for postpetition services. The adequate assurance may take the form of an additional deposit or other security and must be made within twenty days after the commencement of the case. Once aware of the petition filing, utilities typically will send a letter asking for a two-month deposit even if the debtor was current in its bills at the time of the commencement of the case.

The bankruptcy court will ultimately decide what constitutes "adequate assurance of payment." If the utility makes a demand that the trustee or debtor in possession believes to be excessive, the court, after a notice and a hearing, may modify the amount of the deposit or other security demanded by the utility. (See Exhibit 11.6.)

Financial Reports

The United States trustee in each district will require the debtor in possession to furnish the United States trustee with regular reports of postpetition operations. These reports will allow the United States trustee, and any creditor who may wish to examine the reports, to determine if improper payments are being made, if the

■ EXHIBIT 11.5
Sample Pleading

VIDEOS BY JOE, INC.
18 Hollywood Drive
Los Angeles, California 90001
"Here's Looking At You"
October 2, 1995

Manuel Perez, President
Great Film Inc.,
84 Steel Plate Road
City of Industry, California 91744

Re: *In re Videos by Joe, Inc.*

Dear Mr. Perez:

This letter is to inform you that Videos by Joe, Inc. filed a petition for reorganization under Chapter 11 of the Bankruptcy Code on October 1, 1995. The Chapter 11 filing was caused by the bankruptcy of our largest customer who owes us in excess of $100,000.

As you may know, Chapter 11 is designed to enable companies to continue in business under the control and protection of the bankruptcy court while restructuring financial obligations to creditors and taking other actions to enable them to return to profitability. With this in mind, we at Videos by Joe will continue our normal business of selling, producing, and shipping quality products to our customers during the pendency of the Chapter 11 case. We hope to be able to propose a plan of reorganization that provides for meaningful payments to creditors out of future earnings. To this end we would like to continue to buy video film from you.

Videos by Joe will make prompt payment for the goods and services you supply since the date of the commencement of the bankruptcy case. Our lender, First City Bank, has pledged to work with us and continue to finance our operations while we reorganize.

Unfortunately, we are not permitted by law to make payment on any debt owed to you that arose before October 1, 1995 until such time as we have confirmed a plan of reorganization. We sincerely apologize for any inconvenience or harm this may cause you.

Videos by Joe has valued our past relationship and looks forward to a mutually beneficial future. If you have any questions, please give me a call.

Sincerely,

VIDEOS BY JOE, INC.

_____

JOSEPH BUSINESSMAN
President

debtor is paying its taxes as they become due, and whether the debtor is losing money during its Chapter 11 case.

There are two types of reports. The first is often called an interim statement. It is very similar to a sources and uses of cash statement that some companies prepare in the ordinary course of their operations. It is also akin to a check register. The interim statement shows only actual cash, checks, or other cash equivalents that the debtor has received or has paid out during a particular period. If rent became due during that period but was not paid, the payable due to the landlord would not be reflected on the interim statement. The interim statement allows

BANKRUPT C. LAWYER
White Charger Legal Clinic
One Learned Way
Los Angeles, California 90001

Attorneys for Debtor

UNITED STATES BANKRUPTCY COURT
WESTERN DISTRICT OF CALIFORNIA

In re	Case No. 95-00001-JF
VIDEOS BY JOE, INC.,	Chapter 11
Debtor.	
Debtor's Address: 18 Hollywood Drive Los Angeles, California 90001	MOTION FOR ORDER MODIFYING AMOUNT OF DEPOSIT REQUESTED BY UTILITY COMPANY
Debtor's Tax Id. 99-999899	

TO THE HONORABLE JUSTIN FAIR, UNITED STATES BANKRUPTCY JUDGE:

Videos by Joe, Inc. ("Debtor"), through its attorneys, in support of its Motion to Modify Amount of Deposit Requested by Utility Company, respectfully represents as follows:

1. Debtor is a debtor in possession having filed a petition for relief under Chapter 11 of Title 11, United States Code (the "Bankruptcy Code") on October 1, 1995.

2. By a letter dated October 5, 1995, M & M Gas Company (the "Gas Company") made a demand on Debtor, under Section 366 of the Bankruptcy Code, for a cash deposit or other security of $10,000.00 as adequate assurance of future payment. The letter also served as notice of the Gas Company's intent to terminate services to Debtor if such deposit was not made within twenty days of the date of the letter.

3. Debtor believes that the demand made by the Gas Company is unreasonable and unnecessary to provide adequate assurance of payment within the meaning of Section 366 of the Bankruptcy Code. Debtor has contracted for services from the Gas Company for more than ten years. There are no pre- or postpetition payments due to the Gas Company from Debtor. Moreover, the estate is sufficiently liquid to ensure that all administrative claims will be paid in full even in the event that Debtor's case is converted to a case under Chapter 7 of the Bankruptcy Code. In short, adequate assurance of payment in the form of a cash deposit is not necessary under the circumstances of this case.

WHEREFORE, Debtor requests that this Court find that a guarantee of an administrative expense priority for any claim of the Gas Company further supported by Debtor's ability to promptly pay all postpetition obligations is sufficient to constitute adequate assurance of payment for the continuation of the Gas Company's services, and enter its Order that Debtor is not required to post a cash deposit or other security to the Gas Company.

DATED: October 15, 1995

WHITE CHARGER LEGAL CLINIC

BANKRUPT C. LAWYER
Attorneys for Debtor

the reviewers to know whether the debtor is making any improper payments and whether it is writing bad checks.

The second report is commonly known as the operating report. Unlike the interim statement, the operating report reflects all accrued income and liabilities in a particular period. For example, it shows all of the debtor's sales even though some of those sales were on credit and have not yet been paid for. All the debtor's liabilities incurred during the same period, whether or not they have been paid, are also reflected. Outside the bankruptcy context, this type of report is frequently known as a profit and loss statement or an income statement. At the bottom of the operating report, the debtor subtracts its accrued liabilities from its income to show whether it earned a profit or lost money for the period of time covered by the operating report.

The United States trustee for a particular district may have developed other required reports. Full compliance with their requirements can be assured only by reviewing any guidelines issued and by speaking with the analysts or paralegal specialists of the office of the United States trustee. Typically, they will require that an interim statement be filed once every two weeks and an operating report monthly. In the larger or smaller cases, this timing can sometimes be modified.

It is not usually the task of the legal assistant to prepare the interim statements or the operating reports other than to inform the debtor's bookkeeper or accounting staff about what needs to be done and when they need to be filed. A conscientious legal assistant will also check every period to make sure that the reports have not been ignored by a busy debtor.

There is no requirement in the Bankruptcy Code or in the Bankruptcy Rules that the financial reports be filed with the court or served on creditors or other parties in interest. They are usually provided to the secured creditors, whose loan documents may require periodic reports of this type anyway, and to the creditors' committee.

☐ FINANCING AND SALE TRANSACTIONS

Financing Operations

In only the unusual Chapter 11 case will all of the debtor's assets be free from a creditor's security interest or lien. In addition, only rarely will a debtor in possession of a large company be able to continue to operate without some form of financing. Although Section 364(a) of the Bankruptcy Code allows the debtor in possession to incur unsecured debt in the ordinary course of business without bankruptcy court approval, such credit is not always readily available and is often insufficient to meet the debtor's cash needs. Vendors who extended the debtor credit prepetition and were unpaid at the time of commencement of the case may not be willing to extend any more credit even if they would be a priority creditor.

Recognizing the problems debtors in possession have in obtaining unsecured credit, and to facilitate reorganizations, the Bankruptcy Code allows the debtor to use the same two methods to obtain the cash required to continue operations as a Chapter 7 trustee may use to finance a liquidation. As discussed in Chapter 9 of this book, the first method is the use of a secured creditor's *cash collateral*. The second method allows the debtor to obtain new financing by borrowing funds on a secured or on a super priority unsecured basis.

Cash Collateral   *Cash collateral* is "cash, negotiable instruments, documents of title, securities, deposit accounts or other cash equivalents whenever acquired in which the estate and an entity other than the estate have an interest."

To review Chapter 9's discussion, the Bankruptcy Code states that the debtor in possession cannot use cash collateral unless the other party with an interest in the cash collateral consents or unless the court, after notice and a hearing, authorizes its use. If a secured creditor has a lien on the debtor's accounts receivable, as the payments come in, the debtor in possession will not be able to use any of those payments to pay its expenses unless the secured creditor first authorizes the cash collateral to be used or until the court gives its authorization. Pending the authorization, the debtor must put the cash collateral in a separate account and must provide an accounting. This prohibition against uses applies even if the secured creditor allowed the debtor to use all or a portion of the proceeds before the case was commenced.

If an agreement cannot be reached, the debtor in possession must make a motion for authority to use cash collateral. A motion seeking permission to use cash collateral is found in Exhibit 11.7. Bankruptcy Rule 4001(b) provides that such a motion must be served on any creditor that has an interest in the cash collateral, on the committee, or if no committee has been appointed, on the twenty largest unsecured creditors and any other person the court may direct. The hearing must be held no earlier than fifteen days after the motion is served. If the debtor has an immediate need for the use of cash collateral, the court can hold a preliminary hearing before the expiration of the fifteen-day period but may authorize the use of only that amount of cash collateral as is necessary to avoid immediate and irreparable harm to the estate pending the hearing on full notice.

At any contested hearing concerning cash collateral use, the debtor in possession will have the burden of showing that it should be allowed to use the secured creditor's cash collateral because the creditor is adequately protected or, in other words, that the debtor's use of the cash collateral will not harm the creditor. Section 361 establishes three nonexclusive means by which adequate protection may be provided, including:

☐ Periodic payments to the secured creditor to compensate for any cash collateral used.

☐ Additional collateral.

☐ Any other method that gives the creditor the equivalent of the cash collateral used.

For example, the debtor may argue that in consideration for the use of the proceeds of the accounts receivable, it will grant the secured creditor a lien on all new accounts created. Alternatively, the debtor may argue that the *equity cushion*, the difference between the value of the collateral and the amount of the loan, is so large that it alone is sufficient to provide adequate protection. Whether the facts and the debtor's offer point to adequate protection will be for the court to decide.

If the secured creditor and the debtor in possession come to an agreement allowing the use of cash collateral, the agreement must be reduced to writing. Bankruptcy Rule 4001(d) provides that a notice and a motion for approval of such a written agreement must be served on the committee or, if no committee has been appointed, on the twenty largest unsecured creditors and whomever else the court directs. (See Exhibits 11.8 and 11.9.) A copy of the agreement must accompany the motion. If any party in interest objects to the agreement between the debtor and the secured creditor, that party must file and serve an objection within fifteen days of the date of the notice. If no objection is filed, the court can approve or disapprove of the agreement without a hearing. If there is an objection or if the court wants to hold a hearing, the hearing will be held. The debtor, the

■ EXHIBIT 11.7
Sample Pleading

BANKRUPT C. LAWYER
White Charger Legal Clinic
One Learned Way
Los Angeles, California 90001

Attorneys for Debtor

UNITED STATES BANKRUPTCY COURT
WESTERN DISTRICT OF CALIFORNIA

In re	)	Case No. 95-00001-JF
	)	
VIDEOS BY JOE, INC.,	)	Chapter 11
	)	
Debtor.	)	
	)	
Debtor's Address:	)	MOTION FOR ORDER
18 Hollywood Drive	)	AUTHORIZING USE OF CASH
Los Angeles, California 90001	)	COLLATERAL
	)	
Debtor's Tax Id. No. 99-999899	)	
	)	
_____	)	

TO THE HONORABLE JUSTIN FAIR, UNITED STATES BANKRUPTCY JUDGE:

Videos by Joe, Inc. ("Debtor"), through its attorneys, hereby moves for an Order authorizing Debtor to use, in the ordinary course of its business, the income and proceeds received from or on account of its business operations including all cash on hand (the "Cash Collateral"). In support of this Motion, Debtor respectfully represents as follows:

1. Debtor is the debtor in possession. It commenced its case by filing a petition for relief under Chapter 11, Title 11 of the United States Code on October 1, 1995.

2. Debtor was founded in 1990 as a videotaper of weddings, presentations, and other social functions. Today, Debtor is one of the largest independent video filmers in western California, operating from three offices.

3. Debtor employs approximately fifteen people on a daily basis. These employees perform a myriad of services including marketing, filming, processing, shipping, clerical work, and sales.

4. Debtor's major source of funds with which to operate is a $100,000 line of credit with First City Bank ("the Bank"). Under the line of credit, the Bank agreed to lend to Debtor on a formula based on eighty percent (80%) of eligible receivables. As of October 1, 1995, the outstanding balance owed to the Bank, including principal and interest, was approximately $85,000. The Bank asserts a lien on all of Debtor's assets to secure the outstanding balance on the line of credit.

5. As of October 1, 1995, Debtor's major assets had the following approximate value.

Inventory:	$ 5,000
Receivables:	$110,000
Equipment:	$ 30,000

6. If Debtor is unable to use the cash balance on hand at the commencement of its case and the proceeds of receivables during this case, Debtor will be forced to terminate its operations immediately. In contrast to the approximately $145,000 in aggregate of going concern value, Debtor's assets would have an aggregate value of only approximately $103,000 on liquidation, broken down as follows:

Inventory:	$ 3,000
Receivables:	$75,000
Equipment:	$25,000

—continued

■ EXHIBIT 11.7
Sample Pleading—*Continued*

7. If Debtor is forced to terminate its operations, its employees would be laid off, its relationship with its customers would be impaired, and it could be subject to potential damage claims for breach of contracts, many of which are profitable to Debtor. In short, without immediate use of the Cash Collateral, Debtor's ability to reorganize would be severely adversely affected and its estate would suffer immediate and irreparable injury within the meaning of Bankruptcy Rule 4001(b)(2).

8. A debtor in possession is authorized to use cash collateral in the ordinary course of its business operations under Sections 363(c)(2) and 1107 of the Bankruptcy Code, provided that upon a request of a party that has an interest in the cash collateral, the Court shall condition such use as is necessary to provide adequate protection of such interest.

9. If the Bank has a perfected lien on Debtor's assets, its lien is adequately protected within the meaning of 11 U.S.C. § 363 by an equity cushion which exceeds the loan by approximately seventy percent (70%) on a going concern basis and by approximately twenty percent (20%) on a liquidation basis.

10. In addition, Debtor proposes to provide the Bank, concurrently with this Court's granting the relief requested in this Motion, with replacement liens of the same type as its prepetition liens on all cash, inventory, and accounts receivable acquired by Debtor after the filing of its petition to the extent of the Cash Collateral used. Together with the large existing equity cushion, these replacement liens will more than ensure that the Bank's alleged secured claim is adequately protected.

WHEREFORE, Debtor requests that this Court enter an Order:

1. Authorizing Debtor to use, in the ordinary course of business, the Cash Collateral free and clear of any liens or claims of the Bank;

2. Directing the Bank to turn over to Debtor all the Cash Collateral in its possession or control;

3. Granting the Bank replacement liens of the same type as its prepetition liens on Debtor's postpetition inventory and accounts receivable to the extent of the Cash Collateral use;

4. Decreeing that to the extent the Bank has a valid lien in Debtor's assets the Bank is adequately protected by the equity cushion in its collateral and the replacement liens; and

5. Granting such other relief as is appropriate.

DATED: October 1, 1995

WHITE CHARGER LEGAL CLINIC

_____

BANKRUPT C. LAWYER
Attorneys for Debtor

---

objecting party, those who received the motion, and anyone else the court requires must receive at least five days' notice of the hearing.

Section 364 Financing In many cases the debtor in possession will not be able to survive on cash collateral use alone. It may be that its receivables are slow paying or that it needs to borrow based on its inventory value. In such instances the debtor will need to borrow new funds rather than only use cash collateral as it comes in.

As discussed in Chapter 9 of this book, Section 364(b) authorizes the debtor in possession to borrow funds on an unsecured basis other than in the ordinary course of business with repayment entitled to an administrative expense priority.

■ EXHIBIT 11.8
Sample Pleading

BANKRUPT C. LAWYER
White Charger Legal Clinic
One Learned Way
Los Angeles, California 90001

Attorneys for Debtor

UNITED STATES BANKRUPTCY COURT
WESTERN DISTRICT OF CALIFORNIA

In re	Case No. 95-00001-JF
VIDEOS BY JOE, INC.,	Chapter 11
Debtor.	
Debtor's Address:	NOTICE OF FILING OF MOTION
18 Hollywood Drive	FOR ORDER APPROVING
Los Angeles, California 90001	STIPULATION AND STIPULATION
	FOR ORDER AND AUTHORIZING
Debtor's Tax Id. No. 99-999899	USE OF CASH COLLATERAL

TO ALL PARTIES ENTITLED TO NOTICE:

NOTICE IS HEREBY GIVEN that on October 3, 1995 Videos by Joe, Inc., the debtor in possession in the above-referenced case ("Debtor"), and First City Bank, a secured creditor of Debtor (the "Bank"), filed with the United States Bankruptcy Court for the Western District of California their Motion for Order Approving Stipulation and Stipulation for Order Authorizing Use of Cash Collateral (the "Motion"). A complete and accurate copy of the Motion is attached to this Notice.

NOTICE IS FURTHER GIVEN that, pursuant to Bankruptcy Rule 4001, if you wish to object to all or any portion of the Motion, within fifteen (15) days of October 3, 1995 you must file your written objection with the Clerk of the Court and serve a copy of such written objection on: (1) Bankrupt C. Lawyer, Esq., White Charger Legal Clinic, One Learned Way, Los Angeles, California 90001; (2) George G. Snow, Esq., Snow & Porter, 4 Wheel Drive, Los Angeles, California 90017; and (3) the United States Trustee, 300 N. Los Angeles St., Room 3101, Los Angeles, California 90012. Any objection not so served and filed may be deemed waived.

NOTICE IS FINALLY GIVEN that if no objections are filed, the Court may enter its Order approving or disapproving of the Motion without conducting a hearing. If an objection is filed or if the Court determines a hearing is appropriate, the Court will hold a hearing on no less than five (5) days' notice.

DATED: October 3, 1995

WHITE CHARGER LEGAL CLINIC

BANKRUPT C. LAWYER
Attorney for Debtor

The debtor, however, must first obtain an order allowing the loan. Bankruptcy Rule 4001(c) governs the procedure for obtaining an order authorizing borrowing. Under Section 364(c), if the debtor in possession is unable to obtain credit otherwise, it may incur debt with priority over all other administrative expenses (which gives the creditor a super priority claim), secured by a lien on property of

■ EXHIBIT 11.9
Sample Pleading

BANKRUPT C. LAWYER
White Charger Legal Clinic
One Learned Way
Los Angeles, California 90001

Attorneys for Debtor

UNITED STATES BANKRUPTCY COURT
WESTERN DISTRICT OF CALIFORNIA

In re	)	Case No. 95-00001-JF
	)	
VIDEOS BY JOE, INC.,	)	Chapter 11
	)	
Debtor.	)	
	)	
Debtor's Address:	)	MOTION FOR ORDER APPROVING
18 Hollywood Drive	)	STIPULATION AND STIPULATION
Los Angeles, California 90001	)	FOR ORDER AUTHORIZING USE OF
	)	CASH COLLATERAL
Debtor's Tax Id. No. 99-999899	)	
	)	
	)	

TO THE HONORABLE JUSTIN FAIR, UNITED STATES BANKRUPTCY JUDGE:

First City Bank (the "Bank") and Videos by Joe, Inc. ("Debtor"), through their respective attorneys, in support of their Motion for Order Approving Stipulation and Stipulation for Order Authorizing Use of Cash Collateral, respectfully represent, and where appropriate stipulate and agree, as set forth in detail below, that Debtor may use the Bank's cash collateral.

In support of this Motion, the parties respectfully represent as follows:

1. In or about July of 1990, the Bank made certain financial accommodations to Debtor for which Debtor was obligated to the Bank, as of October 1, 1995, in the approximate amount of $85,000 (the "Loan").

2. The terms of the Loan are embodied in a Loan and Security Agreement and a Promissory Note (collectively the "Loan Documents") which are attached to this Motion as Exhibits 1 and 2.

3. As collateral for the Loan, the Bank was granted a security interest in all of Debtor's assets including its inventory and accounts receivable (the "Collateral").

4. The Bank duly perfected its security interests in the Collateral.

5. Certain defaults exist under the Loan Documents.

6. On October 1, 1995 Debtor filed a petition under Chapter 11 of the Bankruptcy Code (thereby commencing the "Case").

7. Debtor desires to use the Bank's cash collateral for general business purposes. The Bank will consent to the use of its cash collateral by Debtor on certain terms and conditions.

Based on the facts set forth above, the Bank and Debtor have and hereby do stipulate and agree, subject to Court approval, as follows:

A. The Bank consents to the use by Debtor of up to sixty percent (60%) of the collections of Debtor's accounts receivable commencing October 5, 1995 provided that the Court approves this Motion and Debtor observes and performs all of its obligations and promises hereunder.

B. As adequate protection for the use of its cash collateral, the Bank is granted liens and security interests in and to all assets of the estate, including all presently existing and hereafter acquired assets, whether real or personal, including but not limited to, the Collateral, general intangibles, causes of action, avoiding powers and the proceeds thereof, equipment and real property owned by or in which Debtor has an interest, and the proceeds therefrom.

—continued

C. In the event that the protection provided by the liens and security interests herein granted turns out, in retrospect, to have been inadequate, the Bank shall be entitled to the priority afforded by Section 507(b) of the Bankruptcy Code to the extent of any deficiency.

D. Upon the occurrence of an event of default under this Stipulation, the voluntary or involuntary dismissal of Debtor's bankruptcy case, the appointment of a trustee, the conversion of the case to one under Chapter 7 of the Bankruptcy Code or the entry of an Order confirming a Chapter 11 Plan of Reorganization, the Bank shall have no obligation to allow the further use of its cash collateral by Debtor and Debtor shall not use the Collateral, including the cash collateral, without the Bank's express written consent.

E. The Bank and Debtor have, in accordance with the requirements of Bankruptcy Rule 4001(d), provided notice of this Motion to the twenty largest creditors holding unsecured claims in Debtor's bankruptcy case. Copies of this Motion have also been provided to the United States Trustee. Debtor believes that there are no other entities with an interest in the Collateral.

DATED: October 3, 1995

WHITE CHARGER LEGAL CLINIC

_____

BANKRUPT C. LAWYER
Attorneys for Debtor

DATED: October 3, 1995

SNOW & PORTER

_____

GEORGE G. SNOW
Attorneys for First
City Bank

the estate that is not otherwise subject to a lien, or secured by a junior lien on property that is already subject to a lien. In the event that even those protections for a lender are insufficient, the debtor in possession may obtain financing secured by a senior or equal lien on property of the estate that is already encumbered.

Bankruptcy Rules 4001(c) and (d) deal with the notice and procedure for obtaining court approval of secured debt financing. The procedure is exactly the same as it is to obtain approval of cash collateral use.

Use, Sale and Lease of Property

Section 363(c)(1), read together with Section 1107, authorizes the debtor in possession to use, sell, or lease any property of the estate in the ordinary course of business without the need for court approval. Accordingly, the debtor may sell its inventory at its regular prices, use its equipment to manufacture goods, and lease delivery trucks if that is what it commonly does in the scope of its operations. This ability to run the business as usual ceases only if the court revokes authorization to operate or otherwise restricts the use, sale, or lease of the assets. For example, a regulatory agency might bring a motion for an order prohibiting the debtor in possession from selling its inventory because it poses a danger.

The debtor in possession may also use, sell, or lease its property out of the ordinary course of business. To do so it must first obtain court approval by follow-

ing the procedures established in Bankruptcy Rule 6004. How property of the estate is sold outside of the ordinary course of business by a Chapter 7 trustee is discussed in Chapter 9 of this book. The section of that chapter on liquidating the estate should be read carefully since it has equal application in a Chapter 11 case. It is the rare case in which the debtor in possession does not seek to sell or lease a portion of its assets during the administration of its bankruptcy case.

Obviously, the distinction between ordinary course and nonordinary course of business is very important. Some things are clearly outside the ordinary course of business: for example, a sale of a division by a manufacturing company or even one piece of machinery for such an operation. Other transactions are not so clear-cut. For example, if the debtor was a car rental agency, the lease of its cars to customers would be in the ordinary course of its business and would not require a bankruptcy court order. But, car agencies typically sell their fleets when they are a few years old and replace them with newer models. Would the sale of the older cars require court approval? If there is any doubt as to whether a particular transaction is or is not within the ordinary course of business, it is best to assume that court approval is required.

Another asset sale issue that arises in Chapter 11 cases is whether a debtor in possession can sell all or substantially all of its assets by following the motion procedure of Section 363(b) and Bankruptcy Rule 6004 or whether major asset sales can be accomplished only through confirmation of a plan of reorganization. The concern is how much information the creditors will be provided. If the sale is through a plan, they will receive a disclosure statement. Outside a plan they will receive only a motion. Under the Act, sales of substantially all of the debtor's assets outside a plan were only allowed if there was an emergency or if the assets were perishable. Under the Bankruptcy Code, the standard is more lax and such sales will usually be approved if there is a good business reason for doing it in the manner the debtor proposes.

☐ THE PLAN

The ideal culmination of a Chapter 11 case is the confirmation of a plan of reorganization. Unfortunately, although few cases are commenced with the idea that they will fail, a plan is confirmed in only a small percentage of cases.

The path towards confirmation can be very arduous. Negotiation and formulation of plans and disclosure statements is usually extremely complicated. Only in the very rare case will any of the documentation be assigned to the legal assistant for preparation. There are, however, many tasks short of actual negotiating or drafting of the plan and disclosure statement that are better done by the legal assistant. These tasks are summarized in this section.

Plan Exclusivity

Section 1121 of the Bankruptcy Code provides that in the first 120 days after a Chapter 11 case is commenced, unless a trustee has been appointed, only the debtor may propose a plan. If the debtor proposes a plan within this time period, it is given another sixty days to have the plan confirmed. These time frames are called the debtor's **exclusivity period.** The court may extend the exclusivity period upon the debtor's motion if the debtor demonstrates cause for the extension. Frequently in large cases the exclusivity period will be extended at least once as a matter of course. A sample motion to extend the exclusivity period is presented in Exhibit 11.10.

Exclusivity Period
In a Chapter 11 case, the period of time in which only the debtor may propose a plan of reorganization.

■ EXHIBIT 11.10
Sample Pleading

BANKRUPT C. LAWYER
White Charger Legal Clinic
One Learned Way
Los Angeles, California 90001

Attorneys for Debtor

UNITED STATES BANKRUPTCY COURT
WESTERN DISTRICT OF CALIFORNIA

In re) VIDEOS BY JOE, INC.,) Debtor.) Debtor's Address:) 18 Hollywood Drive) Los Angeles, California 90001) Debtor's Tax Id. No. 99-999899) _____)	Case No. 95-00001-JF Chapter 11 MOTION FOR ORDER EXTENDING PERIODS OF PLAN EXCLUSIVITY

TO THE HONORABLE JUSTIN FAIR, UNITED STATES BANKRUPTCY JUDGE:

Videos by Joe, Inc. ("Debtor"), through its attorneys, for and in support of its Motion for Order Extending Periods of Plan Exclusivity, respectfully represents that:

1. Debtor filed a petition for relief under Chapter 11 of Title 11, United States Code (the "Bankruptcy Code") on October 1, 1995.

2. As debtor in possession, Debtor has through February 1, 1996 the exclusive right to propose a plan of reorganization (the "Plan") and until approximately April 1, 1996 to have the Plan accepted.

3. For reasons delineated in the accompanying Declaration of Joseph Businessman, proposing a viable Plan capable of acceptance and consummation at this stage in the proceeding is not possible.

4. Debtor submits that its bankruptcy case has too brief an operating history to allow it to propound a meaningful Plan. Moreover, the uncertainty in the negotiations of a purchase of Debtor's assets further reinforces the notion that filing a Plan would be inappropriate at this time.

5. Based upon the foregoing, Debtor submits it is reasonable to extend the plan exclusivity and acceptance periods for two months, respectively, subject to further increase for cause shown.

WHEREFORE, Debtor requests that the Court enter an Order granting the Motion and such other and further relief as the Court shall deem just and proper.

DATED: January 1, 1996

WHITE CHARGER LEGAL CLINIC

_____

BANKRUPT C. LAWYER
Attorney for Debtor

If a trustee has been appointed or if the exclusivity period has expired without being extended, any party in interest may propose a plan. This would include any committee that has been appointed in the case or a trustee. Only the United States trustee is expressly prohibited from proposing a plan. Once exclusivity has lapsed, even if the debtor has proposed a plan, a party in interest can file a plan to compete with the debtor's plan as long as it is filed prior to the hearing on the disclosure statement. After that, court approval is required. Competing plans are not common.

The Disclosure Statement

The Bankruptcy Code requires that every plan of reorganization be accompanied by a disclosure statement that contains **adequate information** sufficient to allow a creditor to make an informed judgment whether to accept or reject the plan. In the words of Section 1125(a) of the Bankruptcy Code,

> adequate information means information of a kind, and in sufficient detail, as far as is reasonably practicable in light of the nature and history of the debtor and the condition of the debtor's books and records, that would enable a hypothetical reasonable investor typical of holders of claims or interests of the relevant class to make an informed judgment about the plan.

Adequate Information
Information in sufficient detail that would enable a reasonable investor to make an informed decision whether to vote for or against a Chapter 11 plan of reorganization.

How much information will be adequate will depend on the facts of each case.

Preparation of a disclosure statement is not something typically assigned to a legal assistant. Nevertheless, the legal assistant can be instrumental by reviewing drafts of the statement and confirming that nothing significant has been omitted. Although there are few mandatory requirements of what the disclosure statement must contain, most disclosure statements contain the following:

☐ A short history of the debtor's business activities.

☐ A description of the debtor's capital structure. This includes the type and number of issued and outstanding shares for corporations and the type and percentage of interests for partnerships.

☐ A list of all parent and subsidiary corporations

☐ A complete description of the debtor's business including competitive conditions, principal products and services, dependence on one or more customers, distribution methods, raw material availability, patents, trademarks, licenses, number of employees, foreign operations, governmental regulatory matters, working capital position, and income and profit both historical and projected.

☐ A complete list of debtor's assets.

☐ A discussion of the debtor's liability.

☐ Information concerning executory contracts and leases.

☐ A description of current and anticipated legal proceedings.

☐ A description of securities being issued.

☐ Information regarding present officers and directors.

☐ An analysis showing that the plan provides a better return to creditors than would a liquidation under Chapter 7.

The Plan

As is true for the disclosure statement, it is unlikely that the plan of reorganization will be drafted by a legal assistant. Yet, as with the disclosure statement, the legal

assistant can be a tremendous help in ensuring that the plan meets the requirements of the Bankruptcy Code and the Bankruptcy Rules.

There are two basic types of plans. The first and easiest is a plan that contemplates the sale of debtor's assets and the proceeds being pooled together and paid to creditors. This type of plan is called a **liquidating** or **pot plan.** A sample of a very simple plan of this type for an estate that has already sold its assets and has no secured debt is presented as Exhibit 11.11. The sale contemplated can be on a piecemeal basis or the debtor can sell all of its assets to a single buyer.

The other type of plan is sometimes called an **earn-out.** It provides that the debtor will continue to operate and will make periodic distributions to creditors from its earnings over a number of years. Often the plan also provides for creditors to receive shares of stock in the debtor. The disclosure statement will contain projections of what the debtor thinks its revenue and expenses will be over the period of time distributions are to be made. This disclosure is intended to demonstrate to creditors that they should receive more in the earn-out than they would if the debtor immediately liquidated. A plan can combine elements of a pot plan and an earn-out plan by providing for the sale of some of the debtor's assets but also for the continued operation of the debtor's business, thereby making two sources of cash available to pay creditors.

Whatever the type, the plan must have the mandatory provisions set out in Section 1123 of the Bankruptcy Code. That section can be used as a checklist. Among its requirements are:

☐ The plan must classify claims and interests.

☐ The plan must identify all classes that are unimpaired.

☐ The plan must specify the treatment of all classes of claims or interests that are impaired.

☐ All claims in the same class must be treated the same.

☐ The plan must contain provisions indicating how it will be carried out (that is, whether it is a pot plan or an earn-out plan).

☐ The plan must contain provisions to protect the voting rights of shareholders.

☐ The plan must disclose the members of the debtor's management after confirmation and how future management will be chosen.

The plan can also contain the optional provisions listed in Section 1123(b). The options include:

☐ Providing for the assumption, assignment or rejection of executory contracts or unexpired leases.

☐ Settling any claim belonging to the estate.

☐ Selling all or substantially all of the property of the estate.

☐ Modifying the rights of secured creditors.

The only prohibition is that any optional provision may not conflict with a mandatory provision.

Approval of the Disclosure Statement

Having the disclosure statement approved by the court is the first step toward plan confirmation. Bankruptcy Rule 3016(c) states that the disclosure statement must be filed with the plan or within such time as the court fixes. There will be a hearing after notice to the debtor, all creditors, equity security holders, and other

---

Liquidating or Pot Plan

A plan of reorganization that provides for the sale or other disposition of all of the assets of the estate or distributes the proceeds of a previous sale or other disposition in the plan.

Earn-out

A plan of reorganization that provides for distributions to creditors to be made from the debtor's future income.

■ EXHIBIT 11.11
Sample Pleading

BANKRUPT C. LAWYER
White Charger Legal Clinic
One Learned Way
Los Angeles, California 90001
Attorneys for Debtor

UNITED STATES BANKRUPTCY COURT
WESTERN DISTRICT OF CALIFORNIA

In re	Case No. 95-00001-JF
VIDEOS BY JOE, INC.,	Chapter 11
Debtor.	
Debtor's Address:	PLAN OF REORGANIZATION
18 Hollywood Drive	March 1, 1996
Los Angeles, California 90001	
Debtor's Tax Id. No. 99-999899	

Videos by Joe, Inc. ("Debtor") proposes the following Plan of Reorganization:

I
DEFINITIONS

A. The following definitions apply in this Plan:

1. "Bankruptcy Code" means 11 U.S.C. § 101, *et seq.*

2. "Bankruptcy Court" means United States Bankruptcy Court for Western District of California.

3. "Confirmation" means entry of an Order of the Bankruptcy Court confirming the Plan.

4. "Distribution" means the pro rata distribution to holders of allowed general unsecured claims.

5. "Effective Date" means the date the Plan takes effect, as described in Article VII of the Plan.

6. "Estate" means the estate created in the Reorganization Case pursuant to Bankruptcy Code Section 541.

7. "Final Order" means an order of the Bankruptcy Court as to which any appeal that has been or may be taken has been resolved or as to which the time for appeal has expired.

8. "Petition Date" means October 1, 1995.

9. "Plan" means this Plan of Reorganization, as it may be modified from time to time.

10. "Reorganization Case" means Case No. 95-00001-JF, in the Bankruptcy Court.

B. Any term used in the Plan that is not specifically defined but that is used in the Bankruptcy Code has the meaning assigned to that term in the Bankruptcy Code.

II
CLASSIFICATION OF CLAIMS AND INTERESTS

A. *Class 1* consists of all allowed claims entitled to expense of administration priority under Section 507(a)(1) of the Bankruptcy Code.

B. *Class 2* consists of all allowed claims against Debtor, if any, allowed under Bankruptcy Code Sections 507(a)(3), 507(a)(4), 507(a)(6), or 507(a)(7).

C. *Class 3* consists of all allowed unsecured claims against Debtor.

D. *Class 4* consists of all allowed interests in Debtor.

—*continued*

III

TREATMENT OF CLASSES OF CLAIMS AND INTERESTS

A. *Pro Rata Distribution.* For any class of claims or interests that the Plan impairs, the property to be distributed to the class under the Plan shall be divided pro rata among the holders of allowed claims or allowed interests of the class, based on the amount of the holders' allowed claims or allowed interests.

B. *Class 1* and *Class 2* are not impaired in that each Class 1 and Class 2 claim that has not already been paid or provided for during the Reorganization Case shall be paid in cash in full on the Effective Date.

C. *Class 3* is impaired. The holders of Class 3 claims will receive a pro rata distribution of the cash available for Distribution after payment of all Class 1 and Class 2 claims.

D. *Class 4* is impaired in that the holders of the Class 4 interests shall receive nothing by reason of their ownership of common stock of Debtor.

IV

EXECUTORY CONTRACTS

Without admitting that any contract or lease is an executory contract or unexpired lease, or that Debtor has any liability under any such contract or lease, all contracts and leases are rejected as of the Effective Date. Any claims arising from the rejection of these executory contracts or unexpired leases shall be classified as Class 3 claims.

V

MEANS OF EXECUTION

A. *Cash Payment to Creditors.* The cash available for the Distribution, after payment of all Class 1 and Class 2 claims, shall be paid pro rata by check mailed to Class 3 creditors within thirty (30) days of the Effective Date or after the last payment to creditors in Classes 1 and 2, whichever later occurs.

B. *Disbursing Agent.* Debtor shall serve as disbursing agent and shall distribute all property to be distributed under the Plan to holders of Class 1, Class 2, and Class 3 claims. In this capacity, Debtor shall serve without bond and shall receive for its services only such fees as the Bankruptcy Court approves.

C. *Disputed Claims.* Debtor shall withhold from property to be distributed under the Plan a sufficient amount to be distributed on account of the face amount of any claim which is disputed and which has not been allowed by a Final Order as of the date of the Distribution under the Plan. Debtor shall invest funds so withheld and shall retain all interest so earned for distribution to the holders of Class 3 claims. As disputed claims, if any, are allowed by a Final Order, Debtor shall distribute property under the Plan to the holders of such disputed claims as soon as practicable. Property remaining after the termination of all disputed claims shall be distributed pro rata among holders of all allowed claims of Class 3.

D. *Additional Property.* To the extent additional property shall come to Debtor after the Distribution, it shall be distributed pro rata by Debtor to holders of allowed Class 3 claims at such time or times when distribution is practical and/or appropriate.

E. *Unclaimed Property.* Any property to be distributed under the Plan that is not claimed by the entity entitled to it before the later of six (6) months after Confirmation and sixty (60) days after an Order allowing the claim or interest of that entity becomes a Final Order shall be redistributed pro rata to Class 3 creditors who have negotiated their checks.

F. *Directors.* Since Debtor will have no corporate existence postconfirmation, there shall be no change in the current composition of the board of directors; Debtor's directors will continue to be Joe Businessman, Myra Businesswoman, and Maximillion Businessman who will oversee the dissolution of Debtor.

G. *Officers.* The officers of Debtor at Confirmation shall serve as the officers of Debtor after Confirmation.

VI

BANKRUPTCY COURT JURISDICTION

After Confirmation, the Bankruptcy Court shall retain such jurisdiction over property of the estate and claims thereto, if any, as is legally permissible.

—*continued*

■ EXHIBIT 11.11
Sample Pleading—*Continued*

VII
EFFECTIVE DATE

   The Plan takes effect on the eleventh day after Confirmation, but the Plan does not take effect if a stay of the Order confirming the Plan is in effect on the eleventh day after Confirmation.

DATED: March 1, 1996

VIDEOS BY JOE, INC.

_____

JOSEPH BUSINESSMAN
President

---

interested parties. Bankruptcy Rule 2002 has proscribed that there must be at least a twenty-five day notice before the hearing to consider approval of the disclosure statement.

   It would be appropriate for the legal assistant to prepare the notice of the hearing and see that it is correctly served. Official Form 12, an order and notice for hearing on disclosure statement can be used. A simple notice will also suffice. The disclosure statement itself will not be sent to creditors and the other parties until it has been approved by the court. A copy will be sent to the debtor, the United States trustee, the Securities and Exchange Commission, and the creditors' committee but otherwise distribution should be limited. Some creditors will want to review the disclosure statement and will ask for a copy of the plan and disclosure statement before the hearing. If they make a request in writing, as is required by Bankruptcy Rule 3017(b), they should be promptly provided with a copy. A list of those creditors who were provided copies should be kept. The reason is that disclosure statements are frequently amended prior to the date of the hearing. The latest versions should be sent to all who had received the earlier version.

   Any party in interest may object to the disclosure statement by alleging that it does not contain adequate information. Unhappy creditors often use the disclosure statement hearing to voice their objections to the plan. While the timing is not correct, it will give the plan proponent forewarning as to possible problems with the plan and an opportunity to either correct any plan defects or prepare for a contested confirmation hearing.

   If it contains adequate information, the court will approve the disclosure statement and will also set the date and time of the confirmation hearing on the plan of reorganization, the date by which any objections to confirmation of the plan must be filed, and the date by which the ballots accepting or rejecting the plan must be submitted. The legal assistant may prepare such an order. It can be modeled after Official Form 13 (which is entitled Order Approving Disclosure Statement and Fixing Time for Filing Acceptance or Rejections of Plan, Combined with Notice Thereof). It should reflect the disclosure statement approval and the dates set by the court.

   As soon as possible after the disclosure statement is approved, a packet of documents must be sent to all creditors, any trustee, all equity security holders, and other parties in interest. The packet must contain:

☐ The plan.

☐ The disclosure statement.

☐ A ballot for recipients to use to vote for or against the plan.

☐ A notice of the date by which objections must be filed and ballots submitted, and the date, time, and place of the confirmation hearing.

☐ Such other information as the court orders.

Often if the debtor is proposing a plan that is a result of successful negotiations with the creditors' committee, the debtor will ask the committee's counsel to prepare a letter to be included in the packet stating that the committee supports the plan and urges creditors to vote for it. Sometimes the packet will also include an addressed and postage-paid envelope for returning the ballot.

The Ballot

Bankruptcy Rule 3017 provides that all creditors and equity security holders entitled to vote for or against a plan are to receive a ballot conforming to Official Form 14. In larger cases, the ballot should be customized for the party to whom it is being sent. The ballot for equity interest holders will be different than the one for creditors since it will speak of number of shares rather than dollar amount of claims. In fact, separate ballots can be drafted for each class provided for in the plan. By doing so, any guesswork as to what class the ballot from a particular creditor or interest holder would fall is eliminated either because the person was sent only one ballot or because it returned only the ballot from a particular class.

When the ballots are received they have to be sorted according to class and counted to see if more than two-thirds in amount and one-half in number of the claimants voting accepted the plan. One method to make the counting much easier is to have the ballots coded by having them photocopied onto different colored paper. For example, Class 1 could have blue ballots; Class 2, green; Class 3, pink; and Class 4, yellow. Although color coding the ballots will take time, sorting time will then be substantially shortened.

Typically, after the packages to creditors have been sent out and while the ballots are being returned, the plan proponent will want to know how the votes are running. The legal assistant should keep a tally by class. When the deadline for voting has passed, the plan proponent must file a declaration or affidavit with the court detailing how many ballots in each class were received and the number of votes for and against the plan. If the tally has been kept, the counting for the purposes of preparing the declaration will already be done. A sample of such a declaration is included as Exhibit 11.12.

The Confirmation Hearing

On the date set by the court and disclosed in the notice sent with the packets, the court will hold a hearing to consider confirmation of the plan of reorganization. Bankruptcy Rule 3020(b)(2) provides that if there have not been any objections and the plan proponent submits evidence that the plan has been accepted by the requisite majority of creditors, the court may enter its order confirming the plan without taking any other evidence. If a party in interest has filed an objection, the court will need to resolve the questions raised in the objection before proceeding to confirmation.

■ EXHIBIT 11.12
Sample Pleading

BANKRUPT C. LAWYER
White Charger Legal Clinic
One Learned Way
Los Angeles, California 90001

Attorneys for Debtor

UNITED STATES BANKRUPTCY COURT
WESTERN DISTRICT OF CALIFORNIA

In re)	Case No. 95-00001-JF
)	
VIDEOS BY JOE, INC.,)	Chapter 11
)	
Debtor.)	
)	
Debtor's Address:)	DECLARATION OF BANKRUPT C.
18 Hollywood Drive)	LAWYER RE BALLOTS ACCEPTING
Los Angeles, California 90001)	OR REJECTING PLAN OF
)	REORGANIZATION
Debtor's Tax Id. NO. 99-999899)	
)	
)	

I, BANKRUPT C. LAWYER, declare as follows:

1. I am an attorney licensed by the State of California and admitted to practice before, *inter alia*, the United States District Court for the Western District of California.

2. I am a partner in White Charger Legal Clinic, attorneys for Videos by Joe, Inc. ("Debtor"). I am the attorney primarily responsible for representing Debtor in its bankruptcy case.

3. In the course of my representation of Debtor, I supervised the receipt of all ballots accepting or rejecting the Debtor's Plan of Reorganization (the "Plan"), the review of those ballots for compliance with appropriate procedures, and the process of recording the ballots so that this Declaration could be generated reflecting the tabulation of the votes. Although only Classes 3 and 4 were impaired under the Plan, all classes were provided with ballots.

4. Attached hereto collectively as Exhibits 1 through 4 are the original ballots received on or before 5:00 P.M. Pacific Standard Time, May 1, 1996, accepting or rejecting the Plan.

5. As evidenced by Exhibit 1, the holders of Class 1 administrative claims voted as follows:

YES VOTES
    COUNT: 2
    AMOUNT: $10,000.00
NO VOTES
    COUNT: 0
    AMOUNT: $0

6. As evidenced by Exhibit 2, the holders of Class 2 priority claims voted as follows:

YES VOTES
    COUNT: 5
    AMOUNT: $17,500.00
NO VOTES
    COUNT: 1
    AMOUNT: $2,000.00

—*continued*

■ EXHIBIT 11.12
Sample Pleading—*Continued*

---

7. As evidenced by Exhibit 3, the holders of Class 3 general unsecured claims voted as follows:

YES VOTES
    COUNT: 10
    AMOUNT: $39,520.64
NO VOTES
    COUNT: 2
    AMOUNT: $8,476.36

8. As evidenced by Exhibit 4, the members of Class 4 equity interest holders voted as follows:

YES VOTES
    COUNT: 0
    NUMBER OF SHARES: 0
NO VOTES
    COUNT: 3
    NUMBER OF SHARES: 10,000

    I declare under penalty of perjury that the foregoing is true and correct, is of my own personal knowledge, and if called as a witness, I would and could testify competently with respect thereto.

Executed at Los Angeles, California, on May 5, 1996.

BANKRUPT C. LAWYER

If the plan is confirmed, the court will enter its order substantially in conformance with Official Form 15. Bankruptcy Rule 3020(c) requires the clerk to give notice of the entry of the order confirming the plan to all creditors, the debtor, equity security holders, and all other parties in interest.

Postconfirmation Matters

Once the plan has been confirmed, its terms are binding on all parties including the debtor, creditors, and equity security holders whether or not they voted for the plan. All assets of the estate, unless the plan provides otherwise, are vested (actually revested) in the debtor, then commonly referred to as the **revested debtor.**

Revested Debtor
A debtor after confirmation of a plan of reorganization if the plan provides that title to the estate's assets will be vested in the debtor upon confirmation.

    Sometimes, despite best intentions, the plan will not work. Usually this happens when the debtor fails to meet its projected sales or profits. At that point the debtor or another party in interest can move to have the case converted to Chapter 7 or dismissed. In the alternative, the plan proponent can move to have the plan modified to make it work under the changed circumstances. Modification can be sought if the plan has not been substantially consummated. The notice and hearing required for any plan modification is governed by the procedures in Bankruptcy Rule 9014.

    Finally, Section 1144 of the Bankruptcy Code allows the court to revoke a confirmation order on a motion by an interested party if confirmation was obtained through fraud. Such a motion must be made within 180 days after the confirmation order is entered.

☐ SPECIAL RULES FOR SPECIAL CHAPTER 11 CASES

The Single Asset Real Estate Case

Many Chapter 11 cases involve an artificial debtor, such as a corporation or a partnership, that has an interest in only one asset, which is usually a piece of real estate. Sometimes these cases are clear abuses of the bankruptcy system. For example, in an effort to stop a foreclosure sale on a parcel of real property, a solvent person transfers the parcel to an empty corporation. The corporation then immediately files a petition to take advantage of the automatic stay. The person's other assets are not brought into the case despite the fact that the creditors may have relied on all the assets in making the credit decision. In other situations the fact that the case involves a single real estate asset is appropriate because the debtor, commonly a limited partnership, was formed for the sole purpose of owning and operating the asset. The creditors relied on only the real property when making their credit decision.

Single asset real estate cases are much easier to administer than cases in which the debtor is involved in manufacturing or other operations. The central concern, other than a secured creditor seeking relief from the stay, is to ensure that any valuable leases to tenants are assumed, tenant security deposits are protected, a management company is authorized to be employed by the court, and insurance is in place.

The reporting requirements that the court or the United States trustee might otherwise require are often inapplicable in single asset real estate cases since they may require information about payroll, inventory levels, and other information for a debtor in possession who operates a business. Upon request, the reporting requirements to the United States trustee will usually be modified so that an initial questionnaire about the property and the debtor's intent with respect to it, as well as monthly narratives about the status, will be sufficient.

Creditor groups frequently complained that single asset real estate cases are improper bankruptcies because they involve simply a two person (the debtor and the lender) dispute better left for the states to deal with. In partial support of creditor dissatisfaction with single asset real estate cases, in the 1994 Amendments Congress singled the smaller of them out for more stringent treatment than that given to other Chapter 11 cases.

First, the 1994 Amendments added a definition for a single asset real estate case. In new Section 101(51B), a single asset real estate case is defined as one involving: (1) real property constituting a single property or project (other than residential real property with less than four units); (2) which generates substantially all of the gross income of a debtor; (3) on which no substantial business is being conducted by the debtor other than the business of operating the real property and incidental activities; and (4) having noncontingent liquidated secured debt of no more than $4 million. If the debt is more than $4 million the new rules will not apply. The new rules will also not apply if the debtor has multiple projects located at different locations, or has businesses other than the operation of the property. Yet, despite these limitations, Congress believed that most real estate related bankruptcy cases would fit within the definition.

The consequence of fitting within the definition of a single asset real estate case is that the secured creditor will be entitled to relief from the automatic stay under Section 362(d)(3) unless within ninety days after the case is commenced either: (1) the debtor files a plan of reorganization that has a reasonable possibility of being confirmed within a reasonable time; or (2) the debtor begins making

monthly interest payments to the secured creditors. This consequence will likely not reduce the amount of time the courts and creditors must devote to these cases. For example, the court will need to determine whether the debtor's plan has a reasonable possibility of being confirmed within a reasonable time. Also, the amount of interest to be paid each month in lieu of a plan is required to be at a "current fair market rate." The court will have to determine that rate if the debtor and the lender cannot agree.

The Small Business Case

Many involved in Chapter 11 cases are concerned about how the rules and regulations make Chapter 11 too expensive and time consuming for those small businesses in need of reorganization that do not qualify for relief under Chapter 12 or 13. Some judges had devised time and cost saving measures designed to speed small businesses through Chapter 11, which were very effective but of questionable legality. Impressed with those efforts Congress decided to formalize and implement them nationally in the 1994 Amendments.

First, the 1994 Amendments added Section 101(51C), which is the definition of a small business. According to that definition, a small business means a person engaged in commercial or business activities other than the ownership or operation of real estate whose secured and unsecured debts total less than $2 million. If a debtor fits within the definition of a small business under Section 101(51C) it can voluntarily opt to be treated as a small business under the Bankruptcy Code. If it does, the special rules discussed below will apply. It need not make that election, however, in which case it will be subject to all of the rules and regulations governing non-small business Chapter 11 cases.

One of the consequences of being a small business is that under Section 1102(a)(3), on request of a party in interest (usually the debtor) and for cause, the court may order that a committee need not be formed. As a result, the debtor will be saved the delay in negotiating the plan with the committee and paying the expenses of the committee as well as the fees and costs of the committee's attorneys and accountants.

In addition, Section 1121(e) has special plan exclusivity rules for those debtors who opt to have their cases treated as small business cases. In those cases, only the debtor may file a plan within the first 100 days, which is down from the 120 days exclusivity given in other Chapter 11 cases. Regardless of who files it, the plan must be filed within the first 160 days. For cause, the Court can reduce either the 100 day or the 160 day period. Conversely, the Court can increase the 100 day period if the debtor shows that its failure to file a plan in the 100 day period was caused by circumstances for which the debtor should not be held accountable. In any event, pressure is added to have the plan filed sooner than would otherwise be true in any other Chapter 11 case.

One of the most helpful consequences of being treated as a small business case is that a court can "conditionally" approve a disclosure statement (presumably without a hearing or notice and presumably without ever seeing it) and then combine the hearing on the disclosure statement with plan confirmation. This should substantially reduce time and costs. To further speed matters up, the conditionally approved disclosure statement need only be mailed ten days before the confirmation hearing. Director's Form B13S is the Order conditionally approving the Disclosure Statement and the Notice for the combined hearing on the Dis-

closure Statement and Plan. Director's Form B15S is the Order Finally Approving Disclosure Statement and Confirming Plan.

In all other respects, small business Chapter 11 cases are treated as regular Chapter 11 cases although in the future the Bankruptcy Rules may be modified to further accelerate the pace of these cases.

☐ EMPLOYMENT AND COMPENSATION OF PROFESSIONALS

Employment of Professionals

In General   As first discussed in Chapter 9 of this book, Section 327 of the Bankruptcy Code provides that the trustee, which also includes the debtor in possession under Section 1107, may employ attorneys, accountants, appraisers, auctioneers, or other professional persons to represent the trustee or assist in the duties listed in the Bankruptcy Code. Similarly, Section 1103 of the Bankruptcy Code allows a creditors' committee to employ attorneys, accountants, or other agents to represent or perform services for the committee.

Conflicts of Interest   As also mentioned in Chapter 9 of this book, whether a professional can accept employment for the trustee, the debtor in possession, or the committee is controlled by some strict rules in the Bankruptcy Code. Section 327(a) allows a person to be employed only if they "do not hold or represent an interest adverse to the estate, and are disinterested." A "disinterested person" is defined in Section 101(14). It excludes a creditor, an equity interest holder, and an insider. Accordingly, creditors, stockholders, and insiders are disqualified from representing the estate. This creates a problem for debtors in possession when their prepetition lawyers or accountants were not paid at the time of the commencement of the bankruptcy case. These professionals are creditors, are not disinterested, and may be disqualified from continuing to represent the debtor. Some courts have taken a strict approach and have refused to authorize the employment of professionals who are prepetition creditors. Others take a more pragmatic approach, and using their discretionary powers, may allow the employment if it is in the best interest of the estate.

Requirement of Court Approval   As indicated earlier, all professionals who will be performing services to the trustee, the debtor in possession, or the committee, and who want to be compensated for those services, must have their employment first approved by the court. When approval has not been obtained before the services are performed, it may be possible to obtain an order approving employment retroactively. Most courts disfavor retroactive employment and it should be relied on only as a last resort.

Procedures   Bankruptcy Rule 2014 gives the procedure for obtaining approval of employment. First, there must be an application of the trustee, the debtor in possession, or the committee. This is one of the few times in bankruptcy practice that relief is properly sought by application. The application should be signed by the person seeking to employ the professional. The other requirements of Rule 2014 were listed in Chapter 9 of this book. Those requirements are shown in Exhibit 11.13, a sample application of a debtor in possession to employ counsel.

BANKRUPT C. LAWYER
White Charger Legal Clinic
One Learned Way
Los Angeles, California 90001

[Proposed] Attorneys for Debtor

UNITED STATES BANKRUPTCY COURT
WESTERN DISTRICT OF CALIFORNIA

In re	)	Case No. 95-00001-JF
	)	
VIDEOS BY JOE, INC.,	)	Chapter 11
	)	
Debtor.	)	
	)	
Debtor's Address:	)	DEBTOR'S APPLICATION TO
18 Hollywood Drive	)	EMPLOY COUNSEL; DECLARATION
Los Angeles, California 90001	)	OF BANKRUPT C. LAWYER IN
	)	SUPPORT THEREOF
Debtor's Tax Id. No. 99-999899	)	
	)	
	)	

Videos by Joe, Inc. ("Debtor"), for and in support of its Application to Employ Counsel, respectfully represents that:

1. Debtor filed a voluntary bankruptcy petition on October 1, 1995 and is the debtor in possession in its Chapter 11 case pursuant to 11 U.S.C. §§ 1107 and 1108.

2. Debtor requires the services of counsel to ensure its compliance with applicable provisions of the Bankruptcy Code, the Bankruptcy Rules, and other applicable statutes and procedural constraints, and to maximize the likelihood of a successful reorganization. Debtor desires to employ White Charger Legal Clinic (the "Firm") for these purposes.

3. In addition to the foregoing, the Firm is needed for the purpose of performing the following professional services:

(a) To advise and consult with Debtor regarding questions arising in its case and concerning the rights and remedies of Debtor with regard to property of the estate, including rights in property which may have been the subject of voidable transfers prior to the filing of Debtor's petition, and in regard to any secured, preferred, or unsecured creditors of the estate;

(b) To appear in, prosecute, and defend suits and proceedings concerning property of the estate;

(c) To take all necessary steps in other matters involving or connected with the affairs of the estate;

(d) To prepare or assist in preparing necessary applications, answers, orders, reports, and other papers, if any, required to be filed in Debtor's case; and

(e) To perform all other legal services for Debtor that may be necessary and appropriate in Debtor's Chapter 11 case or to ensure the retention of such special counsel as may be necessary and proper for such services.

4. The attorneys of the Firm who will appear in Debtor's case are duly admitted to practice before this Court. Debtor has selected the Firm because it has considerable experience in matters of this character and because the Firm has represented Debtor for over five years and has, during that time, become familiar with Debtor's operations.

5. Based upon the foregoing, pursuant to the provisions of 11 U.S.C. § 327 and Rule 2014(a) of the Bankruptcy Rules, Debtor requests this Court's approval of the employment of the Firm.

—continued

6. The Firm proposes to charge fees based upon its prevailing hourly guideline rates which currently range between $80 for the most junior associates to $250 for certain of the more senior partners. The Firm intends to apply to this Court in conformity with 11 U.S.C. §§ 330 and 331 for interim compensation and reimbursement for costs advanced.

7. At the conclusion of Debtor's case the Firm will file an appropriate application seeking allowance of all fees and costs, regardless whether interim compensation has been paid. Upon allowance of such fees and costs Debtor will pay to the Firm the difference between the amounts allowed and any interim compensation paid.

8. Debtor and the Firm understand and agree that the proposed compensation arrangement shall be subject to 11 U.S.C. § 328, which authorizes this Court to allow compensation different from what is provided here if the fee arrangement appears, in retrospect, to have been improvident in light of developments unanticipated at the outset. The Firm understands and agrees that if aggregate interim payments exceed the amount which is ultimately allowed, the Firm will be required to and will promptly repay the difference to the estate.

9. Except as disclosed in the accompanying Declaration of Bankrupt C. Lawyer, Debtor is informed and believes that the Firm is not connected with Debtor, its other attorneys, accountants, or creditors. Debtor is further informed that the Firm represents no other party in interest and that it neither represents nor holds any interest adverse to Debtor or the estate and that the employment of the Firm would be in the best interest of the estate.

WHEREFORE, Debtor requests that it be authorized to employ the Firm at the expense of the estate upon the terms set forth above.

DATED: October 1, 1995

VIDEOS BY JOE, INC.

_____

JOSEPH BUSINESSMAN
President

DECLARATION OF BANKRUPT C. LAWYER

I, Bankrupt C. Lawyer, declare that:

1. I am an attorney at law duly admitted to practice in the State of California and before the United States Bankruptcy Court for the Western District of California.

2. I am a member of White Charger Legal Clinic, the attorneys whom Videos by Joe, Inc. ("Debtor") wishes to have represent it in its Chapter 11 bankruptcy case (the "Firm").

3. I know of no reason why, if the Firm is appointed as Debtor's bankruptcy counsel, it cannot fairly and efficiently discharge all duties required of the Firm to be performed in this case.

4. To the best of my knowledge, information, and belief, and except as stated below, the Firm has no connection with debtor, its other attorneys, accountants, creditors, or any other party in interest; moreover, the Firm neither represents nor holds any interest adverse to the estate in the matters upon which it is to be engaged. It is possible that the Firm may have represented from time to time one or more creditors of Debtor in matters unrelated to this case; however, I am not aware of any conflict which would exist and moreover I warrant that the Firm will not represent any creditor or other party in interest in this case nor will it hereafter represent any person in connection with this case other than Debtor.

5. No agreement exists in violation of the prohibitions of 11 U.S.C. § 504(a) or Rule 2016(b) of the Bankruptcy Rules for a division or sharing of any fees which my be awarded in this case.

6. The Firm has been employed by Debtor in connection with its operations for approximately five years. During that period, the Firm has been paid on a monthly or more often basis. Fees are current through October 1, 1995.

—*continued*

7. The Firm has been paid a retainer of $2,000.00 by Debtor. The retainer will be held pending Orders of the Court under 11 U.S.C. §§ 330 and 331.

I declare under penalty of perjury that the foregoing is true and correct, is based upon personal knowledge except for those matters stated to be on information and belief, and if called as a witness, I could and would testify competently thereto.

Executed at Los Angeles, California, on October 1, 1995.

BANKRUPT C. LAWYER

Court approval of an employment application should be obtained as soon as possible. For the debtor in possession's counsel, the application should be prepared at the same time as the petition so that the employment application can be presented immediately after the case is commenced.

Rule 2016 Statement Whether or not the attorney ultimately applies for compensation, a debtor's attorney in a case under any chapter of the Bankruptcy Code must file with the court a statement of the compensation paid or agreed to be paid if such payment or agreement was made within one year previous to the date of filing of the petition for services rendered or to be rendered in contemplation of or in connection with the case by the attorney. The source of the compensation must also be disclosed. This is required by Bankruptcy Rule 2016 and Official Form B203 can be used.

Compensation of Professionals

Chapter 9 of this book's discussion of professional compensation is equally applicable in Chapter 11 cases. A sample fee application of a debtor in possession's attorneys is shown in Exhibit 11.14. Compare it to Exhibit 9.15 in Chapter 9.

Employment of Insiders

In most bankruptcy cases the salaries and benefits enjoyed by the officers, shareholders, directors, and partners of a debtor will be a sensitive issue to the creditors. More than one company has suffered because of excessive insider payments. Although such payments may be tolerated by the creditors when their checks were merely late in coming, they may not be tolerated at all when, because of the bankruptcy, the creditors may be forced to wait years before they receive any distribution.

In accordance with the debtor in possession's duties to its creditors, it should not be making excessive distributions to insiders. Surprisingly, although compensation and employment of professionals is extensively regulated in the Bankruptcy Code and Rules, there is no such regulation for the employment of insiders. Many jurisdictions have filled in this gap by having local rules on the subject. In addition, the United States trustee has developed guidelines in many jurisdictions.

■ EXHIBIT 11.14
Sample Pleading

BANKRUPT C. LAWYER
White Charger Legal Clinic
One Learned Way
Los Angeles, California 90001

Attorneys for Debtor

UNITED STATES BANKRUPTCY COURT
WESTERN DISTRICT OF CALIFORNIA

In re	Case No. 95-00001-JF
VIDEOS BY JOE, INC.,	Chapter 11
Debtor.	
Debtor's Address:	APPLICATION FOR APPROVAL OF
18 Hollywood Drive	COMPENSATION AND
Los Angeles, California 90001	REIMBURSEMENT OF EXPENSES
Debtor's Tax Id. No. 99-999899	

TO THE HONORABLE JUSTIN FAIR, UNITED STATES BANKRUPTCY JUDGE:

White Charge Legal Clinic (the "Firm"), in support of its Application for Approval of Compensation and Reimbursement of Expenses, respectfully represents that:

1. The Firm was retained by Video's By Joe, Inc. (the "Debtor") to serve as its bankruptcy counsel in preparation for, and during the pendency of, its bankruptcy case. On October 1, 1995, the Firm filed a Chapter 11 petition for the Debtor and on October 5, 1995, the Court issued its order authorizing the employment of the Firm by the Debtor.

2. For the period from October 1, 1995 through and including this date, the Firm has provided legal services to the Debtor in connection with its bankruptcy case. Those services, together with all costs incurred in connection with those services, are particularly described in Exhibit A to the Declaration of Bankrupt C. Lawyer which is filed concurrently (the "Declaration"). Exhibit A identifies the professional who performed the services.

3. A review of Exhibit A indicates the following initials which reflect that time was expended by the following attorney and paralegal:

Initials	Identity
BCL	Bankrupt C. Lawyer
JAM	Julius A. Murray

4. Bankrupt C. Lawyer is, and at all relevant times has been, a member of the Firm. He graduated from the University of California School of Law at Berkeley (Boalt Hall) in 1980 and has practiced law in the insolvency area for almost fifteen years. Mr. Lawyer's billing rate is $200.00 per hour. As set forth in Exhibit A, Mr. Lawyer performed forty hours of professional services to the Debtor since the Firm was retained. During that time, Mr. Lawyer's services ensured that the Debtor was fully, fairly, and adequately represented.

5. Julius A. Murray is an insolvency paralegal whose billing rate is $50.00 per hour. Mr. Murray holds a paralegal certificate from the University of Santa Clara Institute for Paralegal Studies and is experienced and capable in bankruptcy procedure, case management, and administrative matters. Mr. Murray also spent forty hours on the Debtor's case.

—continued

6. The billing rates set forth in paragraphs 4 and 5 are identical to the rates charged all the Firm's clients for whom the referenced individuals performed services during the same period.

7. Billed at the Firm's normal hourly rates, fees total $10,000.00.

8. All of the services for which compensation is requested were performed by the Firm for and on behalf of the Debtor, and not on behalf of any committee, creditor, or any other person.

9. No agreement exists in violation of the prohibitions of 11 U.S.C. § 504(a) or Bankruptcy Rule 2016 for the division or sharing of any fees which may be allowed pursuant to this Application or any future Application.

10. Also attached to the Declaration is a list of all disbursements made by the Firm in connection with its representation of the Debtor. Total costs are $750.00.

11. The Firm believes and represents that the services performed have been beneficial to the estate, and that fees of $10,000.00 and costs of $750.00 are fair and reasonable, represent services or costs actually performed or incurred, and were necessary.

12. As stated in the Debtor's Application to Employ Attorney previously filed, the Firm was paid a $2,000.00 retainer from the Debtor. The retainer has since been residing in the Firm's trust account. No withdrawals have been made.

13. This Application seeks allowance of a claim for $10,750.00; the Firm also requests at this time authorization for the Debtor to pay the allowed amount less the amount of the retainer. The Debtor has ample funds on hand to pay the balance of the amount allowed.

14. The Firm has served a copy of this Application together with the Declaration and its Exhibits upon the Office of the United States Trustee and the Official Creditors' Committee, through counsel.

WHEREFORE, the Firm requests that this Court enter its Order:

1. Approving compensation and reimbursement of expenses for the Firm as follows:

Fees:	$10,000.00
Expense Reimbursement:	$ 750.00
Total:	$10,750.00

2. Authorizing and directing the Debtor to disburse the sum of $8,750.00 to the Firm; and

3. Granting such other and further relief as the Court deems just and proper.

DATED: February 1, 1996

WHITE CHARGER LEGAL CLINIC

_____

BANKRUPT C. LAWYER

If court, United States trustee or creditor approval is required, the debtor would want to emphasize at least some of the following points:

☐ The number of years the individual has been associated with the debtor.

☐ The prepetition salary and benefits as compared to the postpetition salary and benefits.

☐ The responsibilities of the individual.

☐ The benefits the debtor derives from the person's services.

☐ The difficulty in replacing the individual.

☐ The added responsibilities caused by the commencement of the bankruptcy case.

☐ The number of hours devoted by the individual to the debtor.

☐ The lack of other income.

☐ CONVERTING, DISMISSING, OR CLOSING THE CHAPTER 11 CASE

Changing Chapters

Regardless of how much thought went into the decision of filing a Chapter 11 case, during the pendency of the case the question may arise among the debtor and the creditors as to whether the case should have been originally filed under Chapter 7 or whether the case should proceed in the future under Chapter 7. As discussed in Chapter 8 of this book, the act of changing the chapter under which a case is pending is called **conversion.**

According to Section 1112(a) of the Bankruptcy Code, if a Chapter 11 case was commenced voluntarily and no trustee has been appointed, the debtor in possession may convert to a case under Chapter 7, 12 or 13 without interference by the court or any of the creditors. If the case was commenced involuntarily, or was originally other than a Chapter 11 case and was then converted upon the request of a person other than the debtor, or if a trustee has been appointed, this absolute right of the debtor to convert does not exist.

Sometimes the creditors and other parties in interest will prefer the case not remain in Chapter 11 and would just as soon see the estate's assets liquidated. To facilitate those wishes, Section 1112(b) provides that upon request of any party in interest, if cause is shown, the court may convert a Chapter 11 reorganization to a liquidation case under Chapter 7. (See Exhibit 11.15.) A number of examples of cause are given in Section 1112(b) including:

☐ Continuing losses or diminution of the estate, and absence of a reasonable likelihood of rehabilitation.

☐ Inability to effectuate a plan of reorganization.

☐ Unreasonable, prejudicial delay to creditors.

☐ The debtor's failure to propose a plan.

☐ The court's denial or revocation of confirmation of a plan.

☐ The debtor's inability to substantially consummate the plan or the debtor's material default under the terms of the plan.

☐ Termination of the plan because of a failure to meet a specific condition of the plan.

Creditors are not limited to just those acts or omissions mentioned in Section 1112(b) as cause to convert the case to Chapter 7. For example, fraud or gross mismanagement on the part of the debtor could also be grounds for conversion.

Creditors will frequently add to their conversion requests the alternative that the court appoint a trustee. The coupling of these two types of relief is natural because the Bankruptcy Code provides that the court must make the same general findings for each.

Bankruptcy Rule 2002(a)(5) requires that all creditors be given twenty days' notice by mail of a hearing on a motion to convert a Chapter 11 case to a case under any other chapter.

Conversion
The voluntary or involuntary transfer of a bankruptcy case from one chapter of the Bankruptcy Code to a different chapter.

GEORGE SNOW
Snow & Porter
4 Wheel Drive
Los Angeles, California 90017

Attorneys for First City Bank

UNITED STATES BANKRUPTCY COURT
WESTERN DISTRICT OF CALIFORNIA

In re	)	Case No. 95-00001-JF
	)	
VIDEOS BY JOE, INC.,	)	Chapter 11
	)	
Debtor.	)	
	)	
Debtor's Address:	)	MOTION TO CONVERT CASE TO
18 Hollywood Drive	)	CHAPTER 7 OR, IN THE
Los Angeles, California 90001	)	ALTERNATIVE, TO APPOINT A
	)	CHAPTER 11 TRUSTEE
Debtor's Tax Id. No. 99-999899	)	
	)	
	)	

TO THE HONORABLE JUSTIN FAIR, UNITED STATES BANKRUPTCY JUDGE:

First City Bank, a creditor in the above-captioned case (the "Bank"), through its attorneys, hereby moves the Court for an Order converting the above-captioned case from Chapter 11 of the Bankruptcy Code to Chapter 7 of the Bankruptcy Code or, in the alternative, that the Court appoint a Chapter 11 trustee. In support of this Motion, the Bank respectfully represents as follows:

1. Videos by Joe, Inc. ("Debtor") filed a voluntary petition under Chapter 11 of the Bankruptcy Code on October 1, 1995. As shown by the Operating Reports and the Interim Statements Debtor has filed with the Office of the United States Trustee, copies of which are attached to this Motion as Exhibits 1 through 10, Debtor has lost money in each month since the commencement of its case.

2. Debtor's continuing losses operate to the detriment of the creditors by diminishing any value in the estate.

3. In part because of the continuing losses, Debtor has not been able to effectuate a plan of reorganization.

THEREFORE, the Bank respectfully requests that the Court enter its Order converting Debtor's Chapter 11 case to a case under Chapter 7 of the Bankruptcy Code or, in the alternative, appointing a Chapter 11 trustee.

DATED: October 1, 1996

SNOW & PORTER

_____

GEORGE G. SNOW
Attorneys for First City Bank

Section 348 of the Bankruptcy Code details the effects of conversion of a Chapter 11 case to another chapter. As discussed in Chapters 8 and 10 of this book, Section 348(a) provides that conversion constitutes an order for relief but, unless specifically stated otherwise, does not effect a change in the date of the com-

mencement of the case, the filing of the petition or the first order for relief. The fact that these dates do not change is important for such actions as preferences and fraudulent transfers that require the transfer to take place within a set period of time prior to the bankruptcy case being commenced. If the date of conversion was the deciding factor, then most preferences would have taken place more than ninety days prior to the conversion and would not be recoverable for the benefit of the estate. Those items where the date of conversion controls over any earlier date are listed in Section 348(b) and (c). Dates that had no significance in the prior case, such as the deadline to file a complaint to determine the dischargeability of a debt in debtor's Chapter 11 case, would spring to existence in the converted Chapter 7 case.

Upon conversion, the services of any trustee or examiner previously appointed are terminated. Unless creditors have an administrative claim, their claims incurred during the pendency of the earlier case will be treated as prepetition claims. Administrative claims incurred during the earlier case are still entitled to a priority in distribution but will now be paid after the administrative expenses of the case under its new chapter.

In order to facilitate a smooth transition to a Chapter 7 case and the administration of the Chapter 7 trustee, Bankruptcy Rule 1019 requires that when a Chapter 11 case has been converted to Chapter 7, the following must be done:

☐ If the debtor has not filed the schedules, statements, inventories, or any required list, it must do so.

☐ Within twenty days after entry of the order converting the case, notice of the order must be given to all creditors.

☐ Either the debtor in possession or the trustee appointed in the former case must turn over to the Chapter 7 trustee all records and property of the estate in their control.

☐ Within thirty days of the conversion, either the debtor in possession or the trustee appointed in the former case must file with the court a final report and account.

☐ A schedule of the debtor's unpaid debts incurred during the previous chapter must be filed within fifteen days of the conversion.

Any proofs of claims filed by creditors in the previous case are deemed filed in the superseding Chapter 7 case. In a Chapter 11 case, if the creditor is listed in the debtor's schedules and is not scheduled as having a claim that is disputed, contingent, or unliquidated, it need not file a proof of claim. That will not be true upon conversion. Even if the creditor is listed in the correct amount in the debtor's schedules, in most jurisdictions upon conversion the creditor must file a proof of claim to share in any distribution.

Dismissing a Chapter 11 Case The debtor in a Chapter 11 case does not have the absolute right to dismiss its bankruptcy case that Chapters 12 and 13 debtors enjoy. Under Section 1112, the debtor or any creditor who wants the case dismissed must make a motion to the court and establish cause for the dismissal. The types of cause discussed for conversion apply equally to dismissal and the court is charged with finding whichever is in the best interests of the creditors and the estate. If the debtor is ineligible for involuntary Chapter 7 relief because it is a farmer or a charitable organization, when a creditor makes a motion to convert or dismiss, the court's only alternative is to dismiss unless the debtor consents to the conversion.

Bankruptcy Rule 1017(a) governs the procedural aspects of dismissing Chapter 11 cases. The effect of dismissal was discussed in Chapters 8 and 10 of the book, which is equally applicable in Chapter 11 cases.

Closing a Bankruptcy Case

In a Chapter 11 case, where there is a debtor in possession, it will be responsible for seeing that the case is closed. After an estate is fully administered, which usually means that most of the plan payments have been made and all adversary proceedings and contested matters have been completed, the debtor in possession should file a motion with the court stating that the plan has been complied with and the case should be closed. In that motion, the debtor should summarize how the debtor consummated the plan, what claims were allowed in full, what claims were disallowed, what claims were allowed in a reduced amount, and what amounts were paid to creditors. The order closing the case is called a final decree. A sample motion for a final decree is shown in Exhibit 11.16.

■ EXHIBIT 11.16
Sample Pleading

BANKRUPT C. LAWYER
White Charger Legal Clinic
One Learned Way
Los Angeles, California 90001

Attorneys for Debtor

UNITED STATES BANKRUPTCY COURT
WESTERN DISTRICT OF CALIFORNIA

In re	Case No. 95-00001-JF
VIDEOS BY JOE, INC.,	Chapter 11
Debtor.	
Debtor's Address: 18 Hollywood Drive Los Angeles, California 90001	MOTION FOR ENTRY OF FINAL DECREE
Debtor's Tax Id. No. 99-999899	

TO THE HONORABLE JUSTIN FAIR, UNITED STATES BANKRUPTCY JUDGE:

Videos by Joe, Inc., the debtor in possession in the above-captioned case ("Debtor"), through its attorneys, respectfully requests an order of this Court entering the final decree thereby closing Debtor's Chapter 11 case.

I

BACKGROUND AND SUMMARY

On October 1, 1995, Debtor filed a voluntary petition under Chapter 11 of Title 11 of the United States Code. Debtor's plan of reorganization (the "Plan") was confirmed by an order of the court entered on January 31, 1996. Pursuant to the terms of the Plan, Debtor sold all of its assets to Videos by George, Inc.

—continued

■ EXHIBIT 11.16
Sample Pleading—*Continued*

The Plan sets forth four classes of claims against Debtor and the proposed treatment of those classes including the allocation of funds to each class from the proceeds of the sale. Class 1 claims are claims entitled to a priority in payment pursuant to Section 507 of the Bankruptcy Code. Class 2 claims are claims of secured creditors up to the value of their collateral. Class 3 claims are the claims of the prepetition unsecured creditors. Class 4 is the class of interest holders in Debtor.

II
DISTRIBUTIONS

Schedule 1 to this Motion is a list of all of the Class 1 claims and the allowed amount of their claims. Class 1 claim holders received the full amount of their claim on the effective date of the Plan or upon the entry of an Order of the Court allowing their claim.

Schedule 2 to this Motion is a list of all the Class 2 claims and the amount of the value of each secured creditor's collateral. To the extent that a secured creditor's collateral was worth less than the amount of that creditor's claim, the secured creditor also has a Class 3 claim.

Schedule 3 to this Motion is a list of all the Class 3 claims and the allowed amount of those claims. Each holder of a Class 3 claim received a fifty-three percent (53%) distribution on the allowed amount of its claim. The dollar amount of the distribution to each Class 3 claimant is also set forth in Schedule 3.

The names of the interest holders in Debtor are set forth in Schedule 4. No distribution will be made on claims of interest holders.

Claims disallowed in their entirety pursuant to Orders of the Court are set forth on Schedule 5. No payment will be made on these claims.

III
CONCLUSION

Based on the foregoing, Debtor requests that the Court enter its Final Decree closing Debtor's Chapter 11 case.

DATED: March 30, 1996

WHITE CHARGER LEGAL CLINIC

_____

BANKRUPT C. LAWYER
Attorneys for Debtor

SCHEDULE 1

Claimant	Amount of Claim
The Internal Revenue Service	$10,000.00
Board of Equalization	$ 3,000.00
Joseph Businessman	$ 2,000.00
Gerald Cameraman	$ 2,000.00
George and Pamela Wreckers	$ 500.00

SCHEDULE 2

Claimant	Value of Collateral
First City Bank	$75,000.00
B & B Finance Company	$ 9,000.00

—continued

SCHEDULE 3

Claim No.	Claimant	Allowed Claim	Distribution
1	June Film Co.	$ 5,410.71	$ 2,867.68
2	Imperial Processing	$ 2,417.54	$ 1,281.30
3	Ace Trucking	$ 990.00	$ 524.70
5	A–D Motor Freight	$ 6,800.00	$ 3,604.00
6	First City Bank	$20,000.00	$10,600.00
7	Ben's Maintenance	$ 100.00	$ 53.00
8	United Parcel Ser.	$ 1,611.58	$ 854.14
9	Abe's Office Supply	$ 61.65	$ 32.68
11	Shell Oil	$ 149.30	$ 79.13
12	Diamond Radiator	$ 1,479.36	$ 784.06
13	XYZ Advertising	$ 2,000.00	$ 1,060.00
14	Giggie, Inc.	$ 7,000.00	$ 3,710.00

SCHEDULE 4

Interest Holders	Number of Shares
Joseph Businessman	5,000 shares
Myra Businesswoman	3,000 shares
Maximillion Businessman	2,000 shares

SCHEDULE 5

Claim No.	Claimant	Proof of Claim Amount
4	Giggie, Inc.	$ 7,000.00
10	Joseph Businessman	$10,000.00
12	Diamond Radiator	$ 3,666.25

☐ SUMMARY

A debtor will continue to hold and operate its assets in a Chapter 11 case unless it is unable or unqualified to do so. For this reason, a Chapter 11 debtor in a case in which no trustee has been appointed is called a debtor in possession. A debtor in possession has all of the rights and powers of a trustee. These rights and powers include the ability to use cash collateral, obtain financing, employ and compensate professionals, and sell or lease property.

Although a trustee may be appointed to replace the debtor in possession in certain circumstances, such an appointment is rare. Sometimes, an examiner rather than a trustee will be appointed to investigate the debtor's conduct or its business. Also, a creditors' committee, usually comprised of the largest unsecured creditors willing to serve will be appointed to represent the interests of the creditors in the case and review the debtor's performance. Creditor committee members are not paid for their services, although they may employ professionals at the expense of the estate. As a further check, the debtor in possession will be required to submit regular financial statements to the United States trustee for review.

There are several techniques to make a Chapter 11 case proceed more smoothly. These techniques include joint administration or substantive consolidation of related debtors, limiting notice of most proceedings before the Bankruptcy Court, and keeping employees and vendors apprised of developments. Special rules have been implemented to make small Chapter 11 business and real estate cases more efficient and economical. Special rules for the treatment of utilities, such as the power or telephone company, have been created.

The goal of a Chapter 11 case is to confirm a plan of reorganization. For the first four months after a case is commenced, the debtor in possession has the exclusive right to propose a plan, although this time period can be shortened or lengthened by the court. After the period of exclusivity has lapsed, any party in interest other than the United States trustee may propose a plan.

A disclosure statement must accompany a proposed plan of reorganization. The disclosure statement must provide information about the debtor, explain the plan, and give other information creditors need to decide whether to support the plan. Except in small Chapter 11 cases, before the plan is distributed to creditors, the court will review the disclosure statement to insure that it contains the necessary information.

The plan of reorganization will divide creditors into classes and describe their treatment. A plan can provide that the debtor will pay creditors over time from future earnings, provide that creditors will be paid from sale proceeds, or a combination of the two. Once the Bankruptcy Court has approved the disclosure statement, a copy of it, the plan, and a ballot will be sent to creditors. A class of creditors will have accepted the plan if a super majority in each class votes to accept the plan. If all classes accept the plan, it will be confirmed provided all other requirements have been met.

Sometimes a confirmed plan will fail. In other cases, the debtor will be unable to confirm a plan. In those instances, the debtor or the creditors may wish to convert the case to Chapter 7 or dismiss it. The debtor can convert to Chapter 7 at any time but a dismissal or an involuntary conversion requires Court approval.

If a plan is confirmed and there is no need for further Bankruptcy Court involvement, the Chapter 11 case can be closed. This is accomplished by the court's entry of a final decree.

☐ KEY TERMS

Adequate Information	Examiner	Liquidating or Pot Plan
Conversion	Exclusivity Period	Substantive Consolidation
Creditors' Committee	Joint Administration or	
Earn-Out	Administrative Consolidation	

☐ IMPROVE YOUR UNDERSTANDING

1. At a duly held meeting, a majority of the committee votes to require the debtor to sell certain assets. Must the debtor do so?

2. The United States trustee finds only one creditor willing to serve on a committee. Can a committee of one be appointed? Should there be a committee of one?

3. Can a creditor have its attorney serve on a committee on its behalf? If the attorney serves, is the creditor entitled to reimbursement of attorneys' fees?

4. Which of the professionals listed in Section 327(a) is the committee most likely to employ? Why?

For Exercises 5 and 6, assume that the debtor pays its employees on Monday for work through the previous Friday and that the business is closed over the weekends.

5. When should the debtor file its petition?

6. How should the debtor pay the employees to prevent them from being creditors?

7. Does the Bankruptcy Code contain a definition of "utility"?

8. Does Section 366 authorize a utility to take action to collect any prepetition obligation owing from the debtor?

Use the following information in responding to Exercises 9 through 11. XYZ Corporation has a wholly owned subsidiary, Baby XYZ Corporation. Baby XYZ owes $50,000 to XYZ as its share of corporate overhead for their joint headquarters.

9. A partner in a law firm owns stock in XYZ Corporation. Can that law firm represent XYZ in its Chapter 11 case?

10. Can (and if so, should) the same law firm represent XYZ and Baby XYZ? If your answer is yes, give reasons why the same law firm should represent both corporations. If it is no, explain why it should not.

11. Assume that only Baby XYZ will be filing a Chapter 11 case and the law firm's retainer will be paid by XYZ because Baby XYZ is suffering a severe cash flow problem. Must the retainer be disclosed in the firm's employment application?

12. Is there a requirement in the Bankruptcy Code or in the Bankruptcy Rules that retainers must be applied to interim awards?

	CHAPTER 7	CHAPTER 11	CHAPTER 12	CHAPTER 13
CHAPTER 7	X			
CHAPTER 11		X		
CHAPTER 12			X	
CHAPTER 13				X

13. Prepare a table like the example shown here. After reviewing the conversion sections in Chapters 8, 10, and 11 of this book, fill in the boxes with the information necessary to convert (as a matter of right or within the court's discretion, whether a party in interest can move to convert and other pertinent facts) from one chapter (on the vertical axis) to the other (on the horizontal axis).

14. Prepare a table along the lines of the example shown here. After reviewing the dismissal sections in Chapters 8, 10 and 11 of this book fill in the boxes with the information necessary to dismiss.

	Hearing Required	Notice Required	Grounds	Also Move to Convert
CHAPTER 7				
CHAPTER 11				
CHAPTER 12				
CHAPTER 13				

☐ RESEARCH PROJECTS

1. Locate a reported opinion in which a Chapter 11 trustee was appointed and another in which an examiner was appointed. What facts did the courts find important in making their decisions?

2. Find and read at least two decisions of bankruptcy courts discussing substantive consolidation. List the factors the courts considered in support of or in opposition to substantive consolidation.

3. What financial reports are required by the court or the United States trustee in the district in which you live?

4. Locate a reported decision that approved a sale by the debtor in possession of all or substantially all of its assets outside a plan. What factors did the court consider in making its decision?

5. Locate a reported decision that disapproved of the act given in Research Project 4. What factors did the court consider in making its decision?

6. Does Section 1121 discuss how many extensions of the exclusivity period a debtor can obtain?

7. Do any reported decisions discuss how many extensions of the exclusivity period a debtor can obtain?

☐ DRAFTING PROJECTS

1. Draft a motion to limit the notice to be provided on a sale of the debtor's East Coast operations. Develop whatever facts are desired.

2. Draft a letter to a fictional creditor explaining in layperson terms the priority their claim will receive pursuant to Section 503(b)(1) of the Bankruptcy Code if the creditor ships goods or provides services to the debtor in possession.

3. If you did not perform Drafting Project 6 in Chapter 9, go back and do it now for a Chapter 11 debtor in possession.

4. After consulting the materials in Chapter 9 on how a trustee sells assets, Section 363(b), and Bankruptcy Rule 6004, prepare the papers necessary to obtain the bankruptcy court's approval for a debtor in possession to lease new office space.

5. Create a time line for plan confirmation that includes the exclusivity period, the disclosure statement hearing, and confirmation.

6. Compare the sample plan presented in Exhibit 11.11 to Section 1123 of the Bankruptcy Code. For each requirement of Section 1123, indicate where it is satisfied, if at all, in the sample plan.

7. Draft a ballot for Class 4 interest holders to use for the sample plan presented in Exhibit 11.11.

8. Presume that the local rules require that before insiders receive any compensation from the estate, the compensation must be preapproved by the United States trustee. Draft a letter to the United States trustee asking for approval of $5,000 per month compensation for Joe Businessman, the President of Videos by Joe, Inc., a debtor in possession. Create whatever facts you think are necessary.

9. Prepare an application on behalf of a committee to employ counsel.

CHAPTER

THE CREDITORS' PERSPECTIVE

So far, we have focused on the representation of the debtor or the trustee. The rights and remedies of creditors have not been discussed except as they are impacted by the debtor's or the trustee's exercise of his or her rights in the case. This Chapter examines different bankruptcy scenarios from the viewpoint of the creditor, secured and unsecured, priority and non-priority.

☐ THE UNSECURED CREDITOR

Involuntary Cases

In General Most but not all bankruptcy cases are commenced by the debtor filing a petition. Section 303 of the Bankruptcy Code provides a method for creditors to force a debtor into bankruptcy. Creditors may want to do so if the company or person is making preferential transfers to other creditors or insiders, if the debtor is selling off assets and not using the funds to pay creditors, if the debtor has abandoned the business and someone is needed to liquidate the assets, or for a myriad of other reasons.

The eligibility for involuntary relief is more limited than in voluntary cases. First, an **involuntary case** cannot be commenced against anyone who is ineligible to be a voluntary debtor. For example, an involuntary petition could not be filed against an insurance company because insurance companies cannot file voluntary petitions. Second, involuntary cases cannot be commenced against a farmer, defined in Section 101(20) as a person who derived more than eighty percent of its gross income from farming operations in the year before the petition was filed. Finally, any corporation that is not a moneyed, business, or commercial corpora-

---

Involuntary Case
A bankruptcy case commenced by one or more creditors against a debtor.

298

tion, which is generally thought to mean not-for-profit corporations, cannot have an involuntary petition filed against it.

Involuntary cases can be filed only under Chapter 7 or Chapter 11. Chapter 12 cases involve farmers, which cannot be forced into bankruptcy. Since Chapter 13 generally involves wage earners, forcing someone into Chapter 13 would usually mean forcing that person to work. As we have seen, this is thought to violate the prohibition against slavery established in the Thirteenth Amendment to the United States Constitution.

Grounds   A debtor cannot be put into bankruptcy simply on the whim of one of its creditors. If the debtor has twelve or more creditors, at least three must join in the involuntary petition. If the debtor has fewer than twelve creditors, one creditor will suffice. In determining the number of creditors, employees, insiders and those who hold avoidable transfers of the debtor's property are excluded. If there is a danger that one of the creditors will be ineligible, others can join in the petition to cure the numerical defect. Whether one or three or more, the petitioning creditors must hold claims that aggregate at least $10,000 in unsecured or undersecured, noncontingent claims that are not subject to bona fide dispute by the debtor. The last requirement, added by the 1984 Amendments, is designed to prevent creditors who are in litigation with the debtor from compelling a bankruptcy case to obtain an advantage in that litigation.

In order to succeed on their involuntary petition, the petitioning creditors must show that the debtor is generally not paying its debts as they become due or that a custodian has been appointed or has taken possession of substantially all of the debtor's property within 120 days before the filing of the petition. There is no requirement that the debtor be insolvent before it can be the subject of an involuntary case. As long as a debtor is not generally paying its debts as they become due, it is subject to an involuntary case no matter how high its net worth. In contrast, a very insolvent company cannot be forced into bankruptcy if no custodian has been appointed or taken possession of substantially all the assets and if it is paying its bills on a current basis. Since creditors do not usually force a bankruptcy when the debtor is timely paying its debts, meeting this requirement is seldom a problem. But, if the petitioning creditors are wrong, and the involuntary case should never have been brought, the debtor could obtain substantial damages against the petitioning creditors.

Procedure   Bankruptcy Rules 1010, 1011, and 1013 contain the procedures for the commencement and prosecution of involuntary cases. Like voluntary cases, involuntary cases are commenced by the filing of a petition although the petition has different information. Official Form 5 is the involuntary petition. A sample is shown in Exhibit 12.1. The petition is filed with the court along with the appropriate filing fee. The clerk of the court will issue a summons which must then be served on the debtor with a copy of the involuntary petition.

Once the summons and involuntary petition are served, the debtor has twenty days to file an answer or to otherwise respond. If the debtor wishes to contest being in a bankruptcy case, it may deny that it is not generally paying its debts as they become due or may assert that one or more of the creditors who joined in the petition is ineligible because the claim is in bona fide dispute or is contingent. Of course if more than three creditors filed the petition or if other creditors joined in it after it was filed, one creditor's ineligibility will not prevent the petition from being effective.

■ EXHIBIT 12.1
Involuntary Petition

Form B5
(6/90)

FORM 5. INVOLUNTARY PETITION

United States Bankruptcy Court _____ **Western District of** California _____	**INVOLUNTARY PETITION**

IN RE (Name of debtor - If individual, enter: Last, First, Middle) Videos By Joe, Inc.	ALL OTHER NAMES used by debtor in the last 6 years (Include married, maiden, and trade names)

SOC SEC./TAX I.D.NO.(If more than one, state all)
99-999899

STREET ADDRESS OF DEBTOR (No. and street, city, state, and zip code) 18 Hollywood Drive Los Angeles, California 90001	MAILING ADDRESS OF DEBTOR (if different from street address)

COUNTY OR RESIDENCE OR
PRINCIPAL PLACE OF BUSINESS
LOS ANGELES

LOCATION OF PRINCIPAL ASSETS OF BUSINESS DEBTOR (if different from previously listed addresses)

CHAPTER OF BANKRUPTCY CODE UNDER WHICH PETITION IS FILED

[X] Chapter 7   [ ] Chapter 11

INFORMATION REGARDING DEBTOR (Check if applicable boxes)

Petitioners believe
[ ] Debts are primarily consumer debts
[X] Debts are primarily business debts (Complete sections A and B)

TYPE OF DEBTOR
[ ] Individual   [ ] Corporation Publicly Held
[ ] Partnership   [X] Corporation Not Publicly Held
[ ] Other_____

A. TYPE OF BUSINESS (Check one)
[ ] Professional   [ ] Transportation   [ ] Commodity Broker
[ ] Retail/wholesale [ ] Manufacturing/   [ ] Construction
[ ] Railroad   [ ] Mining   [ ] Real Estate
                      [ ] Stockbroker   [X] Other Service.

B. BRIEFLY DESCRIBE NATURE OF BUSINESS
Provides video taping services to
consumers.

VENUE

[X] Debtor has been domiciled or has had a residence, principal place of business, or principal assets in the District for 180 days immediately
preceding the date of this petition or for a longer part of 180 days than in any other District.

[ ] A bankruptcy case concerning debtor's affiliate, general partner or partnership is pending in this District.

PENDING BANKRUPTCY CASE FILED BY OR AGAINST ANY PARTNER OR AFFILIATE OF THIS DEBTOR (Report information for any additional cases on attached sheets.)

Name of Debtor	Case Number	Date
Relationship	District	Judge

ALLEGATIONS
(Check applicable boxes)

1. [X] Petitioner(s) are eligible to file this petition pursuant to 11 U.S.C. §303(b).
2. [X] The debtor is a person against whom an order for relief may be entered under title 11 of
the United States Code.

3.a. [X] The debtor is generally not paying such debtor's debts as they become due, unless such
debts are the subject of a bona fide dispute;

or

b. [ ] Within 120 days preceding the filing of this petition, a custodian, other than trustee,
receiver, or agent appointed or authorized to take charge of less than substantially
all of the property of the debtor for the purpose of enforcing a lien against such property,
was appointed or took possession.

COURT USE ONLY

B5

—continued

Name of Debtor   **Videos By Joe, Inc.**

FORM 5 Involuntary Petition
(10/89)

Case No. _____
(Court use only)

TRANSFER OF CLAIM

☐ Check this box if there has been a transfer of any claim against the debtor by or to any petitioner. Attach all documents evidencing the transfer and any statements that are required under Bankruptcy Rule 1003(a).

REQUEST FOR RELIEF

Petitioner(s) request that an order for relief be entered against the debtor under the chapter of title 11, United States Code, specified in this petition.

Petitioner(s) declare under penalty of perjury that the foregoing is true and correct according to the best of their knowledge, information, and belief.

X _____
Signature of Petitioner or Representative (State title)

Ace Trucking
Name of Petitioner

Name & Mailing
Address of Individual   **Jack Q. King**
Signing in Representative **2309 Mack Street**
Capacity   **Los Angeles, Ca**
                         90001

X _____
Signature of Attorney
Iona Portia
Portia & Carrera
Name of Attorney Firm (If any)

Two Lane Highway
San Diego, CA 92123
Address
(906) 891-5595
Telephone No.

X _____
Signature of Petitioner or Representative (State title)

Imperial Processing
Name of Petitioner

Name & Mailing   **Carl Douglas**
Address of Individual **84 Steel Road**
Signing in Representative **Industry, CA 90050**
Capacity

X _____
Signature of Attorney

Name of Attorney Firm (If any)

Address

Telephone No.

X _____
Signature of Petitioner or Representative (State title)

Abe's Office Supplies
Name of Petitioner

Name & Mailing   **Abe Morrow**
Address of Individual **20 Hollywood Dr.**
Signing in representative **Los Angeles, CA**
Capacity   **90001**

X _____
Signature of Attorney

Name of Attorney Firm (If any)

Address

Telephone No.

PETITIONING CREDITORS

Name and Address of Petitioner	Nature of Claim	Amount of Claim
Ace Trucking 2309 Mack St., L.A., CA 90001	Shipping services provided to debtor.	$990.00
Imperial Processing 84 Steel Rd., Industry, CA	Processing services provided to debtor.	$11,000.00
Abe's Office Supplies 20 Hollywood Dr., L.A., CA	Goods provided to debtor.	$14.50
Note: If there are more than three petitioners, attach additional sheets with the statement under penalty of perjury, petitioner(s) signatures under the statement and the name(s) of attorney(s) and petitioning creditor information in the format above.	Total Amount of Petitioners' Claims	$12,004.50

___0___ continuation sheets attached

The debtor may be willing to be in a bankruptcy case or may realize that fighting it would be senseless. In that case the debtor may file a notice with the court that it consents to the entry of the order for relief. Such a consent is given in Exhibit 12.2. Alternatively, the debtor will do nothing and upon lapse of twenty days' time, the court will take the debtor's default. In either event, the court will enter an order for relief. From then on the case will continue as if it had been commenced voluntarily. If it is a Chapter 7 case, a trustee will be appointed. If it is a Chapter 11 case, the debtor will become the debtor in possession.

If the petition was filed in Chapter 7, in its notice of consent the debtor may elect to convert the case of Chapter 11 or 13 if the debtor is eligible for relief under those chapters. If the creditors want a liquidation, they will then need to move to convert the case back to Chapter 7. The debtor may also elect to convert

■ EXHIBIT 12.2
Sample Pleading

BANKRUPT C. LAWYER
White Charger Legal Clinic
One Learned Way
Los Angeles, California 90001

Attorneys for Debtor

UNITED STATES BANKRUPTCY COURT
WESTERN DISTRICT OF CALIFORNIA

In re) VIDEOS BY JOE, INC.,) Debtor.) Debtor's Address:) 18 Hollywood Drive) Los Angeles, California 90001) Debtor's Tax Id. No. 99-999899) _____)	Case No. 95-00001-JF Chapter 11 CONSENT TO ENTRY OF AN ORDER FOR RELIEF

TO THE HONORABLE JUSTIN FAIR, UNITED STATES BANKRUPTCY JUDGE:

Videos by Joe, Inc. hereby consents to the entry of an Order for Relief under Chapter 11, Title 11 of the United States Code in the case commenced by the Involuntary Case: Creditors' Petition filed against it, the Summons with respect to which was issued on October 1, 1995. Filed concurrently with this Consent as Exhibits A through D are those paper, pleadings, and documents required by Bankruptcy Rules 1007(a)(2), 1007(a)(3), 1007(d), and 2016(b).

DATED: October 20, 1995

VIDEOS BY JOE, INC.

_____

JOE BUSINESSMAN
President

a Chapter 11 petition to Chapter 7 or 13; the creditors have the same right to attempt to convert it back.

If the debtor desires to contest the petition, the matter will be an adversary proceeding governed by the 7000 series of the Bankruptcy Rules. Each side will have the right to engage in discovery and a trial will be held on any of the disputed issues. If the court finds that the petition is well founded, it will enter the order for relief. If it finds for the debtor, it will dismiss the petition and may award damages to the debtor against the petitioning creditors for the debtor's costs, including attorneys' fees, and any damages caused by the improper commencement of the involuntary case.

Dismissal   Once an involuntary petition is filed, it cannot be simply dismissed by the petitioning creditors. The debtor must be given a chance to request damages. Also, to prevent a debtor who properly should be in a bankruptcy case from buying the petitioning creditors' cooperation by paying their debts, the debtor and the petitioning creditors cannot just dismiss the case. Any request for a dismissal must be noticed to all creditors and a court hearing held.

Effect of Filing an Involuntary Petition   Unlike voluntary cases, the order for relief is not entered upon the filing of the involuntary petition. However, the bankruptcy case has officially been commenced. Whenever the Bankruptcy Code speaks of the commencement of the case, it will mean the filing of the involuntary petition. If, instead, it speaks of the entry of the order for relief, it will not apply in involuntary cases as soon as the petition is filed. For example, Section 362(a) provides that the automatic stay takes effect upon the commencement of the case. Thus, the debtor that has just had an involuntary petition filed against it is protected by the automatic stay. On the other hand, the time limit by which executory contracts and unexpired leases must be assumed or rejected begins upon the entry of the order for relief. Therefore, a debtor subject to an involuntary case need not worry about losing valuable contracts or leases while fighting an involuntary petition.

There are a number of rules that govern the debtor's conduct pending the entry of the order for relief in an involuntary case. Section 303(f) of the Bankruptcy Code allows the debtor to operate its business and to use, acquire, and dispose of its property as if the case had not been commenced. Any debt incurred between the filing of the petition and the entry of the order for relief, which is called the "gap" period, is entitled to a priority in payment over any prepetition claim under Section 507(a)(2). In addition, Section 549 permits the trustee or the debtor in possession to recover any assets transferred during this time if an order for relief is ultimately entered. While that power provides certain protections, it is not as good as preventing the transfer from taking place. Pursuant to Section 303(g), if necessary to preserve or protect the debtor's property against loss, the court has the power to appoint an interim trustee to take possession of the debtor's business pending the hearing on the involuntary petition. The debtor can defeat the appointment of a trustee by posting a bond. If the appointment of a trustee would be too harsh, the court may otherwise restrict the debtor's operations by, for example, preventing it from making transfers out of the ordinary course of business. A simple motion seeking just such a restriction is found in Exhibit 12.3.

Compensation   Creditors who hire counsel to bring an involuntary petition may file a motion with the court to be reimbursed for the attorneys' fees and costs they incurred.

■ EXHIBIT 12.3
Sample Pleading

SARAH PORTIA
Portia & Carrera
Two Lane Highway
San Diego, California 92123

Attorneys for Petitioning Creditors

UNITED STATES BANKRUPTCY COURT
WESTERN DISTRICT OF CALIFORNIA

In re	)	Case No. 95-00001-JF
	)	
VIDEOS BY JOE, Inc.,	)	Chapter 11
	)	
Debtor.	)	MOTION FOR ORDER RESTRICTING
	)	OPERATIONS OF DEBTOR PENDING
Debtor's Address:	)	TRIAL ON INVOLUNTARY
18 Hollywood Drive	)	PETITION
Los Angeles, California 90001	)	
	)	
Debtor's Tax Id. No. 99-999899	)	
	)	

TO THE HONORABLE JUSTIN FAIR, UNITED STATES BANKRUPTCY JUDGE:

Imperial Processing, Act Trucking, and Abe's Office Supply (the "Petitioning Creditors"), through their attorneys, hereby move the Court for its order restricting the operations of the debtor pending trial of the issue of whether an Order for Relief should be entered. In support of this Motion, the Petitioning Creditors respectfully represent as follows:

1. Videos by Joe, Inc. (the "Debtor") is the debtor in the above-captioned involuntary Chapter 11 case which was commenced on October 1, 1995 by the filing of an Involuntary Case: Creditors' Petition against Debtor by Petitioning Creditors. Petitioning Creditors hold claims against Debtor in the aggregate amount of approximately $50,000.

2. Petitioning Creditors understand that on or about September 20, 1995, Debtor transferred to certain of its film vendors unexposed video film valued at approximately $10,000. This transfer was made in partial satisfaction to the indebtedness of Debtor to such vendors. Petitioning Creditors believe that additional transfers of film inventory are contemplated and suspect that similar transactions may be occurring with other vendors.

3. Such transfers are prejudicial to unsecured creditors. From the standpoint of creditors, Debtor receives no value for the inventory. The transfer may be avoidable as a preference, but creditors then bear the expense and risk of litigation, including the risk that the transferees will be unable to respond to a judgment. Furthermore, the depletion of inventory may impact negatively on Debtor's ability to make future sales.

4. Bankruptcy Code Section 303(f) provides that

Notwithstanding Section 363 of this title, *except to the extent that the court orders otherwise,* and until an order for relief in the case, any business of the debtor may continue to operate, and the debtor may continue to use, acquire or dispose of property as if an involuntary case concerning the debtor had not been commenced (emphasis added).

5. An order imposing upon Debtor the requirements of Section 363(b)(1) of the Bankruptcy Code and prohibiting the payment of prepetition debts should be entered. Such an order is only minimally burdensome on Debtor. Debtor will remain in control of its business and can operate in the ordinary course. Transactions that are outside the ordinary course of business are permissible, but only after notice to creditors and an opportunity for them to be heard.

—continued

■ EXHIBIT 12.3
Sample Pleading—*Continued*

---

6. Such an order will have important benefits to unsecured creditors. Transfers of inventory, with the resulting prejudice, will cease. The core business will be preserved for the benefit of all creditors, not just the preferred few.

WHEREFORE, Petitioning Creditors request that the Court enter its order imposing the requirements of Bankruptcy Code Section 363(b)(1) upon Debtor and prohibiting Debtor from making any transfers on account of any prepetition indebtedness.

DATED: October 3, 1995

PORTIA & CARRERA

SARAH PORTIA
Attorneys for Petitioning Creditors

Proofs of Claim

In General   A **claim** is defined in Section 101(5) to be any right to payment, whether or not secured, liquidated, contingent, disputed, or matured. Payments or distributions in bankruptcy cases are made on allowed claims. There are several different ways in which a claim becomes allowed but the most common is through the creditor filing a **proof of claim.**

A proof of claim is a relatively simple document that is usually filed with the court by a creditor. It is fairly simple because it is designed to be completed by creditors without the assistance of an attorney. Attorneys can file proofs of claim on behalf of their clients. Non-attorneys can also file proofs of claim on behalf of creditors, but if they do so a power of attorney in the form of Official Form 11A should be used.

Official Form 10 is the proof of claim that can be used by all creditors whether they are unsecured, secured, prepetition, priority, or non-priority. Official Form 10 can also be used in cases under every chapter of the Bankruptcy Code. Exhibit 12.4 is a blank Official Form 10 proof of claim. The discussion below corresponds to the circled numbers in each part of Exhibit 12.4.

Section 1: The Caption   In the same manner as other papers filed in a bankruptcy case, a proof of claim must indicate the bankruptcy court in which the case is pending, the name of the debtor, and the case number. Unlike other papers, however, the creditor need not indicate whether the case is a Chapter 7, 11, 12, or 13.

Section 2: The Creditor's Identification   After the caption, the three boxes marked "2" in Exhibit 12.4 ask for the creditor's name and address as well as the account or other number by which the creditor identifies the debtor. This will help the debtor or the trustee communicate with the creditor in the future. If the creditor wants all communication to be handled through its lawyers, the creditor's address can be filled in with the name and address of the lawyer (See Exhibit 12.9).

Section 3: Notices   In the box marked "3" in Exhibit 12.4, the creditor should indicate if it is aware whether anyone else has filed a proof of claim relating to

Claim
A right to payment or performance, whether or not liquidated, contingent, disputed, or secured.

Proof of Claim
The form completed and filed by a creditor in order to protect its right to payment or performance in a bankruptcy case.

■ EXHIBIT 12.4
Proof of Claim

B10 (Official Form 10)
(Rev. 12/94)

United States Bankruptcy Court

_____ District of _____

PROOF OF CLAIM

In re (Name of Debtor)	Case Number

NOTE: This form should not be used to make a claim for an administrative expense arising after the commencement of the case. A "request" for payment of an administrative expense may be filed pursuant to 11 U.S.C. § 503.

Name of Creditor
(The person or other entity to whom the debtor owes money or property)

☐ Check box if you are aware that anyone else has filed a proof of claim relating to your claim. Attach copy of statement giving particulars.

Name and Address Where Notices Should be Sent

☐ Check box if you have never received any notices from the bankruptcy court in this case.

☐ Check box if the address differs from the address on the envelope sent to you by the court.

THIS SPACE IS FOR COURT USE ONLY

Telephone Number

ACCOUNT OR OTHER NUMBER BY WHICH CREDITOR IDENTIFIES DEBTOR:

Check here if this claim ☐ replaces ☐ amends a previously filed claim, dated: _____

1. BASIS FOR CLAIM
☐ Goods sold
☐ Services performed
☐ Money loaned
☐ Personal injury/wrongful death
☐ Taxes
☐ Other (Describe briefly)

☐ Retiree benefits as defined in 11 U.S.C. § 1114 (a)
☐ Wages, salaries, and compensations (Fill out below)
Your social security number _____
Unpaid compensation for services performed
from _____ to _____
(date) (date)

2. DATE DEBT WAS INCURRED

3. IF COURT JUDGMENT, DATE OBTAINED:

4. CLASSIFICATION OF CLAIM. Under the Bankruptcy Code all claims are classified as one or more of the following: (1) Unsecured nonpriority, (2) Unsecured Priority, (3) Secured. It is possible for part of a claim to be in one category and part in another.
CHECK THE APPROPRIATE BOX OR BOXES that best describe your claim and STATE THE AMOUNT OF THE CLAIM AT TIME CASE FILED.

☐ SECURED CLAIM $ _____
Attach evidence of perfection of security interest
Brief Description of Collateral:
☐ Real Estate ☐ Motor Vehicle ☐ Other (Describe briefly)

Amount of arrearage and other charges at time case filed included in secured claim above, if any $ _____

☐ UNSECURED NONPRIORITY CLAIM $ _____
A claim is unsecured if there is no collateral or lien on property of the debtor securing the claim or to the extent that the value of such property is less than the amount of the claim.

☐ UNSECURED PRIORITY CLAIM $ _____
Specify the priority of the claim.

☐ Wages, salaries, or commissions (up to $4000)*, earned not more than 90 days before filing of the bankruptcy petition or cessation of the debtor's business, whichever is earlier - 11 U.S.C. § 507(a)(3)
☐ Contributions to an employee benefit plan - 11 U.S.C. § 507(a)(4)
☐ Up to $1,800* of deposits toward purchase, lease, or rental of property or services for personal, family, or household use - 11 U.S.C. § 507(a)(6)
☐ Alimony, maintenance, or support owed to a spouse, former spouse, or child - 11 U.S.C. § 507(a)(7)
☐ Taxes or penalties of governmental units - 11 U.S.C. § 507 (a)(8)
☐ Other - Specify applicable paragraph of 11 U.S.C. § 507(a) _____ .
* Amounts are subject to adjustment on 4/1/98 and every 3 years thereafter with respect to cases commenced on or after the date of adjustment.

5. TOTAL AMOUNT OF CLAIM AT TIME CASE FILED:
$ _____ (Unsecured) $ _____ (Secured) $ _____ (Priority) $ _____ (Total)

☐ Check this box if claim includes charges in addition to the principal amount of the claim. Attach itemized statement of all additional charges.

THIS SPACE IS FOR COURT USE ONLY

6. CREDITS AND SETOFFS: The amount of all payments on this claim has been credited and deducted for the purpose of making this proof of claim. In filing this claim, claimant has deducted all amounts that claimant owes to debtor.

7. SUPPORTING DOCUMENTS: *Attach copies of supporting documents*, such as promissory notes, purchase orders, invoices, itemized statements of running accounts, contracts, court judgments, or evidence of security interests. If the documents are not available, explain. If the documents are voluminous, attach a summary.

8. TIME-STAMPED COPY: To receive an acknowledgment of the filing of your claim, enclose a stamped, self-addressed envelope and copy of this proof of claim.

Date	Sign and print the name and title, if any, of the creditor or other person authorized to file this claim (attach copy of power of attorney, if any)

Penalty for presenting fraudulent claim: Fine of up to $500,000 or imprisonment for up to 5 years, or both. 18 U.S.C. §§ 152 and 3571.

the same claim, if it has never received any notices from the bankruptcy court, or if there has been a change of address. The last two items should insure that the clerk fulfills its duties in Bankruptcy Rule 2002(g) to update the mailing list in the case by substituting the address provided by a creditor on a proof of claim if that address is different from the one supplied by the debtor. This form also helps identify duplicate claims filed by different entities.

Section 4: Replaced or Amended Claims In the box marked "4" in Exhibit 12.4, creditors are to check whether the proof of claim replaces or amends a previously filed claim. This will also help the trustee or debtor avoid counting duplicate or superseded claims.

Section 5: Claim Information Exhibit 12.4 has three boxes marked "5" that are numbered paragraphs 1, 2, and 3 of Official Form 10. The first of these boxes gives various alternatives for creditors to use to state the basis of their claim, such as "goods sold," "services provided," and "money loaned." The information required for "Wages, salaries and compensation," the last alternative, will assist the trustee or debtor to make the appropriate withholding calculations and reports as well as help determine whether any priority amount is properly claimed.

The boxes marked "5" in Exhibit 12.4 also require the date the debt was incurred and, if applicable, the date of any court judgment. This requirement is a mystery. This information is largely irrelevant to any claim determination unless the debt was incurred postpetition. In that event the proof of claim is not the appropriate paper to file. As the note at the top of the form states, it should not be used to make a claim for an administrative expense.

Section 6: Classification and Amount of Claim The box marked "6", which is box 4 in Official Form 10, requires the creditor to classify its claim into secured, unsecured nonpriority, and unsecured priority, and to give the amount of each type. For secured creditors, the form requests a brief description of the collateral, evidence of the perfection of the security interest, and the amount of any past due amounts (arrearages) and other charges included in the secured claim. A sample proof of claim for a secured creditor is shown in Exhibit 12.11.

For unsecured priority creditors, the form requires the creditor to state under which provision of Section 507(a) it claims to be entitled to a priority. The form was revised after the 1994 Amendments to include the renumbering caused by the addition of the new Section 507(a)(7) priority for alimony and support. A claim filed by a partial priority creditor is given in Exhibit 12.9.

If a creditor has different types of claims, information can be put in more than one category. For example, a secured creditor whose collateral is worth less than the amount of the debt will have a secured claim up to the value of the collateral and an unsecured nonpriority claim for the deficiency. An employee might have an unsecured priority claim for $4,000 in back wages and an unsecured nonpriority claim for the balance due.

Section 7: Summary In the box marked "7" the information found in box "6" will be summarized and totaled. It also requires the creditors to check a box if the amounts claimed include things like interest, penalties, attorneys' fees and other charges. An itemized statement of these charges must be attached.

Section 8: Documentation In the box marked "8" in Exhibit 12.4, the creditor is instructed to make all credits and setoffs due to the debtor, attach copies of all supporting documentation unless voluminous in which case a summary will do, and submit a copy and a self-addressed stamped envelope in order to receive a conformed copy. For a secured creditor the supporting documentation would include the note and security agreement in addition to the perfection proof required earlier. For a trade creditor the documentation might include an invoice, proof of delivery, or statement.

Section 9: Signature Proofs of claim should be signed by the creditor or by its authorized agent. This could include a corporate officer, credit manager, or attorney.

Exhibit 12.5 is a proof of claim prepared by a trade creditor with a simple claim.

Who Can File Obviously, proofs of claim are usually filed by creditors. Sometimes they can be filed by other parties. If a creditor fails to file a proof of claim, Section 501(c) and Bankruptcy Rule 3004 allow the debtor or the trustee to do so in the name of the creditor. The debtor may want to file a claim on behalf of a creditor to ensure that the creditor is paid, especially if there is an affiliate of the debtor that is also obligated on the debt or the debt is not dischargeable and will survive the bankruptcy case. The trustee may file a claim on behalf of a creditor if, perhaps, the trustee believes the creditor should be paid but for some reason the creditor did not file the claim. For example, sometimes the trustee will file proofs of claim on behalf of unpaid employees who did not understand their right to file proofs of claim.

Bankruptcy Code Section 501 and Bankruptcy Rule 3005 allow any person who is liable with the debtor on a debt, such as a guarantor or co-borrower, or who has given security for the debt to file a proof of claim for a creditor if the creditor has not filed one. If an entity other than the creditor files a claim on behalf of that creditor, the creditor may later file its own claim; this claim will supersede any claim filed for it.

Filing and Service Proofs of claim are generally filed with the clerk of the court. In some jurisdictions they will be filed with the Chapter 13 trustee. In addition, in some very large cases, the court will order that they be sent directly to the debtor or the trustee. In those cases, usually an employee of the debtor or the trustee, or an employee of their attorney, will be made a special deputy clerk.

There is no requirement in the Bankruptcy Code or in the Bankruptcy Rules that proofs of claim be served on any party in interest. Some local rules may require that they be served on the debtor and the trustee, if any. Even if the local rules do not require any service, it is often customary to provide a copy to the debtor in possession or the trustee as a matter of courtesy.

Timing Pursuant to Bankruptcy Rule 3002(c), in all cases except those under Chapter 11, proofs of claim must be filed within ninety days after the first date set for the meeting of creditors. Even if the first meeting of creditors is continued to another date, the claim filing deadline will be determined by reference to the date on which it was first set. This is a very important date to calendar when the legal assistant first learns of the commencement of the case because if a claim is not filed in a timely manner, it is unlikely that the creditor will receive a distribution. It is always a good idea to prepare and file the proof of claim as soon as is possible in the case to ensure that the task does not fall between the cracks.

Some claims, although treated as prepetition claims, cannot be filed within the deadline provided in Bankruptcy Rule 3002(c). One example is claims arising from the rejection of an executory contract, which may not happen until after the claims filing deadline has passed. Bankruptcy Rule 3002(c)(4) provides that those claims must be filed within the time set by the court. Claims that arise because of the result of a judgment, such as claims of creditors who had to pay back a preference, must be filed within thirty days after the judgment becomes final. Bankruptcy Rule

■ EXHIBIT 12.5
Completed Proof of Claim

B10 (Official Form 10)
(Rev. 12/94)

United States Bankruptcy Court	
___Western___ District of ___California___	**PROOF OF CLAIM**

In re (Name of Debtor)
Videos by Joe, Inc.

Case Number
95-00001-JF

NOTE: This form should not be used to make a claim for an administrative expense arising after the commencement of the case. A "request" for payment of an administrative expense may be filed pursuant to 11 U.S.C. § 503.

Name of Creditor
(The person or other entity to whom the debtor owes money or property)
Ace Trucking

☐ Check box if you are aware that anyone else has filed a proof of claim relating to your claim. Attach copy of statement giving particulars.

Name and Address Where Notices Should be Sent
Ace Trucking
2309 Mack Street
Los Angeles, California 90001
Attn: Jack Q. King
Telephone Number (213) 891-0700

☐ Check box if you have never received any notices from the bankruptcy court in this case.

☐ Check box if the address differs from the address on the envelope sent to you by the court.

THIS SPACE IS FOR
COURT USE ONLY

ACCOUNT OR OTHER NUMBER BY WHICH CREDITOR IDENTIFIES DEBTOR:
X11144

Check here if this claim ☐ replaces ☐ amends   a previously filed claim, dated: _____

1. BASIS FOR CLAIM

☐ Goods sold
☒ Services performed
☐ Money loaned
☐ Personal injury/wrongful death
☐ Taxes
☐ Other (Describe briefly)

☐ Retiree benefits as defined in 11 U.S.C. § 1114 (a)
☐ Wages, salaries, and compensations (Fill out below)
Your social security number _____
Unpaid compensation for services performed
from _____ to _____
(date)   (date)

2.   DATE DEBT WAS INCURRED
September 15, 1995

3.   IF COURT JUDGMENT, DATE OBTAINED:

4.   CLASSIFICATION OF CLAIM. Under the Bankruptcy Code all claims are classified as one or more of the following: (1) Unsecured nonpriority, (2) Unsecured Priority, (3) Secured. It is possible for part of a claim to be in one category and part in another. CHECK THE APPROPRIATE BOX OR BOXES that best describe your claim and STATE THE AMOUNT OF THE CLAIM AT TIME CASE FILED.

☐ SECURED CLAIM $ _____
Attach evidence of perfection of security interest
Brief Description of Collateral:
☐ Real Estate ☐ Motor Vehicle ☐ Other (Describe briefly)

Amount of arrearage and other charges at time case filed included
in secured claim above, if any $ _____

☒ UNSECURED NONPRIORITY CLAIM $ 990.00
A claim is unsecured if there is no collateral or lien on property of the debtor securing the claim or to the extent that the value of such property is less than the amount of the claim.

☐ UNSECURED PRIORITY CLAIM $ _____
Specify the priority of the claim.

☐ Wages, salaries, or commissions (up to $4000)*, earned not more than 90 days before filing of the bankruptcy petition or cessation of the debtor's business, whichever is earlier - 11 U.S.C. § 507(a)(3)

☐ Contributions to an employee benefit plan - 11 U.S.C. § 507(a)(4)

☐ Up to $1,800* of deposits toward purchase, lease, or rental of property or services for personal, family, or household use - 11 U.S.C. § 507(a)(6)

☐ Alimony, maintenance, or support owed to a spouse, former spouse, or child - 11 U.S.C. § 507(a)(7)

☐ Taxes or penalties of governmental units - 11 U.S.C. § 507 (a)(8)

☐ Other - Specify applicable paragraph of 11 U.S.C. § 507(a) _____ .
* Amounts are subject to adjustment on 4/1/98 and every 3 years thereafter with respect to cases commenced on or after the date of adjustment.

5.   TOTAL AMOUNT OF CLAIM AT TIME CASE FILED:

$ 990.00 (Unsecured) $ _____ (Secured) $ _____ (Priority) $ 990.00 (Total)

☐ Check this box if claim includes charges in addition to the principal amount of the claim. Attach itemized statement of all additional charges.

THIS SPACE IS FOR
COURT USE ONLY

6.   CREDITS AND SETOFFS: The amount of all payments on this claim has been credited and deducted for the purpose of making this proof of claim. In filing this claim, claimant has deducted all amounts that claimant owes to debtor.

7.   SUPPORTING DOCUMENTS: *Attach copies of supporting documents*, such as promissory notes, purchase orders, invoices, itemized statements of running accounts, contracts, court judgments, or evidence of security interests. If the documents are not available, explain. If the documents are voluminous, attach a summary.

8.   TIME-STAMPED COPY: To receive an acknowledgment of the filing of your claim, enclose a stamped, self-addressed envelope and copy of this proof of claim.

Date

Oct. 15, 1995

Sign and print the name and title, if any, of the creditor or other person authorized to file this claim (attach copy of power of attorney, if any)

Jack Q. King, Owner

Penalty for presenting fraudulent claim: Fine of up to $500,000 or imprisonment for up to 5 years, or both. 18 U.S.C. §§ 152 and 3571.

3005 allows a codebtor to file a claim only within the thirty-day period following expiration of the time for creditor filings. There is no deadline for claims filed by the debtor or the trustee.

Chapter 11 cases are very different from other chapters when it comes to the filing of proofs of claim. Bankruptcy Rule 3003(c) and Bankruptcy Code Section 1111 provide that if a creditor or equity security holder is listed in the schedules and the debtor does not list the claim as disputed, contingent, or unliquidated, the claim is deemed filed and the creditor need not file a proof of claim if the amount scheduled is correct. If the claim is scheduled as disputed, contingent, or unliquidated, the creditor must file a proof of claim to participate in the distribution to creditors. If the amount is wrong, unless the creditor files a proof of claim, the wrong amount will be deemed correct. If a proof of claim is filed, it will supersede the scheduled amount.

Although a creditor need not file a claim if its claim has been deemed filed, there is no prohibition against it doing so. In fact, it is usually easier to simply file a proof of claim than to try to learn how a creditor is scheduled and in what amount.

There is no ninety-day deadline for the filing of a proof of claim in a Chapter 11 case as there is in other cases. However, sometime before plan confirmation, the court will set a date by which required proofs of claim must be filed.

If a proof of claim is filed in a Chapter 11 case that is later converted to a Chapter 7 case, the creditor need not file another proof of claim. Although at least one case has held that a creditor whose claim was deemed filed in a Chapter 11 case need not file a claim in the converted case, the better practice is to file a proof of claim.

Amendments and Withdrawals Once a claim is timely filed, regardless of the chapter in which the case is pending, it can be later amended to correct any mistakes in amount. The power to amend should not be relied on too heavily since not all courts will allow amendments if the debtor or the trustee has relied on the amount in the original claim or if the amendment is substantially different than the original claim.

The creditor may withdraw its claim simply by filing a notice of withdrawal at any time prior to an objection being filed. A creditor may want to withdraw a claim if it was contingent and the contingency never happened or it might agree to withdraw its claim as part of a settlement of any dispute with the debtor.

The No-Asset Case

In most consumer and many business Chapter 7 cases, there are no assets or there are insufficient assets for the trustee to administer. In a consumer case, usually all of the debtor's property is exempt. What other property there is may not be worth the cost of its liquidation and it will be abandoned by the trustee. In a business case, there might be a secured creditor who has a lien on all the assets, which are worth less than the amount owed. In those very common scenarios, unsecured creditors will not receive any distribution from the estate in exchange for the discharge of the debt due them.

Often the trustee will examine the debtor's schedules and if it appears that there is nothing to be administered, the trustee will issue what is commonly referred to as a **no-asset report.** There is no reason for proofs of claim to be filed since there will not be any distribution. The clerk will issue a notice informing

No Asset Report
A report filed by a Chapter 7 trustee upon determining that there are no assets to be administered by the trustee and no likelihood of a distribution to creditors.

creditors that they should not file proofs of claim. Later, the trustee may discover that there are assets to administer and will determine whether a distribution could be made. If the trustee decides a distribution could be made, creditors will be so informed and told to file their proofs of claim by the date set in the notice. This date, as provided in Bankruptcy Rule 3002(c)(5), will be ninety days after the mailing of the notice telling of the possible distribution.

If no assets are ever located, the case will be closed without creditors receiving a distribution.

Case Monitoring

Bankruptcy cases have many players, some of whom have major roles (such as the debtor, the trustee, or the creditors' committee). Most of the players have very minor roles (such as small unsecured creditors). If the office in which a legal assistant works is representing one of the major players, the status of the case and the events that are taking place in it will be easily known because of direct and frequent communication between the parties. The legal assistant will not be called on to do much monitoring of the case as a whole, but may be asked to watch the progress of a particular adversary proceeding.

When the client has a minor role in a case, the legal assistant will be most effectively used as a cost-efficient method of obtaining information. Depending on the client's desires and budget, the legal assistant can take on the following tasks:

☐ Obtain copies of the schedules and provide the client with a list of the major liabilities and assets and any other information that may be of use to the client, such as whether the client's claim is scheduled.

☐ Early in the case prepare and file a request for special notice (see Exhibit 12.6) so that all papers served by the parties in the case are received by the legal assistant's office. The request for special notice should be served on the debtor, the trustee, the committee, and any other known major players in the case.

☐ The legal assistant can summarize the pleadings received in a weekly, monthly, or quarterly status letter for the client.

☐ Periodically call or write to the trustee or counsel for the debtor in possession for an update as to the status of the case and plan negotiations or distributions to creditors. A friendly relationship with the trustee's administrator or the debtor's counsel's legal assistant will usually facilitate receipt of those answers.

☐ Obtain a docket of the papers filed and orders entered from the clerk's office in the case and in any adversary proceeding of interest. If information concerning the claims filed in the case is important to the client, a copy of the claim's register should be ordered as well.

Priority Creditors

Sections 507(a)(2) through (a)(9) of the Bankruptcy Code list nine types of unsecured, prepetition claims that are entitled to be paid in full before any distribution is made to other unsecured prepetition creditors. These claims, which are fully detailed in the section on the schedules in Chapter 7, are known as **priority claims** and the entity that holds one is known as a *priority creditor*.

If the client is a priority creditor, the proof of claim should be clearly marked that the claimant is entitled to priority in payment. If only part of the claim is entitled to be paid ahead of other creditors, the portion entitled to the priority

Priority Claim
A type of claim that Congress has decided should receive special treatment. Priority claims must be paid in full before general unsecured creditors receive a distribution.

■ EXHIBIT 12.6
Sample Pleading

GEORGE G. SNOW
Snow & Porter
4 Wheel Drive
Los Angeles, California 90017
Attorneys for First City Bank

UNITED STATES BANKRUPTCY COURT
WESTERN DISTRICT OF CALIFORNIA

In re	) Case No. 95-00001-JF
	)
VIDEOS BY JOE, INC.,	) Chapter 7
	)
Debtor.	)
	)
Debtor's Address:	) REQUEST FOR SPECIAL NOTICE
18 Hollywood Drive	) AND INCLUSION IN MAILING LIST
Los Angeles, California 90001	)
	)
Debtor's Tax Id No. 99-999899	)
	)

TO THE CLERK OF THE BANKRUPTCY COURT AND PARTIES IN INTEREST:

PLEASE TAKE NOTICE that First City Bank, a creditor of the debtor in the above-captioned case, hereby requests special notice of all matters that must be noticed to creditors, or other parties in interest and further requests that for all notice purposes the following address be added:

SNOW & PORTER
4 Wheel Drive
Los Angeles, California 90017
Attention: George G. Snow

This request includes the type of notice referred to in Bankruptcy Rules 2002(i) and 3017(a) and also includes without limitation, all schedules, notices of any orders, applications, complaints, demands, hearings, motions, petitions, pleadings or requests, any other documents brought before the Court in this case, whether formal or informal, whether written or oral, and whether transmitted or conveyed by mail, delivery, telephone, telegraph, telex, or otherwise.

DATED: October 5, 1995

SNOW & PORTER

_____

GEORGE G. SNOW
Attorneys for First City Bank

should be clearly indicated. A proof of claim for a debt that is entitled to a partial priority in payment because a portion of it was incurred in the involuntary gap period is presented as Exhibit 12.7.

In some cases, if it has sufficient assets to do so, the debtor or the trustee may move the court for permission to pay all or some of the priority creditors early so that they are not required to wait until plan confirmation or the closing of the

■ EXHIBIT 12.7
Proof of Claim

B10 (Official Form 10)
(Rev. 12/94)

United States Bankruptcy Court	**PROOF OF CLAIM**

Western District of _California_

In re (Name of Debtor)
Videos by Joe, Inc.

Case Number
95-00001-JF

NOTE: This form should not be used to make a claim for an administrative expense arising after the commencement of the case. A "request" for payment of an administrative expense may be filed pursuant to 11 U.S.C. § 503.

Name of Creditor
(The person or other entity to whom the debtor owes money or property)
Great Film, Inc.

Name and Address Where Notices Should be Sent
Great Film, Inc.
84 Steel Plate Road
City of Industry, California 90050
Attn: Manuel Perez
Telephone Number (213) 891-5595

☐ Check box if you are aware that anyone else has filed a proof of claim relating to your claim. Attach copy of statement giving particulars.

☐ Check box if you have never received any notices from the bankruptcy court in this case.

☐ Check box if the address differs from the address on the envelope sent to you by the court.

THIS SPACE IS FOR COURT USE ONLY

ACCOUNT OR OTHER NUMBER BY WHICH CREDITOR IDENTIFIES DEBTOR:

Check here if this claim ☐ replaces a previously filed claim, dated: _____
                          ☐ amends

1. BASIS FOR CLAIM
   ☒ Goods sold
   ☐ Services performed
   ☐ Money loaned
   ☐ Personal injury/wrongful death
   ☐ Taxes
   ☐ Other (Describe briefly)

   ☐ Retiree benefits as defined in 11 U.S.C. § 1114 (a)
   ☐ Wages, salaries, and compensations (Fill out below)
   Your social security number _____
   Unpaid compensation for services performed
   from _____ to _____
        (date)   (date)

2. DATE DEBT WAS INCURRED
   August 1, 1995, September 15, 1995

3. IF COURT JUDGMENT, DATE OBTAINED:

4. CLASSIFICATION OF CLAIM. Under the Bankruptcy Code all claims are classified as one or more of the following: (1) Unsecured nonpriority, (2) Unsecured Priority, (3) Secured. It is possible for part of a claim to be in one category and part in another. CHECK THE APPROPRIATE BOX OR BOXES that best describe your claim and STATE THE AMOUNT OF THE CLAIM AT TIME CASE FILED.

   ☐ SECURED CLAIM $ _____
   Attach evidence of perfection of security interest
   Brief Description of Collateral:
   ☐ Real Estate ☐ Motor Vehicle ☐ Other (Describe briefly)

   Amount of arrearage and other charges at time case filed included
   in secured claim above, if any $ _____

   ☒ UNSECURED NONPRIORITY CLAIM $ 500.00
   A claim is unsecured if there is no collateral or lien on property of the debtor securing the claim or to the extent that the value of such property is less than the amount of the claim.

   ☒ UNSECURED PRIORITY CLAIM $ 200.00
   Specify the priority of the claim.

   ☐ Wages, salaries, or commissions (up to $4000)✱, earned not more than 90 days before filing of the bankruptcy petition or cessation of the debtor's business, whichever is earlier - 11 U.S.C. § 507(a)(3)

   ☐ Contributions to an employee benefit plan - 11 U.S.C. § 507(a)(4)

   ☐ Up to $1,800✱ of deposits toward purchase, lease, or rental of property or services for personal, family, or household use - 11 U.S.C. § 507(a)(6)

   ☐ Alimony, maintenance, or support owed to a spouse, former spouse, or child - 11 U.S.C. § 507(a)(7)

   ☐ Taxes or penalties of governmental units - 11 U.S.C. § 507(a)(8)

   ☒ Other - Specify applicable paragraph of 11 U.S.C. § 507(a) 507.(a)(2)
   ✱ Amounts are subject to adjustment on 4/1/98 and every 3 years thereafter with respect to cases commenced on or after the date of adjustment.

5. TOTAL AMOUNT OF CLAIM AT TIME CASE FILED:

$ 500.00	$ _____	$ 200.00	$ 700.00
(Unsecured)	(Secured)	(Priority)	(Total)

☐ Check this box if claim includes charges in addition to the principal amount of the claim. Attach itemized statement of all additional charges.

THIS SPACE IS FOR COURT USE ONLY

6. CREDITS AND SETOFFS: The amount of all payments on this claim has been credited and deducted for the purpose of making this proof of claim. In filing this claim, claimant has deducted all amounts that claimant owes to debtor.

7. SUPPORTING DOCUMENTS: _Attach copies of supporting documents,_ such as promissory notes, purchase orders, invoices, itemized statements of running accounts, contracts, court judgments, or evidence of security interests. If the documents are not available, explain. If the documents are voluminous, attach a summary.

8. TIME-STAMPED COPY: To receive an acknowledgment of the filing of your claim, enclose a stamped, self-addressed envelope and copy of this proof of claim.

Date	Sign and print the name and title, if any, of the creditor or other person authorized to file this claim (attach copy of power of attorney, if any)
Oct. 15, 1995	Manuel Perez, President

Penalty for presenting fraudulent claim: Fine of up to $500,000 or imprisonment for up to 5 years, or both. 18 U.S.C. §§ 152 and 3571.

case to be paid. This is certainly true if the debtor owes its employees for unpaid payroll and is attempting to reorganize. Since employee cooperation and high morale may be crucial to the success of that reorganization, the debtor is likely to want to see that there is no delay in payment to its workers. If the estate is prepared to pay priority creditors ahead of time, the procedure to be followed is to make a motion to the court for the necessary authority. A sample of such a motion was included in Chapter 11 as Exhibit 11.4

There is nothing in the Bankruptcy Code or the Bankruptcy Rules that allows a priority creditor to be paid early. The making of such a motion rests with the representative of the estate; however, the creditor certainly could and should ask the debtor in possession or the trustee to consider it.

Administrative Creditors

During the course of a bankruptcy case the trustee and the debtor in possession will incur debts. The debts could range from professionals' fees, rent, wages, liquidation costs, or goods purchased. Debts incurred subsequent to the commencement of the case are typically called **administrative claims** because they were incurred during the administration of the case.

Administrative Claim
A claim incurred after the commencement of the bankruptcy case that is a reasonable and necessary expense of the estate.

Administrative claims of the type specified in Section 503(b) of the Bankruptcy Code are entitled to a first-in-line priority in payment under Section 507(a)(1). With the exception of payments to professionals, administrative claims are, or at least usually should be, paid when due in the ordinary course of the administration of the case. No court order is required. Sometimes they are not paid promptly, usually because the debtor in possession has no better ability to pay its bills after it filed its bankruptcy case than it did before. It may also be that the claim is disputed.

When the estate has failed to pay an administrative claim, the creditor has several alternatives. It may simply file a priority proof of claim, although Official Form 10 indicates that only priority creditors under Sections 502(a)(2) through 502(a)(8) should use the proof of claim. If only the proof of claim is filed, the creditor must wait to be paid at the close of the case or plan confirmation or for a party in interest to file an objection to the proof of claim.

The creditor may also file suit in the appropriate state court. That lawsuit would not be subject to the automatic stay since it does not involve a claim that arose before the commencement of the case. Such a lawsuit would not be worthwhile since any judgment could not be enforced because all the property of the estate is also given the protection of the automatic stay. Any levy or attachment of a judgment lien by the administrative creditor would violate that stay.

The best alternative is for the administrative creditor to file an action in the bankruptcy court to compel payment. Section 503(a) specifically provides that an administrative creditor may do so. Since it would be an action to recover money, it would be an adversary proceeding commenced by the filing of a complaint as required by Bankruptcy Rule 7001.

Lessors

There are few bankruptcy cases in which the estate does not have real or personal leased property. In fact, it is very common for the debtor to have rented its business premises and all the equipment in it. The successful representation of lessors, for both real and personal property, is dependent in large measure on vigilance and

on moving quickly. The legal assistant's completion of a number of tasks that will need to be done shortly after the petition is filed can ensure successful representation of the lessor.

Expired Leases The only part of leased property that comes into the estate is the debtor's interest in it. If the lease has expired or has otherwise terminated prepetition, the debtor no longer has a legally recognized interest in the property and no right to use it. Not all terminations will be effective and any termination based only on the debtor's financial condition or its commencing a bankruptcy case is never effective. But, if there has been a proper termination of the lease, the debtor or the trustee must surrender the property.

If the debtor refuses to surrender the property, the lessor's recourse is different depending on the type of property involved. For business real property, Section 362 provides that the automatic stay does not apply to attempts to regain possession if the term of the lease expired. In those situations, the landlord is free to pursue its unlawful detainer claims in the state courts. For residential real property, nonresidential real property with an unexpired term, and all personal property, there is no automatic stay exemption and the lessor must either file a motion to obtain relief from the automatic stay (see Exhibit 12.8) before pursuing the rights and remedies granted by the lease and state law or file a complaint for the turnover of property in the bankruptcy court. The lessor should move quickly to regain possession because any delay may be deemed to be consent to the estate's continued use.

Administrative Claim If the estate continues to use leased property after the commencement of the bankruptcy case, it is only fair that the estate should have to pay for the use. The compensation must only be reasonable. It need not necessarily be the amount called for in the lease, although most courts will hold the contract rate to be strong evidence of a reasonable rate. The estate will be able to argue for a lower figure if, for example, it is using only a portion of the premises or the equipment or if what it formerly used for manufacturing operations is now being used for storage (which usually rents for a lower amount).

For whatever the amount the estate is liable, the lessor will have an administrative claim in that amount. Again the rules are very different as to how that amount gets paid between nonresidential real and other property.

With respect to business real property, Section 365 provides that the trustee or the debtor in possession must pay the amount due to the landlord on a timely basis. The estate may obtain an extension of time to comply with that requirement, but the court is prevented from granting any extension beyond sixty days after the entry of the order for relief. If the payments are not timely received and no motion to extend the time for performance is made, the landlord will be required to bring the matter to the court's attention by filing either a motion for relief from the automatic stay, so as to begin unlawful detainer proceedings, or an action to compel payment of the accruing administrative claim.

For residential real property, there is no statutory requirement that the estate make all lease payments timely. It is much more important in these situations for the lessor to be diligent in having the administrative claim paid by making demands and going to court to compel payment.

The 1994 Amendments added special rules for personal property leases other than leases for property used primarily for personal, family, or household uses. New Section 365(d)(10) provides that the trustee or debtor in possession must perform

■ EXHIBIT 12.8
Sample Pleading

HAROLD SCHWARTZ
Schwartz & Schwartz
1800 Development Way
Thousand Oaks, California 92017

Attorneys for Leona Properties

UNITED STATES BANKRUPTCY COURT
WESTERN DISTRICT OF CALIFORNIA

In re	Case No. 95-00001-JF
VIDEOS BY JOE, INC.,	Chapter 11
Debtor.	
Debtor's Address: 18 Hollywood Drive Los Angeles, California 90001	
Debtor's Tax Id. No. 99-999899	
LEONA PROPERTIES,	MOTION FOR ORDER GRANTING RELIEF FROM THE AUTOMATIC STAY
Movant,	
v.	
VIDEOS BY JOE, INC.,	
Respondent.	

TO THE HONORABLE JUSTIN FAIR, UNITED STATES BANKRUPTCY JUDGE:

Leona Properties ("Lessor"), through its attorneys, in support of its Motion for Order Granting Relief from the Automatic Stay, respectfully represents as follows:

1. Lessor is the owner and lessor of real property commonly known as 19890 Santa Clara Avenue, Rancho Dominguez, County of Los Angeles, State of California (the "Property").

2. On or about September 16, 1990, Lessor and Videos by Joe, Inc., the debtor in possession in the above-captioned case ("Debtor"), entered into a written lease agreement (the "Lease"). The Lease provided that Debtor would lease the Property from Lessor for a period of ten (10) years commencing on October 15, 1990 and ending on October 15, 2000.

3. Under the terms of the Lease, Debtor was to make monthly payments to Lessor in the amount of $2,000.00 on or before the fifteenth of every month.

4. Debtor has refused and failed to pay the required monthly rent for the Property since August 1, 1995.

5. Pursuant to paragraph 10.1 of the Lease, Debtor was obligated to pay all real property taxes for the Property. Debtor has refused and failed to pay these taxes due for the period of July 12, 1994 through October 1, 1995.

6. As of September 1, 1995, Debtor was indebted to Lessor in the total amount of $6,700.00 for rent, late charges, and real property taxes.

—continued

■ EXHIBIT 12.8
Sample Pleading—*Continued*

7. On or about September 1, 1995, Lessor served upon Debtor a Three-Day Notice to Pay Rent or Quit (the "Notice"). The Notice demanded that Debtor pay the delinquent rent and real property taxes due within three days after service of the Notice or surrender possession of the Property. The Notice further provided that Lessor elected to declare the forfeiture of the Lease if all unpaid amounts were not paid within the required time period.

8. Debtor failed and refused to tender the unpaid rent and real property taxes within three days after service of the Notice and the Lease was thereby terminated by Lessor pursuant to relevant state law.

9. On September 10, 1995, Lessor filed its Complaint for Unlawful Detainer in Superior Court of the State of California for the County of Los Angeles, entitled *Leona Properties v. Videos by Joe, Inc.* (the "Complaint").

10. On October 1, 1995, Debtor filed its voluntary petition under Chapter 11 of the Bankruptcy Code.

11. Pursuant to Section 362(a) of the Bankruptcy Code, Lessor is precluded from continuing its action on the Complaint. By this Motion, Lessor seeks relief from the automatic stay imposed in Debtor's bankruptcy case.

12. Lessor submits that relief from the automatic stay is mandated under Section 362(d) of the Bankruptcy Code for cause. Lessor effectively terminated the Lease prior to the commencement of Debtor's bankruptcy case. Therefore, Debtor has no legal interest in the Lease or the Property.

WHEREFORE, Lessor requests that this Court enter its Order as follows:

1. That the automatic stay arising under Section 362(a) of the Bankruptcy Code be vacated so that Lessor may continue with its unlawful detainer proceedings in the State Court and proceed to obtain possession of the Property;

2. That the Court order that the subsequent filing by Debtor of any case under the Bankruptcy Code or the conversion of Debtor's present case will not operate as an automatic stay against Lessor's rights and remedies with respect to the Property; and

3. For such other and further relief as this Court may deem to be just and proper.

DATED: October 5, 1995

SCHWARTZ & SCHWARTZ

_____

HAROLD SCHWARTZ
Attorneys for Leona Properties

the debtor's obligations under a lease of business personal property beginning sixty days after the case is commenced and continuing until the lease is assumed or rejected unless the court, based on the equities of the case, orders otherwise. Lessors of property used primarily for personal, family, or household uses will need to move the court to compel payments if the debtor is not making timely payments.

Assumption and Rejection In a Chapter 7 case for real and personal property, the trustee must decide to either assume or reject an unexpired lease within sixty days after the entry of the order for relief or obtain a court order extending the time to make the decision. A lessor is entitled to ask the court to have the trustee make its decision earlier than the sixty days if the landlord has a good reason. Since the trustee has a duty to investigate whether the lease has any value to the estate, the court will not require the trustee to make any rash judgments. As a result, motions to shorten the sixty-day period are not usually granted.

In Chapter 11 cases, leases of business real property must also be assumed or rejected within the first sixty days unless an extension is granted. The only deadline

for assumption or rejection of all other types of leases is upon plan confirmation. While the estate may reject leases as soon as it can determine they have little or no value, unless there is an intended assignment, the debtor in possession has no motivation to assume leases any sooner than is necessary. Because assumption will mean the curing of all defaults and rejection will mean the return of the property, the personal property lessor should move quickly to have a deadline sooner than plan confirmation set for the assumption or rejection of the lease. However, the lessor might not want to incur the expense of such a motion if the lease is not in default or if it has little chance of releasing the property.

Damages   If the estate ultimately assumes a lease, all defaults will be cured and lessor will have no remaining prepetition claim in the bankruptcy case. If a lease is assumed and then breached, the lessor will have an administrative claim for all of its damages. These must be paid in full before the prepetition creditors are paid. If a lease is assumed in a Chapter 11 case and then rejected in the superseding Chapter 7 case, the lessor's damage claim will be a Chapter 11 administrative claim paid ahead of prepetition claims but behind Chapter 7 administrative claims.

If a lease is rejected, the lessor may have three different types of claims. First, it may have a prepetition claim for any defaults that existed at the time of the commencement of the bankruptcy case. Second, it may have a claim for any rent that became due while the estate was still in possession of the leased property that has not been paid. Third, it will have a claim arising from the rejection of the lease; this is treated like a breach of the lease. Under Section 502(g), this last claim is deemed to be a prepetition claim. There is also a statutory limit as to its amount. Section 502(b)(6) states that it cannot exceed the greater of one year's future rent under the lease or, for long-term leases, fifteen percent of the remaining term as long as fifteen percent of the remaining term is not greater than three years. Proofs of claim for the damages caused by the rejection of the lease should be filed no later than thirty days after the rejection.

Security Deposits   In many leases the lessor holds a deposit from the debtor to secure lease payments. Because the automatic stay prevents setoffs, if there are prepetition defaults, the lessor will need to obtain relief from the automatic stay in order to apply the deposit to the defaults. Some debtors would prefer that the landlord under a rejected lease apply the deposit to any postpetition amounts that are due and let the landlord have a claim for the prepetition defaults. If under the plan creditors will not be paid in full, the benefit to the debtor of such an application is obvious. However, courts have been disinclined to require the lessor to follow the debtor's preference.

Exhibit 12.9 is an example of a proof of claim filed by a landlord who had a $2,000 prepetition claim secured by a $2,000 security deposit, $2,000 administrative claim for the one month the trustee used the property, and a prepetition claim for one year's rent caused by the trustee's rejection.

Reclamation

Reclamation
The right of a person to seek to obtain possession of its property in the hands of the estate.

Chapter 9 of this book discussed the right of a trustee to compel turnover of property of the estate in the hands of third persons. The opposite side of the coin is the right of a third party to recover its property in the hands of the bankruptcy estate. This is called **reclamation.** The grounds for reclamation can include any theory of ownership or title that is better than the title of the estate.

■ EXHIBIT 12.9
Proof of Claim

B10 (Official Form 10)
(Rev. 12/94)

United States Bankruptcy Court

<u>Western</u> District of <u>California</u>

PROOF OF CLAIM

In re (Name of Debtor)
Videos by Joe, Inc.

Case Number
95-00001-JF

NOTE: This form should not be used to make a claim for an administrative expense arising after the commencement of the case. A "request" for payment of an administrative expense may be filed pursuant to 11 U.S.C. § 503.

Name of Creditor
(The person or other entity to whom the debtor owes money or property)
Leona Properties

Name and Address Where Notices Should be Sent
Leona Properties
c/o Harold Schwartz
1800 Development Way
Thousand Oaks, California   92017
Telephone Number **(818) 667-4300**

[ ] Check box if you are aware that anyone else has filed a proof of claim relating to your claim. Attach copy of statement giving particulars.

[ ] Check box if you have never received any notices from the bankruptcy court in this case.

[X] Check box if the address differs from the address on the envelope sent to you by the court.

THIS SPACE IS FOR
COURT USE ONLY

ACCOUNT OR OTHER NUMBER BY WHICH CREDITOR IDENTIFIES DEBTOR:

Check here if this claim [ ] replaces / [X] amends a previously filed claim, dated: **October 15, 1995**

1.   BASIS FOR CLAIM

[ ] Goods sold
[ ] Services performed
[ ] Money loaned
[ ] Personal injury/wrongful death
[ ] Taxes
[X] Other (Describe briefly) **Rental of Real Property**

[ ] Retiree benefits as defined in 11 U.S.C. § 1114 (a)
[ ] Wages, salaries, and compensations (Fill out below)
Your social security number _____
Unpaid compensation for services performed
from _____ to _____
(date)   (date)

2.   DATE DEBT WAS INCURRED
Sept. 1, 1995 to Nov. 1, 1995

3.   IF COURT JUDGMENT, DATE OBTAINED:

4.   CLASSIFICATION OF CLAIM. Under the Bankruptcy Code all claims are classified as one or more of the following: (1) Unsecured nonpriority, (2) Unsecured Priority, (3) Secured. It is possible for part of a claim to be in one category and part in another.
CHECK THE APPROPRIATE BOX OR BOXES that best describe your claim and STATE THE AMOUNT OF THE CLAIM AT TIME CASE FILED.

[X] SECURED CLAIM $ **2,000.00**
Attach evidence of perfection of security interest
Brief Description of Collateral: **Security Deposit**
[ ] Real Estate [ ] Motor Vehicle [X] Other (Describe briefly)
Cash Security Deposit
Amount of arrearage and other charges at time case filed included
in secured claim above, if any $ **2,000.00**

[X] UNSECURED NONPRIORITY CLAIM $ **24,000.00**
A claim is unsecured if there is no collateral or lien on property of the debtor securing the claim or to the extent that the value of such property is less than the amount of the claim.

[X] UNSECURED PRIORITY CLAIM $ **2,000.00**
Specify the priority of the claim.

[ ] Wages, salaries, or commissions (up to $4000)*, earned not more than 90 days before filing of the bankruptcy petition or cessation of the debtor's business, whichever is earlier - 11 U.S.C. § 507(a)(3)

[ ] Contributions to an employee benefit plan - 11 U.S.C. § 507(a)(4)

[ ] Up to $1,800* of deposits toward purchase, lease, or rental of property or services for personal, family, or household use - 11 U.S.C. § 507(a)(6)

[ ] Alimony, maintenance, or support owed to a spouse, former spouse, or child - 11 U.S.C. § 507(a)(7)

[ ] Taxes or penalties of governmental units - 11 U.S.C. § 507 (a)(8)

[X] Other - Specify applicable paragraph of 11 U.S.C. § 507(a) **507.(a)(1)**
* Amounts are subject to adjustment on 4/1/98 and every 3 years thereafter with respect to cases commenced on or after the date of adjustment.

5.   TOTAL AMOUNT OF CLAIM AT TIME CASE FILED:

$ **24,000.00** (Unsecured) $ **2,000.00** (Secured) $ **2,000.00** (Priority) $ **28,000.00** (Total)

[ ] Check this box if claim includes charges in addition to the principal amount of the claim. Attach itemized statement of all additional charges.

THIS SPACE IS FOR
COURT USE ONLY

6.   CREDITS AND SETOFFS: The amount of all payments on this claim has been credited and deducted for the purpose of making this proof of claim. In filing this claim, claimant has deducted all amounts that claimant owes to debtor.

7.   SUPPORTING DOCUMENTS: *Attach copies of supporting documents,* such as promissory notes, purchase orders, invoices, itemized statements of running accounts, contracts, court judgments, or evidence of security interests. If the documents are not available, explain. If the documents are voluminous, attach a summary.

8.   TIME-STAMPED COPY: To receive an acknowledgment of the filing of your claim, enclose a stamped, self-addressed envelope and copy of this proof of claim.

Date

Sign and print the name and title, if any, of the creditor or other person authorized to file this claim (attach copy of power of attorney, if any)

Nov. 15, 1995   **Harold Schwartz, Attorney**

Penalty for presenting fraudulent claim: Fine of up to $500,000 or imprisonment for up to 5 years, or both. 18 U.S.C. §§ 152 and 3571.

In addition to the grounds for reclamation just discussed, there is a statutory basis of reclamation that can be very significant to unsecured creditors. Uniform Commercial Code Section 2-702 provides a right of reclamation to a seller of goods on credit who discovers that its buyer is insolvent. Section 2-702 allows the seller to reclaim the goods simply by making a demand within ten days of the buyer's receipt of the goods.

Section 546 of the Bankruptcy Code preserves the seller's right to reclaim when the buyer is in bankruptcy. Specifically, Section 546(c) provides that the rights of a trustee are subject to any statutory or common law right of a seller of goods that has sold goods to the debtor in the ordinary course of the seller's business if the buyer receives the goods while insolvent and the seller makes demand on the goods in writing within ten days after receipt of the goods. Section 546(c) was amended in the 1994 Amendments to provide that if the ten–day reclamation period expires after the bankruptcy case is commenced, the writing need only be made before twenty days after receipt of the goods. For example, if the goods were delivered on September 23, and the bankruptcy case was filed on October 1, the seller would have until October 13 to make the reclamation demand. A sample of such a demand follows as Exhibit 12.10.

Under the Uniform Commercial Code, if the seller properly makes the demand, it is entitled to the goods. However, under Section 546's reclamation, the right to obtain the goods is not absolute. If the trustee or the debtor in possession wants to keep the goods it may do so; however, it must either give the seller an administrative claim for the value of the goods subject to reclamation or a lien to secure the claim. Also, a new Section 546(g) was added in the 1994 Amendments that allows the court to permit a debtor to return goods to a seller and let the seller credit the purchase price of the goods to its prepetition claim.

Obviously, reclamation is an important right for suppliers who were unaware of the debtor's pending bankruptcy: it means the difference between being paid in full or receiving only what other prepetition unsecured creditors receive. For it to

■ EXHIBIT 12.10
Sample Pleading

October 3, 1995
DEMAND FOR RETURN OF GOODS

TO:　　　VIDEOS BY JOE, INC.
　　　　　18 Hollywood Drive
　　　　　Los Angeles, California 90017

FROM:　 GREAT FILM, INC.
　　　　　84 Steel Plate Road
　　　　　City of Industry, California 91744

NOTICE IS HEREBY GIVEN THAT pursuant to California Uniform Commercial Code Section 2702 and Bankruptcy Code Section 546(c), and by reason of your insolvency, Great Film, Inc. hereby demands the return of all goods delivered to you on and after September 23, 1995.

　　GREAT FILM, INC.

MANUEL PEREZ
President

be effective, however, the supplier must act immediately because the ten and twenty-day periods pass quickly. Further, if the seller's goods have already been sold by the debtor in the ordinary course of its business before it receives the reclamation notice, the seller's exercise of its reclamation rights will be too late.

If the seller gives the required notice and the debtor in possession or trustee does not respond, the creditor will have to file a complaint to enforce its reclamation rights and recover the property.

Seeking a Discharge or Dischargeability Determination

Perhaps the greatest result an attorney representing an unsecured creditor could obtain in a case in which creditors will not be paid in full is to obtain a judgment determining that the client's claim will not be discharged. Second best—but far more detrimental to the debtor—is a judgment determining that the debtor is not entitled to a discharge at all and all debts will be enforceable despite the bankruptcy case. The grounds for denying the debtor a discharge on a particular debt or on all debts were set out in Chapter 8 of this book (in the section on discharge). To review, the grounds for dischargeability that require a court determination are obtaining money or property by fraud, certain consumer debts incurred just before bankruptcy, fraud or defalcation while acting as a fiduciary, embezzlement, larceny, or willful and malicious injury. The debtor's bad acts that could prevent a discharge from any claim include transfers or concealment of assets, unjustifiable destruction or concealment of books and records, fraudulent false oaths or false claims, fraudulently attempting to obtain an advantage by acting or forebearing to act, failure to satisfactorily explain a loss of assets, willful refusal to obey an order of the court, and improper actions with respect to the bankruptcy case of an insider.

In a Chapter 7 case, if the creditor is entitled to have its claim declared nondischargeable or to deny the debtor a discharge, Bankruptcy Rules 4004 and 4007 require the creditor to file a complaint and commence an adversary proceeding within sixty days of the date first set for the Section 341(a) meeting of creditors. As is true with the deadline for filing proofs of claim, even if the meeting is continued to another date, the sixty days will be measured from the original date. The sixty-day time limit is very strict and the deadline should be calendared as soon as notice of the Section 341(a) meeting is received. The time period may be extended, but only if a motion to do so is brought before the end of the sixty days.

Sometimes the debtor's bad acts that give rise to a claim that the debtor should not receive a discharge do not occur until after the sixty days have passed or even until after the debtor has received the discharge. In those circumstances, the creditor's remedy is to attempt to revoke the discharge. Revocation is allowed in Section 727(d).

In a Chapter 11 case of an individual, an objection to discharge need not be filed until confirmation of the plan. A complaint to determine the dischargeability of a debt is the same as in Chapter 7 cases.

In order to discourage baseless dischargeability litigation that a debtor may not be able to afford to defend, Section 523(d) of the Bankruptcy Code states that if a creditor seeks to have a consumer debt allegedly incurred through fraud or certain consumer debts incurred on the eve of bankruptcy deemed nondischargeable, and the debt is discharged, the debtor may be entitled to costs and expenses of suit, including attorneys' fees, if the creditor did not have a good faith belief that the debt was not entitled to be discharged.

☐ THE SECURED CREDITOR

Proofs of Claim

Unlike other creditors, there is no requirement that a secured creditor file a proof of claim in order to retain its lien on the debtor's property. It would be prudent, however, for the secured creditor to file a proof of claim if it wants notices directed a particular way or to put the debtor or trustee on notice of its lien. Further, if there is a risk that the collateral is not worth the amount of the debt, the secured creditor will need to file a proof of claim in order to preserve the right to share as an unsecured creditor for its deficiency claim. A sample proof of claim for a secured creditor is given in Exhibit 12.11.

Cash Collateral Use

As mentioned in Chapters 9 and 11 of this book, Section 363 of the Bankruptcy Code defines *cash collateral* to mean property of the estate that is cash, negotiable instruments, deposit accounts, and other cash equivalents in which a creditor has a security interest. If a creditor has a security interest in the debtor's accounts receivable, as the accounts are collected the checks and the cash will become the creditor's cash collateral.

As discussed in Chapters 9 and 11 in the sections on financing liquidations and operations, once the petition is filed, the trustee or the debtor in possession may not use a creditor's cash collateral without its consent or an order of the court authorizing the use. If the secured creditor consents to the use of cash collateral, whatever terms and conditions it has negotiated with the debtor or the trustee should be placed in writing. A sample of such a written agreement was found in Chapter 11, as Exhibit 11.9. Bankruptcy Rule 4001(d) contains the procedure for obtaining bankruptcy court approval of the agreement. Generally, with limited notice, the court may approve a stipulation to allow the use of cash collateral for a short period of time and only so much cash collateral as is necessary to avoid harm to the debtor's operations. To obtain an order approving continuing use, the parties must bring a motion that sets out the terms of the agreement and provide no less than fifteen days' notice of the motion to the creditors' committee or, if there is no committee, to the twenty largest unsecured creditors and such other parties as the court may direct. If any party with notice of the motion files an objection, the court will hold a hearing to determine the matters raised in the objection and to see if the motion should be granted. If no objection is made, there need not be a hearing and the court can grant the motion without one.

If the secured creditor does not consent to the use of its cash collateral, then Section 363(c) obligates the trustee or the debtor in possession to segregate and account for all cash collateral coming within the possession or other control of the estate. It is common for the secured creditor's counsel to inform a Chapter 11 debtor's counsel in writing that the creditor has not consented and the cash collateral should be segregated. A sample of such a letter follows as Exhibit 12.12.

In real life, sometimes debtors in possession do use cash collateral without consent and without court authorization. In some cases debtors, usually guided by incompetent counsel, use cash collateral for days or even weeks before the secured creditor is even informed of the filing of the bankruptcy petition. In those situations, which bode very ill for a cooperative reorganization, the secured creditor must quickly file a motion that requests that the court prevent the use of cash

■ EXHIBIT 12.11
Proof of Claim for Secured Creditor

B10 (Official Form 10)
(Rev. 12/94)

United States Bankruptcy Court	PROOF OF CLAIM

__Western__ District of __California__

In re (Name of Debtor)
Videos by Joe, Inc.

Case Number
95-00001-JF

NOTE: This form should not be used to make a claim for an administrative expense arising after the commencement of the case. A "request" for payment of an administrative expense may be filed pursuant to 11 U.S.C. § 503.

Name of Creditor
(The person or other entity to whom the debtor owes money or property)
First City Bank

Name and Address Where Notices Should be Sent
First City Bank
c/o George G. Snow, Esq.
4 Wheel Drive
Los Angeles, California   90017
Telephone Number (213) 891-5595

□ Check box if you are aware that anyone else has filed a proof of claim relating to your claim. Attach copy of statement giving particulars.

□ Check box if you have never received any notices from the bankruptcy court in this case.

[X] Check box if the address differs from the address on the envelope sent to you by the court.

THIS SPACE IS FOR
COURT USE ONLY

ACCOUNT OR OTHER NUMBER BY WHICH CREDITOR IDENTIFIES DEBTOR:

Check here if this claim   □ replaces   a previously filed claim, dated: _____
                            □ amends

1.   BASIS FOR CLAIM
□ Goods sold
□ Services performed
[X] Money loaned
□ Personal injury/wrongful death
□ Taxes
□ Other (Describe briefly)

□ Retiree benefits as defined in 11 U.S.C. § 1114 (a)
□ Wages, salaries, and compensations (Fill out below)
Your social security number _____
Unpaid compensation for services performed
from _____ to _____
      (date)   (date)

2.   DATE DEBT WAS INCURRED
October 1, 1990

3.   IF COURT JUDGMENT, DATE OBTAINED:

4.   CLASSIFICATION OF CLAIM. Under the Bankruptcy Code all claims are classified as one or more of the following: (1) Unsecured nonpriority, (2) Unsecured Priority, (3) Secured. It is possible for part of a claim to be in one category and part in another.
CHECK THE APPROPRIATE BOX OR BOXES that best describe your claim and STATE THE AMOUNT OF THE CLAIM AT TIME CASE FILED.

[X] SECURED CLAIM $50,000.00
Attach evidence of perfection of security interest
Brief Description of Collateral: Video Equipment
□ Real Estate □ Motor Vehicle [X] Other (Describe briefly)
Video Equipment
Amount of arrearage and other charges at time case filed included
in secured claim above, if any $2,700.00

□ UNSECURED NONPRIORITY CLAIM $ _____
A claim is unsecured if there is no collateral or lien on property of the debtor securing the claim or to the extent that the value of such property is less than the amount of the claim.

□ UNSECURED PRIORITY CLAIM $ _____
Specify the priority of the claim.

□ Wages, salaries, or commissions (up to $4000)*, earned not more than 90 days before filing of the bankruptcy petition or cessation of the debtor's business, whichever is earlier - 11 U.S.C. § 507(a)(3)

□ Contributions to an employee benefit plan - 11 U.S.C. § 507(a)(4)

□ Up to $1,800* of deposits toward purchase, lease, or rental of property or services for personal, family, or household use - 11 U.S.C. § 507(a)(6)

□ Alimony, maintenance, or support owed to a spouse, former spouse, or child - 11 U.S.C. § 507(a)(7)

□ Taxes or penalties of governmental units - 11 U.S.C. § 507 (a)(8)

□ Other - Specify applicable paragraph of 11 U.S.C. § 507(a) _____ .
* Amounts are subject to adjustment on 4/1/98 and every 3 years thereafter with respect to cases commenced on or after the date of adjustment.

5.   TOTAL AMOUNT OF
CLAIM AT TIME
CASE FILED:

$ _____ $ 50,000.00 $ _____ $ 50,000.00
   (Unsecured)   (Secured)   (Priority)   (Total)

[X] Check this box if claim includes charges in addition to the principal amount of the claim. Attach itemized statement of all additional charges.

THIS SPACE IS FOR
COURT USE ONLY

6.   CREDITS AND SETOFFS: The amount of all payments on this claim has been credited and deducted for the purpose of making this proof of claim. In filing this claim, claimant has deducted all amounts that claimant owes to debtor.

7.   SUPPORTING DOCUMENTS: *Attach copies of supporting documents*, such as promissory notes, purchase orders, invoices, itemized statements of running accounts, contracts, court judgments, or evidence of security interests. If the documents are not available, explain. If the documents are voluminous, attach a summary.

8.   TIME-STAMPED COPY: To receive an acknowledgment of the filing of your claim, enclose a stamped, self-addressed envelope and copy of this proof of claim.

Date

Sign and print the name and title, if any, of the creditor or other person authorized to file this claim (attach copy of power of attorney, if any)

Oct. 15, 1995   George G. Snow, Attorney

Penalty for presenting fraudulent claim: Fine of up to $500,000 or imprisonment for up to 5 years, or both. 18 U.S.C. §§ 152 and 3571.

■ EXHIBIT 12.12
Sample Pleading

SNOW & PORTER
Attorneys at Law
4 Wheel Drive
Los Angeles, California 90017
October 2,1995

Bankrupt C. Lawyer, Esq.
White Charger Legal Clinic
One Learned Way
Los Angeles, California 90001

     Re: *In re Videos by Joe, Inc. ("VBJ")*
             Case No. 95-00001-JF

Dear Mr. Lawyer:

    As you know, this law firm represents First City Bank (the "Bank"), a secured creditor of VBJ with a duly perfected lien on its inventory, equipment, accounts receivable, and all proceeds of the foregoing. As a result, all funds coming into the possession of VBJ constitute the Bank's "cash collateral" as that term is defined in 11 U.S.C. § 363(a).

    This letter will serve to inform you and VBJ that the Bank does not consent to the use of its cash collateral by VBJ. Further, the Bank will expect VBJ to strictly comply with the requirements of 11 U.S.C. § 363(c)(4). Please call me immediately with the location of the Bank's segregated cash collateral and when the Bank might expect an accounting of its cash collateral.

Very truly yours,

SNOW & PORTER

_____

George G. Snow

Adequate Protection
Property, lien, conduct, or other asset or act that is sufficient to ensure that a creditor with an interest in property to be used, sold or leased by the estate will not be disadvantaged.

collateral. Bankruptcy Rule 4001(a) provides the procedures. Courts are usually willing to hear these motions on an emergency basis.

    If the secured creditor refuses to consent to the use of cash collateral, the proper procedure is to file a motion and notice a hearing for permission to use the cash collateral. Since very few debtors with secured creditors can operate without the use of cash collateral to buy inventory and pay payroll and other operating expenses, the hearing will usually be held on very short notice. If there is a sufficient showing of an emergency, the court may even authorize the use without a hearing. A sample motion seeking authority to use cash collateral is found in Chapter 11, as Exhibit 11.7.

    At a hearing of a motion to use cash collateral, the trustee or the debtor in possession will be required to prove that the secured creditor will not be harmed by the estate's use of cash collateral. To do so the estate must show that the creditor is or can be adequately protected. There is no definition of **adequate protection** in the Bankruptcy Code but examples are given in Section 361. They include periodic cash payments, replacement liens, and other actions that will ensure that a secured creditor receives what it is entitled to. Commonly, the debtor in possession or the trustee will attempt to make this showing by offering the secured creditor replacement liens on all assets acquired after the filing of the

bankruptcy case and demonstrating through projections of sales and expenses that the creditor's pool of collateral will increase by virtue of continued operations. It may offer to turn over to the creditor all cash collateral received that is not necessary for operations. It may offer a lien on previously unencumbered property.

The court will make the ultimate determination as to whether the estate should be allowed to use cash collateral and on what terms. The secured creditor should keep in mind that the court is not likely to compel the debtor to terminate operations if the evidence is close on the issue of adequate protection. Often the creditor is better served by attempting to negotiate a stipulation that has protection rather than relying on the court to agree with its position. There is, however, at least one benefit of contesting cash collateral use. If the court determines that the creditor is adequately protected and at the end of the case it turns out that the creditor suffers a deficiency, Section 507(b) provides that the deficiency is entitled to a priority in payment ahead of all other administrative claims, including attorneys' fees.

Finally, faced with the debtor's use of cash collateral, the creditor, especially one that has been providing account receivable financing for the debtor prepetition, should investigate providing financing to the debtor under Section 364 rather than cash collateral use under Section 363. Financing can offer even greater protections for the secured creditor, including a priority lien even ahead of the creditors who suffer a deficiency after a court determination that they are adequately protected. Financing and the procedure for obtaining the required court approval were discussed in Chapters 9 and 11.

Relief From the Automatic Stay

In General The scope of the automatic stay was covered in Chapter 4. With respect to secured creditors, the automatic stay prevents them from taking any action to foreclose or in any other way enforce their security interests in their collateral. Although the automatic stay usually remains in effect until the case is closed, the secured creditor may have the stay terminated earlier by requesting that the court grant it relief from the automatic stay.

The effect of an order granting a secured creditor relief from the automatic stay is that it may proceed to enforce its rights and remedies with respect to its collateral as if the bankruptcy case was over. The creditor could commence or renew foreclosure proceedings, demand turnover of collateral and the like. The secured creditor also may ask the court to annul the automatic stay; this would have the same effect as if no bankruptcy case had ever been commenced. A creditor might want to seek annulment rather than termination when some act was performed in violation of the automatic stay prior to the creditor obtaining relief and the creditor wants that act to be valid.

Grounds Section 362(d) of the Bankruptcy Code sets out three grounds for relief from the automatic stay. If any of the grounds can be established, the Bankruptcy Code provides that the creditor must be given relief from the stay.

The first ground is for cause. Cause is not defined in Section 362(d) or anywhere else in the Bankruptcy Code. All Section 362(d) states is that it includes a lack of adequate protection of a secured creditor's interest in its collateral. Adequate protection is not defined in the Bankruptcy Code but examples of it are given in Section 361. The examples provided are periodic cash payments equal to at least the amount by which the collateral is depreciating, replacement liens in assets that

are not encumbered or in which the existing liens are less than the property's worth, and any other method of providing the secured creditor with the equivalent of the property being used by the debtor. The list is not exhaustive and the ways in which secured creditors can assert that they are not adequately protected is limited only by the extent of their creativity. Possible other reasons why the creditor is not adequately protected and cause exists for relief from the automatic stay are a lack of insurance on the property, unpaid taxes, a deteriorating condition with insufficient upkeep, and the like.

The second ground for relief is that the debtor has no equity in the property and the property is not necessary for an effective reorganization. Both elements of this second ground must exist for relief to be granted.

The third ground for relief, which is only applicable in single asset real estate cases, as that phrase is defined in Section 101(51B) of the Bankruptcy Code, is that ninety days has passed since the case was commenced and the debtor has neither: (1) filed a plan of reorganization that has a reasonable possibility of being confirmed within a reasonable time; nor (2) begun making monthly interest payments to the secured creditor.

If they can, secured creditors will allege more than one ground as reasons why they should be granted relief from the automatic stay. This is usually not difficult because they overlap. For example, cause is commonly alleged because of the lack of equity in the property.

Defenses   In response to a request for relief from the automatic stay for lack of adequate protection, the debtor will allege that the creditor is, in fact, adequately protected. The debtor may assert that the value of the property itself is more than enough to adequately protect the secured creditor. This method of adequate protection is usually referred to as the **equity cushion** and the courts differ as to whether it alone is sufficient and, if it is, the size or percentage of the cushion necessary to provide adequate protection.

If there is an insufficient equity cushion, the debtor may also offer a different method of adequate protection to defeat the creditor's relief from stay action such as monthly payments to decrease the size of the debt. The debtor may also be willing to stipulate to a grant of relief from the automatic stay at a date in the future if the debtor has not restructured the debt through a plan or sold the collateral and paid the creditor off.

If the relief from stay request is based on the second ground, the debtor may assert that it does have equity in the collateral and that even if it does not, the property is necessary to an effective reorganization.

Burdens   Pursuant to Section 362(g), in any hearing on a motion for relief from the stay, the burden is on the secured creditor to establish the debtor's equity in the property. The party opposing the relief (usually the debtor or the trustee) has the burden on all other issues such as adequate protection. While this statement may seem to suggest that the debtor or the trustee has the more difficult burden, as a practical matter, it is just the opposite. Because adequate protection is so linked with value and equity, if the secured creditor has the burden on equity it also has at least some of the burden on adequate protection.

Procedure   Obtaining relief from stay is discussed in Bankruptcy Rule 4001; it in turn references Rule 9014; relief from the automatic stay is obtained by the filing of a motion (see Exhibit 12.13). Any additional procedures that need to be adhered to are left to local rule.

Equity Cushion

The excess of the value of property over the claims secured by it.

■ EXHIBIT 12.13
Sample Pleading

GEORGE G. SNOW
Snow & Porter
4 Wheel Drive
Los Angeles, California 90017

Attorneys for First City Bank

UNITED STATES BANKRUPTCY COURT
WESTERN DISTRICT OF CALIFORNIA

In re	Case No. 95-00001-JF
VIDEOS BY JOE, INC.,	Chapter 11
Debtor.	
Debtor's Address: 18 Hollywood Drive Los Angeles, California 90001	
Debtor's Tax Id. No. 99-999899	
FIRST CITY BANK,	MOTION FOR ORDER GRANTING RELIEF FROM AUTOMATIC STAY
Movant,	
v.	
VIDEOS BY JOE, INC.,	
Respondent.	

First City Bank (the "Bank"), through its attorneys, in support of its Motion for Order Granting Relief from the Automatic Stay, respectfully represents as follows:

1. Videos by Joe, Inc. is the debtor in the within case, having filed a petition for relief under Chapter 11 of the Bankruptcy Code on October 1, 1995 ("Debtor").

2. Among the assets of Debtor's estate is that real property commonly known as 18 Hollywood Drive, situated in the City and County of Los Angeles, State of California, more particularly described as follows:

Lot 18 of Parcel 64 recorded in the records of the County of Los Angeles, State of California on Page 59–10562.

3. On or about October 1, 1994, Debtor made, executed, and delivered a written promissory note to the Bank in the principal sum of $100,000 together with interest thereon at the rate of 10 percent per annum (the "Note"). The Note called for monthly installment payments of interest only in the sum of $835.00 to be paid on the first day of every month, commencing on November 1, 1994, and continuing on the first day of every month for 35 months thereafter at which time the principal and any unpaid interest was to be all due and payable. A complete and accurate copy of the Note is attached as Exhibit 1 of the concurrently filed Declaration of Horace Hardman.

—continued

4. As part of the same transaction described in the preceding paragraph, to secure payment and performance of the Note, Debtor made, executed, and delivered to the Bank a Deed of Trust and Assignment of Rents pertaining to the Property, a complete and accurate copy of which is attached to the Hardman Declaration as Exhibit 2 (the "Deed of Trust"). The Deed of Trust was duly recorded in the Official Records of the County of Los Angeles, State of California, on October 3, 1994, as instrument No. 88–64321.

5. Debtor has defaulted in the performance of its obligations under the Note and the Deed of Trust. The defaults include, but are not limited to, the following:

(a) Debtor has failed to make the monthly payments required under the Note since March 1, 1995;

(b) The Note is now all due and payable;

(c) Debtor has not maintained insurance in an amount sufficient to protect the interest of the Bank under the Note and Deed of Trust; and

(d) Debtor has failed to pay real property taxes pertaining to the Property for fiscal year 1994–1995, which taxes have become delinquent.

6. As of November 1, 1995, the following sums had become due and owing under the Note:

(a) Principal balance	$100,000
(b) Interest	$ 9,174
(c) Late Charges	$ 459
Total	$109,633

7. The Bank is informed and believes that the Property is additionally encumbered by a deed of trust in favor of Big Bank securing repayment of a promissory note having a principal balance of approximately $50,000 recorded *prior* to the date of the recordation of the Deed of Trust.

8. Debtor has not offered to provide adequate protection to the Bank of its interest in the Property.

9. In addition to the foregoing, cause for relief from the automatic stay exists in that Debtor has not paid current real property taxes pertaining to the Property and has not adequately insured the Property. By virtue of the foregoing, the Bank is entitled to relief from the automatic stay to proceed with foreclosure as authorized by Section 362(d)(1) of the Bankruptcy Code.

10. The indebtedness owing to the Bank under the Note, and to the holders of senior deeds of trust is in excess of $164,000. Filed concurrently with this Motion is the Declaration of O. Pinion, a certified real estate appraiser, declaring that the fair market value of the Property is less than $165,000. The Bank is, therefore, of the informed opinion that after payment of all amounts due, including attorneys' fees and costs, Debtor will not have any equity in the Property and the Property is not necessary to an effective reorganization. By virtue thereof, the Bank is entitled to relief from the automatic stay to proceed with foreclosure as authorized by Section 362(d)(2) of the Bankruptcy Code.

WHEREFORE, the Bank requests that this Court enter its Order:

1. Vacating the automatic stay arising under Section 362(a) of the Bankruptcy Code under either Section 362(d)(1) or 362(d)(2) of the Bankruptcy Code and authorizing the Bank to proceed according to law to foreclose upon its lien encumbering the Property;

2. Directing that no additional motion to this Court for any further relief from the automatic stay will be required in the event it becomes necessary to initiate unlawful detainer proceedings against Debtor after a foreclosure sale pertaining to the Property; and

3. Granting such other and further relief as the Court deems appropriate.

DATED: November 1, 1995

SNOW & PORTER

GEORGE G. SNOW
Attorneys for First City Bank

One of the returns Congress has provided to creditors in exchange for imposing the automatic stay is that relief from stay actions against property are to be given expedited treatment by the courts. Section 362(e) provides that a stay against property of the estate terminates thirty days after a motion for relief has been made unless the court orders the stay to be continued at a hearing held before the end of the thirty-day period. This hearing need not be a final hearing on the motion but if it is a preliminary hearing, in order to continue the stay in effect, the court must find that there is a reasonable likelihood that the party opposing the relief will prevail at the final hearing. In addition, the final hearing must be completed within thirty days after the preliminary hearing unless the parties consent to extend the thirty–day deadline or the court extends it for a specific time because of compelling circumstances.

Bankruptcy Rule 4001(b) provides that the stay against property expires thirty days after the final hearing unless, within that time, the court denies the motion. In short, at the longest, the entire matter must be heard and decided no later than sixty days after the motion is filed unless there is an agreement or compelling circumstances.

Even given the expedited pace of relief from stay actions, there may be situations in which the creditor believes that it needs relief earlier. If the creditor can establish that its collateral will be irreparably harmed before it can be heard on the normal time schedule, Section 362(f) allows it to bring its motion on an *ex parte* basis. Bankruptcy Rule 4001(c) provides that oral and written notice must be given to the debtor or the trustee of the *ex parte* motion. They also have the right to seek to reinstate the stay on two days' notice.

Stipulations   Often the creditor and the debtor or the trustee will reach an agreement as to the appropriate level of adequate protection for the creditor prior to any hearing. Bankruptcy Rule 4001(d) provides the method for having such an agreement approved by the court. In order to prevent collusion between the creditor and a friendly debtor, one of the parties must file a motion that discloses the terms of the agreement. (See Exhibit 12.14.) The motion must be served on the committee if there is one and, if not, on the debtor's twenty largest unsecured creditors. A party in interest then has fifteen days to file an objection to the motion. If an objection is filed there will be a hearing and the court will determine whether the stipulation should be approved or not. If there is no objection, the court can enter its order granting the motion and approving the stipulation without a hearing.

Chapter 12 and 13 Cases   Unlike Chapters 7 and 11, in Chapter 12 and 13, the automatic stay is extended to creditor actions to collect consumer debts from those individuals who are obligated on the debt with the debtor. These individuals are called codebtors. To obtain relief from the stay in order to proceed against a codebtor, the creditor follows the normal procedure. The grounds are set out in Section 1201(c) and 1301(c); they are as follows:

☐ The codebtor is really the principal debtor because it received the consideration that gave rise to the claim.

☐ The debtor's plan does not propose to pay the claim. If it only proposes to pay a percentage of the debt, the creditor may obtain relief from the stay but only to collect the deficiency against the codebtor.

☐ Continuing the stay against the codebtor until the case is closed would cause irreparable harm to the creditor.

■ EXHIBIT 12.14
Sample Pleading

GEORGE G. SNOW
Snow & Porter
4 Wheel Drive
Los Angeles, California 90017

Attorneys for First City Bank

UNITED STATES BANKRUPTCY COURT
WESTERN DISTRICT OF CALIFORNIA

In re	)	Case No. 95-00001-JF
	)	
VIDEOS BY JOE, INC.,	)	Chapter 11
	)	
Debtor.	)	
	)	
Debtor's Address:	)	NOTICE OF MOTION AND MOTION
18 Hollywood Drive	)	FOR APPROVAL OF AGREEMENT
Los Angeles, California 90001	)	FOR RELIEF FROM THE AUTOMATIC
	)	STAY
Debtor's Tax Id. No. 99-999899	)	
	)	

First City Bank (the "Bank") and Videos by Joe, Inc., the debtor in possession in the above-captioned case (the "Debtor"), in support of their Motion for Approval of Agreement for Relief from the Automatic Stay, state as follows:

1. The Bank and the Debtor have entered into a stipulation for relief from automatic stay (the "Stipulation"), a complete and accurate copy of which is attached to this Motion as Exhibit 1.

2. This Motion seeks approval of the Stipulation as required by Bankruptcy Rule 4001. Grounds for approval of the Stipulation are that the debtor has no equity in the Property as that term is defined in the Stipulation; the Property is not necessary to an effective reorganization; and the Bank is not adequately protected as that phrase is defined in Section 361 of the Bankruptcy Code since the value of the Property does not exceed the amount of the debt owing to the Bank and other secured creditors.

3. Objections to this Motion and the Stipulation must be filed within fifteen (15) days of the date on which the Motion was mailed. Objections must be in writing, filed with the Court and served upon the attorneys identified in the left-hand corner of page 1 of the Motion and upon attorneys for the Debtor. Objections must be accompanied by a written request for a hearing thereon.

4. If no objection is filed, the Court may enter an Order approving or disapproving this Motion and the Stipulation without conducting a hearing. If an objection is filed or if the Court determines a hearing is appropriate, the Court will hold a hearing on no less than five (5) days' notice to the objector, the Bank, the Debtor, and upon any other entities as the Court may direct.

DATED: November 15, 1995

SNOW & PORTER

_____

GEORGE G. SNOW
Attorneys for First City Bank

—continued

■ EXHIBIT 12.14
Sample Pleading—*Continued*

Exhibit 1

GEORGE G. SNOW
Snow & Porter
4 Wheel Drive
Los Angeles, California 90017

Attorneys for First City Bank

UNITED STATES BANKRUPTCY COURT
WESTERN DISTRICT OF CALIFORNIA

In re)	Case No. 95-00001-JF
)	
VIDEOS BY JOE, INC.,)	Chapter 11
)	
Debtor.)	
)	
Debtor's Address:)	
18 Hollywood Drive)	
Los Angeles, California 90001)	STIPULATION FOR ORDER
)	GRANTING RELIEF FROM THE
Debtor's Tax Id. No. 99-999899)	AUTOMATIC STAY
)	

First City Bank (the "Bank") and Videos by Joe, Inc., the debtor in possession in the above-captioned case (the "Debtor"), through their attorneys, hereby stipulate and agree, subject to Court approval, as follows:

1. The Debtor is the owner of improved real property located at 18 Hollywood Drive, Los Angeles, California (the "Property").

2. The Property is encumbered by a first in priority deed of trust in favor of Big Bank securing repayment of a note with a balance due, as of November 1, 1995, of approximately $50,000. The Property is additionally encumbered by a second in priority deed of trust in favor of the Bank securing repayment of a note with a balance due, as of November 1, 1995, of approximately $110,000.

3. The fair market value of the Property does not exceed $170,000.

4. The Debtor uses the Property in order to operate its business. The Debtor will move to new premises to operate its business on March 1, 1996.

Based on the foregoing facts, the Bank and the Debtor agree as follows:

A. Except as provided in Paragraph B of this Stipulation, the Bank shall be entitled to relief from the automatic stay of Section 362(a) of the Bankruptcy Code effective upon the entry of the Order approving this Stipulation and shall thereafter be entitled to take such acts as may be necessary to foreclose its interest in the Property.

B. Provided the Debtor pays to the Bank the sum of $835.00 per month for each of the months of December 1995, January 1996, and February 1996, this Bank shall not conduct a foreclosure sale of its interest in the Property until on or after March 1, 1996. In the event that the Debtor fails to make any of the payments provided in this paragraph, the Bank shall be entitled to conduct its foreclosure sale at the earliest time provided by law.

DATED: November 15, 1995

SNOW & PORTER

_____

GEORGE G. SNOW
Attorneys for First City Bank

—continued

■ EXHIBIT 12.14
Sample Pleading—*Continued*

DATED: November 15, 1995

WHITE CHARGER LEGAL CLINIC

_____

BANKRUPT C. LAWYER
Attorneys for Debtor

Surcharge of Collateral

The general rule in bankruptcy cases is that a secured creditor is entitled to be paid an amount equal to the value of its interest in its collateral. One exception is if it agrees to receive less. Another exception discussed in Chapter 9 of this book is found in Section 506(c) of the Bankruptcy Code, which states that the costs of preserving, protecting, and disposing of the collateral may be assessed against the creditor to the extent the creditor is benefited. The exception is based on fairness. If the trustee incurs costs and expenses in performing some service that benefited the secured creditor, it is only fair that the secured creditor pay those costs and expenses. If, for example, the trustee incurred auctioneer fees and costs in liquidating equipment that secured the debt owed to a creditor, then the Bankruptcy Code provides a method in Section 506(c) for the trustee to recoup those fees and costs from the proceeds of the equipment sold. This is especially true if the secured creditor consented to the trustee's actions.

There are many open questions in the application of Section 506(c). One question is whether any entity other than the trustee or the debtor in possession can use Section 506(c) to collect claims from the secured creditor. A similar question is whether the estate is first required to pay the claim and then seek reimbursement from the creditor. Another issue that is being considered by the courts is whether a secured creditor should have to pay the debtor in possession's attorneys' fees if a Chapter 11 case is administratively insolvent and the secured creditor has a lien on all the assets. Because of these and other open questions, and a creditor's inherent dislike of giving up a part of the proceeds of its collateral, actions brought under Section 506(c) are usually very hotly contested.

Another section in the Bankruptcy Code provides an alternative method of surcharging secured creditors. Section 552(b) provides that if the debtor granted to the creditor a security interest in certain assets and the proceeds of those assets, then after the commencement of the bankruptcy case the creditor's security interest will continue in the proceeds unless the court, for a good reason, orders otherwise. More and more trustees and debtors in possession are arguing that if their time, effort, and expenses added value to collateral that created those proceeds, the creditor's security interest should not extend to all of the proceeds.

Whatever the theory used to try to force the secured creditor to fund at least some of the costs of administration of the case, if a party in interest wishes to surcharge a secured creditor's collateral, it must commence an adversary proceeding by the filing of a complaint. A sample complaint for surcharge of collateral was found in Chapter 9, as Exhibit 9.12.

□ SUMMARY

Bankruptcy cases can be commenced voluntarily by the debtor or involuntarily by creditors. An involuntary case cannot be filed against a farmer or a charitable institution; in addition, an involuntary case can only be brought under Chapters 7 and 11. If the debtor has more than twelve creditors, the petition can be filed by as few as three creditors so long as those creditors have unsecured claims that total at least $10,000. If the debtor has less than twelve creditors, an involuntary petition can be filed by only one creditor. If an involuntary petition is filed, the debtor may either consent or fight the petition on the ground that the creditors are ineligible or that the debtor is paying its debts. If the court finds that the petition was properly filed, it will enter an order for relief and the case will proceed in the same manner as a case filed by the debtor.

A creditor presents its claim in a bankruptcy case by filing a proof of claim. A proof of claim is a simple form designed to be completed and filed by a non-attorney. The same form can be used by secured, unsecured, and priority creditors. Unpaid administrative creditors should file a complaint for payment rather than a proof of claim. The deadline for filing a proof of claim varies among the chapters of the Bankruptcy Code.

Special rules apply to lessors of real and personal property. A lessor under an expired lease may need to bring a motion for relief from the automatic stay if the trustee or debtor will not surrender the leased property. When the lease must be assumed or rejected will vary based on the type of property, the type of lease, and the chapter of the case.

Other rights of unsecured creditors include reclamations—recovering property sold to a debtor on the eve of the filing of its bankruptcy case—and having a claim determined non-dischargeable.

A secured creditor will face issues of cash collateral use, financing, and relief from the stay. There are three grounds for relief from the stay: cause; the debtor has no equity in the property and it is not necessary for an effective reorganization; and in a small real estate Chapter 11 case ninety days has passed and the debtor has not filed a plan that has a reasonable possibility of confirmation and has not begun making payments to the secured creditor. On a hearing on a motion for relief from the stay the debtor will have the burden on all issues other than the existence in equity in the property. Motions for relief from stay will be heard on an expedited basis. If the debtor and the secured creditor settle their dispute, notice of the settlement must be given to creditors.

□ KEY TERMS

Adequate Protection
Administrative Claim
Claim

Equity Cushion
Involuntary Case
No Asset Report

Priority Claim
Proof of Claim
Reclamation

□ IMPROVE YOUR UNDERSTANDING

1. Creditor A is owed $5.00 from the debtor. Creditor B is owed $9,995.00 from the debtor. Creditor C is owed $1,000.00 from the debtor but that debt is secured by the debtor's real estate worth twice that amount. If the debtor has more than twelve creditors, can creditors A, B, and C alone be petitioning creditors?

2. In determining the number of creditors a debtor has, are governmental units included?

3. May an insider be a petitioning creditor?

4. May an involuntary Chapter 11 debtor convert its case to Chapter 7? If so, how could the petitioning creditors respond?

5. Create a table indicating the last date to file claims in Chapter 7, 11, 12, and 13 cases by the creditor, the debtor, the trustee, and by a co-obligor.

6. If a priority creditor's claim is correctly described as such in the debtor's Schedule E, need the priority creditor file a proof of claim in order to participate in the estate?

7. What other types of priority claims might a debtor want to pay prior to the end of the case? Why?

8. Review Sections 503(b) and 507(a)(1) of the Bankruptcy Code. Are there any claims incurred in the administration of the case that are not entitled to a priority in payment?

In responding to Exercises 9 through 11, rely on the following information:

A company has the following leases:

□ A lease for its building premises. This lease expires in the year 2015 and calls for rent of $10,000 per month. Rent is now three months behind.

□ A five-year lease for an automatic photograph development machine. This lease requires monthly payments of $1,000. All payments are current.

□ A lease for six vans at $100 each per month. This lease is automatically renewed each month unless there is a thirty-day notice of termination given. Such a notice has not been given but three months of payments have been missed.

9. What are the debtor in possession's deadlines for assuming or rejecting each of these leases? If a Chapter 11 trustee is appointed, what are the trustee's deadlines for assuming or rejecting each of these leases?

10. How can each of the lessors most diligently guard their rights? In what situation would the most diligent solution be the most uneconomic?

11. The Chapter 11 case proceeds for three months and the debtor in possession does not assume any of the leases. The case converts to Chapter 7 and thirty days later the trustee rejects all leases. What is the measure of each lessor's claim and what portion of it is prepetition, Chapter 11 administrative, and Chapter 7 administrative?

Uniform Commercial Code Section 2-702 requires the seller to have sold the goods to the buyer on credit. Bankruptcy Code Section 546(c) does not have this provision.

12. Can a seller of goods only use Section 546(c) if it sold the goods on credit?

13. Can you think of any set of circumstances where a right to reclaim would exist if the sale was not on credit terms?

14. Review the section in Chapter 8 on discharge and dischargeability. If you did not complete the Improve Your Understanding exercises and the Drafting Project then, do them now.

15. Give four examples of cash collateral.

16. A lender has a security interest in a debtor's inventory and its proceeds. Postpetition, the debtor obtains inventory on credit and sells it for a check. Is the check the lender's cash collateral? Consider Section 552(a) in your response.

17. If the secured creditor does not consent to the use of its cash collateral, pending a court hearing, must the trustee turn over the cash collateral to the secured creditor?

18. If the trustee is holding a secured creditor's cash collateral, must the trustee provide the creditor with adequate protection?

19. In order for there to be cash collateral, does the creditor need to have a consensual lien?

20. The debtor is the owner and developer of an eighteen hole golf course scheduled to open in six months. Three of the holes are located on a parcel of real property the debtor purchased in 1994 for $1,000,000. The debtor borrowed the money to purchase the parcel from First City Bank; this financing required monthly payments of $5,000. Debtor had failed to make any of the payments when it filed its Chapter 11 case on October 1, 1995, the day before the Bank's scheduled foreclosure sale. The Bank is now owed $1,100,000 due to accrued interest and costs. The entire golf course recently has been appraised at $9,000,000 when completed. The parcel (of three holes) by itself has been appraised at only $900,000 since by itself it has a lesser value.

Is this a "single asset real estate" case? Construct arguments for the debtor and for the Bank in the relief from stay litigation the Bank brings.

21. Why do you think there is a codebtor stay in Chapter 12 and 13 cases but not in Chapter 7 cases of individuals?

22. A secured creditor files and serves its motion for relief from the stay and the debtor responds. At the hearing the parties agree to a settlement. Does Bankruptcy Rule 4001(d) apply? Should it?

23. Think of three acts or omissions by a debtor not mentioned in this chapter that may constitute cause for the real property secured creditor to obtain relief from the automatic stay.

24. Are all relief from stay motions entitled to expedited treatment? Think of two examples that might not be entitled to such treatment.

☐ RESEARCH PROJECTS

1. Locate one case in which the court allowed a creditor to file an untimely claim that would be treated as timely. What was the basis for the court's decision?

2. The debtor in possession wants to assume a business real property lease and files a motion to do so on the fiftieth day after it commenced its case. The hearing is set for the seventieth day after the case is commenced. On day sixty-one, the landlord moves for relief from stay on the ground that the lease has been rejected because it was not assumed within the first sixty days. Find a reported decision that tells you who will win.

3. Locate two cases involving operating companies in which the court refused to authorize the use of cash collateral. To the extent you can tell from the opinion, what was the impact on operations?

4. Find two reported decisions discussing when annulment of the automatic stay is appropriate.

5. If you did not do the Research Project at the end of the section in Chapter 9 on financing the liquidation, do so now.

☐ DRAFTING PROJECT

1. In a Chapter 7 case, the Internal Revenue Service failed to file a proof of claim for debtor's $10,000.00 prepetition income tax liability. Prepare a proof of claim on behalf of the debtor for such a claim.

CHAPTER 13

TAXES IN BANKRUPTCY

During the course of any bankruptcy case tax issues will arise. Although tax laws and regulations are well beyond the scope of this book, this Chapter addresses some of the more common tax issues in bankruptcy cases such as the priority and discharge of tax claims. It also summarizes some of the rules and procedural provisions relating to taxes owed by the debtor and the estate.

☐ TAXES ON THE ESTATE

The trustee or debtor in possession is liable for all federal, state, and local taxes incurred in operating the debtor's business, subject to the limitations and the rules set forth in the Bankruptcy Code. For example, the debtor in possession must pay income taxes on profits earned after it filed its bankruptcy case. The trustee and the debtor in possession must also withhold from any payments made to creditors all taxes required to be withheld by nonbankruptcy law. Section 346(f) of the Bankruptcy Code states that the trustee must pay the withheld taxes to the appropriate taxing agency "at the time and in the manner required by such tax law."

☐ DETERMINATION OF TAXES

Bankruptcy Court Jurisdiction Over Tax Claims

Section 157 of Title 28 of the United States Code authorizes bankruptcy judges to determine core proceedings. Core proceedings include "matters concerning the administration of the estate . . . allowance or disallowance of claims against the estate . . . determination as to the dischargeability of particular debts [and] other

proceedings affecting . . . the adjustment of the debtor-creditor . . . relationship."
Determination of tax claims against the debtor or the estate should be included
within this list of core proceedings. Accordingly, tax disputes may properly be
resolved by bankruptcy courts.

The Procedure for Determining the Estate's Liability

Postpetition Taxes Section 505 sets out the procedure to determine the amount
of most taxes against the debtor and the estate. Briefly, it provides that the trustee
can file a tax return and ask for an expedited determination of the estate's tax
liability. Unless the trustee hears from the taxing agency within a relatively short
period of time, the return will be deemed correct and there will be no future
liability. Section 505 is discussed in more detail below.

Prepetition Taxes The bankruptcy court may determine prepetition taxes in the
same way it determines other claims unless they have been determined by a different court before the commencement of the bankruptcy case. If that has happened, the bankruptcy court cannot make a new determination. The one exception
is where the taxes were determined without a contest before the bankruptcy case
was commenced. In those circumstances the bankruptcy court can make a new
determination.

Chapter 11 and 12 Plans Sections 1146(d) and 1231(d) provide that the court
may authorize a plan proponent to seek a determination, limited to legal issues,
from a state or local governmental income taxing agency of the effect of the plan.
If there is a controversy, the bankruptcy court can resolve the controversy on the
earlier of when the governmental unit has responded or 270 days after the determination request is made.

The Proper Forum for Determining the Estate's Liability

Just because the bankruptcy court can determine tax claims does not necessarily
mean that it will want to or that it will be the best place for the determinations.
What the bankruptcy court may do is direct traffic among the various courts and
other tribunals that might have jurisdiction to determine taxes. This ability is
implemented by granting relief from the automatic stay. Section 362(a)(6) stays
the assessment of taxes after commencement of the case. Section 362(a)(8) stays
the "commencement or continuation of a proceeding before the United States
Tax Court concerning the debtor." In addition, Section 362(a)(1) stays "the commencement or continuation . . . of a judicial, administrative, or other action or
proceeding against the debtor . . . to recover a claim against the debtor." Since
only the bankruptcy court may grant relief from the automatic stay, any litigation
in another court or administrative tribunal regarding taxes must first be approved
by the bankruptcy court.

This is not to suggest that the taxing agencies cannot do anything without
relief from the automatic stay. Since the 1994 Amendments, Section 362(b)(9)
has provided that the following acts by a taxing agency are not covered by the
automatic stay: (1) an audit by a governmental unit to determine tax liability; (2)
the issuance to the debtor by a governmental unit of a notice of tax deficiency;
(3) a demand for tax returns; and (4) the making of an assessment for any tax
and issuance of a notice and demand for payment. This last exemption will allow

a tax lien to be created unless the tax is a debt of the debtor that will not be discharged and the property or its proceeds are transferred out of the estate or otherwise revested in the debtor.

If the bankruptcy court grants relief from the automatic stay to permit postpetition tax litigation in other forums, it may not later redetermine the amount or legality of those taxes after the other court has ruled.

Prepetition Taxes

There are two issues in the postpetition determination of prepetition taxes: whether the tax is a claim against the estate or just against the debtor and whether the debtor is liable for a nondischargeable tax.

One reason the Bankruptcy Code makes the bankruptcy court the traffic director over tax claims is to permit the debtor the advantage in the choice of the forum for the determination of tax claims and to prevent the debtor from being bound on the issues of dischargeability and amount of the tax by a determination against the estate. The estate and the debtor have different interests in contesting tax claims, especially in a situation where the estate will not be able to pay the tax because it has insufficient assets and the taxing agency will look to the debtor for payment. If, however, a tax liability is determined against the debtor before bankruptcy, that determination will bind the estate, which is a successor to the debtor.

Allowability Against the Estate　If there is an administrative or judicial tax proceeding pending when the bankruptcy case commences, it will involve only the debtor and will be stayed by Section 362 except as noted above. The trustee may consent to a lifting of the stay and may intervene in the proceeding. In that event, the estate will be bound by any determination made.

The trustee may oppose relief from the automatic stay to prevent a determination of the debtor's tax liability by the nonbankruptcy forum or may seek to have the bankruptcy court limit the effect of the other court's determination as a condition for granting relief from the automatic stay. The trustee may also object to the tax claim in the bankruptcy court while the other proceeding is pending. If the bankruptcy court grants relief from the automatic stay to let the other proceeding continue but reaches a determination on the trustee's objection to the tax claim before the other forum makes its determination, then the trustee will not be bound by the ruling of the other forum. Conversely, the debtor will not be bound by the bankruptcy court's ruling, because the debtor is not a party to the claim objection proceeding.

Debtor's Liability　As discussed in Chapter 8 of this book, many taxes are not dischargeable. Any question concerning whether the tax is nondischargeable may be determined in an action in the bankruptcy court brought by the taxing agency or by the debtor. If neither party acts, then the debtor's liability for the tax and the tax's nondischargeability will be determined after bankruptcy in the usual administrative or judicial forum.

Administrative Expense Taxes

Expedited Determination　The statute of limitations on tax issues may be as long as seven years. Pursuant to Section 505, the trustee may obtain an expedited

determination of the estate's liability for administrative expense taxes by submitting the tax return to the appropriate taxing agency along with a request for a determination of liability. The trustee is discharged from liability upon payment of the tax shown on the return if the taxing agency does not select the return for examination within sixty days and complete such an examination within 180 days after the trustee's request. A sample request is shown in Exhibit 13.1. If the taxing agency completes its examination, the trustee will be discharged upon payment of the tax determined by the taxing agency or, if the trustee disputes the results of the taxing agency's examination, by the amount determined by the court. If the return is fraudulent or contains a material misrepresentation, however, the trustee will not be discharged.

Individuals The bankruptcy estate of an individual debtor is a separate taxable entity. The debtor's tax year ceases on the entry of the order for relief, and the estate's tax year then commences. The estate will not be liable as an administrative expense for any tax on income earned by and paid to the debtor before the case was commenced.

As shown in Exhibit 13.2, the trustee is required to file tax returns in a liquidation case of an individual only if during the entire period of administration of the case there is taxable gain. In a reorganization case, the trustee must file a tax return for each postpetition taxable period during the case.

■ EXHIBIT 13.1
Sample Request of Tax Determination

Mildred Pierce, Trustee
700 Flower Street
Los Angeles, California 90001

October 15, 1996

Internal Revenue Service
Special Procedures Department
Laguna Niguel, California 90003

    Re: In re Videos by Joe, Inc.
       Case No. LA95-00001-JF
       United States Bankruptcy Court
       Western District of California

Ladies and Gentlemen:

The undersigned is the duly appointed, acting and qualified Chapter 7 trustee of the above-referenced bankruptcy estate. Enclosed is the final tax return in connection with the estate. Also enclosed is the estate's check in the amount of $1,200.00, representing the full tax liability shown in the return.

Pursuant to 11 U.S.C. §505(b), I request a prompt determination by you of any unpaid liability of the estate for any tax incurred during its administration. Unless you notify me within sixty days that the return has been selected for examination, I will be discharged from any liability for such tax.

Very truly yours,

Mildred Pierce
Trustee

Must They File A Tax Return?		
Chapter 7		
Debtor		No, except for individual debtors with nonestate income.
Trustee		
	Individual Debtor	Yes, but only if there is net taxable income during the Chapter 7 case.
	Corporate Debtor	Yes, but only if there is net taxable income during the Chapter 7 case.
	Partnership Debtor	Yes.
Chapter 11		
Debtor in possession or trustee		Yes.
Debtor out of possession		No, except for individual debtor with nonestate income.
Chapter 12		
Debtor in possession or trustee		Yes.
Debtor out of possession		No, except for individual debtor with nonestate income.
Chapter 13		
Debtor		Yes.

Partnerships In the case of a partnership debtor there is no change in the tax-payer's status and the trustee must file returns in the same form and same manner as the partnership. As shown in Exhibit 13.2, in liquidation as well as reorganization cases, a return is required for each taxable period, whether or not there is gain or loss during that time period.

Corporations Like partnerships, there is no change in the status of a corporation for tax purposes upon the filing of the petition, and the trustee must file returns in the same form and manner as the corporation. (See Exhibit 13.2.) As in an individual case, however, the trustee must file an income tax return in a liquidation case only if there is taxable gain over the entire period of the administration of the case.

☐ PRIORITIES OF TAXES

In General

Unsecured claims for taxes may be entitled to a first priority in payment as an administrative expense under Section 503(b), an eighth priority under Section 507(a)(8), general unsecured status without priority, subordination in Chapter 7 under Section 726(a)(4), or any priority as a withholding tax, the same as the claim from which the tax is withheld. Secured tax claims are treated like other

secured claims up to the value of the taxing agency's collateral. The chart in Exhibit 13.3 summarizes the following discussion.

Postpetition Income Taxes

Income taxes include any taxes on or measured by gross receipts. Pursuant to Section 503(b)(1)(B)(i), income taxes are entitled to a first-in priority payment as administrative expenses if the taxes are incurred by the estate.

Income Tax
Any tax on or measured by gross receipts.

Unsecured Prepetition Income Taxes

An unsecured tax on or measured by income or gross receipts is entitled to a eighth in priority payment under Section 507(a)(8)(A) if:

☐ The tax year ended on or before the date of bankruptcy and the tax return was last due within three years before the date of bankruptcy or was due after bankruptcy;

☐ The tax has not yet been assessed at the date of the bankruptcy but is still subject to being assessed under applicable tax law; or

☐ The tax was assessed within 240 days before bankruptcy.

■ EXHIBIT 13.3
Tax Priority

Priority Taxes		
Common Types of Taxes		Priority?
Incurred Postpetition		Yes, Sections 503(b) and 507(a)(1).
Income Taxes	For a tax period more than three years prepetition	No, unless fits within one of the other categories.
	For a tax period less than three years prepetition	Yes, Section 507(a)(8)(A)(i).
	Assessed within 240 days prepetition	Yes, Section 507(a)(8)(A)(ii).
	Assessable postpetition by law or agreement	Yes, Section 507(a)(8)(A)(iii).
Property Taxes	Payable more than one year prepetition	No, but it may be a secured claim.
	Payable within one year prepetition	Yes, Section 507(a)(8)(B).
Taxes Debtor is Required to Collect or Withhold		Yes, Section 507(a)(8)(C).
Employment Taxes Earned from the Debtor	For a tax period more than three years prepetition	No.
	For a tax period less than three years prepetition	Yes, Section 507(a)(8)(D).
Penalties		Only if related to a priority tax and in compensation for actual monetary loss.
Interest		Unclear. Some jurisdictions allow if on a priority tax claim; some do not allow.

If the tax does not fit within one of these categories, and is not an administrative expense or withholding tax, it will be treated the same as other nonpriority prepetition claims.

Property Taxes

Property Tax
Tax imposed on the ownership or real or personal property based on the property's value, number, weight or size.

Property taxes are taxes imposed on the ownership of real or personal property, and may be based on value or on number, weight, size, and so on. Section 507(a)(8)(B) grants priority status to a property tax claim assessed prepetition and payable in the year before the petition was filed. Any tax assessed for a postpetition period will be an administrative claim.

Excise Taxes

Excise Tax
A tax on a transaction, event, or occurrence.

An **excise tax** is a tax on a transaction, event, or occurrence. Examples of excise taxes are sales taxes, estate and gift taxes, and gasoline and special fuel taxes. Except as discussed here, an excise tax is entitled to administrative expense status if the transaction, event, or occurrence on which the tax is based occurs after the commencement of the case and the tax is incurred by the estate. Thus, if the trustee is operating the retail sales business of the debtor, any sales tax imposed by the state will be entitled to administrative expense priority. A sales or use tax imposed directly on the trustee for goods that the trustee purchases will also be entitled to administrative expense status as an excise tax.

If the transaction, event, or occurrence happened before bankruptcy, then the related excise tax will be a prepetition claim, even though the return or the tax may not be due until after the commencement of the bankruptcy case. Under Section 507(a)(8)(E), the excise tax will be entitled to priority only if the return was due, including extensions, within three years before bankruptcy or after bankruptcy. If no return is required, then the tax is entitled to priority if the transaction on which the tax is imposed occurred within three years before bankruptcy.

Penalties

There are two kinds of penalties for nonpayment of taxes. One is strictly punitive in nature and is intended to penalize the taxpayer for failure to pay on time. The other is compensatory and is designed to help the taxing authority to collect the tax from a different source. An example of the latter is the 100 percent penalty imposed on a responsible officer for failure to withhold and pay over to the taxing agency the employees' share of income and social security taxes.

A prepetition tax penalty will be entitled to eighth in priority treatment along with other taxes only if the penalty is a compensatory penalty. Punitive claims are subordinated and paid only after the claims of all general unsecured creditors in liquidation cases.

☐ NONDISCHARGEABLE TAXES

The Bankruptcy Code generally implements the policy that all taxes that are nondischargeable in an individual's case should also be entitled to priority. This policy gives some relief to a debtor with nondischargeable taxes by increasing the probability that all or a portion of the taxes will be paid from the estate. If the priority nondischargeable tax claim is $100 and the trustee has enough assets to distribute

$50 to the taxing agency, the debtor will have a remaining liability of only $50. If it was not entitled to a priority in payment, the debtor's remaining liability would probably be much greater.

There are some taxes that are not entitled to priority but are also excepted from discharge under Section 523(a)(1). If the debtor fails to file a required return or files the return so late that the taxing agency did not have a fair opportunity to collect the tax before bankruptcy, or if the debtor made a fraudulent return or willfully attempted in any manner to evade or defeat the tax, then the tax is excepted from discharge even though it may not be entitled to priority. Giving such taxes a priority in payment would penalize other creditors by reducing the amount of assets available to satisfy unsecured claims. That prejudice to other creditors is not fair when the action was the result of the debtor's wrongdoing.

Interest and penalties on nondischargeable taxes are also not dischargeable. In contrast, interest and penalties on dischargeable taxes are discharged.

□ PAYMENT OF TAXES

Most taxes are entitled to a priority in payment and therefore will be paid, assuming sufficient assets, in any case under the Bankruptcy Code. The rules for the timing of payment of priority taxes differ slightly for administrative expense taxes and prepetition priority taxes and differ among the various chapters of the Bankruptcy Code. Under all chapters, nonpriority unsecured taxes are treated the same as all other general unsecured claims and secured tax claims are treated just like other secured claims.

Chapter 7

In a Chapter 7 case, taxes entitled to administrative expense priority are paid first under Sections 726(a)(1) and 507(a)(1) with all other administrative expenses. Prepetition taxes that are entitled to a priority in payment under Section 507(a)(8) will be satisfied after the Section 507(a)(1) through Section 507(a)(7) priority claims are paid and immediately before payment of Section 507(a)(9) and general unsecured claims.

Chapter 11

Administrative expense taxes must be paid in cash in full on confirmation of a Chapter 11 reorganization plan. Unsecured priority taxes must also be paid in full but the cash payments may stretch over a period of six years beginning upon the date of the assessment of the tax. A fair market rate of interest must be paid on the principal amount to the taxing agency.

Chapters 12 and 13

A Chapter 12 or 13 plan must provide for the full payment of all priority tax claims. Payments can be deferred and paid in installments over the life of the plan. Interest on the tax claim is not required, except to the extent that Sections 1225(a)(4) and 1325(a)(4) require otherwise. Under those provisions, the debtor must pay interest under the plan on any unsecured claim if the creditor would be paid interest in a Chapter 7 liquidation case.

☐ SUMMARY

Being a debtor or a trustee in a bankruptcy case does not excuse the need to file tax returns or pay taxes incurred by the estate. The one general exception is that in a Chapter 7 case of an individual or a corporation, the trustee will not have to file a tax return if there is no taxable income during the case.

Bankruptcy courts have the ability to determine the estate's liability for pre and postpetition taxes. The bankruptcy court can, however, lift the automatic stay and let any dispute over the taxes owed proceed in the tax courts. For prepetition taxes, a tax court may determine the debtor's liability, which would not be binding on the trustee unless he or she participated in the tax court proceedings. The Bankruptcy Code establishes procedures for a trustee or debtor in possession to obtain an expedited determination of the estate's tax liability so that the estate can be closed without the fear that the Internal Revenue Service will later claim that additional taxes are due.

Postpetition taxes will need to be paid as an administrative priority in the bankruptcy case. Most prepetition taxes, unless they were due at least three years before the bankruptcy case was commenced, are treated as eighth priority claims. Property taxes may be secured claims in addition to being priority taxes. Most priority taxes will also be nondischargeable.

In a Chapter 11, 12, or 13 plan, priority tax claims can be stretched out for up to as long as six years. Interest must be paid.

☐ KEY TERMS

Excise Tax   Income Tax   Property Tax

☐ IMPROVE YOUR UNDERSTANDING

1. What is the priority of the debtor in possession's portion of employment taxes incurred after the commencement of its bankruptcy case?

2. If the debtor in possession fails to pay income taxes accrued postpetition, will the automatic stay prevent the Internal Revenue Service from assessing the tax? Will it prevent the IRS from taking steps to collect the tax?

3. Just before it filed its Chapter 7 case, the debtor lost a hearing before the tax court that resulted in a judgment. Is the debtor bound by the tax court's determination? Is the trustee?

4. If the debtor was in the midst of trial at the tax court when it filed its Chapter 7 case, could it continue the trial? What would it have to do? How could the trustee react?

5. Are there any taxes entitled to a priority in payment under Section 507(a)(8) that are dischargeable?

6. Why do you think Congress gave trustees the right to an expedited determination of tax liability?

7. The debtor fails to file any tax returns for the three years prior to the filing of its Chapter 7 case. The Internal Revenue Service discovers this fact one year later while the case is still open. What could the IRS do? If the IRS found liability in each of the three years, what priority would the taxes be entitled to under the Bankruptcy Code? Are they dischargeable?

8. Must interest be paid on priority taxes in a Chapter 7 case? In a Chapter 11 case? In a Chapter 12 or 13 case?

9. A taxing agency with a nondischargeable tax fails to timely file a proof of claim in an individual debtor's Chapter 7 case. Should the debtor be concerned on behalf of the taxing agency? If so, what can the debtor do?

☐ RESEARCH PROJECT

1. Are there any Bankruptcy Rules specifically concerning tax issues?

BANKRUPTCY CODE

CHAPTER 1—GENERAL PROVISIONS

§ 101. Definitions

In this title—

(1) "accountant" means accountant authorized under applicable law to practice public accounting, and includes professional accounting association, corporation, or partnership, if so authorized;

(2) "affiliate" means—

(A) entity that directly or indirectly owns, controls, or holds with power to vote, 20 percent or more of the outstanding voting securities of the debtor, other than an entity that holds such securities—

(i) in a fiduciary or agency capacity without sole discretionary power to vote such securities; or

(ii) solely to secure a debt, if such entity has not in fact exercised such power to vote;

(B) corporation 20 percent or more of whose outstanding voting securities are directly or indirectly owned, controlled, or held with power to vote, by the debtor, or by an entity that directly or indirectly owns, controls, or holds with power to vote, 20 percent or more of the outstanding voting securities of the debtor, other than an entity that holds such securities—

(i) in a fiduciary or agency capacity without sole discretionary power to vote such securities; or

(ii) solely to secure a debt, if such entity has not in fact exercised such power to vote;

(C) person whose business is operated under a lease or operating agreement by a debtor, or person substantially all of whose property is operated under an operating agreement with the debtor; or

(D) entity that operates the business or substantially all of the property of the debtor under a lease or operating agreement;

(4) "attorney" means attorney, professional law association, corporation, or partnership, authorized under applicable law to practice law;

(5) "claim" means—

(A) right to payment, whether or not such right is reduced to judgment, liquidated, unliquidated, fixed, contingent, matured, unmatured, disputed, undisputed, legal, equitable, secured, or unsecured; or

(B) right to an equitable remedy for breach of performance if such breach gives rise to a right to payment, whether or not such right to an equitable remedy is reduced to judgment, fixed, contingent, matured, unmatured, disputed, undisputed, secured, or unsecured;

(6) "commodity broker" means futures commission merchant, foreign futures commission merchant, clearing organization, leverage transaction merchant, or commodity options dealer, as defined in section 761 or this title, with respect to which there is a customer, as defined in section 761 of this title;

(7) "community claim" means claim that arose before the commencement of the case concerning the debtor for which property of the kind specified in section 541(a)(2) of this title is liable, whether or not there is any such property at the time of the commencement of the case;

(8) "consumer debt" means debt incurred by an individual primarily for a personal, family, or household purpose;

(9) "corporation"—

(A) includes—

(i) association having a power or privilege that a private corporation, but not an individual or a partnership, possesses;

(ii) partnership association organized under a law that makes only the capital subscribed responsible for the debts of such association;

(iii) joint-stock company;

(iv) unincorporated company or association; or

(v) business trust; but

(B) does not include limited partnership;

(10) "creditor" means—

(A) entity that has a claim against the debtor that arose at the time of or before the order for relief concerning the debtor;

(B) entity that has a claim against the estate of a kind specified in section 348(d), 502(f), 502(g), 502(h) or 502(i) of this title; or

(C) entity that has a community claim;

(11) "custodian" means—

(A) receiver or trustee of any of the property of the debtor, appointed in a case or proceeding not under this title;

(B) assignee under a general assignment for the benefit of the debtor's creditors; or

(C) trustee, receiver, or agent under applicable law, or under a contract, that is appointed or authorized to take charge of property of the debtor for the purpose of enforcing a lien against such property, or for the purpose of general administration of such property for the benefit of the debtor's creditors;

(12) "debt" means liability on a claim;

(12A) "debt for child support" means a debt of a kind specified in section 523(a)(5) of this title for maintenance or support of a child of the debtor;

(13) "debtor" means person or municipality concerning which a case under this title has been commenced;

(14) "disinterested person" means person that—

(A) is not a creditor, an equity security holder, or an insider;

(B) is not and was not an investment banker for any outstanding security of the debtor;

(C) has not been, within three years before the date of the filing of the petition, an investment banker for a security of the debtor, or an attorney for such an investment banker in connection with the offer, sale, or issuance of a security of the debtor;

(D) is not and was not, within two years before the date of the filing of the petition, a director, officer, or employee of the debtor or of an investment banker specified in subparagraph (B) or (C) of this paragraph; and

(E) does not have an interest materially adverse to the interest of the estate or of any class of creditors or equity security holders, by reason of any direct or indirect relationship to, connection with, or interest in, the debtor or an investment banker specified in sub-

paragraph (B) or (C) of this paragraph, or for any other reason;

(15) "entity" includes person, estate, trust, governmental unit, and United States trustee;

(16) "equity security" means—

(A) share in a corporation, whether or not transferable or denominated "stock", or similar security;

(B) interest of a limited partner in a limited partnership; or

(C) warrant or right, other than a right to convert, to purchase, sell, or subscribe to a share, security, or interest of a kind specified in subparagraph (A) or (B) of this paragraph;

(17) "equity security holder" means holder of an equity security of the debtor;

(18) "family farmer" means—

(A) individual or individual and spouse engaged in a farming operation whose aggregate debts do not exceed $1,500,000 and not less than 80 percent of whose aggregate noncontingent, liquidated debts (excluding a debt for the principal residence of such individual or such individual and spouse unless such debt arises out of a farming operation), on the date the case is filed, arise out of a farming operation owned or operated by such individual or such individual and spouse, and such individual or such individual and spouse receive from such farming operation more than 50 percent of such individual's or such individual and spouse's gross income for the taxable year preceding the taxable year in which the case concerning such individual or such individual and spouse was filed; or

(B) corporation or partnership in which more than 50 percent of the outstanding stock or equity is held by one family, or by one family and the relatives of the members of such family; and such family or such relatives conduct the farming operation; and

(i) more than 80 percent of the value of its assets consists of assets related to the farming operation;

(ii) its aggregate debts do not exceed $1,500,000 and not less than 80 percent of its aggregate noncontingent, liquidated debts (excluding a debt for one dwelling which is owned by such corporation or partnership and which a shareholder or partner maintains as a principal residence, unless such debt arises out of a farming operation), on the date the case is filed, arise out of the farming operation owned or operated by such corporation or such partnership; and

(iii) if such corporation issues stock, such stock is not publicly traded;

(19) "family farmer with regular annual income" means family farmer whose annual income is sufficiently stable and regular to enable such family farmer to make payments under a plan under chapter 12 of this title;

(20) "farmer" means (except when such term appears in the term "family farmer") person that received more than 80 percent of such person's gross income during the

taxable year of such person immediately preceding the tax-able year of such person during which the case under this title concerning such person was commenced from a farm-ing operation owned or operated by such person;

(21) "farming operation" includes farming, tillage of the soil, dairy farming, ranching, production or raising of crops, poultry, or livestock, and production of poultry or livestock products in an unmanufactured state;

(21A) "farmout agreement" means a written agreement in which—

(A) the owner of a right to drill, produce, or operate liquid or gaseous hydrocarbons on property agrees or has agreed to transfer or assign all or a part of such right to another entity; and

(B) such other entity (either directly or through its agents or its assigns), as consideration, agrees to perform drilling, reworking, recompleting, testing, or similar or related operations, to develop or produce liquid or gas-eous hydrocarbons on the property;

(21B) "Federal depository institutions regulatory agency" means—

(A) with respect to an insured depository institution (as defined in section 3(c)(2) of the Federal Deposit Insurance Act) for which no conservator or receiver has been appointed, the appropriate Federal banking agency (as defined in section 3(q) or such Act);

(B) with respect to an insured credit union (includ-ing an insured credit union for which the National Credit Union Administration has been appointed con-servator or liquidating agent), the National Credit Un-ion Administration;

(C) with respect to any insured depository institu-tion for which the Resolution Trust Corporation has been appointed conservator or receiver, the Resolution Trust Corporation; and

(D) with respect to any insured depository institu-tion for which the Federal Deposit Insurance Corpora-tion has been appointed conservator or receiver, the Federal Deposit Insurance Corporation;

(22) "financial institution" means a person that is a commercial or savings bank, industrial savings bank, sav-ings and loan association, or trust company and, when any such person is acting as agent or custodian for a customer in connection with a securities contract, as defined in sec-tion 741 of this title, such customer;

(23) "foreign proceeding" means proceeding, whether judicial or administrative and whether or not under bank-ruptcy law, in a foreign country in which the debtor's dom-icile, residence, principal place of business, or principal assets were located at the commencement of such proceed-ing, for the purpose of liquidating an estate, adjusting debts by composition, extension, or discharge, or effecting a reorganization;

(24) "foreign representative" means duly selected trus-tee, administrator, or other representative of an estate in a foreign proceeding;

(25) "forward contract" means a contract (other than a commodity contract) for the purchase, sale, or transfer of a commodity, as defined in section 761(8) of this title, or any similar good, article, service, right, or interest which is presently or in the future becomes the subject of dealing in the forward contract trade, or product or byproduct thereof, with a maturity date more than two days after the date the contract is entered into, including, but not limited to, a repurchase transaction, reverse repurchase transaction, consignment, lease, swap, hedge transaction, deposit, loan, option, allocated transaction, unallocated transaction, or any combination thereof or option thereon;

(26) "forward contract merchant" means a person whose business consists in whole or in part of entering into forward contracts as or with merchants in a commodity, as defined in section 761(8) of this title, or any similar good, article, service, right, or interest which is presently or in the future becomes the subject of dealing in the forward contract trade;

(27) "governmental unit" means United States; State; Commonwealth; District; Territory; municipality; foreign state; department, agency, or instrumentality of the United States (but not a United States trustee while serving as a trustee in a case under this title), a State, a Common-wealth, a District, a Territory, a municipality, or a foreign state; or other foreign or domestic government;

(28) "indenture" means mortgage, deed of trust, or in-denture, under which there is outstanding a security, other than a voting-trust certificate, constituting a claim against the debtor, a claim secured by a lien on any of the debtor's property, or an equity security of the debtor;

(29) "indenture trustee" means trustee under an indenture;

(30) "individual with regular income" means individ-ual whose income is sufficiently stable and regular to enable such individual to make payments under a plan under chapter 13 of this title, other than a stockbroker or a com-modity broker;

(31) "insider" includes—

(A) if the debtor is an individual—

(i) relative of the debtor or of a general partner of the debtor;

(ii) partnership in which the debtor is a general partner;

(iii) general partner of the debtor; or

(iv) corporation of which the debtor is a direc-tor, officer, or person in control;

(B) if the debtor is a corporation—

(i) director of the debtor;

(ii) officer of the debtor;

(iii) person in control of the debtor;

(iv) partnership in which the debtor is a general partner;

(v) general partner of the debtor; or

(vi) relative of a general partner, director, offi-cer, or person in control of the debtor;

(C) if the debtor is a partnership—

(i) general partner in the debtor;

(ii) relative of a general partner in, general partner of, or person in control of the debtor;

(iii) partnerhsip in which the debtor is a general partner;

(iv) general partner of the debtor; or

(v) person in control of the debtor;

(D) if the debtor is a municipality, elected official of the debtor or relative of an elected official of the debtor;

(E) affiliate, or insider of an affiliate as if such affiliate were the debtor; and

(F) managing agent of the debtor;

(32) "insolvent" means—

(A) with reference to an entity other than a partnership and a municipality, financial condition such that the sum of such entity's debts is greater than all of such entity's property, at a fair valuation, exclusive of—

(i) property transferred, concealed, or removed with intent to hinder, delay, or defraud such entity's creditors; and

(ii) property that may be exempted from property of the estate under section 522 of this title;

(B) with reference to a partnership, financial condition such that the sum of such partnership's debts is greater than the aggregate of, at a fair valuation—

(i) all of such partnership's property, exclusive of property of the kind specified in subparagraph (A)(i) of this paragraph; and

(ii) the sum of the excess of the value of each general partners' nonpartnership property, exclusive of property of the kind specified in subparagraph (A) of this paragraph, over such partner's nonpartnership debts; and

(C) with reference to a municipality, financial condition such that the municipality is—

(i) generally not paying its debts as they become due unless such debts are the subject of a bona fide dispute; or

(ii) unable to pay its debts as they become due;

(33) "institution-affiliated party"—

(A) with respect to an insured depository institution (as defined in section 3(c)(2) of the Federal Deposit Insurance Act), has the meaning given it in section 3(u) of the Federal Deposit Insurance Act; and

(B) with respect to an insured credit union, has the meaning given it in section 206(r) of the Federal Credit Unit Act;

(34) "insured credit union" has the meaning given it in section 101(7) of the Federal Credit Union Act;

(35) "insured depository institution"—

(A) has the meaning given it in section 3(c)(2) of the Federal Deposit Insurance Act; and

(B) includes an insured credit union (except in the case of paragraphs (21B) and (33)(A) of this subsection);

(35A) "intellectual property" means—

(A) trade secret;

(B) invention, process, design, or plant protected under title 35;

(C) patent application;

(D) plant variety;

(E) work of authorship protected under title 17; or

(F) mask work protected under chapter 9 of title 17; to the extent protected by applicable nonbankruptcy law; and

(36) "judicial lien" means lien obtained by judgment, levy, sequestration, or other legal or equitable process or proceeding;

(37) "lien" means charge against or interest in property to secure payment of a debt or performance of an obligation;

(38) "margin payment" means, for purposes of the forward contract provisions of this title, payment or deposit of cash, a security or other property, that is commonly known in the forward contract trade as original margin, initial margin, maintenance margin, or variation margin, including mark-to-market payments, or variation payments; and

(39) "mask work" has the meaning given it in section 901(a)(2) of title 17.

(40) "municipality" means political subdivision or public agency or instrumentality of a State;

(41) "person" includes individual, partnership, and corporation, but does not include governmental unit, except that a governmental unit that—

(A) acquires an asset from a person—

(i) as a result of the operation of a loan guarantee agreement; or

(ii) as receiver or liquidating agent of a person;

(B) is a guarantor of a pension benefit payable by or on behalf of the debtor or an affiliate of the debtor; or

(C) is the legal or beneficial owner of an asset of—

(i) an employee pension benefit plan that is a governmental plan, as defined in section 414(d) of the Internal Revenue Code of 1986; or

(ii) an eligible deferred compensation plan, as defined in section 457(b) of the Internal Revenue Code of 1986;

shall be considered, for purposes of section 1102 of this title, to be a person with respect to such asset or such benefit;

(42) "petition" means petition filed under section 301, 302, 303, or 304 of this title, as the case may be, commencing a case under this title;

(42A) "production payment" means a term overriding royalty satisfiable in cash or in kind—

(A) contingent on the production of a liquid or gaseous hydrocarbon from particular real property; and

(B) from a specified volume, or a specified value, from the liquid or gaseous hydrocarbon produced from such property, and determined without regard to production costs;

(43) "purchaser" means transferee of a voluntary transfer, and includes immediate or mediate transferee of such a transferee;

(44) "railroad" means common carrier by railroad engaged in the transportation of individuals or property or owner of trackage facilities leased by such a common carrier;

(45) "relative" means individual related by affinity or consanguinity within the third degree as determined by the common law, or individual in a step or adoptive relationship within such a third degree;

(46) "repo participant" means an entity that, on any day during the period beginning 90 days before the date of the filing of the petition, has an outstanding repurchase agreement with the debtor;

(47) "repurchase agreement" (which definition also applies to a reverse repurchase agreement) means an agreement, including related terms, which provides for the transfer of certificates of deposit, eligible bankers' acceptances, or securities that are direct obligations of, or that are fully guaranteed as to principal and interest by, the United States or any agency of the United States against the transfer of funds by the transferee of such certificates of deposit, eligible bankers' acceptances, or securities with a simultaneous agreement by such transferee to transfer to the transferor thereof certificates of deposit, eligible bankers' acceptances, or securities as described above, at a date certain not later than one year after such transfers or on demand, against the transfer of funds;

(48) "securities clearing agency" means person that is registered as a clearing agency under section 17A of the Securities Exchange Act of 1934 or whose business is confined to the performance of functions of a clearing agency with respect to exempted securities, as defined in section 3(a)(12) of such Act for the purposes of such section 17A;

(49) "security"—

(A) includes—

(i) note;

(ii) stock;

(iii) treasury stock;

(iv) bond;

(v) debenture;

(vi) collateral trust certificate;

(vii) pre-organization certificate or subscription;

(viii) transferable share;

(ix) voting-trust certificate

(x) certificate of deposit;

(xi) certificate of deposit for security;

(xii) investment contract or certificate of interest or participation in a profit-sharing agreement or in an oil, gas, or mineral royalty or lease, if such contract or interest is required to be the subject of a registration statement filed with the Securities and Exchange Commission under the provisions of the Securities Act of 1933, or is exempt under section 3(b) of such Act from the requirement to file such a statement;

(xiii) interest of a limited partner in a limited partnership;

(xiv) other claim or interest commonly known as "security"; and

(xv) certificate of interest or participation in, temporary or interim certificate for, receipt for, or warrant or right to subscribe to or purchase or sell, a security; but

(B) does not include—

(i) currency, check, draft, bill of exchange, or bank letter of credit;

(ii) leverage transaction, as defined in section 761 of this title;

(iii) commodity futures contract or forward contract;

(iv) option, warrant, or right to subscribe to or purchase or sell a commodity futures contract;

(v) option to purchase or sell a commodity;

(vi) contract or certificate of a kind specified in subparagraph (A)(xii) of this paragraph that is not required to be the subject of a registration statement filed with the Securities and Exchange Commission and is not exempt under section 3(b) of the Securities Act of 1933 from the requirement to file such a statement; or

(vii) debt or evidence of indebtedness for goods sold and delivered or services rendered;

(50) "security agreement" means agreement that creates or provides for a security interest;

(51) "security interest" means lien created by an agreement;

(51A) "settlement payment" means, for purposes of the forward contract provisions of this title, a preliminary settlement payment, a partial settlement payment, an interim settlement payment, a settlement payment on account, a final settlement payment, a net settlement payment, or any other similar payment commonly used in the forward contract trade;

(51B) "single asset real estate" means real property constituting a single property or project, other than residential real property with fewer than 4 residential units, which generates substantially all of the gross income of a debtor and on which no substantial business is being conducted by a debtor other than the business of operating the real property and activities incidental thereto having aggregate noncontingent, liquidated secured debts in an amount no more than $4,000,000;

(51C) "small business" means a person engaged in commercial or business activities (but does not include a person whose primary activity is the business of owning or operating real property and activities incidental thereto) whose aggregate noncontingent liquidated secured and unsecured debts as of the date of the petition do not exceed $2,000,000;

(52) "State" includes the District of Columbia and Puerto Rico, except for the purpose of defining who may be a debtor under chapter 9 of this title;

(53) "statutory lien" means lien arising solely by force of a statute on specified circumstances or conditions, or lien of distress for rent, whether or not statutory, but does not include security interest or judicial lien, whether or not such interest or lien is provided by or is dependent on a statute and whether or not such interest or lien is made fully effective by statute;

(53A) "stockbroker" means person—

(A) with respect to which there is a customer, as defined in section 741 of this title; and

(B) that is engaged in the business of effecting transactions in securities—

(i) for the account of others; or

(ii) with members of the general public, from or for such person's own account;

(53B) "swap agreement" means—

(A) an agreement (including terms and conditions incorporated by reference therein) which is a rate swap agreement, basis swap, forward rate agreement, commodity swap, interest rate option, forward foreign exchange agreement, spot foreign exchange agreement, rate cap agreement, rate floor agreement, rate collar agreement, currency swap agreement, cross-currency rate swap agreement, currency option, any other similar agreement (including any option to enter into any of the foregoing);

(B) any combination of the foregoing; or

(C) a master agreement for any of the foregoing together with all supplements;

(53C) "swap participant" means an entity that, at any time before the filing of the petition, has an outstanding swap agreement with the debtor;

(53D) "timeshare plan" means and shall include that interest purchased in any arrangement, plan, scheme, or similar device, but not including exchange programs, whether by membership, agreement, tenancy in common, sale, lease, deed, rental agreement, license, right to use agreement, or by any other means, whereby a purchaser, in exchange for consideration, receives a right to use accommodations, facilities, or recreational sites, whether improved or unimproved, for a specific period of time less than a full year during any given year, but not necessarily for consecutive years, and which extends for a period of more than three years. A "timeshare interest" is that interest purchased in a timeshare plan which grants the purchaser the right to use and occupy accommodations, facilities, or recreational sites, whether improved or unimproved, pursuant to a timeshare plan;

(54) "transfer" means every mode, direct or indirect, absolute or conditional, voluntary or involuntary, of disposing of or parting with property or with an interest in property, including retention of title as a security interest and foreclosure of the debtor's equity of redemption;

(55) "United States", when used in a geographical sense, includes all locations where the judicial jurisdiction of the United States extends, including territories and possessions of the United States;

(56A) "term overriding royalty" means an interest in liquid or gaseous hydrocarbons in place or to be produced from particular real property that entitles the owner thereof to a share of production, or the value thereof, for a term limited by time, quantity, or value realized;

§ 102. Rules of construction

In this title—

(1) "after notice and a hearing", or a similar phrase—

(A) means after such notice as is appropriate in the particular circumstances, and such opportunity for a hearing as is appropriate in the particular circumstances; but

(B) authorizes an act without an actual hearing if such notice is given property and if—

(i) such a hearing is not requested timely by a party in interest;

(ii) there is insufficient time for a hearing to be commenced before such act must be done, and the court authorizes such act;

(2) "claim against the debtor" includes claim against property of the debtor;

(3) "includes" and "including" are not limiting;

(4) "may not" is prohibitive, and not permissive;

(5) "or" is not exclusive;

(6) "order for relief" means entry of an order for relief;

(7) the singular includes the plural;

(8) a definition, contained in a section of this title that refers to another section of this title, does not, for the purpose of such reference, affect the meaning of a term used in such other section; and

(9) United States trustee includes a designee of the United States trustee.

§ 103. Applicability of chapters

(a) Except as provided in section 1161 of this title, chapters 1, 3, and 5 of this title apply in a case under chapter 7, 11, 12, or 13 of this title.

(b) Subchapters I and II of chapter 7 of this title apply only in a case under such chapter.

(c) Subchapter III of chapter 7 of this title applies only in a case under such chapter concerning a stockbroker.

(d) Subchapter IV of chapter 7 of this title applies only in a case under such chapter concerning a commodity broker.

(e) Except as provided in section 901 of this title, only chapters 1 and 9 of this title apply in a case under such chapter 9.

(f) Except as provided in section 901 of this title, subchapters I, II, and III of chapter 11 of this title apply only in a case under such chapter.

(g) Subchapter IV of chapter 11 of this title applies

only in a case under such chapter concerning a railroad.

(h) Chapter 13 of this title applies only in a case under such chapter.

(i) Chapter 12 of this title applies only in a case under such chapter.

§ 104. Adjustment of dollar amounts

(a) The Judicial Conference of the United States shall transmit to the Congress and to the President before May 1, 1985, and before May 1 of every sixth year after May 1, 1985, a recommendation for the uniform percentage adjustment of each dollar amount in this title and in section 1930 of title 28.

(b)(1) On April 1, 1998, and at each 3-year interval ending on April 1 thereafter, each dollar amount in effect under sections 109(e), 303(b), 507(a), 522(d), and 523(a)(2)(C) immediately before such April 1 shall be adjusted—

(A) to reflect the changes in the Consumer Price Index for All Urban Consumers, published by the Department of Labor, for the most recent 3-year period ending immediately before January 1 preceding such April 1, and

(B) to round to the nearest $25 the dollar amount that represents such change.

(2) Not later than March 1, 1998, and at each 3-year interval ending on March 1 thereafter, the Judicial Conference of the United States shall publish in the Federal Register the dollar amounts that will become effective on such April 1 under sections 109(e), 303(b), 507(a), 522(d), and 523(a)(2)(C) of this title.

(3) Adjustments made in accordance with paragraph (1) shall not apply with respect to cases commenced before the date of such adjustments.

§ 105. Power of court

(a) The court may issue any order, process, or judgment that is necessary or appropriate to carry out the provisions of this title. No provision of this title providing for the raising of an issue by a party in interest shall be construed to preclude the court from, sua sponte, taking any action or making any determination necessary or appropriate to enforce or implement court orders or rules, or to prevent an abuse of process.

(b) Notwithstanding subsection (a) of this section, a court may not appoint a receiver in a case under this title.

(c) The ability of any district judge or other officer or employee of a district court to exercise any of the authority or responsibilities conferred upon the court under this title shall be determined by reference to the provisions relating to such judge, officer, or employee set forth in title 28. This subsection shall not be interpreted to exclude bankruptcy judges and other officers or employees appointed pursuant to chapter 6 of title 28 from its operation.

(d) The court, on its own motion or on the request of a party in interest, may—

(1) hold a status conference regarding any case or proceeding under this title after notice to the parties in interest; and

(2) unless inconsistent with another provision of this title or with applicable Federal Rules of Bankruptcy Procedure, issue an order at any such conference prescribing such limitations and conditions as the court deems appropriate to ensure that the case is handled expeditiously and economically, including an order that—

(A) sets the date by which the trustee must assume or reject an executory contract or unexpired lease; or

(B) in a case under chapter 11 of this title—

(i) sets a date by which the debtor, or trustee if one has been appointed, shall file a disclosure statement and plan;

(ii) sets a date by which the debtor, or trustee if one has been appointed, shall solicit acceptances of a plan;

(iii) sets the date by which a party in interest other than a debtor may file a plan;

(iv) sets a date by which a proponent of a plan, other than the debtor, shall solicit acceptances of such plan;

(v) fixes the scope and format of the notice to be provided regarding the hearing on approval of the disclosure statement; or

(vi) provides that the hearing on approval of the disclosure statement may be combined with the hearing on confirmation of the plan.

§ 106. Waiver of sovereign immunity

(a) Notwithstanding an assertion of sovereign immunity, sovereign immunity is abrogated as to a governmental unit to the extent set forth in this section with respect to the following:

(1) Sections 105, 106, 107, 108, 303, 346, 362, 363, 364, 365, 366, 502, 503, 505, 506, 510, 522, 523, 524, 525, 542, 543, 544, 545, 546, 547, 548, 549, 550, 551, 552, 553, 722, 724, 726, 728, 744, 749, 764, 901, 922, 926, 928, 929, 944, 1107, 1141, 1142, 1143, 1146, 1201, 1203, 1205, 1206, 1227, 1231, 1301, 1303, 1305, and 1327 of this title.

(2) The court may hear and determine any issue arising with respect to the application of such sections to governmental units.

(3) The court may issue against a governmental unit an order, process, or judgment under such sections or the Federal Rules of Bankruptcy Procedure, including an order or judgment awarding a money recovery, but not including an award of punitive damages. Such order or judgment for costs or fees under this title or the Federal Rules of Bankruptcy Procedure against any govern-

mental unit shall be consistent with the provisions and limitations of section 2412(d)(2)(A) of title 28.

(4) The enforcement of any such order, process, or judgment against any governmental unit shall be consistent with appropriate nonbankruptcy law applicable to such governmental unit and, in the case of a money judgment against the United States, shall be paid as if it is a judgment rendered by a district court of the United States.

(5) Nothing in this section shall create any substantive claim for relief or cause of action not otherwise existing under this title, the Federal Rules of Bankruptcy Procedure, or nonbankruptcy law.

(b) A governmental unit that has filed a proof of claim in the case is deemed to have waived sovereign immunity with respect to a claim against such governmental unit that is property of the estate and that arose out of the same transaction or occurrence out of which the claim of such governmental unit arose.

(c) Notwithstanding any assertion of sovereign immunity by a governmental unit, there shall be offset against a claim or interest of a governmental unit any claim against such governmental unit that is property of the estate.

§ 107. Public access to papers

(a) Except as provided in subsection (b) of this section, a paper filed in a case under this title and the dockets of a bankruptcy court are public records and open to examination by an entity at reasonable times without charge.

(b) On request of a party in interest, the bankruptcy court shall, and on the bankruptcy court's own motion, the bankruptcy court may—

(1) protect an entity with respect to a trade secret or confidential research, development, or commercial information; or

(2) protect a person with respect to scandalous or defamatory matter contained in a paper filed in a case under this title.

§ 108. Extension of time

(a) If applicable nonbankruptcy law, an order entered in a nonbankruptcy proceeding, or an agreement fixes a period within which the debtor may commence an action, and such period has not expired before the date of the filing of the petition, the trustee may commence such action only before the later of—

(1) the end of such period, including any suspension of such period occurring on or after the commencement of the case; or

(2) two years after the order for relief.

(b) Except as provided in subsection (a) of this section, if applicable nonbankruptcy law, an order entered in a nonbankruptcy proceeding, or an agreement fixes a period within which the debtor or an individual protected under section 1201 or 1301 of this title may file any pleading,

demand, notice, or proof of claim or loss, cure a default, or perform any other similar act, and such period has not expired before the date of the filing of the petition, the trustee may only file, cure, or perform, as the case may be, before the later of—

(1) the end of such period, including any suspension of such period occurring on or after the commencement of the case; or

(2) 60 days after the order for relief.

(c) Except as provided in section 524 of this title, if applicable nonbankruptcy law, an order entered in a nonbankruptcy proceeding, or an agreement fixes a period for commencing or continuing a civil action in a court other than a bankruptcy court on a claim against the debtor, or against an individual with respect to which such individual is protected under section 1201 or 1301 of this title, and such period has not expired before the date of the filing of the petition, then such period does not expire until the later of—

(1) the end of such period, including any suspension of such period occurring on or after the commencement of the case; or

(2) 30 days after notice of the termination or expiration of the stay under section 362, 922, 1201, or 1301 of this title, as the case may be, with respect to such claim.

§ 109. Who may be a debtor

(a) Notwithstanding any other provision of this section, only a person that resides or has a domicile, a place of business, or property in the United States, or a municipality, may be a debtor under this title.

(b) A person may be a debtor under chapter 7 of this title only if such person is not—

(1) a railroad;

(2) a domestic insurance company, bank, savings bank, cooperative bank, savings and loan association, building and loan association, homestead association, a small business investment company licensed by the Small Business Administration under subsection (c) or (d) of section 301 of the Small Business Investment Act of 1958, credit union, or industrial bank or similar institution which is an insured bank as defined in section 3(h) of the Federal Deposit Insurance Act; or

(3) a foreign insurance company, bank, savings bank, cooperative bank, savings and loan association, building and loan association, homestead association, or credit union, engaged in such business in the United States.

(c) An entity may be a debtor under chapter 9 of this title if and only if such entity—

(1) is a municipality;

(2) is specifically authorized, in its capacity as a municipality or by name, to be a debtor under such chapter by State law, or by a governmental officer or organiza-

tion empowered by State law to authorize such entity to be a debtor under such chapter;

(3) is insolvent;

(4) desires to effect a plan to adjust such debts; and

(5)(A) has obtained the agreement of creditors holding at least a majority in amount of the claims of each class that such entity intends to impair under a plan in a case under such chapter;

(B) has negotiated in good faith with creditors and has failed to obtain the agreement of creditors holding at least a majority in amount of the claims of each class that such entity intends to impair under a plan in a case under such chapter;

(C) is unable to negotiate with creditors because such negotiation is impracticable; or

(D) reasonably believes that a creditor may attempt to obtain a transfer that is avoidable under section 547 of this title.

(d) Only a person that may be a debtor under chapter 7 of this title, except a stockbroker or a commodity broker, and a railroad may be a debtor under chapter 11 of this title.

(e) Only an individual with regular income that owes, on the date of the filing of the petition, noncontingent, liquidated, unsecured debts of less than $250,000 and noncontingent, liquidated, secured debts of less than $750,000, or an individual with regular income and such individual's spouse, except a stockbroker or a commodity broker, that owe, on the date of the filing of the petition, noncontingent, liquidated, unsecured debts that aggregate less than $250,000 and noncontingent, liquidated, secured debts of less than $750,000 may be a debtor under chapter 13 of this title.

(f) Only a family farmer with regular annual income may be a debtor under chapter 12 of this title.

(g) Notwithstanding any other provision of this section, no individual or family farmer may be a debtor under this title who has been a debtor in a case pending under this title at any time in the preceding 180 days if—

(1) the case was dismissed by the court for willful failure of the debtor to abide by orders of the court, or to appear before the court in proper prosecution of the case; or

(2) the debtor requested and obtained the voluntary dismissal of the case following the filing of a request for relief from the automatic stay provided by section 362 of this title.

§ 110. Penalty for persons who negligently or fraudulently prepare bankruptcy petitions

(a) In this section—

(1) "bankruptcy petition preparer" means a person, other than an attorney or an employee of an attorney, who prepares for compensation a document for filing; and

(2) "document for filing" means a petition or any other document prepared for filing by a debtor in a United States bankruptcy court or a United States district court in connection with a case under this title.

(b)(1) A bankruptcy petition preparer who prepares a document for filing shall sign the document and print on the document the preparer's name and address.

(2) A bankruptcy petition preparer who fails to comply with paragraph (1) may be fined not more than $500 for each such failure unless the failure is due to reasonable cause.

(c)(1) A bankruptcy petition preparer who prepares a document for filing shall place on the document, after the preparer's signature, an identifying number that identifies individuals who prepared the document.

(2) For purposes of this section, the identifying number of a bankruptcy petition preparer shall be the Social Security account number of each individual who prepared the document or assisted in its preparation.

(3) A bankruptcy petition preparer who fails to comply with paragraph (1) may be fined not more than $500 for each such failure unless the failure is due to reasonable cause.

(d)(1) A bankruptcy petition preparer shall, not later than the time at which a document for filing is presented for the debtor's signature, furnish to the debtor a copy of the document.

(2) A bankruptcy petition preparer who fails to comply with paragraph (1) may be fined not more than $500 for each such failure unless the failure is due to reasonable cause.

(e)(1) A bankruptcy petition preparer shall not execute any document on behalf of the debtor.

(2) A bankruptcy petition preparer may be fined not more than $500 for each document executed in violation of paragraph (1).

(f)(1) A bankruptcy petition preparer shall not use the word "legal" or any similar term in any advertisements, or advertise under any category that includes the word "legal" or any similar term.

(2) A bankruptcy petition preparer shall be fined not more than $500 for each violation of paragraph (1).

(g)(1) A bankruptcy petition preparer shall not collect or receive any payment from the debtor or on behalf of the debtor for the court fees in connection with filing the petition.

(2) A bankruptcy petition preparer shall be fined not more than $500 for each violation of paragraph (1).

(h)(1) Within 10 days after the date of the filing of a petition, a bankruptcy petition preparer shall file a declaration under penalty of perjury disclosing any fee received from or on behalf of the debtor within 12 months immediately prior to the filing of the case, and any unpaid fee charged to the debtor.

(2) The court shall disallow and order the immediate turnover to the bankruptcy trustee of any fee referred to in paragraph (1) found to be in excess of the value of services

rendered for the documents prepared. An individual debtor may exempt any funds so recovered under section 522(b).

(3) The debtor, the trustee, a creditor, or the United States trustee may file a motion for an order under paragraph (2).

(4) A bankruptcy petition preparer shall be fined not more than $500 for each failure to comply with a court order to turn over funds within 30 days of service of such order.

(i)(1) If a bankruptcy case or related proceeding is dismissed because of the failure to file bankruptcy papers, including papers specified in section 521(1) of this title, the negligence or intentional disregard of this title or the Federal Rules of Bankruptcy Procedure by a bankruptcy petition preparer, or if a bankruptcy petition preparer violates this section or commits any fraudulent, unfair, or deceptive act, the bankruptcy court shall certify that fact to the district court, and the district court, on motion of the debtor, the trustee, or a creditor and after a hearing, shall order the bankruptcy petition preparer to pay to the debtor—

(A) the debtor's actual damages;

(B) the greater of—

(i) $2,000; or

(ii) twice the amount paid by the debtor to the bankruptcy petition preparer for the preparer's services; and

(C) reasonable attorneys' fees and costs in moving for damages under this subsection.

(2) If the trustee or creditor moves for damages on behalf of the debtor under this subsection, the bankruptcy petition preparer shall be ordered to pay the movant the additional amount of $1,000 plus reasonable attorneys' fees and costs incurred.

(j)(1) A debtor for whom a bankruptcy petition preparer has prepared a document for filing, the trustee, a creditor, or the United States trustee in the district in which the bankruptcy petition prepare resides, has conducted business, or the United States trustee in any other district in which the debtor resides may bring a civil action to enjoin a bankruptcy petition preparer from engaging in any conduct in violation of this section or from further acting as a bankruptcy petition preparer.

(2)(A) In an action under paragraph (1), if the court finds that—

(i) a bankruptcy petition preparer has—

(I) engaged in conduct in violation of this section or of any provision of this title a violation of which subjects a person to criminal penalty;

(II) misrepresented the preparer's experience or education as a bankruptcy petition preparer; or

(III) engaged in any other fraudulent, unfair, or deceptive conduct; and

(ii) injunctive relief is appropriate to prevent the recurrence of such conduct,

the court may enjoin the bankruptcy petition preparer from engaging in such conduct.

(B) If the court finds that a bankruptcy petition preparer has continually engaged in conduct described in subclause (I), (II), or (III) of clause (i) and that an injunction prohibiting such conduct would not be sufficient to prevent such person's interference with the proper administration of this title, or has not paid a penalty imposed under this section, the court may enjoin the person from acting as a bankruptcy petition preparer.

(3) The court shall award to a debtor, trustee, or creditor that brings a successful action under this subsection reasonable attorney's fees and costs of the action, to be paid by the bankruptcy petition preparer.

(k) Nothing in this section shall be construed to permit activities that are otherwise prohibited by law, including rules and laws that prohibit the unauthorized practice of law.

CHAPTER 3—CASE ADMINISTRATION

SUBCHAPTER I—COMMENCEMENT OF A CASE

SUBCHAPTER I—COMMENCEMENT OF A CASE

§ 301. Voluntary cases

A voluntary case under a chapter of this title is commenced by the filing with the bankruptcy court of a petition under such chapter by an entity that may be a debtor under such chapter. The commencement of a voluntary case under a chapter of this title constitutes an order for relief under such chapter.

§ 302. Joint cases

(a) A joint case under a chapter of this title is commenced by the filing with the bankruptcy court of a single petition under such chapter by an individual that may be a debtor under such chapter and such individual's spouse. The commencement of a joint base under a chapter of this title constitutes an order for relief under such chapter.

(b) After the commencement of a joint case, the court shall determine the extent, if any, to which the debtors' estates shall be consolidated.

§ 303. Involuntary cases

(a) An involuntary case may be commenced only under chapter 7 or 11 of this title, and only against a person, except a farmer, family farmer, or a corporation that is not a moneyed, business, or commercial corporation, that may be a debtor under the chapter under which such case is commenced.

(b) An involuntary case against a person is commenced by the filing with the bankruptcy court of a petition under chapter 7 or 11 of this title—

(1) by three or more entities, each of which is either a holder of a claim against such person that is not contingent as to liability or the subject of a bona fide dispute, or an indenture trustee representing such a holder, if such claims aggregate at least $10,000 more than the value of any lien on property of the debtor securing such claims held by the holders of such claims;

(2) if there are fewer than 12 such holders, excluding any employee or insider of such person and any transferee of a transfer that is voidable under section 544, 545, 547, 548, 549, or 724(a) of this title, by one or more of such holders that hold in the aggregate at least $10,000 of such claims;

(3) if such person is a partnership—

(A) by fewer than all of the general partners in such partnership; or

(B) if relief has been ordered under this title with respect to all of the general partners in such partnership, by a general partner in such partnership, the trustee of such a general partner, or a holder of a claim against such partnership; or

(4) by a foreign representative of the estate in a foreign proceeding concerning such a person.

(c) After the filing of a petition under this section but before the case is dismissed or relief is ordered, a creditor holding an unsecured claim that is not contingent, other than a creditor filing under subsection (b) of this section, may join in the petition with the same effect as if such joining creditor were a petitioning creditor under subsection (b) of this section.

(d) The debtor, or a general partner in a partnership debtor that did not join in the petition, may file an answer to a petition under this section.

(e) After notice and a hearing, and for cause, the court may require the petitioners under this section to file a bond to indemnify the debtor for such amounts as the court may later allow under subsection (i) of this section.

(f) Notwithstanding section 363 of this title, except to the extent that the court orders otherwise, and until an order for relief in the case, any business of the debtor may continue to operate, and the debtor may continue to use, acquire, or dispose of property as if an involuntary case concerning the debtor had not been commenced.

(g) At any time after the commencement of an involuntary case under chapter 7 of this title but before an order for relief in the case, the court, on request of a party in interest, after notice to the debtor and a hearing, and if necessary to preserve the property of the estate or to prevent loss to the estate, may order the United States trustee to appoint an interim trustee under section 701 of this title to take possession of the property of the estate and to operate any business of the debtor. Before an order for relief, the debtor may regain possession of property in the possession of a trustee ordered appointed under this subsection if the debtor files such bond as the court requires, conditioned on the debtor's accounting for and delivering to the trustee, if there is an order for relief in the case, such property, or the value, as of the date the debtor regains possession, of such property.

(h) If the petition is not timely controverted, the court shall order relief against the debtor in an involuntary case under the chapter under which the petition was filed. Otherwise, after trial, the court shall order relief against the debtor in an involuntary case under the chapter under which the petition was filed, only if—

(1) the debtor is generally not paying such debtor's

debts as such debts become due unless such debts are the subject of a bona fide dispute; or

(2) within 120 days before the date of the filing of the petition, a custodian, other than a trustee, receiver, or agent appointed or authorized to take charge of less than substantially all of the property of the debtor for the purpose of enforcing a lien against such property, was appointed or took possession.

(i) If the court dismisses a petition under this section other than on consent of all petitioners and the debtor, and if the debtor does not waive the right to judgment under this subsection, the court may grant judgment—

(1) against the petitioners and in favor of the debtor for—

(A) costs; or

(B) a reasonable attorney's fee; or

(2) against any petitioner that filed the petition in bad faith, for—

(A) any damages proximately caused by such filing; or

(B) punitive damages

(j) Only after notice to all creditors and a hearing may the court dismiss a petition filed under this section—

(1) on the motion of a petitioner;

(2) on consent of all petitioners and the debtor; or

(3) for want of prosecution.

(k) Notwithstanding subsection (a) of this section, an involuntary case may be commenced against a foreign bank that is not engaged in such business in the United States only under chapter 7 of this title and only if a foreign proceeding concerning such bank is pending.

§ 304. Cases ancillary to foreign proceedings

(a) A case ancillary to a foreign proceeding is commenced by the filing with the bankruptcy court of a petition under this section by a foreign representative.

(b) Subject to the provisions of subsection (c) of this section, if a party in interest does not timely controvert the petition, or after trial, the court may—

(1) enjoin the commencement or continuation of—

(A) any action against—

(i) a debtor with respect to property involved in such foreign proceeding; or

(ii) such property; or

(B) the enforcement of any judgment against the debtor with respect to such property, or any act or the commencement or continuation of any judicial proceeding to create or enforce a lien against the property of such estate;

(2) order turnover of the property of such estate, or the proceeds of such property, to such foreign representative; or

(3) order other appropriate relief.

(c) In determining whether to grant relief under subsection (b) of this section, the court shall be guided by what will best assure an economical and expeditious ad-ministration of such estate, consistent with—

(1) just treatment of all holders of claims against or interests in such estate;

(2) protection of claim holders in the United States against prejudice and inconvenience in the processing of claims in such foreign proceeding;

(3) prevention of preferential or fraudulent dispositions of property of such estate;

(4) distribution of proceeds of such estate substantially in accordance with the order prescribed by this title;

(5) comity; and

(6) if appropriate, the provision of an opportunity for a fresh start for the individual that such foreign proceeding concerns.

§ 305. Abstention

(a) The court, after notice and a hearing, may dismiss a case under this title, or may suspend all proceedings in a case under this title, at any time if—

(1) the interests of creditors and the debtor would be better served by such dismissal or suspension; or

(2)(A) there is pending a foreign proceeding; and

(B) the factors specified in section 304(c) of this title warrant such dismissal or suspension.

(b) A foreign representative may seek dismissal or suspension under subsection (a)(2) of this section.

(c) An order under subsection (a) of this section dismissing a case or suspending all proceedings in a case, or a decision not so to dismiss or suspend, is not reviewable by appeal or otherwise by the court of appeals under section 158(d), 1291, or 1292 of title 28 or by the Supreme Court of the United States under section 1254 of title 28.

§ 306. Limited appearance

An appearance in a bankruptcy court by a foreign representative in connection with a petition or request under section 303, 304, or 305 of this title does not submit such foreign representative to the jurisdiction of any court in the United States for any other purpose, but the bankruptcy court may condition any order under section 303, 304, or 305 of this title on compliance by such foreign representative with the orders of such bankruptcy court.

§ 307. United States trustee

The United States trustee may raise and may appear and be heard on any issue in any case proceeding under this title but may not file a plan pursuant to section 1121(c) of this title.

SUBCHAPTER II—OFFICERS

§ 321. Eligibility to serve as trustee

(a) A person may serve as trustee in a case under this title only if such person is—

(1) an individual that is competent to perform the duties of trustee and, in a case under chapter 7, 12, or 13 of this title, resides or has an office in the judicial district within which the case is pending, or in any judicial district adjacent to such district; or

(2) a corporation authorized by such corporation's charter or bylaws to act as trustee, and, in a case under chapter 7, 12, or 13 of this title, having an office in at least one of such districts.

(b) A person that has served as an examiner in the case may not serve as trustee in the case.

(c) The United States trustee for the judicial district in which the case is pending is eligible to serve as trustee in the case if necessary.

§ 322. Qualification of trustee

(a) Except as provided in subsection (b)(1), a person selected under section 701, 702, 703, 1104, 1163, 1202, or 1302 of this title to serve as trustee in a case under this title qualifies if before five days after such selection, and before beginning official duties, such person has filed with the court a bond in favor of the United States conditioned on the faithful performance of such official duties.

(b)(1) The United States trustee qualifies wherever such trustee serves as trustee in a case under this title.

(2) The United States trustee shall determine—

(A) the amount of a bond required to be filed under subsection (a) of this section; and

(B) the sufficiency of the surety on such bond.

(c) A trustee is not liable personally or on such trustee's bond in favor of the United States for any penalty or forfeiture incurred by the debtor.

(d) A proceeding on a trustee's bond may not be commenced after two years after the date on which such trustee was discharged.

§ 323. Role and capacity of trustee

(a) The trustee in a case under this title is the representative of the estate.

(b) The trustee in a case under this title has capacity to sue and be sued.

§ 324. Removal of trustee or examiner

(a) The court, after notice and a hearing, may remove a trustee, other than the United States trustee, or an examiner, for cause.

(b) Whenever the court removes a trustee or examiner under subsection (a) in a case under this title, such trustee or examiner shall thereby be removed in all other cases under this title in which such trustee or examiner is then serving unless the court orders otherwise.

§ 325. Effect of vacancy

A vacancy in the office of trustee during a case does not abate any pending action or proceeding, and the suc-cessor trustee shall be substituted as a party in such action or proceeding.

§ 326. Limitation on compensation of trustee

(a) In a case under chapter 7 or 11, the court may allow reasonable compensation under section 330 of this title of the trustee for the trustee's services, payable after the trustee renders such services, not to exceed 25 percent on the first $5,000 or less, 10 percent on any amount in excess of $5,000 but not in excess of $50,000, 5 percent on any amount in excess of $50,000 but not in excess of $1,000,000, and reasonable compensation not to exceed 3 percent of such moneys in excess of $1,000,000 upon all moneys disbursed or turned over in the case by the trustee to parties in interest, excluding the debtor, but including holders of secured claims.

(b) In a case under chapter 12 or 13 of this title, the court may not allow compensation for services or reimbursement of expenses of the United States trustee or of a standing trustee appointed under section 586(b) of title 28, but may allow reasonable compensation under section 330 of this title of a trustee appointed under section 1202(a) or 1302(a) of this title for the trustee's services, payable after the trustee renders such services, not to exceed five percent upon all payments under the plan.

(c) If more than one person serves as trustee in the case, the aggregate compensation of such persons for such service may not exceed the maximum compensation prescribed for a single trustee by subsection (a) or (b) of this section, as the case may be.

(d) The court may deny allowance of compensation for services or reimbursement of expenses of the trustee if the trustee failed to make diligent inquiry into facts that would permit denial of allowance under section 328(c) or this title, or, with knowledge of such facts, employed a professional person under section 327 of this title.

§ 327. Employment of professional persons

(a) Except as otherwise provided in this section, the trustee, with the court's approval, may employ one or more attorneys, accountants, appraisers, auctioneers, or other professional persons, that do not hold or represent an interest adverse to the estate, and that are disinterested persons, to represent or assist the trustee in carrying out the trustee's duties under this title.

(b) If the trustee is authorized to operate the business of the debtor under section 721, 1202 or 1108 of this title, and if the debtor has regularly employed attorneys, accountants, or other professional persons on salary, the trustee may retain or replace such professional persons if necessary in the operation of such business.

(c) In a case under chapter 7, 11 or 12 of this title, a person is not disqualified for employment under this section solely because of such person's employment by or representation of a creditor, unless there is objection by another

creditor or the United States trustee, in which case the court shall disapprove such employment if there is an actual conflict of interest.

(d) The court may authorize the trustee to act as attorney or accountant for the estate if such authorization is in the best interest of the estate.

(e) The trustee, with the court's approval, may employ, for a specified special purpose, other than to represent the trustee in conducting the case, an attorney that has represented the debtor, if in the best interest of the estate, and if such attorney does not represent or hold any interest adverse to the debtor or to the estate with respect to the matter on which such attorney is to be employed.

(f) The trustee may not employ a person that has served as an examiner in the case.

§ 328. Limitation on compensation of professional persons

(a) The trustee, or a committee appointed under section 1102 of this title, with the court's approval, may employ or authorize the employment of a professional person under section 327 or 1103 of this title, as the case may be, on any reasonable terms and conditions of employment, including on a retainer, on an hourly basis, or on a contingent fee basis. Notwithstanding such terms and conditions, the court may allow compensation different from the compensation provided under such terms and conditions after the conclusion of such employment, if such terms and conditions prove to have been improvident in light of developments not capable of being anticipated at the time of the fixing of such terms and conditions.

(b) If the court has authorized a trustee to serve as an attorney or accountant for the estate under section 327(d) of this title, the court may allow compensation for the trustee's services as such attorney or accountant only to the extent that the trustee performed services as attorney or accountant for the estate and not for performance of any of the trustee's duties that are generally performed by a trustee without the assistance of an attorney or accountant for the estate.

(c) Except as provided in section 327(c), 327(e), or 1107(b) of this title, the court may deny allowance of compensation for services and reimbursement of expenses of a professional person employed under section 327 or 1103 of this title if, at any time during such professional person's employment under section 327 or 1103 of this title, such professional person is not a disinterested person, or represents or holds an interest adverse to the interest of the estate with respect to the matter on which such professional person is employed.

§ 329. Debtor's transactions with attorneys

(a) Any attorney representing a debtor in a case under this title, or in connection with such a case, whether or not such attorney applies for compensation under this title, shall file with the court a statement of the compensation paid or agreed to be paid, if such payment or agreement was made after one year before the date of the filing of the petition, for services rendered or to be rendered in contemplation of or in connection with the case by such attorney, and the source of such compensation.

(b) If such compensation exceeds the reasonable value of any such services, the court may cancel any such agreement, or order the return of any such payment, to the extent excessive, to—

(1) the estate, if the property transferred—

(A) would have been property of the estate; or

(B) was to be paid by or on behalf of the debtor under a plan under chapter 11, 12 or 13 of this title; or

(2) the entity that made such payment.

§ 330. Compensation of officers

(a)(1) After notice to the parties in interest and the United States Trustee and a hearing, and subject to sections 326, 328, and 329, the court may award to a trustee, an examiner, a professional person employed under section 327 or 1103—

(A) reasonable compensation for actual, necessary services rendered by the trustee, examiner, professional person, or attorney and by any paraprofessional person employed by any such person; and

(B) reimbursement for actual, necessary expenses.

(2) The court may, on its own motion or on the motion of the United States Trustee, the United States Trustee for the District or Region, the trustee for the estate, or any other party in interest, award compensation that is less than the amount of compensation that is requested.

(3)(A) In determining the amount of reasonable compensation to be awarded, the court shall consider the nature, the extent, and the value of such services, taking into account all relevant factors, including—

(A) the time spent on such services;

(B) the rates charged for such services;

(C) whether the services were necessary to the administration of, or beneficial at the time at which the service was rendered toward the completion of, a case under this title;

(D) whether the services were performed within a reasonable amount of time commensurate with the complexity, importance, and nature of the problem, issue, or task addressed; and

(E) whether the compensation is reasonable, based on the customary compensation charged by comparably skilled practitioners in cases other than cases under this title.

(4)(A) Except as provided in subparagraph (B), the court shall not allow compensation for—

(i) unnecessary duplication of services; or

(ii) services that were not—

(I) reasonably likely to benefit the debtor's estate; or

(II) necessary to the administration of the case.

(B) In a chapter 12 or chapter 13 case in which the debtor is an individual, the court may allow reasonable compensation to the debtor's attorney for representing the interests of the debtor in connection with the bankruptcy case based on a consideration of the benefit and necessity of such services to the debtor and the other factors set forth in this section.

(5) The court shall reduce the amount of compensation awarded under this section by the amount of any interim compensation awarded under section 331, and, if the amount of such interim compensation exceeds the amount of compensation awarded under this section, may order the return of the excess to the estate.

(6) Any compensation awarded for the preparation of a fee application shall be based on the level and skill reasonably required to prepare the application.

(b)(1) There shall be paid from the filing fee in a case under chapter 7 of this title $45 to the trustee serving in such case, after such trustee's services are rendered.

(2) The Judicial Conference of the United States—

(A) shall prescribe additional fees of the same kind as prescribed under section 1914(b) of title 28; and

(B) may prescribe notice of appearance fees and fees charged against distributions in cases under this title;

to pay $15 to trustees serving in cases after such trustees' services are rendered. Beginning 1 year after the date of the enactment of the Bankruptcy Reform Act of 1994, such $15 shall be paid in addition to the amount paid under paragraph (1).

(c) Unless the court orders otherwise, in a case under chapter 12 or 13 of this title the compensation paid to the trustee serving in the case shall not be less than $5 per month from any distribution under the plan during the administration of the plan.

(d) In a case in which the United States trustee serves as trustee, the compensation of the trustee under this section shall be paid to the clerk of the bankruptcy court and deposited by the clerk into the United States Trustee System Fund established by section 589a of title 28.

§ 331. Interim compensation

A trustee, an examiner, a debtor's attorney, or any professional person employed under section 327 or 1103 of this title may apply to the court not more than once every 120 days after an order for relief in a case under this title, or more often if the court permits, for such compensation for services rendered before the date of such an application or reimbursement for expenses incurred before such date as is provided under section 330 of this title. After notice and a hearing, the court may allow and disburse to such applicant such compensation or reimbursement.

SUBCHAPTER III—ADMINISTRATION

§ 341. Meetings of creditors and equity security holders

(a) Within a reasonable time after the order for relief in a case under this title, the United States trustee shall convene and preside at a meeting of creditors.

(b) The United States trustee may convene order a meeting of any equity security holders.

(c) The court may not preside at, and may not attend, any meeting under this section including any final meeting of creditors.

(d) Prior to the conclusion of the meeting of creditors or equity security holders, the trustee shall orally examine the debtor to ensure that the debtor in a case under chapter 7 of this title is aware of—

(1) the potential consequences of seeking a discharge in bankruptcy, including the effects on credit history;

(2) the debtor's ability to file a petition under a different chapter of this title;

(3) the effect of receiving a discharge of debts under this title; and

(4) the effect of reaffirming a debt, including the debtor's knowledge of the provisions of section 524(d) of this title.

§ 342. Notice

(a) There shall be given such notice as is appropriate, including notice to any holder of a community claim, of an order for relief in a case under this title.

(b) Prior to the commencement of a case under this title by an individual whose debts are primarily consumer debts, the clerk shall give written notice to such individual that indicates each chapter of this title under which such individual may proceed.

(c) If notice is required to be given by the debtor to a creditor under this title, any rule, any applicable law, or any order of the court, such notice shall contain the name, address, and taxpayer identification number of the debtor, but the failure of such notice to contain such information shall not invalidate the legal effect of such notice.

§ 343. Examination of the debtor

The debtor shall appear and submit to examination under oath at the meeting of creditors under section 341(a) of this title. Creditors, any indenture trustee, any trustee or examiner in the case, or the United States trustee may examine the debtor. The United States trustee may administer the oath required under this section.

§ 344. Self-incrimination; immunity

Immunity for persons required to submit to examination, to testify, or to provide information in a case under this title may be granted under part V of title 18.

§ 345. Money of estates

(a) A trustee in a case under this title may make such deposit or investment of the money of the estate for which such trustee serves as will yield the maximum reasonable net return on such money, taking into account the safety of such deposit or investment.

(b) Except with respect to a deposit or investment that is insured or guaranteed by the United States or by a department, agency, or instrumentality of the United States or backed by the full faith and credit of the United States, the trustee shall require from an entity with which such money is deposited or invested—

(1) a bond—

(A) in favor of the United States;

(B) secured by the undertaking of a corporate surety approved by the United States trustee for the district in which the case is pending; and

(C) conditioned on—

(i) a proper accounting for all money so deposited or invested and for any return on such money;

(ii) prompt repayment of such money and return; and

(iii) faithful performance of duties as a depository; or

(2) the deposit of securities of the kind specified in section 9303 of title 31;

unless the court for cause orders otherwise.

(c) An entity with which such moneys are deposited or invested is authorized to deposit or invest such moneys as may be required under this section.

§ 346. Special tax provisions

(a) Except to the extent otherwise provided in this section, subsections (b), (c), (d), (e), (g), (h), (i), and (j) of this section apply notwithstanding any State or local law imposing a tax, but subject to the Internal Revenue Code of 1986.

(b)(1) In a case under chapter 7, 12 or 11 of this title concerning an individual, any income of the estate may be taxed under a State or local law imposing a tax on or measured by income only to the estate, and may not be taxed to such individual. Except as provided in section 728 of this title, if such individual is a partner in a partnership, any gain or loss resulting from a distribution of property from such partnership, or any distributive share of income, gain, loss, deduction, or credit of such individual that is distributed, or considered distributed, from such partnership, after the commencement of the case is gain, loss, income, deduction, or credit, as the case may be, of the estate.

(2) Except as otherwise provided in this section and in section 728 of this title, any income of the estate in such a case, and any State or local tax on or measured by such income, shall be computed in the same manner as the income and the tax of an estate.

(3) The estate in such a case shall use the same accounting method as the debtor used immediately before the commencement of the case.

(c)(1) The commencement of a case under this title concerning a corporation or a partnership does not effect a change in the status of such corporation or partnership for the purposes of any State or local law imposing a tax on or measured by income. Except as otherwise provided in this section and in section 728 of this title, any income of the estate in such case may be taxed only as though such case had not been commenced.

(2) In such a case, except as provided in section 728 of this title, the trustee shall make any tax return otherwise required by State or local law to be filed by or on behalf of such corporation or partnership in the same manner and form as such corporation or partnership, as the case may be, is required to make such return.

(d) In a case under chapter 13 of this title, any income of the estate or the debtor may be taxed under a State or local law imposing a tax on or measured by income only to the debtor, and may not be taxed to the estate.

(e) A claim allowed under section 502(f) or 503 of this title, other than a claim for a tax that is not otherwise deductible or a capital expenditure that is not otherwise deductible, is deductible by the entity to which income of the estate is taxed unless such claim was deducted by another entity, and a deduction for such a claim is deemed to be a deduction attributable to a business.

(f) The trustee shall withhold from any payment of claims for wages, salaries, commissions, dividends, interest, or other payments, or collect, any amount required to be withheld or collected under applicable State or local tax law, and shall pay such withheld or collected amount to the appropriate governmental unit at the time and in the manner required by such tax law, and with the same priority as the claim from which such amount was withheld was paid.

(g)(1) Neither gain nor loss shall be recognized on a transfer—

(A) by operation of law, of property to the estate;

(B) other than a sale, of property from the estate to the debtor; or

(C) in a case under chapter 11 or 12 of this title concerning a corporation, of property from the estate to a corporation that is an affiliate participating in a joint plan with the debtor, or that is a successor to the debtor under the plan, except that gain or loss may be recognized to the same extent that such transfer results in

the recognition of gain or loss under section 371 of the Internal Revenue Code of 1986.

(2) The transferee of a transfer of a kind specified in this subsection shall take the property transferred with the same character, and with the transferor's basis, as adjusted under subsection (j)(5) of this section, and holding period.

(h) Notwithstanding sections 728(a) and 1146(a) of this title, for the purpose of determining the number of taxable periods during which the debtor or the estate may use a loss carryover or a loss carryback, the taxable period of the debtor during which the case is commenced is deemed not to have been terminated by such commencement.

(i)(1) In a case under chapter 7, 12, or 11 of this title concerning an individual, the estate shall succeed to the debtor's tax attributes, including—

   (A) any investment credit carryover;

   (B) any recovery exclusion;

   (C) any loss carryover;

   (D) any foreign tax credit carryover;

   (E) any capital loss carryover; and

   (F) any claim of right.

(2) After such a case is closed or dismissed, the debtor shall succeed to any tax attribute to which the estate succeeded under paragraph (1) of this subsection but that was not utilized by the estate. The debtor may utilize such tax attributes as though any applicable time limitations on such utilization by the debtor were suspended during the time during which the case was pending.

(3) In such a case, the estate may carry back any loss of the estate to a taxable period of the debtor that ended before the order for relief under such chapter the same as the debtor could have carried back such loss had the debtor incurred such loss and the case under this title had not been commenced, but the debtor may not carry back any loss of the debtor from a taxable period that ends after such order to any taxable period of the debtor that ended before such order until after the case is closed.

(j)(1) Except as otherwise provided in this subsection, income is not realized by the estate, the debtor, or a successor to the debtor by reason of forgiveness or discharge of indebtedness in a case under this title.

(2) For the purposes of any State or local law imposing a tax on or measured by income, a deduction with respect to a liability may not be allowed for any taxable period during or after which such liability is forgiven or discharged under this title. In this paragraph, "a deduction with respect to a liability" includes a capital loss incurred on the disposition of a capital asset with respect to a liability that was incurred in connection with the acquisition of such asset.

(3) Except as provided in paragraph (4) of this subsection, for the purpose of any State or local law imposing a tax on or measured by income, any net operating loss of an individual or corporate debtor, including a net operating loss carryover to such debtor, shall be reduced by the amount of indebtedness forgiven or discharged in a case under this title, except to the extent that such forgiveness or discharge resulted in a disallowance under paragraph (2) of this subsection.

(4) A reduction of a net operating loss or a net operating loss carryover under paragraph (3) of this subsection or of basis under paragraph (5) of this subsection is not required to the extent that the indebtedness of an individual or corporate debtor forgiven or discharged—

   (A) consisted of items of a deductible nature that were not deducted by such debtor; or

   (B) resulted in an expired net operating loss carryover or other deduction that—

      (i) did not offset income for any taxable period; and

      (ii) did not contribute to a net operating loss in or a net operating loss carryover to the taxable period during or after which such indebtedness was discharged.

(5) For the purposes of a State or local law imposing a tax on or measured by income, the basis of the debtor's property or of property transferred to an entity required to use the debtor's basis in whole or in part shall be reduced by the lesser of—

   (A)(i) the amount by which the indebtedness of the debtor has been forgiven or discharged in a case under this title; minus

      (ii) the total amount of adjustments made under paragraphs (2) and (3) of this subsection; and

   (B) the amount by which the total basis of the debtor's assets that were property of the estate before such forgiveness or discharge exceeds that debtor's total liabilities that were liabilities both before and after such forgiveness or discharge.

(6) Notwithstanding paragraph (5) of this subsection, basis is not required to be reduced to the extent that the debtor elects to treat as taxable income, of the taxable period in which indebtedness is forgiven or discharged, the amount of indebtedness forgiven or discharged that otherwise would be applied in reduction of basis under paragraph (5) of this subsection.

(7) For the purposes of this subsection, indebtedness with respect to which an equity security, other than an interest of a limited partner in a limited partnership, is issued to the creditor to whom such indebtedness was owed, or that is forgiven as a contribution to capital by an equity security holder other than a limited partner in the debtor, is not forgiven or discharged in a case under this title—

   (A) to any extent that such indebtedness did not consist of items of a deductible nature; or

   (B) if the issuance of such equity security has the same consequences under a law imposing a tax on or measured by income to such creditor as a payment in cash to such creditor in an amount equal to the fair market value of

such equity security, then to the lesser of—

    (i) the extent that such issuance has the same such consequences; and

    (ii) the extent of such fair market value.

§ 347. Unclaimed property

(a) Ninety days after the final distribution under section 726, 1226, or 1326 of this title in a case under chapter 7, 12, or 13 of this title, as the case maybe, the trustee shall stop payment on any check remaining unpaid, and any remaining property of the estate shall be paid into the court and disposed of under chapter 129 of title 28.

(b) Any security, money, or other property remaining unclaimed at the expiration of the time allowed in a case under chapter 9, 11, or 12 of this title for the presentation of a security or the performance of any other act as a condition to participation in the distribution under any plan confirmed under section 943(b), 1129, 1173, or 1225 of this title, as the case may be, becomes the property of the debtor or of the entity acquiring the assets of the debtor under the plan, as the case may be.

§ 348. Effect of conversion

(a) Conversion of a case from a case under one chapter of this title to a case under another chapter of this title constitutes an order for relief under the chapter to which the case is converted, but, except as provided in subsections (b) and (c) of this section, does not effect a change in the date of the filing of the petition, the commencement of the case, or the order for relief.

(b) Unless the court for cause orders otherwise, in sections 701(a), 727(a)(10), 727(b), 728(a), 728(b), 1102(a), 1110(a)(1), 1121(b), 1121(c), 1141(d)(4), 1146(a), 1146(b), 1201(a), 1221, 1228(a), 1301(a), and 1305(a), of this title, "the order for relief under this chapter" in a chapter to which a case has been converted under section 706, 1112, 1208, or 1307 of this title means the conversion of such case to such chapter.

(c) Sections 342 and 365(d) of this title apply in a case that has been converted under section 706, 1112, 1208, or 1307 of this title, as if the conversion order were the order for relief.

(d) A claim against the estate or the debtor that arises after the order for relief but before conversion in a case that is converted under section 1112, 1208, or 1307 of this title, other than a claim specified in section 503(b) of this title, shall be treated for all purposes as if such claim had arisen immediately before the date of the filing of the petition.

(e) Conversion of a case under section 706, 1112, 1208, or 1307 of this title terminates the service of any trustee or examiner that is serving in the case before such conversion.

(f)(1) Except as provided in paragraph (2), when a case under chapter 13 of this title is converted to a case under another chapter under this title—

    (A) property of the estate in the converted case shall consist of property of the estate, as of the date of filing of the petition, that remains in the possession of or is under the control of the debtor on the date of conversion; and

    (B) valuations of property and of allowed secured claims in the chapter 13 case shall apply in the converted case, with allowed secured claims reduced to the extent that they have been paid in accordance with the chapter 13 plan.

(2) If the debtor converts a case under chapter 13 of this title to a case under another chapter under this title in bad faith, the property in the converted case shall consist of the property of the estate as of the date of conversion.

§ 349. Effect of dismissal

(a) Unless the court, for cause, orders otherwise, the dismissal of a case under this title does not bar the discharge, in a later case under this title, of debts that were dischargeable in the case dismissed; nor does the dismissal of a case under this title prejudice the debtor with regard to the filing of a subsequent petition under this title, except as provided in section 109(g) of this title.

(b) Unless the court, for cause, orders otherwise, a dismissal of a case other than under section 742 of this title—

    (1) reinstates—

        (A) any proceeding or custodianship superseded under section 543 of this title;

        (B) any transfer avoided under section 522, 544, 545, 547, 548, 549, or 724(a) of this title, or preserved under section 510(c)(2), 522(i)(2), or 551 of this title; and

        (C) any lien voided under section 506(d) of this title;

    (2) vacates any order, judgment, or transfer ordered, under section 522(i)(1), 542, 550, or 553 of this title; and

    (3) revests the property of the estate in the entity in which such property was vested immediately before the commencement of the case under this title.

§ 350. Closing and reopening cases

(a) After an estate is fully administered and the court has discharged the trustee, the court shall close the case.

(b) A case may be reopened in the court in which such case was closed to administer assets, to accord relief to the debtor, or for other cause.

SUBCHAPTER IV—ADMINISTRATIVE POWERS

§ 361. Adequate protection

When adequate protection is required under section 362, 363, or 364 of this title of an interest of an entity in

property, such adequate protection may be provided by—

(1) requiring the trustee to make a cash payment or periodic case payments to such entity, to the extent that the stay under section 362 of this title, use, sale, or lease under section 363 of this title, or any grant of a lien under section 364 of this title results in a decrease in the value of such entity's interest in such property;

(2) providing to such entity an additional or replacement lien to the extent that such stay, use, sale, lease, or grant results in a decrease in the value of such entity's interest in such property; or

(3) granting such other relief, other than entitling such entity to compensation allowable under section 503(b)(1) of this title as an administrative expense, as will result in the realization by such entity of the indubitable equivalent of such entity's interest in such property.

§ 362. Automatic stay

(a) Except as provided in subsection(b) of this section, a petition filed under section 301, 302, or 303 of this title, or an application filed under section 5(a)(3) of the Securities Investor Protection Act of 1970, operates as a stay, applicable to all entities, of—

(1) the commencement or continuation, including the issuance or employment of process, of a judicial, administrative, or other action or proceeding against the debtor that was or could have been commenced before the commencement of the case under this title, or to recover a claim against the debtor that arose before the commencement of the case under this title;

(2) the enforcement, against the debtor or against property of the estate, of a judgment obtained before the commencement of the case under this title;

(3) any act to obtain possession of property of the estate or of property from the estate or to exercise control over property of the estate;

(4) any act to create, perfect, or enforce any lien against property of the estate;

(5) any act to create, perfect, or enforce against property of the debtor any lien to the extent that such lien secures a claim that arose before the commencement of the case under this title;

(6) any act to collect, assess, or recover a claim against the debtor that arose before the commencement of the case under this title;

(7) the setoff of any debt owing to the debtor that arose before the commencement of the case under this title against any claim against the debtor; and

(8) the commencement or continuation of a proceeding before the United States Tax Court concerning the debtor.

(b) The filing of a petition under section 301, 302, or 303 of this title, or of an application under section 5(a)(3) of the Securities Investor Protection Act of 1970, does not operate as a stay—

(1) under subsection (a) of this section, of the commencement or continuation of a criminal action or proceeding against the debtor;

(2) under subsection (a) of this section—

(A) of the commencement or continuation of an action or proceeding for—

(i) the establishment of paternity; or

(ii) the establishment or modification of an order for alimony, maintenance, or support; or

(B) of the collection of alimony, maintenance, or support from property that is not property of the estate;

(3) under subsection (a) of this section, of any act to perfect, or to maintain or continue the perfection of, an interest in property to the extent that the trustee's rights and powers are subject to such perfection under section 546(b) of this title or to the extent that such act is accomplished within the period provided under section 547(e)(2)(A) of this title;

(4) under subsection (a)(1) of this section, of the commencement or continuation of an action or proceeding by a governmental unit to enforce such governmental unit's police or regulatory power;

(5) under subsection (a)(2) of this section, of the enforcement of a judgment, other than a money judgment, obtained in an action or proceeding by a governmental unit to enforce such governmental unit's police or regulatory power;

(6) under subsection (a) of this section, of the setoff by a commodity broker, forward contract merchant, stockbroker, financial institutions, or securities clearing agency of any mutual debt and claim under or in connection with commodity contracts, as defined in section 761 of this title, forward contracts, or securities contracts, as defined in section 741 of this title, that constitutes the setoff of a claim against the debtor for a margin payment, as defined in section 101, 741, or 761 of this title, or settlement payment, as defined in section 101 or 741 of this title, arising out of commodity contracts, forward contracts, or securities contracts against cash, securities, or other property held by or due from such commodity broker, forward contract merchant, stockbroker, financial institutions, or securities clearing agency to margin, guarantee, secure, or settle commodity contracts, forward contracts, or securities contracts;

(7) under subsection (a) of this section, of the setoff by a repo participant, of any mutual debt and claim under or in connection with repurchase agreements that constitutes the setoff of a claim against the debtor for a margin payment, as defined in section 741 or 761 of this title, or settlement payment, as defined in section 741 of this title, arising out of repurchase agreements against cash, securities, or other property held by or due from such repo participant to margin, guarantee, secure or settle repurchase agreements;

(8) under subsection (a) of this section, of the com-

mencement of any action by the Secretary of Housing and Urban Development to foreclose a mortgage or deed of trust in any case in which the mortgage or deed of trust held by the Secretary is insured or was formerly insured under the National Housing Act and covers property, or combinations of property, consisting of five or more living units;

(9) under subsection (a), of—

(A) an audit by a governmental unit to determine tax liability;

(B) the issuance to the debtor by a governmental unit of a notice of tax deficiency;

(C) a demand for tax returns; or

(D) the making of an assessment for any tax and issuance of a notice and demand for payment of such an assessment (but any tax lien that would otherwise attach to property of the estate by reason of such an assessment shall not take effect unless such tax is a debt of the debtor that will not be discharged in the case and such property or its proceeds are transferred out of the estate to, or otherwise revested in, the debtor).

(10) under subsection (a) of this section, of any act by a lessor to the debtor under a lease of nonresidential real property that has terminated by the expiration of the stated term of the lease before the commencement of or during a case under this title to obtain possession of such property;

(11) under subsection (a) of this section, of the presentment of a negotiable instrument and the giving of notice of and protesting dishonor of such an instrument;

(12) under subsection (a) of this section, after the date which is 90 days after the filing of such petition, of the commencement or continuation, and conclusion to the entry of final judgment, of an action which involves a debtor subject to reorganization pursuant to chapter 11 of this title and which was brought by the Secretary of Transportation under section 31325 of title 46 (including distribution of any proceeds of sale) to foreclose a preferred ship or fleet mortgage, or a security interest in or relating to a vessel or vessel under construction, held by the Secretary of Transportation under section 207 or title XI of the Merchant Marine Act, 1936, or under applicable State law;

(13) under subsection (a) of this section, after the date which is 90 days after the filing of such petition, of the commencement of continuation, and conclusion to the entry of final judgment, of an action which involves a debtor subject to reorganization pursuant to chapter 11 of this title and which was brought by the Secretary of Commerce under section 31325 of title 46 (including distribution of any proceeds of sale) to foreclose a preferred ship or fleet mortgage in a vessel or a mortgage, deed of trust, or other security interest in a fishing facility held by the Secretary of Commerce un-

der section 207 or title XI of the Merchant Marine Act, 1936;

(14) under subsection (a) of this section, of any action by an accrediting agency regarding the accreditation status of the debtor as an educational institution;

(15) under subsection (a) of this section, of any action by a State licensing body regarding the licensure of the debtor as an educational institution;

(16) under subsection (a) of this section, of any action by a guaranty agency, as defined in section 435(j) of the Higher Education Act of 1965 or the Secretary of Education regarding the eligibility of the debtor to participate in programs authorized under such Act;

(17) under subsection (a) of this section, of the setoff by a swap participant, of any mutual debt and claim under or in connection with any swap agreement that constitutes the setoff of a claim against the debtor for any payment due from the debtor under or in connection with any swap agreement against any payment due to the debtor from the swap participant under or in connection with any swap agreement or against cash, securities, or other property of the debtor held by or due from such swap participant to guarantee, secure or settle any swap agreement; or

(18) under subsection (a) of the creation or perfection of a statutory lien for an ad valorem property tax imposed by the District of Columbia, or a political subdivision of a State, if such tax comes due after the filing of the petition.

The provisions of paragraphs (12) and (13) of this subsection shall apply with respect to any such petition filed on or before December 31, 1989.

(c) Except as provided in subsections (d), (e), and (f) of this section—

(1) the stay of an act against property of the estate under subsection (a) of this section continues until such property is no longer property of the estate; and

(2) the stay of any other act under subsection (a) of this section continues until the earliest of–

(A) the time the case is closed;

(B) the time the case is dismissed; or

(C) if the case is a case under chapter 7 of this title concerning an individual or a case under chapter 9, 11, 12, or 13 of this title, the time a discharge is granted or denied.

(d) On request of a party in interest and after notice and a hearing, the court shall grant relief from the stay provided under subsection (a) of this section, such as by terminating, annulling, modifying, or conditioning such stay—

(1) for cause, including the lack of adequate protection of an interest in property of such party in interest;

(2) with respect to a stay of an act against property under subsection (a) of this section, if—

(A) the debtor does not have an equity in such

property; and

　(B) such property is not necessary to an effective reorganization; or

(3) with respect to a stay of an act against single asset real estate under subsection (a), by a creditor whose claim is secured by an interest in such real estate, unless, not later than the date that is 90 days after the entry of the order of relief (or such later date as the court may determine for cause by order entered within that 90-day period)—

　(A) the debtor has filed a plan of reorganization that has a reasonable possibility of being confirmed within a reasonable time; or

　(B) the debtor has commenced monthly payments to each creditor whose claim is secured by such real estate(other than a claim secured by a judgment lien or by an unmatured statutory lien), which payments are in an amount equal to interest at a current fair market rate on the value of the creditor's interest in the real estate.

(e) Thirty days after a request under subsection (d) of this section for relief from the stay of any act against property of the estate under subsection (a) of this section, such stay is terminated with respect to the party in interest making such request, unless the court, after notice and a hearing, orders such stay continued in effect pending the conclusion of, or as a result of, a final hearing and determination under subsection (d) of this section. A hearing under this subsection may be a preliminary hearing, or may be consolidated with the final hearing under subsection (d) of this section. The court shall order such stay continued in effect pending the conclusion of the final hearing under subsection (d) of this section if there is a reasonable likelihood that the party opposing relief from such stay will prevail at the conclusion of such final hearing. If the hearing under this subsection is a preliminary hearing, then such final hearing shall be concluded not later than thirty days after the conclusion of such preliminary hearing, unless the 30-day period is extended with the consent of the parties in interest or for a specific time which the court finds is required by compelling circumstances.

(f) Upon request of a party in interest, the court, with or without a hearing, shall grant such relief from the stay provided under subsection (a) of this section as is necessary to prevent irreparable damage to the interest of an entity in property, if such interest will suffer such damage before there is an opportunity for notice and a hearing under subsection (d) or (e) of this section.

(g) In any hearing under subsection (d) or (e) of this section concerning relief from the stay of any act under subsection (a) of this section—

　(1) the party requesting such relief has the burden of proof on the issue of the debtor's equity in property; and

　(2) the party opposing such relief has the burden of proof on all other issues.

(h) An individual injured by any willful violation of a stay provided by this section shall recover actual damages, including costs and attorneys' fees, and, in appropriate circumstances, may recover punitive damages.

§ 363. Use, sale, or lease of property

(a) In this section, "cash collateral" means cash, negotiable instruments, documents of title, securities, deposit accounts, or other cash equivalents whenever acquired in which the estate and an entity other than the estate have an interest and includes the proceeds, products, offspring, rents, or profits of property and the fees, charges, accounts or other payments for the use or occupancy of rooms and other public facilities in hotels, motels, or other lodging properties subject to a security interest as provided in section 552(b) of this title, whether existing before or after the commencement of a case under this title.

(b)(1) The trustee, after notice and a hearing, may use, sell, or lease, other than in the ordinary course of business, property of the estate.

(2) If notification is required under subsection (a) of section 7A of the Clayton Act in the case of a transaction under this subsection, then—

　(A) notwithstanding subsection (a) of such section, the notification required by such subsection to be given by the debtor shall be given by the trustee; and

　(B) notwithstanding subsection (b) of such section, the required waiting period shall end on the 15th day after the date of the receipt, by the Federal Trade Commission and the Assistant Attorney General in charge of the Antitrust Division of the Department of Justice, of the notification required under such subsection (a), unless such waiting period is extended—

　　(i) pursuant to subsection (e)(2) of such section, in the same manner as such subsection (e)(2) applies to a cash tender offer;

　　(ii) pursuant to subsection (g)(2) of such section; or

　　(iii) by the court after notice and a hearing.

(c)(1) If the business of the debtor is authorized to be operated under section 721, 1108, 1203, 1204, or 1304 of this title and unless the court orders otherwise, the trustee may enter into transactions, including the sale or lease of property of the estate, in the ordinary course of business, without notice or a hearing, and may use property of the estate in the ordinary course of business without notice or a hearing.

(2) The trustee may not use, sell, or lease cash collateral under paragraph (1) of this subsection unless—

　(A) each entity that has an interest in such cash collateral consents; or

　(B) the court, after notice and a hearing, authorizes such use, sale, or lease in accordance with the provisions of this section.

(3) Any hearing under paragraph (2)(B) of this subsection may be a preliminary hearing or may be consolidated with a hearing under subsection (e) of this section, but shall be scheduled in accordance with the needs of the debtor. If the hearing under paragraph (2)(B) of this subsection is a preliminary hearing, the court may authorize such use, sale, or lease only if there is a reasonable likelihood that the trustee will prevail at the final hearing under subsection (e) of this section. The court shall act promptly on any request for authorization under paragraph (2)(B) of this subsection.

(4) Except as provided in paragraph (2) of this subsection, the trustee shall segregate and account for any cash collateral in the trustee's possession, custody, or control.

(d) The trustee may use, sell, or lease property under subsection (b) or (c) of this section only to the extent not inconsistent with any relief granted under section 362(c), 362(d), 362(e), or 362(f) of this title.

(e) Notwithstanding any other provision of this section, at any time, on request of an entity that has an interest in property used, sold, or leased, or proposed to be used, sold, or leased, by the trustee, the court, with or without a hearing, shall prohibit or condition such use, sale, or lease as is necessary to provide adequate protection of such interest. This subsection also applies to property that is subject to any unexpired lease of personal property (to the exclusion of such property being subject to an order to grant relief from the stay under section 362).

(f) The trustee may sell property under subsection (b) or (c) of this section free and clear of any interest in such property of an entity other than the estate, only if—

(1) applicable nonbankruptcy law permits sale of such property free and clear of such interest;

(2) such entity consents;

(3) such interest is a lien and the price at which such property is to be sold is greater than the aggregate value of all liens on such property;

(4) such interest is in bona fide dispute; or

(5) such entity could be compelled, in a legal or equitable proceeding, to accept a money satisfaction of such interest.

(g) Notwithstanding subsection (f) of this section, the trustee may sell property under interest (b) or (c) of this section free and clear of any vested or contingent right in the nature of dower or curtesy.

(h) Notwithstanding subsection (f) of this section, the trustee may sell both the estate's interest, under subsection (b) or (c) of this section, and the interest of any co-owner in property in which the debtor had, at the time of the commencement of the case, an undivided interest as a tenant in common, joint tenant, or tenant by the entirety, only if—

(1) partition in kind of such property among the estate and such co-owners is impracticable;

(2) sale of the estate's undivided interest in such property would realize significantly less for the estate than sale of such property free of the interests of such co-owners;

(3) the benefit to the estate of a sale of such property free of the interests of co-owners outweighs the detriment, if any, to such co-owners; and

(4) such property is not used in the production, transmission, or distribution, for sale, of electric energy or of natural or synthetic gas for heat, light, or power.

(i) Before the consummation of a sale of property to which subsection (g) or (h) of this section applies, or of property of the estate that was community property of the debtor and the debtor's spouse immediately before the commencement of the case, the debtor's spouse, or a co-owner of such property, as the case may be, may purchase such property at the price at which such sale is to be consummated.

(j) After a sale of property to which subsection (g) or (h) of this section applies, the trustee shall distribute to the debtor's spouse or the co-owners of such property, as the case may be, and to the estate, the proceeds of such sale, less the costs and expenses, not including any compensation of the trustee, of such sale, according to the interests of such spouse or co-owners, and of the estate.

(k) At a sale under subsection (b) of this section of property that is subject to a lien that secures an allowed claim, unless the court for cause orders otherwise the holder of such claim may bid at such sale, and, if the holder of such claim purchases such property, such holder may offset such claim against the purchase price of such property.

(l) Subject to the provisions of section 365, the trustee may use, sell, or lease property under subsection (b) or (c) of this section, or a plan under chapter 11, 12, or 13 of this title may provide for the use, sale, or lease of property, notwithstanding any provision in a contract, a lease, or applicable law that is conditioned on the insolvency or financial condition of the debtor, on the commencement of a case under this title concerning the debtor, or on the appointment of or the taking possession by a trustee in a case under this title or a custodian, and that effects, or gives an option to effect, a forfeiture, modification, or termination of the debtor's interest in such property.

(m) The reversal or modification on appeal of an authorization under subsection (b) or (c) of this section of a sale or lease of property does not affect the validity of a sale or lease under such authorization to an entity that purchased or leased such property in good faith, whether or not such entity knew of the pendency of the appeal, unless such authorization and such sale or lease were stayed pending appeal.

(n) The trustee may avoid a sale under this section if the sale price was controlled by an agreement among potential bidders at such sale, or may recover from a party to such agreement any amount by which the value of the property sold exceeds the price at which such sale was consummated, and may recover any costs, attorneys' fees, or

expenses incurred in avoiding such sale or recovering such amount. In addition to any recovery under the preceding sentence, the court may grant judgment for punitive damages in favor of the estate and against any such party that entered into such an agreement in willful disregard of this subsection.

(o) In any hearing under this section—

(1) the trustee has the burden of proof on the issue of adequate protection; and

(2) the entity asserting an interest in property has the burden of proof on the issue of the validity, priority, or extent of such interest.

§ 364. Obtaining credit

(a) If the trustee is authorized to operate the business of the debtor under section 721, 1108, 1203, 1204, or 1304 of this title, unless the court orders otherwise, the trustee may obtain unsecured credit and incur unsecured debt in the ordinary course of business allowable under section 503(b)(1) of this title as an administrative expense.

(b) The court, after notice and a hearing, may authorize the trustee to obtain unsecured credit or to incur unsecured debt other than under subsection(a) of this section, allowable under section 503(b)(1) of this title as an administrative expense.

(c) If the trustee is unable to obtain unsecured credit allowable under section 503(b)(1) of this title as an administrative expense, the court, after notice and a hearing, may authorize the obtaining of credit or the incurring of debt—

(1) with priority over any or all administrative expenses of the kind specified in section 503(b) or 507(b) of this title;

(2) secured by a lien on property of the estate that is not otherwise subject to a lien; or

(3) secured by a junior lien on property of the estate that is subject to a lien.

(d)(1) The court, after notice and a hearing, may authorize the obtaining of credit or the incurring of debt secured by a senior or equal lien on property of the estate that is subject to a lien only if—

(A) the trustee is unable to obtain such credit otherwise; and

(B) there is adequate protection of the interest of the holder of the lien on the property of the estate on which such senior or equal lien is proposed to be granted.

(2) In any hearing under this subsection, the trustee has the burden of proof on the issue of adequate protection.

(e) The reversal or modification on appeal of an authorization under this section to obtain credit or incur debt, or of a grant under this section of a priority or a lien, does not affect the validity of any debt so incurred, or any priority or lien so granted, to an entity that extended such credit in good faith, whether or not such entity knew of the pendency of the appeal, unless such authorization and the incurring of such debt, or the granting of such priority or lien, were stayed pending appeal.

(f) Except with respect to an entity that is an underwriter as defined in section 1145(b) of this title, section 5 of the Securities Act of 1933, the Trust Indenture Act of 1939, and any State or local law requiring registration for offer or sale of a security or registration or licensing of an issuer of, underwriter of, or broker or dealer in, a security does not apply to the offer or sale under this section of a security that is not an equity security.

§ 365. Executory contracts and unexpired leases

(a) Except as provided in sections 765 and 766 of this title and in subsections (b), (c), and (d) of this section, the trustee, subject to the court's approval, may assume or reject any executory contract or unexpired lease of the debtor.

(b)(1) If there has been a default in an executory contract or unexpired lease of the debtor, the trustee may not assume such contract or lease unless, at the time of assumption of such contract or lease, the trustee—

(A) cures, or provides adequate assurance that the trustee will promptly cure, such default;

(B) compensates, or provides adequate assurance that the trustee will promptly compensate, a party other than the debtor to such contract or lease, for any actual pecuniary loss to such party resulting from such default; and

(C) provides adequate assurance of future performance under such contract or lease.

(2) Paragraph (1) of this subsection does not apply to a default that is a breach of a provision relating to—

(A) the insolvency or financial condition of the debtor at any time before the closing of the case;

(B) the commencement of a case under this title;

(C) the appointment of or taking possession by a trustee in a case under this title or a custodian before such commencement; or

(D) the satisfaction of any penalty rate or provision relating to a default arising from any failure by the debtor to perform nonmonetary obligations under the executory contract or unexpired lease.

(3) For the purposes of paragraph (1) of this subsection and paragraph (2)(B) of subsection (f), adequate assurance of future performance of a lease of real property in a shopping center includes adequate assurance—

(A) of the source of rent and other consideration due under such lease, and in the case of an assignment, that the financial condition and operating performance of the proposed assignee and its guarantors, if any, shall be similar to the financial condition and operating performance of the debtor and its guarantors, if any, as of the time the debtor became the lessee under the lease;

(B) that any percentage rent due under such lease will not decline substantially;

(C) that assumption or assignment of such lease is subject to all the provisions thereof, including (but not limited to) provisions such as a radius, location, use, or exclusivity provision, and will not breach any such provision contained in any other lease, financing agreement, or master agreement relating to such shopping center; and

(D) that assumption or assignment of such lease will not disrupt any tenant mix or balance in such shopping center.

(4) Notwithstanding any other provision of this section, if there has been a default in an unexpired lease of the debtor, other than a default of a kind specified in paragraph (2) of this subsection, the trustee may not require a lessor to provide services or supplies incidental to such lease before assumption of such lease unless the lessor is compensated under the terms of such lease for any services and supplies provided under such lease before assumption of such lease.

(c) The trustee may not assume or assign any executory contract or unexpired lease of the debtor, whether or not such contract or lease prohibits or restricts assignment of rights or delegation of duties, if—

(1)(A) applicable law excuses a party, other than the debtor, to such contract or lease from accepting performance from or rendering performance to an entity other than the debtor or the debtor in possession whether or not such contract, or lease, prohibits or restricts assignment of rights or delegation of duties; and

(B) such party does not consent to such assumption or assignment; or

(2) such contract is a contract to make a loan, or extend other debt financing or financial accommodations, to or for the benefit of the debtor, or to issue a security of the debtor;

(3) such lease is of nonresidential real property and has been terminated under applicable bankruptcy law prior to the order for relief; or

(4) such lease is of nonresidential real property under which the debtor is the lessee of an aircraft terminal or aircraft gate at an airport at which the debtor is the lessee under one or more additional nonresidential leases of an aircraft terminal or aircraft gate and the trustee, in connection with such assumption or assignment, does not assume all such leases or does not assume and assign all of such leases to the same person, except that the trustee may assume or assign less than all of such leases with the airport operator's written consent.

(d)(1) In a case under chapter 7 of this title, if the trustee does not assume or reject an executory contract or unexpired lease of residential real property or of personal property of the debtor within 60 days after the order for relief, or within such additional time as the court, for cause, within such 60-day period, fixes, then such contract or lease is deemed rejected.

(2) In a case under chapter 9, 11, 12, or 13 of this title, the trustee may assume or reject an executory contract or unexpired lease of residential real property or of personal property of the debtor at any time before the confirmation of a plan but the court, on the request of any party to such contract or lease, may order the trustee to determine within a specified period of time whether to assume or reject such contract or lease.

(3) The trustee shall timely perform all the obligations of the debtor, except those specified in section 365(b)(2), arising from and after the order for relief under any unexpired lease of nonresidential real property, until such lease is assumed or rejected, notwithstanding section 503(b)(1) of this title. The court may extend, for cause, the time for performance of any such obligation that arises within 60 days after the date of the order for relief, but the time for performance shall not be extended beyond such 60-day period. This subsection shall not be deemed to affect the trustee's obligations under the provisions of subsection (b) or (f) of this section. Acceptance of any such performance does not constitute waiver or relinquishment of the lessor's rights under such lease or under this title.

(4) Notwithstanding paragraphs (1) and (2), in a case under any chapter of this title, if the trustee does not assume or reject an unexpired lease of nonresidential real property under which the debtor is the lessee within 60 days after the date of the order for relief, or within such additional time as the court, for cause, within such 60-day period, fixes, then such lease is deemed rejected, and the trustee shall immediately surrender such nonresidential real property to the lessor.

(5) Notwithstanding paragraphs (1) and (4) of this subsection, in a case under any chapter of this title, if the trustee does not assume or reject an unexpired lease of nonresidential real property under which the debtor is an affected air carrier that is the lessee of an aircraft terminal or aircraft gate before the occurrence of a termination event, then (unless the court orders the trustee to assume such unexpired leases within 5 days after the termination event), at the option of the airport operator, such lease is deemed rejected 5 days after the occurrence of a termination event and the trustee shall immediately surrender possession of the premises to the airport operator; except that the lease shall not be deemed to be rejected unless the airport operator first waives the right to damages related to the rejection. In the event that the lease is deemed to be rejected under this paragraph, the airport operator shall provide the affected air carrier adequate opportunity after the surrender of the premises to remove the fixtures and equipment installed by the affected air carrier.

(6) For the purposes of paragraph (5) of this subsection and paragraph (f)(1) of this section, the occurrence of a termination event means, with respect to a debtor which is an affected air carrier that is the lessee of an aircraft terminal or aircraft gate—

(A) the entry under section 301 or 302 of this title of an order for relief under chapter 7 of this title;

(B) the conversion of a case under any chapter of this title to a case under chapter 7 of this title; or

(C) the granting of relief from the stay provided under section 362(a) of this title with respect to aircraft, aircraft engines, propellers, applicances, or spare parts, as defined in section 101 of section 40102 of title 49, except for property of the debtor found by the court not to be necessary to an effective reorganization.

(7) Any order entered by the court pursuant to paragraph (4) extending the period within which the trustee of an affected air carrier must assume or reject an unexpired lease of nonresidential real property shall be without prejudice to—

(A) the right of the trustee to seek further extensions within such additional time period granted by the court pursuant to paragraph (4); and

(B) the right of any lessor or any other party in interest to request, at any time, a shortening or termination of the period within which the trustee must assume or reject an unexpired lease of nonresidential real property.

(8) The burden of proof for establishing cause for an extension by an affected air carrier under paragraph (4) or the maintenance of a previously granted extension under paragraph (7)(A)and (B) shall at all times remain with the trustee.

(9) For purposes of determining cause under paragraph (7) with respect to an unexpired lease of nonresidential real property between the debtor that is an affected air carrier and an airport operator under which such debtor is the lessee of an airport terminal or an airport gate, the court shall consider, among other relevant factors, whether substantial harm will result to the airport operator or airline passengers as a result of the extension or the maintenance of a previously granted extension. In making the determination of substantial harm, the court shall consider, among other relevant factors, the level of actual use of the terminals or gates which are the subject of the lease, the public interest in actual use of such terminals or gates, the existence of competing demands for the use of such terminals or gates, the effect of the court's extension or termination of the period of time to assume or reject the lease on such debtor's ability to successfully reorganize under chapter 11 of this title, and whether the trustee of the affected air carrier is capable of continuing to comply with its obligations under section 365(d)(3) of this title.

(10) The trustee shall timely perform all of the obligations of the debtor, except those specified in section 365(b)(2), first arising from or after 60 days after the order for relief in a case under chapter 11 of this title under an unexpired lease of personal property (other than personal property leased to an individual primarily for personal, family, or household purposes), until such lease is assumed or rejected notwithstanding section 503(b)(1) of this title,

unless the court, after notice and a hearing and based on the equities of the case, orders otherwise with respect to the obligations or timely performance thereof. This subsection shall not be deemed to affect the trustee's obligations under the provisions of subsection (b) or (f). Acceptance of any such performance does not constitute waiver or relinquishment of the lessor's rights under such lease or under this title.

(e)(1) Notwithstanding a provision in an executory contract or unexpired lease, or in applicable law, an executory contract or unexpired lease of the debtor may not be terminated or modified, and any right or obligation under such contract or lease may not be terminated or modified, at any time after the commencement of the case solely because of a provision in such contract or lease that is conditioned on—

(A) the insolvency or financial condition of the debtor at any time before the closing of the case;

(B) the commencement of a case under this title; or

(C) the appointment of or taking possession by a trustee in a case under this title or a custodian before such commencement.

(2) Paragraph (1) of this subsection does not apply to an executory contract or unexpired lease of the debtor, whether or not such contract or lease prohibits or restricts assignment of rights or delegation of duties, if—

(A)(i) applicable law excuses a party, other than the debtor, to such contract or lease from accepting performance from or rendering performance to the trustee or to an assignee of such contract or lease, whether or not such contract or lease prohibits or restricts assignment of rights or delegation of duties; and

(ii) such party does not consent to such assumption or assignment; or

(B) such contract is a contract to make a loan, or extend other debt financing or financial accommodations, to or for the benefit of the debtor, or to issue a security of the debtor.

This subsection also applies to property that is subject to any unexpired lease of personal property (to the exclusion of such property being subject to an order to grant relief from the stay under section 362).

(f)(1) Except as provided in subsection (c) of this section, notwithstanding a provision in an executory contract or unexpired lease of the debtor, or in applicable law, that prohibits, restricts, or conditions the assignment of such contract or lease, the trustee may assign such contract or lease under paragraph (2) of this subsection; except that the trustee may not assign an unexpired lease of nonresidential real property under which the debtor is an affected air carrier that is the lessee of an aircraft terminal or aircraft gate is there has occurred a termination event.

(2) The trustee may assign an executory contract or unexpired lease of the debtor only if—

(A) the trustee assumes such contract or lease in accordance with the provisions of this section; and

(B) adequate assurance of future performance by the assignee of such contract or lease is provided, whether or not there has been a default in such contract or lease.

(3) Notwithstanding a provision in an executory contract or unexpired lease of the debtor, or in applicable law that terminates or modifies, or permits a party other than the debtor to terminate or modify, such contract or lease or a right or obligation under such contract or lease on account of an assignment of such contract or lease, such contract, lease, right, or obligation may not be terminated or modified under such provision because of the assumption or assignment of such contract or lease by the trustee.

(g) Except as provided in subsections (h)(2) and (i)(2) of this section, the rejection of an executory contract or unexpired lease of the debtor constitutes a breach of such contract or lease—

(1) if such contract or lease has not been assumed under this section or under a plan confirmed under chapter 9, 11, 12, or 13 of this title, immediately before the date of the filing of the petition; or

(2) if such contract or lease has been assumed under this section or under a plan confirmed under chapter 9, 11, 12, or 13 of this title—

(A) if before such rejection the case has not been converted under section 1112, 1208, or 1307 of this title, at the time of such rejection; or

(B) if before such rejection the case has been converted under section 1112, 1208, or 1307 of this title—

(i) immediately before the date of such conversion, if such contract or lease was assumed before such conversion; or

(ii) at the time of such rejection, if such contract or lease was assumed after such conversion.

(h)(1)(A) If the trustee rejects an unexpired lease of real property under which the debtor is the lessor and—

(i) if the rejection by the trustee amounts to such a breach as would entitle the lessee to treat such lease as terminated by virtue of its terms, applicable nonbankruptcy law, or any agreement made by the lessee, then the lessee under such lease may treat such lease as terminated by the rejection; or

(ii) if the term of such lease has commenced, the lessee may retain its rights under such lease (including rights such as those relating to the amount and timing of payment of rent and other amounts payable by the lessee and any right of use, possession, quiet enjoyment, subletting, assignment, or hypothecation) that are in or appurtenant to the real property for the balance of the term of such lease and for any renewal or extension of such rights to the extent that such rights are enforceable under applicable nonbankruptcy law.

(B) If the lessee retains its rights under subparagraph (A)(ii), the lessee may offset against the rent reserved under such lease for the balance of the term after the date of the rejection of such lease and for the term of any renewal or extension of such lease, the value of any damage caused by the nonperformance after the date of such rejection, of any obligation of the debtor under such lease, but the lessee shall not have any other right against the estate or the debtor on account of any damage occurring after such date caused by such nonperformance.

(C) The rejection of a lease of real property in a shopping center with respect to which the lessee elects to retain its rights under subparagraph (A)(ii) does not affect the enforceability under applicable nonbankruptcy law of any provision in the lease pertaining to radius, location, use, exclusivity, or tenant mix or balance.

(D) In this paragraph, "lessee" includes any successor, assign, or mortgagee permitted under the terms of such lease.

(2)(A) If the trustee rejects a timeshare interest under a timeshare plan under which the debtor is the timeshare interest seller and—

(i) if the rejection amounts to such a breach as would entitle the timeshare interest purchaser to treat the timeshare plan as terminated under its terms, applicable nonbankruptcy law, or any agreement made by timeshare interest purchaser, the timeshare interest purchaser under the timeshare plan may treat the timeshare plan as terminated by such rejection; or

(ii) if the term of such timeshare interest has commenced, then the timeshare interest purchaser may retain its rights in such timeshare interest for the balance of such term and for any term of renewal or extension of such timeshare interest to the extent that such rights are enforceable under applicable nonbankruptcy law.

(B) If the timeshare interest purchaser retains its rights under subparagraph (A), such timeshare interest purchaser may offset against the moneys due for such timeshare interest for the balance of the term after the date of the rejection of such timeshare interest, and the term of any renewal or extension of such timeshare interest, the value of any damage caused by the nonperformance after the date of such rejection, of any obligation of the debtor under such timeshare plan, but the timeshare interest purchaser shall not have any right against the estate or the debtor on account of any damage occurring after such date caused by such nonperformance.

(i)(1) If the trustee rejects an executory contract of the debtor for the sale of real property or for the sale of a timeshare interest under a timeshare plan, under which the purchaser is in possession, such purchaser may treat such contract as terminated, or, in the alternative, may remain in possession of such real property or timeshare interest.

(2) If such purchaser remains in possession—

(A) such purchaser shall continue to make all payments due under such contract, but may, offset against such payments any damages occurring after the date of the rejection of such contract caused by the nonperformance of any obligation of the debtor after such date, but such purchaser does not have any rights against the estate on account of any damages arising after such date from such rejection, other than such offset; and

(B) the trustee shall deliver title to such purchaser in accordance with the provisions of such contract, but is relieved of all other obligations to perform under such contract.

(j) A purchaser that treats an executory contract as terminated under subsection (i) of this section, or a party whose executory contract to purchase real property from the debtor is rejected and under which such party is not in possession, has a lien on the interest of the debtor in such property for the recovery of any portion of the purchase price that such purchaser or party has paid.

(k) Assignment by the trustee to an entity of a contract or lease assumed under this section relieves the trustee and the estate from any liability for any breach of such contract or lease occurring after such assignment.

(l) If an unexpired lease under which the debtor is the lessee is assigned pursuant to this section, the lessor of the property may require a deposit or other security for the performance of the debtor's obligations under the lease substantially the same as would have been required by the landlord upon the initial leasing to a similar tenant.

(m) For purposes of this section 365 and sections 541(b)(2) and 362(b)(10), leases of real property shall include any rental agreement to use real property.

(n)(1) If the trustee rejects an executory contract under which the debtor is a licensor of a right to intellectual property, the licensee under such contract may elect—

(A) to treat such contract as terminated by such rejection if such rejection by the trustee amounts to such a breach as would entitle the licensee to treat such contract as terminated by virtue of its own terms, applicable nonbankruptcy law, or an agreement made by the licensee with another entity; or

(B) to retain its rights (including a right to enforce any exclusivity provision of such contract, but excluding any other right under applicable nonbankruptcy law to specific performance of such contract) under such contract and under any agreement supplementary to such contract, to such intellectual property (including any embodiment of such intellectual property to the extent protected by applicable nonbankruptcy law), as such rights existed immediately before the case commenced, for—

(i) the duration of such contract; and

(ii) any period for which such contract may be extended by the licensee as of right under applicable

nonbankruptcy law.

(2) If the licensee elects to retain its rights, as described in paragraph (1)(B) of this subsection, under such contract—

(A) the trustee shall allow the licensee to exercise such rights;

(B) the licensee shall make all royalty payments due under such contract for the duration of such contract and for any period described in paragraph (1)(B) of this subsection for which the licensee extends such contract; and

(C) the licensee shall be deemed to waive—

(i) any right of setoff it may have with respect to such contract under this title or applicable nonbankruptcy law; and

(ii) any claim allowable under section 503(b) of this title arising from the performance of such contract.

(3) If the licensee elects to retain its rights, as described in paragraph (1)(B) of this subsection, then on the written request of the licensee the trustee shall—

(A) to the extent provided in such contract, or any agreement supplementary to such contract, provide to the licensee any intellectual property (including such embodiment) held by the trustee; and

(B) not interfere with the rights of the licensee as provided in such contract, or any agreement supplementary to such contract, to such intellectual property (including such embodiment) including any right to obtain such intellectual property (or such embodiment) from another entity.

(4) Unless and until the trustee rejects such contract, on the written request of the licensee the trustee shall—

(A) to the extent provided in such contract or any agreement supplementary to such contract—

(i) perform such contract; or

(ii) provide to the licensee such intellectual property (including any embodiment of such intellectual property to the extent protected by applicable nonbankruptcy law) held by the trustee; and

(B) not interfere with the rights of the licensee as provided in such contract, or any agreement supplementary to such contract, to such intellectual property (including such embodiment), including any right to obtain such intellectual property (or such embodiment) from another entity.

(o) In a case under chapter 11 of this title, the trustee shall be deemed to have assumed (consistent with the debtor's other obligations under section 507), and shall immediately cure any deficit under, any commitment by the debtor to a Federal depository institutions regulatory agency (or predecessor to such agency) to maintain the capital of an insured depository institution, and any claim for a subsequent breach of the obligations thereunder shall be entitled to priority under section 507. This subsection shall not extend any com-

mitment that would otherwise be terminated by any act of such an agency.

§ 366. Utility service

(a) Except as provided in subsection (b) of this section, a utility may not alter, refuse, or discontinue service to, or discriminate against, the trustee or the debtor solely on the basis of the commencement of a case under this title or that a debt owed by the debtor to such utility for service rendered before the order for relief was not paid when due.

(b) Such utility may alter, refuse, or discontinue service if neither the trustee nor the debtor, within 20 days after the date of the order for relief, furnishes adequate assurance of payment, in the form of a deposit or other security, for service after such date. On request of a party in interest and after notice and a hearing, the court may order reasonable modification of the amount of the deposit or other security necessary to provide adequate assurance of payment.

CHAPTER 5—CREDITORS, DEBTOR, AND THE ESTATE

SUBCHAPTER I—CREDITORS AND CLAIMS

Sec.

SUBCHAPTER I—CREDITORS AND CLAIMS

§ 501. Filing of proofs of claims or interests

(a) A creditor or an indenture trustee may file a proof of claim. An equity security holder may file a proof of interest.

(b) If a creditor does not timely file a proof of such creditor's claim, an entity that is liable to such creditor with the debtor, or that has secured such creditor, may file a proof of such claim.

(c) If a creditor does not timely file a proof of such creditor's claim, the debtor or the trustee may file a proof of such claim.

(d) A claim of a kind specified in section 502(e)(2), 502(f), 502(g), 502(h) or 502(i) of this title may be filed under subsection (a), (b), or (c) of this section the same as if such claim were a claim against the debtor and had arisen before the date of the filing of the petition.

§ 502. Allowance of claims or interests

(a) A claim or interest, proof of which is filed under section 501 of this title, is deemed allowed, unless a party in interest, including a creditor of a general partner in a partnership that is a debtor in a case under chapter 7 of this title, objects.

(b) Except as provided in subsections (e)(2), (f), (g), (h) and (i) of this section, if such objection to a claim is made, the court, after notice and a hearing, shall determine the amount of such claim in lawful currency of the United States as of the date of the filing of the petition, and shall allow such claim in such amount except to the extent that—

(1) such claim is unenforceable against the debtor and property of the debtor, under any agreement or applicable law for a reason other than because such claim is contingent or unmatured;

(2) such claim is for unmatured interest;

(3) if such claim is for a tax assessed against property of the estate, such claim exceeds the value of the interest of the estate in such property;

(4) if such claim is for services of an insider or attorney of the debtor, such claim exceeds the reasonable value of such services;

(5) such claim is for a debt that is unmatured on the date of the filing of the petition and that is excepted from discharge under section 523(a)(5) of this title;

(6) if such claim is the claim of a lessor for damages resulting from the termination of a lease of real property, such claim exceeds—

(A) the rent reserved by such lease, without acceleration, for the greater of one year, or 15 percent, not to exceed three years, of the remaining term of such lease, following the earlier of—

(i) the date of the filing of the petition; and

(ii) the date on which such lessor repossessed, or the lessee surrendered, the leased property; plus

(B) any unpaid rent due under such lease, without acceleration, on the earlier of such dates;

(7) if such claim is the claim of an employee for damages resulting from the termination of an employment contract, such claim exceeds—

(A) the compensation provided by such contract, without acceleration, for one year following the earlier of—

(i) the date of the filing of the petition; or

(ii) the date on which the employer directed the employee to terminate, or such employee terminated, performance under such contact; plus

(B) any unpaid compensation due under such contract, without acceleration, on the earlier of such dates;

(8) such claim results from a reduction, due to late payment, in the amount of an otherwise applicable credit available to the debtor in connection with an employment tax on wages, salaries, or commissions earned from the debtor; or

(9) proof of such claim is not timely filed, except to the extent tardily filed as permitted under paragraph (1), (2), or (3) of section 726(a) of this title or under the Federal Rules of Bankruptcy Procedure, except that a claim of a governmental unit shall be timely filed if it is filed before 180 days after the date of the order for relief or such later time as the Federal Rules of Bankruptcy Procedure may provide.

(c) There shall be estimated for purpose of allowance under this section—

(1) any contingent or unliquidated claim, the fixing or liquidation of which, as the case may be, would unduly delay the administration of the case; or

(2) any right to payment arising from a right to an equitable remedy for breach of performance.

(d) Notwithstanding subsections (a) and (b) of this section, the court shall disallow any claim of any entity from which property is recoverable under section 542, 543, 550, or 553 of this title or that is a transferee of a transfer avoidable under section 522(f), 522(h), 544, 545, 547, 548, 549, or 724(a) of this title, unless such entity or transferee has paid the amount, or turned over any such property, for which such entity or transferee is liable under section 522(i), 542, 543, 550, or 553 of this title.

(e)(1) Notwithstanding subsections (a), (b), and (c) of this section and paragraph (2) of this subsection, the court shall disallow any claim for reimbursement or contribution of an entity that is liable with the debtor on or has secured the claim of a creditor, to the extent that—

(A) such creditor's claim against the estate is disallowed;

(B) such claim for reimbursement or contribution is contingent as of the time of allowance or disallowance of such claim for reimbursement or contribution; or

(C) such entity asserts a right of subrogation to the rights of such creditor under section 509 of this title.

(2) A claim for reimbursement or contribution of such an entity that becomes fixed after the commencement of the case shall be determined, and shall be allowed under subsection (a), (b), or (c) of this section, or disallowed under subsection (d) of this section, the same as if such claim had become fixed before the date of the filing of the petition.

(f) If an involuntary case, a claim arising in the ordinary course of the debtor's business or financial affairs after the commencement of the case but before the earlier of the appointment of a trustee and the order for relief shall be determined as of the date such claim arises, and shall be allowed under subsection (a), (b), or (c) of this section or disallowed under subsection (d) or (e) of this section, the same as if such claim had arisen before the date of the filing of the petition.

(g) A claim arising from the rejection, under section 365 of this title or under a plan under chapter 9, 11, 12, or 13 of this title, of an executory contract or unexpired lease of the debtor that has not been assumed shall be determined, and shall be allowed under subsection (a), (b), or (c) of this section or disallowed under subsection (d) or (e) of this section, the same as if such claim had arisen before the date of the filing of the petition.

(h) A claim arising from the recovery of property under section 522, 550, or 553 of this title shall be determined, and shall be allowed under subsection (a),

(b), or (c) of this section, or disallowed under subsection (d) or (e) of this section, the same as if such claim had arisen before the date of the filing of the petition.

(i) A claim that does not arise until after commencement of the case for a tax entitled to priority under section 507(a)(8) of this title shall be determined, and shall be allowed under subsection (a), (b), or (c) of this section, or disallowed under subsection (d) or (e) of this section, the same as if such claim had arisen before the date of the filing of the petition.

(j) A claim that has been allowed or disallowed may be reconsidered for cause. A reconsidered claim may be allowed or disallowed according to the equities of the case. Reconsideration of a claim under this subsection does not affect the validity of any payment or transfer from the estate made to a holder of an allowed claim on account of such allowed claim that is not reconsidered, but if a reconsidered claim is allowed and is of the same class as such holder's claim, such holder may not receive any additional payment or transfer from the estate on account of such holder's allowed claim until the holder of such reconsidered and allowed claim receives payment on account of such claim proportionate in value to that already received by such other holder. This subsection does not alter or modify the trustee's right to recover from a creditor any excess payment or transfer made to such creditor.

§ 503. Allowance of administrative expenses

(a) An entity may timely file a request for payment of an administrative expense, or may tardily file such request if permitted by the court for cause.

(b) After notice and a hearing, there shall be allowed administrative expenses, other than claims allowed under section 502(f) of this title, including—

(1)(A) the actual, necessary costs and expenses of preserving the estate, including wages, salaries, or commissions for services rendered after the commencement of the case;

(B) any tax—

(i) incurred by the estate, except a tax of a kind specified in section 507(a)(8) of this title; or

(ii) attributable to an excessive allowance of a tentative carryback adjustment that the estate received, whether the taxable year to which such adjustment relates ended before or after the commencement of the case; and

(C) any fine, penalty, or reduction in credit relating to a tax of a kind specified in subparagraph (B) of this paragraph;

(2) compensation and reimbursement awarded under section 330(a) of this title;

(3) the actual, necessary expenses, other than compensation and reimbursement specified in paragraph (4) of this subsection, incurred by—

(A) a creditor that files a petition under section 303 of this title;

(B) a creditor that recovers, after the court's approval, for the benefit of the estate any property transferred or concealed by the debtor;

(C) a creditor in connection with the prosecution of a criminal offense relating to the case or to the business or property of the debtor;

(D) a creditor, an indenture trustee, an equity security holder, or a committee representing creditors or equity security holders other than a committee appointed under section 1102 of this title, in making a substantial contribution in a case under chapter 9 or 11 of this title;

(E) a custodian superseded under section 543 of this title, and compensation for the services of such custodian; or

(F) a member of a committee appointed under section 1102 of this title, if such expenses are incurred in the performance of the duties of such committee;

(4) reasonable compensation for professional services rendered by an attorney or an accountant of an entity whose expense is allowable under paragraph (3) of this subsection, based on the time, the nature, the extent, and the value of such services, and the cost of comparable services other than in a case under this title, and reimbursement for actual, necessary expenses incurred by such attorney or accountant;

(5) reasonable compensation for services rendered by an indenture trustee in making a substantial contribution in a case under chapter 9 or 11 of this title, based on the time, the nature, the extent, and the value of such services, and the cost of comparable services other than in a case under this title; and

(6) the fees and mileage payable under chapter 119 of title 28.

§ 504. Sharing of compensation

(a) Except as provided in subsection (b) of this section, a person receiving compensation or reimbursement under section 503(b)(2) or 503(b)(4) of this title may not share or agree to share—

(1) any such compensation or reimbursement with another person; or

(2) any compensation or reimbursement received by another person under such sections.

(b)(1) A member, partner, or regular associate in a professional association, corporation, or partnership may share compensation or reimbursement received under section 503(b)(2) or 503(b)(4) of this title with another member, partner, or regular associate in such association, corporation, or partnership, and may share in any compensation or reimbursement received under such sections by another

member, partner, or regular associate in such association, corporation, or partnership.

(2) An attorney for a creditor that files a petition under section 303 of this title may share compensation and reimbursement received under section 503(b)(4) of this title with any other attorney contributing to the services rendered or expenses incurred by such creditor's attorney.

§ 505. Determination of tax liability

(a)(1) Except as provided in paragraph (2) of this subsection, the court may determine the amount or legality of any tax, any fine or penalty relating to a tax, or any addition to tax, whether or not previously assessed, whether or not paid, and whether or not contested before and adjudicated by a judicial or administrative tribunal of competent jurisdiction.

(2) The court may not so determine—

(A) the amount or legality of a tax, fine, penalty, or addition to tax if such amount or legality was contested before and adjudicated by a judicial or administrative tribunal of competent jurisdiction before the commencement of the case under this title; or

(B) any right of the estate to a tax refund, before the earlier of—

(i) 120 days after the trustee properly requests such refund from the governmental unit from which such refund is claimed; or

(ii) a determination by such governmental unit of such request.

(b) A trustee may request a determination of any unpaid liability of the estate for any tax incurred during the administration of the case by submitting a tax return for such tax and a request for such a determination to the governmental unit charged with responsibility for collection or determination of such tax. Unless such return is fraudulent, or contains a material misrepresentation, the trustee, the debtor, and any successor to the debtor are discharged from any liability for such tax—

(1) upon payment of the tax shown on such return, if—

(A) such governmental unit does not notify the trustee, within 60 days after such request, that such return has been selected for examination; or

(B) such governmental unit does not complete such an examination and notify the trustee of any tax due, within 180 days after such request or within such additional time as the court, for cause, permits;

(2) upon payment of the tax determined by the court, after notice and a hearing, after completion by such governmental unit of such examination; or

(3) upon payment of the tax determined by such governmental unit to be due.

(c) Notwithstanding section 362 of this title, after determination by the court of a tax under this section, the governmental unit charged with responsibility for collection of such tax may assess such tax against the estate, the debtor, or a successor to the debtor, as the case may be, subject to any otherwise applicable law.

§ 506. Determination of secured status

(a) An allowed claim of a creditor secured by a lien on property in which the estate has an interest, or that is subject to setoff under section 553 of this title, is a secured claim to the extent of the value of such creditor's interest in the estate's interest in such property, or to the extent of the amount subject to setoff, as the case may be, and is an unsecured claim to the extent that the value of such creditor's interest or the amount so subject to setoff is less than the amount of such allowed claim. Such value shall be determined in light of the purpose of the valuation and of the proposed disposition or use of such property, and in conjunction with any hearing on such disposition or use or on a plan affecting such creditor's interest.

(b) To the extent that an allowed secured claim is secured by property the value of which, after any recovery under subsection (c) of this section, is greater than the amount of such claim, there shall be allowed to the holder of such claim, interest on such claim, and any reasonable fees, costs, or charges provided for under the agreement under which such claim arose.

(c) The trustee may recover from property securing an allowed secured claim the reasonable, necessary costs and expenses of preserving, or disposing of, such property to the extent of any benefit to the holder of such claim.

(d) To the extent that a lien secures a claim against the debtor that is not an allowed secured claim, such lien is void, unless—

(1) such claim was disallowed only under section 502(b)(5) or 502(e) of this title; or

(2) such claim is not an allowed secured claim due only to the failure of any entity to file a proof of such claim under section 501 of this title.

§ 507. Priorities

(a) The following expenses and claims have priority in the following order:

(1) First, administrative expenses allowed under section 503(b) of this title, and any fees and charges assessed against the estate under chapter 123 of title 28.

(2) Second, unsecured claims allowed under section 502(f) of this title.

(3) Third, allowed unsecured claims, but only to the extent of $4,000 for each individual or corporation, as the case may be, earned within 90 days before the date of the filing of the petition or the date of the cessation of the debtor's business, whichever occurs first, for—

(A) wages, salaries, or commissions, including vacation, severance, and sick leave pay earned by an individual; or

(B) sales commissions earned by an individual or by a corporation with only 1 employee, acting as an independent contractor in the sale of goods or services for the debtor in the ordinary course of the debtor's business if, and only if, during the 12 months preceding that date, at least 75 percent of the amount that the individual or corporation earned by acting as an independent contractor in the sale of goods or services was earned from the debtor;

(4) Fourth, allowed unsecured claims for contributions to an employee benefit plan—

(A) arising from services rendered within 180 days before the date of the filing of the petition or the date of the cessation of the debtor's business, whichever occurs first; but only

(B) for each such plan, to the extent of—

(i) the number of employees covered by each such plan multiplied by $4,000; less

(ii) the aggregate amount paid to such employees under paragraph (3) of this subsection, plus the aggregate amount paid by the estate on behalf of such employees to any other employees benefit plan.

(5) Fifth, allowed unsecured claims of persons—

(A) engaged in the production or raising of grain, as defined in section 557(b) of this title, against a debtor who owns or operates a grain storage facility, as defined in section 557(b) of this title, for grain or the proceeds of grain, or

(B) engaged as a United States fisherman against a debtor who has acquired fish or fish produce from a fisherman through a sale or conversion, and who is engaged in operating a fish produce storage or processing facility—

but only to the extent of $4,000 for each such individual.

(6) Sixth, allowed unsecured claims of individuals, to the extent of $1,800 for each such individual, arising from the deposit, before the commencement of the case, of money in connection with the purchase, lease, or rental of property, or the purchase of services, for the personal, family, or household use of such individuals, that were not delivered or provided.

(7) Seventh, allowed claims for debts to a spouse, former spouse, or child of the debtor, for alimony to, maintenance for, or support of such spouse or child, in connection with a separation agreement, divorce decree or other order of a court of record, determination made in accordance with State or territorial law by a governmental unit, or property settlement agreement, but not to the extent that such debt—

(A) is assigned to another entity, voluntarily, by operation of law, or otherwise; or

(B) includes a liability designated as alimony, maintenance, or support, unless such liability is actually in the nature of alimony, maintenance or support.

(8) Eighth, allowed unsecured claims of governmental units; only to the extent that such claims are for—

(A) a tax on or measured by income or gross receipts—

(i) for a taxable year ending on or before the date of the filing of the petition for which a return, if required, is last due, including extensions, after three years before the date of the filing of the petition;

(ii) assessed within 240 days, plus any time plus 30 days during which an offer in compromise with respect to such tax that was made within 240 days after such assessment was pending, before the date of the filing of the petition; or

(iii) other than a tax of a kind specified in section 523(a)(1)(B) or 523(a)(1)(C) of this title, not assessed before, but assessable, under applicable law or by agreement, after, the commencement of the case;

(B) a property tax assessed before the commencement of the case and last payable without penalty after one year before the date of the filing of the petition;

(C) a tax required to be collected or withheld and for which the debtor is liable in whatever capacity;

(D) an employment tax on a wage, salary, or commission of a kind specified in paragraph (3) of this subsection earned from the debtor before the date of the filing of the petition, whether or not actually paid before such date, for which a return is last due, under applicable law or under any extension, after three years before the date of the filing of the petition;

(E) an excise tax on—

(i) a transaction occurring before the date of the filing of the petition for which a return, if required, is last due, under applicable law or under any extension, after three years before the date of the filing of the petition; or

(ii) if a return is not required, a transaction occurring during the three years immediately preceding the date of the filing of the petition;

(F) a customs duty arising out of the importation of merchandise—

(i) entered for consumption within one year before the date of the filing of the petition;

(ii) covered by an entry liquidated or reliquidated within one year before the date of the filing of the petition; or

(iii) entered for consumption within four years before the date of the filing of the petition but unliquidated on such date, if the Secretary of

the Treasury certifies that failure to liquidate such entry was due to an investigation pending on such date into assessment of antidumping or countervailing duties or fraud, or if information needed for the proper appraisement or classification of such merchandise was not available to the appropriate customs officer before such date; or

(G) a penalty related to a claim of a kind specified in this paragraph and in compensation for actual pecuniary loss.

(9) Ninth, allowed unsecured claims based upon any commitment by the debtor to a Federal depository institutions regulatory agency (or predecessor to such agency) to maintain the capital of an insured depository institution.

(b) If the trustee, under section 362, 363, or 364 of this title, provides adequate protection of the interest of a holder of a claim secured by a lien on property of the debtor and if, notwithstanding such protection, such creditor has a claim allowable under subsection (a)(1) of this section arising from the stay of action against such property under section 362 of this title, from the use, sale, or lease of such property under section 363 of this title, or from the granting of a lien under section 364(d) of this title, then such creditor's claim under such subsection shall have priority over every other claim allowable under such subsection.

(c) For the purpose of subsection (a) of this section, a claim of a governmental unit arising from an erroneous refund or credit of a tax has the same priority as a claim for the tax to which such refund or credit relates.

(d) An entity that is subrogated to the rights of a holder of a claim of a kind specified in subsection (a)(3), (a)(4), (a)(5), (a)(6), (a)(7), (a)(8), or (a)(9) of this section is not subrogated to the right of the holder of such claim to priority under such subsection.

§ 508. Effect of distribution other than under this title

(a) If a creditor receives, in a foreign proceeding, payment of, or a transfer of property on account of, a claim that is allowed under this title, such creditor may not receive any payment under this title on account of such claim until each of the other holders of claims on account of which such holders are entitled to share equally with such creditor under this title has received payment under this title equal in value to the consideration received by such creditor in such foreign proceeding.

(b) If a creditor of a partnership debtor receives, from a general partner that is not a debtor in a case under chapter 7 of this title, payment of, or a transfer of property on account of, a claim that is allowed under this title and that is not secured by a lien on property of such partner, such creditor may not receive any payment under this title on account of such claim until each of the other holders of claims on account of which such holders are entitled to share equally with such creditor under this title has received payment under this title equal in value to the consideration received by such creditor from such general partner.

§ 509. Claims of codebtors

(a) Except as provided in subsection (b) or (c) of this section, an entity that is liable with the debtor on, or that has secured, a claim of a creditor against the debtor, and that pays such claim, is subrogated to the rights of such creditor to the extent of such payment.

(b) Such entity is not subrogated to the rights of such creditor to the extent that—

(1) a claim of such entity for reimbursement or contribution on account of such payment of such creditor's claim is—

(A) allowed under section 502 of this title;

(B) disallowed other than under section 502(e) of this title; or

(C) subordinated under section 510 of this title; or

(2) as between the debtor and such entity, such entity received the consideration for the claim held by such creditor.

(c) The court shall subordinate to the claim of a creditor and for the benefit of such creditor an allowed claim, by way of subrogation under this section, or for reimbursement or contribution, of an entity that is liable with the debtor on, or that has secured, such creditor's claim, until such creditor's claim is paid in full, either through payments under this title or otherwise.

§ 510. Subordination

(a) A subordination agreement is enforceable in a case under this title to the same extent that such agreement is enforceable under applicable nonbankruptcy law.

(b) For the purpose of distribution under this title, a claim arising from rescission of a purchase or sale of a security of the debtor or of an affiliate of the debtor, for damages arising from the purchase or sale of such a security, or for reimbursement or contribution allowed under section 502 on account of such a claim, shall be subordinated to all claims or interests that are senior to or equal the claim or interest represented by such security, except that if such security is common stock, such claim has the same priority as common stock.

(c) Notwithstanding subsections (a) and (b) of this section, after notice and a hearing, the court may—

(1) under principles of equitable subordination, subordinate for purposes of distribution all or part of an allowed claim to all or part of another allowed claim or all or part of an allowed interest to all or part of another allowed interest; or

(2) order that any lien securing such a subordinated claim be transferred to the estate.

SUBCHAPTER II—DEBTOR'S DUTIES AND BENEFITS

§ 521. Debtor's duties

The debtor shall—

(1) file a list of creditors, and unless the court orders otherwise, a schedule of assets and liabilities, a schedule of current income and current expenditures, and a statement of the debtor's financial affairs;

(2) if an individual debtor's schedule of assets and liabilities includes consumer debts which are secured by property of the estate—

(A) within thirty days after the date of the filing of a petition under chapter 7 of this title or on or before the date of the meeting of creditors, whichever is earlier, or within such additional time as the court, for cause, within such period fixes, the debtor shall file with the clerk a statement of his intention with respect to the retention or surrender of such property and, if applicable, specifying that such property is claimed as exempt, that the debtor intends to redeem such property, or that the debtor intends to reaffirm debts secured by such property;

(B) within forty-five days after the filing of a notice of intent under this section, or within such additional time as the court, for cause, within such forty-five day period fixes, the debtor shall perform his intention with respect to such property, as specified by subparagraph (A) of this paragraph; and

(C) nothing in subparagraphs (A) and (B) of this paragraph shall alter the debtor's or the trustee's rights with regard to such property under this title;

(3) if a trustee is serving in the case, cooperate with the trustee as necessary to enable the trustee to perform the trustee's duties under this title;

(4) if a trustee is serving in the case, surrender to the trustee all property of the estate and any recorded information, including books, documents, records, and papers, relating to property of the estate, whether or not immunity is granted under section 344 of this title; and

(5) appear at the hearing required under section 524(d) of this title.

§ 522. Exemptions

(a) In this section—

(1) "dependent" includes spouse, whether or not actually dependent; and

(2) "value" means fair market value as of the date of the filing of the petition or, with respect to property that becomes property of the estate after such date, as

of the date such property becomes property of the estate.

(b) Notwithstanding section 541 of this title, an individual debtor may exempt from property of the estate the property listed in either paragraph (1) or, in the alternative, paragraph (2) of this subsection. In joint cases filed under section 302 of this title and individual cases filed under section 301 or 303 of this title by or against debtors who are husband and wife, and whose estates are ordered to be jointly administered under Rule 1015(b) of the Federal Rules of Bankruptcy Procedure, one debtor may not elect to exempt property listed in paragraph (1) and the other debtor elect to exempt property listed in paragraph (2) of this subsection. If the parties cannot agree on the alternative to be elected, they shall be deemed to elect paragraph (1), where such election is permitted under the law of the jurisdiction where the case is filed. Such property is—

(1) property that is specified under subsection (d) of this section, unless the State law that is applicable to the debtor under paragraph (2)(A) of this subsection specifically does not so authorize; or, in the alternative,

(2)(A) any property that is exempt under Federal law, other than subsection (d) of this section, or State or local law that is applicable on the date of the filing of the petition at the place in which the debtor's domicile has been located for the 180 days immediately preceding the date of the filing of the petition, or for a longer portion of such 180-day period than in any other place; and

(B) any interest in property in which the debtor had, immediately before the commencement of the case, an interest as a tenant by the entirety or joint tenant to the extent that such interest as a tenant by the entirety or joint tenant is exempt from process under applicable nonbankruptcy law.

(c) Unless the case is dismissed, property exempted under this section is not liable during or after the case for any debt of the debtor that arose, or that is determined under section 502 of this title as if such debt had risen, before the commencement of the case, except—

(1) a debt of a kind specified in section 523(a)(1) or 523(a)(5) of this title;

(2) a debt secured by a lien that is—

(A)(i) not avoided under subsection (f) or (g) of this section or under section 544, 545, 547, 548, 549, or 724(a) of this title; and

(ii) not void under section 506(d) of this title; or

(B) a tax lien, notice of which is properly filed; or

(3) a debt of a kind specified in section 523(a)(4) or 523(a)(6) of this title owed by an institution-affiliated party of an insured depository institution to a Federal depository institutions regulatory agency acting in its capacity as conservator, receiver, or liquidating agent for such institution.

(d) The following property may be exempted under

subsection (b)(1) of this section:

(1) The debtor's aggregate interest, not to exceed $15,000 in value, in real property or personal property that the debtor or a dependent of the debtor uses as a residence, in a cooperative that owns property that the debtor or a dependent of the debtor uses as a residence, or in a burial plot for the debtor or a dependent of the debtor.

(2) The debtor's interest, not to exceed $2,400 in value, in one motor vehicle.

(3) The debtor's interest, not to exceed $400 in value in any particular item or $8,000 in aggregate value, in household furnishings, household goods, wearing apparel, appliances, books, animals, crops, or musical instruments, that are held primarily for the personal, family, or household use of the debtor or a dependent of the debtor.

(4) The debtor's aggregate interest, not to exceed $1,000 in value, in jewelry held primarily for the personal, family, or household use of the debtor or a dependent of the debtor.

(5) The debtor's aggregate interest in any property, not to exceed in value $800 plus up to $7,500 of any unused amount of the exemption provided under paragraph (1) of this subsection.

(6) The debtor's aggregate interest, not to exceed $1,500 in value, in any implements, professional books, or tools, of the trade of the debtor or the trade of a dependent of the debtor.

(7) Any unmatured life insurance contract owned by the debtor, other than a credit life insurance contract.

(8) The debtor's aggregate interest, not to exceed in value $8,000 less any amount of property of the estate transferred in the manner specified in section 542(d) of this title, in any accrued dividend or interest under, or loan value of, any unmatured life insurance contract owned by the debtor under which the insured is the debtor or an individual of whom the debtor is a dependent.

(9) Professionally prescribed health aids for the debtor or a dependent of the debtor.

(10) The debtor's right to receive—

(A) a social security benefit, unemployment compensation, or a local public assistance benefit;

(B) a veteran's benefit;

(C) a disability, illness, or unemployment benefit;

(D) alimony, support, or separate maintenance, to the extent reasonably necessary for the support of the debtor and any dependent of the debtor;

(E) a payment under a stock bonus, pension, profitsharing, annuity, or similar plan or contract on account of illness, disability, death, age, or length of service, to the extent reasonably necessary for the support of the debtor and any dependent of the debtor, unless—

(i) such plan or contract was established by or under the auspices of an insider that employed the debtor at the time the debtor's rights under such plan or contract arose;

(ii) such payment is on account of age or length of service; and

(iii) such plan or contract does not qualify under section 401(a), 403(a), 403(b), or 408 of the Internal Revenue Code of 1986.

(11) The debtor's right to receive, or property that is traceable to—

(A) an award under a crime victim's reparation law;

(B) a payment on account of the wrongful death of an individual of whom the debtor was a dependent, to the extent reasonably necessary for the support of the debtor and any dependent of the debtor;

(C) a payment under a life insurance contract that insured the life of an individual of whom the debtor was a dependent on the date of such individual's death, to the extent reasonably necessary for the support of the debtor and any dependent of the debtor;

(D) a payment, not to exceed $15,000, on account of personal bodily injury, not including pain and suffering or compensation for actual pecuniary loss, of the debtor or an individual of whom the debtor is a dependent; or

(E) a payment in compensation of loss of future earnings of the debtor or an individual of whom the debtor is or was a dependent, to the extent reasonably necessary for the support of the debtor and any dependent of the debtor.

(e) A waiver of an exemption executed in favor of a creditor that holds an unsecured claim against the debtor is unenforceable in a case under this title with respect to such claim against property that the debtor may exempt under subsection (b) of this section. A waiver by the debtor of a power under subsection (f) or (h) of this section to avoid a transfer, under subsection (g) or (i) of this section to exempt property, or under subsection (i) of this section to recover property or to preserve a transfer, is unenforceable in a case under this title.

(f)(1) Notwithstanding any waiver of exemptions, but subject to paragraph (3), the debtor may avoid the fixing of a lien on an interest of the debtor in property to the extent that such lien impairs an exemption to which the debtor would have been entitled under subsection (b) of this section, if such lien is—

(A) a judicial lien, other than a judicial lien that secures a debt—; or

(i) to a spouse, former spouse, or child of the debtor, for alimony to, maintenance for, or support

of such spouse or child, in connection with a separation agreement, divorce decree or other order of a court of record, determination made in accordance with State or territorial law by a governmental unit, or property settlement agreement; and

(ii) to the extent that such debt—

(I) is not assigned to another entity, voluntarily, by operation of law, or otherwise; and

(II) includes a liability designated as alimony, maintenance, or support, unless such liability is actually in the nature of alimony, maintenance or support.

(B) a nonpossessory, nonpurchase-money security interest in any—

(i) household furnishings, household goods, wearing apparel, appliances, books, animals, crops, musical instruments, or jewelry that are held primarily for the personal, family, or household use of the debtor or a dependent of the debtor;

(ii) implements, professional books, or tools, of the trade of the debtor or the trade of a dependent of the debtor; or

(iii) professionally prescribed health aids for the debtor or a dependent of the debtor.

(2)(A) For the purposes of this subsection, a lien shall be considered to impair an exemption to the extent that the sum of—

(i) the lien,

(ii) all other liens on the property; and

(iii) the amount of the exemption that the debtor could claim if there were no liens on the property; exceeds the value that the debtor's interest in the property would have in the absence of any liens.

(B) In the case of a property subject to more than 1 lien, a lien that has been avoided shall not be considered in making the calculation under subparagraph (A) with respect to other liens.

(C) This paragraph shall not apply with respect to a judgment arising out of a mortgage foreclosure.

(3) In a case in which State law that is applicable to the debtor—

(A) permits a person to voluntarily waive a right to claim exemptions under subsection (d) or prohibits a debtor from claiming exemptions under subsection (d); and

(B) either permits the debtor to claim exemptions under State law without limitation in amount, except to the extent that the debtor has permitted the fixing of a consensual lien on any property or prohibits avoidance of a consensual lien on property otherwise eligible to be claimed as exempt property; the debtor may not avoid the fixing of a lien on an interest of the debtor or a dependent of the debtor in property if the lien is a nonpossessory, nonpurchase-money security interest in implements, professional books, or tools of the trade of the debtor or a dependent of the debtor or farm

animals or crops of the debtor or a dependent of the debtor to the extent the value of such implements, professional books, tools of the trade, animals, and crops exceeds $5,000.

(g) Notwithstanding sections 550 and 551 of this title, the debtor may exempt under subsection (b) of this section property that the trustee recovers under section 501(c)(2), 542, 543, 550, 551, or 553 of this title, to the extent that the debtor could have exempted such property under subsection (b) of this section if such property had not been transferred, if—

(1)(A) such transfer was not a voluntary transfer of such property by the debtor; and

(B) the debtor did not conceal such property; or

(2) the debtor could have avoided such transfer under subsection (f)(2) of this section.

(h) The debtor may avoid a transfer of property of the debtor or recover a setoff to the extent that the debtor could have exempted such property under subsection (g)(1) of this section if the trustee had avoided such transfer, if—

(1) such transfer is avoidable by the trustee under section 544, 545, 547, 548, 549, or 724(a) of this title or recoverable by the trustee under section 553 of this title; and

(2) the trustee does not attempt to avoid such transfer.

(i)(1) If the debtor avoids a transfer or recovers a setoff under subection (f) or (h) of this section, the debtor may recover in the manner prescribed by, and subject to the limitations of, section 550 of this title, the same as if the trustee had avoided such transfer, and may exempt any property so recovered under subsection (b) of this section.

(2) Notwithstanding section 551 of this title, a transfer avoided under section 544, 545, 547, 548, 549, or 724(a) of this title, under subsection (f) or (h) of this section, or property recovered under section 553 of this title, may be preserved for the benefit of the debtor to the extent that the debtor may exempt such property under subsection (g) of this section or paragraph (1) of this subsection.

(j) Notwithstanding subsections (g) and (i) of this section, the debtor may exempt a particular kind of property under subsections (g) and (i) of this section only to the extent that the debtor has exempted less property in value of such kind than that to which the debtor is entitled under subsection (b) of this section.

(k) Property that the debtor exempts under this section is not liable for payment of any administrative expense except—

(1) the aliquot share of the costs and expenses of avoiding a transfer of property that the debtor exempts under subsection (g) of this section, or of recovery of such property, that is attributable to the value of the portion of such property exempted in relation to the value of the property recovered; and

(2) any costs and expenses of avoiding a transfer

under subsection (f) or (h) of this section, or of recovery of property under subsection (i)(1) of this section, that the debtor has not paid.

(*l*) The debtor shall file a list of property that the debtor claims as exempt under subsection (b) of this section. If the debtor does not file such a list, a dependent of the debtor may file such a list, or may claim property as exempt from property of the estate on behalf of the debtor. Unless a party in interest objects, the property claimed as exempt on such list is exempt.

(m) Subject to the limitation in subsection (b), this section shall apply separately with respect to each debtor in a joint case.

§ 523. Exceptions to discharge

(a) A discharge under section 727, 1141, 1228(a), 1228(b), or 1328(b) of this title does not discharge an individual debtor from any debt—

(1) for a tax or a customs duty—

(A) of the kind and for the periods specified in section 507(a)(2) or 507(a)(8) of this title, whether or not a claim for such tax was filed or allowed;

(B) with respect to which a return, if required—

(i) was not filed; or

(ii) was filed after the date on which such return was last due, under applicable law or under any extension, and after two years before the date of the filing of the petition; or

(C) with respect to which the debtor made a fraudulent return or willfully attempted in any manner to evade or defeat such tax;

(2) for money, property, services, or an extension, renewal, or refinancing of credit, to the extent obtained by—

(A) false pretenses, a false representation, or actual fraud, other than a statement respecting the debtor's or an insider's financial condition;

(B) use of a statement in writing—

(i) that is materially false;

(ii) respecting the debtor's or an insider's financial condition;

(iii) on which the creditor to whom the debtor is liable for such money, property, services, or credit reasonably relied; and

(iv) that the debtor caused to be made or published with intent to deceive; or

(C) for purposes of subparagraph (A) of this paragraph, consumer debts owed to a single creditor and aggregating more than $1,000 for "luxury goods or services" incurred by an individual debtor on or within 60 days before the order for relief under this title, or cash advances aggregating more than $1,000 that are extensions of consumer credit under an open end credit plan obtained by an individual debtor on or within 60 days before the order for

relief under this title, are presumed to be nondischargeable; "luxury goods or services" do not include goods or services reasonably acquired for the support or maintenance of the debtor or a dependent of the debtor; an extension of consumer credit under an open end credit plan is to be defined for purposes of this subparagraph as it is defined in the Consumer Credit Protection Act;

(3) neither listed nor scheduled under section 521(1) of this title, with the name, if known to the debtor, of the creditor to whom such debt is owed, in time to permit—

(A) if such debt is not of a kind specified in paragraph (2), (4), or (6) of this subsection, timely filing of a proof of claim, unless such creditor had notice or actual knowledge of the case in time for such timely filing; or

(B) if such debt is of a kind specified in paragraph (2), (4), or (6) of this subsection, timely filing of a proof of claim and timely request for a determination of dischargeability of such debt under one of such paragraphs, unless such creditor had notice or actual knowledge of the case in time for such timely filing and request;

(4) for fraud or defalcation while acting in a fiduciary capacity, embezzlement, or larceny;

(5) to a spouse, former spouse, or child of the debtor, for alimony to, maintenance for, or support of such spouse or child, in connection with a separation agreement, divorce decree or other order of a court of record, determination made in accordance with state or territorial law by a governmental unit, or property settlement agreement, but not to the extent that—

(A) such debt is assigned to another entity, voluntarily, by operation of law, or otherwise (other than debts assigned pursuant to section 402(a)(26) of the Social Security Act, or any such debt which has been assigned to the Federal Government or to a State or any political subdivision of such State); or

(B) such debt includes a liability designated as alimony, maintenance, or support, unless such liability is actually in the nature of alimony, maintenance, or support;

(6) for willful and malicious injury by the debtor to another entity or to the property of another entity;

(7) to the extent such debt is for a fine, penalty, or forfeiture payable to and for the benefit of a governmental unit, and is not compensation for actual pecuniary loss, other than a tax penalty—

(A) relating to a tax of a kind not specified in paragraph (1) of this subsection; or

(B) imposed with respect to a transaction or event that occurred before three years before the date of the filing of the petition;

(8) for an educational benefit overpayment or loan made, insured or guaranteed by a governmental unit, or

made under any program funded in whole or in part by a governmental unit or nonprofit institution, or for an obligation to repay funds received as an educational benefit, scholarship or stipend, unless—

(A) such loan, benefit, scholarship, or stipend overpayment first became due more than 7 years (exclusive of any applicable suspension of the repayment period) before the date of the filing of the petition; or

(B) excepting such debt from discharge under this paragraph will impose an undue hardship on the debtor and the debtor's dependents;

(9) for death or personal injury caused by the debtor's operation of a motor vehicle if such operation was unlawful because the debtor was intoxicated from using alcohol, a drug, or another substance;

(10) that was or could have been listed or scheduled by the debtor in a prior case concerning the debtor under this title or under the Bankruptcy Act in which the debtor waived discharge, or was denied a discharge under section 727(a)(2), (3), (4), (5), (6), or (7) of this title, or under section 14c(1), (2), (3), (4), (6), or (7) of such Act;

(11) provided in any final judgment, unreviewable order, or consent order or decree entered in any court of the United States or of any State, issued by a Federal depository institutions regulatory agency, or contained in any settlement agreement entered into by the debtor, arising from any act of fraud or defalcation while acting in a fiduciary capacity committed with respect to any depository institution or insured credit union; or

(12) for malicious or reckless failure to fulfill any commitment by the debtor to a Federal depository institutions regulatory agency to maintain the capital of an insured depository institution, except that this paragraph shall not extend any such commitment which would otherwise be terminated due to any act of such agency;

(13) for any payment of an order of restitution issued under title 18, United States Code;

(14) incurred to pay a tax to the United States that would be nondischargeable pursuant to paragraph (1);

(15) not of the kind described in paragraph (5) that is incurred by the debtor in the course of a divorce or separation or in connection with a separation agreement, divorce decree or other order of a court of record, a determination made in accordance with State or territorial law by a governmental unit unless—

(A) the debtor does not have the ability to pay such debt from income or property of the debtor not reasonably necessary to be expended for the maintenance or support of the debtor or a dependent of the debtor and, if the debtor is engaged in a business, for the payment of expenditures necessary for the continuation, preservation, and operation of such business; or

(B) discharging such debt would result in a ben-

efit to the debtor that outweighs the detrimental consequences to a spouse, former spouse, or child of the debtor;

(16) for a fee or assessment that becomes due and payable after the order for relief to a membership association with respect to the debtor's interest in a dwelling unit that has condominium ownership or in a share of a cooperative housing corporation, but only if such fee or assessment is payable for a period during which—

(A) the debtor physically occupied a dwelling unit in the condominium or cooperative project; or

(B) the debtor rented the dwelling unit to a tenant and received payments from the tenant for such period,

but nothing in this paragraph shall except from discharge the debt of a debtor for a membership association fee or assessment for a period arising before entry of the order for relief in a pending or subsequent bankruptcy case.

(b) Notwithstanding subsection (a) of this section, a debt that was excepted from discharge under subsection (a)(1), (a)(3), or (a)(8) of this section, under section 17a(1), 17a(3), or 17a(5) of the Bankruptcy Act, under section 439A of the Higher Education Act of 1965, or under section 733(g) of the Public Health Service Act in a prior case concerning the debtor under this title, or under the Bankruptcy Act, is dischargeable in a case under this title unless, by the terms of subsection (a) of this section, such debt is not dischargeable in the case under this title.

(c)(1) Except as provided in subsection (a)(3)(B) of this section, the debtor shall be discharged from a debt of a kind specified in paragraph (2), (4), (6), or (15) of subsection (a) of this section, unless, on request of the creditor to whom such debt is owed, and after notice and a hearing, the court determines such debt to be excepted from discharge under paragraph (2), (4), (6), or (15), as the case may be, of subsection (a) of this section.

(2) Paragraph (1) shall not apply in the case of a Federal depository institutions regulatory agency seeking, in its capacity as conservator, receiver, or liquidating agent for an insured depository institution, to recover a debt described in subsection (a)(2), (a)(4), (a)(6), or (a)(11) owed to such institution by an institution-affiliated party unless the receiver, conservator, or liquidating agent was appointed in time to reasonably comply, or for a Federal depository institutions regulatory agency acting in its corporate capacity as a successor to such receiver, conservator, or liquidating agent to reasonably comply, with subsection (a)(3)(B) as a creditor of such institution-affiliated party with respect to such debt.

(d) If a creditor requests a determination of dischargeability of a consumer debt under subsection (a)(2) of this section, and such debt is discharged, the court shall grant judgment in favor of the debtor for the costs of, and a reasonable attorney's fee for, the proceeding if the court finds that the position of the creditor was not substantially justified, except that the court shall not award such costs

and fees if special circumstances would make the award unjust.

(e) Any institution-affiliated party of an insured depository institution shall be considered to be acting in a fiduciary capacity with respect to the purposes of subsection (a)(4) or (11).

§ 524. Effect of discharge

(a) A discharge in a case under this title—

(1) voids any judgment at any time obtained, to the extent that such judgment is a determination of the personal liability of the debtor with respect to any debt discharged under section 727, 944, 1141, 1228, or 1328 of this title, whether or not discharge of such debt is waived;

(2) operates as an injunction against the commencement or continuation of an action, the employment of process, or an act, to collect, recover or offset any such debt as a personal liability of the debtor, whether or not discharge of such debt is waived; and

(3) operates as an injunction against the commencement or continuation of an action, the employment of process, or an act, to collect or recover from, or offset against, property of the debtor of the kind specified in section 541(a)(2) of this title that is acquired after the commencement of the case, on account of any allowable community claim, except a community claim that is excepted from discharge under section 523, 1228(a)(1), or 1328(a)(1) of this title, or that would be so excepted, determined in accordance with the provisions of sections 523(c) and 523(d) of this title, in a case concerning the debtor's spouse commenced on the date of the filing of the petition in the case concerning the debtor, whether or not discharge of the debt based on such community claim is waived.

(b) Subsection (a)(3) of this section does not apply if—

(1)(A) the debtor's spouse is a debtor in a case under this title, or a bankrupt or a debtor in a case under the Bankruptcy Act, commenced within six years of the date of the filing of the petition in the case concerning the debtor; and

(B) the court does not grant the debtor's spouse a discharge in such case concerning the debtor's spouse; or

(2)(A) the court would not grant the debtor's spouse a discharge in a case under chapter 7 of this title concerning such spouse commenced on the date of the filing of the petition in the case concerning the debtor; and

(B) a determination that the court would not so grant such discharge is made by the bankruptcy court within the time and in the manner provided for a determination under section 727 of this title of whether a debtor is granted a discharge.

(c) An agreement between a holder of a claim and the debtor, the consideration for which, in whole or in part, is based on a debt that is dischargeable in a case under this title is enforceable only to any extent enforceable under applicable nonbankruptcy law, whether or not discharge of such debt is waived, only if—

(1) such agreement was made before the granting of the discharge under section 727, 1141, 1228, or 1328 of this title;

(2)(A) such agreement contains a clear and conspicuous statement which advises the debtor that the agreement may be rescinded at any time prior to discharge or within sixty days after such agreement is filed with the court, whichever occurs later, by giving notice of rescission to the holder of such claim; and

(B) such agreement contains a clear and conspicuous statement which advises the debtor that such agreement is not required under this title, under nonbankruptcy law, or under any agreement not in accordance with the provisions of this subsection;

(3) such agreement has been filed with the court and, if applicable, accompanied by a declaration or an affidavit of the attorney that represented the debtor during the course of negotiating an agreement under this subsection, which states that—

(A) such agreement represents a fully informed and voluntary agreement by the debtor;

(B) such agreement does not impose an undue hardship on the debtor or a dependent of the debtor; and

(C) the attorney fully advised the debtor of the legal effect and consequences of—

(i) an agreement of the kind specified in this subsection; and

(ii) any default under such an agreement;

(4) the debtor has not rescinded such agreement at any time prior to discharge or within sixty days after such agreement is filed with the court, whichever occurs later, by giving notice of rescission to the holder of such claim;

(5) the provisions of subsection (d) of this section have been complied with; and

(6)(A) in a case concerning an individual who was not represented by an attorney during the course of negotiating an agreement under this subsection, the court approves such agreement as—

(i) not imposing an undue hardship on the debtor or a dependent of the debtor; and

(ii) in the best interest of the debtor.

(B) Subparagraph (A) shall not apply to the extent that such debt is a consumer debt secured by real property.

(d) In a case concerning an individual, when the court has determined whether to grant or not to grant a discharge under section 727, 1141, 1228, or 1328 of this title, the court may hold a hearing at which the debtor shall appear in person. At any such hearing, the court may inform the debtor that a discharge has been granted or the reason why a discharge has not been granted. If a discharge has been granted and if the debtor desires to make an agreement of the kind specified in subsection (c) of this section and was

not represented by an attorney during the course of negotiating such agreement, then the court shall hold a hearing at which the debtor shall appear in person and at such hearing the court shall

(1) inform the debtor—

(A) that such an agreement is not required under this title, under nonbankruptcy law, or under any agreement not made in accordance with the provisions of subsection (c) of this section; and

(B) of the legal effect and consequences of—

(i) an agreement of the kind specified in subsection (c) of this section; and

(ii) a default under such an agreement; and

(2) determine whether the agreement that the debtor desires to make complies with the requirements of subsection (c)(6) of this section, if the consideration for such agreement is based in whole or in part on a consumer debt that is not secured by real property of the debtor.

(e) Except as provided in subsection (a)(3) of this section, discharge of a debt of the debtor does not affect the liability of any other entity on, or the property of any other entity for, such debt.

(f) Nothing contained in subsection (c) or (d) of this section prevents a debtor from voluntarily repaying any debt.

(g)(1)(A) After notice and hearing, a court that enters an order confirming a plan of reorganization under chapter 11 may issue, in connection with such order, an injunction in accordance with this subsection to supplement the injunctive effect of a discharge under this section.

(B) An injunction may be issued under subparagraph (A) to enjoin entities from taking legal action for the purpose of directly or indirectly collecting, recovering, or receiving payment or recovery with respect to any claim or demand that, under a plan of reorganization, is to be paid in whole or in part by a trust described in paragraph (2)(B)(i), except such legal actions as are expressly allowed by the injunction, the confirmation order, or the plan of reorganization.

(2)(A) Subject to subsection (h), if the requirements of subparagraph (B) are met at the time an injunction described in paragraph (1) is entered, then after entry of such injunction, any proceeding that involves the validity, application, construction, or modification of such injunction, or of this subsection with respect to such injunction, may be commenced only in the district court in which such injunction was entered, and such court shall have exclusive jurisdiction over any such proceeding without regard to the amount in controversy.

(B) The requirements of this subparagraph are that—

(i) the injunction is to be implemented in connection with a trust that, pursuant to the plan or reorganization—

(I) is to assume the liabilities of a debtor

which at the time of entry of the order for relief has been named as a defendant in personal injury, wrongful death, or property-damage actions seeking recovery for damages allegedly caused by the presence of, or exposure to, asbestos or asbestos-containing products;

(II) is to be funded in whole or in part by the securities of 1 or more debtors involved in such plan and by the obligation of such debtor or debtors to make future payments, including dividends;

(III) is to own, or by the exercise of rights granted under such plan would be entitled to own if specified contingencies occur, or majority of the voting shares of—

(aa) each such debtor;

(bb) the parent corporation of each such debtor; or

(cc) a subsidiary of each such debtor that is also a debtor; and

(IV) is to use its assets or income to pay claims and demands; and

(ii) subject to subsection (h), the court determines that—

(I) the debtor is likely to be subject to substantial future demands for payment arising out of the same or similar conduct or events that gave rise to the claims that are addressed by the injunction;

(II) the actual amounts, numbers, and timing of such future demands cannot be determined;

(III) pursuit of such demands outside the procedures prescribed by such plan is likely to threaten the plan's purpose to deal equitably with claims and future demands;

(IV) as part of the process of seeking confirmation of such plan—

(aa) the terms of the injunction proposed to be issued under paragraph (1)(A), including any provisions barring actions against third parties pursuant to paragraph (4)(A), are set out in such plan and in any disclosure statement supporting the plan; and

(bb) a separate class or classes or the claimants whose claims are to be addressed by a trust described in clause (i) is established and votes, by at least 75 percent of those voting, in favor of the plan; and

(V) subject to subsection (h), pursuant to court orders or otherwise, the trust will operate through mechanisms such as structured, periodic, or supplemental payments, pro rata distributions, matrices, or periodic review of estimates of the numbers and values of present claims and future demands, or other comparable mechanisms, that provide reasonable assurance that the trust will value, and be in a financial position to pay, pres-

ent claims and future demands that involve similar claims in substantially the same manner.

(3)(A) If the requirements of paragraph (2)(B) are met and the order confirming the plan or reorganization was issued or affirmed by the district court that has jurisdiction over the reorganization case, then after the time for appeal of the order that issues or affirms the plan—

(i) the injunction shall be valid and enforceable and may not be revoked or modified by any court except through appeal in accordance with paragraph (6);

(ii) no entity that pursuant to such plan or thereafter becomes a direct or indirect transferee of, or successor to any assets of, a debtor or trust that is the subject of the injunction shall be liable with respect to any claim or demand made against such entity by reason of its becoming such a transferee or successor; and

(iii) no entity that pursuant to such plan or thereafter makes a loan to such a debtor or trust or to such a successor or transferee shall, by reason of making the loan, be liable with respect to any claim or demand made against such entity, nor shall any pledge of assets made in connection with such a loan be upset or impaired for that reason;

(B) Subparagraph (A) shall not be construed to—

(i) imply that an entity described in subparagraph (A)(ii) or (iii) would, if this paragraph were not applicable, necessarily be liable to any entity by reason of any of the acts described in subparagraph (A);

(ii) relieve any such entity of the duty to comply with, or of liability under, any Federal or State law regarding the making of a fraudulent conveyance in a transaction described in subparagraph (A)(ii) or (iii); or

(iii) relieve a debtor of the debtor's obligation to comply with the terms of the plan of reorganization, or affect the power of the court to exercise its authority under sections 1141 and 1142 to compel the debtor to do so.

(4)(A)(i) Subject to subparagraph (B), an injunction described in paragraph (1) shall be valid and enforceable against all entities that it addresses.

(ii) Notwithstanding the provisions of section 524(e), such an injunction may bar any action directed against a third party who is identifiable from the terms of such injunction (by name or as part of an identifiable group) and is alleged to be directly or indirectly liable for the conduct of, claims against, or demands on the debtor to the extent such alleged liability of such third party arises by reason of—

(I) the third party's ownership of a financial interest in the debtor, a past or present affiliate of the debtor, or a predecessor in interest of the debtor;

(II) the third party's involvement in the management of the debtor or a predecessor in interest of the debtor, or service as an officer, director or employee of the debtor or a related party;

(III) the third party's provision of insurance to the debtor or a related party; or

(IV) the third party's involvement in a transaction changing the corporate structure, or in a loan or other financial transaction affecting the financial condition, of the debtor or a related party, including but not limited to—

(aa) involvement in providing financing (debt or equity), or advice to an entity involved in such a transaction; or

(bb) acquiring or selling a financial interest in an entity as part of such a transaction.

(iii) As used in this subparagraph, the term 'related party' means—

(I) a past or present affiliate of the debtor;

(II) a predecessor in interest of the debtor; or

(III) any entity that owned a financial interest in—

(aa) the debtor;

(bb) a past or present affiliate of the debtor; or

(cc) a predecessor in interest of the debtor.

(B) Subject to subsection (h), if, under a plan or reorganization, a kind of demand described in such plan is to be paid in whole or in part by a trust described in paragraph (2)(B)(i) in connection with which an injunction described in paragraph (1) is to be implemented, then such injunction shall be valid and enforceable with respect to a demand of such kind made, after such plan is confirmed, against the debtor or debtors involved, or against a third party described in subparagraph (A)(ii), if—

(i) as part of the proceedings leading to issuance of such injunction, the court appoints a legal representative for the purpose of protecting the rights of persons that might subsequently assert demands for such kind, and

(ii) the court determines, before entering the order confirming such plan, that identifying such debtor or debtors, or such third party (by name or as part of an identifiable group), in such injunction with respect to such demands for purposes of this subparagraph is fair and equitable with respect to the persons that might subsequently assert such demands, in light of the benefits provided, or to be provided, to such trust on behalf of such debtor or debtors or such third party.

(5) In this subsection, the term "demand" means a demand for payment, present or future, that—

(A) was not a claim during the proceedings leading to the confirmation of a plan of reorganization;

(B) arises out of the same or similar conduct or

events that gave rise to the claims addressed by the injunction issued under paragraph (1); and

(C) pursuant to the plan, is to be paid by a trust described in paragraph (2)(B)(i).

(6) Paragraph (3)(A)(i) does not bar an action taken by or at the direction of an appellate court on appeal of an injunction issued under paragraph (1) or of the order of confirmation that relates to the injunction.

(7) This subsection does not affect the operation of section 1144 or the power of the district court to refer a proceeding under section 157 of title 28 or any reference of a proceeding made prior to the date of the enactment of this subsection.

(h) Application to Existing Injunctions.—For purposes of subsection (g)—

(1) subject to paragraph (2), if an injunction of the kind described in subsection (g)(1)(B) was issued before the date of the enactment of this Act, as part of a plan or reorganization confirmed by an order entered before such date, then the injunction shall be considered to meet the requirements of subsection (g)(2)(B) for purposes of subsection (g)(2)(A), and to satisfy subsection (g)(4)(A)(ii), if—

(A) the court determined at the time the plan was confirmed that the plan was fair and equitable in accordance with the requirements of section 1129(b);

(B) as part of the proceedings leading to issuance of such injunction and confirmation of such plan, the court had appointed a legal representative for the purpose of protecting the rights of persons that might subsequently assert demands described in subsection (g)(4)(B) with respect to such plan; and

(C) such legal representative did not object to confirmation of such plan or issuance of such injunction; and

(2) for purposes of paragraph (1), if a trust described in subsection (g)(2)(B)(i) is subject to a court order on the date of the enactment of this Act staying such trust from settling or paying further claims—

(A) the requirements of subsection (g)(2)(B)(ii)(V) shall not apply with respect to such trust until such stay is lifted or dissolved; and

(B) if such trust meets such requirements on the date such stay is lifted or dissolved, such trust shall be considered to have met such requirements continuously from the date of the enactment of this Act.

§ 525. Protection against discriminatory treatment

(a) Except as provided in the Perishable Agricultural Commodities Act, 1930, the Packers and Stockyards Act, 1921, and section 1 of the Act entitled "An Act making appropriations for the Department of Agriculture for the fiscal year ending June 30, 1944, and for other purposes,"

approved July 12, 1943, a governmental unit may not deny, revoke, suspend, or refuse to renew a license, permit, charter, franchise, or other similar grant to, condition such a grant to, discriminate with respect to such a grant against, deny employment to, terminate the employment of, or discriminate with respect to employment against, a person that is or has been a debtor under this title or a bankrupt or a debtor under the Bankruptcy Act, or another person with whom such bankrupt or debtor has been associated, solely because such bankrupt or debtor is or has been a debtor under this title or a bankrupt or debtor under the Bankruptcy Act, has been insolvent before the commencement of the case under this title, or during the case but before the debtor is granted or denied a discharge, or has not paid a debt that is dischargeable in the case under this title or that was discharged under the Bankruptcy Act.

(b) No private employer may terminate the employment of, or discriminate with respect to employment against, an individual who is or has been a debtor under this title, a debtor or bankrupt under the Bankruptcy Act, or an individual associated with such debtor or bankrupt, solely because such debtor or bankrupt—

(1) is or has been a debtor under this title or a debtor or bankrupt under the Bankruptcy Act;

(2) has been insolvent before the commencement of a case under this title or during the case but before the grant or denial of a discharge; or

(3) has not paid a debt that is dischargeable in a case under this title or that was discharged under the Bankruptcy Act.

(c)(1) A governmental unit that operates a student grant or loan program and a person engaged in a business that includes the making of loans guaranteed or insured under a student loan program may not deny a grant, loan, loan guarantee, or loan insurance to a person that is or has been a debtor under this title or a bankrupt or debtor under the Bankruptcy Act, or another person with whom the debtor or bankrupt has been associated, because the debtor or bankrupt is or has been a debtor under this title or a bankrupt or debtor under the Bankruptcy Act, has been insolvent before the commencement of a case under this title or during the pendency of the case but before the debtor is granted or denied a discharge, or has not paid a debt that is dischargeable in the case under this title or that was discharged under the Bankruptcy Act.

(2) In this section, "student loan program" means the program operated under part B, D, or E of title IV of the Higher Education Act of 1965 or a similar program operated under State or local law.

SUBCHAPTER III—THE ESTATE

§ 541. Property of the estate

(a) The commencement of a case under section 301, 302, or 303 of this title creates an estate. Such estate is

comprised of all the following property, wherever located and by whomever held:

(1) Except as provided in subsections (b) and (c)(2) of this section, all legal or equitable interests of the debtor in property as of the commencement of the case.

(2) All interests of the debtor and the debtor's spouse in community property as of the commencement of the case that is—

(A) under the sole, equal, or joint management and control of the debtor; or

(B) liable for an allowable claim against the debtor, or for both an allowable claim against the debtor and an allowable claim against the debtor's spouse, to the extent that such interest is so liable.

(3) Any interest in property that the trustee recovers under section 329(b), 363(n), 543, 550, 553, of 723 of this title.

(4) Any interest in property preserved for the benefit of or ordered transferred to the estate under section 510(c) or 551 of this title.

(5) Any interest in property that would have been property of the estate if such interest had been an interest of the debtor on the date of the filing of the petition, and that the debtor acquires or becomes entitled to acquire within 180 days after such date—

(A) by bequest, devise, or inheritance;

(B) as a result of a property settlement agreement with the debtor's spouse, or of an interlocutory or final divorce decree; or

(C) as a beneficiary of a life insurance policy or of a death benefit plan.

(6) Proceeds, product, offspring, rents, or profits of or from property of the estate, except such as are earnings from services performed by an individual debtor after the commencement of the case.

(7) Any interest in property that the estate acquires after the commencement of the case.

(b) Property of the estate does not include—

(1) any power that the debtor may exercise solely for the benefit of an entity other than the debtor;

(2) any interest of the debtor as a lessee under a lease of nonresidential real property that has terminated at the expiration of the stated term of such lease before the commencement of the case under this title, and ceases to include any interest of the debtor as a lessee under a lease of nonresidential real property that has terminated at the expiration of the stated term of such lease during the case;

(3) any eligibility of the debtor to participate in programs authorized under the Higher Education Act of 1965 (20 U.S.C. 1001 et seq.; 42 U.S.C. 2751 et seq.), or any accreditation status or State licensure of the debtor as an educational institution;

(4) any interest of the debtor in liquid or gaseous hydrocarbons to the extent that—

(A)(i) the debtor has transferred or has agreed to transfer such interest pursuant to a farmout agreement or any written agreement directly related to a farmout agreement; and

(ii) but for the operation of this paragraph, the estate could include the interest referred to in clause (i) only by virtue of section 365 or 544(a)(3) of this title; or

(B)(i) the debtor has transferred such interest pursuant to a written conveyance of a production payment to an entity that does not participate in the operation of the property from which such production payment is transferred; and

(ii) but for the operation of this paragraph, the estate could include the interest referred to in clause (i) only by virtue of section 542 of this title;

Paragraph (4) shall not be construed to exclude from the estate any consideration the debtor retains, receives, or is entitled to receive for transferring an interest in liquid or gaseous hydrocarbons pursuant to a farmout agreement; or

(5) any interest in cash or cash equivalents that constitute proceeds of a sale by the debtor of a money order that is made—

(A) on or after the date that is 14 days prior to the date on which the petition is filed; and

(B) under an agreement with a money order issuer that prohibits the commingling of such proceeds with property of the debtor (notwithstanding that, contrary to the agreement, the proceeds may have been commingled with property of the debtor),

unless the money order issuer had not taken action, prior to the filing of the petition, to require compliance with the prohibition.

(c)(1) Except as provided in paragraph (2) of this subsection, an interest of the debtor in property becomes property of the estate under subsection (a)(1), (a)(2), or (a)(5) of this section notwithstanding any provision in an agreement, transfer instrument, or applicable nonbankruptcy law—

(A) that restricts or conditions transfer of such interest by the debtor; or

(B) that is conditioned on the insolvency or financial condition of the debtor, on the commencement of a case under this title, or on the appointment of or taking possession by a trustee in a case under this title or a custodian before such commencement and that effects or gives an option to effect a forfeiture, modification, or termination of the debtor's interest in property.

(2) A restriction on the transfer of a beneficial interest of the debtor in a trust that is enforceable under applicable nonbankruptcy law is enforceable in a case under this title.

(d) Property in which the debtor holds, as of the commencement of the case, only legal title and not an equitable interest, such as a mortgage secured by real property, or an interest in such a mortgage, sold by the debtor but as to which the debtor retains legal title to service or supervise the servicing of such mortgage or interest, becomes property of the estate under subsection (a)(1) or (2) of this

section only to the extent of the debtor's legal title to such property, but not to the extent of any equitable interest in such property that the debtor does not hold.

§ 542. Turnover of property to the estate

(a) Except as provided in subsection (c) or (d) of this section, an entity, other than a custodian, in possession, custody, or control, during the case, of property that the trustee may use, sell, or lease under section 363 of this title, or that the debtor may exempt under section 522 of this title, shall deliver to the trustee, and account for, such property or the value of such property, unless such property is of inconsequential value or benefit to the estate.

(b) Except as provided in subsection (c) or (d) of this section, an entity that owes a debt that is property of the estate and that is matured, payable on demand, or payable on order, shall pay such debt to, or on the order of, the trustee, except to the extent that such debt may be offset under section 553 of this title against a claim against the debtor.

(c) Except as provided in section 362(a)(7) of this title, an entity that has neither actual notice nor actual knowledge of the commencement of the case concerning the debtor may transfer property of the estate, or pay a debt owing to the debtor, in good faith and other than in the manner specified in subsection (d) of this section, to an entity other than the trustee, with the same effect as to the entity making such transfer or payment as if the case under this title concerning the debtor had not been commenced.

(d) A life insurance company may transfer property of the estate or property of the debtor to such company in good faith, with the same effect with respect to such company as if the case under this title concerning the debtor had not been commenced, if such transfer is to pay a premium or to carry out a nonforfeiture insurance option, and is required to be made automatically, under a life insurance contract with such company that was entered into before the date of the filing of the petition and that is property of the estate.

(e) Subject to any applicable privilege, after notice and a hearing, the court may order an attorney, accountant, or other person that holds recorded information, including books, documents, records, and papers, relating to the debtor's property or financial affairs, to turn over or disclose such recorded information to the trustee.

§ 543. Turnover of property by a custodian

(a) A custodian with knowledge of the commencement of a case under this title concerning the debtor may not make any disbursement from, or take any action in the administration of, property of the debtor, proceeds, product, offspring, rents, or profits of such property, or property of the estate, in the possession, custody, or control of such custodian, except such action as is necessary to preserve such property.

(b) A custodian shall—

(1) deliver to the trustee any property of the debtor held by or transferred to such custodian, or proceeds, product, offspring, rents, or profits of such property, that is in such custodian's possession, custody, or control on the date that such custodian acquires knowledge of the commencement of the case; and

(2) file an accounting of any property of the debtor, or proceeds, product, offspring, rents, or profits of such property, that, at any time, came into the possession, custody, or control of such custodian.

(c) The court, after notice and a hearing, shall—

(1) protect all entities to which a custodian has become obligated with respect to such property or proceeds, product, offspring, rents, or profits of such property;

(2) provide for the payment of reasonable compensation for services rendered and costs and expenses incurred by such custodian; and

(3) surcharge such custodian, other than an assignee for the benefit of the debtor's creditors that was appointed or took possession more than 120 days before the date of the filing of the petition, for any improper or excessive disbursement, other than a disbursement that has been made in accordance with applicable law or that has been approved, after notice and a hearing, by a court of competent jurisdiction before the commencement of the case under this title.

(d) After notice and hearing, the bankruptcy court—

(1) may excuse compliance with subsection (a), (b), or (c) of this section if the interests of creditors and, if the debtor is not insolvent, of equity security holders would be better served by permitting a custodian to continue in possession, custody, or control of such property, and

(2) shall excuse compliance with subsections (a) and (b)(1) of this section if the custodian is an assignee for the benefit of the debtor's creditors that was appointed or took possession more than 120 days before the date of the filing of the petition, unless compliance with such subsections is necessary to prevent fraud or injustice.

§ 544. Trustee as lien creditor and as successor to certain creditors and purchasers

(a) The trustee shall have, as of the commencement of the case, and without regard to any knowledge of the trustee or of any creditor, the rights and powers of, or may avoid any transfer of property of the debtor or any obligation incurred by the debtor that is voidable by—

(1) a creditor that extends credit to the debtor at the time of the commencement of the case, and that

obtains, at such time and with respect to such credit, a judicial lien on all property on which a creditor on a simple contract could have obtained such a judicial lien, whether or not such a creditor exists;

(2) a creditor that extends credit to the debtor at the time of the commencement of the case, and obtains, at such time and with respect to such credit, an execution against the debtor that is returned unsatisfied at such time, whether or not such a creditor exists; or

(3) a bona fide purchaser of real property, other than fixtures, from the debtor, against whom applicable law permits such transfer to be perfected, that obtains the status of a bona fide purchaser and has perfected such transfer at the time of the commencement of the case, whether or not such a purchaser exists.

(b) The trustee may avoid any transfer of an interest of the debtor in property or any obligation incurred by the debtor that is voidable under applicable law by a creditor holding an unsecured claim that is allowable under section 502 of this title or that is not allowable only under section 502(e) of this title.

§ 545. Statutory liens

The trustee may avoid the fixing of a statutory lien on property of the debtor to the extent that such lien—

(1) first becomes effective against the debtor—

(A) when a case under this title concerning the debtor is commenced;

(B) when an insolvency proceeding other than under this title concerning the debtor is commenced;

(C) when a custodian is appointed or authorized to take or takes possession;

(D) when the debtor becomes insolvent;

(E) when the debtor's financial condition fails to meet a specified standard; or

(F) at the time of an execution against property of the debtor levied at the instance of an entity other than the older of such statutory lien;

(2) is not perfected or enforceable at the time of the commencement of the case against a bona fide purchaser that purchases such property at the time of the commencement of the case, whether or not such a purchaser exists;

(3) is for rent; or

(4) is a lien of distress for rent.

§ 546. Limitations on avoiding powers

(a) An action or proceeding under section 544, 545, 547, 548, or 553 of this title may not be commenced after the earlier of—

(1) the later of—

(A) 2 years after the entry of the order for relief; or

(B) 1 year after the appointment or election of the first trustee under section 702, 1104, 1163, 1202, or 1302 of this title if such appointment or such election occurs before the expiration of the period specified in subparagraph (A); or

(2) the time the case is closed or dismissed.

(b)(1) The rights and powers of a trustee under sections 544, 545, and 549 of this title are subject to any generally applicable law that—

(A) permits perfection of an interest in property to be effective against an entity that acquires rights in such property before the date of perfection; or

(B) provides for the maintenance or continuation of perfection of an interest in property to be effective against an entity that acquires rights in such property before the date on which action is taken to effect such maintenance or continuation.

(2) If—

(A) a law described in paragraph (1) requires seizure of such property or commencement of an action to accomplish such perfection, or maintenance or continuation of perfection of an interest in property; and

(B) such property has not been seized or such an action has not been commenced before the date of the filing of the petition;

such interest in such property shall be perfected, or perfection of such interest shall be maintained or continued, by giving notice within the time fixed by such law for such seizure or such commencement.

(c) Except as provided in subsection (d) of this section, the rights and powers of a trustee under sections 544(a), 545, 547, and 549 of this title are subject to any statutory or common-law right of a seller of goods that has sold goods to the debtor, in the ordinary course of such seller's business, to reclaim such goods if the debtor has received such goods while insolvent, but—

(1) such a seller may not reclaim any such goods unless such seller demands in writing reclamation of such goods—

(A) before 10 days after receipt of such goods by the debtor; or

(B) if such 10-day period expires after the commencement of the case, before 20 days after receipt of such goods by the debtor; and

(2) the court may deny reclamation to a seller with such a right of reclamation that has made such a demand only if the court—

(A) grants the claim of such a seller priority as a claim of a kind specified in section 503(b) of this title; or

(B) secures such claim by a lien.

(d) In the case of a seller who is a producer of grain sold to a grain storage facility, owned or operated by the debtor, in the ordinary course of such seller's business (as such terms are defined in section 557 of this title) or in the case of a United States fisherman who has caught fish

sold to a fish processing facility owned or operated by the debtor in the ordinary course of such fisherman's business, the rights and powers of the trustee under sections 544(a), 545, 547, and 549 of this title are subject to any statutory or common law right of such producer or fisherman to reclaim such grain or fish if the debtor has received such grain or fish while insolvent, but—

(1) such producer or fisherman may not reclaim any grain or fish unless such producer or fisherman demands, in writing, reclamation of such grain or fish before ten days after receipt thereof by the debtor; and

(2) the court may deny reclamation to such a producer or fisherman with a right of reclamation that has been made such a demand only if the court secures such claim by a lien.

(e) Notwithstanding sections 544, 545, 547, 548(a)(2), and 548(b) of this title, the trustee may not avoid a transfer that is a margin payment, as defined in section 101, 741, or 761 of this title, or settlement payment, as defined in section 101 or 741 of this title, made by or to a commodity broker, forward contract merchant, stockbroker, financial institution, or securities clearing agency, that is made before the commencement of the case, except under section 548(a)(1) of this title.

(f) Notwithstanding sections 544, 545, 547, 548(a)(2), and 548(b) of this title, the trustee may not avoid a transfer that is a margin payment, as defined in section 741 or 761 of this title, or settlement payment, as defined in section 741 of this title, made by or to a repo participant, in connection with a repurchase agreement and that is made before the commencement of the case, except under section 548(a)(1) of this title.

(g) Notwithstanding sections 544, 545, 547, 548(a)(2) and 548(b) of this title, the trustee may not avoid a transfer under a swap agreement, made by or to a swap participant, in connection with a swap agreement and that is made before the commencement of the case, except under section 548(a)(1) of this title.

(g)[1] Notwithstanding the rights and powers of a trustee under sections 544(a), 545, 547, 549, and 553, if the court determines on a motion by the trustee made not later than 120 days after the date of the order for relief in a case under chapter 11 of this title and after notice and a hearing, that a return is in the best interests of the estate, the debtor, with the consent of a creditor, may return goods shipped to the debtor by the creditor before the commencement of the case, and the creditor may offset the purchase price of such goods against any claim of the creditor against the debtor that arose before the commencement of the case.

§ 547. Preferences

(a) In this section—

(1) "inventory" means personal property leased or furnished, held for sale or lease, or to be furnished under a contract for service, raw materials, work in process, or materials used or consumed in a business, including farm products such as crops or livestock, held for sale or lease;

(2) "new value" means money or money's worth in goods, services, or new credit, or release by a transferee of property previously transferred to such transferee in a transaction that is neither void nor voidable by the debtor or the trustee under any applicable law, including proceeds of such property, but does not include an obligation substituted for an existing obligation;

(3) "receivable" means right to payment, whether or not such right has been earned by performance; and

(4) a debt for a tax is incurred on the day when such tax is last payable without penalty, including any extension.

(b) Except as provided in subsection (c) of this section, the trustee may avoid any transfer of an interest of the debtor in property—

(1) to or for the benefit of a creditor;

(2) for or on account of an antecedent debt owed by the debtor before such transfer was made;

(3) made while the debtor was insolvent;

(4) made—

(A) on or within 90 days before the date of the filing of the petition; or

(B) between ninety days and one year before the date of the filing of the petition, if such creditor at the time of such transfer was an insider; and

(5) that enables such creditor to receive more than such creditor would receive if—

(A) the case were a case under chapter 7 of this title;

(B) the transfer had not been made; and

(C) such creditor received payment of such debt to the extent provided by the provisions of this title.

(c) The trustee may not avoid under this section a transfer—

(1) to the extent that such transfer was—

(A) intended by the debtor and the creditor to or for whose benefit such transfer was made to be a contemporaneous exchange for new value given to the debtor; and

(B) in fact a substantially contemporaneous exchange;

(2) to the extent that such transfer was—

(A) in payment of a debt incurred by the debtor in the ordinary course of business or financial affairs of the debtor and the transferee;

(B) made in the ordinary course of business or financial affairs of the debtor and the transferee; and

(C) made according to ordinary business terms;

(3) that creates a security interest in property acquired by the debtor—

(A) to the extent such security interest secures new value that was—

---

1. Should probably be designated as subsection (h).

(i) given at or after the signing of a security agreement that contains a description of such property as collateral;

(ii) given by or on behalf of the secured party under such agreement;

(iii) given to enable the debtor to acquire such property; and

(iv) in fact used by the debtor to acquire such property; and

(B) that is perfected on or before 20 days after the debtor receives possession of such property;

(4) to or for the benefit of a creditor, to the extent that, after such transfer, such creditor gave new value to or for the benefit of the debtor—

(A) not secured by an otherwise unavoidable security interest; and

(B) on account of which new value the debtor did not make an otherwise unavoidable transfer to or for the benefit of such creditor;

(5) that creates a perfected security interest in inventory or a receivable or the proceeds of either, except to the extent that the aggregate of all such transfers to the transferee caused a reduction, as of the date of the filing of the petition and to the prejudice of other creditors holding unsecured claims, of any amount by which the debt secured by such security interest exceeded the value of all security interests for such debt on the later of—

(A)(i) with respect to a transfer to which subsection (b)(4)(A) of this section applies, 90 days before the date of the filing of the petition; or

(ii) with respect to a transfer to which subsection (b)(4)(B) of this section applies, one year before the date of the filing of the petition; or

(B) the date on which new value was first given under the security agreement creating such security interest;

(6) that is the fixing of a statutory lien that is not avoidable under section 545 of this title;

(7) to the extent such transfer was a bona fide payment of a debt to a spouse, former spouse, or child of the debtor, for alimony to, maintenance for, or support of such spouse or child, in connection with a separation agreement, divorce decree or other order of a court of record, determination made in accordance with State or territorial law by a governmental unit, or property settlement agreement, but not to the extent that such debt—

(A) is assigned to another entity, voluntarily, by operation of law, or otherwise; or

(B) includes a liability designated as alimony, maintenance, or support, unless such liability is actually in the nature of alimony, maintenance or support; or

(8) if, in a case filed by an individual debtor whose debts are primarily consumer debts, the aggregate value of all property that constitutes or is affected by such

transfer is less than $600.

(d) The trustee may avoid a transfer of an interest in property of the debtor transferred to or for the benefit of a surety to secure reimbursement of such a surety that furnished a bond or other obligation to dissolve a judicial lien that would have been avoidable by the trustee under subsection (b) of this section. The liability of such surety under such bond or obligation shall be discharged to the extent of the value of such property recovered by the trustee or the amount paid to the trustee.

(e)(1) For the purpose of this section—

(A) a transfer of real property other than fixtures, but including the interest of a seller or purchaser under a contract for the sale of real property, is perfected when a bona fide purchaser of such property from the debtor against whom applicable law permits such transfer to be perfected cannot acquire an interest that is superior to the interest of the transferee; and

(B) a transfer of a fixture or property other than real property is perfected when a creditor on a simple contract cannot acquire a judicial lien that is superior to the interest of the transferee.

(2) For the purposes of this section, except as provided in paragraph (3) of this subsection, a transfer is made—

(A) at the time such transfer takes effect between the transferor and the transferee, if such transfer is perfected at, or within 10 days after, such time, except as provided in subsection (c)(3)(B);

(B) at the time such transfer is perfected, if such transfer is perfected after such 10 days; or

(C) immediately before the date of the filing of the petition, if such transfer is not perfected at the later of—

(i) the commencement of the case; or

(ii) 10 days after such transfer takes effect between the transferor and the transferee.

(3) For the purposes of this section, a transfer is not made until the debtor has acquired rights in the property transferred.

(f) For the purposes of this section, the debtor is presumed to have been insolvent on and during the 90 days immediately preceding the date of the filing of the petition.

(g) For the purposes of this section, the trustee has the burden of proving the avoidability of a transfer under subsection (b) of this section, and the creditor or party in interest against whom recovery or avoidance is sought has the burden of proving the nonavoidability of a transfer under subsection (c) of this section.

§ 548. Fraudulent transfers and obligations

(a) The trustee may avoid any transfer of an interest of the debtor in property, or any obligation incurred by the debtor, that was made or incurred on or within one year before the date of the filing of the petition, if the debtor voluntarily or involuntarily—

(1) made such transfer or incurred such obligation

with actual intent to hinder, delay, or defraud any entity to which the debtor was or became, on or after the date that such transfer was made or such obligation was incurred, indebted; or

(2)(A) received less than a reasonably equivalent value in exchange for such transfer or obligation; and

(B)(i) was insolvent on the date that such transfer was made or such obligation was incurred, or became insolvent as a result of such transfer or obligation;

(ii) was engaged in business or a transaction, or was about to engage in business or a transaction, for which any property remaining with the debtor was an unreasonably small capital; or

(iii) intended to incur, or believed that the debtor would incur, debts that would be beyond the debtor's ability to pay as such debts matured.

(b) The trustee of a partnership debtor may avoid any transfer of an interest of the debtor in property, or any obligation incurred by the debtor, that was made or incurred on or within one year before the date of the filing of the petition, to a general partner in the debtor, if the debtor was insolvent on the date such transfer was made or such obligation was incurred, or became insolvent as a result of such transfer or obligation.

(c) Except to the extent that a transfer or obligation voidable under this section is voidable under section 544, 545, or 547 of this title, a transferee or obligee of such a transfer or obligation that takes for value and in good faith has a lien on or may retain any interest transferred or may enforce any obligation incurred, as the case may be, to the extent that such transferee or obligee gave value to the debtor in exchange for such transfer or obligation.

(d)(1) For the purposes of this section, a transfer is made when such transfer is so perfected that a bona fide purchaser from the debtor against whom applicable law permits such transfer to be perfected cannot acquire an interest in the property transferred that is superior to the interest in such property of the transferee, but if such transfer is not so perfected before the commencement of the case, such transfer is made immediately before the date of the filing of the petition.

(2) In this section—

(A) "value" means property, or satisfaction or securing of a present or antecedent debt of the debtor, but does not include an unperformed promise to furnish support to the debtor or to a relative of the debtor;

(B) a commodity broker, forward contract merchant, stockbroker, financial institution, or securities clearing agency that receives a margin payment, as defined in section 101, 741 or 761 of this title, or settlement payment, as defined in section 101 or 741 of this title, takes for value to the extent of such payment;

(C) a repo participant that receives a margin payment, as defined in section 741 or 761 of this title, or settlement payment, as defined in section 741 of this title, in connection with a repurchase agreement, takes for value to the extent of such payment; and

(D) a swap participant that receives a transfer in connection with a swap agreement takes for value to the extent of such transfer.

§ 549. Postpetition transactions

(a) Except as provided in subsection (b) or (c) of this section, the trustee may avoid a transfer of property of the estate—

(1) that occurs after the commencement of the case; and

(2)(A) that is authorized only under section 303(f) or 542(c) of this title; or

(B) that is not authorized under this title or by the court.

(b) In an involuntary case, the trustee may not avoid under subsection (a) of this section a transfer made after the commencement of such case but before the order for relief to the extent any value, including services, but not including satisfaction or securing of a debt that arose before the commencement of the case, is given after the commencement of the case in exchange for such transfer, notwithstanding any notice or knowledge of the case that the transferee has.

(c) The trustee may not avoid under subsection (a) of this section a transfer of real property to a good faith purchaser without knowledge of the commencement of the case and for present fair equivalent value unless a copy or notice of the petition was filed, where a transfer of such real property may be recorded to perfect such transfer, before such transfer is so perfected that a bona fide purchaser of such property, against whom applicable law permits such transfer to be perfected, could not acquire an interest that is superior to the interest of such good faith purchaser. A good faith purchaser without knowledge of the commencement of the case and for less than present fair equivalent value has a lien on the property transferred to the extent of any present value given, unless a copy or notice of the petition was so filed before such transfer was so perfected.

(d) An action or proceeding under this section may not be commenced after the earlier of—

(1) two years after the date of the transfer sought to be avoided; or

(2) the time the case is closed or dismissed.

§ 550. Liability of transferee of avoidable transfer

(a) Except as otherwise provided in this section, to the extent that a transfer is avoided under section 544, 545, 547, 548, 549, 553(b), or 724(a) of this title, the trustee may recover, for the benefit of the estate, the property transferred, or, if the court so orders, the value of such property, from—

(1) the initial transferee of such transfer or the entity for whose benefit such transfer was made; or

(2) any immediate or mediate transferee of such initial transferee.

(b) The trustee may not recover under section (a)(2) of this section from—

(1) a transferee that takes for value, including satisfaction or securing of a present or antecedent debt, in good faith, and without knowledge of the voidability of the transfer avoided; or

(2) any immediate or mediate good faith transferee of such transferee.

(c) If a transfer made between 90 days and one year before the filing of the petition—

(1) is avoided under section 547(b) of this title; and

(2) was made for the benefit of a creditor that at the time of such transfer was an insider;

the trustee may not recover under subsection (a) from a transferee that is not an insider.

(d) The trustee is entitled to only a single satisfaction under subsection (a) of this section.

(e)(1) A good faith transferee from whom the trustee may recover under subsection (a) of this section has a lien on the property recovered to secure the lessor of—

(A) the cost, to such transferee, of any improvement made after the transfer, less the amount of any profit realized by or accruing to such transferee from such property; and

(B) any increase in the value of such property as a result of such improvement, of the property transferred.

(2) In this subsection, "improvement" includes—

(A) physical additions or changes to the property transferred;

(B) repairs to such property;

(C) payment of any tax on such property;

(D) payment of any debt secured by a lien on such property that is superior or equal to the rights of the trustee; and

(E) preservation of such property.

(f) An action or proceeding under this section may not be commenced after the earlier of—

(1) one year after the avoidance of the transfer on account of which recovery under this section is sought; or

(2) the time the case is closed or dismissed.

§ 551. Automatic preservation of avoided transfer

Any transfer avoided under section 522, 544, 545, 547, 548, 549, or 724(a) of this title, or any lien void under section 506(d) of this title, is preserved for the benefit of the estate but only with respect to property of the estate.

§ 552. Postpetition effect of security interest

(a) Except as provided in subsection (b) of this section, property acquired by the estate or by the debtor after the

commencement of the case is not subject to any lien resulting from any security agreement entered into by the debtor before the commencement of the case.

(b)(1) Except as provided in section 363, 506(c), 522, 544, 545, 547, and 548 of this title, if the debtor and an entity entered into a security agreement before the commencement of the case and if the security interest created by such security agreement extends to property of the debtor acquired before the commencement of the case and to proceeds, product, offspring, or profits of such property, then such security interest extends to such proceeds, product, offspring, or profits acquired by the estate after the commencement of the case to the extent provided by such security agreement and by applicable non-bankruptcy law, except to any extent that the court, after notice and a hearing and based on the equities of the case, orders otherwise.

(2) Except as provided in sections 363, 506(c), 522, 544, 545, 547, and 548 of this title, and notwithstanding section 546(b) of this title, if the debtor and an entity entered into a security agreement before the commencement of the case and if the security interest created by such security agreement extends to property of the debtor acquired before the commencement of the case and to amounts paid as rents of such property or the fees, charges, accounts, or other payments for the use or occupancy of rooms and other public facilities in hotels, motels, or other lodging properties, then such security interest extends to such rents and such fees, charges, accounts, or other payments acquired by the estate after the commencement of the case to the extent provided in such security agreement, except to any extent that the court, after notice and a hearing and based on the equities of the case, orders otherwise.

§ 553. Setoff

(a) Except as otherwise provided in this section and in sections 362 and 363 of this title, this title does not affect any right of a creditor to offset a mutual debt owing by such creditor to the debtor that arose before the commencement of the case under this title against a claim of such creditor against the debtor that arose before the commencement of the case, except to the extent that—

(1) the claim of such creditor against the debtor is disallowed;

(2) such claim was transferred, by an entity other than the debtor, to such creditor—

(A) after the commencement of the case; or

(B)(i) after 90 days before the date of the filing of the petition; and

(ii) while the debtor was insolvent; or

(3) the debt owed to the debtor by such creditor was incurred by such creditor—

(A) after 90 days before the date of the filing of the petition;

(B) while the debtor was insolvent; and

(C) for the purpose of obtaining a right of setoff against the debtor.

(b)(1) Except with respect to a setoff of a kind described in section 362(b)(6), 362(b)(7), 362(b)(14), 365(h), or 365(i)(2) of this title, if a creditor offsets a mutual debt owing to the debtor against a claim against the debtor on or within 90 days before the date of the filing of the petition, then the trustee may recover from such creditor the amount so offset to the extent that any insufficiency on the date of such setoff is less than the insufficiency on the later of—

(A) 90 days before the date of the filing of the petition; and

(B) the first date during the 90 days immediately preceding the date of the filing of the petition on which there is an insufficiency.

(2) In this subsection, "insufficiency" means amount, if any, by which a claim against the debtor exceeds a mutual debt owing to the debtor by the holder of such claim.

(c) For the purposes of this section, the debtor is presumed to have been insolvent on and during the 90 days immediately preceding the date of the filing of the petition.

§ 554. Abandonment of property of the estate

(a) After notice and a hearing, the trustee may abandon any property of the estate that is burdensome to the estate or that is of inconsequential value and benefit to the estate.

(b) On request of a party in interest and after notice and a hearing, the court may order the trustee to abandon any property of the estate that is burdensome to the estate or that is of inconsequential value and benefit to the estate.

(c) Unless the court orders otherwise, any property scheduled under section 521(1) of this title not otherwise administered at the time of the closing of a case is abandoned to the debtor and administered for purposes of section 350 of this title.

(d) Unless the court orders otherwise, property of the estate that is not abandoned under this section and that is not administered in the case remains property of the estate.

§ 555. Contractual right to liquidate a securities contract

The exercise of a contractual right of a stockbroker, financial institution, or securities clearing agency to cause the liquidation of a securities contract, as defined in section 741 of this title, because of a condition of the kind specified in section 365(e)(1) of this title shall not be stayed, avoided, or otherwise limited by operation of any provision of this title or by order of a court or administrative agency in any proceeding under this title unless such order is authorized under the provisions of the Securities Investor Protection Act of 1970 or any statute administered by the Securities and Exchange Commission. As used in this section, the term "contractual right" includes a right set forth in a rule or bylaw of a national securities exchange, a national securities association, or a securities clearing agency.

§ 556. Contractual right to liquidate a commodities contract or forward contract

The contractual right of a commodity broker or forward contract merchant to cause the liquidation of a commodity contract, as defined in section 761, or forward contract because of a condition of the kind specified in section 365(e)(1) of this title, and the right to a variation or maintenance margin payment received from a trustee with respect to open commodity contracts or forward contracts, shall not be stayed, avoided, or otherwise limited by operation of any provision of this title or by the order of a court in any proceeding under this title. As used in this section, the term "contractual right" includes a right set forth in a rule or bylaw of a clearing organization or contract market or in a resolution of the governing board thereof and a right, whether or not evidenced in writing, arising under common law, under law merchant or by reason of normal business practice.

§ 557. Expedited determination of interests in, and abandonment or other disposition of grain assets

(a) This section applies only in a case concerning a debtor that owns or operates a grain storage facility and only with respect to grain and the proceeds of grain. This section does not affect the application of any other section of this title to property other than grain and proceeds of grain.

(b) In this section—

(1) "grain" means wheat, corn, flaxseed, grain sorghum, barley, oats, rye, soybeans, other dry edible beans, or rice;

(2) "grain storage facility" means a site or physical structure regularly used to store grain for producers, or to store grain acquired from producers for resale; and

(3) "producer" means an entity which engages in the growing of grain.

(c)(1) Notwithstanding sections 362, 363, 365, and 554 of this title, on the court's own motion the court may, and on the request of the trustee or an entity that claims an interest in grain or the proceeds of grain the court shall, expedite the procedures for the determination of interests in and the disposition of grain and the proceeds of grain, by shortening to the greatest extent feasible such time periods as are otherwise applicable for such procedures and by establishing, by order, a timetable having a duration of not to exceed 120 days for the completion of the applicable procedure specified in subsection (d) of this section. Such time periods and such timetable may be modified by the court, for cause, in accordance with subsection (f) of this section.

(2) The court shall determine the extent to which such time periods shall be shortened, based upon—

(A) any need of an entity claiming an interest in such grain or the proceeds of grain for a prompt determination of such interest;

(B) any need of such entity for a prompt disposition of such grain;

(C) the market for such grain;

(D) the conditions under which such grain is stored;

(E) the costs of continued storage or disposition of such grain;

(F) the orderly administration of the estate;

(G) the appropriate opportunity for an entity to assert an interest in such grain; and

(H) such other considerations as are relevant to the need to expedite such procedures in the case.

(d) The procedures that may be expedited under subsection (c) of this section include—

(1) the filing of and response to—

(A) a claim of ownership;

(B) a proof of claim;

(C) a request for abandonment;

(D) a request for relief from the stay of action against property under section 362(a) of this title;

(E) a request for determination of secured status;

(F) a request for determination of whether such grain or the proceeds of grain—

(i) is property of the estate;

(ii) must be turned over to the estate; or

(iii) may be used, sold, or leased; and

(G) any other request for determination of an interest in such grain or the proceeds of grain;

(2) the disposition of such grain or the proceeds of grain, before or after determination of interests in such grain of the proceeds of grain, by way of—

(A) sale of such grain;

(B) abandonment;

(C) distribution; or

(D) such other method as is equitable in the case;

(3) subject to sections 701, 702, 703, 1104, 1202, and 1302 of this title, the appointment of a trustee or examiner and the retention and compensation of any professional person required to assist with respect to matters relevant to the determination of interests in or disposition of such grain or the proceeds of grain; and

(4) the determination of any dispute concerning a matter specified in paragraph (1), (2), or (3) of this subsection.

(e)(1) Any governmental unit that has regulatory jurisdiction over the operation or liquidation of the debtor or the debtor's business shall be given notice of any request made or order entered under subsection (c) of this section.

(2) Any such governmental unit may raise, and may appear and be heard on, any issue relating to grain or the proceeds of grain in a case in which a request is made, or an order is entered, under subsection (c) of this section.

(3) The trustee shall consult with such governmental unit before taking any action relating to the disposition of grain in the possession, custody, or control of the debtor or the estate.

(f) The court may extend the period for final disposition of grain or the proceeds of grain under this section beyond 120 days if the court finds that—

(1) the interests of justice so require in light of the complexity of the case; and

(2) the interests of those claimants entitled to distribution of grain or the proceeds of grain will not be materially injured by such additional delay.

(g) Unless an order establishing an expedited procedure under subsection (c) of this section, or determining any interest in or approving any disposition of grain or the proceeds of grain, is stayed pending appeal—

(1) the reversal or modification of such order on appeal does not affect the validity of any procedure, determination, or disposition that occurs before such reversal or modification, whether or not any entity knew of the pendency of the appeal; and

(2) neither the court nor the trustee may delay, due to the appeal of such order, any proceeding in the case in which such order is used.

(h)(1) The trustee may recover from grain and the proceeds of grain the reasonable and necessary costs and expenses allowable under section 503(b) of this title attributable to preserving or disposing of grain or the proceeds of grain, but may not recover from such grain or the proceeds of grain any other costs or expenses.

(2) Notwithstanding section 326(a) of this title, the dollar amounts of money specified in such section include the value, as of the date of disposition, of any grain that the trustee distributes in kind.

(i) In all cases where the quantity of a specific type of grain held by a debtor operating a grain storage facility exceeds ten thousand bushels, such grain shall be sold by the trustee and the assets thereof distributed in accordance with the provisions of this section.

§ 558. Defenses of the estate

The estate shall have the benefit of any defense available to the debtor as against any entity other than the estate, including statutes of limitation, statutes of frauds, usury, and other personal defenses. A waiver of any such defense by the debtor after the commencement of the case does not bind the estate.

§ 559. Contractual right to liquidate a repurchase agreement

The exercise of a contractual right of a repo participant to cause the liquidation of a repurchase agreement because of a condition of the kind specified in section 365(e)(1) of this title shall not be stayed, avoided, or otherwise limited by operation of any provision of this title or by order of a court or administrative agency in any proceeding under this title, unless, where the debtor is a stockbroker or securities

clearing agency, such order is authorized under the provisions of the Securities Investor Protection Act of 1970 or any statute administered by the Securities and Exchange Commission. In the event that a repo participant liquidates one or more repurchase agreements with a debtor and under the terms of one or more such agreements has agreed to deliver assets subject to repurchase agreements to the debtor, any excess of the market prices received on liquidation of such assets (or if any such assets are not disposed of on the date of liquidation of such repurchase agreements, at the prices available at the time of liquidation of such repurchase agreements from a generally recognized source or the most recent closing bid quotation from such a source) over the sum of the stated repurchase prices and all expenses in connection with the liquidation of such repurchase agreements shall be deemed property of the estate, subject to the available rights of setoff. As used in this section, the term "contractual right" includes a right set forth in a rule or bylaw, applicable to each party to the repurchase agreement, or a national securities exchange, a national securities association, or a securities clearing agency, and a right, whether or not evidenced in writing, arising under common law, under law merchant or by reason of normal business practice.

§ 560. Contractual right to terminate a swap agreement

The exercise of any contractual right of any swap participant to cause the termination of a swap agreement because of a condition of the kind specified in section 365(e)(1) of this title or to offset or net out any termination values or payment amounts arising under or in connection with any swap agreement shall not be stayed, avoided, or otherwise limited by operation of any provision of this title or by order of a court or administrative agency in any proceeding under this title. As used in this section, the term "contractual right" includes a right, whether or not evidenced in writing, arising under common law, under law merchant, or by reason of normal business practice.

CHAPTER 7—LIQUIDATION

SUBCHAPTER I—OFFICERS AND ADMINISTRATION

SUBCHAPTER II—COLLECTION, LIQUIDATION, AND DISTRIBUTION OF THE ESTATE

SUBCHAPTER III—STOCKBROKER LIQUIDATION

SUBCHAPTER IV—COMMODITY BROKER LIQUIDATION

SUBCHAPTER I—OFFICERS AND ADMINISTRATION

§ 701. Interim trustee

(a)(1) Promptly after the order for relief under this chapter, the United States trustee shall appoint one disinterested person that is a member of the panel of private trustees established under section 586(a)(1) of title 28 or that is serving as trustee in the case immediately before the order for relief under this chapter to serve as interim trustee in the case.

(2) If none of the members of such panel is willing to serve as interim trustee in the case, then the United States trustee may serve as interim trustee in the case.

(b) The service of an interim trustee under this section

terminates when a trustee elected or designated under section 702 of this title to serve as trustee in the case qualifies under section 322 of this title.

(c) An interim trustee serving under this section is a trustee in a case under this title.

§ 702. Election of trustee

(a) A creditor may vote for a candidate for trustee only if such creditor—

(1) holds an allowable, undisputed, fixed, liquidated, unsecured claim of a kind entitled to distribution under section 726(a)(2), 726(a)(3), 726(a)(4), 752(a), 766(h), or 766(i) of this title;

(2) does not have an interest materially adverse, other than an equity interest that is not substantial in relation to such creditor's interest as a creditor, to the interest or creditors entitled to such distribution; and

(3) is not an insider.

(b) At the meeting of creditors held under section 341 of this title, creditors may elect one person to serve as trustee in the case if election of a trustee is requested by creditors that may vote under subsection (a) of this section, and that hold at least 20 percent in amount of the claims specified in subsection (a)(1) of this section that are held by creditors that may vote under subsection (a) of this section.

(c) A candidate for trustee is elected trustee if—

(1) creditors holding at least 20 percent in amount of the claims of a kind specified in subsection (a)(1) of this section that are held by creditors that may vote under subsection (a) of this section vote; and

(2) such candidate receives the votes of creditors holding a majority in amount of claims specified in subsection (a)(1) of this section that are held by creditors that vote for a trustee.

(d) If a trustee is not elected under this section, then the interim trustee shall serve as trustee in the case.

§ 703. Successor trustee

(a) If a trustee dies or resigns during a case, fails to qualify under section 322 of this title, or is removed under section 324 of this title, creditors may elect, in the manner specified in section 702 of this title, a person to fill the vacancy in the office of trustee.

(b) Pending election of a trustee under subsection (a) of this section, if necessary to preserve or prevent loss to the estate, the United States trustee may appoint an interim trustee in the manner specified in section 701(a).

(c) If creditors do not elect a successor trustee under subsection (a) of this section or if a trustee is needed in a case reopened under section 350 of this title, then the United States trustee—

(1) shall appoint one disinterested person that is a member of the panel of private trustees established under section 586(a)(1) of title 28 to serve as trustee in the case; or

(2) may, if none of the disinterested members of such panel is willing to serve as trustee, serve as trustee in the case.

§ 704. Duties of trustee

The trustee shall—

(1) collect and reduce to money the property of the estate for which such trustee serves, and close such estate as expeditiously as is compatible with the best interests of parties in interest;

(2) be accountable for all property received;

(3) ensure that the debtor shall perform his intention as specified in section 521(2)(B) of this title;

(4) investigate the financial affairs of the debtor;

(5) if a purpose would be served, examine proofs of claims and object to the allowance of any claim that is improper;

(6) if advisable, oppose the discharge of the debtor;

(7) unless the court orders otherwise, furnish such information concerning the estate and the estate's administration as is requested by a party in interest;

(8) if the business of the debtor is authorized to be operated, file with the court, with the United States trustee, and with any governmental unit charged with responsibility for collection or determination of any tax arising out of such operation, periodic reports and summaries of the operation of such business, including a statement of receipts and disbursements, and such other information as, with the United States trustee or the court requires; and

(9) make a final report and file a final account of the administration of the estate with the court and with the United States trustee.

§ 705. Creditors' committee

(a) At the meeting under section 341(a) of this title, creditors that may vote for a trustee under section 702(a) of this title may elect a committee of not fewer than three, and not more than eleven, creditors, each of whom holds an allowable unsecured claim of a kind entitled to distribution under section 726(a)(2) of this title.

(b) A committee elected under subsection (a) of this section may consult with the trustee or the United States trustee in connection with the administration of the estate, make recommendations to the trustee or the United States trustee respecting the performance of the trustee's duties, and submit to the court or the United States trustee any question affecting the administration of the estate.

§ 706. Conversion

(a) The debtor may convert a case under this chapter to a case under chapter 11, 12, or 13 of this title at any time, if the case has not been converted under section

1112, 1208, or 1307 of this title. Any waiver of the right to convert a case under this subsection is unenforceable.

(b) On request of a party in interest and after notice and a hearing, the court may convert a case under this chapter to a case under chapter 11 of this title at any time.

(c) The court may not convert a case under this chapter to a case under chapter 12 or 13 of this title unless the debtor requests such conversion.

(d) Notwithstanding any other provision of this section, a case may not be converted to a case under another chapter of this title unless the debtor may be a debtor under such chapter.

§ 707. Dismissal

(a) The court may dismiss a case under this chapter only after notice and a hearing and only for cause, including—

(1) unreasonable delay by the debtor that is prejudicial to creditors;

(2) nonpayment of any fees or charges required under chapter 123 of title 28; and

(3) failure of the debtor in a voluntary case to file, within fifteen days or such additional time as the court may allow after the filing of the petition commencing such case, the information required by paragraph (1) of section 521, but only on a motion by the United States trustee.

(b) After notice and a hearing, the court, on its own motion or on a motion by the United States Trustee, but not at the request or suggestion or any party in interest, may dismiss a case filed by an individual debtor under this chapter whose debts are primarily consumer debts if it finds that the granting of relief would be a substantial abuse of the provisions of this chapter. There shall be a presumption in favor of granting the relief requested by the debtor.

SUBCHAPTER II—COLLECTION, LIQUIDATION, AND DISTRIBUTION OF THE ESTATE

§ 721. Authorization to operate business

The court may authorize the trustee to operate the business of the debtor for a limited period, if such operation is in the best interest of the estate and consistent with the orderly liquidation of the estate.

§ 722. Redemption

An individual debtor may, whether or not the debtor has waived the right to redeem under this section, redeem tangible personal property intended primarily for personal, family, or household use, from a lien securing a dischargeable consumer debt, if such property is exempted under section 522 of this title or has been abandoned under section 554 of this title, by paying the holder of such lien the amount of the allowed secured claim of such holder that it secured by such lien.

§ 723. Rights of partnership trustee against general partners

(a) If there is a deficiency of property of the estate to pay in full all claims which are allowed in a case under this chapter concerning a partnership and with respect to which a general partner of the partnership is personally liable, the trustee shall have a claim against such general partner to the extent that under applicable nonbankruptcy law such general partner is personally liable for such deficiency.

(b) To the extent practicable, the trustee shall first seek recovery of such deficiency from any general partner in such partnership that is not a debtor in a case under this title. Pending determination of such deficiency, the court may order any such partner to provide the estate with indemnity for, or assurance of payment of, any deficiency recoverable from such partner, or not to dispose of property.

(c) Notwithstanding section 728(c) of this title, the trustee has a claim against the estate of each general partner in such partnership that is a debtor in a case under this title for the full amount of all claims of creditors allowed in the case concerning such partnership. Notwithstanding section 502 of this title, there shall not be allowed in such partner's case a claim against such partner on which both such partner and such partnership are liable, except to any extent that such claim is secured only by property of such partner and not by property of such partnership. The claim of the trustee under this subsection is entitled to distribution in such partner's case under section 726(a) of this title the same as any other claim of a kind specified in such section.

(d) If the aggregate that the trustee recovers from the estates of general partners under subsection (c) of this section is greater than any deficiency not recovered under subsection (b) of this section, the court, after notice and a hearing, shall determine an equitable distribution of the surplus so recovered, and the trustee shall distribute such surplus to the estates of the general partners in such partnership according to such determination.

§ 724. Treatment of certain liens

(a) The trustee may avoid a lien that secures a claim of a kind specified in section 726(a)(4) of this title.

(b) Property in which the estate has an interest and that is subject to a lien that is not avoidable under this title and that secures an allowed claim for a tax, or proceeds of such property, shall be distributed—

(1) first, to any holder of an allowed claim secured by a lien on such property that is not avoidable under this title and that is senior to such tax lien;

(2) second, to any holder of a claim of a kind spec-

ified in section 507(a)(1), 507(a)(2), 507(a)(3), 507(a)(4), 507(a)(5), 507(a)(6), or 507(a)(7) of this title, to the extent of the amount of such allowed tax claim that is secured by such tax lien;

(3) third, to the holder of such tax lien, to any extent that such holder's allowed tax claim that is secured by such tax lien exceeds any amount distributed under paragraph (2) of this subsection;

(4) fourth, to any holder of an allowed claim secured by a lien on such property that is not avoidable under this title and that is junior to such tax lien;

(5) fifth, to the holder of such tax lien, to the extent that such holder's allowed claim secured by such tax lien is not paid under paragraph (3) of this subsection; and

(6) sixth, to the estate.

(c) If more than one holder of a claim is entitled to distribution under a particular paragraph of subsection (b) of this section, distribution to such holders under such paragraph shall be in the same order as distribution to such holders would have been other than under this section.

(d) A statutory lien the priority of which is determined in the same manner as the priority of a tax lien under section 6323 of the Internal Revenue Code of 1986 shall be treated under subsection (b) of this section the same as if such lien were a tax lien.

§ 725. Disposition of certain property

After the commencement of a case under this chapter, but before final distribution of property of the estate under section 726 of this title, the trustee, after notice and a hearing, shall dispose of any property in which an entity other than the estate has an interest, such as a lien, and that has not been disposed of under another section of this title.

§ 726. Distribution of property of the estate

(a) Except as provided in section 510 of this title, property of the estate shall be distributed—

(1) first, in payment of claims of the kind specified in, and in the order specified in, section 507 of this title, proof of which is timely filed under section 501 of this title or tardily filed before the date on which the trustee commences distribution under this section;

(2) second, in payment of any allowed unsecured claim, other than a claim of a kind specified in paragraph (1), (3), or (4) of this subsection, proof of which is—

(A) timely filed under section 501(a) of this title;

(B) timely filed under section 501(b) or 501(c) of this title; or

(C) tardily filed under section 501(a) of this title, if—

(i) the creditor that holds such claim did not have notice or actual knowledge of the case in time for timely filing of a proof of such claim under section 501(a) of this title; and

(ii) proof of such claim is filed in time to permit payment of such claim;

(3) third, in payment of any allowed unsecured claim proof of which is tardily filed under section 501(a) of this title, other than a claim of the kind specified in paragraph (2)(C) of this subsection;

(4) fourth, in payment of any allowed claim, whether secured or unsecured, for any fine, penalty, or forfeiture, or for multiple, exemplary, or punitive damages, arising before the earlier of the order for relief or the appointment of a trustee, to the extent that such fine, penalty, forfeiture, or damages are not compensation for actual pecuniary loss suffered by the holder of such claim;

(5) fifth, in payment of interest at the legal rate from the date of the filing of the petition, on any claim paid under paragraph (1), (2), (3), or (4) of this subsection; and

(6) sixth, to the debtor.

(b) Payment on claims of a kind specified in paragraph (1), (2), (3), (4), (5), (6), (7), or (8) of section 507(a) of this title, or in paragraph (2), (3), (4), or (5) of subsection (a) of this section, shall be made pro rata among claims of the kind specified in each such particular paragraph, except that in a case that has been converted to this chapter under section 1009,[1] 1112, 1208, or 1307 of this title, a claim allowed under section 503(b) of this title incurred under this chapter after such conversion has priority over a claim allowed under section 503(b) of this title incurred under any other chapter of this title or under this chapter before such conversion and over any expenses of a custodian superseded under section 543 of this title.

(c) Notwithstanding subsections (a) and (b) of this section, if there is property of the kind specified in section 541(a)(2) of this title, or proceeds of such property, in the estate, such property or proceeds shall be segregated from other property of the estate, and such property or proceeds and other property of the estate shall be distributed as follows:

(1) Claims allowed under section 503 of this title shall be paid either from property of the kind specified in section 541(a)(2) of this title, or from other property of the estate, as the interest of justice requires.

(2) Allowed claims, other than claims allowed under section 503 of this title, shall be paid in the order specified in subsection (a) of this section, and, with respect to claims of a kind specified in a particular paragraph of section 507 of this title or subsection (a) of this section, in the following order and manner:

(A) First, community claims against the debtor or the debtor's spouse shall be paid from property of

---

1. So in original.

the kind specified in section 541(a)(2) of this title, except to the extent that such property is solely liable for debts of the debtor.

(B) Second, to the extent that community claims against the debtor are not paid under subparagraph (A) of this paragraph, such community claims shall be paid from property of the kind specified in section 541(a)(2) of this title that is solely liable for debts of the debtor.

(C) Third, to the extent that all claims against the debtor including community claims against the debtor are not paid under subparagraph (A) or (B) of this paragraph such claims shall be paid from property of the estate other than property of the kind specified in section 541(a)(2) of this title.

(D) Fourth, to the extent that community claims against the debtor or the debtor's spouse are not paid under subparagraph (A), (B), or (C) of this paragraph, such claims shall be paid from all remaining property of the estate.

§ 727. Discharge

(a) The court shall grant the debtor a discharge, unless—

(1) the debtor is not an individual;

(2) the debtor, with intent to hinder, delay, or defraud a creditor or an officer of the estate charged with custody of property under this title, has transferred, removed, destroyed, mutilated, or concealed, or has permitted to be transferred, removed, destroyed, mutilated, or concealed—

(A) property of the debtor, within one year before the date of the filing of the petition; or

(B) property of the estate, after the date of the filing of the petition;

(3) the debtor has concealed, destroyed, mutilated, falsified, or failed to keep or preserve any recorded information, including books, documents, records, and papers, from which the debtor's financial condition or business transactions might be ascertained, unless such act or failure to act was justified under all of the circumstances of the case;

(4) the debtor knowingly and fraudulently, in or in connection with the case—

(A) made a false oath or account;

(B) presented or used a false claim;

(C) gave, offered, received, or attempted to obtain money, property, or advantage, or a promise of money, property, or advantage, for acting or forbearing to act; or

(D) withheld from an officer of the estate entitled to possession under this title, any recorded information, including books, documents, records, and papers, relating to the debtor's property or financial affairs;

(5) the debtor has failed to explain satisfactorily, before determination of denial of discharge under this paragraph, any loss of assets or deficiency of assets to meet the debtor's liabilities;

(6) the debtor has refused, in the case—

(A) to obey any lawful order of the court, other than an order to respond to a material question or to testify;

(B) on the ground of privilege against self-incrimination, to respond to a material question approved by the court or to testify, after the debtor has been granted immunity with respect to the matter concerning which such privilege was invoked; or

(C) on a ground other than the properly invoked privilege against self-incrimination, to respond to a material question approved by the court or to testify;

(7) the debtor has committed any act specified in paragraph (2), (3), (4), (5), or (6) of this subsection, on or within one year before the date of the filing of the petition, or during the case, in connection with another case, under this title or under the Bankruptcy Act, concerning an insider;

(8) the debtor has been granted a discharge under this section, under section 1141 of this title, or under section 14, 371, or 476 of the Bankruptcy Act, in a case commenced within six years before the date of the filing of the petition;

(9) the debtor has been granted a discharge under section 1228 or 1328 of this title, or under section 660 or 661 of the Bankruptcy Act, in a case commenced within six years before the date of the filing of the petition, unless payments under the plan in such case totaled at least—

(A) 100 percent of the allowed unsecured claims in such case; or

(B)(i) 70 percent of such claims; and

(ii) the plan was proposed by the debtor in good faith, and was the debtor's best effort; or

(10) the court approves a written waiver of discharge executed by the debtor after the order for relief under this chapter.

(b) Except as provided in section 523 of this title, a discharge under subsection (a) of this section discharges the debtor from all debts that arose before the date of the order for relief under this chapter, and any liability on a claim that is determined under section 502 of this title as if such claim had arisen before the commencement of the case, whether or not a proof of claim based on any such debt or liability is filed under section 501 of this title, and whether or not a claim based on any such debt or liability is allowed under section 502 of this title.

(c)(1) The trustee, a creditor, or the United States trustee may object to the granting of a discharge under subsection (a) of this section.

(2) On request of a party in interest, the court may order the trustee to examine the acts and conduct of the

debtor to determine whether a ground exists for denial of discharge.

(d) On request of the trustee, a creditor, or the United States trustee, and after notice and a hearing, the court shall revoke a discharge granted under subsection (a) of this section if—

(1) such discharge was obtained through the fraud of the debtor, and the requesting party did not know of such fraud until after the granting of such discharge;

(2) the debtor acquired property that is property of the estate, or became entitled to acquire property that would be property of the estate, and knowingly and fraudulently failed to report the acquisition of or entitlement to such property, or to deliver or surrender such property to the trustee; or

(3) the debtor committed an act specified in subsection (a)(6) of this section.

(e) The trustee, a creditor, or the United States trustee may request a revocation of a discharge—

(1) under subsection (d)(1) of this section within one year after such discharge is granted; or

(2) under subsection (d)(2) or (d)(3) of this section before the later of—

(A) one year after the granting of such discharge; and

(B) the date the case is closed.

§ 728. Special tax provisions

(a) For the purposes of any State or local law imposing a tax on or measured by income, the taxable period of a debtor that is an individual shall terminate on the date of the order for relief under this chapter, unless the case was converted under section 1112 or 1208 of this title.

(b) Notwithstanding any State or local law imposing a tax on or measured by income, the trustee shall make tax returns of income for the estate of an individual debtor in a case under this chapter or for a debtor that is a corporation in a case under this chapter only if such estate or corporation has net taxable income for the entire period after the order for relief under this chapter during which the case is pending. If such entity has such income, or if the debtor is a partnership, then the trustee shall make and file a return of income for each taxable period during which the case was pending after the order for relief under this chapter.

(c) If there are pending a case under this chapter concerning a partnership and a case under this chapter concerning a partner in such partnership, a governmental unit's claim for any unpaid liability of such partner for a State or local tax on or measured by income, to the extent that such liability arose from the inclusion in such partner's taxable income of earnings of such partnership that were not withdrawn by such partner, is a claim only against such partnership.

(d) Notwithstanding section 541 of this title, if there

are pending a case under this chapter concerning a partnership and a case under this chapter concerning a partner in such partnership, then any State or local tax refund or reduction of tax of such partner that would have otherwise been property of the estate of such partner under section 541 of this title—

(1) is property of the estate of such partnership to the extent that such tax refund or reduction of tax is fairly apportionable to losses sustained by such partnership and not reimbursed by such partner; and

(2) is otherwise property of the estate of such partner.

§ 741. Definitions for this subchapter

In this subchapter—

(1) "Commission" means Securities and Exchange Commission;

(2) "customer" includes—

(A) entity with whom a person deals as principal or agent and that has a claim against such person on account of a security received, acquired, or held by such person in the ordinary course of such person's business as a stockbroker, from or for the securities account or accounts of such entity—

(i) for safekeeping;

(ii) with a view to sale;

(iii) to cover a consummated sale;

(iv) pursuant to a purchase;

(v) as collateral under a security agreement; or

(vi) for the purpose of effecting registration of transfer; and

(B) entity that has a claim against a person arising out of—

(i) a sale or conversion of a security received, acquired, or held as specified in subparagraph (A) of this paragraph; or

(ii) a deposit of cash, a security, or other property with such person for the purpose of purchasing or selling a security;

(3) "customer name security" means security—

(A) held for the account of a customer on the date of the filing of the petition by or on behalf of the debtor;

(B) registered in such customer's name on such date or in the process of being so registered under instructions from the debtor; and

(C) not in a form transferable by delivery on such date;

(4) "customer property" means cash, security, or other property, and proceeds of such case, security, or property, received, acquired, or held by or for the account of the debtor, from or for the securities account of a customer—

(A) including—

(i) property that was unlawfully converted from and that is the lawful property of the estate;

(ii) a security held as property of the debtor to

the extent such security is necessary to meet a net equity claim of a customer based on a security of the same class and series of an issuer;

(iii) resources provided through the user or realization of a customer's debit cash balance or a debit item includible in the Formula for Determination of Reserve Requirement for Brokers and Dealers as promulgated by the Commission under the Securities Exchange Act of 1934; and

(iv) other property of the debtor that any applicable law, rule, or regulation requires to be set aside or held for the benefit of a customer, unless including such property as customer property would not significantly increase customer property; but

(B) not including—

(i) a customer name security delivered to or reclaimed by a customer under section 751 of this title; or

(ii) property to the extent that a customer does not have a claim against the debtor based on such property;

(5) "margin payment" means payment or deposit of cash, a security, or other property, that is commonly known to the securities trade as original margin, initial margin, maintenance margin, or variation margin, or as a mark-to-market payment, or that secures an obligation of a participant in a securities clearing agency;

(6) "net equity" means, with respect to all accounts of a customer that such customer has in the same capacity—

(A)(i) aggregate dollar balance that would remain in such accounts after the liquidation, by sales or purchase, at the time of the filing of the petition, of all securities positions in all such accounts, except any customer name securities of such customer; minus

(ii) any claim of the debtor against such customer in such capacity that would have been owing immediately after such liquidation; plus

(B) any payment by such customer to the trustee, within 60 days after notice under section 342 of this title, of any business related claim of the debtor against such customer in such capacity;

(7) "securities contract" means contract for the purchase, sale, or loan of a security, including an option for the purchase or sale of a security, certificate of deposit, or group or index of securities (including any interest therein or based on the value thereof), or any option entered into on a national securities exchange relating to foreign currencies, or the guarantee of any settlement of cash or securities by or to a securities clearing agency;

(8) "settlement payment" means a preliminary settlement payment, a partial settlement payment, an interim settlement payment, a settlement payment on account, a final settlement payment, or any other similar payment commonly used in the securities trade; and

(9) "SIPC" means Securities Investor Protection Corporation.

§ 742. Effect on section 362 of this title in this subchapter

Notwithstanding section 362 of this title, SIPC may file an application for a protective decree under the Securities Investor Protection Act of 1970. The filing of such application stays all proceedings in the case under this title unless and until such application is dismissed. If SIPC completes the liquidation of the debtor, then the court shall dismiss the case.

§ 743. Notice

The clerk shall give the notice required by section 342 of this title to SIPC and to the Commission.

§ 744. Executory contracts

Notwithstanding section 365(d)(1) of this title, the trustee shall assume or reject, under section 365 of this title, any executory contract of the debtor for the purchase or sale of a security in the ordinary course of the debtor's business, within a reasonable time after the date of the order for relief, but not to exceed 30 days. If the trustee does not assume such a contract within such time, such contract is rejected.

§ 745. Treatment of accounts

(a) Accounts held by the debtor for a particular customer in separate capacities shall be treated as accounts of separate customers.

(b) If a stockbroker or a bank holds a customer net equity claim against the debtor that arose out of a transaction for a customer of such stockbroker or bank, each such customer of such stockbroker or bank shall be treated as a separate customer of the debtor.

(c) Each trustee's account specified as such on the debtor's books, and supported by a trust deed filed with, and qualified as such by, the Internal Revenue Service, and under the Internal Revenue Code of 1986, shall be treated as a separate customer account for each beneficiary under such trustee account.

§ 746. Extent of customer claims

(a) If, after the date of the filing of the petition, an entity enters into a transaction with the debtor, in a manner that would have made such entity a customer had such transaction occurred before the date of the filing of the petition, and such transaction was entered into by such entity in good faith and before the qualification under section 322 of this title of a trustee, such entity shall be deemed a customer, and the date of such transaction shall be deemed to be the date of the filing of the petition for the purpose of determining such entity's net equity.

(b) An entity does not have a claim as a customer to the extent that such entity transferred to the debtor cash

or a security that, by contract, agreement, understanding, or operation of law, is—

    (1) part of the capital of the debtor; or

    (2) subordinated to the claims of any or all creditors.

§ 747. Subordination of certain customer claims

Except as provided in section 510 of this title, unless all other customer net equity claims have been paid in full, the trustee may not pay in full or pay in part, directly or indirectly, any net equity claim of a customer that was, on the date the transaction giving rise to such claim occurred—

    (1) an insider;

    (2) a beneficial owner of at least five percent of any class of equity securities of the debtor, other than—

        (A) nonconvertible stock having fixed preferential dividend and liquidation rights; or

        (B) interests of limited partners in a limited partnership;

    (3) a limited partner with a participation of at least five percent in the net assets or net profits of the debtor; or

    (4) an entity that, directly or indirectly, through agreement or otherwise, exercised or had the power to exercise control over the management or policies of the debtor.

§ 748. Reduction of securities to money

As soon as practicable after the date of the order for relief, the trustee shall reduce to money, consistent with good market practice, all securities held as property of the estate, except for customer name securities delivered or reclaimed under section 751 of this title.

§ 749. Voidable transfers

(a) Except as otherwise provided in this section, any transfer of property that, but for such transfer, would have been customer property, may be avoided by the trustee, and such property shall be treated as customer property, if and to the extent that the trustee avoids such transfer under section 544, 545, 547, 548, or 549 of this title. For the purpose of such sections, the property so transferred shall be deemed to have been property of the debtor and, if such transfer was made to a customer or for a customer's benefit, such customer shall be deemed, for the purposes of this section, to have been a creditor.

(b) Notwithstanding sections 544, 545, 547, 548, and 549 of this title, the trustee may not avoid a transfer made before five days after the order for relief if such transfer is approved by the Commission by rule or order, either before or after such transfer, and if such transfer is—

    (1) a transfer of a securities contract entered into or carried by or through the debtor on behalf of a customer, and of any cash, security, or other property margining or securing such securities contract; or

    (2) the liquidation of a securities contract entered into or carried by or through the debtor on behalf of a customer.

§ 750. Distribution of securities

The trustee may not distribute a security except under section 751 of this title.

§ 751. Customer name securities

The trustee shall deliver any customer name security to or on behalf of the customer entitled to such security, unless such customer has a negative net equity. With the approval of the trustee, a customer may reclaim a customer name security after payment to the trustee, within such period as the trustee allows, of any claim of the debtor against such customer to the extent that such customer will not have a negative net equity after such payment.

§ 752. Customer property

(a) The trustee shall distribute customer property ratably to customers on the basis and to the extent of such customers' allowed net equity claims and in priority to all other claims, except claims of the kind specified in section 507(a)(1) of this title that are attributable to the administration of such customer property.

(b)(1) The trustee shall distribute customer property in excess of that distributed under subsection (a) of this section in accordance with section 726 of this title.

(2) Except as provided in section 510 of this title, if a customer is not paid the full amount of such customer's allowed net equity claim from customer property, the unpaid portion of such claim is a claim entitled to distribution under section 726 of this title.

(c) Any cash or security remaining after the liquidation of a security interest created under a security agreement made by the debtor, excluding property excluded under section 741(4)(B) of this title, shall be apportioned between the general estate and customer property in the same proportion as the general estate of the debtor and customer property were subject to such security interest.

SUBCHAPTER IV—COMMODITY BROKER LIQUIDATION

§ 761. Definitions for the subchapter

In this subchapter—

    (1) "Act" means Commodity Exchange Act;

    (2) "clearing organization" means organization that clears commodity contracts made on, or subject to the rules of, a contract market or board of trade;

    (3) "Commission" means Commodity Futures Trading Commission;

    (4) "commodity contract" means—

(A) with respect to a futures commission merchant, contract for the purchase or sale of a commodity for future delivery on, or subject to the rules of, a contract market or board of trade;

(B) with respect to a foreign futures commission merchant, foreign future;

(C) with respect to a leverage transaction merchant, leverage transaction;

(D) with respect to a clearing organization, contract for the purchase or sale of a commodity for future delivery on, or subject to the rules of, a contract market or board of trade that is cleared by such clearing organization, or commodity option traded on, or subject to the rules of, a contract market or board of trade that is cleared by such clearing organization, or

(E) with respect to a commodity options dealer, commodity option;

(5) "commodity option" means agreement or transaction subject to regulation under section 4c(b) of the Act;

(6) "commodity options dealer" means person that extends credit to, or that accepts cash, a security, or other property from, a customer of such person for the purchase or sale of an interest in a commodity option;

(7) "contract market" means board of trade designated as a contract market by the Commission under the Act;

(8) "contract of sale", "commodity", "future delivery", "board of trade", and "futures commission merchant" have the meanings assigned to those terms in the Act;

(9) "customer" means—

(A) with respect to a futures commission merchant—

(i) entity for or with whom such futures commission merchant deals and that holds a claim against such futures commission merchant on account of a commodity contract made, received, acquired, or held by or through such futures commission merchant in the ordinary course of such futures commission merchant's business as a futures commission merchant from or for the commodity futures account of such entity; or

(ii) entity that holds a claim against such futures commission merchant arising out of—

(I) the making, liquidation, or change in the value of a commodity contract of a kind specified in clause (i) of this subparagraph;

(II) a deposit or payment of cash, a security, or other property with such futures commission merchant for the purpose of making or margining such a commodity contract; or

(III) the making or taking of delivery on such a commodity contract;

(B) with respect to a foreign futures commission merchant—

(i) entity for or with whom such foreign futures commission merchant deals and that holds a claim against such foreign futures commission merchant on account of a commodity contract made, received, acquired, or held by or through such foreign futures commission merchant in the ordinary course of such foreign futures commission merchant's business as a foreign futures commission merchant from or for the foreign futures account of such entity; or

(ii) entity that holds a claim against such foreign futures commission merchant arising out of—

(I) the making, liquidation, or change in value of a commodity contract of a kind specified in clause (i) of this subparagraph;

(II) a deposit or payment of cash, a security, or other property with such foreign futures commission merchant for the purpose of making or margining such a commodity contract; or

(III) the making or taking of delivery on such a commodity contract;

(C) with respect to a leverage transaction merchant—

(i) entity for or with whom such leverage transaction merchant deals and that holds a claim against such leverage transaction merchant on account of a commodity contract engaged in by or with such leverage transaction merchant in the ordinary course of such leverage transaction merchant's business as a leverage transaction merchant from or for the leverage account of such entity; or

(ii) entity that holds a claim against such leverage transaction merchant arising out of—

(I) the making, liquidation, or change in value of a commodity contract of a kind specified in clause (i) of this subparagraph;

(II) a deposit or payment of cash, a security, or other property with such leverage transaction merchant for the purpose of entering into or margining such a commodity contract; or

(III) the making or taking of delivery on such a commodity contract;

(D) with respect to a clearing organization, clearing member of such clearing organization with whom such clearing organization deals and that holds a claim against such clearing organization on account of cash, a security, or other property received by such clearing organization to margin, guarantee, or secure a commodity contract in such clearing member's proprietary account or customers'

account; or

(E) with respect to a commodity options dealer—

(i) entity for or with whom such commodity options dealer deals and that holds a claim on account of a commodity contract made, received, acquired, or held by or through such commodity options dealer in the ordinary course of such commodity options dealer's business as a commodity options dealer from or for the commodity options account of such entity; or

(ii) entity that holds a claim against such commodity options dealer arising out of—

(I) the making of, liquidation of, exercise of, or a change in value of, a commodity contract of a kind specified in clause (i) of this subparagraph; or

(II) a deposit or payment of cash, a security, or other property with such commodity options dealer for the purpose of making, exercising, or margining such a commodity contract;

(10) "customer property" means cash, a security, or other property, or proceeds of such cash, security, or property, received, acquired, or held by or for the account of the debtor, from or for the account of a customer—

(A) including—

(i) property received, acquired, or held to margin, guarantee, secure, purchase, or sell a commodity contract;

(ii) profits or contractual or other rights accruing to a customer as a result of a commodity contract;

(iii) an open commodity contract;

(iv) specifically identifiable customer property;

(v) warehouse receipt or other document held by the debtor evidencing ownership of or title to property to be delivered to fulfill a commodity contract from or for the account of a customer;

(vi) cash, a security, or other property received by the debtor as payment for a commodity to be delivered to fulfill a commodity contract from or for the account of a customer;

(vii) a security held as property of the debtor to the extent such security is necessary to meet a net equity claim based on a security of the same class and series of an issuer;

(viii) property that was unlawfully converted from and that is the lawful property of the estate; and

(ix) other property of the debtor that any applicable law, rule, or regulation requires to be set aside or held for the benefit of a customer, unless

including such property as customer property would not significantly increase customer property; but

(B) not including to the extent that a customer does not have a claim against the debtor based on such property;

(11) "foreign future" means contract for the purchase or sale of a commodity for future delivery on, or subject to the rules of, a board of trade outside the United States;

(12) "foreign futures commission merchant" means entity engaged in soliciting or accepting orders for the purchase or sale of a foreign future or that, in connection with such a solicitation or acceptance, accepts cash, a security, or other property, or extends credit to margin, guarantee, or secure any trade or contract that results from such a solicitation or acceptance;

(13) "leverage transaction" means agreement that is subject to regulation under section 19 of the Commodity Exchange Act, and that is commonly known to the commodities trade as a margin account, margin contract, leverage account, or leverage contract;

(14) "leverage transaction merchant" means person in the business of engaging in leverage transactions;

(15) "margin payment" means payment or deposit of cash, a security, or other property, that is commonly known to the commodities trade as original margin, initial margin, maintenance margin, or variation margin, including mark-to-market payments, settlement payments, variation payments, daily settlement payments, and final settlement payments made as adjustments to settlement prices;

(16) "member property" means customer property received, acquired, or held by or for the account of a debtor that is a clearing organization, from or for the proprietary account of a customer that is a clearing member of the debtor; and

(17) "net equity" means, subject to such rules and regulations as the Commission promulgates under the Act, with respect to the aggregate of all of a customer's accounts that such customer has in the same capacity—

(A) the balance remaining in such customer's accounts immediately after—

(i) all commodity contracts of such customer have been transferred, liquidated, or become identified for delivery; and

(ii) all obligations of such customer in such capacity to the debtor have been offset; plus

(B) the value, as of the date of return under section 766 of this title, of any specifically identifiable customer property actually returned to such customer before the date specified in subparagraph (A) of this paragraph; plus

(C) the value, as of the date of transfer, of—

(i) any commodity contract to which such

customer is entitled that is transferred to another person under section 766 of this title; and

(ii) any cash, security, or other property of such customer transferred to such other person under section 766 of this title to margin or secure such transferred commodity contract.

§ 762. Notice to the Commission and right to be heard

(a) The clerk shall give the notice required by section 342 of this title to the Commission.

(b) The Commission may raise and may appear and be heard on any issue in a case under this chapter.

§ 763. Treatment of accounts

(a) Accounts held by the debtor for a particular customer in separate capacities shall be treated as accounts of separate customers.

(b) A member of a clearing organization shall be deemed to hold such member's proprietary account in a separate capacity from such member's customers' account.

(c) The net equity in a customer's account may not be offset against the net equity in the account of any other customer.

§ 764. Voidable transfers

(a) Except as otherwise provided in this section, any transfer by the debtor of property that, but for such transfer, would have been customer property, may be avoided by the trustee, and such property shall be treated as customer property, if and to the extent that the trustee avoids such transfer under section 544, 545, 547, 548, 549, or 724(a) of this title. For the purpose of such sections, the property so transferred shall be deemed to have been property of the debtor, and, if such transfer was made to a customer or for a customer's benefit, such customer shall be deemed, for the purposes of this section, to have been a creditor.

(b) Notwithstanding sections 544, 545, 547, 548, 549, and 724(a) of this title, the trustee may not avoid a transfer made before five days after the order for relief, if such transfer is approved by the Commission by rule or order, either before or after such transfer, and if such transfer is—

(1) a transfer of a commodity contract entered into or carried by or through the debtor on behalf of a customer, and of any cash, securities, or other property margining or securing such commodity contract; or

(2) the liquidation of a commodity contract entered into or carried by or through the debtor on behalf of a customer.

§ 765. Customer instructions

(a) The notice required by section 342 of this title to customers shall instruct each customer—

(1) to file a proof of such customer's claim promptly,

and to specify in such claim any specifically identifiable security, property, or commodity contract; and

(2) to instruct the trustee of such customer's desired disposition, including transfer under section 766 of this title or liquidation, of any commodity contract specifically identified to such customer.

(b) The trustee shall comply, to the extent practicable, with any instruction received from a customer regarding such customer's desired disposition of any commodity contract specifically identified to such customer. If the trustee has transferred, under section 766 of this title, such a commodity contract, the trustee shall transmit any such instruction to the commodity broker to whom such commodity contract was so transferred.

§ 766. Treatment of customer property

(a) The trustee shall answer all margin calls with respect to a specifically identifiable commodity contract of a customer until such time as the trustee returns or transfers such commodity contract, but the trustee may not make a margin payment that has the effect of a distribution to such customer of more than that to which such customer is entitled under subsection (h) or (i) of this section.

(b) The trustee shall prevent any open commodity contract from remaining open after the last day of trading in such commodity contract, or into the first day on which notice of intent to deliver on such commodity contract may be tendered, whichever occurs first. With respect to any commodity contract that has remained open after the last day of trading in such commodity contract or with respect to which delivery must be made or accepted under the rules of the contract market on which such commodity contract was made, the trustee may operate the business of the debtor for the purpose of—

(1) accepting or making tender of notice of intent to deliver the physical commodity underlying such commodity contract;

(2) facilitating delivery of such commodity; or

(3) disposing of such commodity if a party to such commodity contract defaults.

(c) The trustee shall return promptly to a customer any specifically identifiable security, property, or commodity contract to which such customer is entitled, or shall transfer, on such customer's behalf, such security, property, or commodity contract to a commodity broker that is not a debtor under this title, subject to such rules or regulations as the Commission may prescribe, to the extent that the value of such security, property, or commodity contract does not exceed the amount to which such customer would be entitled under subsection (h) or (i) of this section if such security, property, or commodity contract were not returned or transferred under this subsection.

(d) If the value of a specifically identifiable security, property, or commodity contract exceeds the amount to which the customer of the debtor is entitled under subsec-

tion (h) or (i) of this section, then such customer to whom such security, property, or commodity contract is specifically identified may deposit cash with the trustee equal to the difference between the value of such security, property, or commodity contract and such amount, and the trustee then shall—

(1) return promptly such security, property, or commodity contract to such customer; or

(2) transfer, on such customer's behalf, such security, property, or commodity contract to a commodity broker that is not a debtor under this title, subject to such rules or regulations as the Commission may prescribe.

(e) Subject to subsection (b) of this section, the trustee shall liquidate any commodity contract that—

(1) is identified to a particular customer and with respect to which such customer has not timely instructed the trustee as to the desired disposition of such commodity contract;

(2) cannot be transferred under subsection (c) of this section; or

(3) cannot be identified to a particular customer.

(f) As soon as practicable after the commencement of the case, the trustee shall reduce to money, consistent with good market practice, all securities and other property, other than commodity contracts, held as property of the estate, except for specifically identifiable securities or property distributable under subsection (h) or (i) of this section.

(g) The trustee may not distribute a security or other property except under subsection (h) or (i) of this section;

(h) Except as provided in subsection (b) of this section, the trustee shall distribute customer property ratably to customers on the basis and to the extent of such customers' allowed net equity claims, and in priority to all other claims, except claims of a kind specified in section 507(a)(1) of this title that are attributable to the administration of customer property. Such distribution shall be in the form of—

(1) cash;

(2) the return or transfer, under subsection (c) or (d) of this section, of specifically identifiable customer securities, property, or commodity contracts; or

(3) payment of margin calls under subsection (a) of this section.

Notwithstanding any other provision of this subsection, a customer net equity claim based on a proprietary account, as defined by Commission rule, regulation, or order, may not be paid either in whole or in part, directly or indirectly, out of customer property unless all other customer net equity claims have been paid in full.

(i) If the debtor is a clearing organization, the trustee shall distribute—

(1) customer property, other than member property, ratably to customers on the basis and to the extent of such customers' allowed net equity claims based on such customers' accounts other than proprietary accounts,

and in priority to all other claims, except claims of a kind specified in section 507(a)(1) of this title that are attributable to the administration of such customer property; and

(2) member property ratably to customers on the basis and to the extent of such customers' allowed net equity claims based on such customers' proprietary accounts, and in priority to all other claims, except claims of a kind specified in section 507(a)(1) of this title that are attributable to the administration of member property or customer property.

(j)(1) The trustee shall distribute customer property in excess of that distributed under subsection (h) or (i) of this section in accordance with section 726 of this title.

(2) Except as provided in section 510 of this title, if a customer is not paid the full amount of such customer's allowed net equity claim from customer property, the unpaid portion of such claim is a claim entitled to distribution under section 726 of this title.

CHAPTER 9—ADJUSTMENT OF DEBTS OF A MUNICIPALITY

SUBCHAPTER I—GENERAL PROVISIONS

SUBCHAPTER II—ADMINISTRATION

SUBCHAPTER III—THE PLAN

SUBCHAPTER I—GENERAL PROVISIONS

§ 901. Applicability of other sections of this title

(a) Sections 301, 344, 347(b), 349, 350(b), 361, 362, 364(c), 364(d), 364(e), 364(f), 365, 366, 501, 502, 503, 504, 506, 507(a)(1), 509, 510, 524(a)(1), 524(a)(2), 544, 545, 546, 547, 548, 549(a), 549(c), 549(d), 550, 551, 552, 553, 557, 1102, 1103, 1109, 1111(b), 1122, 1123(a)(1), 1123(a)(2), 1123(a)(3), 1123(a)(4), 1123(a)(5), 1123(b), 1124, 1125, 1126(a), 1126(b), 1126(c), 1126(e), 1126(f), 1126(g), 1127(d), 1128, 1129(a)(2), 1129(a)(3), 1129(a)(6), 1129(a)(8), 1129(a)(10), 1129(b)(1), 1129(b)(2)(A), 1129(b)(2)(B), 1142(b), 1143, 1144, and 1145 of this title apply in a case under this chapter.

(b) A term used in a section of this title made applicable in a case under this chapter by subsection (a) of this section or section 103(e) of this title has the meaning defined for such term for the purpose of such applicable section, unless such term is otherwise defined in section 902 of this title.

(c) A section made applicable in a case under this chapter by subsection (a) of this section that is operative if the business of the debtor is authorized to be operated is operative in a case under this chapter.

§ 902. Definitions for this chapter

In this chapter—

(1) "property of the estate", when used in a section that is made applicable in a case under this chapter by section 103(e) or 901 of this title, means property of the debtor;

(2) "special revenues" means—

(A) receipts derived from the ownership, operation, or disposition of projects or systems of the debtor that are primarily used or intended to be used primarily to provide transportation, utility, or other services, including the proceeds of borrowings to finance the projects or systems;

(B) special excise taxes imposed on particular activities or transactions;

(C) incremental tax receipts from the benefited area in the case of tax-increment financing;

(D) other revenues or receipts derived from particular functions of the debtor, whether or not the debtor has other functions; or

(E) taxes specifically levied to finance one or more projects or systems, excluding receipts from general property, sales, or income taxes (other than tax-increment financing) levied to finance the general purposes of the debtor;

(3) "special tax payer" means record owner or holder of legal or equitable title to real property against which a special assessment or special tax has been levied the proceeds of which are the sole source of payment of an obligation issued by the debtor to defray the cost of an improvement relating to such real property;

(4) "special tax payer affected by the plan" means special tax payer with respect to whose real property the plan proposes to increase the proportion of special assessments or special taxes referred to in paragraph (2) of this section assessed against such real property; and

(5) "trustee", when used in a section that is made applicable in a case under this chapter by section 103(e) or 901 of this title, means debtor, except as provided in section 926 of this title.

§ 903. Reservation of State power to control municipalities

This chapter does not limit or impair the power of a State to control, by legislation or otherwise, a municipality of or in such State in the exercise of the political or governmental powers of such municipality, including expenditures for such exercise, but—

(1) a State law prescribing a method of composition of indebtedness of such municipality may not bind any creditor that does not consent to such composition; and

(2) a judgment entered under such a law may not bind a creditor that does not consent to such compensation.

§ 904. Limitation on jurisdiction and powers of court

Notwithstanding any power of the court, unless the debtor consents or the plan so provides, the court may not, by any stay, order, or decree, in the case or otherwise, interfere with—

(1) any of the political or governmental powers of the debtor;

(2) any of the property or revenues of the debtor; or

(3) the debtor's use or enjoyment of any income-producing property.

SUBCHAPTER II—ADMINISTRATION

§ 921. Petition and proceedings relating to petition

(a) Notwithstanding sections 109(d) and 301 of this title, a case under this chapter concerning an unincorporated tax or special assessment district that does not have such district's own officials is commenced by the filing under section 301 of this title of a petition under this chapter by such district's governing authority or the board or body having authority to levy taxes or assessments to meet the obligations of such district.

(b) The chief judge of the court of appeals for the circuit embracing the district in which the case is commenced shall designate the bankruptcy judge to conduct the case.

(c) After any objection to the petition, the court, after

notice and a hearing, may dismiss the petition if the debtor did not file the petition in good faith or if the petition does not meet the requirements of this title.

(d) If the petition is not dismissed under subsection (c) of this section, the court shall order relief under this chapter.

(e) The court may not, on account of an appeal from an order for relief, delay any proceeding under this chapter in the case in which the appeal is being taken; nor shall any court order a stay of such proceeding pending such appeal. The reversal on appeal of a finding of jurisdiction does not affect the validity of any debt incurred that is authorized by the court under section 364(c) or 364(d) of this title.

§ 922. Automatic stay of enforcement of claims against the debtor

(a) A petition filed under this chapter operates as a stay, in addition to the stay provided by section 362 of this title, applicable to all entities, of—

(1) the commencement or continuation, including the issuance or employment of process, of a judicial, administrative, or other action or proceeding against an officer or inhabitant of the debtor that seeks to enforce a claim against the debtor; and

(2) the enforcement of a lien on or arising out of taxes or assessments owed to the debtor.

(b) Subsections (c), (d), (e), (f), and (g) of section 362 of this title apply to a stay under subsection (a) of this section the same as such subsections apply to a stay under section 362(a) of this title.

(c) If the debtor provides, under section 362, 364, or 922 of this title, adequate protection of the interest of the holder of a claim secured by a lien on property of the debtor and if, notwithstanding such protection such creditor has a claim arising from the stay of action against such property under section 362 or 922 of this title or from the granting of a lien under section 364(d) of this title, then such claim shall be allowable as an administrative expense under section 503(b) of this title.

(d) Notwithstanding section 362 of this title and subsection (a) of this section, a petition filed under this chapter does not operate as a stay of application of pledged special revenues in a manner consistent with section 927 of this title to payment of indebtedness secured by such revenues.

§ 923. Notice

There shall be given notice of the commencement of a case under this chapter, notice of an order for relief under this chapter, and notice of the dismissal of a case under this chapter. Such notice shall also be published at least once a week for three successive weeks in at least one newspaper of general circulation published within the district in which the case is commenced, and in such other newspaper having a general circulation among bond dealers and bondholders as the court designates.

§ 924. List of creditors

The debtor shall file a list of creditors.

§ 925. Effect of list of claims

A proof of claim is deemed filed under section 501 of this title for any claim that appears in the list filed under section 924 of this title, except a claim that is listed as disputed, contingent, or unliquidated.

§ 926. Avoiding powers

(a) If the debtor refuses to pursue a cause of action under section 544, 545, 547, 548, 549(a), or 550 of this title, then on request of a creditor, the court may appoint a trustee to pursue such cause of action.

(b) A transfer of property of the debtor to or for the benefit of any holder of a bond or note, on account of such bond or note, may not be avoided under section 547 of this title.

§ 927. Limitation on recourse

The holder of a claim payable solely from special revenues of the debtor under applicable nonbankruptcy law shall not be treated as having recourse against the debtor on account of such claim pursuant to section 1111(b) of this title.

§ 928. Post petition effect of security interest

(a) Notwithstanding section 522(a) of this title and subject to subsection (b) of this section, special revenues acquired by the debtor after the commencement of the case shall remain subject to any lien resulting from any security agreement entered into by the debtor before the commencement of the case.

(b) Any such lien on special revenues, other than municipal betterment assessments, derived from a project or system shall be subject to the necessary operating expenses of such project or system, as the case may be.

§ 929. Municipal leases

A lease to a municipality shall not be treated as an executory contract or unexpired lease for the purposes of section 365 or 502(b)(6) of this title solely by reason of its being subject to termination in the event the debtor fails to appropriate rent.

§ 930. Dismissal

(a) After notice and a hearing, the court may discuss a case under this chapter for cause, including—

(1) want of prosecution;

(2) unreasonable delay by the debtor that is prejudicial to creditors;

(3) failure to propose a plan within the time fixed under section 941 of this title;

(4) if a plan is not accepted within any time fixed by the court;

(5) denial of confirmation of a plan under section 943(b) of this title and denial of additional time for filing another plan or a modification of a plan; or

(6) if the court has retained jurisdiction after confirmation of a plan—

(A) material default by the debtor with respect to a term of such plan; or

(B) termination of such plan by reason of the occurrence of a condition specified in such plan.

(b) The court shall dismiss a case under this chapter if confirmation of a plan under this chapter is refused.

SUBCHAPTER III—THE PLAN

§ 941. Filing of plan

The debtor shall file a plan for the adjustment of the debtor's debts. If such a plan is not filed with the petition, the debtor shall file such a plan at such later time as the court fixes.

§ 942. Modification of plan

The debtor may modify the plan at any time before confirmation, but may not modify the plan so that the plan as modified fails to meet the requirements of this chapter. After the debtor files a modification, the plan as modified becomes the plan.

§ 943. Confirmation

(a) A special tax payer may object to confirmation of a plan.

(b) The court shall confirm the plan if—

(1) the plan complies with the provisions of this title made applicable by sections 103(e) and 901 of this title;

(2) the plan complies with the provisions of this chapter;

(3) all amounts to be paid by the debtor or by any person for services or expenses in the case or incident to the plan have been fully disclosed and are reasonable;

(4) the debtor is not prohibited by law from taking any action necessary to carry out the plan;

(5) except to the extent that the holder of a particular claim has agreed to a different treatment of such claim, the plan provides that on the effective date of the plan each holder of a claim of a kind specified in section 507(a)(1) of this title will receive on account of such claim cash equal to the allowed amount of such claim;

(6) any regulatory or electoral approval necessary under applicable nonbankruptcy law in order to carry out any provision of the plan has been obtained, or such provision is expressly conditioned on such approval; and

(7) the plan is in the best interests of creditors and is feasible.

§ 944. Effect of confirmation

(a) The provisions of a confirmed plan bind the debtor and any creditor, whether or not—

(1) a proof of such creditor's claim is filed or deemed filed under section 501 of this title;

(2) such claim is allowed under section 502 of this title; or

(3) such creditor has accepted the plan.

(b) Except as provided in subsection (c) of this section, the debtor is discharged from all debts as of the time when—

(1) the plan is confirmed;

(2) the debtor deposits any consideration to be distributed under the plan with a disbursing agent appointed by the court; and

(3) the court has determined

(A) that any security so deposited will constitute, after distribution, a valid legal obligation of the debtor; and

(B) that any provision made to pay or secure payment of such obligation is valid.

(c) The debtor is not discharged under subsection (b) of this section from any debt—

(1) excepted from discharge by the plan or order confirming the plan; or

(2) owed to an entity that, before confirmation of the plan, had neither notice nor actual knowledge of the case.

§ 945. Continuing jurisdiction and closing of the case

(a) The court may retain jurisdiction over the case for such period of time as is necessary for the successful implementation of the plan.

(b) Except as provided in subsection (a) of this section, the court shall close the case when administration of the case has been completed.

§ 946. Effect of exchange of securities before the date of the filing of the petition

The exchange of a new security under the plan for a claim covered by the plan, whether such exchange occurred before or after the date of the filing of the petition, does not limit or impair the effectiveness of the plan or of

any provision of this chapter. The amount and number specified in section 1126(c) of this title include the amount and number of claims formerly held by a creditor that has participated in any such exchange.

CHAPTER 11—REORGANIZATION

SUBCHAPTER I—OFFICERS AND ADMINISTRATION

SUBCHAPTER I—OFFICERS AND ADMINISTRATION

§ 1101. Definitions for this chapter

In this chapter—

(1) "debtor in possession" means debtor except when a person that has qualified under section 322 of this title is serving as trustee in the case;

(2) "substantial consummation" means—

(A) transfer of all or substantially all of the property proposed by the plan to be transferred;

(B) assumption by the debtor or by the successor to the debtor under the plan of the business or of the management of all or substantially all of the property dealt with by the plan; and

(C) commencement of distribution under the plan.

§ 1102. Creditors' and equity security holders' committees

(a)(1) Except as provided in paragraph (3), as soon as practicable after the order for relief under chapter 11 of this title, the United States trustee shall appoint a committee of creditors holding unsecured claims and may appoint additional committees of creditors or of equity security holders as the United States trustee deems appropriate.

(2) On request of a party in interest, the court may order the appointment of additional committees of creditors or of equity security holders if necessary to assure adequate representation of creditors or of equity security holders. The United States trustee shall appoint any such committee.

(3) On request of a party in interest in a case in which the debtor is a small business and for cause, the court may order that a committee of creditors not be appointed.

(b)(1) A committee of creditors appointed under subsection (a) of this section shall ordinarily consist of the

persons, willing to serve, that hold the seven largest claims against the debtor of the kinds represented on such committee, or of the members of a committee organized by creditors before the commencement of the case under this chapter, if such committee was fairly chosen and is representative of the different kinds of claims to be represented.

(2) A committee of equity security holders appointed under subsection (a)(2) of this section shall ordinarily consist of the persons, willing to serve, that hold the seven largest amounts of equity securities of the debtor of the kinds represented on such committee.

§ 1103. Powers and duties of committees

(a) At a scheduled meeting of a committee appointed under section 1102 of this title, at which a majority of the members of such committee are present, and with the court's approval, such committee may select and authorize the employment by such committee of one or more attorneys, accountants, or other agents, to represent or perform services for such committee.

(b) An attorney or accountant employed to represent a committee appointed under section 1102 of this title may not, while employed by such committee, represent any other entity having an adverse interest in connection with the case. Representation of one or more creditors of the same class as represented by the committee shall not per se constitute the representation of an adverse interest.

(c) A committee appointed under section 1102 of this title may—

(1) consult with the trustee or debtor in possession concerning the administration of the case;

(2) investigate the acts, conduct, assets, liabilities, and financial condition of the debtor, the operation of the debtor's business and the desirability of the continuance of such business, and any other matter relevant to the case or to the formulation of a plan;

(3) participate in the formulation of a plan, advise those represented by such committee of such committee's determinations as to any plan formulated, and collect and file with the court acceptances or rejections of a plan;

(4) request the appointment of a trustee or examiner under section 1104 of this title; and

(5) perform such other services as are in the interest of those represented.

(d) As soon as practicable after the appointment of a committee under section 1102 of this title, the trustee shall meet with such committee to transact such business as may be necessary and proper.

§ 1104. Appointment of trustee or examiner

(a) At any time after the commencement of the case but before confirmation of a plan, on request of a party in interest or the United States trustee, and after notice and

a hearing, the court shall order the appointment of a trustee—

(1) for cause, including fraud, dishonesty, incompetence, or gross mismanagement of the affairs of the debtor by current management, either before or after the commencement of the case, or similar case, but not including the number of holders of securities of the debtor or the amount of assets or liabilities of the debtor; or

(2) if such appointment is in the interests of creditors, any equity security holders, and other interests of the estate, without regard to the number of holders of securities of the debtor or the amount of assets or liabilities of the debtor.

(b) Except as provided in section 1163 of this title, on the request of a party in interest made not later than 30 days after the court orders the appointment of a trustee under subsection (a), the United States trustee shall convene a meeting of creditors for the purpose of electing one disinterested person to serve as trustee in the case. The election of a trustee shall be conducted in the manner provided in subsections (a), (b), and (c) of section 702 of this title.

(c) If the court does not order the appointment of a trustee under this section, then at any time before the confirmation of a plan, on request of a party in interest or the United States trustee, and after notice and a hearing, the court shall order the appointment of an examiner to conduct such an investigation of the debtor as is appropriate, including an investigation of any allegations of fraud, dishonesty, incompetence, misconduct, mismanagement, or irregularity in the management of the affairs of the debtor of or by current or former management of the debtor, if—

(1) such appointment is in the interests of creditors, any equity security holders, and other interests of the estate; or

(2) the debtor's fixed, liquidated, unsecured debts, other than debts for goods, services, or taxes, or owing to an insider, exceed $5,000,000.

(d) If the court orders the appointment of a trustee or an examiner, if a trustee or an examiner dies or resigns during the case or is removed under section 324 of this title, or if a trustee fails to qualify under section 322 of this title, then the United States trustee, after consultation with parties in interest, shall appoint, subject to the court's approval, one disinterested person other than the United States trustee to serve as trustee or examiner, as the case may be, in the case.

§ 1105. Termination of trustee's appointment

At any time before confirmation of a plan, on request of a party in interest or the United States trustee, and after notice and a hearing, the court may terminate the trustee's appointment and restore the debtor to possession and man-

agement of the property of the estate and of the operation of the debtor's business.

§ 1106. Duties of trustee and examiner

(a) A trustee shall—

(1) perform the duties of a trustee specified in sections 704(2), 704(5), 704(7), 704(8), and 704(9) of this title;

(2) if the debtor has not done so, file the list, schedule, and statement required under section 521(1) of this title;

(3) except to the extent that the court orders otherwise, investigate the acts, conduct, assets, liabilities, and financial condition of the debtor, the operation of the debtor's business and the desirability of the continuance of such business, and any other matter relevant to the case or to the formulation of a plan;

(4) as soon as practicable—

(A) file a statement of any investigation conducted under paragraph (3) of this subsection, including any fact ascertained pertaining to fraud, dishonesty, incompetence, misconduct, mismanagement, or irregularity in the management of the affairs of the debtor, or to a cause of action available to the estate; and

(B) transmit a copy or a summary of any such statement to any creditors' committee or equity security holders' committee, to any indenture trustee, and to such other entity as the court designates;

(5) as soon as practicable, file a plan under section 1121 of this title, file a report of why the trustee will not file a plan, or recommend conversion of the case to a case under chapter 7, 12, or 13 of this title or dismissal of the case;

(6) for any year for which the debtor has not filed a tax return required by law, furnish, without personal liability, such information as may be required by the governmental unit with which such tax return was to be filed, in light of the condition of the debtor's books and records and the availability of such information; and

(7) after confirmation of a plan, file such reports as are necessary or as the court orders.

(b) An examiner appointed under section 1104(d) of this title shall perform the duties specified in paragraphs (3) and (4) of subsection (a) of this section, and, except to the extent that the court orders otherwise, any other duties of the trustee that the court orders the debtor in possession not to perform.

§ 1107. Rights, powers, and duties of debtor in possession

(a) Subject to any limitations on a trustee serving in a case under this chapter, and to such limitations or conditions as the court prescribes, a debtor in possession shall have all the rights, other than the right to compensation under section 330 of this title, and powers, and shall perform all the functions and duties, except the duties specified in sections 1106(a)(2), (3), and (4) of this title, of a trustee serving in a case under this chapter.

(b) Notwithstanding section 327(a) of this title, a person is not disqualified for employment under section 327 of this title by a debtor in possession solely because of such person's employment by or representation of the debtor before the commencement of the case.

§ 1108. Authorization to operate business

Unless the court, on request of a party in interest and after notice and a hearing, orders otherwise, the trustee may operate the debtor's business.

§ 1109. Right to be heard

(a) The Securities and Exchange Commission may raise and may appear and be heard on any issue in a case under this chapter, but the Securities and Exchange Commission may not appeal from any judgment, order, or decree entered in the case.

(b) A party in interest, including the debtor, the trustee, a creditors' committee, an equity security holders' committee, a creditor, an equity security holder, or any indenture trustee, may raise and may appear and be heard on any issue in a case under this chapter.

§ 1110. Aircraft equipment and vessels

(a)(1) The right of a secured party with a security interest in equipment described in paragraph (2) or of a lessor or conditional vendor of such equipment to take possession of such equipment in compliance with a security agreement, lease, or conditional sale contract is not affected by section 362, 363, or 1129 or by any power of the court to enjoin the taking of possession unless—

(A) before the date that is 60 days after the date of the order for relief under this chapter, the trustee, subject to the court's approval, agrees to perform all obligations of the debtor that become due on or after the date of the order under such security agreement, lease, or conditional sale contract; and

(B) any default, other than a default of a kind specified in section 365(b)(2), under such security agreement, lease, or conditional sale contract—

(i) that occurs before the date of the order is cured before the expiration of such 60-day period; and

(ii) that occurs after the date of the order is cured before the later of—

(I) the date that is 30 days after the date of the default; and

(II) the expiration of such 60-day period.

(2) Equipment is described in this paragraph if it is—

(A) an aircraft, aircraft engine, propeller, appliance, or spare part (as defined in section 40102 of title 49) that is subject to a security interest granted by, leased to, or conditionally sold to a debtor that is a citizen of the United States (as defined in 40102 of title 49) holding an air carrier operating certificate issued by the Secretary of Transportation pursuant to chapter 447 of title 49 for aircraft capable of carrying 10 or more individuals or 6,000 pounds or more of cargo; or

(B) a documented vessel (as defined in section 30101(1) of title 46) that is subject to a security interest granted by, leased to, or conditionally sold to a debtor that is a water carrier that holds a certificate of public convenience and necessity or permit issued by the Interstate Commerce Commission.

(3) Paragraph (1) applies to a secured party, lessor, or conditional vendor acting in its own behalf or acting as trustee or otherwise in behalf of another party.

(b) The trustee and the secured party, lessor, or conditional vendor whose right to take possession is protected under subsection (a) may agree, subject to the court's approval, to extend the 60-day period specified in subsection (a)(1).

(c) With respect to equipment first placed in service on or prior to the date of enactment of this subsection, for purposes of this section—

(1) the term "lease" includes any written agreement with respect to which the lessor and the debtor, as lessee, have expressed in the agreement or in a substantially contemporaneous writing that the agreement is to be treated as a lease for Federal income tax purposes; and

(2) the term "security interest" means a purchase-money equipment security interest.

§ 1111. Claims and interests

(a) A proof of claim or interest is deemed filed under section 501 of this title for any claim or interest that appears in the schedules filed under section 521(1) or 1106(a)(2) of this title, except a claim or interest that is scheduled as disputed, contingent, or unliquidated.

(b)(1)(A) A claim secured by a lien on property of the estate shall be allowed or disallowed under section 502 of this title the same as if the holder of such claim had recourse against the debtor on account of such claim, whether or not such holder has such recourse, unless—

(i) the class of which such claim is a part elects, by at least two-thirds in amount and more than half in number of allowed claims of such class, application of paragraph (2) of this subsection; or

(ii) such holder does not have such recourse and such property is sold under section 363 of this title or is to be sold under the plan.

(B) A class of claims may not elect application of paragraph (2) of this subsection if—

(i) the interest on account of such claims of the holders of such claims in such property is of inconsequential value; or

(ii) the holder of a claim of such class has recourse against the debtor on account of such claim and such property is sold under section 363 of this title or is to be sold under the plan.

(2) If such an election is made, then notwithstanding section 506(a) of this title, such claim is a secured claim to the extent that such claim is allowed.

§ 1112. Conversion or dismissal

(a) The debtor may convert a case under this chapter to a case under chapter 7 of this title unless—

(1) the debtor is not a debtor in possession;

(2) the case originally was commenced as an involuntary case under this chapter; or

(3) the case was converted to a case under this chapter other than on the debtor's request.

(b) Except as provided in subsection (c) of this section, on request of a party in interest or the United States trustee or bankruptcy administrator, and after notice and a hearing, the court may convert a case under this chapter to a case under chapter 7 of this title or may dismiss a case under this chapter, whichever is in the best interest of creditors and the estate, for cause, including—

(1) continuing loss to or diminution of the estate and absence of a reasonable likelihood of rehabilitation;

(2) inability to effectuate a plan;

(3) unreasonable delay by the debtor that is prejudicial to creditors;

(4) failure to propose a plan under section 1121 of this title within any time fixed by the court;

(5) denial of confirmation of every proposed plan and denial of a request made for additional time for filing another plan or a modification of a plan;

(6) revocation of an order of confirmation under section 1144 of this title, and denial of confirmation of another plan or a modified plan under section 1129 of this title;

(7) inability to effectuate substantial consummation of a confirmed plan;

(8) material default by the debtor with respect to a confirmed plan;

(9) termination of a plan by reason of the occurrence of a condition specified in the plan; or

(10) nonpayment of any fees or charges required under chapter 123 of title 28.

(c) The court may not convert a case under this chapter to a case under chapter 7 of this title of the debtor is a farmer or a corporation that is not a moneyed, business, or commercial corporation, unless the debtor requests such conversion.

(d) The court may convert a case under this chapter to a case under chapter 12 or 13 of this title only if—

(1) the debtor requests such conversion;

(2) the debtor has not been discharged under section 1141(d) of this title; and

(3) if the debtor requests conversion to chapter 12 of this title, such conversion is equitable.

(e) Except as provided in subsections (c) and (f), the court, on request of the United States trustee, may convert a case under this chapter to a case under chapter 7 of this title or may dismiss a case under this chapter, whichever is in the best interest of creditors and the estate if the debtor in a voluntary case fails to file, within fifteen days after the filing of the petition commencing such case or such additional time as the court may allow, the information required by paragraph (1) of section 521, including a list containing the names and addresses of the holders of the twenty largest unsecured claims (or of all unsecured claims if there are fewer than twenty unsecured claims), and the approximate dollar amounts of each of such claims.

(f) Notwithstanding any other provision of this section, a case may not be converted to a case under another chapter of this title unless the debtor may be a debtor under such chapter.

§ 1113. Rejection of collective bargaining agreements

(a) The debtor in possession, or the trustee if one has been appointed under the provisions of this chapter, other than a trustee in a case covered by subchapter IV of this chapter and by title I of the Railway Labor Act, may assume or reject a collective bargaining agreement only in accordance with the provisions of this section.

(b)(1) Subsequent to filing a petition and prior to filing an application seeking rejection of a collective bargaining agreement, the debtor in possession or trustee (hereinafter in this section, "trustee" shall include a debtor in possession), shall—

(A) make a proposal to the authorized representative of the employees covered by such agreement, based on the most complete and reliable information available at the time of such proposal, which provides for those necessary modifications in the employees benefits and protections that are necessary to permit the reorganization of the debtor and assures that all creditors, the debtor and all of the affected parties are treated fairly and equitably; and

(B) provide, subject to subsection (d)(3), the representative of the employees with such relevant information as is necessary to evaluate the proposal.

(2) During the period beginning on the date of the making of a proposal provided for in paragraph (1) and ending on the date of the hearing provided for in subsection (d)(1), the trustee shall meet, at reasonable times, with the authorized representative to confer in good faith in attempting to reach mutually satisfactory modifications of such agreement.

(c) The court shall approve an application for rejection of a collective bargaining agreement only if the court finds that—

(1) the trustee has, prior to the hearing, made a proposal that fulfills the requirements of subsection (b)(1);

(2) the authorized representative of the employees has refused to accept such proposal without good cause; and

(3) the balance of the equities clearly favors rejection of such agreement.

(d)(1) Upon the filing of an application for rejection the court shall schedule a hearing to be held not later than fourteen days after the date of the filing of such application. All interested parties may appear and be heard at such hearing. Adequate notice shall be provided to such parties at least ten days before the date of such hearing. The court may extend the time for the commencement of such hearing for a period not exceeding seven days where the circumstances of the case, and the interests of justice require such extension, or for additional periods of time to which the trustee and representative agree.

(2) The court shall rule on such application for rejection within thirty days after the date of the commencement of the hearing. In the interests of justice, the court may extend such time for ruling for such additional period as the trustee and the employees' representative may agree to. If the court does not rule on such application within thirty days after the date of the commencement of the hearing, or within such additional time as the trustee and the employees' representative may agree to, the trustee may terminate or alter any provisions of the collective bargaining agreement pending the ruling of the court on such application.

(3) The court may enter such protective orders, consistent with the need of the authorized representative of the employee to evaluate the trustee's proposal and the application for rejection, as may be necessary to prevent disclosure of information provided to such representative where such disclosure could compromise the position of the debtor with respect to its competitors in the industry in which it is engaged.

(e) If during a period when the collective bargaining agreement continues in effect, and if essential to the continuation of the debtor's business, or in order to avoid irreparable damage to the estate, the court, after notice and a hearing, may authorize the trustee to implement interim changes in the terms, conditions, wages, benefits, or work rules provided by a collective bargaining agreement. Any hearing under this paragraph shall be scheduled in accordance with the needs of the trustee. The implementation of such interim changes shall not render the application for rejection moot.

(f) No provision of this title shall be construed to permit a trustee to unilaterally terminate or alter any provisions of a collective bargaining agreement prior to compliance with the provisions of this section.

§ 1114. Payment of insurance benefits to retired employees

(a) For purposes of this section, the term "retiree benefits" means payments to any entity or person for the purpose of providing or reimbursing payments for retired employees and their spouse and dependents, for medical, surgical, or hospital care benefits, or benefits in the event

of sickness, accident, disability, or death under any plan, fund, or program (through the purchase of insurance or otherwise) maintained or established in whole or in part by the debtor prior to filing a petition commencing a case under this title.

(b)(1) For purposes of this section, the term "authorized representative" means the authorized representative designated pursuant to subsection (c) for persons receiving any retiree benefits covered by a collective bargaining agreement or subsection (d) in the case of persons receiving retiree benefits not covered by such an agreement.

(2) Committees of retired employees appointed by the court pursuant to this section shall have the same rights, powers, and duties as committees appointed under sections 1102 and 1103 of this title for the purpose of carrying out the purposes of sections 1114 and 1129(a)(13) and, as permitted by the court, shall have the power to enforce the rights of persons under this title as they relate to retiree benefits.

(c)(1) A labor organization shall be, for purposes of this section, the authorized representative of those persons receiving any retiree benefits covered by any collective bargaining agreement to which that labor organization is signatory, unless (A) such labor organization elects not to serve as the authorized representative of such persons, or (B) the court, upon a motion by any party in interest, after notice and hearing, determines that different representation of such persons is appropriate.

(2) In cases where the labor organization referred to in paragraph (1) elects not to serve as the authorized representative of those persons receiving any retiree benefits covered by any collective bargaining agreement to which that labor organization is signatory, or in cases where the court, pursuant to paragraph (1) finds different representation of such persons appropriate, the court, upon a motion by any party in interest, and after notice and a hearing, shall appoint a committee of retired employees if the debtor seeks to modify or not pay the retiree benefits or if the court otherwise determines that it is appropriate, from among such persons, to serve as the authorized representative of such persons under this section.

(d) The court, upon a motion by any party in interest, and after notice and a hearing, shall appoint a committee of retired employees if the debtor seeks to modify or not pay the retiree benefits or if the court otherwise determines that it is appropriate, to serve as the authorized representative, under this section, of those persons receiving any retiree benefits not covered by a collective bargaining agreement.

(e)(1) Notwithstanding any other provision of this title, the debtor in possession, or the trustee if one has been appointed under the provisions of this chapter (hereinafter in this section "trustee" shall include a debtor in possession), shall timely pay and shall not modify any retiree benefits, except that—

(A) the court, on motion of the trustee or author-ized representative, and after notice and a hearing, may order modification of such payments, pursuant to the provisions of subsections (g) and (h) of this section, or

(B) the trustee and the authorized representative of the recipients of those benefits may agree to modification of such payments,

after which such benefits as modified shall continue to be paid by the trustee.

(2) Any payment for retiree benefits required to be made before a plan confirmed under section 1129 of this title is effective has the status of an allowed administrative expense as provided in section 503 of this title.

(f)(1) Subsequent to filing a petition and prior to filing an application seeking modification of the retiree benefits, the trustee shall—

(A) make a proposal to the authorized representative of the retirees, based on the most complete and reliable information available at the time of such proposal, which provides for those necessary modifications in the retiree benefits that are necessary to permit the reorganization of the debtor and assures that all creditors, the debtor and all of the affected parties are treated fairly and equitably; and

(B) provide, subject to subsection (k)(3), the representative of the retirees with such relevant information as is necessary to evaluate the proposal.

(2) During the period beginning on the date of the making of a proposal provided for in paragraph (1), and ending on the date of the hearing provided for in subsection (k)(1), the trustee shall meet, at reasonable times, with the authorized representative to confer in good faith in attempting to reach mutually satisfactory modifications of such retiree benefits.

(g) The court shall enter an order providing for modification in the payment of retiree benefits if the court finds that—

(1) the trustee has, prior to the hearing, made a proposal that fulfills the requirements of subsection (f);

(2) the authorized representative of the retirees has refused to accept such proposal without good cause; and

(3) such modification is necessary to permit the reorganization of the debtor and assures that all creditors, the debtor, and all of the affected parties are treated fairly and equitably, and is clearly favored by the balance of the equities;

except that in no case shall the court enter an order providing for such modification which provides for a modification to a level lower than that proposed by the trustee in the proposal found by the court to have complied with the requirements of this subsection and subsection (f): *Provided, however,* That at any time after an order is entered providing for modification in the payment of retiree benefits, or at any time after an agreement modifying such benefits is made between the trustee and the authorized representative of the recipients of such benefits, the authorized representative may apply to the court for an order

increasing those benefits which order shall be granted if the increase in retiree benefits sought is consistent with the standard set forth in paragraph (3): *Provided further,* That neither the trustee nor the authorized representative is precluded from making more than one motion for a modification order governed by this subsection.

(h)(1) Prior to a court issuing a final order under subsection (g) of this section, if essential to the continuation of the debtor's business, or in order to avoid irreparable damage to the estate, the court, after notice and a hearing, may authorize the trustee to implement interim modifications in retiree benefits.

(2) Any hearing under this subsection shall be scheduled in accordance with the needs of the trustee.

(3) The implementation of such interim changes does not render the motion for modification moot.

(i) No retiree benefits paid between the filing of the petition and the time a plan confirmed under section 1129 of this title becomes effective shall be deducted or offset from the amounts allowed as claims for any benefits which remain unpaid, or from the amounts to be paid under the plan with respect to such claims for unpaid benefits, whether such claims for unpaid benefits are based upon or arise from a right to future unpaid benefits or from any benefits not paid as a result of modifications allowed pursuant to this section.

(j) No claim for retiree benefits shall be limited by section 502(b)(7) of this title.

(k)(1) Upon the filing of an application for modifying retiree benefits, the court shall schedule a hearing to be held not later than fourteen days after the date of the filing of such application. All interested parties may appear and be heard at such hearing. Adequate notice shall be provided to such parties at least ten days before the date of such hearing. The court may extend the time for the commencement of such hearing for a period not exceeding seven days where the circumstances of the case, and the interests of justice require such extension, or for additional periods of time to which the trustee and the authorized representative agree.

(2) The court shall rule on such application for modification within ninety days after the date of the commencement of the hearing. In the interests of justice, the court may extend such time for ruling for such additional period as the trustee and the authorized representative may agree to. If the court does not rule on such application within ninety days after the date of the commencement of the hearing, or within such additional time as the trustee and the authorized representative may agree to, the trustee may implement the proposed modifications pending the ruling of the court on such application.

(3) The court may enter such protective orders, consistent with the need of the authorized representative of the retirees to evaluate the trustee's proposal and the application for modification, as may be necessary to prevent disclosure of information provided to such representative where such disclosure could compromise the position of the debtor with respect to its competitors in the industry in which it is engaged.

(*l*) This section shall not apply to any retiree, or the spouse or dependents of such retiree, if such retiree's gross income for the twelve months preceding the filing of the bankruptcy petition equals or exceeds $250,000, unless such retiree can demonstrate to the satisfaction of the court that he is unable to obtain health, medical, life, and disability coverage for himself, his spouse, and his dependents who would otherwise be covered by the employer's insurance plan, comparable to the coverage provided by the employer on the day before the filing of a petition under this title.

SUBCHAPTER II—THE PLAN

§ 1121. Who may file a plan

(a) The debtor may file a plan with a petition commencing a voluntary case, or at any time in a voluntary case or an involuntary case.

(b) Except as otherwise provided in this section, only the debtor may file a plan until after 120 days after the date of the order for relief under this chapter.

(c) Any party in interest, including the debtor, the trustee, a creditors' committee, an equity security holders' committee, a creditor, an equity security holder, or any indenture trustee, may file a plan if and only if—

(1) a trustee has been appointed under this chapter;

(2) the debtor has not filed a plan before 120 days after the date of the order for relief under this chapter; or

(3) the debtor has not filed a plan that has been accepted, before 180 days after the date of the order for relief under this chapter, by each class of claims or interests that is impaired under the plan.

(d) On request of a party in interest made within the respective periods specified in subsections (b) and (c) of this section and after notice and a hearing, the court may for cause reduce or increase the 120-day period or the 180-day period referred to in this section.

(e) In a case in which the debtor is a small business and elects to be considered a small business—

(1) only the debtor may file a plan until after 100 days after the date of the order for relief under this chapter;

(2) all plans shall be filed within 160 days after the date of the order for relief; and

(3) on request of a party in interest made within the respective periods specified in paragraphs (1) and (2) and after notice and a hearing, the court may—

(A) reduce the 100-day period or the 160-day period specified in paragraph (1) or (2) for cause; and

(B) increase the 100-day period specified in paragraph (1) if the debtor shows that the need for an

increase is caused by circumstances for which the debtor should not be held accountable.

§ 1122. Classification of claims or interests

(a) Except as provided in subsection (b) of this section, a plan may place a claim or an interest in a particular class only if such claim or interest is substantially similar to the other claims or interests of such class.

(b) A plan may designate a separate class of claims consisting only of every unsecured claim that is less than or reduced to an amount that the court approves as reasonable and necessary for administrative convenience.

§ 1123. Contents of plan

(a) Notwithstanding any otherwise applicable non-bankruptcy law, a plan shall—

(1) designate, subject to section 1122 of this title, classes of claims, other than claims of a kind specified in section 507(a)(1), 507(a)(2), or 507(a)(8) of this title, and classes of interests;

(2) specify any class of claims or interests that is not impaired under the plan;

(3) specify the treatment of any class of claims or interests that is impaired under the plan;

(4) provide the same treatment for each claim or interest of a particular class, unless the holder of a particular claim or interest agrees to a less favorable treatment of such particular claim or interest;

(5) provide adequate means for the plan's implementation, such as—

(A) retention by the debtor of all or any part of the property of the estate;

(B) transfer of all or any part of the property of the estate to one or more entities, whether organized before or after the confirmation of such plan;

(C) merger or consolidation of the debtor with one or more persons;

(D) sale of all or any part of the property of the estate, either subject to or free of any lien, or the distribution of all or any part of the property of the estate among those having an interest in such property of the estate;

(E) satisfaction or modification of any lien;

(F) cancellation or modification of any indenture or similar instrument;

(G) curing or waiving of any default;

(H) extension of a maturity date or a change in an interest rate or other term of outstanding securities;

(I) amendment of the debtor' charter; or

(J) issuance of securities of the debtor, or of any entity referred to in subparagraph (B) or (C) of this paragraph, for cash, for property, for existing securities, or in exchange for claims or interests, or for any other appropriate purpose;

(6) provide for the inclusion in the charter of the debtor, if the debtor is a corporation, or of any corporation referred to in paragraph (5)(B) or (5)(C) of this subsection, of a provision prohibiting the issuance of nonvoting equity securities, and providing, as to the several classes of securities possessing voting power, an appropriate distribution of such power among such classes, including, in the case of any class of equity securities having a preference over another class of equity securities with respect to dividends, adequate provisions for the election of directors representing such preferred class in the event of default in the payment of such dividends; and

(7) contain only provisions that are consistent with the interests of creditors and equity security holders and with public policy with respect to the manner of selection of any officer, director, or trustee under the plan and any successor to such officer, director, or trustee.

(b) Subject to subsection (a) of this section, a plan may—

(1) impair or leave unimpaired any class of claims, secured or unsecured, or of interests;

(2) subject to section 365 of this title, provide for the assumption, rejection, or assignment of any executory contract or unexpired lease of the debtor not previously rejected under such section;

(3) provide for—

(A) the settlement or adjustment of any claim or interest belonging to the debtor or to the estate; or

(B) the retention and enforcement by the debtor, by the trustee, or by a representative of the estate appointed for such purpose, of any such claim or interest;

(4) provide for the sale of all or substantially all of the property of the estate, and the distribution of the proceeds of such sale among holders of claims or interests;

(5) modify the rights of holders of secured claims, other than a claim secured only by a security interest in real property that is the debtor's principal residence, or of holders of unsecured claims, or leave unaffected the rights of holders of any class of claims; and

(6) include any other appropriate provision not inconsistent with the applicable provisions of this title.

(c) In a case concerning an individual, a plan proposed by an entity other than the debtor may not provide for the use, sale, or lease of property exempted under section 522 of this title, unless the debtor consents to such use, sale, or lease.

(d) Notwithstanding subsection (a) of this section and sections 506(b), 1129(a)(7), and 1129(b) of this title, if it is proposed in a plan to cure a default the amount necessary to cure the default shall be determined in accordance with the underlying agreement and applicable nonbankruptcy law.

§ 1124. Impairment of claims or interests

Except as provided in section 1123(a)(4) of this title, a class of claims or interests is impaired under a plan unless, with respect to each claim or interest of such class, the plan—

(1) leaves unaltered the legal, equitable, and contractual rights to which such claim or interest entitles the holder of such claim or interest; or

(2) notwithstanding any contractual provision or applicable law that entitles the holder of such claim or interest to demand or receive accelerated payment of such claim or interest after the occurrence of a default—

(A) cures any such default that occurred before or after the commencement of the case under this title, other than a default of a kind specified in section 365(b)(2) of this title;

(B) reinstates the maturity of such claim or interest as such maturity existed before such default;

(C) compensates the holder of such claim or interest for any damages incurred as a result of any reasonable reliance by such holder on such contractual provision or such applicable law; and

(D) does not otherwise alter the legal, equitable, or contractual rights to which such claim or interest entitles the holder of such claim or interest.

§ 1125. Postpetition disclosure and solicitation

(a) In this section—

(1) "adequate information" means information of a kind, and in sufficient detail, as far as is reasonably practicable in light of the nature and history of the debtor and the condition of the debtor's books and records, that would enable a hypothetical reasonable investor typical of holders of claims or interests of the relevant class to make an informed judgment about the plan, but adequate information need not include such information about any other possible or proposed plan; and

(2) "investor typical of holders of claims or interests of the relevant class" means investor having—

(A) a claim or interest of the relevant class;

(B) such a relationship with the debtor as the holders of other claims or interests of such class generally have; and

(C) such ability to obtain such information from sources other than the disclosure required by this section as holders of claims or interest in such class generally have.

(b) An acceptance or rejection of a plan may not be solicited after the commencement of the case under this title from a holder of a claim or interest with respect to such claim or interest, unless, at the time of or before such solicitation, there is transmitted to such holder the plan or a summary of the plan, and a written disclosure statement approved, after notice and a hearing, by the court as con-

taining adequate information. The court may approve a disclosure statement without a valuation of the debtor or an appraisal of the debtor's assets.

(c) The same disclosure statement shall be transmitted to each holder of a claim or interest of a particular class, but there may be transmitted different disclosure statements, differing in amount, detail, or kind of information, as between classes.

(d) Whether a disclosure statement required under subsection (b) of this section contains adequate information is not governed by any otherwise applicable nonbankruptcy law, rule, or regulation, but an agency or official whose duty is to administer or enforce such a law, rule, or regulation may be heard on the issue of whether a disclosure statement contains adequate information. Such an agency or official may not appeal from, or otherwise seek review of, an order approving a disclosure statement.

(e) A person that solicits acceptance or rejection of a plan, in good faith and in compliance with the applicable provisions of this title, or that participates, in good faith and in compliance with the applicable provisions of this title, in the offer, issuance, sale, or purchase of a security, offered or sold under the plan, of the debtor, of an affiliate participating in a joint plan with the debtor, or of a newly organized successor to the debtor under the plan, is not liable, on account of such solicitation or participation, for violation of any applicable law, rule, or regulation governing solicitation of acceptance or rejection of a plan or the offer, issuance, sale, or purchase of securities.

(f) Notwithstanding subsection (b), in a case in which the debtor has elected under section 1121(e) to be considered a small business—

(1) the court may conditionally approve a disclosure statement subject to final approval after notice and a hearing;

(2) acceptances and rejections of a plan may be solicited based on a conditionally approved disclosure statement as long as the debtor provides adequate information to each holder of a claim or interest that is solicited, but a conditionally approved disclosure statement shall be mailed at least 10 days prior to the date of the hearing on confirmation of the plan; and

(3) a hearing on the disclosure statement may be combined with a hearing on confirmation of a plan.

§ 1126. Acceptance of plan

(a) The holder of a claim or interest allowed under section 502 of this title may accept or reject a plan. If the United States is a creditor or equity security holder, the Secretary of the Treasury may accept or reject the plan on behalf of the United States.

(b) For the purposes of subsections (c) and (d) of this section, a holder of a claim or interest that has accepted or rejected the plan before the commencement of the case

under this title is deemed to have accepted or rejected such plan, as the case may be, if—

(1) the solicitation of such acceptance or rejection was in compliance with any applicable nonbankruptcy law, rule, or regulation governing the adequacy of disclosure in connection with such solicitation; or

(2) if there is not any such law, rule, or regulation, such acceptance or rejection was solicited after disclosure to such holder of adequate information, as defined in section 1125(a) of this title.

(c) A class of claims has accepted a plan if such plan has been accepted by creditors, other than any equity designated under subsection (e) of this section, that hold at least two-thirds in amount and more than one-half in number of the allowed claims of such class held by creditors, other than any equity designated under subsection (e) of this section, that have accepted or rejected such plan.

(d) A class of interests has accepted a plan if such plan has been accepted by holders of such interests, other than any entity designated under subsection (e) of this section, that hold at least two-thirds in amount of the allowed interests of such class held by holders of such interests, other than any entity designated under subsection (e) of this section, that have accepted or rejected such plan.

(e) On request of a party in interest, and after notice and a hearing, the court may designate any entity whose acceptance or rejection of such plan was not in good faith, or was not solicited or procured in good faith or in accordance with the provisions of this title.

(f) Notwithstanding any other provision of this section, a class that is not impaired under a plan, and each holder of a claim or interest of such class, are conclusively presumed to have accepted the plan, and solicitation of acceptances with respect to such class from the holders of claims or interests of such class is not required.

(g) Notwithstanding any other provision of this section, a class is deemed not to have accepted a plan if such plan provides that the claims or interests of such class do not entitle the holders of such claims or interests to receive or retain any property under the plan on account of such claims or interests.

§ 1127. Modification of plan

(a) The proponent of a plan may modify such plan at any time before confirmation, but may not modify such plan so that such plan as modified fails to meet the requirements of sections 1122 and 1123 of this title. After the proponent of a plan files a modification of such plan with the court, the plan as modified becomes the plan.

(b) The proponent of a plan or the reorganized debtor may modify such plan at any time after confirmation of such plan and before substantial consummation of such plan, but may not modify such plan so that such plan as modified fails to meet the requirements of sections 1122 and 1123 of this title. Such plan as modified under this

subsection becomes the plan only if circumstances warrant such modification and the court, after notice and a hearing, confirms such plan as modified, under section 1129 of this title.

(c) The proponent of a modification shall comply with section 1125 of this title with respect to the plan as modified.

(d) Any holder of a claim or interest that has accepted or rejected a plan is deemed to have accepted or rejected, as the case may be, such plan as modified, unless, within the time fixed by the court, such holder changes such holder's previous acceptance or rejection.

§ 1128. Confirmation hearing

(a) After notice, the court shall hold a hearing on confirmation of a plan.

(b) A party in interest may object to confirmation of a plan.

§ 1129. Confirmation of plan

(a) The court shall confirm a plan only if all of the following requirements are met:

(1) The plan complies with the applicable provisions of this title.

(2) The proponent of the plan complies with the applicable provisions of this title.

(3) The plan has been proposed in good faith and not by any means forbidden by law.

(4) Any payment made or to be made by the proponent, by the debtor, or by a person issuing securities or acquiring property under the plan, for services or for costs and expenses in or in connection with the case, or in connection with the plan and incident to the case, has been approved by, or is subject to the approval of, the court as reasonable.

(5)(A)(i) The proponent of the plan has disclosed the identity and affiliations of any individual proposed to serve, after confirmation of the plan, as a director, officer, or voting trustee of the debtor, an affiliate of the debtor participating in a joint plan with the debtor, or a successor to the debtor under the plan; and

(ii) the appointment to, or continuance in, such office of such individual, is consistent with the interests of creditors and equity security holders and with public policy; and

(B) the proponent of the plan has disclosed the identity of any insider that will be employed or retained by the reorganized debtor, and the nature of any compensation for such insider.

(6) Any governmental regulatory commission with jurisdiction, after confirmation of the plan, over the rates of the debtor has approved any rate change provided for in the plan, or such rate change is expressly conditioned on such approval.

(7) With respect to each impaired class of claims or interests—

(A) each holder of a claim or interest of such class—

(i) has accepted the plan; or

(ii) will receive or retain under the plan on account of such claim or interest property of a value, as of the effective date of the plan, that is not less than the amount that such holder would so receive or retain if the debtor were liquidated under chapter 7 of this title on such date; or

(B) if section 1111(b)(2) of this title applies to the claims of such class, each holder of a claim of such class will receive or retain under the plan on account of such claim property of a value, as of the effective date of the plan, that is not less than the value of such holder's interest in the estate's interest in the property that secures such claims.

(8) With respect to each class of claims or interests—

(A) such class has accepted the plan; or

(B) such class is not impaired under the plan.

(9) Except to the extent that the holder of a particular claim has agreed to a different treatment of such claim, the plan provides that—

(A) with respect to a claim of a kind specified in section 507(a)(1) or 507(a)(2) of this title, on the effective date of the plan, the holder of such claim will receive on account of such claim cash equal to the allowed amount of such claim;

(B) with respect to a class of claims of a kind specified in section 507(a)(3), 507(a)(4), 507(a)(5), 507(a)(6), or 507(a)(7) of this title, each holder of a claim of such class will receive—

(i) if such class has accepted the plan, deferred cash payments of a value, as of the effective date of the plan, equal to the allowed amount of such claim; or

(ii) if such class has not accepted the plan, cash on the effective date of the plan equal to the allowed amount of such claim; and

(C) with respect to a claim of a kind specified in section 507(a)(8) of this title, the holder of such claim will receive on account of such claim deferred cash payments, over a period not exceeding six years after the date of assessment of such claim, of a value, as of the effective date of the plan, equal to the allowed amount of such claim.

(10) If a class of claims is impaired under the plan, at least one class of claims that is impaired under the plan has accepted the plan, determined without including any acceptance of the plan by any insider.

(11) Confirmation of the plan is not likely to be followed by the liquidation, or the need for further financial reorganization, of the debtor or any successor to the debtor under the plan, unless such liquidation or reorganization is proposed in the plan.

(12) All fees payable under section 1930 of title 28, as determined by the court at the hearing on confirmation of the plan, have been paid or the plan provides for the payment of all such fees on the effective date of the plan.

(13) The plan provides for the continuation after its effective date of payment of all retiree benefits, as that term is defined in section 1114 of this title, at the level established pursuant to subsection (e)(1)(B) or (g) of section 1114 of this title, at any time prior to confirmation of the plan, for the duration of the period the debtor has obligated itself to provide such benefits.

(b)(1) Notwithstanding section 510(a) of this title, if all of the applicable requirements of subsection (a) of this section other than paragraph (8) are met with respect to a plan, the court, on request of the proponent of the plan, shall confirm the plan notwithstanding the requirements of such paragraph if the plan does not discriminate unfairly, and is fair and equitable, with respect to each class of claims or interests that is impaired under, and has not accepted, the plan.

(2) For the purpose of this subsection, the condition that a plan be fair and equitable with respect to a class includes the following requirements:

(A) With respect to a class of secured claims; the plan provides—

(i)(I) that the holders of such claims retain the liens securing such claims, whether the property subject to such liens is retained by the debtor or transferred to another entity, to the extent of the allowed amount of such claims; and

(II) that each holder of a claim of such class receive on account of such claim deferred cash payments totaling at least the allowed amount of such claim, of a value, as of the effective date of the plan, of at least the value of such holder's interest in the estate's interest in such property;

(ii) for the sale, subject to section 363(k) of this title, of any property that is subject to the liens securing such claims, free and clear of such liens, with such liens to attach to the proceeds of such sale, and the treatment of such liens on proceeds under clause (i) or (iii) of this subparagraph; or

(iii) for the realization by such holders of the indubitable equivalent of such claims.

(B) With respect to a class of unsecured claims—

(i) the plan provides that each holder of a claim of such class receive or retain on account of such claim property of a value, as of the effective date of the plan, equal to the allowed amount of such claim; or

(ii) the holder of any claim or interest that is junior to the claims of such class will not receive or retain under the plan on account of such junior claim or interest any property.

(C) With respect to a class of interests—

(i) the plan provides that each holder of an interest of such class receive or retain on account of such interest property of a value, as of the effective date of the plan, equal to the greatest of the allowed amount of any fixed liquidation preference to which such holder is entitled, any fixed redemption price to which such holder is entitled, or the value of such interest; or

(ii) the holder of any interest that is junior to the interests of such class will not receive or retain under the plan on account of such junior interest any property.

(c) Notwithstanding subsections (a) and (b) of this section and except as provided in section 1127(b) of this title, the court may confirm only one plan, unless the order of confirmation in the case has been revoked under section 1144 of this title. If the requirements of subsections (a) and (b) of this section are met with respect to more than one plan, the court shall consider the preferences of creditors and equity security holders in determining which plan to confirm.

(d) Notwithstanding any other provision of this section, on request of a party in interest that is a governmental unit, the court may not confirm a plan if the principal purpose of the plan is the avoidance of taxes or the avoidance of the application of section 5 of the Securities Act of 1933. In any hearing under this subsection, the governmental unit has the burden of proof on the issue of avoidance.

SUBCHAPTER III—POSTCONFIRMATION MATTERS

§ 1141. Effect of confirmation

(a) Except as provided in subsections (d)(2) and (d)(3) of this section, the provisions of a confirmed plan bind the debtor, any entity issuing securities under the plan, any entity acquiring property under the plan, and any creditor, equity security holder, or general partner in the debtor, whether or not the claim or interest of such creditor, equity security holder, or general partner is impaired under the plan and whether or not such creditor, equity security holder, or general partner has accepted the plan.

(b) Except as otherwise provided in the plan or the order confirming the plan, the confirmation of a plan vests all of the property of the estate in the debtor.

(c) Except as provided in subsections (d)(2) and (d)(3) of this section and except as otherwise provided in the plan or in the order confirming the plan, after confirmation of a plan, the property dealt with by the plan is free and clear of all claims and interests of creditors, equity security holders, and of general partners in the debtor.

(d)(1) Except as otherwise provided in this subsection,

in the plan, or in the order confirming the plan, the confirmation of a plan—

(A) discharges the debtor from any debt that arose before the date of such confirmation, and any debt of a kind specified in section 502(g), 502(h), or 502(i) of this title, whether or not—

(i) a proof of the claim based on such debt is filed or deemed filed under section 501 of this title;

(ii) such claim is allowed under section 502 of this title; or

(iii) the holder of such claim has accepted the plan; and

(B) terminates all rights and interests of equity security holders and general partners provided for by the plan.

(2) The confirmation of a plan does not discharge an individual debtor from any debt excepted from discharge under section 523 of this title.

(3) The confirmation of a plan does not discharge a debtor if—

(A) the plan provides for the liquidation of all or substantially all of the property of the estate;

(B) the debtor does not engage in business after consummation of the plan; and

(C) the debtor would be denied a discharge under section 727(a) of this title if the case were a case under chapter 7 of this title.

(4) The court may approve a written waiver of discharge executed by the debtor after the order for relief under this chapter.

§ 1142. Implementation of plan

(a) Notwithstanding any otherwise applicable nonbankruptcy law, rule, or regulation relating to financial condition, the debtor and any entity organized or to be organized for the purpose of carrying out the plan shall carry out the plan and shall comply with any orders of the court.

(b) The court may direct the debtor and any other necessary party to execute or deliver or to join in the execution or delivery of any instrument required to effect a transfer of property dealt with by a confirmed plan, and to perform any other act, including the satisfaction of any lien, that is necessary for the consummation of the plan.

§ 1143. Distribution

If a plan requires presentment or surrender of a security or the performance of any other act as a condition to participation in distribution under the plan, such action shall be taken not later than five years after the date of the entry of the order of confirmation. Any entity that has not within such time presented or surrendered such entity's security or taken any such other action that the plan requires may not participate in distribution under the plan.

§ 1144. Revocation of an order of confirmation

On request of a party in interest at any time before 180 days after the date of the entry of the order of confirmation, and after notice and a hearing, the court may revoke such order if and only if such order was procured by fraud. An order under this section revoking an order of confirmation shall—

(1) contain such provisions as are necessary to protect any entity acquiring rights in good faith reliance on the order of confirmation; and

(2) revoke the discharge of the debtor.

§ 1145. Exemption from securities laws

(a) Except with respect to an entity that is an underwriter as defined in subsection (b) of this section, section 5 of the Securities Act of 1933 and any State or local law requiring registration for offer or sale of a security or registration or licensing of an issuer of, underwriter of, or broker or dealer in, a security do not apply to—

(1) the offer or sale under a plan of security of the debtor, of an affiliate participating in a joint plan with the debtor, or of a successor to the debtor under the plan—

(A) in exchange for a claim against, an interest in, or a claim for an administrative expense in the case concerning, the debtor or such affiliate; or

(B) principally in such exchange and partly for cash or property;

(2) the offer of a security through any warrant, option, right to subscribe, or conversion privilege that was sold in the manner specified in paragraph (1) of this subsection, or the sale of a security upon the exercise of such a warrant, option, right, or privilege;

(3) the offer or sale, other than under a plan, of a security of an issuer other than the debtor or an affiliate, if—

(A) such security was owned by the debtor on the date of the filing of the petition;

(B) the issuer of such security is—

(i) required to file reports under section 13 of 15(d) of the Securities Exchange Act of 1934; and

(ii) in compliance with the disclosure and reporting provision of such applicable section; and

(C) such offer or sale is of securities that do not exceed—

(i) during the two-year period immediately following the date of the filing of the petition, four percent of the securities of such class outstanding on such date; and

(ii) during any 180-day period following such two-year period, one percent of the securities outstanding at the beginning of such 180-day period; or

(4) a transaction by a stockbroker in a security that is executed after a transaction of a kind specified in paragraph (1) or (2) of this subsection in such security and before the expiration of 40 days after the first date on which such security was bona fide offered to the public by the issuer or by or through an underwriter, if such stockbroker provides, at the time of or before such transaction by such stockbroker, a disclosure statement approved under section 1125 of this title, and, if the court orders, information supplementing such disclosure statement.

(b)(1) Except as provided in paragraph (2) of this subsection and except with respect to ordinary trading transactions of an entity that is not an issuer, an entity is an underwriter under section 2(11) of the Securities Act of 1933, if such entity—

(A) purchases a claim against, interest in, or claim for an administrative expense in the case concerning, the debtor, if such purchase is with a view to distribution of any security received or to be received in exchange for such a claim or interest;

(B) offers to sell securities offered or sold under the plan for the holders of such securities;

(C) offers to buy securities offered or sold under the plan from the holders of such securities, if such offer to buy is—

(i) with a view to distribution of such securities; and

(ii) under an agreement made in connection with the plan, with the consummation of the plan, or with the offer or sale of securities under the plan; or

(D) is an issuer, as used in such section 2(11), with respect to such securities.

(2) An entity is not an underwriter under section 2(11) of the Securities Act of 1933 or under paragraph (1) of this subsection with respect to an agreement that provides only for—

(A)(i) the matching or combining of fractional interests in securities offered or sold under the plan into whole interests; or

(ii) the purchase or sale of such fractional interests from or to entities receiving such fractional interests under the plan; or

(B) the purchase or sale for such entities of such fractional or whole interests as are necessary to adjust for any remaining fractional interests after such matching.

(3) An entity other than an entity of the kind specified in paragraph (1) of this subsection is not an underwriter under section 2(11) of the Securities Act of 1933 with respect to any securities offered or sold to such entity in the manner specified in subsection (a)(1) of this section.

(c) An offer or sale of securities of the kind and in the manner specified under subsection (a)(1) of this section is deemed to be a public offering.

(d) The Trust Indenture Act of 1939 does not apply to a note issued under the plan that matures not later than one year after the effective date of the plan.

§ 1146. Special tax provisions

(a) For the purposes of any State or local law imposing a tax on or measured by income, the taxable period of a debtor that is an individual shall terminate on the date of the order for relief under this chapter, unless the case was converted under section 706 of this title.

(b) The trustee shall make a State or local tax return of income for the estate of an individual debtor in a case under this chapter for each taxable period after the order for relief under this chapter during which the case is pending.

(c) The issuance, transfer, or exchange of a security, or the making or delivery of an instrument of transfer under a plan confirmed under section 1129 of this title, may not be taxed under any law imposing a stamp tax or similar tax.

(d) The court may authorize the proponent of a plan to request a determination, limited to questions of law, by a State or local governmental unit charged with responsibility for collection or determination of a tax on or measured by income, of the tax effects, under section 346 of this title and under the law imposing such tax, of the plan. In the event of an actual controversy, the court may declare such effects after the earlier of—

(1) the date on which such governmental unit responds to the request under this subsection; or

(2) 270 days after such request.

SUBCHAPTER IV—RAILROAD REORGANIZATION

§ 1161. Inapplicability of other sections

Sections 341, 343, 1102(a)(1), 1104, 1105, 1107, 1129(a)(7), and 1129(c) of this title do not apply in a case concerning a railroad.

§ 1162. Definition

In this subchapter, "Commission" means Interstate Commerce Commission.

§ 1163. Appointment of trustee

As soon as practicable after the order for relief the Secretary of Transportation shall submit a list of five disinterested persons that are qualified and willing to serve as trustees in the case. The United States trustee shall appoint one of such persons to serve as trustee in the case.

§ 1164. Right to be heard

The Commission, the Department of Transportation, and any State or local commission having regulatory juris-

diction over the debtor may raise and may appear and be heard on any issue in a case under this chapter, but may not appeal from any judgment, order, or decree entered in the case.

§ 1165. Protection of the public interest

In applying sections 1166, 1167, 1169, 1170, 1171, 1172, 1173, and 1174 of this title, the court and the trustee shall consider the public interest in addition to the interests of the debtor, creditors, and equity security holders.

§ 1166. Effect of subtitle IV of title 49 and of Federal, State, or local regulations

Except with respect to abandonment under section 1170 of this title, or merger, modification of the financial structure of the debtor, or issuance or sale of securities under a plan, the trustee and the debtor are subject to the provisions of subtitle IV of title 49 that are applicable to railroads, and the trustee is subject to orders of any Federal, State, or local regulatory body to the same extent as the debtor would be if a petition commencing the case under this chapter had not been filed, but—

(1) any such order that would require the expenditure, or the incurring of an obligation for the expenditure, of money from the estate is not effective unless approved by the court; and

(2) the provisions of this chapter are subject to section 601(b) of the Regional Rail Reorganization Act of 1973.

§ 1167. Collective bargaining agreements

Notwithstanding section 365 of this title, neither the court nor the trustee may change the wages or working conditions of employees of the debtor established by a collective bargaining agreement that is subject to the Railway Labor Act except in accordance with section 6 of such Act.

§ 1168. Rolling stock equipment

(a)(1) The right of a secured party with a security interest in or of a lessor or conditional vendor of equipment described in paragraph (2) to take possession of such equipment in compliance with an equipment security agreement, lease, or conditional sale contract is not affected by section 362, 363, or 1129 or by any power of the court to enjoin the taking of possession, unless—

(A) before the date that is 60 days after the date of commencement of a case under this chapter, the trustee, subject to the court's approval, agrees to perform all obligations of the debtor that become due on or after the date of commencement of the case under such security agreement, lease, or conditional sale contract; and

(B) any default, other than a default of a kind described in section 365(b)(2), under such security agreement, lease, or conditional sale contract—

(i) that occurs before the date of commencement of the case and is an event of default therewith is cured before the expiration of such 60-day period; and

(ii) that occurs or becomes an event of default after the date of commencement of the case is cured before the later of—

(I) the date that is 30 days after the date of the default or event of default; or

(II) the expiration of such 60-day period.

(2) Equipment is described in this paragraph if it is rolling stock equipment or accessories used on such equipment, including superstructures and racks, that is subject to a security interest granted by, leased to, or conditionally sold to the debtor.

(3) Paragraph (1) applies to a secured party, lessor, or conditional vendor acting in its own behalf or acting as trustee or otherwise in behalf of another party.

(b) The trustee and the secured party, lessor, or conditional vendor whose right to take possession is protected under subsection (a) may agree, subject to the court's approval, to extend the 60-day period specified in subsection (a)(1).

(c) With respect to equipment first placed in service on or prior to the date of enactment of this subsection, for purposes of this section—

(1) the term "lease" includes any written agreement with respect to which the lessor and the debtor, as lessee, have expressed in the agreement or in a substantially contemporaneous writing that the agreement is to be treated as a lease for Federal income tax purposes; and

(2) the term "security interest" means a purchase-money equipment security interest.

(d) With respect to equipment first placed in service after the date of enactment of this subsection, for purposes of this section, the term "rolling stock equipment" includes rolling stock equipment that is substantially rebuilt and accessories used on such equipment.

§ 1169. Effect of rejection of lease of railroad line

(a) Except as provided in subsection (b) of this section, if a lease of a line of railroad under which the debtor is the lessee is rejected under section 365 of this title, and if the trustee, within such time as the court fixes, and with the court's approval, elects not to operate the leased line, the lessor under such lease, after such approval, shall operate the line.

(b) If operation of such line by such lessor is impracticable or contrary to the public interest, the court, on request of such lessor, and after notice and a hearing, shall order the trustee to continue operation of such line for the account of such lessor until abandonment is ordered under section 1170 of this title, or until such operation is otherwise lawfully terminated, whichever occurs first.

(c) During any such operation, such lessor is deemed a carrier subject to the provisions of subtitle IV of title 49 that are applicable to railroads.

§ 1170. Abandonment of railroad line

(a) The court after notice and a hearing, may authorize the abandonment of all or a portion of a railroad line if such abandonment is—

(1)(A) in the best interest of the estate; or

(B) essential to the formulation of a plan; and

(2) consistent with the public interest.

(b) If, except for the pendency of the case under this chapter, such abandonment would require approval by the Commission under a law of the United States, the trustee shall initiate an appropriate application for such abandonment with the Commission. The court may fix a time within which the Commission shall report to the court on such application.

(c) After the court receives the report of the Commission, or the expiration of the time fixed under subsection (b) of this section, whichever occurs first, the court may authorize such abandonment, after notice to the Commission, the Secretary of Transportation, the trustee, any party in interest that has requested notice, any affected shipper or community, and any other entity prescribed by the court, and a hearing.

(d)(1) Enforcement of an order authorizing such abandonment shall be stayed until the time for taking an appeal has expired, or, if an appeal is timely taken, until such order has become final.

(2) If an order authorizing such abandonment is appealed, the court, on request of a party in interest, may authorize suspension of service on a line or a portion of a line pending the determination of such appeal, after notice to the Commission, the Secretary of Transportation, the trustee, any party in interest that has requested notice, any affected shipper or community, and any other entity prescribed by the court, and a hearing. An appellant may not obtain a stay of the enforcement of an order authorizing such suspension by the giving of a supersedeas bond or otherwise, during the pendency of such appeal.

(e)(1) In authorizing any abandonment of a railroad line under this section, the court shall require the rail carrier to provide a fair arrangement at least as protective of the interests of employees as that established under section 11347 of title 49.

(2) Nothing in this subsection shall be deemed to affect the priorities or timing of payment of employee protection which might have existed in the absence of this subsection.

§ 1171. Priority claims

(a) There shall be paid as an administrative expense any claim of an individual or of the personal representative of a deceased individual against the debtor or the estate, for personal injury to or death of such individual arising out of the operation of the debtor or the estate, whether such claim arose before or after the commencement of the case.

(b) Any unsecured claim against the debtor that would have been entitled to priority if a receiver in equity of the

property of the debtor had been appointed by a Federal court on the date of the order for relief under this title shall be entitled to the same priority in the case under this chapter.

§ 1172. Contents of plan

(a) In addition to the provisions required or permitted under section 1123 of this title, a plan—

(1) shall specify the extent to and the means by which the debtor's rail service is proposed to be continued, and the extent to which any of the debtor's rail service is proposed to be terminated; and

(2) may include a provision for—

(A) the transfer of any or all of the operating railroad lines of the debtor to another operating railroad; or

(B) abandonment of any railroad line in accordance with section 1170 of this title.

(b) If, except for the pendency of the case under this chapter, transfer of, or operation of or over, any of the debtor's rail lines by an entity other than the debtor or a successor to the debtor under the plan would require approval by the Commission under a law of the United States, then a plan may not propose such a transfer or such operation unless the proponent of the plan initiates an appropriate application for such a transfer or such operation with the Commission and, within such time as the court may fix, not exceeding 180 days, the Commission, with or without a hearing, as the Commission may determine, and with or without modification or condition, approves such application, or does not act on such application. Any action or order of the Commission approving, modifying, conditioning, or disapproving such application is subject to review by the court only under sections 706(2)(A), 706(2)(B), 706(2)(C), and 706(2)(D) of title 5.

(c)(1) In approving an application under subsection (b) of this section, the Commission shall require the rail carrier to provide a fair arrangement at least as protective of the interests of employees as that established under section 11347 of title 49.

(2) Nothing in this subsection shall be deemed to affect the priorities or timing of payment of employee protection which might have existed in the absence of this subsection.

§ 1173. Confirmation of plan

(a) The court shall confirm a plan if—

(1) the applicable requirements of section 1129 of this title have been met;

(2) each creditor or equity security holder will receive or retain under the plan property of a value, as of the effective date of the plan, that is not less than the value of property that each such creditor or equity security holder would so receive or retain if all of the operating railroad lines of the debtor were sold, and the

proceeds of such sale, and the other property of the estate, were distributed under chapter 7 of this title on such date;

(3) in light of the debtor's past earnings and the probable prospective earnings of the reorganized debtor, there will be adequate coverage by such prospective earnings of any fixed charges, such as interest on debt, amortization of funded debt, and rent for leased railroads, provided for by the plan; and

(4) the plan is consistent with the public interest.

(b) If the requirements of subsection (a) of this section are met with respect to more than one plan, the court shall confirm the plan that is most likely to maintain adequate rail service in the public interest.

§ 1174. Liquidation

On request of a party in interest and after notice and a hearing, the court may, or, if a plan has not been confirmed under section 1173 of this title before five years after the date of the order for relief, the court shall, order the trustee to cease the debtor's operation and to collect and reduce to money all of the property of the estate in the same manner as if the case were a case under chapter 7 of this title.

CHAPTER 12—ADJUSTMENT OF DEBTS OF A FAMILY FARMER WITH REGULAR ANNUAL INCOME

SUBCHAPTER I—OFFICERS, ADMINISTRATION, AND THE ESTATE

SUBCHAPTER I—OFFICERS, ADMINISTRATION, AND THE ESTATE

§ 1201. Stay of action against codebtor

(a) Except as provided in subsections (b) and (c) of this section, after the order for relief under this chapter, a creditor may not act, or commence or continue any civil action, to collect all or any part of a consumer debt of the debtor from any individual that is liable on such debt with the debtor, or that secured such debt, unless—

(1) such individual became liable on or secured such debt in the ordinary course of such individual's business; or

(2) the case is closed, dismissed, or converted to a case under chapter 7 of this title.

(b) A creditor may present a negotiable instrument, and may give notice of dishonor of such an instrument.

(c) On request of a party in interest and after notice and a hearing, the court shall grant relief from the stay provided by subsection (a) of this section with respect to a creditor, to the extent that—

(1) as between the debtor and the individual protected under subsection (a) of this section, such individual received the consideration for the claim held by such creditor;

(2) the plan filed by the debtor proposes not to pay such claim; or

(3) such creditor's interest would be irreparably harmed by continuation of such stay.

(d) Twenty days after the filing of a request under subsection (c)(2) of this section for relief from the stay provided by subsection (a) of this section, such stay is terminated with respect to the party in interest making such request, unless the debtor or any individual that is liable on such debt with the debtor files and serves upon such party in interest a written objection to the taking of the proposed action.

§ 1202. Trustee

(a) If the United States trustee has appointed an individual under section 586(b) of title 28 to serve as standing trustee in cases under this chapter and if such individual qualifies as a trustee under section 322 of this title, then such individual shall serve as trustee in any case filed under this chapter. Otherwise, the United States trustee shall appoint one disinterested person to serve as trustee in the case or the United States trustee may serve as trustee in the case if necessary.

(b) The trustee shall—

(1) perform the duties specified in sections 704(2), 704(3), 704(5), 704(6), 704(7) and 704(9) of this title;

(2) perform the duties specified in section 1106(a)(3) and 1106(a)(4) of this title if the court, for cause and on request of a party in interest, the trustee, or the United States trustee, so orders;

(3) appear and be heard at any hearing that concerns—

(A) the value of property subject to a lien;

(B) confirmation of a plan;

(C) modification of the plan after confirmation; or

(D) the sale of property of the estate;

(4) ensure that the debtor commences making timely payments required by a confirmed plan; and

(5) if the debtor ceases to be a debtor in possession, perform the duties specified in sections 704(8), 1106(a)(1), 1106(a)(2), 1106(a)(6), 1106(a)(7), and 1203.

§ 1203. Rights and powers of debtor

Subject to such limitations as the court may prescribe, a debtor in possession shall have all the rights, other than the right to compensation under section 330, and powers, and shall perform all the functions and duties, except the duties specified in paragraphs (3) and (4) of section 1106(a), of a trustee serving in a case under chapter 11, including operating the debtor's farm.

§ 1204. Removal of debtor as debtor in possession

(a) On request of a party in interest, and after notice and a hearing, the court shall order that the debtor shall not be a debtor in possession for cause, including fraud, dishonesty, incompetence, or gross mismanagement of the affairs of the debtor, either before or after the commencement of the case.

(b) On request of a party in interest, and after notice and a hearing, the court may reinstate the debtor in possession.

§ 1205. Adequate protection

(a) Section 361 does not apply in a case under this chapter.

(b) In a case under this chapter, when adequate protection is required under section 362, 363, or 364 of this title of an interest of an entity in property, such adequate protection may be provided by—

(1) requiring the trustee to make a cash payment or periodic cash payments to such entity, to the extent that the stay under section 362 of this title, use, sale, or lease under section 363 of this title, or any grant of a lien under section 364 of this title results in a decrease in the value of property securing a claim or of an entity's ownership interest in property;

(2) providing to such entity an additional or replacement lien to the extent that such stay, use, sale,

lease, or grant results in a decrease in the value of property securing a claim or of an entity's ownership interest in property;

(3) paying to such entity for the use of farmland the reasonable rent customary in the community where the property is located, based upon the rental value, net income, and earning capacity of the property; or

(4) granting such other relief, other than entitling such entity to compensation allowable under section 503(b)(1) of this title as an administrative expense, as will adequately protect the value of property securing a claim or of such entity's ownership interest in property.

§ 1206. Sales free of interests

After notice and a hearing, in addition to the authorization contained in section 363(f), the trustee in a case under this chapter may sell property under section 363(b) and (c) free and clear of any interest in such property of an entity other than the estate if the property is farmland or farm equipment, except that the proceeds of such sale shall be subject to such interest.

§ 1207. Property of the estate

(a) Property of the estate includes, in addition to the property specified in section 541 of this title—

(1) all property of the kind specified in such section that the debtor acquires after the commencement of the case but before the case is closed, dismissed, or converted to a case under chapter 7 of this title, whichever occurs first; and

(2) earnings from services performed by the debtor after the commencement of the case but before the case is closed, dismissed, or converted to a case under chapter 7 of this title, whichever occurs first.

(b) Except as provided in section 1204, a confirmed plan, or an order confirming a plan, the debtor shall remain in possession of all property of the estate.

§ 1208. Conversion or dismissal

(a) The debtor may convert a case under this chapter to a case under chapter 7 of this title at any time. Any waiver of the right to convert under this subsection is unenforceable.

(b) On request of the debtor at any time, if the case has not been converted under section 706 or 1112 of this title, the court shall dismiss a case under this chapter. Any waiver of the right to dismiss under this subsection is unenforceable.

(c) On request of a party in interest, and after notice and a hearing, the court may dismiss a case under this chapter for cause, including—

(1) unreasonable delay, or gross mismanagement, by the debtor that is prejudicial to creditors;

(2) nonpayment of any fees and charges required

under chapter 123 of title 28;

(3) failure to file a plan timely under section 1221 of this title;

(4) failure to commence making timely payments required by a confirmed plan;

(5) denial of confirmation of a plan under section 1225 of this title and denial of a request made for additional time for filing another plan or a modification of a plan;

(6) material default by the debtor with respect to a term of a confirmed plan;

(7) revocation of the order of confirmation under section 1230 of this title, and denial of confirmation of a modified plan under section 1229 of this title;

(8) termination of a confirmed plan by reason of the occurrence of a condition specified in the plan; or

(9) continuing loss to or diminution of the estate and absence of a reasonable likelihood of rehabilitation.

(d) On request of a party in interest, and after notice and a hearing, the court may dismiss a case under this chapter or convert a case under this chapter to a case under chapter 7 of this title upon a showing that the debtor has committed fraud in connection with the case.

(e) Notwithstanding any other provision of this section, a case may not be converted to a case under another chapter of this title unless the debtor may be a debtor under such chapter.

SUBCHAPTER II—THE PLAN

§ 1221. Filing of plan

The debtor shall file a plan not later than 90 days after the order for relief under this chapter, except that the court may extend such period if the need for an extension is attributable to circumstances for which the debtor should not justly be held accountable.

§ 1222. Contents of plan

(a) The plan shall—

(1) provide for the submission of all or such portion of future earnings or other future income of the debtor to the supervision and control of the trustee as is necessary for the execution of the plan;

(2) provide for the full payment, in deferred cash payments, of all claims entitled to priority under section 507 of this title, unless the holder of a particular claim agrees to a different treatment of such clam; and

(3) if the plan classifies claims and interests, provide the same treatment for each claim or interest within a particular class unless the holder of a particular claim or interest agrees to less favorable treatment.

(b) Subject to subsections (a) and (c) of this section, the plan may—

(1) designate a class or classes of unsecured claims,

as provided in section 1122 of this title, but may not discriminate unfairly against any class so designated; however, such plan may treat claims for a consumer debt of the debtor if an individual is liable on such consumer debt with the debtor differently than other unsecured claims;

(2) modify the rights of holders of secured claims, or of holders of unsecured claims, or leave unaffected the rights of holders of any class of claims;

(3) provide for the curing or waiving of any default;

(4) provide for payments on any unsecured claim to be made concurrently with payments on any secured claim or any other unsecured claim;

(5) provide for the curing of any default within a reasonable time and maintenance of payments while the case is pending on any unsecured claim or secured claim on which the last payment is due after the date on which the final payment under the plan is due;

(6) subject to section 365 of this title, provide for the assumption, rejection, or assignment of any executory contract or unexpired lease of the debtor not previously rejected under such section;

(7) provide for the payment of all or part of a claim against the debtor from property of the estate or property of the debtor;

(8) provide for the sale of all or any part of the property of the estate or the distribution of all or any part of the property of the estate among those having an interest in such property.

(9) provide for payment of allowed secured claims consistent with section 1225(a)(5) of this title, over a period exceeding the period permitted under section 1222(c);

(10) provide for the vesting of property of the estate, on confirmation of the plan or at a later time, in the debtor or in any other entity; and

(11) include any other appropriate provision not inconsistent with this title.

(c) Except as provided in subsections (b)(5) and (b)(9), the plan may not provide for payments over a period that is longer than three years unless the court for cause approves a longer period, but the court may not approve a period that is longer than five years.

(d) Notwithstanding subsection (b)(2) of this section and sections 506(b) and 1225(a)(5) of this title, if it is proposed in a plan to cure a default, the amount necessary to cure the default, shall be determined in accordance with the underlying agreement and applicable nonbankruptcy law.

§ 1223. Modification of plan before confirmation

(a) The debtor may modify the plan at any time before confirmation, but may not modify the plan so that the plan as modified fails to meet the requirements of section 1222 of this title.

(b) After the debtor files a modification under this section, the plan as modified becomes the plan.

(c) Any holder of a secured claim that has accepted or rejected the plan is deemed to have accepted or rejected, as the case may be, the plan as modified, unless the modification provides for a change in the rights of such holder from what such rights were under the plan before modification, and such holder changes such holder's previous acceptance or rejection.

§ 1224. Confirmation hearing

After expedited notice, the court shall hold a hearing on confirmation of the plan. A party in interest, the trustee, or the United States trustee may object to the confirmation of the plan. Except for cause, the hearing shall be concluded not later than 45 days after the filing of the plan.

§ 1225. Confirmation of plan

(a) Except as provided in subsection (b), the court shall confirm a plan if—

(1) the plan complies with the provisions of this chapter and with the other applicable provisions of this title;

(2) any fee, charge, or amount required under chapter 123 of title 28, or by the plan, to be paid before confirmation, has been paid;

(3) the plan has been proposed in good faith and not by any means forbidden by law;

(4) the value, as of the effective date of the plan, of property to be distributed under the plan on account of each allowed unsecured claim is not less than the amount that would be paid on such claim if the estate of the debtor were liquidated under chapter 7 of this title on such date;

(5) with respect to each allowed secured claim provided for by the plan—

(A) the holder of such claim has accepted the plan;

(B)(i) the plan provides that the holder of such claim retain the lien securing such claim; and

(ii) the value, as of the effective date of the plan, of property to be distributed by the trustee or the debtor under the plan on account of such claim is not less than the allowed amount of such claim; or

(C) the debtor surrenders the property securing such claim to such holder; and

(6) the debtor will be able to make all payments under the plan and to comply with the plan.

(b)(1) If the trustee or the holder of an allowed unsecured claim objects to the confirmation of the plan, then the court may not approve the plan unless, as of the effective date of the plan—

(A) the value of the property to be distributed under the plan on account of such claim is not less than the amount of such claim; or

(B) the plan provides that all of the debtor's projected disposable income to be received in the three-year period, or such longer period as the court may approve under section 1222(c), beginning on the date that the first payment is due under the plan will be applied to make payments under the plan.

(2) For purposes of this subsection, "disposable income" means income which is received by the debtor and which is not reasonably necessary to be expended—

(A) for the maintenance or support of the debtor or a dependent of the debtor; or

(B) for the payment of expenditures necessary for the continuation, preservation, and operation of the debtor's business.

(c) After confirmation of a plan, the court may order any entity from whom the debtor receives income to pay all or any part of such income to the trustee.

§ 1226. Payments

(a) Payments and funds received by the trustee shall be retained by the trustee until confirmation or denial of confirmation of a plan. If a plan is confirmed, the trustee shall distribute any such payment in accordance with the plan. If a plan is not confirmed, the trustee shall return any such payments to the debtor, after deducting—

(1) any unpaid claim allowed under section 503(b) of this title; and

(2) if a standing trustee is serving in the case, the percentage fee fixed for such standing trustee.

(b) Before or at the time of each payment to creditors under the plan, there shall be paid—

(1) any unpaid claim of the kind specified in section 507(a)(1) of this title; and

(2) if a standing trustee appointed under section 1202(c) of this title is serving in the case, the percentage fee fixed for such standing trustee under section 1202(d) of this title.

(c) Except as otherwise provided in the plan or in the order confirming the plan, the trustee shall make payments to creditors under the plan.

§ 1227. Effect of confirmation

(a) Except as provided in section 1228(a) of this title, the provisions of a confirmed plan bind the debtor, each creditor, each equity security holder, and each general partner in the debtor, whether or not the claim of such creditor, such equity security holder, or such general partner in the debtor is provided for by the plan, and whether or not such creditor, such equity security holder, or such general partner in the debtor has objected to, has accepted, or has rejected the plan.

(b) Except as otherwise provided in the plan or the order confirming the plan, the confirmation of a plan vests all of the property of the estate in the debtor.

(c) Except as provided in section 1228(a) of this title and

except as otherwise provided in the plan or in the order confirming the plan, the property vesting in the debtor under subsection (b) of this section is free and clear of any claim or interest of any creditor provided for by the plan.

§ 1228. Discharge

(a) As soon as practicable after completion by the debtor of all payments under the plan, other than payments to holders of allowed claims provided for under section 1222(b)(5) or 1222(b)(10) of this title, unless the court approves a written waiver of discharge executed by the debtor after the order for relief under this chapter, the court shall grant the debtor a discharge of all debts provided for by the plan allowed under section 503 of this title or disallowed under section 502 of this title, except any debt—

(1) provided for under section 1222(b)(5) or 1222(b)(10) of this title; or

(2) of the kind specified in section 523(a) of this title.

(b) At any time after the confirmation of the plan and after notice and a hearing, the court may grant a discharge to a debtor that has not completed payments under the plan only if—

(1) the debtor's failure to complete such payments is due to circumstances for which the debtor should not justly be held accountable;

(2) the value, as of the effective date of the plan, of property actually distributed under the plan on account of each allowed unsecured claim is not less than the amount that would have been paid on such claim if the estate of the debtor had been liquidated under chapter 7 of this title on such date; and

(3) modification of the plan under section 1229 of this title is not practicable.

(c) A discharge granted under subsection (b) of this section discharges the debtor from all unsecured debts provided for by the plan or disallowed under section 502 of this title, except any debt—

(1) provided for under section 1222(b)(5) or 1222(b)(10) of this title; or

(2) of a kind specified in section 523(a) of this title.

(d) On request of a party in interest before one year after a discharge under this section is granted, and after notice and a hearing, the court may revoke such discharge only if—

(1) such discharge was obtained by the debtor through fraud; and

(2) the requesting party did not know of such fraud until after such discharge was granted.

(e) After the debtor is granted a discharge, the court shall terminate the services of any trustee serving in the case.

§ 1229. Modification of plan after confirmation

(a) At any time after confirmation of the plan but before the completion of payments under such plan, the plan

may be modified, on request of the debtor, the trustee, or the holder of an allowed unsecured claim, to—

(1) increase or reduce the amount of payments on claims of a particular class provided for by the plan;

(2) extend or reduce the time for such payments; or

(3) alter the amount of the distribution to a creditor whose claim is provided for by the plan to the extent necessary to take account of any payment of such claim other than under the plan.

(b)(1) Sections 1222(a), 1222(b), and 1223(c) of this title and the requirements of section 1225(a) of this title apply to any modification under subsection (a) of this section.

(2) The plan as modified becomes the plan unless, after notice and a hearing, such modification is disapproved.

(c) A plan modified under this section may not provide for payments over a period that expires after three years after the time that the first payment under the original confirmed plan was due, unless the court, for cause, approves a longer period, but the court may not approve a period that expires after five years after such time.

§ 1230. Revocation of an order of confirmation

(a) On request of a party in interest at any time within 180 days after the date of the entry of an order of confirmation under section 1225 of this title, and after notice and a hearing, the court may revoke such order if such order was procured by fraud.

(b) If the court revokes an order of confirmation under subsection (a) of this section, the court shall dispose of the case under section 1207 of this title, unless, within the time fixed by the court, the debtor proposes and the court confirms a modification of the plan under section 1229 of this title.

§ 1231. Special tax provisions

(a) For the purpose of any State or local law imposing a tax on or measured by income, the taxable period of a debtor that is an individual shall terminate on the date of the order for relief under this chapter, unless the case was converted under section 706 of this title.

(b) The trustee shall make a State or local tax return of income for the estate of an individual debtor in a case under this chapter for each taxable period after the order for relief under this chapter during which the case is pending.

(c) The issuance, transfer, or exchange of a security, or the making or delivery of an instrument of transfer under a plan confirmed under section 1225 of this title, may not be taxed under any law imposing a stamp tax or similar tax.

(d) The court may authorize the proponent of a plan to request a determination, limited to questions of law, by a State or local governmental unit charged with responsibility for collection, or determination of a tax on or measured by income, of the tax effects, under section 346 of this title and under the law imposing such tax, of the plan. In the event of an actual controversy, the court may declare such effects after the earlier of—

(1) the date on which such governmental unit responds to the request under this subsection; or

(2) 270 days after such request.

CHAPTER 13—ADJUSTMENT OF DEBTS OF AN INDIVIDUAL WITH REGULAR INCOME

SUBCHAPTER I—OFFICERS, ADMINISTRATION, AND THE ESTATE

SUBCHAPTER I—OFFICERS, ADMINISTRATION, AND THE ESTATE

§ 1301. Stay of action against codebtor

(a) Except as provided in subsections (b) and (c) of this section, after the order for relief under this chapter, a creditor may not act, or commence or continue any civil action, to collect all or any part of a consumer debt of the debtor from any individual that is liable on such debt with the debtor, or that secured such debt, unless—

(1) such individual became liable on or secured such debt in the ordinary course of such individual's business; or

(2) the case is closed, dismissed, or converted to a case under chapter 7 or 11 of this title.

(b) A creditor may present a negotiable instrument,

and may give notice of dishonor of such an instrument.

(c) On request of a party in interest and after notice and a hearing, the court shall grant relief from the stay provided by subsection (a) of this section with respect to a creditor, to the extent that—

(1) as between the debtor and the individual protected under subsection (a) of this section, such individual received the consideration for the claim held by such creditor;

(2) the plan filed by the debtor proposes not to pay such claim; or

(3) such creditor's interest would be irreparably harmed by continuation of such stay.

(d) Twenty days after the filing of a request under subsection (c)(2) of this section for relief from the stay provided by subsection (a) of this section, such stay is terminated with respect to the party in interest making such request, unless the debtor or any individual that is liable on such debt with the debtor files and serves upon such party in interest a written objection to the taking of the proposed action.

§ 1302. Trustee

(a) If the United States trustee appoints an individual under section 586(b) of title 28 to serve as standing trustee in cases under this chapter and if such individual qualifies under section 322 of this title, then such individual shall serve as trustee in the case. Otherwise, the United States trustee shall appoint one disinterested person to serve as trustee in the case or the United States trustee may serve as a trustee in the case.

(b) The trustee shall—

(1) perform the duties specified in sections 704(2), 704(3), 704(4), 704(5), 704(6), 704(7), and 704(9) of this title;

(2) appear and be heard at any hearing that concerns—

(A) the value of property subject to a lien;

(B) confirmation of a plan; or

(C) modification of the plan after confirmation;

(3) dispose of, under regulations issued by the Director of the Administrative Office of the United States Courts, moneys received or to be received in a case under chapter XIII of the Bankruptcy Act;

(4) advise, other than on legal matters, and assist the debtor in performance under the plan; and

(5) ensure that the debtor commences making timely payments under section 1326 of this title.

(c) If the debtor is engaged in business, then in addition to the duties specified in subsection (b) of this section, the trustee shall perform the duties specified in sections 1106(a)(3) and 1106(a)(4) of this title.

§ 1303. Rights and powers of debtor

Subject to any limitations on a trustee under this chapter, the debtor shall have, exclusive of the trustee, the rights and powers of a trustee under sections 363(b), 363(d), 363(e), 363(f), and 363(l), of this title.

§ 1304. Debtor engaged in business

(a) A debtor that is self-employed and incurs trade credit in the production of income from such employment is engaged in business.

(b) Unless the court orders otherwise, a debtor engaged in business may operate the business of the debtor and, subject to any limitations on a trustee under sections 363(c) and 364 of this title and to such limitations or conditions as the court prescribes, shall have, exclusive of the trustee, the rights and powers of the trustee under such sections.

(c) A debtor engaged in business shall perform the duties of the trustee specified in section 704(8) of this title.

§ 1305. Filing and allowance of postpetition claims

(a) A proof of claim may be filed by any entity that holds a claim against the debtor—

(1) for taxes that become payable to a governmental unit while the case is pending; or

(2) that is a consumer debt, that arises after the date of the order for relief under this chapter, and that is for property or services necessary for the debtor's performance under the plan.

(b) Except as provided in subsection (c) of this section, a claim filed under subsection (a) of this section shall be allowed or disallowed under section 502 of this title, but shall be determined as of the date such claim arises, and shall be allowed under section 502(a), 502(b), or 502(c) of this title, or disallowed under section 502(d) or 502(e) of this title, the same as if such clam had arisen before the date of the filing of the petition.

(c) A claim filed under subsection (a)(2) of this section shall be disallowed if the holder of such claim knew or should have known that prior approval by the trustee of the debtor's incurring the obligation was practicable and was not obtained.

§ 1306. Property of the estate

(a) Property of the estate includes, in addition to the property specified in section 541 of this title—

(1) all property of the kind specified in such section that the debtor acquires after the commencement of the case but before the case is closed, dismissed, or converted to a case under chapter 7, 11, or 12 of this title, whichever occurs first; and

(2) earnings from services performed by the debtor after the commencement of the case but before the case is closed, dismissed, or converted to a case under chapter 7, 11, or 12 of this title, whichever occurs first.

(b) Except as provided in a confirmed plan or order confirming a plan, the debtor shall remain in possession of all property of the estate.

§ 1307. Conversion or dismissal

(a) The debtor may convert a case under this chapter to a case under chapter 7 of this title at any time. Any waiver of the right to convert under this subsection is unenforceable.

(b) On request of the debtor at any time, if the case has not been converted under section 706, 112, or 1208 of this title, the court shall dismiss a case under this chapter. Any waiver of the right to dismiss under this subsection is unenforceable.

(c) Except as provided in subsection (e) of this section, on request of a party in interest or the United States trustee and after notice and a hearing, the court may convert a case under this chapter to a case under chapter 7 of this title, or may dismiss a case under this chapter, whichever is in the best interests of creditors and the estate, for cause, including—

(1) unreasonable delay by the debtor that is prejudicial to creditors;

(2) nonpayment of any fees and charges required under chapter 123 of title 28;

(3) failure to file a plan timely under section 1321 of this title;

(4) failure to commence making timely payments under section 1326 of this title;

(5) denial of confirmation of a plan under section 1325 of this title and denial of a request made for additional time for filing another plan or a modification of a plan;

(6) material default by the debtor with respect to a term of a confirmed plan;

(7) revocation of the order of confirmation under section 1330 of this title, and denial of confirmation of a modified plan under section 1329 of this title;

(8) termination of a confirmed plan by reason of the occurence of a condition specified in the plan other than completion of payments under the plan;

(9) only on request of the United States trustee, failure of the debtor to file, within fifteen days, or such additional time as the court may allow, after the filing of the petition commencing such case, the information required by paragraph (1) of section 521; or

(10) only on request of the United States trustee, failure to timely file the information required by paragraph (2) of section 521.

(d) Except as provided in subsection (e) of this section, at any time before the confirmation of a plan under section 1325 of this title, on request of a party in interest or the United States trustee and after notice and a hearing, the court may convert a case under this chapter to a case under chapter 11 or 12 of this title.

(e) The court may not convert a case under this chapter to a case under chapter 7, 11, or 12 of this title if the debtor is a farmer, unless the debtor requests such conversion.

(f) Notwithstanding any other provision of this section, a case may not be converted to a case under another chapter of this title unless the debtor may be a debtor under such chapter.

SUBCHAPTER II—THE PLAN

§ 1321. Filing of plan

The debtor shall file a plan.

§ 1322. Contents of plan

(a) The plan shall—

(1) provide for the submission of all or such portion of future earnings or other future income of the debtor to the supervision and control of the trustee as is necessary for the execution of the plan;

(2) provide for the full payment, in deferred cash payments, of all claims entitled to priority under section 507 of this title, unless the holder of a particular claim agrees to a different treatment of such claim; and

(3) if the plan classifies claims, provide the same treatment for each claim within a particular class.

(b) Subject to subsections (a) and (c) of this section, the plan may—

(1) designate a class or classes of unsecured claims, as provided in section 1122 of this title, but may not discriminate unfairly against any class so designated; however, such plan may treat claims for a consumer debt of the debtor if an individual is liable on such consumer debt with the debtor differently than other unsecured claims;

(2) modify the rights of holders of secured claims, other than a claim secured only by a security interest in real property that is the debtor's principal residence, or of holders of unsecured claims, or leave unaffected the rights of holders of any class of claims;

(3) provide for the curing or waiving of any default;

(4) provide for payments on any unsecured claim to be made concurrently with payments on any secured claim or any other unsecured claim;

(5) notwithstanding paragraph (2) of this subsection, provide for the curing of any default within a reasonable time and maintenance of payments while the case is pending on any unsecured claim or secured claim on which the last payment is due after the date on which the final payment under the plan is due;

(6) provide for the payment of all or any part of any claim allowed under section 1305 of this title;

(7) subject to section 365 of this title, provide for the assumption, rejection, or assignment of any executory contract or unexpired lease of the debtor not previously rejected under such section;

(8) provide for the payment of all or part of a claim against the debtor from property of the estate or property of the debtor;

(9) provide for the vesting of property of the estate, on confirmation of the plan or at a later time, in the debtor or in any other entity; and

(10) include any other appropriate provision not inconsistent with this title.

(c) Notwithstanding subsection (b)(2) and applicable nonbankruptcy law—

(1) a default with respect to, or that gave rise to, a lien on the debtor's principal residence may be cured under paragraph (3) or (5) of subsection (b) until such residence is sold at a foreclosure sale that is conducted in accordance with applicable nonbankruptcy law; and

(2) in a case in which the last payment on the original payment schedule for a claim secured only by a security interest in real property that is the debtor's principal residence is due before the date on which the final payment under the plan is due, the plan may provide for the payment of the claim as modified pursuant to section 1325(a)(5) of this title.

(d) The plan may not provide for payments over a period that is longer than three years, unless the court, for cause, approves a longer period, but the court may not approve a period that is longer than five years.

(e) Notwithstanding subsection (b)(2) of this section and sections 506(b) and 1325(a)(5) of this title, if it is proposed in a plan to cure a default, the amount necessary to cure the default, shall be determined in accordance with the underlying agreement and applicable nonbankruptcy law.

§ 1323. Modification of plan before confirmation

(a) The debtor may modify the plan at any time before confirmation, but may not modify the plan so that the plan as modified fails to meet the requirements of section 1322 of this title.

(b) After the debtor files a modification under this section, the plan as modified becomes the plan.

(c) Any holder of a secured claim that has accepted or rejected the plan is deemed to have accepted or rejected, as the case may be, the plan as modified, unless the modification provides for a change in the rights of such holder from what such rights were under the plan before modification, and such holder changes such holder's previous acceptance or rejection.

§ 1324. Confirmation hearing

After notice, the court shall hold a hearing on confirmation of the plan. A party in interest may object to confirmation of the plan.

§ 1325. Confirmation of plan

(a) Except as provided in subsection (b), the court shall confirm a plan if—

(1) the plan complies with the provisions of this chapter and with the other applicable provisions of this title;

(2) any fee, charge, or amount required under chapter 123 of title 28, or by the plan, to be paid before confirmation, has been paid;

(3) the plan has been proposed in good faith and not by any means forbidden by law;

(4) the value, as of the effective date of the plan, of property to be distributed under the plan on account of each allowed unsecured claim is not less than the amount that would be paid on such claim if the estate of the debtor were liquidated under chapter 7 of this title on such date;

(5) with respect to each allowed secured claim provided for by the plan—

(A) the holder of such claim has accepted the plan;

(B)(i) the plan provides that the holder of such claim retain the lien securing such claim; and

(ii) the value, as of the effective date of the plan, of property to be distributed under the plan on account of such claim is not less than the allowed amount of such claim; or

(C) the debtor surrenders the property securing such claim to such holder; and

(6) the debtor will be able to make all payments under the plan and to comply with the plan.

(b)(1) If the trustee or the holder of an allowed unsecured claim objects to the confirmation of the plan, then the court may not approve the plan unless, as of the effective date of the plan—

(A) the value of the property to be distributed under the plan on account of such claim is not less than the amount of such claim; or

(B) the plan provides that all of the debtor's projected disposable income to be received in the three-year period beginning on the date that the first payment is due under the plan will be applied to make payments under the plan.

(2) For purposes of this subsection, "disposable income" means income which is received by the debtor and which is not reasonably necessary to be expended—

(A) for the maintenance or support of the debtor or a dependent of the debtor; and

(B) if the debtor is engaged in business, for the payment of expenditures necessary for the continuation, preservation, and operation of such business.

(c) After confirmation of a plan, the court may order any entity from whom the debtor receives income to pay all or any part of such income to the trustee.

§ 1326. Payments

(a)(1) Unless the court orders otherwise, the debtor shall commence making the payments proposed by a plan

within 30 days after the plan is filed.

(2) A payment made under this subsection shall be retained by the trustee until confirmation or denial of confirmation of a plan. If a plan is confirmed, the trustee shall distribute any such payment in accordance with the plan as soon as practicable. If a plan is not confirmed, the trustee shall return any such payment to the debtor, after deducting any unpaid claim allowed under section 503(b) of this title.

(b) Before or at the time of each payment to creditors under the plan, there shall be paid—

(1) any unpaid claim of the kind specified in section 507(a)(1) of this title; and

(2) if a standing trustee appointed under section 586(b) of title 28 is serving in the case, the percentage fee fixed for such standing trustee under section 586(e)(1)(B) of title 28.

(c) Except as otherwise provided in the plan or in the order confirming the plan, the trustee shall make payments to creditors under the plan.

§ 1327. Effect of confirmation

(a) The provisions of a confirmed plan bind the debtor and each creditor, whether or not the claim of such creditor is provided for by the plan, and whether or not such creditor has objected to, has accepted, or has rejected the plan.

(b) Except as otherwise provided in the plan or the order confirming the plan, the confirmation of a plan vests all of the property of the estate in the debtor.

(c) Except as otherwise provided in the plan or in the order confirming the plan, the property vesting in the debtor under subsection (b) of this section is free and clear of any claim or interest of any creditor provided for by the plan.

§ 1328. Discharge

(a) As soon as practicable after completion by the debtor of all payments under the plan, unless the court approves a written waiver of discharge executed by the debtor after the order for relief under this chapter, the court shall grant the debtor a discharge of all debts provided for by the plan or disallowed under section 502 of this title, except any debt—

(1) provided for under section 1322(b)(5) of this title;

(2) of the kind specified in paragraph (5), (8), or (9) of section 523(a) or 523(a)(9) of this title; or

(b) At any time after the confirmation of the plan and after notice and a hearing, the court may grant a discharge to a debtor that has not completed payments under the plan only if—

(1) the debtor's failure to complete such payments is due to circumstances for which the debtor should not justly be held accountable;

(2) the value, as of the effective date of the plan, of property actually distributed under the plan on account of each allowed unsecured claim is not less than the amount that would have been paid on such claim if the estate of the debtor had been liquidated under chapter 7 of this title on such date; and

(3) modification of the plan under section 1329 of this title is not practicable.

(c) A discharge granted under subsection (b) of this section discharges the debtor for all unsecured debts provided for by the plan or disallowed under section 502 of this title, except any debt—

(1) provided for under section 1322(b)(5) of this title; or

(2) of a kind specified in section 523(a) of this title.

(d) Notwithstanding any other provision of this section, a discharge granted under this section does not discharge the debtor from any debt based on an allowed claim filed under section 1305(a)(2) of this title if prior approval by the trustee of the debtor's incurring such debt was practicable and was not obtained.

(e) On request of a party in interest before one year after a discharge under this section is granted, and after notice and a hearing, the court may revoke such discharge only if—

(1) such discharge was obtained by the debtor through fraud; and

(2) the requesting party did not know of such fraud until after such discharge was granted.

§ 1329. Modification of plan after confirmation

(a) At any time after confirmation of the plan but before the completion of payments under such plan, the plan may be modified, upon request of the debtor, the trustee, or the holder of an allowed unsecured claim, to—

(1) increase or reduce the amount of payments on claims of a particular class provided for by the plan;

(2) extend or reduce the time for such payments; or

(3) alter the amount of the distribution to a creditor whose claim is provided for by the plan to the extent necessary to take account of any payment of such claim other than under the plan.

(b)(1) Sections 1322(a), 1322(b), and 1323(c) of this title and the requirements of section 1325(a) of this title apply to any modification under subsection (a) of this section.

(2) The plan as modified becomes the plan unless, after notice and a hearing, such modification is disapproved.

(c) A plan modified under this section may not provide for payments over a period that expires after three years after the time that the first payment under the original confirmed plan was due, unless the court, for cause, approves a longer period, but the court may not approve a period that expires after five years after such time.

§ 1330. Revocation of an order of confirmation

(a) On request of a party in interest at any time within 180 days after the date of the entry of an order of confirmation under section 1325 of this title, and after notice and a hearing, the court may revoke such order if such order was procured by fraud.

(b) If the court revokes an order of confirmation under subsection (a) of this section, the court shall dispose of the case under section 1307 of this title, unless, within the time fixed by the court, the debtor proposes and the court confirms a modification of the plan under section 1329 of this title.

FEDERAL RULES OF
BANKRUPTCY PROCEDURE

Rule 1001

SCOPE OF RULES AND FORMS; SHORT TITLE

The Bankruptcy Rules and Forms govern procedure in cases under title 11 of the United States Code. The rules shall be cited as the Federal Rules of Bankruptcy Procedure and the forms as the Official Bankruptcy Forms. These rules shall be construed to secure the just, speedy, and inexpensive determination of every case and proceeding.

PART I
COMMENCEMENT OF CASE;
PROCEEDINGS RELATING TO
PETITION AND ORDER FOR RELIEF

Rule 1002

COMMENCEMENT OF CASE

(a) Petition. A petition commencing a case under the Code shall be filed with the clerk.

(b) Transmission to United States Trustee. The clerk shall forthwith transmit to the United States trustee a copy of the petition filed pursuant to subdivision (a) of this rule.

Rule 1003

INVOLUNTARY PETITION

(a) Transferor or Transferee of Claim. A transferor or transferee of a claim shall annex to the original and each copy of the petition a copy of all documents evidencing the transfer, whether transferred unconditionally, for security, or otherwise, and a signed statement that the claim was not transferred for the purpose of commencing the case and setting forth the consideration for and terms of the transfer. An entity that has transferred or acquired a claim for the purpose of commencing a case for liquidation under

chapter 7 or for reorganization under chapter 11 shall not be a qualified petitioner.

(b) Joinder of Petitioners After Filing. If the answer to an involuntary petition filed by fewer than three creditors avers the existence of 12 or more creditors, the debtor shall file with the answer a list of all creditors with their addresses, a brief statement of the nature of their claims, and the amounts thereof. If it appears that there are 12 or more creditors as provided in § 303(b) of the Code, the court shall afford a reasonable opportunity for other creditors to join in the petition before a hearing is held thereon.

Rule 1004

PARTNERSHIP PETITION

(a) Voluntary Petition. A voluntary petition may be filed on behalf of the partnership by one or more general partners if all general partners consent to the petition.

(b) Involuntary Petition; Notice and Summons. After filing of an involuntary petition under § 303(b)(3) of the Code, (1) the petitioning partners or other petitioners shall cause forthwith a copy of the petition to be sent to or served on each general partner who is not a petitioner; and (2) the clerk shall issue forthwith a summons for service on each general partner who is not a petition. Rule 1010 applies to the form and service of the summons.

Rule 1005

CAPTION OF PETITION

The caption of a petition commencing a case under the Code shall contain the name of the court, the title of the case, and the docket number. The title of the case shall include the name, social security number and employer's tax identification number of the debtor and all other names used by the debtor within six years before filing the petition. If the petition is not filed by the debtor, it shall include all names used by the debtor which are known to petitioners.

Rule 1006

FILING FEE

(a) General Requirement. Every petition shall be accompanied by the prescribed filing fee except as provided in subdivision (b) of this rule.

(b) Payment of Filing Fee in Installments.

(1) *Application for Permission to Pay Filing Fee in Installments.* A voluntary petition by an individual shall be accepted for filing if accompanied by the debtor's signed application stating that the debtor is unable to pay the filing fee except in installments. The application shall state

the proposed terms of the installment payments and that the applicant has neither paid any money nor transferred any property to an attorney for services in connection with the case.

(2) *Action on Application.* Prior to the meeting of creditors, the court may order the filing fee paid to the clerk or grant leave to pay in installments and fix the number, amount and dates of payment. The number of installments shall not exceed four, and the final installment shall be payable not later than 120 days after filing the petition. For cause shown, the court may extend the time of any installment, provided the last installment is paid not later than 180 days after filing the petition.

(3) *Postponement of Attorney's Fees.* The filing fee must be paid in full before the debtor or chapter 13 trustee may pay an attorney or any other person who renders services to the debtor in connection with the case.

Rule 1007

LISTS, SCHEDULES, AND STATEMENTS; TIME LIMITS

(a) List of Creditors and Equity Security Holders.

(1) *Voluntary Case.* In a voluntary case, the debtor shall file with the petition a list containing the name and address of each creditor unless the petition is accompanied by a schedule of liabilities.

(2) *Involuntary Case.* In an involuntary case, the debtor shall file within 15 days after entry of the order for relief, a list containing the name and address of each creditor unless a schedule of liabilities has been filed.

(3) *Equity Security Holders.* In a chapter 11 reorganization case, unless the court orders otherwise, the debtor shall file within 15 days after entry of the order for relief a list of the debtor's equity security holders of each class showing the number and kind of interests registered in the name of each holder, and the last known address or place of business of each holder.

(4) *Extension of Time.* Any extension of time for the filing of the lists required by this subdivision may be granted only on motion for cause shown and on notice to the United States trustee and to any trustee, committee elected pursuant to § 705 or appointed pursuant to § 1102 of the Code, or other party as the court may direct.

(b) Schedules and Statements Required.

(1) Except in a chapter 9 municipality case, the debtor, unless the court orders otherwise, shall file schedules of assets and liabilities, a schedule of current income and expenditures, a schedule of executory contracts and unexpired leases, and a statement of financial affairs, prepared as prescribed by the appropriate Official Forms.

(2) An individual debtor in a chapter 7 case shall file a statement of intention as required by § 521(2) of the Code, prepared as prescribed by the appropriate Official

Form. A copy of the statement of intention shall be served on the trustee and the creditors named in the statement on or before the filing of the statement.

(c) Time Limits. The schedules and statements, other than the statement of intention, shall be filed with the petition in a voluntary case, or if the petition is accompanied by a list of all the debtor's creditors and their addresses, within 15 days thereafter, except as otherwise provided in subdivisions (d), (e), and (h) of this rule. In an involuntary case the schedules and statements, other than the statement of intention, shall be filed by the debtor within 15 days after entry of the order for relief. Schedules and statements previously filed in a pending chapter 7 case shall be deemed filed in a superseding case unless the court directs otherwise. Any extension of time for the filing of the schedules and statements may be granted only on motion for cause shown and on notice to the United States trustee and to any committee elected pursuant to § 705 or appointed pursuant to § 1102 of the Code, trustee, examiner, or other party as the court may direct. Notice of an extension shall be given to the United States trustee and to any committee, trustee, or other party as the court may direct.

(d) List of 20 Largest Creditors in Chapter 9 Municipality Case or Chapter 11 Reorganization Case. In addition to the list required by subdivision (a) of this rule, a debtor in a chapter 9 municipality case or a debtor in a voluntary chapter 11 reorganization case shall file with the petition a list containing the name, address and claim of the creditors that hold the 20 largest unsecured claims, excluding insiders, as prescribed by the appropriate Official Form. In an involuntary chapter 11 reorganization case, such list shall be filed by the debtor within 2 days after entry of the order for relief under § 303(h) of the Code.

(e) List in Chapter 9 Municipality Cases. The list required by subdivision (a) of this rule shall be filed by the debtor in a chapter 9 municipality case within such time as the court shall fix. If a proposed plan requires a revision of assessments so that the proportion of special assessments or special taxes to be assessed against some real property will be different from the proportion in effect at the date the petition is filed, the debtor shall also file a list showing the name and address of each known holder of title, legal or equitable, to real property adversely affected. On motion for cause shown, the court may modify the requirements of this subdivision and subdivision (a) of this rule.

(f) [Abrogated].

(g) Partnership and Partners. The general partners of a debtor partnership shall prepare and file the schedules of the assets and liabilities, schedule of current income and expenditures, schedule of executory contracts and unexpired leases, and statement of financial affairs of the partnership. The court may order any general partner to file a statement of personal assets and liabilities within such time as the court may fix.

(h) Interests Acquired or Arising After Petition. If, as provided by § 541(a)(5) of the Code, the debtor acquires or becomes entitled to acquire any interest in property, the debtor shall within 10 days after the information comes to the debtor's knowledge or within such further time the court may allow, file a supplemental schedule in the chapter 7 liquidation case, chapter 11 reorganization case, chapter 12 family farmer's debt adjustment case, or chapter 13 individual debt adjustment case. If any of the property required to be reported under this subdivision is claimed by the debtor as exempt, the debtor shall claim the exemptions in the supplemental schedule. The duty to file a supplemental schedule in accordance with this subdivision continues notwithstanding the closing of the case, except that the schedule need not be filed in a chapter 11, chapter 12, or chapter 13 case with respect to property acquired after entry of the order confirming a chapter 11 plan or discharging the debtor in a chapter 12 or chapter 13 case.

(i) Disclosure of List of Security Holders. After notice and hearing and for cause shown, the court may direct an entity other than the debtor or trustee to disclose any list of security holders of the debtor in its possession or under its control, indicating the name, address and security held by any of them. The entity possessing this list may be required either to produce the list or a true copy thereof, or permit inspection or copying, or otherwise disclose the information contained on the list.

(j) Impounding of Lists. On motion of a party in interest and for cause shown the court may direct the impounding of the lists filed under this rule, and may refuse to permit inspection by any entity. The court may permit inspection or use of the lists, however, by any party in interest on terms prescribed by the court.

(k) Preparation of Lists, Schedules, or Statements on Default of Debtor. If a list, schedule, or statement, other than a statement of intention, is not prepared and filed as required by this rule, the court may order the trustee, a petitioning creditor, committee, or other party to prepare and file any of these papers within a time fixed by the court. The court may approve reimbursement of the cost incurred in complying with such an order as an administrative expense.

(l) Transmission to United States Trustee. The clerk shall forthwith transmit to the United States trustee a copy of every list, schedule, and statement filed pursuant to subdivision (a)(1), (a)(2), (b), (d), or (h) of this rule.

Rule 1008

VERIFICATION OF PETITIONS AND ACCOMPANYING PAPERS

All petitions lists, schedules, statements and amendments thereto shall be verified or contain an unsworn declaration as provided in 28 U.S.C. § 1746.

Rule 1009

AMENDMENTS OF VOLUNTARY PETITIONS, LISTS, SCHEDULES AND STATEMENTS

(a) General Right to Amend. A voluntary petition, list, schedule, or statement may be amended by the debtor as a matter of course at any time before the case is closed. The debtor shall give notice of the amendment to the trustee and to any entity affected thereby. On motion of a party in interest, after notice and a hearing, the court may order any voluntary petition, list, schedule, or statement to be amended and the clerk shall give notice of the amendment to entities designated by the court.

(b) Statement of Intention. The statement of intention may be amended by the debtor at any time before the expiration of the period provided in § 521(2)(B) of the Code. The debtor shall give notice of the amendment to the trustee and to any entity affected thereby.

(c) Transmission to United States Trustee. The clerk shall forthwith transmit to the United States trustee a copy of every amendment filed pursuant to subdivision (a) or (b) of this rule.

Rule 1010

SERVICE OF INVOLUNTARY PETITION AND SUMMONS; PETITION COMMENCING ANCILLARY CASE

On the filing of an involuntary petition or a petition commencing a case ancillary to a foreign proceeding the clerk shall forthwith issue a summons for service. When an involuntary petition is filed, service shall be made on the debtor. When a petition commencing an ancillary case is filed, service shall be made on the parties against whom relief is sought pursuant to § 304(b) of the Code and on any other parties as the court may direct. The summons shall be served with a copy of the petition in the manner provided for service of a summons and complaint by Rule 7004(a) or (b). If service cannot be so made, the court may order that the summons and petition be served by mailing copies to the party's last known address, and by at least one publication in a manner and form directed by the court. The summons and petition may be served on the party anywhere. Rule 7004(f) and Rule 4(g) and (h) F.R.Civ.P. apply when service is made or attempted under this rule.

Rule 1011

RESPONSIVE PLEADING OR MOTION IN INVOLUNTARY AND ANCILLARY CASES

(a) Who May Contest Petition. The debtor named in an involuntary petition or a party in interest to a petition commencing a case ancillary to a foreign proceeding may contest the petition. In the case of a petition against a partnership under Rule 1004(b), a nonpetitioning general partner, or a person who is alleged to be a general partner but denies the allegation, may contest the petition.

(b) Defenses and Objections; When Presented. Defenses and objections to the petition shall be presented in the manner prescribed by Rule 12 F.R.Civ.P. and shall be filed and served within 20 days after service of the summons, except that if service is made by publication on a party or partner not residing or found within the state in which the court sits, the court shall prescribe the time for filing and serving the response.

(c) Effect of Motion. Service of a motion under Rule 12(b) F.R.Civ.P. shall extend the time for filing and serving a responsive pleading as permitted by Rule 12(a) F.R.Civ.P.

(d) Claims Against Petitioners. A claim against a petitioning creditor may not be asserted in the answer except for the purpose of defeating the petition.

(e) Other Pleadings. No other pleadings shall be permitted, except that the court may order a reply to an answer and prescribe the time for filing and service.

Rule 1012

[ABROGATED]

Rule 1013

HEARING AND DISPOSITION OF A PETITION IN AN INVOLUNTARY CASE

(a) Contested Petition. The court shall determine the issues of a contested petition at the earliest practicable time and forthwith enter an order for relief, dismiss the petition, or enter any other appropriate order.

(b) Default. If no pleading or other defense to a petition is filed within the time provided by Rule 1011, the court, on the next day, or as soon thereafter as practicable, shall enter an order for the relief requested in the petition.

(c) [Abrogated]

Rule 1014

DISMISSAL AND CHANGE OF VENUE

(a) Dismissal and Transfer of Cases.

(1) *Cases Filed in Proper District.* If a petition is filed in a proper district, on timely motion of a party in interest, and after hearing on notice to the petitioners, the United States trustee, and other entities as directed by the court, the case may be transferred to any other district if the court determines that the transfer is in the interest of justice or for the convenience of the parties.

(2) *Cases Filed in Improper District.* If a petition is filed in an improper district, on timely motion of a party in interest and after hearing on notice to the petitioners, the United States trustee, and other entities as directed by the court, the case may be dismissed or transferred to any other

district if the court determines that transfer is in the interest of justice or for the convenience of the parties.

(b) Procedure When Petitions Involving the Same Debtor or Related Debtors are Filed in Different Courts. If petitions commencing cases under the Code are filed in different districts by or against (1) the same debtor, or (2) a partnership and one or more of its general partners, or (3) two or more general partners, or (4) a debtor and an affiliate, on motion filed in the district in which the petition filed first is pending and after hearing on notice to the petitioners, the United States trustee, and other entities as directed by the court, the court may determine, in the interest of justice or for the convenience of the parties, the district or districts in which the case or cases should proceed. Except as otherwise ordered by the court in the district in which the petition filed first is pending, the proceedings on the other petitions shall be stayed by the courts in which they have been filed until the determination is made.

Rule 1015

CONSOLIDATION OR JOINT ADMINISTRATION OF CASES PENDING IN SAME COURT

(a) Cases Involving Same Debtor. If two or more petitions are pending in the same court by or against the same debtor, the court may order consolidation of the cases.

(b) Cases Involving Two or More Related Debtors. If a joint petition or two or more petitions are pending in the same court by or against (1) a husband and wife, or (2) a partnership and one or more of its general partners, or (3) two or more general partners, or (4) a debtor and an affiliate, the court may order a joint administration of the estates. Prior to entering an order the court shall give consideration to protecting creditors of different estates against potential conflicts of interest. An order directing joint administration of individual cases of a husband and wife shall, if one spouse has elected the exemptions under § 522(b)(1) of the Code and the other has elected the exemptions under § 522(b)(2), fix a reasonable time within which either may amend the election so that both shall have elected the same exemptions. The order shall notify the debtors that unless they elect the same exemptions within the time fixed by the court, they will be deemed to have elected the exemptions provided by § 522(b)(1).

(c) Expediting and Protective Orders. When an order for consolidation or joint administration of a joint case or two or more cases is entered pursuant to this rule, while protecting the rights of the parties under the Code, the court may enter orders as may tend to avoid unnecessary costs and delay.

Rule 1016

DEATH OR INCOMPETENCY OF DEBTOR

Death or incompetency of the debtor shall not abate a liquidation case under chapter 7 of the Code. In such event the estate shall be administered and the case concluded in the same manner, so far as possible, as though the death or incompetency had not occurred. If a reorganization, family farmer's debt adjustment, or individual's debt adjustment case is pending under chapter 11, chapter 12, or chapter 13, the case may be dismissed; or if further administration is possible and in the best interest of the parties, the case may proceed and be concluded in the same manner, so far as possible, as though the death or incompetency had not occurred.

Rule 1017

DISMISSAL OR CONVERSION OF CASE; SUSPENSION

(a) Voluntary Dismissal; Dismissal for Want of Prosecution or Other Cause. Except as provided in §§ 707(b), 1208(b), and 1307(b) of the Code, a case shall not be dismissed on motion of the petitioner or for want of prosecution or other cause or by consent of the parties prior to a hearing on notice as provided in Rule 2002. For such notice the debtor shall file a list of all creditors with their addresses within the time fixed by the court unless the list was previously filed. If the debtor fails to file the list, the court may order the preparing and filing by the debtor or other entity.

(b) Dismissal for Failure to Pay Filing Fee.

(1) For failure to pay any installment of the filing fee, the court may after hearing on notice to the debtor and the trustee dismiss the case.

(2) If the case is dismissed or the case closed without full payment of the filing fee, the installments collected shall be distributed in the same manner and proportions as if the filing fee had been paid in full.

(3) Notice of dismissal for failure to pay the filing fee shall be given within 30 days after the dismissal to creditors appearing on the list of creditors and to those who have filed claims, in the manner provided in Rule 2002.

(c) Suspension. A case shall not be dismissed or proceedings suspended pursuant to § 305 of the Code prior to a hearing on notice as provided in Rule 2002(a).

(d) Procedure for Dismissal or Conversion. A proceeding to dismiss a case or convert a case to another chapter, except pursuant to §§ 706(a), 707(b), 1112(a), 1208(a) or (b), or 1307(a) or (b) of the Code, is governed by Rule 9014. Conversion or dismissal pursuant to §§ 706(a), 1112(a), 1208(b), or 1307(b) shall be on motion filed and served as required by Rule 9013. A chapter 12 or chapter 13 case shall be converted without court order on the filing by the debtor of a notice of conversion pursuant to §§ 1208(a) or 1307(a), and the filing date of the notice shall be deemed the date of the conversion order for the purposes of applying § 348(c) of the Code and Rule 1019. The clerk shall forwith transmit to the United States trustee a copy of the notice.

(e) Dismissal of Individual Debtor's Chapter 7 Case for Substantial Abuse. An individual debtor's case may be dismissed for substantial abuse pursuant to § 707(b) only on motion by the United States trustee or on the court's own motion and after a hearing on notice to the debtor, the trustee, the United States trustee, and such other parties in interest as the court directs.

(1) A motion by the United States trustee shall be filed not later than 60 days following the first date set for the meeting of creditors held pursuant to § 341(a), unless, before such time has expired, the court for cause extends the time for filing the motion. The motion shall advise the debtor of all matters to be submitted to the court for its consideration at the hearing.

(2) If the hearing is on the court's own motion, notice thereof shall be served on the debtor not later than 60 days following the first date set for the meeting of creditors pursuant to § 341(a). The notice shall advise the debtor of all matters to be considered by the court at the hearing.

Rule 1018

CONTESTED INVOLUNTARY PETITIONS; CONTESTED PETITIONS COMMENCING ANCILLARY CASES; PROCEEDINGS TO VACATE ORDER FOR RELIEF; APPLICABILITY OF RULES IN PART VII GOVERNING ADVERSARY PROCEEDINGS

The following rules in Part VII apply to all proceedings relating to a contested involuntary petition, to proceedings relating to a contested petition commencing a case ancillary to a foreign proceeding, and to all proceedings to vacate an order for relief: Rules 7005, 7008–7010, 7015, 7016, 7024–7026, 7028–7037, 7052, 7054, 7056, and 7062, except as otherwise provided in Part I of these rules and unless the court otherwise directs. The court may direct that other rules in Part VII shall also apply. For the purposes of this rule a reference in the Part VII rules to adversary proceedings shall be read as a reference to proceedings relating to a contested involuntary petition, or contested ancillary petition, or proceedings to vacate an order for relief. Reference in the Federal Rules of Civil Procedure to the complaint shall be read as a reference to the petition.

Rule 1019

CONVERSION OF CHAPTER 11 REORGANIZATION CASE, CHAPTER 12 FAMILY FARMER'S DEBT ADJUSTMENT CASE, OR CHAPTER 13 INDIVIDUAL'S DEBT ADJUSTMENT CASE TO CHAPTER 7 LIQUIDATION CASE

When a chapter 11, chapter 12, or chapter 13 case has been converted or reconverted to a chapter 7 case:

(1) *Filing of Lists, Inventories, Schedules, Statements.*

(A) Lists, inventories, schedules, and statements of financial affairs theretofore filed shall be deemed to be filed in the chapter 7 case, unless the court directs otherwise. If they have not been previously filed, the debtor shall comply with Rule 1007 as if an order for relief had been entered on an involuntary petition on the date of the entry of the order directing that the case continue under chapter 7.

(B) The statement of intention, if required, shall be filed within 30 days following entry of the order of conversion or before the first date set for the meeting of creditors, whichever is earlier. An extension of time may be granted for cause only on motion made before the time has expired. Notice of an extension shall be given to the United States trustee and to any committee, trustee, or other party as the court may direct.

(2) *New Filing Periods.* A new time period for filing claims, a complaint objecting to discharge, or a complaint to obtain a determination of dischargeability of any debt shall commence pursuant to Rules 3002, 4004, or 4007, provided that a new time period shall not commence if a chapter 7 case had been converted to a chapter 11, 12, or 13 case and thereafter reconverted to a chapter 7 case and the time for filing claims, a complaint objecting to discharge, or a complaint to obtain a determination of the dischargeability of any debt, or any extension thereof, expired in the original chapter 7 case.

(3) *Claims Filed in Superseded Cases.* All claims actually filed by a creditor in the superseded case shall be deemed filed in the chapter 7 case.

(4) *Turnover of Records and Property.* After qualification of, or assumption of duties by the chapter 7 trustee, any debtor in possession or trustee previously acting in the chapter 11, 12, or 13 case shall, forthwith, unless otherwise ordered, turn over to the chapter 7 trustee all records and property of the estate in the possession or control of the debtor in possession or trustee.

(5) *Filing Final Report and Schedule of Postpetition Debts.* Unless the court directs otherwise, each debtor in possession or trustee in the superseded case shall; (A) within 15 days following the entry of the order of conversion of a chapter 11 case, file a schedule of unpaid debts incurred after commencement of the superseded case including the name and address of each creditor; and (B) within 30 days following the entry of the order of conversion of a chapter 11, chapter 12, or chapter 13 case, file and transmit to the United States trustee a final report and account. Within 15 days following the entry of the order of conversion, unless the court directs otherwise, a chapter 13 debtor shall file a schedule of unpaid debts incurred after the commencement of a chapter 13 case, and a chapter 12 debtor in possession or, if the chapter 12 debtor is not in possession, the trustee shall file a schedule of unpaid debts incurred after the commencement of a chapter 12 case. If the conversion order is entered after confirmation of a plan, the debtor shall file (A) a schedule of property not listed in the final report and account acquired after the filing of

the original petition but before entry of the conversion order; (B) a schedule of unpaid debts not listed in the final report and account incurred after confirmation but before entry of the conversion order; and (C) a schedule of executory contracts and unexpired leases entered into or assumed after the filing of the original petition but before entry of the conversion order. The clerk shall forthwith transmit to the United States trustee a copy of every schedule filed pursuant to this paragraph.

(6) *Filing of Postpetition Claims; Notice.* On the filing of the schedule of unpaid debts, the clerk, or some other person as the court may direct, shall give notice to those entities, including the United States, any state, or any subdivision thereof, that their claims may be filed pursuant to Rules 3001(a)–(d) and 3002. Unless a notice of insufficient assets to pay a dividend is mailed pursuant to Rule 2002(e), the court shall fix the time for filing claims arising from the rejection of executory contracts or unexpired leases under §§ 348(c) and 365(d) of the Code.

(7) *Extension of Time to File Claims Against Surplus.* Any extension of time for the filing of claims against a surplus granted pursuant to Rule 3002(c)(6), shall apply to holders of claims who failed to file their claims within the time prescribed, or fixed by the court pursuant to paragraph (6) of this rule, and notice shall be given as provided in Rule 2002.

PART II
OFFICERS AND ADMINISTRATION; NOTICES; MEETINGS; EXAMINATIONS; ELECTIONS; ATTORNEYS AND ACCOUNTANTS

Rule

Rule 2001

APPOINTMENT OF INTERIM TRUSTEE BEFORE ORDER FOR RELIEF IN A CHAPTER 7 LIQUIDATION CASE

(a) Appointment. At any time following the commencement of an involuntary liquidation case and before an order for relief, the court on written motion of a party in interest may order the appointment of an interim trustee under § 303(g) of the Code. The motion shall set forth the necessity for the appointment and may be granted only after hearing on notice to the debtor, the petitioning creditors, the United States trustee, and other parties in interest as the court may designate.

(b) Bond of Movant. An interim trustee may not be appointed under this rule unless the movant furnishes a bond in an amount approved by the court, conditioned to indemnify the debtor for costs, attorney's fee, expenses, and damages allowable under § 303(i) of the Code.

(c) Order of Appointment. The order directing the appointment of an interim trustee shall state the reason the appointment is necessary and shall specify the trustee's duties.

(d) Turnover and Report. Following qualification of the trustee selected under § 702 of the Code, the interim trustee, unless otherwise ordered, shall (1) forthwith deliver to the trustee all the records and property of the estate in possession or subject to control of the interim trustee and, (2) within 30 days thereafter file a final report and account.

Rule 2002

NOTICES TO CREDITORS, EQUITY SECURITY HOLDERS, UNITED STATES, AND UNITED STATES TRUSTEE

(a) Twenty-Day Notices to Parties in Interest. Except as provided in subdivisions (h), (i) and (*l*) of this rule, the

clerk, or some other person as the court may direct, shall give the debtor, the trustee, all creditors and indenture trustees not less than 20 days notice by mail of (1) the meeting of creditors pursuant to § 341 of the Code; (2) a proposed use, sale, or lease of property of the estate other than in the ordinary course of business, unless the court for cause shown shortens the time or directs another method of giving notice; (3) the hearing on approval of a compromise or settlement or a controversy other than approval of an agreement pursuant to Rule 4001(d), unless the court for cause shown directs that notice not be sent; (4) the date fixed for the filing of claims against a surplus in an estate as provided in Rule 3002(c)(6); (5) in a chapter 7 liquidation, a chapter 11 reorganization case, and a chapter 12 family farmer debt adjustment case, the hearing on the dismissal of the case, unless the hearing is pursuant to § 707(b) of the Code, or the conversion of the case to another chapter; (6) the time fixed to accept or reject a proposed modification of a plan; (7) hearings on all applications for compensation or reimbursement of expenses totalling in excess of $500; (8) the time fixed for filing proofs of claims pursuant to Rule 3003(c); and (9) the time fixed for filing objections and the hearing to consider confirmation of a chapter 12 plan.

(b) Twenty-Five-Day Notices to Parties in Interest. Except as provided in subdivision (*l*) of this rule, the clerk, or some other person as the court may direct, shall give the debtor, the trustee, all creditors and indenture trustees not less than 25 days notice by mail of (1) the time fixed for filing objections and the hearing to consider approval of a disclosure statement; and (2) the time fixed for filing objections and the hearing to consider confirmation of a chapter 9, chapter 11, or chapter 13 plan.

(c) Content of Notice.

(1) *Proposed Use, Sale, or Lease of Property.* Subject to Rule 6004 the notice of a proposed use, sale, or lease of property required by subdivision (a)(2) of this rule shall include the time and place of any public sale, the terms and conditions of any private sale and the time fixed for filing objections. The notice of a proposed use, sale, or lease of property, including real estate, is sufficient if it generally describes the property.

(2) *Notice of Hearing on Compensation.* The notice of a hearing on an application for compensation or reimbursement of expenses required by subdivision (a)(7) of this rule shall identify the applicant and the amounts requested.

(d) Notice to Equity Security Holders. In a chapter 11 reorganization case, unless otherwise ordered by the court, the clerk, or some other person as the court may direct, shall in the manner and form directed by the court give notice to all equity security holders of (1) the order for relief; (2) any meeting of equity security holders held pursuant to § 341 of the Code; (3) the hearing on the proposed sale of all or substantially all of the debtor's assets; (4) the hearing on the dismissal or conversion of a case to another chapter; (5) the time fixed for filing objections to and the hearing to

consider approval of a disclosure statement; (6) the time fixed for filing objections to and the hearing to consider confirmation of a plan; and (7) the time fixed to accept or reject a proposed modification of a plan.

(e) Notice of No Dividend. In a chapter 7 liquidation case, if it appears from the schedules that there are no assets from which a dividend can be paid, the notice of the meeting of creditors may include a statement to that effect; that it is unnecessary to file claims; and that if sufficient assets become available for the payment of a dividend, further notice will be given for the filing of claims.

(f) Other Notices. Except as provided in subdivision (*l*) of this rule, the clerk, or some other person as the court may direct, shall give the debtor, all creditors, and indenture trustees notice by mail of (1) the order for relief; (2) the dismissal or the conversion of the case to another chapter; (3) the time allowed for filing claims pursuant to Rule 3002; (4) the time fixed for filing a complaint objecting to the debtor's discharge pursuant to § 727 of the Code as provided in Rule 4004; (5) the time fixed for filing a complaint to determine the dischargeability of a debt pursuant to § 523 of the Code as provided in Rule 4007; (6) the waiver, denial, or revocation of a discharge as provided in Rule 4006; (7) entry of an order confirming a chapter 9, 11, or 12 plan; and (8) a summary of the trustee's final report and account in a chapter 7 case if the net proceeds realized exceed $1,500. Notice of the time fixed for accepting or rejecting a plan pursuant to Rule 3017(c) shall be given in accordance with Rule 3017(d).

(g) Addresses of Notices. All notices required to be mailed under this rule to a creditor, equity security holder, or indenture trustee shall be addressed as such entity or an authorized agent may direct in a filed request; otherwise, to the address shown in the list of creditors or the schedule whichever is filed later. If a different address is stated in a proof of claim duly filed, that address shall be used unless a notice of no dividend has been given.

(h) Notices to Creditors Whose Claims Are Filed. In a chapter 7 case, the court may, after 90 days following the first date set for the meeting of creditors pursuant to § 341 of the Code, direct that all notices required by subdivision (a) of this rule, except clause (4) thereof, be mailed only to creditors whose claims have been filed and creditors, if any, who are still permitted to file claims by reason of an extension granted under Rule 3002(c)(6).

(i) Notices to Committees. Copies of all notices required to be mailed under this rule shall be mailed to the committees elected pursuant to § 705 or appointed pursuant to § 1102 of the Code or to their authorized agents. Notwithstanding the foregoing subdivisions, the court may order that notices required by subdivision (a)(2), (3) and (7) of this rule be transmitted to the United States trustee and be mailed only to the committees elected pursuant to § 705 or appointed pursuant to § 1102 of the Code or to their authorized agents and to the creditors and equity security holders who serve on the trustee or debtor in pos-

session and file a request that all notices be mailed to them. A committee appointed pursuant to § 1114 shall receive copies of all notices required by subdivisions (a)(1), (a)(6), (b), (f)(2), and (f)(7), and such other notices as the court may direct.

(j) Notices to the United States. Copies of notices required to be mailed to all creditors under this rule shall be mailed (1) in a chapter 11 reorganization case, to the Securities and Exchange Commission at any place the Commission designates, if the Commission has filed either a notice of appearance in the case or a written request to receive notices; (2) in a commodity broker case, to the Commodity Future Trading Commission at Washington, D.C.; (3) in a chapter 11 case to the District Director of Internal Revenue for the district in which the case is pending; (4) if the papers in the case disclose a debt to the United States other than for taxes, to the United States attorney for the district in which the case is pending and to the department, agency, or instrumentality of the United States through which the debtor became indebted; or if the filed papers disclose a stock interest of the United States, to the Secretary of the Treasury at Washington, D.C.

(k) Notices to United States Trustee. Unless the case is a chapter 9 municipality case or unless the United States trustee otherwise requests, the clerk, or some other person as the court may direct, shall transmit to the United States trustee notice of the matters described in subdivisions (a)(2), (a)(3), (a)(5), (a)(9), (b), (f)(1), (f)(2), (f)(4), (f)(6), (f)(7), and (f)(8) of this rule and notice of hearings on all applications for compensation or reimbursement of expenses. Notices to the United States trustee shall be transmitted within the time prescribed in subdivision (a) or (b) of this rule. The United States trustee shall also receive notice of any other matter if such notice is requested by the United States trustee or ordered by the court. Nothing in these rules shall require the clerk or any other person to transmit to the United States trustees any notice, schedule, report, application or other document in a case under the Securities Investor Protection Act, 15 U.S.C. § 78aaa et seq.

(l) Notice by Publication. The court may order notice by publication if it finds that notice by mail is impracticable or that it is desirable to supplement the notice.

(m) Orders Designating Matter of Notices. The court may from time to time enter orders designating the matters in respect to which, the entity to whom, and the form and manner in which notices shall be sent except as otherwise provided by these rules.

(n) Caption. The caption of every notice given under this rule shall comply with Rule 1005.

(o) Notice of Order for Relief in Consumer Case. In a voluntary case commenced by an individual debtor whose debts are primarily consumer debts, the clerk or some other person as the court may direct shall give the trustee and all creditors notice by mail of the order for relief within 20 days from the date thereof.

Rule 2003

MEETING OF CREDITORS OR EQUITY SECURITY HOLDERS

(a) Date and Place. In a chapter 7 liquidation or a chapter 11 reorganization case, the United States trustee shall call a meeting of creditors to be held no fewer than 20 and no more than 40 days after the order for relief. In a chapter 12 family farmer debt adjustment case, the United States trustee shall call a meeting of creditors to be held no fewer than 20 and no more than 35 days after the order for relief. In a chapter 13 individual's debt adjustment case, the United States trustee shall call a meeting of creditors to be held no fewer than 20 and no more than 50 days after the order for relief. If there is an appeal from or a motion to vacate the order for relief, or if there is a motion to dismiss the case, the United States trustee may set a later date for the meeting. The meeting may be held at a regular place for holding court or at any other place designated by the United States trustee within the district convenient for the parties in interest. If the United States trustee designates a place for the meeting which is not regularly staffed by the United States trustee or an assistant who may preside at the meeting, the meeting may be held not more than 60 days after the order for relief.

(b) Order of Meeting

(1) *Meeting of Creditors.* The United States trustee shall preside at the meeting of creditors. The business of the meeting shall include the examination of the debtor under oath and, in a chapter 7 liquidation case, may include the election of a trustee or of a creditors' committee. The presiding officer shall have the authority to administer oaths.

(2) *Meeting of Equity Security Holders.* If the United States trustee convenes a meeting of equity security holders pursuant to § 341(b) of the Code, the United States trustee shall fix a date for the meeting and shall preside.

(3) *Right to Vote.* In a chapter 7 liquidation case, a creditor is entitled to vote at a meeting if, at or before the meeting, the creditor has filed a proof of claim or a writing setting forth facts evidencing a right to vote pursuant to § 702(a) of the Code unless objection is made to the claim or the proof of claim is insufficient on its face. A creditor of a partnership may file a proof of claim or writing evidencing a right to vote for the trustee for the estate of a general partner notwithstanding that a trustee for the estate of the partnership has previously qualified. In the event of an objection to the amount or allowability of a claim for the purpose of voting, unless the court orders otherwise, the United States trustee shall tabulate the votes for each alternative presented by the dispute and, if resolution of such dispute is necessary to determine the result of the election, the tabulations for each alternative shall be reported to the court.

(c) Record of Meeting. Any examination under oath at the meeting of creditors held pursuant to § 341(a) of the Code shall be recorded verbatim by the United States trus-

tee using electronic sound recording equipment or other means of recording, and such record shall be preserved by the United States trustee and available for public access until two years after the conclusion of the meeting of creditors. Upon request of any entity, the United States trustee shall certify and provide a copy or transcript of such recording at the entity's expense.

(d) Report to the Court. The presiding officer shall transmit to the court the name and address of any person elected trustee or entity elected a member of a creditors' committee. If an election is disputed, the presiding officer shall promptly inform the court in writing that a dispute exists. Pending disposition by the court of a disputed election for trustee, the interim trustee shall continue in office. If no motion for the resolution of such election dispute is made to the court within 10 days after the date of the creditors' meeting, the interim trustee shall serve as trustee in the case.

(e) Adjournment. The meeting may be adjourned from time to time by announcement at the meeting of the adjourned date and time without further written notice.

(f) Special Meetings. The United States trustee may call a special meeting of creditors on request of a party in interest or on the United States trustee's own initiative.

(g) Final Meeting. If the United States trustee calls a final meeting of creditors in a case in which the net proceeds realized exceed $1,500, the clerk shall mail a summary of the trustee's final account to the creditors with a notice of the meeting, together with a statement of the amount of the claims allowed. The trustee shall attend the final meeting and shall, if requested, report on the administration of the estate.

Rule 2004

EXAMINATION

(a) Examination on Motion. On motion of any party in interest, the court may order the examination of any entity.

(b) Scope of Examination. The examination of an entity under this rule or of the debtor under § 343 of the Code may relate only to the acts, conduct, or property or to the liabilities and financial condition of the debtor, or to any matter which may affect the administration of the debtor's estate, or to the debtor's right to a discharge. In a family farmer's debt adjustment case under chapter 12, an individual's debt adjustment case under chapter 13, or a reorganization case under chapter 11 of the Code, other than for the reorganization of a railroad, the examination may also relate to the operation of any business and the desirability of its continuance, the source of any money or property acquired or to be acquired by the debtor for purpose of consummating a plan and the consideration given or offered therefor, and any other matter relevant to the case or to the formulation of a plan.

(c) Compelling Attendance and Production of Documentary Evidence. The attendance of an entity for examination and the production of documentary evidence may be compelled in the manner provided in Rule 9016 for the attendance of witnesses at a hearing or trial.

(d) Time and Place of Examination of Debtor. The court may for cause shown and on terms as it may impose order the debtor to be examined under this rule at any time or place it designates, whether within or without the district wherein the case is pending.

(e) Mileage. An entity other than a debtor shall not be required to attend as a witness unless lawful mileage and witness fee for one day's attendance shall be first tendered. If the debtor resides more than 100 miles from the place of examination when required to appear for an examination under this rule, the mileage allowed by law to a witness shall be tendered for any distance more than 100 miles from the debtor's residence at the date of the filing of the first petition commencing a case under the Code or the residence at the time the debtor is required to appear for the examination, whichever is the lesser.

Rule 2005

APPREHENSION AND REMOVAL OF DEBTOR TO COMPEL ATTENDANCE FOR EXAMINATION

(a) Order to Compel Attendance for Examination. On motion of any party in interest supported by an affidavit alleging (1) that the examination of the debtor is necessary for the proper administration of the estate and that there is reasonable cause to believe that the debtor is about to leave or has left the debtor's residence or principal place of business to avoid examination, or (2) that the debtor has evaded service of a subpoena or of an order to attend for examination, or (3) that the debtor has willfully disobeyed a subpoena or order to attend for examination, duly served, the court may issue to the marshal, or some other officer authorized by law, an order directing the officer to bring the debtor before the court without unnecessary delay. If, after hearing, the court finds the allegations to be true, the court shall thereupon cause the debtor to be examined forthwith. If necessary, the court shall fix conditions for further examination and for the debtor's obedience to all orders made in reference thereto.

(b) Removal. Whenever any order to bring the debtor before the court is issued under this rule and the debtor is found in a district other than that of the court issuing the order, the debtor may be taken into custody under the order and removed in accordance with the following rules:

(1) If the debtor taken into custody under the order at a place less than 100 miles from the place of issue of the order, the debtor shall be brought forthwith before the court that issued the order.

(2) If the debtor taken into custody under the order at a place 100 miles or more from the place of issue of the

order, the debtor shall be brought without unnecessary delay before the nearest available United States magistrate judge, bankruptcy judge, or district judge. If, after hearing, the magistrate judge, bankruptcy judge, or district judge finds that an order has issued under this rule and that the person in custody is the debtor, or if the person in custody waives a hearing, the magistrate judge, bankruptcy judge, or district judge shall order removal, and the person in custody shall be released on conditions ensuring prompt appearance before the court that issued the order to compel the attendance.

(c) Conditions of Release. In determining what conditions will reasonably assure attendance or obedience under subdivision (a) of this rule or appearance under subdivision (b) of this rule, the court shall be governed by the provisions and policies of title 18, U.S.C., § 3146(a) and (b).

Rule 2006

SOLICITATION AND VOTING OF PROXIES IN CHAPTER 7 LIQUIDATION CASES

(a) Applicability. This rule applies only in a liquidation case pending under chapter 7 of the Code.

(b) Definitions.

(1) *Proxy.* A proxy is a written power of attorney authorizing any entity to vote the claim or otherwise act as the owner's attorney in fact in connection with the administration of the estate.

(2) *Solicitation of Proxy.* The solicitation of a proxy is any communication, other than one from an attorney to a regular client who owns a claim or from an attorney to the owner of a claim who has requested the attorney to represent the owner, by which a creditor is asked, directly or indirectly, to give a proxy after or in contemplation of the filing of a petition by or against the debtor.

(c) Authorized Solicitation.

(1) A proxy may be solicited only by (A) a creditor owning an allowable unsecured claim against the estate on the date of the filing of the petition; (B) a committee elected pursuant to § 705 of the Code; (C) a committee of creditors selected by a majority in number and amount of claims of creditors (i) whose claims are not contingent or unliquidated, (ii) who are not disqualified from voting under § 702(a) of the Code and (iii) who were present or represented at a meeting of which all creditors having claims of over $500 or the 100 creditors having the largest claims had at least five days notice in writing and of which meeting written minutes were kept and are available reporting the names of the creditors present or represented and voting and the amounts of their claims; or (D) a bona fide trade or credit association, but such association may solicit only creditors who were its members of subscribers in good standing and had allowable unsecured claims on the date of the filing of the petition.

(2) A proxy may be solicited only in writing.

(d) Solicitation Not Authorized. This rule does not permit solicitation (1) in any interest other than that of general creditors; (2) by or on behalf of any custodian; (3) by the interim trustee or by or on behalf of any entity not qualified to vote under § 702(a) of the Code; (4) by or on behalf of an attorney at law; or (5) by or on behalf of a transferee of a claim for collection only.

(e) Data Required From Holders of Multiple Proxies. At any time before the voting commences at any meeting of creditors pursuant to § 341(a) of the Code, or at any other time as the court may direct, a holder of two or more proxies shall file and transmit to the United States trustee a verified list of the proxies to be voted and a verified statement of the pertinent facts and circumstances in connection with the execution and delivery of each proxy, including:

(1) a copy of the solicitation;

(2) identification of the solicitor, the forwarder, if the forwarder is neither the solicitor nor the owner of the claim, and the proxyholder, including their connections with the debtor and with each other. If the solicitor, forwarder, or proxyholder is an association, there shall also be included a statement that the creditors whose claims have been solicited and the creditors whose claims are to be voted were members or subscribers in good standing and had allowable unsecured claims on the date of the filing of the petition. If the solicitor, forwarder, or proxyholder is a committee of creditors, the statement shall also set forth the date and place the committee was organized, that the committee was organized in accordance with clause (B) or (C) of paragraph (c)(1) of this rule, the members of the committee, the amounts of their claims, when the claims were acquired, the amounts paid therefor, and the extent to which the claims of the committee members are secured or entitled to priority;

(3) a statement that no consideration has been paid or promised by the proxyholder for the proxy;

(4) a statement as to whether there is any agreement and, if so, the particulars thereof, between the proxyholder and any other entity for the payment of any consideration in connection with voting the proxy, or for the sharing of compensation with any entity, other than a member or regular associate of the proxyholder's law firm, which may be allowed the trustee or any entity for services rendered in the case, or for the employment of any person as attorney, accountant, appraiser, auctioneer, or other employee for the estate;

(5) if the proxy was solicited by an entity other than the proxyholder, or forwarded to the holder by an entity who is neither a solicitor of the proxy nor the owner of the claim, a statement signed and verified by the solicitor or forwarder that no consideration has been paid or promised for the proxy, and whether there is any agreement, and, if so, the particulars thereof, between the solicitor or

forwarder and any other entity for the payment of any consideration in connection with voting the proxy, or for sharing compensation with any entity, other than a member or regular associate of the solicitor's or forwarder's law firm which may be allowed the trustee or any entity for services rendered in the case, or for the employment of any person as attorney, accountant, appraiser, auctioneer, or other employee for the estate;

(6) if the solicitor, forwarder, or proxyholder is a committee, a statement signed and verified by each member as to the amount and source of any consideration paid or to be paid to such member in connection with the case other than by way of dividend on the member's claim.

(f) Enforcement of Restrictions on Solicitation. On motion of any party in interest or on its own initiative, the court may determine whether there has been a failure to comply with the provisions of this rule or any other impropriety in connection with the solicitation or voting of a proxy. After notice and a hearing the court may reject any proxy for cause, vacate any order entered in consequence of the voting of any proxy which should have been rejected, or take any other appropriate action.

Rule 2007

REVIEW OF APPOINTMENT OF CREDITORS' COMMITTEE ORGANIZED BEFORE COMMENCEMENT OF THE CASE

(a) Motion to Review Appointment. If a committee appointed by the United States trustee pursuant to § 1102(a) of the Code consists of the members of a committee organized by creditors before the commencement of a chapter 9 or chapter 11 case, on motion of a party in interest and after a hearing on notice to the United States trustee and other entities as the court may direct, the court may determine whether the appointment of the committee satisfies the requirements of § 1102(b)(1) of the Code.

(b) Selection of Members of Committee. The court may find that a committee organized by unsecured creditors before the commencement of a chapter 9 or chapter 11 case was fairly chosen if:

(1) it was selected by a majority in number and amount of claims of unsecured creditors who may vote under § 702(a) of the Code and were present in person or represented at a meeting of which all creditors having unsecured claims of over $1,000 or the 100 unsecured creditors having the largest claims had at least five days notice in writing, and of which meeting written minutes reporting the names of the creditors present or represented and voting and the amounts of their claims were kept and are available for inspection;

(2) all proxies voted at the meeting for the elected committee were solicited pursuant to Rule 2006 and the lists and statements required by subdivision (e) thereof have been transmitted to the United States trustee; and

(3) the organization of the committee was in all other respects fair and proper.

(c) Failure to Comply With Requirements for Appointment. After a hearing on notice pursuant to subdivision (a) of this rule, the court shall direct the United States trustee to vacate the appointment of the committee and may order other appropriate action if the court finds that such appointment failed to satisfy the requirements of § 1102(b)(1) of the Code.

Rule 2007.1

APPOINTMENT OF TRUSTEE OR EXAMINER IN A CHAPTER 11 REORGANIZATION CASE

(a) Order to Appoint Trustee or Examiner. In a chapter 11 reorganization case, a motion for an order to appoint a trustee or an examiner pursuant to § 1104(a) or § 1104(b) of the Code shall be made in accordance with Rule 9014.

(b) Approval of Appointment. An order approving the appointment of a trustee or examiner pursuant to § 1104(c) of the Code shall be made only on application of the United States trustee, stating the name of the person appointed, the names of the parties in interest with whom the United States trustee consulted regarding the appointment, and, to the best of the applicant's knowledge, all the person's connections with the debtor, creditors, any other parties in interest, their respective attorneys and accountants, the United States trustee, and persons employed in the office of the United States trustee. The application shall be accompanied by a verified statement of the person appointed setting forth the person's connections with the debtor, creditors, any other party in interest, their respective attorneys and accountants, the United States trustee, and any person employed in the office of the United States trustee.

Rule 2008

NOTICE TO TRUSTEE OF SELECTION

The United States trustee shall immediately notify the person selected as trustee how to qualify and, if applicable, the amount of the trustee's bond. A trustee that has filed a blanket bond pursuant to Rule 2010 and has been selected as trustee in a chapter 7, chapter 12, or chapter 13 case that does not notify the court and the United States trustee in writing of rejection of the office within five days after receipt of notice of selection shall be deemed to have accepted the office. Any other person selected as trustee shall notify the court and the United States trustee in writing of acceptance of the office within five days after receipt of notice of selection or shall be deemed to have rejected the office.

Rule 2009

TRUSTEES FOR ESTATES WHEN JOINT ADMINISTRATION ORDERED

(a) Election of Single Trustee for Estates Being Jointly Administered. If the court orders a joint administration of two or more estates pursuant to Rule 1015(b), creditors may elect a single trustee for the estates being jointly administered.

(b) Right of Creditors to Elect Separate Trustee. Notwithstanding entry of an order for joint administration pursuant to Rule 1015(b) the creditors of any debtor may elect a separate trustee for the estate of the debtor as provided in § 702 of the Code.

(c) Appointment of Trustees for Estates Being Jointly Administered.

(1) *Chapter 7 Liquidation Cases.* The United States trustee may appoint one or more interim trustees for estates being jointly administered in chapter 7 cases.

(2) *Chapter 11 Reorganization Cases.* If the appointment of a trustee is ordered, the United States trustee may appoint one or more trustees for estates being jointly administered in chapter 11 cases.

(3) *Chapter 12 Family Farmer's Debt Adjustment Cases.* The United States trustee may appoint one or more trustees for estates being jointly administered in chapter 12 cases.

(4) *Chapter 13 Individual's Debt Adjustment Cases.* The United States trustee may appoint one or more trustees for estates being jointly administered in chapter 13 cases.

(d) Potential Conflicts of Interest. On a showing that creditors or equity security holders of the different estates will be prejudiced by conflicts of interest of a common trustee who has been elected or appointed, the court shall order the selection of separate trustees for estates being jointly administered.

(e) Separate Accounts. The trustee or trustees of estates being jointly administered shall keep separate accounts of the property and distribution of each estate.

Rule 2010

QUALIFICATION BY TRUSTEE; PROCEEDING ON BOND

(a) Blanket Bond. The United States trustee may authorize a blanket bond in favor of the United States conditioned on the faithful performance of official duties by the trustee or trustees to cover (1) a person who qualifies as trustee in a number of cases, and (2) a number of trustees each of whom qualifies in a different case.

(b) Proceeding on Bond. A proceeding on the trustee's bond may be brought by any party in interest in the name of the United States for the use of the entity injured by the breach of the condition.

Rule 2011

EVIDENCE OF DEBTOR IN POSSESSION OR QUALIFICATION OF TRUSTEE

(a) Whenever evidence is required that a debtor is a debtor in possession or that a trustee has qualified, the clerk may so certify and the certificate shall constitute conclusive evidence of that fact.

(b) If a person elected or appointed as trustee does not qualify within the time prescribed by § 322(a) of the Code, the clerk shall so notify the court and the United States trustee.

Rule 2012

SUBSTITUTION OF TRUSTEE OR SUCCESSOR TRUSTEE; ACCOUNTING

(a) Trustee. If a trustee is appointed in a chapter 11 case or the debtor is removed as debtor in possession in a chapter 12 case, the trustee is substituted automatically for the debtor in possession as a party in any pending action, proceeding, or matter.

(b) Successor trustee. When a trustee dies, resigns, is removed, or otherwise ceases to hold office during the pendency of a case under the Code (1) the successor is automatically substituted as a party in any pending action, proceeding, or matter; and (2) the successor trustee shall prepare, file, and transmit to the United States trustee an accounting of the prior administration of the estate.

Rule 2013

PUBLIC RECORD OF COMPENSATION AWARDED TO TRUSTEES, EXAMINERS, AND PROFESSIONALS

(a) Record to Be Kept. The clerk shall maintain a public record listing fees awarded by the court (1) to trustees and attorneys, accountants, appraisers, auctioneers and other professionals employed by trustees, and (2) to examiners. The record shall include the name and docket number of the case, the name of the individual or firm receiving the fee and the amount of the fee awarded. The record shall be maintained chronologically and shall be kept current and open to examination by the public without charge. "Trustees," as used in this rule, does not include debtors in possession.

(b) Summary of Record. At the close of each annual period, the clerk shall prepare a summary of the public record by individual or firm name, to reflect total fees awarded during the preceding year. The summary shall be open to examination by the public without charge. The clerk shall transmit a copy of the summary to the United States trustee.

Rule 2014

EMPLOYMENT OF PROFESSIONAL PERSONS

(a) **Application for an Order of Employment.** An order approving the employment of attorneys, accountants, appraisers, auctioneers, agents, or other professionals pursuant to § 327, § 1103, or § 1114 of the Code shall be made only on application of the trustee or committee. The application shall be filed and, unless the case is a chapter 9 municipality case, a copy of the application shall be transmitted by the applicant to the United States trustee. The application shall state the specific facts showing the necessity for the employment, the name of the person to be employed, the reasons for the selection, the professional services to be rendered, any proposed arrangement for compensation, and, to the best of the applicant's knowledge, all of the person's connections with the debtor, creditors, any other party in interest, their respective attorneys and accountants, the United States trustee, or any person employed in the office of the United States trustee. The application shall be accompanied by a verified statement of the person to be employed setting forth the person's connections with the debtor, creditors, any other party in interest, their respective attorneys and accountants, the United States trustee, or any person employed in the office of the United States trustee.

(b) **Services Rendered by Member or Associate of Firm of Attorneys or Accountants.** If, under the Code and this rule, a law partnership or corporation is employed as an attorney, or an accounting partnership or corporation is employed as an accountant, or if a named attorney or accountant is employed, any partner, member, or regular associate of the partnership, corporation or individual may act as attorney or accountant so employed, without further order of the court.

Rule 2015

DUTY TO KEEP RECORDS, MAKE REPORTS, AND GIVE NOTICE OF CASE

(a) **Trustee or Debtor in Possession.** A trustee or debtor in possession shall (1) in a chapter 7 liquidation case and, if the court directs, in a chapter 11 reorganization case file and transmit to the United States trustee a complete inventory of the property of the debtor within 30 days after qualifying as a trustee or debtor in possession, unless such an inventory has already been filed; (2) keep a record of receipts and the disposition of money and property received; (3) file the reports and summaries required by § 704(8) of the Code which shall include a statement, if payments are made to employees, of the amounts of deductions for all taxes required to be withheld or paid for and in behalf of employees and the place where these amounts are deposited; (4) as soon as possible after the commencement of the case, give notice of the case to every entity known to be holding money or property subject to withdrawal or order of the debtor, including every bank, savings or building and loan association, public utility company, and landlord with whom the debtor has a deposit, and to every insurance company which has issued a policy having a cash surrender value payable to the debtor, except that notice need not be given to any entity who has knowledge or has previously been notified of the case; (5) in a chapter 11 reorganization case, on or before the last day of the month after each calendar quarter until a plan is confirmed or the case is converted or dismissed, file and transmit to the United States trustee a statement of disbursements made during such calendar quarter and a statement of the amount of the fee required pursuant to 28 U.S.C. § 1930(a)(6) that has been paid for such calendar quarter.

(b) **Chapter 12 Trustee and Debtor in Possession.** In a chapter 12 family farmer's debt adjustment case, the debtor in possession shall perform the duties prescribed in clauses (1)–(4) of subdivision (a) of this rule. If the debtor is removed as debtor in possession, the trustee shall perform the duties of the debtor in possession prescribed in this paragraph.

(c) **Chapter 13 Trustee and Debtor.**

(1) *Business Cases.* In a chapter 13 individual's debt adjustment case, when the debtor is engaged in business, the debtor shall perform the duties prescribed by clauses (1)–(4) of subdivision (a) of this rule.

(2) *Nonbusiness Cases.* In a chapter 13 individual's debt adjustment case, when the debtor is not engaged in business, the trustee shall perform the duties prescribed by clause (2) of subdivision (a) of this rule.

(d) **Transmission of Reports.** In a chapter 11 case the court may direct that copies or summaries of annual reports and copies or summaries of other reports shall be mailed to the creditors, equity security holders, and indenture trustees. The court may also direct the publication of summaries of any such reports. A copy of every report or summary mailed or published pursuant to this subdivision shall be transmitted to the United States trustee.

Rule 2016

COMPENSATION FOR SERVICES RENDERED AND REIMBURSEMENT OF EXPENSES

(a) **Application for Compensation or Reimbursement.** An entity seeking interim or final compensation for services, or reimbursement of necessary expenses, from the estate shall file an application setting forth a detailed statement of (1) the services rendered, time expended and expenses incurred, and (2) the amounts requested. An application for compensation shall include a statement as to what payments have theretofore been made or promised

to the applicant for services rendered or to be rendered in any capacity whatsoever in connection with the case, the source of the compensation so paid or promised, whether any compensation previously received has been shared and whether an agreement or understanding exists between the applicant and any other entity for the sharing of compensation received or to be received for services rendered in or in connection with the case, and the particulars of any sharing of compensation or agreement or understanding therefor, except that details of any agreement by the applicant for the sharing of compensation as a member or regular associate of a firm of lawyers or accountants shall not be required. The requirements of this subdivision shall apply to an application for compensation for services rendered by an attorney or accountant even though the application is filed by a creditor or other entity. Unless the case is a chapter 9 municipality case, the applicant shall transmit to the United States trustee a copy of the application.

(b) Disclosure of Compensation Paid or Promised to Attorney for Debtor. Every attorney for a debtor, whether or not the attorney applies for compensation, shall file and transmit to the United States trustee within 15 days after the order for relief, or at another time as the court may direct, the statement required by § 329 of the Code including whether the attorney has shared or agreed to share the compensation with any other entity. The statement shall include the particulars of any such sharing or agreement to share by the attorney, but the details of any agreement for the sharing of the compensation with a member or regular associate of the attorney's law firm shall not be required. A supplemental statement shall be filed and transmitted to the United States trustee within 15 days after any payment or agreement not previously disclosed.

Rule 2017

EXAMINATION OF DEBTOR'S TRANSACTIONS WITH DEBTOR'S ATTORNEY

(a) Payment or Transfer to Attorney Before Order for Relief. On motion by any party in interest or on the court's own initiative, the court after notice and a hearing may determine whether any payment of money or any transfer of property by the debtor, made directly or indirectly and in contemplation of the filing of a petition under the Code by or against the debtor or before entry of the order for relief in an involuntary case, to an attorney for services rendered or to be rendered is excessive.

(b) Payment or Transfer to Attorney After Order for Relief. On motion by the debtor, the United States trustee, or on the court's own initiative, the court after notice and a hearing may determine whether any payment of money or any transfer of property, or any agreement therefor, by the debtor to an attorney after entry of an order for relief in a case under the Code is excessive, whether the payment or transfer is made or is to be made directly or indirectly, if the payment, transfer, or agreement therefor is for services in any way related to the case.

Rule 2018

INTERVENTION; RIGHT TO BE HEARD

(a) Permissive Intervention. In a case under the Code, after hearing on such notice as the court directs and for cause shown, the court may permit any interested entity to intervene generally or with respect to any specified matter.

(b) Intervention by Attorney General of a State. In a chapter 7, 11, 12, or 13 case, the Attorney General of a State may appear and be heard on behalf of consumer creditors if the court determines the appearance is in the public interest, but the Attorney General may not appeal from any judgment, order, or decree in the case.

(c) Chapter 9 Municipality Case. The Secretary of the Treasury of the United States may, or if requested by the court shall, intervene in a chapter 9 case. Representatives of the state in which the debtor is located may intervene in a chapter 9 case with respect to matter specified by the court.

(d) Labor Unions. In a chapter 9, 11, or 12 case, a labor union or employees' association, representative of employees of the debtor, shall have the right to be heard on the economic soundness of a plan affecting the interests of the employees. A labor union or employees' association which exercises its right to be heard under this subdivision shall not be entitled to appeal any judgment, order, or decree relating to the plan, unless otherwise permitted by law.

(e) Service on Entities Covered by This Rule. The court may enter orders governing the service of notice and papers on entities permitted to intervene or be heard pursuant to this rule.

Rule 2019

REPRESENTATION OF CREDITORS AND EQUITY SECURITY HOLDERS IN CHAPTER 9 MUNICIPALITY AND CHAPTER 11 REORGANIZATION CASES

(a) Data Required. In a chapter 9 municipality or chapter 11 reorganization case, except with respect to a committee appointed pursuant to § 1102 or 1114 of the Code, every entity or committee representing more than one creditor or equity security holder and, unless otherwise directed by the court, every indenture trustee, shall file a verified statement setting forth (1) the name and address of the creditor or equity security holder; (2) the nature and amount of the claim or interest and the time of acquisition thereof unless it is alleged to have been acquired more than one year prior to the filing of the petition; (3) a recital of the pertinent facts and circumstances in connection with the employment of the entity or indenture trustee, and, in

the case of a committee, the name or names of the entity or entities at whose instance, directly or indirectly, the employment was arranged or the committee was organized or agreed to act; and (4) with reference to the time of the employment of the entity, the organization or formation of the committee, or the appearance in the case of any indenture trustee, the amounts of claims or interests owned by the entity, the members of the committee or the indenture trustee, the times when acquired, the amounts paid therefor, and any sales or other disposition thereof. The statement shall include a copy of the instrument, if any, whereby the entity, committee, or indenture trustee is empowered to act on behalf of creditors or equity security holders. A supplemental statement shall be filed promptly, setting forth any material changes in the facts contained in the statement filed pursuant to this subdivision.

(b) Failure to Comply; Effect. On motion of any party in interest or on its own initiative, the court may (1) determine whether there has been a failure to comply with the provisions of subdivision (a) of this rule or with any other applicable law regulating the activities and personnel of any entity, committee, or indenture trustee or any other impropriety in connection with any solicitation and, if it so determines, the court may refuse to permit that entity, committee, or indenture trustee to be heard further or to intervene in the case; (2) examine any representation provision of a deposit agreement, proxy, trust mortgage, trust indenture, or deed of trust, or committee or other authorization, and any claim or interest acquired by any entity or committee in contemplation or in the course of a case under the Code and grant appropriate relief; and (3) hold invalid any authority, acceptance, rejection, or objection given, procured, or received by an entity or committee who has not complied with this rule or with § 1125(b) of the Code.

Rule 2020

REVIEW OF ACTS BY UNITED STATES TRUSTEE

A proceeding to contest any act or failure to act by the United States trustee is governed by Rule 9014.

PART III
CLAIMS AND DISTRIBUTION TO CREDITORS AND EQUITY INTEREST HOLDERS; PLANS

Rule

Rule 3001

PROOF OF CLAIM

(a) Form and Content. A proof of claim is a written statement setting forth a creditor's claim. A proof of claim shall conform substantially to the appropriate Official Form.

(b) Who May Execute. A proof of claim shall be executed by the creditor or the creditor's authorized agent except as provided in Rules 3004 and 3005.

(c) Claim Based on a Writing. When a claim, or an interest in property of the debtor securing the claim, is based on a writing, the original or a duplicate shall be filed with the proof of claim. If the writing has been lost or destroyed, a statement of the circumstances of the loss or destruction shall be filed with the claim.

(d) Evidence of Perfection of Security Interest. If a security interest in property of the debtor is claimed, the proof of claim shall be accompanied by evidence that the security interest has been perfected.

(e) Transferred Claim

(1) *Transfer of Claim Other Than for Security Before Proof Filed.* If a claim has been transferred other than for security before proof of the claim has been filed, the proof of claim may be filed only by the transferee or an indenture trustee.

(2) *Transfer of Claim Other Than for Security After Proof Filed.* If a claim other than one based on a publicly traded note, bond, or debenture has been transferred other than for security after the proof of claim has been filed, evidence of the transfer shall be filed by the transferee. The clerk shall immediately notify the alleged transferor by mail of the filing of the evidence of transfer and that objection thereto, if any, must be filed within 20 days of the mailing of the notice or within any additional time allowed by the court. If the alleged transferor files a timely objection and the court finds, after notice and a hearing, that the claim has been transferred other than for security, it shall enter an order substituting the transferee for the transferor. If a timely objection is not filed by the alleged transferor, the transferee shall be substituted for the transferor.

(3) *Transfer of Claim for Security Before Proof Filed.* If a claim other than one based on a publicly traded note, bond, or debenture has been transferred for security before proof of the claim has been filed, the transferor or transferee or both may file a proof of claim for the full amount. The proof shall be supported by a statement setting forth the terms of the transfer. If either the transferor or the transferee files a proof of claim, the clerk shall immediately notify the other by mail of the right to join in the filed claim. If both transferor and transferee file proofs of the same claim, the proofs shall be consolidated. If the transferor or transferee does not file an agreement regarding its relative rights respecting voting of the claim, payment of dividends thereon, or participation in the administration of the estate, on motion by a party in interest and after notice and a hearing, the court shall enter such orders respecting these matters as may be appropriate.

(4) *Transfer of Claims for Security After Proof Filed.* If a claim other than one based on a publicly traded note, bond, or debenture has been transferred for security after the proof of claim has been filed, evidence of the terms of the transfer shall be filed by the transferee. The clerk shall immediately notify the alleged transferor by mail of the filing of the evidence of transfer and that objection thereto, if any, must be filed within 20 days of the mailing of the notice or within any additional time allowed by the court. If a timely objection is filed by the alleged transferor, the court, after notice and a hearing, shall determine whether the claim has been transferred for security. If the transferor or transferee does not file an agreement regarding its relative rights respecting voting of the claim, payment of div-

idends thereon, or participation in the administration of the estate, on motion by a party in interest and after notice and a hearing, the court shall enter such orders respecting these matters as may be appropriate.

(5) *Service of Objection or Motion; Notice of Hearing.* A copy of an objection filed pursuant to paragraph (2) or (4) or a motion filed pursuant to paragraph (3) or (4) of this subdivision together with a notice of a hearing shall be mailed or otherwise delivered to the transferor or transferee, whichever is appropriate, at least 30 days prior to the hearing.

(f) Evidentiary Effect. A proof of claim executed and filed in accordance with these rules shall constitute prima facie evidence of the validity and amount of the claim.

(g) To the extent not inconsistent with the United States Warehouse Act or applicable State law, a warehouse receipt, scale ticket, or similar document of the type routinely issued as evidence of title by a grain storage facility, as defined in section 557 of title 11, shall constitute prima facie evidence of the validity and amount of a claim of ownership of a quantity of grain.

Rule 3002

FILING PROOF OF CLAIM OR INTEREST

(a) Necessity for Filing. An unsecured creditor or an equity security holder must file a proof of claim or interest in accordance with this rule for the claim or interest to be allowed, except as provided in Rules 1019(3), 3003, 3004 and 3005.

(b) Place of Filing. A proof of claim or interest shall be filed in accordance with Rule 5005.

(c) Time for Filing.

In a chapter 7 liquidation, chapter 12 family farmer's debt adjustment, or chapter 13 individual's debt adjustment case, a proof of claim shall be filed within 90 days after the first date set for the meeting of creditors called pursuant to § 341(a) of the Code, except as follows:

(1) On motion of the United States, a state, or subdivision thereof before the expiration of such period and for cause shown, the court may extend the time for filing of a claim by the United States, a state, or subdivision thereof.

(2) In the interest of justice and if it will not unduly delay the administration of the case, the court may extend the time for filing a proof of claim by an infant or incompetent person or the representative of either.

(3) An unsecured claim which arises in favor of an entity or becomes allowable as a result of a judgment may be filed within 30 days after the judgment becomes final if the judgment is for the recovery of money or property from that entity or denies or avoids the entity's interest in property. If the judgment imposes a liability which is not satisfied, or a duty which is not performed within such period or such further time as the court may permit, the claim shall not be allowed.

(4) A claim arising from the rejection of an executory contract or unexpired lease of the debtor may be filed within such time as the court may direct.

(5) If notice of insufficient assets to pay a dividend was given to creditors pursuant to Rule 2002(e), and subsequently the trustee notifies the court that payment of a dividend appears possible, the clerk shall notify the creditors of that fact and that they may file proofs of claim within 90 days after the mailing of the notice.

(6) In a chapter 7 liquidation case, if a surplus remains after all claims allowed have been paid in full, the court may grant an extension of time for the filing of claims against the surplus not filed within the time hereinabove prescribed.

Rule 3003

FILING PROOF OF CLAIM OR EQUITY SECURITY INTEREST IN CHAPTER 9 MUNICIPALITY OR CHAPTER 11 REORGANIZATION CASES

(a) Applicability of Rule. This rule applies in chapter 9 and 11 cases.

(b) Schedule of Liabilities and List of Equity Security Holders.

(1) Schedule of Liabilities. The schedule of liabilities filed pursuant to § 521(1) of the Code shall constitute prima facie evidence of the validity and amount of the claims of creditors, unless they are scheduled as disputed, contingent, or unliquidated. It shall not be necessary for a creditor or equity security holder to file a proof of claim or interest except as provided in subdivision (c)(2) of this rule.

(2) List of Equity Security Holders. The list of equity security holders filed pursuant to Rule 1007(a)(3) shall constitute prima facie evidence of the validity and amount of the equity security interests and it shall not be necessary for the holders of such interests to file a proof of interest.

(c) Filing Proof of Claim.

(1) Who May File. Any creditor or indenture trustee may file a proof of claim within the time prescribed by subdivision (c)(3) of this rule.

(2) Who Must File. Any creditor or equity security holder whose claim or interest is not scheduled or scheduled as disputed, contingent, or unliquidated shall file a proof of claim or interest within the time prescribed by subdivision (c)(3) of this rule; any creditor who fails to do so shall not be treated as a creditor with respect to such claim for the purposes of voting and distribution.

(3) Time for Filing. The court shall fix and for cause shown may extend the time within which proofs of claim or interest may be filed. Notwithstanding the expiration of such time, a proof of claim may be filed to the extent and under the conditions stated in Rule 3002(c)(2), (c)(3), and (c)(4).

(4) Effect of Filing Claim or Interest. A proof of claim or interest executed and filed in accordance with this sub-division shall supersede any scheduling of that claim or interest pursuant to § 521(1) of the Code.

(5) Filing by Indenture Trustee. An indenture trustee may file a claim on behalf of all known or unknown holders of securities issued pursuant to the trust instrument under which it is trustee.

(d) Proof of Right to Record Status. For the purposes of Rules 3017, 3018 and 3021 and for receiving notices, an entity who is not the record holder of a security may file a statement setting forth facts which entitle that entity to be treated as the record holder. An objection to the statement may be filed by any party in interest.

Rule 3004

FILING OF CLAIMS BY DEBTOR OR TRUSTEE

If a creditor fails to file a proof of claim on or before the first date set for the meeting of creditors called pursuant to § 341(a) of the Code, the debtor or trustee may do so in the name of the creditor, within 30 days after expiration of the time for filing claims prescribed by Rule 3002(c) or 3003(c), whichever is applicable. The clerk shall forthwith mail notice of the filing to the creditor, the debtor and the trustee. A proof of claim filed by a creditor pursuant to Rule 3002 or Rule 3003(c), shall supersede the proof filed by the debtor or trustee.

Rule 3005

FILING OF CLAIM, ACCEPTANCE, OR REJECTION BY GUARANTOR, SURETY, INDORSER, OR OTHER CODEBTOR

(a) Filing of Claim. If a creditor has not filed a proof of claim pursuant to Rule 3002 or 3003(c), an entity that is nor may be liable with the debtor to that creditor, or who has secured that creditor, may, within 30 days after the expiration of the time for filing claims prescribed by Rule 3002(c) or 3003(c) whichever is applicable, execute and file a proof of claim in the name of the creditor, if known, or if unknown, in the entity's own name. No distribution shall be made on the claim except on satisfactory proof that the original debt will be diminished by the amount of distribution. A proof of claim filed by a creditor pursuant to Rule 3002 or 3003(c) shall supersede the proof of claim filed pursuant to the first sentence of this subdivision.

(b) Filing of Acceptance or Rejection; Substitution of Creditor. An entity which has filed a claim pursuant to the first sentence of subdivision (a) of this rule may file an acceptance or rejection of a plan in the name of the creditor, if known, or if unknown, in the entity's own name but if the creditor files a proof of claim within the time permitted by Rule 3003(c) or files a notice prior to confirmation of a plan of the creditor's intention to act in the creditor's own behalf, the creditor shall be substituted for the obligor with respect to that claim.

Rule 3006

WITHDRAWAL OF CLAIM; EFFECT ON ACCEPTANCE OR REJECTION OF PLAN

A creditor may withdraw a claim as of right by filing a notice of withdrawal, except as provided in this rule. If after a creditor has filed a proof of claim an objection is filed thereto or a complaint is filed against the creditor in an adversary proceeding, or the creditor has accepted or rejected the plan or otherwise has participated significantly in the case, the creditor may not withdraw the claim except on order of the court after a hearing on notice to the trustee or debtor in possession, and any creditors' committee elected pursuant to § 705(a) or appointed pursuant to § 1102 of the Code. The order of the court shall contain such terms and conditions as the court deems proper. Unless the court orders otherwise, an authorized withdrawal of a claim shall constitute withdrawal of any related acceptance or rejection of a plan.

Rule 3007

OBJECTIONS TO CLAIMS

An objection to the allowance of a claim shall be in writing and filed. A copy of the objection with notice of the hearing thereon shall be mailed or otherwise delivered to the claimant, the debtor or debtor in possession and the trustee at least 30 days prior to the hearing. If an objection to a claim is joined with a demand for relief of the kind specified in Rule 7001, it becomes an adversary proceeding.

Rule 3008

RECONSIDERATION OF CLAIMS

A party in interest may move for reconsideration of an order allowing or disallowing a claim against the estate. The court after a hearing on notice shall enter an appropriate order.

Rule 3009

DECLARATION AND PAYMENT OF DIVIDENDS IN A CHAPTER 7 LIQUIDATION CASE

In a chapter 7 case, dividends to creditors shall be paid as promptly as practicable. Dividend checks shall be made payable to and mailed to each creditor whose claim has been allowed, unless a power of attorney authorizing another entity to receive dividends has been executed and filed in accordance with Rule 9010. In that event, dividend checks shall be made payable to the creditor and to the other entity and shall be mailed to the other entity.

Rule 3010

SMALL DIVIDENDS AND PAYMENTS IN CHAPTER 7 LIQUIDATION, CHAPTER 12 FAMILY FARMER'S DEBT ADJUSTMENT, AND CHAPTER 13 INDIVIDUAL'S DEBT ADJUSTMENT CASES

(a) **Chapter 7 Cases.** In a chapter 7 case no dividend in an amount less than $5 shall be distributed by the trustee to any creditor unless authorized by local rule or order of the court. Any dividend not distributed to a creditor shall be treated in the same manner as unclaimed funds as provided in § 347 of the Code.

(b) **Chapter 12 and Chapter 13 Cases.** In a chapter 12 or chapter 13 case no payment in an amount less than $15 shall be distributed by the trustee to any creditor unless authorized by local rule or order of the court. Funds not distributed because of this subdivision shall accumulate and shall be paid whenever the accumulation aggregates $15. Any funds remaining shall be distributed with the final payment.

Rule 3011

UNCLAIMED FUNDS IN CHAPTER 7 LIQUIDATION, CHAPTER 12 FAMILY FARMER'S DEBT ADJUSTMENT, AND CHAPTER 13 INDIVIDUAL'S DEBT ADJUSTMENT CASES

The trustee shall file a list of all known names and addresses of the entities and the amounts which they are entitled to be paid from remaining property of the estate that is paid into court pursuant to § 347(a) of the Code.

Rule 3012

VALUATION OF SECURITY

The court may determine the value of a claim secured by a lien on property in which the estate has an interest on motion of any party in interest and after a hearing on notice to the holder of the secured claim and any other entity as the court may direct.

Rule 3013

CLASSIFICATION OF CLAIMS AND INTERESTS

For the purposes of the plan and its acceptance, the court may, on motion after hearing on notice as the court may direct, determine classes of creditors and equity security holders pursuant to §§ 1122, 1222(b)(1), and 1322(b)(1) of the Code.

Rule 3014

ELECTION PURSUANT TO § 1111(b) BY SECURED CREDITOR IN CHAPTER 9 MUNICIPALITY AND CHAPTER 11 REORGANIZATION CASES

An election of application of § 1111(b)(2) of the Code by a class of secured creditors in a chapter 9 or 11 case may be made at any time prior to the conclusion of the hearing on the disclosure statement or within such later

time as the court may fix. The election shall be in writing and signed unless made at the hearing on the disclosure statement. The election, if made by the majorities required by § 1111(b)(1)(A)(i), shall be binding on all members of the class with respect to the plan.

Rule 3015

FILING, OBJECTION TO CONFIRMATION, AND MODIFICATION OF A PLAN IN A CHAPTER 12 FAMILY FARMER'S DEBT ADJUSTMENT OR A CHAPTER 13 INDIVIDUAL'S DEBT ADJUSTMENT CASE

(a) **Chapter 12 Plan.** The debtor may file a chapter 12 plan with the petition. If a plan is not filed with the petition, it shall be filed within the time prescribed by § 1221 of the Code.

(b) **Chapter 13 Plan.** The debtor may file a chapter 13 plan with the petition. If a plan is not filed with the petition, it shall be filed within 15 days thereafter, and such time may not be further extended except for cause shown and on notice as the court may direct. If a case is converted to chapter 13, a plan shall be filed within 15 days thereafter, and such time may not be further extended except for cause shown and on notice as the court may direct.

(c) **Dating.** Every proposed plan and any modification thereof shall be dated.

(d) **Notice and Copies.** The plan or a summary of the plan shall be included with each notice of the hearing on confirmation mailed pursuant to Rule 2002(b). If required by the court, the debtor shall furnish a sufficient number of copies to enable the clerk to include a copy of the plan with the notice of the hearing.

(e) **Transmission to United States Trustee.** The clerk shall forthwith transmit to the United States trustee a copy of the plan and any modification thereof filed pursuant to subdivision (a) or (b) of this rule.

(f) **Objection to Confirmation; Determination of Good Faith in the Absence of an Objection.** An objection to confirmation of a plan shall be filed and served on the debtor, the trustee, and any other entity designated by the court, and shall be transmitted to the United States trustee, before confirmation of the plan. An objection to confirmation is governed by Rule 9014. If no objection is timely filed, the court may determine that the plan has been proposed in good faith and not by any means forbidden by law without receiving evidence on such issues.

(g) **Modification of Plan After Confirmation.** A request to modify a plan pursuant to § 1229 or § 1329 of the Code shall identify the proponent and shall be filed together with the proposed modification. The clerk, or some other person as the court may direct, shall give the debtor, the trustee, and all creditors not less than 20 days notice by mail of the time fixed for filing objections and, if an objection is filed, the hearing to consider the proposed modification, unless the court orders otherwise with respect

to creditors who are not affected by the proposed modification. A copy of the notice shall be transmitted to the United States trustee. A copy of the proposed modification, or a summary thereof, shall be included with the notice. If required by the court, the proponent shall furnish a sufficient number of copies of the proposed modification, or a summary thereof, to enable the clerk to include a copy with each notice. Any objection to the proposed modification shall be filed and served on the debtor, the trustee, and any other entity designated by the court, and shall be transmitted to the United States trustee. An objection to a proposed modification is governed by Rule 9014.

Rule 3016

FILING OF PLAN AND DISCLOSURE STATEMENT IN CHAPTER 9 MUNICIPALITY AND CHAPTER 11 REORGANIZATION CASES

(a) **Time for Filing Plan.** A party in interest, other than the debtor, who is authorized to file a plan under § 1121(c) of the Code may not file a plan after entry of an order approving a disclosure statement unless confirmation of the plan relating to the disclosure statement has been denied or the court otherwise directs.

(b) **Identification of Plan.** Every proposed plan and any modification thereof shall be dated and, in a chapter 11 case, identified with the name of the entity or entities submitting or filing it.

(c) **Disclosure Statement.** In a chapter 9 or 11 case, a disclosure statement pursuant to § 1125 or evidence showing compliance with § 1126(b) of the Code shall be filed with the plan or within a time fixed by the court.

Rule 3017

COURT CONSIDERATION OF DISCLOSURE STATEMENT IN CHAPTER 9 MUNICIPALITY AND CHAPTER 11 REORGANIZATION CASES

(a) **Hearing on Disclosure Statement and Objections Thereto.** Following the filing of a disclosure statement as provided in Rule 3016(c), the court shall hold a hearing on not less than 25 days notice to the debtor, creditors, equity security holders and other parties in interest as provided in Rule 2002 to consider such statement and any objections or modifications thereto. The plan and the disclosure statement shall be mailed with the notice of the hearing only to the debtor, any trustee or committee appointed under the Code, the Securities and Exchange Commission and any party in interest who requests in writing a copy of the statement or plan. Objections to the disclosure statement shall be filed and served on the debtor, the trustee, any committee appointed under the Code and such other entity as may be designated by the court, at any time prior to approval of the disclosure statement or by such earlier date as the court may fix. In a chapter 11 re-

organization case, every notice, plan, disclosure statement, and objection required to be served or mailed pursuant to this subdivision shall be transmitted to the United States trustee within the time provided in this subdivision.

(b) Determination on Disclosure Statement. Following the hearing the court shall determine whether the disclosure statement should be approved.

(c) Dates Fixed for Voting on Plan and Confirmation. On or before approval of the disclosure statement, the court shall fix a time within which the holders of claims and interests may accept or reject the plan and may fix a date for the hearing on confirmation.

(d) Transmission and Notice to United States Trustee, Creditors and Equity Security Holders. On approval of a disclosure statement, unless the court orders otherwise with respect to one or more unimpaired classes of creditors or equity security holders, the debtor in possession, trustee, proponent of the plan, or clerk as ordered by the court shall mail to all creditors and equity security holders, and in a chapter 11 reorganization case shall transmit to the United States trustee, (1) the plan, or a court approved summary of the plan; (2) the disclosure statement approved by the court; (3) notice of the time within which acceptances and rejections of such plan may be filed; and (4) such other information as the court may direct including any opinion of the court approving the disclosure statement or a court approved summary of the opinion. In addition, notice of the time fixed for filing objections and the hearing on confirmation shall be mailed to all creditors and equity security holders pursuant to Rule 2002(b), and a form of ballot conforming to the appropriate Official Form shall be mailed to creditors and equity security holders entitled to vote on the plan. In the event the opinion of the court is not transmitted or only a summary of the plan is transmitted, the opinion of the court or the plan shall be provided on request of a party in interest at the expense of the proponent of the plan. If the court orders that the disclosure statement and the plan or a summary of the plan shall not be mailed to any unimpaired class, notice that the class is designated in the plan as unimpaired and notice of the name and address of the person from whom the plan or summary of the plan and disclosure statement may be obtained upon request and at the expense of the proponent of the plan, shall be mailed to members of the unimpaired class together with the notice of the time fixed for filing objections to and the hearing on confirmation. For the purposes of this subdivision, creditors and equity security holders shall include holders of stock, bonds, debentures, notes, and other securities of record at the date the order approving the disclosure statement was entered.

(e) Transmission to Beneficial Holders of Securities. At the hearing held pursuant to subdivision (a) of this rule the court shall consider the procedures for transmitting the documents and information required by subdivision (d) of this rule to beneficial holders of stock, bonds, debentures, notes and other securities and determine the adequacy of such procedures and enter such orders as the court deems appropriate.

Rule 3018

ACCEPTANCE OR REJECTION OF PLAN IN A CHAPTER 9 MUNICIPALITY OR A CHAPTER 11 REORGANIZATION CASE

(a) Entities Entitled to Accept or Reject Plan; Time for Acceptance or Rejection. A plan may be accepted or rejected in accordance with § 1126 of the Code within the time fixed by the court pursuant to Rule 3017. Subject to subdivision (b) of this rule, an equity security holder or creditor whose claim is based on a security of record shall not be entitled to accept or reject a plan unless the equity security holder or creditor is the holder of record of the security on the date the order approving the disclosure statement is entered. For cause shown, the court after notice and hearing may permit a creditor or equity security holder to change or withdraw an acceptance or rejection. Notwithstanding objection to a claim or interest, the court after notice and hearing may temporarily allow the claim or interest in an amount which the court deems proper for the purpose of accepting or rejecting a plan.

(b) Acceptances or Rejections Obtained Before Petition. An equity security holder or creditor whose claim is based on a security of record who accepted or rejected the plan before the commencement of the case shall not be deemed to have accepted or rejected the plan pursuant to § 1126(b) of the Code unless the equity security holder or creditor was the holder of record of the security on the date specified in the solicitation of such acceptance or rejection for the purposes of such solicitation. A holder of a claim or interest who has accepted or rejected a plan before the commencement of the case under the Code shall not be deemed to have accepted or rejected the plan if the court finds after notice and hearing that the plan was not transmitted to substantially all creditors and equity security holders of the same class, that an unreasonably short time was prescribed for such creditors and equity security holders to accept or reject the plan, or that the solicitation was not in compliance with § 1126(b) of the Code.

(c) Form of Acceptance or Rejection. An acceptance or rejection shall be in writing, identify the plan or plans accepted or rejected, be signed by the creditor or equity security holder or an authorized agent, and conform to the appropriate Official Form. If more than one plan is transmitted pursuant to Rule 3017, an acceptance or rejection may be filed by each creditor or equity security holder for any number of plans transmitted and if acceptances are filed for more than one plan, the creditor or equity security holder may indicate a preference or preferences among the plans so accepted.

(d) Acceptance or Rejection by Partially Secured Creditor. A creditor whose claim has been allowed in part

as a secured claim and in part as an unsecured claim shall be entitled to accept or reject a plan in both capacities.

Rule 3019

MODIFICATION OF ACCEPTED PLAN BEFORE CONFIRMATION IN A CHAPTER 9 MUNICIPALITY OR A CHAPTER 11 REORGANIZATION CASE

In a chapter 9 or chapter 11 case, after a plan has been accepted and before its confirmation, the proponent may file a modification of the plan. If the court finds after hearing on notice to the trustee, any committee appointed under the Code and any other entity designated by the court that the proposed modification does not adversely change the treatment of the claim of any creditor or the interest of any equity security holder who has not accepted in writing the modification, it shall be deemed accepted by all creditors and equity security holders who have previously accepted the plan.

Rule 3020

DEPOSIT; CONFIRMATION OF PLAN IN A CHAPTER 9 MUNICIPALITY OR A CHAPTER 11 REORGANIZATION CASE

(a) Deposit. In a chapter 11 case, prior to entry of the order confirming the plan, the court may order the deposit with the trustee or debtor in possession of the consideration required by the plan to be distributed on confirmation. Any money deposited shall be kept in a special account established for the exclusive purpose of making the distribution.

(b) Objection to and Hearing on Confirmation in a Chapter 9 or Chapter 11 Case.

(1) *Objection.* An objection to confirmation of the plan shall be filed and served on the debtor, the trustee, the proponent of the plan, any committee appointed under the Code, and any other entity designated by the court, within a time fixed by the court. Unless the case is a chapter 9 municipality case, a copy of every objection to confirmation shall be transmitted by the objecting party to the United States trustee within the time fixed for filing objections. An objection to confirmation is governed by Rule 9014.

(2) *Hearing.* The court shall rule on confirmation of the plan after notice and hearing as provided in Rule 2002. If no objection is timely filed, the court may determine that the plan has been proposed in good faith and not by any means forbidden by law without receiving evidence on such issues.

(c) Order of Confirmation. The order of confirmation shall conform to the appropriate Official Form and notice of entry thereof shall be mailed promptly as provided in Rule 2002(f) to the debtor, the trustee, creditors, equity security holders, and other parties in interest. Except in a chapter 9 municipality case, notice of entry of the order of

confirmation shall be transmitted to the United States trustee as provided in Rule 2002(k).

(d) Retained Power. Notwithstanding the entry of the order of confirmation, the court may issue any other order necessary to administer the estate.

Rule 3021

DISTRIBUTION UNDER PLAN

After confirmation of a plan, distribution shall be made to creditors whose claims have been allowed, to holders of stock, bonds, debentures, notes, and other securities of record at the time of commencement of distribution whose claims or equity security interests have not been disallowed and to indenture trustees who have filed claims pursuant to Rule 3003(c)(5) and which have been allowed.

Rule 3022

FINAL DECREE IN CHAPTER 11 REORGANIZATION CASE

After an estate is fully administered in a chapter 11 reorganization case, the court, on its own motion or on motion of a party in interest, shall enter a final decree closing the case.

PART IV
THE DEBTOR: DUTIES AND BENEFITS

Rule

4001.	Relief From Automatic Stay; Prohibiting or Conditioning the Use, Sale, or Lease of Property; Use of Cash Collateral; Obtaining Credit; Agreements
4002.	Duties of Debtor
4003.	Exemptions
4004.	Grant or Denial of Discharge
4005.	Burden of Proof in Objecting to Discharge
4006.	Notice of No Discharge
4007.	Determination of Dischargeability of a Debt
4008.	Discharge and Reaffirmation Hearing

Rule 4001

RELIEF FROM AUTOMATIC STAY; PROHIBITING OR CONDITIONING THE USE, SALE, OR LEASE OF PROPERTY; USE OF CASH COLLATERAL; OBTAINING CREDIT; AGREEMENTS

(a) Relief From Stay; Prohibiting or Conditioning the Use, Sale, or Lease of Property.

(1) *Motion.* A motion for relief from an automatic stay provided by the Code or a motion to prohibit or condition the use, sale, or lease of property pursuant to § 363(e) shall be made in accordance with Rule 9014 and shall be served

on any committee elected pursuant to § 705 or appointed pursuant to § 1102 of the Code or its authorized agent, or, if the case is a chapter 9 municipality case or a chapter 11 reorganization case and no committee of unsecured creditors has been appointed pursuant to § 1102, on the creditors included on the list filed pursuant to Rule 1007(d), and on such other entities as the court may direct.

(2) *Ex Parte Relief.* Relief from a stay under § 362(a) or a request to prohibit or condition the use, sale, or lease of property pursuant to § 363(e) may be granted without prior notice only if (A) it clearly appears from specific facts shown by affidavit or by a verified motion that immediate and irreparable injury, loss, or damage will result to the movant before the adverse party or the attorney for the adverse party can be heard in opposition, and (B) the movant's attorney certifies to the court in writing the efforts, if any, which have been made to give notice and the reasons why notice should not be required. The party obtaining relief under this subdivision and § 362(f) or § 363(e) shall immediately give oral notice thereof to the trustee or debtor in possession and to the debtor and forthwith mail or otherwise transmit to such adverse party or parties a copy of the order granting relief. On two days notice to the party who obtained relief from the stay without notice or on shorter notice to that party as the court may prescribe, the adverse party may appear and move reinstatement of the stay or reconsideration of the order prohibiting or conditioning the use, sale, or lease of property. In that event, the court shall proceed expeditiously to hear and determine the motion.

(b) Use of Cash Collateral.

(1) *Motion; Service.* A motion for authorization to use cash collateral shall be made in accordance with Rule 9014 and shall be served on any entity which has an interest in the cash collateral, on any committee elected pursuant to § 705 or appointed pursuant to § 1102 of the Code or its authorized agent, or, if the case is a chapter 9 municipality case or a chapter 11 reorganization case and no committee of unsecured creditors has been appointed pursuant to § 1102, on the creditors included on the list filed pursuant to Rule 1007(d), and on such other entities as the court may direct.

(2) *Hearing.* The court may commence a final hearing on a motion for authorization to use cash collateral no earlier than 15 days after service of the motion. If the motion so requests, the court may conduct a preliminary hearing before such 15 day period expires, but the court may authorize the use of only that amount of cash collateral as is necessary to avoid immediate and irreparable harm to the estate pending a final hearing.

(3) *Notice.* Notice of hearing pursuant to this subdivision shall be given to the parties on whom service of the motion is required by paragraph (1) of this subdivision and to such other entities as the court may direct.

(c) Obtaining Credit.

(1) *Motion; Service.* A motion for authority to obtain credit shall be made in accordance with Rule 9014 and shall be served on any committee elected pursuant to § 705 or appointed pursuant to § 1102 of the Code or its authorized agent, or, if the case is a chapter 9 municipality case or a chapter 11 reorganization case and no committee of unsecured creditors has been appointed pursuant to § 1102, on the creditors included on the list filed pursuant to Rule 1007(d), and on such other entities as the court may direct. The motion shall be accompanied by a copy of the agreement.

(2) *Hearing.* The court may commence a final hearing on a motion for authority to obtain credit no earlier than 15 days after service of the motion. If the motion so requests, the court may conduct a hearing before such 15 day period expires, but the court may authorize the obtaining of credit only to the extent necessary to void immediate and irreparable harm to the estate pending a final hearing.

(3) *Notice.* Notice of hearing pursuant to this subdivision shall be given to the parties on whom service of the motion is required by paragraph (1) of this subdivision and to such other entities as the court may direct.

(d) Agreement Relating to Relief From the Automatic Stay, Prohibiting or Conditioning the Use, Sale, or Lease of Property, Providing Adequate Protection, Use of Cash Collateral, and Obtaining Credit.

(1) *Motion; Service.* A motion for approval of an agreement (A) to provide adequate protection, (B) to prohibit or condition the use, sale, or lease of property, (C) to modify or terminate the stay provided for in § 362, (D) to use cash collateral, or (E) between the debtor and an entity that has a lien or interest in property of the estate pursuant to which the entity consents to the creation of a lien senior or equal to the entity's lien or interest in such property shall be served on any committee elected pursuant to § 705 or appointed pursuant to § 1102 of the Code or its authorized agent, or, if the case is a chapter 9 municipality case or a chapter 11 reorganization case and no committee of unsecured creditors has been appointed pursuant to § 1102, on the creditors included on the list filed pursuant to Rule 1007(d), and on such other entities as the court may direct. The motion shall be accompanied by a copy of the agreement.

(2) *Objection.* Notice of the motion and the time within which objections may be filed and served on the debtor in possession or trustee shall be mailed to the parties on whom service is required by paragraph (1) of this subdivision and to such other entities as the court may direct. Unless the court fixes a different time, objections may be filed within 15 days of the mailing of notice.

(3) *Disposition; Hearing.* If no objection is filed, the court may enter an order approving or disapproving the agreement without conducting a hearing. If an objection is filed or if the court determines a hearing is appropriate, the court shall hold a hearing on no less than five days' notice

to the objector, the movant, the parties on whom service is required by paragraph (1) of this subdivision and such other entities as the court may direct.

(4) *Agreement in Settlement of Motion.* The court may direct that the procedures prescribed in paragraphs (1), (2), and (3) of this subdivision shall not apply and the agreement may be approved without further notice if the court determines that a motion made pursuant to subdivisions (a), (b), or (c) of this rule was sufficient to afford reasonable notice of the material provisions of the agreement and opportunity for a hearing.

Rule 4002

DUTIES OF DEBTOR

In addition to performing other duties prescribed by the Code and rules, the debtor shall (1) attend and submit to an examination at the times ordered by the court; (2) attend the hearing on a complaint objecting to discharge and testify, if called as a witness; (3) inform the trustee immediately in writing as to the location of real property in which the debtor has an interest and the name and address of every person holding money or property subject to the debtor's withdrawal or order if a schedule of property has not yet been filed pursuant to Rule 1007; (4) cooperate with the trustee in the preparation of an inventory, the examination of proofs of claim, and the administration of the estate, and (5) file a statement of change of the debtor's address.

Rule 4033

EXEMPTIONS

(a) **Claim of Exemptions.** A debtor shall list the property claimed as exempt under § 522 of the Code on the schedule of assets required to be filed by Rule 1007. If the debtor fails to claim exemptions or file the schedule within the time specified in Rule 1007, a dependent of the debtor may file the list within 30 days thereafter.

(b) **Objections to Claim of Exemptions.** The trustee or any creditor may file objections to the list of property claimed as exempt within 30 days after the conclusion of the meeting of creditors held pursuant to Rule 2003(a) of the filing of any amendment to the list or supplemental schedules unless, within such period, further time is granted by the court. Copies of the objections shall be delivered or mailed to the trustee and to the person filing the list and the attorney for such person.

(c) **Burden of Proof.** In any hearing under this rule, the objecting party has the burden of proving that the exemptions are not properly claimed. After hearing on notice, the court shall determine the issues presented by the objections.

(d) **Avoidance by Debtor of Transfers of Exempt Property.** A proceeding by the debtor to avoid a lien or other transfer of property exempt under § 522(f) of the Code shall be by motion in accordance with Rule 9014.

Rule 4004

GRANT OR DENIAL OF DISCHARGE

(a) **Time for Filing Complaint Objecting to Discharge; Notice of Time Fixed.** In a chapter 7 liquidation case a complaint objecting to the debtor's discharge under § 727(a) of the Code shall be filed not later than 60 days following the first date set for the meeting of creditors held pursuant to § 341(a). In a chapter 11 reorganization case, such complaint shall be filed not later than the first date set for the hearing on confirmation. Not less than 25 days notice of the time so fixed shall be given to the United States trustee and all creditors as provided in Rule 2002(f) and (k) and to the trustee and the trustee's attorney.

(b) **Extension of Time.** On motion of any party in interest, after hearing on notice, the court may extend for cause the time for filing a complaint objecting to discharge. The motion shall be made before such time has expired.

(c) **Grant of Discharge.** In a chapter 7 case, on expiration of the time fixed for filing a complaint objecting to discharge and the time fixed for filing a motion to dismiss the case pursuant to Rule 1017(e), the court shall forthwith grant the discharge unless (1) the debtor is not an individual, (2) a complaint objecting to the discharge has been filed, (3) the debtor has filed a waiver under § 727(a)(10), or (4) a motion to dismiss the case under Rule 1017(e) is pending. Notwithstanding the foregoing, on motion of the debtor, the court may defer the entry of an order granting a discharge for 30 days and, on motion within such period, the court may defer entry of the order to a date certain.

(d) **Applicability of Rules in Part VII.** A proceeding commenced by a complaint objecting to discharge is governed by Part VII of these rules.

(e) **Order of Discharge.** An order of discharge shall conform to the appropriate Official Form.

(f) **Registration in Other Districts.** An order of discharge that has become final may be registered in any other district by filing a certified copy of the order in the office of the clerk of that district. When so registered the order of discharge shall have the same effect as an order of the court of the district where registered.

(g) **Notice of Discharge.** The clerk shall promptly mail a copy of the final order of discharge to those specified in subdivision (a) of this rule.

Rule 4005

BURDEN OF PROOF IN OBJECTING TO DISCHARGE

At the trial on a complaint objecting to a discharge, the plaintiff has the burden of proving the objection.

Rule 4006

NOTICE OF NO DISCHARGE

If an order is entered denying or revoking a discharge or if a waiver of discharge is filed, the clerk, after the order becomes final or the waiver is filed, shall promptly give notice thereof to all creditors in the manner provided in Rule 2002.

Rule 4007

DETERMINATION OF DISCHARGEABILITY OF A DEBT

(a) Persons Entitled to File Complaint. A debtor or any creditor may file a complaint to obtain a determination of the dischargeability of any debt.

(b) Time for Commencing Proceeding Other Than Under § 523(c) of the Code. A complaint other than under § 523(c) may be filed at any time. A case may be reopened without payment of an additional filing fee for the purpose of filing a complaint to obtain a determination under this rule.

(c) Time for Filing Complaint Under § 523(c) in Chapter 7 Liquidation, Chapter 11 Reorganization, and Chapter 12 Family Farmer's Debt Adjustment Cases; Notice of Time Fixed. A complaint to determine the dischargeability of any debt pursuant to § 523(c) of the Code shall be filed not later than 60 days following the first date set for the meeting of creditors held pursuant to § 341(a). The court shall give all creditors not less than 30 days notice of the time so fixed in the manner provided in Rule 2002. On motion of any party in interest, after hearing on notice, the court may for cause extend the time fixed under this subdivision. The motion shall be made before the time has expired.

(d) Time for Filing Complaint Under § 523(c) in Chapter 13 Individual's Debt Adjustment Cases; Notice of Time Fixed. On motion by a debtor for a discharge under § 1328(b), the court shall enter an order fixing a time for the filing of a complaint to determine the dischargeability of any debt pursuant to § 523(c) and shall give not less than 30 days notice of the time fixed to all creditors in the manner provided in Rule 2002. On motion of any party in interest after hearing on notice the court may for cause extend the time fixed under this subdivision. The motion shall be made before the time has expired.

(e) Applicability of Rules in Part VII. A proceeding commenced by a complaint filed under this rule is governed by Part VII of these rules.

Rule 4008

DISCHARGE AND REAFFIRMATION HEARING

Not more than 30 days following the entry of an order granting or denying a discharge, or confirming a plan in a chapter 11 reorganization case concerning an individual debtor and on not less than 10 days notice to the debtor and the trustee, the court may hold a hearing as provided in § 524(d) of the Code. A motion by the debtor for approval of a reaffirmation agreement shall be filed before or at the hearing.

PART V
COURTS AND CLERKS

Rule 5001

COURTS AND CLERKS' OFFICES

(a) Courts Always Open. The courts shall be deemed always open for the purpose of filing any pleading or other proper paper, issuing and returning process, and filing, making, or entering motions, orders and rules.

(b) Trials and Hearings; Orders in Chambers. All trials and hearings shall be conducted in open court and so far as convenient in a regular court room. All other acts or proceedings may be done or conducted by a judge in chambers and at any place either within or without the district; but no hearing, other than one ex parte, shall be conducted outside the district without the consent of all parties affected thereby.

(c) Clerk's Office. The clerk's office with the clerk or a deputy in attendance shall be open during business hours on all days except Saturdays, Sundays and the legal holidays listed in Rule 9006(a).

Rule 5002

RESTRICTIONS ON APPROVAL OF APPOINTMENTS

(a) Approval of Appointment of Relatives Prohibited. The appointment of an individual as a trustee or examiner pursuant to § 1104 of the Code shall not be approved by

the court if the individual is a relative of the bankruptcy judge approving the appointment or the United States trustee in the region in which the case is pending. The employment of an individual as attorney, accountant, appraiser, auctioneer, or other professional person pursuant to §§ 327, 1103, or 1114 shall not be approved by the court if the individual is a relative of the bankruptcy judge approving the employment. The employment of an individual as attorney, accountant, appraiser, auctioneer, or other professional person pursuant to §§ 327, 1103, or 1114 may be approved by the court if the individual is a relative of the United States trustee in the region in which the case is pending, unless the court finds that the relationship with the United States trustee renders the employment improper under the circumstances of the case. Whenever under this subdivision an individual may not be approved for appointment or employment, the individual's firm, partnership, corporation, or any other form of business association or relationship, and all members, associates and professional employees thereof also may not be approved for appointment or employment.

(b) Judicial Determination That Approval of Appointment or Employment is Improper. A bankruptcy judge may not approve the appointment of a person as a trustee or examiner pursuant to § 1104 of the Code or approve the employment of a person as an attorney, accountant, appraiser, auctioneer, or other professional person pursuant to §§ 327, 1103, or 1114 of the Code if that person is or has been so connected with such judge or the United States trustee as to render the appointment or employment improper.

Rule 5003

RECORDS KEPT BY THE CLERK

(a) Bankruptcy Dockets. The clerk shall keep a docket in each case under the Code and shall enter thereon each judgment, order, and activity in that case as prescribed by the Director of the Administrative Office of the United States Courts. The entry of a judgment or order in a docket shall show the date the entry is made.

(b) Claims Register. The clerk shall keep in a claims register a list of claims filed in a case when it appears that there will be distribution to unsecured creditors.

(c) Judgments and Orders. The clerk shall keep, in the form and manner as the Director of the Administrative Office of the United States Courts may prescribe, a correct copy of every final judgment or order affecting title to or lien on real property or for the recovery of money or property, and any other order which the court may direct to be kept. On request of the prevailing party, a correct copy of every judgment or order affecting title to or lien upon real or personal property or for the recovery of money or property shall be kept and indexed with the civil judgments of the district court.

(d) Index of Cases; Certificate of Search. The clerk shall keep indices of all cases and adversary proceedings as prescribed by the Director of the Administrative Office of the United States Courts. On request, the clerk shall make a search of any index and papers in the clerk's custody and certify whether a case or proceeding has been filed in or transferred to the court or if a discharge has been entered in its records.

(e) Other Books and Records of the Clerk. The clerk shall also keep such other books and records as may be required by the Director of the Administrative Office of the United States Courts.

Rule 5004

DISQUALIFICATION

(a) Disqualification of Judge. A bankruptcy judge shall be governed by 28 U.S.C. § 455, and disqualified from presiding over the proceeding or contested matter in which the disqualifying circumstance arises or, if appropriate, shall be disqualified from presiding over the case.

(b) Disqualification of Judge From Allowing Compensation. A bankruptcy judge shall be disqualified from allowing compensation to a person who is a relative of the bankruptcy judge or with whom the judge is so connected as to render it improper for the judge to authorize such compensation.

Rule 5005

FILING AND TRANSMITTAL OF PAPERS

(a) Filing. The lists, schedules, statements, proofs of claim or interest, complaints, motions, applications, objections and other papers required to be filed by these rules, except as provided in 28 U.S.C. § 1409, shall be filed with the clerk in the district where the case under the Code is pending. The judge of that court may permit the papers to be filed with the judge, in which event the filing date shall be noted thereon, and they shall be forthwith transmitted to the clerk. The clerk shall not refuse to accept for filing any petition or other paper presented for the purpose of filing solely because it is not presented in proper form as required by these rules or any local rules or practices.

(b) Transmittal to the United States Trustee.

(1) The complaints, motions, applications, objections and other papers required to be transmitted to the United States trustee by these rules shall be mailed or delivered to an office of the United States trustee, or to another place designated by the United States trustee, in the district where the case under the Code is pending.

(2) The entity, other than the clerk, transmitting a paper to the United States trustee shall promptly file as proof of such transmittal a verified statement identifying the paper and stating the date on which it was transmitted to the United States trustee.

(3) Nothing in these rules shall require the clerk to transmit any paper to the United States trustee if the United States trustee requests in writing that the paper not be transmitted.

(c) **Error in Filing or Transmittal.** A paper intended to be filed with the clerk but erroneously delivered to the United States trustee, the trustee, the attorney for the trustee, a bankruptcy judge, a district judge, or the clerk of the district court shall, after the date of its receipt has been noted thereon, be transmitted forthwith to the clerk of the bankruptcy court. A paper intended to be transmitted to the United States trustee but erroneously delivered to the clerk, the trustee, the attorney for the trustee, a bankruptcy judge, or the clerk of the district court shall, after the date of its receipt has been noted thereon, be transmitted forthwith to the United States trustee. In the interest of justice, the court may order that a paper erroneously delivered shall be deemed filed with the clerk or transmitted to the United States trustee as of the date of its original delivery.

Rule 5006

CERTIFICATION OF COPIES OF PAPERS

The clerk shall issue a certified copy of the record of any proceeding in a case under the Code or of any paper filed with the clerk on payment of any prescribed fee.

Rule 5007

RECORD OF PROCEEDINGS AND TRANSCRIPTS

(a) **Filing of Record or Transcript.** The reporter or operator of a recording device shall certify the original notes of testimony, tape recording, or other original record of the proceeding and promptly file them with the clerk. The person preparing any transcript shall promptly file a certified copy.

(b) **Transcript Fees.** The fees for copies of transcripts shall be charged at rates prescribed by the Judicial Conference of the United States. No fee may be charged for the certified copy filed with the clerk.

(c) **Admissibility of Record in Evidence.** A certified sound recording or a transcript of a proceeding shall be admissible as prima facie evidence to establish the record.

Rule 5008

[ABROGATED]

Rule 5009

CLOSING CHAPTER 7 LIQUIDATION, CHAPTER 12 FAMILY FARMER'S DEBT ADJUSTMENT, AND CHAPTER 13 INDIVIDUAL'S DEBT ADJUSTMENT CASES

If in a chapter 7, chapter 12, or chapter 13 case the trustee has filed a final report and final account and has certified that the estate has been fully administered, and if

within 30 days no objection has been filed by the United States trustee or a party in interest, there shall be a presumption that the estate has been fully administered.

Rule 5010

REOPENING CASES

A case may be reopened on motion of the debtor or other party in interest pursuant to § 350(b) of the Code. In a chapter 7, 12, or 13 case a trustee shall not be appointed by the United States trustee unless the court determines that a trustee is necessary to protect the interests of creditors and the debtor or to insure efficient administration of the case.

Rule 5011

WITHDRAWAL AND ABSTENTION FROM HEARING A PROCEEDING

(a) **Withdrawal.** A motion for withdrawal of a case or proceeding shall be heard by a district judge.

(b) **Abstention From Hearing a Proceeding.** A motion for abstention pursuant to 28 U.S.C. § 1334(c) shall be governed by Rule 9014 and shall be served on the parties to the proceeding.

(c) **Effect of Filing of Motion for Withdrawal or Abstention.** The filing of a motion for withdrawal of a case or proceeding or for abstention pursuant to 28 U.S.C. § 1334(c) shall not stay the administration of the case or any proceeding therein before the bankruptcy judge except that the bankruptcy judge may stay, on such terms and conditions as are proper, proceedings pending disposition of the motion. A motion for a stay ordinarily shall be presented to the bankruptcy judge. A motion for a stay or relief from a stay filed in the district court shall state why it has not been presented to or obtained from the bankruptcy judge. Relief granted by the district judge shall be on such terms and conditions as the judge deems proper.

PART VI
COLLECTION AND LIQUIDATION OF THE ESTATE

Rule 6001

BURDEN OF PROOF AS TO VALIDITY OF POSTPETITION TRANSFER

Any entity asserting the validity of a transfer under § 549 of the Code shall have the burden of proof.

Rule 6002

ACCOUNTING BY PRIOR CUSTODIAN OF PROPERTY OF THE ESTATE

(a) Accounting Required. Any custodian required by the Code to deliver property in the custodian's possession or control to the trustee shall promptly file and transmit to the United States trustee a report and account with respect to the property of the estate and the administration thereof.

(b) Examination of Administration. On the filing and transmittal of the report and account required by subdivision (a) of this rule and after an examination has been made into the superseded administration, after notice and a hearing, the court shall determine the propriety of the administration, including the reasonableness of all disbursements.

Rule 6003

[ABROGATED]

Rule 6004

USE, SALE, OR LEASE OF PROPERTY

(a) Notice of Proposed Use, Sale, or Lease of Property. Notice of a proposed use, sale, or lease of property, other than cash collateral, not in the ordinary course of business shall be given pursuant to Rule 2002(a)(2), (c)(1), (i), and (k) and, if applicable, in accordance with § 363(b)(2) of the Code.

(b) Objection to Proposal. Except as provided in subdivisions (c) and (d) of this rule, an objection to a proposed use, sale, or lease of property shall be filed and served not less than five days before the date set for the proposed action or within the time fixed by the court. An objection to the proposed use, sale, or lease of property is governed by Rule 9014.

(c) Sale Free and Clear of Liens and Other Interests. A motion for authority to sell property free and clear of liens or other interests shall be made in accordance with Rule 9014 and shall be served on the parties who have liens or other interests in the property to be sold. The notice required by subdivision (a) of this rule shall include

the date of the hearing on the motion and the time within which objections may be filed and served on the debtor in possession or trustee.

(d) Sale of Property Under $2,500. Notwithstanding subdivision (a) of this rule, when all of the nonexempt property of the estate has an aggregate gross value less than $2,500, it shall be sufficient to give a general notice of intent to sell such property other than in the ordinary course of business to all creditors, indenture trustees, committees appointed or elected pursuant to the Code, the United States trustee and other persons as the court may direct. An objection to any such sale may be filed and served by a party in interest within 15 days of the mailing of the notice, or within the time fixed by the court. An objection is governed by Rule 9014.

(e) Hearing. If a timely objection is made pursuant to subdivision (b) or (d) of this rule, the date of the hearing thereon may be set in the notice given pursuant to subdivision (a) of this rule.

(f) Conduct of Sale Not In The Ordinary Course of Business.

(1) *Public or Private Sale.* All sales not in the ordinary course of business may be by private sale or by public auction. Unless it is impracticable, an itemized statement of the property sold, the name of each purchaser, and the price received for each item or lot or for the property as a whole if sold in bulk shall be filed on completion of a sale. If the property is sold by an auctioneer, the auctioneer shall file the statement, transmit a copy thereof to the United States trustee, and furnish a copy to the trustee, debtor in possession, or chapter 13 debtor. If the property is not sold by an auctioneer, the trustee, debtor in possession, or chapter 13 debtor shall file the statement and transmit a copy thereof to the United States trustee.

(2) *Execution of Instruments.* After a sale in accordance with this rule the debtor, the trustee, or debtor in possession, as the case may be, shall execute any instrument necessary or ordered by the court to effectuate the transfer to the purchaser.

Rule 6005

APPRAISERS AND AUCTIONEERS

The order of the court approving the employment of an appraiser or auctioneer shall fix the amount or rate of compensation. No officer or employee of the Judicial Branch of the United States or the United States Department of Justice shall be eligible to act as appraiser or auctioneer. No residence or licensing requirement shall disqualify an appraiser or auctioneer from employment.

Rule 6006

ASSUMPTION, REJECTION AND ASSIGNMENT OF EXECUTORY CONTRACTS AND UNEXPIRED LEASES

(a) Proceeding to Assume, Reject, or Assign. A proceeding to assume, reject, or assign an executory contract or unexpired lease, other than as part of a plan, is governed by Rule 9014.

(b) Proceeding to Require Trustee to Act. A proceeding by a party to an executory contract or unexpired lease in a chapter 9 municipality case, chapter 11 reorganization case, chapter 12 family farmer's debt adjustment case, or chapter 13 individual's debt adjustment case, to require the trustee, debtor in possession, or debtor to determine whether to assume or reject the contract or lease is governed by Rule 9014.

(c) Notice. Notice of a motion made pursuant to subdivision (a) or (b) of this rule shall be given to the other party to the contract or lease, to other parties in interest as the court may direct, and, except in a chapter 9 municipality case, to the United States trustee.

Rule 6007

ABANDONMENT OR DISPOSITION OF PROPERTY

(a) Notice of Proposed Abandonment or Disposition; Objections; Hearing. Unless otherwise directed by the court, the trustee or debtor in possession shall give notice of a proposed abandonment or disposition of property to the United States trustee, all creditors, indenture trustees and committees elected pursuant to § 705 or appointed pursuant to § 1102 of the Code. A party in interest may file and serve an objection within 15 days of the mailing of the notice, or within the time fixed by the court. If a timely objection is made, the court shall set a hearing on notice to the United States trustee and to other entities as the court may direct.

(b) Motion by Party In Interest. A party in interest may file and serve a motion requiring the trustee or debtor in possession to abandon property of the estate.

(c) [Abrogated].

Rule 6008

REDEMPTION OF PROPERTY FROM LIEN OR SALE

On motion by the debtor, trustee, or debtor in possession and after hearing on notice as the court may direct, the court may authorize the redemption of property from a lien or from a sale to enforce a lien in accordance with applicable law.

Rule 6009

PROSECUTION AND DEFENSE OF PROCEEDINGS BY TRUSTEE OR DEBTOR IN POSSESSION

With or without court approval, the trustee or debtor in possession may prosecute or may enter an appearance and defend any pending action or proceeding by or against the debtor, or commence and prosecute any action or proceeding in behalf of the estate before any tribunal.

Rule 6010

PROCEEDING TO AVOID INDEMNIFYING LIEN OR TRANSFER TO SURETY

If a lien voidable under § 547 of the Code has been dissolved by the furnishing of a bond or other obligation and the surety thereon has been indemnified by the transfer of, or the creation of a lien upon, nonexempt property of the debtor, the surety shall be joined as a defendant in any proceeding to avoid the indemnifying transfer or lien. Such proceeding is governed by the rules in Part VII.

PART VII
ADVERSARY PROCEEDINGS

Rule 7001

SCOPE OF RULES OF PART VII

An adversary proceeding is governed by the rules of this Part VII. It is a proceeding (1) to recover money or property, except a proceeding to compel the debtor to deliver property to the trustee, or a proceeding under § 554(b) or § 725 of the Code, Rule 2017, or Rule 6002, (2) to determine the validity, priority, or extent of a lien or other interest in property, other than a proceeding under Rule 4003(d), (3) to obtain approval pursuant to § 363(h) for the sale of both the interest of the estate and of a co-owner in property, (4) to object to or revoke a discharge, (5) to revoke an order of confirmation of a chapter 11, chapter 12, or chapter 13 plan, (6) to determine the dischargeability of a debt, (7) to obtain an injunction or other equitable relief, (8) to subordinate any allowed claim or interest, except when subordination is provided in a chapter 9, 11, 12, or 13 plan, (9) to obtain a declaratory judgment relating to any of the foregoing, or (10) to determine a claim or cause of action removed pursuant to 28 U.S.C. § 1452.

Rule 7002

REFERENCES TO FEDERAL RULES OF CIVIL PROCEDURE

Whenever a Federal Rule of Civil Procedure applicable to adversary proceedings makes reference to another Federal Rule of Civil Procedure, the reference shall be read as a reference to the Federal Rule of Civil Procedure as modified in this Part VII.

Rule 7003

COMMENCEMENT OF ADVERSARY PROCEEDING

Rule 3 F.R.Civ.P. applies in adversary proceedings.

Rule 7004

PROCESS; SERVICE OF SUMMONS, COMPLAINT

(a) Summons; Service; Proof of Service. Rule 4(a), (b), (c)(2)(C)(i), (d), (e) and (g)–(j) F.R.Civ.P. applies in adversary proceedings. Personal service pursuant to Rule 4(d) F.R.Civ.P. may be made by any person not less than 18 years of age who is not a party and the summons may be delivered by the clerk to any such person.

(b) Service by First Class Mail. Except as provided in subdivision (h), in addition to the methods of service authorized by Rule 4(c)(2)(C)(i) and (d) F.R.Civ.P., service may be made within the United States by first class mail postage prepaid as follows:

(1) Upon an individual other than an infant or incompetent, by mailing a copy of the summons and complaint to the individual's dwelling house or usual place of abode or to the place where the individual regularly conducts a business or profession.

(2) Upon an infant or an incompetent person, by mailing a copy of the summons and complaint to the person upon whom process is prescribed to be served by the law of the state in which service is made when an action is brought against such defendant in the courts of general jurisdiction of that state. The summons and complaint in such case shall be addressed to the person required to be served at that person's dwelling house or usual place of abode or at the place where the person regularly conducts a business or profession.

(3) Upon a domestic or foreign corporation or upon a partnership or other unincorporated association, by mailing a copy of the summons and complaint to the attention of an officer, a managing or general agent, or to any other agent authorized by appointment or by law to receive service of process and, if the agent is one authorized by statute to receive service and the statute so requires, by also mailing a copy to the defendant.

(4) Upon the United States, by mailing a copy of the

summons and complaint to the United States attorney for the district in which the action is brought and also the Attorney General of the United States at Washington, District of Columbia, and in any action attacking the validity of an order of an officer or an agency of the United States not made a party, by also mailing a copy of the summons and complaint to such officer or agency.

(5) Upon any officer or agency of the United States, by mailing a copy of the summons and complaint to the United States as prescribed in paragraph (4) of this subdivision and also to the officer or agency. If the agency is a corporation, the mailing shall be as prescribed in paragraph (3) of this subdivision of this rule. If the United States trustee is the trustee in the case and service is made upon the United States trustee solely as trustee, service may be made as prescribed in paragraph (10) of this subdivision of this rule.

(6) Upon a state or municipal corporation or other governmental organization thereof subject to suit, by mailing a copy of the summons and complaint to the person or office upon whom process is prescribed to be served by the law of the state in which service is made when an action is brought against such a defendant in the courts of general jurisdiction of that state, or in the absence of the designation of any such person or office by state law, then to the chief executive officer thereof.

(7) Upon a defendant of any class referred to in paragraph (1) or (3) of this subdivision of this rule, it is also sufficient if a copy of the summons and complaint is mailed to the entity upon whom service is prescribed to be served by any statute of the United States or by the law of the state in which service is made when an action is brought against such defendant in the court of general jurisdiction of that state.

(8) Upon any defendant, it is also sufficient if a copy of the summons and complaint is mailed to an agent of such defendant authorized by appointment or by law to receive service of process, at the agent's dwelling house or usual place of abode or at the place where the agent regularly carries on a business or profession and, if the authorization so requires, by mailing also a copy of the summons and complaint to the defendant as provided in this subdivision.

(9) Upon the debtor, after a petition has been filed by or served upon the debtor and until the case is dismissed or closed, by mailing copies of the summons and complaint to the debtor at the address shown in the petition or statement of affairs or to such other address as the debtor may designate in a filed writing and, if the debtor is represented by an attorney, to the attorney at the attorney's post-office address.

(10) Upon the United States trustee, when the United States trustee is the trustee in the case and service is made upon the United States trustee solely as trustee, by mailing a copy of the summons and complaint to an office of the

United States trustee or another place designated by the United States trustee in the district where the case under the Code is pending.

(c) Service by Publication. If a party to an adversary proceeding to determine or protect rights in property in the custody of the court cannot be served as provided in Rule 4(d) or (i) F.R.Civ.P. or subdivision (b) of this rule, the court may order the summons and complaint to be served by mailing copies thereof by first class mail postage prepaid, to the party's last known address and by at least one publication in such manner and form as the court may direct.

(d) Nationwide Service of Process. The summons and complaint and all other process except a subpoena may be served anywhere in the United States.

(e) Service on Debtor and Others in Foreign Country. The summons and complaint and all other process except a subpoena may be served as provided in Rule 4(d)(1) and (d)(3) F.R.Civ.P. in a foreign country (A) on the debtor, any person required to perform the duties of a debtor, any general partner of a partnership debtor, or any attorney who is a party to a transaction subject to examination under Rule 2017; or (B) on any party to an adversary proceeding to determine or protect rights in property in the custody of the court; or (C) on any person whenever such service is authorized by a federal or state law referred to in Rule 4(c)(2)(C)(i) or (e) F.R.Civ.P.

(f) Summons: Time Limit for Service. If service is made pursuant to Rule 4(d)(1)–(6) F.R.Civ.P. it shall be made by delivery of the summons and complaint within 10 days following issuance of the summons. If service is made by any authorized form of mail, the summons and complaint shall be deposited in the mail within 10 days following issuance of the summons. If a summons is not timely delivered or mailed, another summons shall be issued and served.

(g) Effect of Amendment to Rule 4 F.R.Civ.P. The subdivisions of Rule 4 F.R.Civ.P. made applicable by these rules shall be the subdivisions of Rule 4 F.R.Civ.P. in effect on January 1, 1990, notwithstanding any amendment to Rule 4 F.R.Civ.P. subsequent thereto.

(h) Service of Process on an Insured Depository Institution. Service on an insured depository institution (as defined in section 3 of the Federal Deposit Insurance Act) in a contested matter or adversary proceeding shall be made by certified mail addressed to an officer of the institution unless—

(1) the institution has appeared by its attorney, in which case the attorney shall be served by first class mail;

(2) the court orders otherwise after service upon the institution by certified mail of notice of an application to permit service on the institution by first class mail sent to an officer of the institution designated by the institution; or

(3) the institution has waived in writing its entitlement to service by certified mail by designating an officer to receive service.

Rule 7005

SERVICE AND FILING OF PLEADINGS AND OTHER PAPERS

Rule 5 F.R.Civ.P. applies in adversary proceedings.

Rule 7007

PLEADINGS ALLOWED

Rule 7 F.R.Civ.P. applies in adversary proceedings.

Rule 7008

GENERAL RULES OF PLEADING

(a) **Applicability of Rule 8 F.R.Civ.P.** Rule 8 F.R.Civ.P. applies in adversary proceedings. The allegation of jurisdiction required by Rule 8(a) shall also contain a reference to the name, number, and chapter of the case under the Code to which the adversary proceeding relates and to the district and division where the case under the Code is pending. In an adversary proceeding before a bankruptcy judge, the complaint, counterclaim, cross-claim, or third-party complaint shall contain a statement that the proceeding is core or non-core and, if non-core, that the pleader does or does not consent to entry of final orders or judgment by the bankruptcy judge.

(b) **Attorney's Fees.** A request for an award of attorney's fees shall be pleaded as a claim in a complaint, cross-claim, third-party complaint, answer, or reply as may be appropriate.

Rule 7009

PLEADING SPECIAL MATTERS

Rule 9 F.R.Civ.P. applies in adversary proceedings.

Rule 7010

FORM OF PLEADINGS

Rule 10 F.R.Civ.P. applies in adversary proceedings, except that the caption of each pleading in such a proceeding shall conform substantially to the appropriate Official Form.

Rule 7012

DEFENSES AND OBJECTIONS—WHEN AND HOW PRESENTED—BY PLEADING OR MOTION— MOTION FOR JUDGMENT ON THE PLEADINGS

(a) **When Presented.** If a complaint is duly served, the defendant shall serve an answer within 30 days after the issuance of the summons, except when a different time is prescribed by the court. The court shall prescribe the time for service of the answer when service of a complaint is made by publication or upon a party in a foreign country. A party served with a pleading stating a cross-claim shall serve an answer thereto within 20 days after service. The plaintiff shall serve a reply to a counterclaim in the answer within 20 days after service of the answer or, if a reply is ordered by the court, within 20 days after service of the order, unless the order otherwise directs. The United States or an officer or agency thereof shall serve an answer to a complaint within 35 days after the issuance of the summons, and shall serve an answer to a cross-claim, or a reply to a counterclaim, within 35 days after service upon the United States attorney of the pleading in which the claim is asserted. The service of a motion permitted under this rule alters these periods of time as follows, unless a different time is fixed by order of the court: (1) if the court denies the motion or postpones its disposition until the trial on the merits, the responsive pleading shall be served within 10 days after notice of the court's action; (2) if the court grants a motion for a more definite statement, the responsive pleading shall be served within 10 days after the service of a more definite statement.

(b) **Applicability of Rule 12(b)–(h) F.R.Civ.P.** Rule 12(b)–(h) F.R.Civ.P. applies in adversary proceedings. A responsive pleading shall admit or deny an allegation that the proceeding is core or non-core. If the response is that the proceeding is non-core, it shall include a statement that the party does or does not consent to entry of final orders or judgment by the bankruptcy judge. In non-core proceedings final orders and judgments shall not be entered on the bankruptcy judge's order except with the express consent of the parties.

Rule 7013

COUNTERCLAIM AND CROSS-CLAIM

Rule 13 F.R.Civ.P. applies in adversary proceedings, except that a party sued by a trustee or debtor in possession need not state as a counterclaim any claim that the party has against the debtor, the debtor's property, or the estate, unless the claim arose after the entry of an order for relief. A trustee or debtor in possession who fails to plead a counterclaim through oversight, inadvertence, or excusable neglect, or when justice so requires, may by leave of court amend the pleading, or commence a new adversary proceeding or separate action.

Rule 7014

THIRD-PARTY PRACTICE

Rule 14 F.R.Civ.P. applies in adversary proceedings.

Rule 7015

AMENDED AND SUPPLEMENTAL PLEADINGS

Rule 15 F.R.Civ.P. applies in adversary proceedings.

Rule 7016

PRE-TRIAL PROCEDURE; FORMULATING ISSUES

Rule 16 F.R.Civ.P. applies in adversary proceedings.

Rule 7017

PARTIES PLAINTIFF AND DEFENDANT; CAPACITY

Rule 17 F.R.Civ.P. applies in adversary proceedings, except as provided in Rule 2010(b).

Rule 7018

JOINDER OF CLAIMS AND REMEDIES

Rule 18 F.R.Civ.P. applies in adversary proceedings.

Rule 7019

JOINDER OF PERSONS NEEDED FOR JUST DETERMINATION

Rule 19 F.R.Civ.P. applies in adversary proceedings, except that (1) if an entity joined as a party raises the defense that the court lacks jurisdiction over the subject matter and the defense is sustained, the court shall dismiss such entity from the adversary proceeding and (2) if an entity joined as a party properly and timely raises the defense of improper venue, the court shall determine, as provided in 28 U.S.C. § 1412, whether that part of the proceeding involving the joined party shall be transferred to another district, or whether the entire adversary proceeding shall be transferred to another district.

Rule 7020

PERMISSIVE JOINDER OF PARTIES

Rule 20 F.R.Civ.P. applies in adversary proceedings.

Rule 7021

MISJOINDER AND NON-JOINDER OF PARTIES

Rule 21 F.R.Civ.P. applies in adversary proceedings.

Rule 7022

INTERPLEADER

Rule 22(1) F.R.Civ.P. applies in adversary proceedings.

Rule 7023

CLASS PROCEEDINGS

Rule 23 F.R.Civ.P. applies in adversary proceedings.

Rule 7023.1

DERIVATIVE PROCEEDINGS BY SHAREHOLDERS

Rule 23.1 F.R.Civ.P. applies in adversary proceedings.

Rule 7023.2

ADVERSARY PROCEEDINGS RELATING TO UNINCORPORATED ASSOCIATIONS

Rule 23.2 F.R.Civ.P. applies in adversary proceedings.

Rule 7024

INTERVENTION

Rule 24 F.R.Civ.P. applies in adversary proceedings.

Rule 7025

SUBSTITUTION OF PARTIES

Subject to the provisions of Rule 2012, Rule 25 F.R.Civ.P. applies in adversary proceedings.

Rule 7026

GENERAL PROVISIONS GOVERNING DISCOVERY

Rule 26 F.R.Civ.P. applies in adversary proceedings.

Rule 7027

DEPOSITIONS BEFORE ADVERSARY PROCEEDINGS OR PENDING APPEAL

Rule 27 F.R.Civ.P. applies to adversary proceedings.

Rule 7028

PERSONS BEFORE WHOM DEPOSITIONS MAY BE TAKEN

Rule 28 F.R.Civ.P. applies in adversary proceedings.

Rule 7029

STIPULATIONS REGARDING DISCOVERY PROCEDURE

Rule 29 F.R.Civ.P. applies in adversary proceedings.

Rule 7030

DEPOSITIONS UPON ORAL EXAMINATION

Rule 30 F.R.Civ.P. applies in adversary proceedings.

Rule 7031

DEPOSITION UPON WRITTEN QUESTIONS

Rule 31 F.R.Civ.P. applies in adversary proceedings.

Rule 7032

USE OF DEPOSITIONS IN ADVERSARY PROCEEDINGS

Rule 32 F.R.Civ.P. applies in adversary proceedings.

Rule 7033

INTERROGATORIES TO PARTIES

Rule 33 F.R.Civ.P. applies in adversary proceedings.

Rule 7034

PRODUCTION OF DOCUMENTS AND THINGS AND ENTRY UPON LAND FOR INSPECTION AND OTHER PURPOSES

Rule 34 F.R.Civ.P. applies in adversary proceedings.

Rule 7035

PHYSICAL AND MENTAL EXAMINATION OF PERSONS

Rule 35 F.R.Civ.P. applies in adversary proceedings.

Rule 7036

REQUESTS FOR ADMISSION

Rule 36 F.R.Civ.P. applies in adversary proceedings.

Rule 7037

FAILURE TO MAKE DISCOVERY: SANCTIONS

Rule 37 F.R.Civ.P. applies in adversary proceedings.

Rule 7040

ASSIGNMENT OF CASES FOR TRIAL

Rule 40 F.R.Civ.P. applies in adversary proceedings.

Rule 7041

DISMISSAL OF ADVERSARY PROCEEDINGS

Rule 41 F.R.Civ.P. applies in adversary proceedings, except that a complaint objecting to the debtor's discharge shall not be dismissed at the plaintiff's instance without notice to the trustee, the United States trustee, and such other persons as the court may direct, and only on order of the court containing terms and conditions which the court deems proper.

Rule 7042

CONSOLIDATION OF ADVERSARY PROCEEDINGS; SEPARATE TRIALS

Rule 42 F.R.Civ.P. applies in adversary proceedings.

Rule 7052

FINDINGS BY THE COURT

Rule 52 F.R.Civ.P. applies in adversary proceedings.

Rule 7054

JUDGMENTS; COSTS

(a) **Judgments.** Rule 54(a)–(c) F.R.Civ.P. applies in adversary proceedings.

(b) **Costs.** The court may allow costs to the prevailing party except when a statute of the United States or these rules otherwise provides. Costs against the United States, its officers and agencies shall be imposed only to the extent permitted by law. Costs may be taxed by the clerk on one day's notice; on motion served within five days thereafter, the action of the clerk may be reviewed by the court.

Rule 7055

DEFAULT

Rule 55 F.R.Civ.P. applies in adversary proceedings.

Rule 7056

SUMMARY JUDGMENT

Rule 56 F.R.Civ.P. applies in adversary proceedings.

Rule 7062

STAY OF PROCEEDINGS TO ENFORCE A JUDGMENT

Rule 62 F.R.Civ.P. applies in adversary proceedings. An order granting relief from an automatic stay provided by § 362, § 922, § 1201, or § 1301 of the Code, an order authorizing or prohibiting the use of cash collateral or the use, sale or lease of property of the estate under § 363, an order authorizing the trustee to obtain credit pursuant to § 364, and an order authorizing the assumption or assignment of an executory contract or unexpired lease pursuant to § 365 shall be additional exceptions to Rule 62(a).

Rule 7064

SEIZURE OF PERSON OR PROPERTY

Rule 64 F.R.Civ.P. applies in adversary proceedings.

Rule 7065

INJUNCTIONS

Rule 65 F.R.Civ.P. applies in adversary proceedings, except that a temporary restraining order or preliminary injunction may be issued on application of a debtor, trustee, or debtor in possession without compliance with Rule 65(c).

Rule 7067

DEPOSIT IN COURT

Rule 67 F.R.Civ.P. applies in adversary proceedings.

Rule 7068

OFFER OF JUDGMENT

Rule 68 F.R.Civ.P. applies in adversary proceedings.

Rule 7069

EXECUTION

Rule 69 F.R.Civ.P. applies in adversary proceedings.

Rule 7070

JUDGMENT FOR SPECIFIC ACTS; VESTING TITLE

Rule 70 F.R.Civ.P. applies in adversary proceedings and the court may enter a judgment divesting the title of any party and vesting title in others whenever the real or personal property involved is within the jurisdiction of the court.

Rule 7071

PROCESS IN BEHALF OF AND AGAINST PERSONS NOT PARTIES

Rule 71 F.R.Civ.P. applies in adversary proceedings.

Rule 7087

TRANSFER OF ADVERSARY PROCEEDING

On motion and after a hearing, the court may transfer an adversary proceeding or any part thereof to another district pursuant to 28 U.S.C. § 1412, except as provided in Rule 7019(2).

PART VIII
APPEALS TO DISTRICT COURT OR BANKRUPTCY APPELLATE PANEL

Rule 8001

MANNER OF TAKING APPEAL; VOLUNTARY DISMISSAL

(a) Appeal as of Right; How Taken. An appeal from a final judgment, order, or decree of a bankruptcy judge to a district court or bankruptcy appellate panel shall be taken by filing a notice of appeal with the clerk within the time allowed by Rule 8002. Failure of an appellant to take any step other than the timely filing of a notice of appeal does not affect the validity of the appeal, but is ground only for such action as the district court or bankruptcy appellate panel deems appropriate, which may include dismissal of the appeal. The notice of appeal shall conform substantially to the appropriate Official Form, shall contain the names of all parties to the judgment, order, or decree appealed from and the names, addresses and telephone numbers of their respective attorneys, and be accompanied by the prescribed fee. Each appellant shall file a sufficient number of copies of the notice of appeal to enable the clerk to comply promptly with Rule 8004.

(b) Appeal by Leave; How Taken. An appeal from an interlocutory judgment, order or decree of a bankruptcy judge as permitted by 28 U.S.C. § 158(a) shall be taken by filing a notice of appeal, as prescribed in subdivision (a) of this rule, accompanied by a motion for leave to appeal prepared in accordance with Rule 8003 and with proof of service in accordance with Rule 8008.

(c) Voluntary Dismissal.

(1) *Before Docketing.* If an appeal has not been docketed, the appeal may be dismissed by the bankruptcy judge on the filing of a stipulation for dismissal signed by all the parties, or on motion and notice by the appellant.

(2) *After Docketing.* If an appeal has been docketed and the parties to the appeal sign and file with the clerk of the district court or the clerk of the bankruptcy appellate panel an agreement that the appeal be dismissed and pay any court costs or fees that may be due, the clerk of the district court or the clerk of the bankruptcy appellate panel shall

enter an order dismissing the appeal. An appeal may also be dismissed on motion of the appellant on terms and conditions fixed by the district court or bankruptcy appellate panel.

(d) **[Abrogated]**

(e) **Consent to Appeal to Bankruptcy Appellate Panel.** Unless otherwise provided by a rule promulgated pursuant to Rule 8018, consent to have an appeal heard by a bankruptcy appellate panel may be given in a separate statement of consent executed by a party or contained in the notice of appeal or cross appeal. The statement of consent shall be filed before the transmittal of the record pursuant to Rule 8007(b) or within 30 days of the filing of the notice of appeal, whichever is later.

Rule 8002

TIME FOR FILING NOTICE OF APPEAL

(a) **Ten-day Period.** The notice of appeal shall be filed with the clerk within 10 days of the date of the entry of the judgment, order, or decree appealed from. If a timely notice of appeal is filed by a party, any other party may file a notice of appeal within 10 days of the date on which the first notice of appeal was filed, or within the time otherwise prescribed by this rule, whichever period last expires. A notice of appeal filed after the announcement of a decision or order but before entry of the judgment, order, or decree shall be treated as filed after such entry and on the day thereof. If a notice of appeal is mistakenly filed with the district court or the bankruptcy appellate panel, the clerk of the district court or the clerk of the bankruptcy appellate panel shall note thereon the date on which it was received and transmit it to the clerk and it shall be deemed filed with the clerk on the date so noted.

(b) **Effect of Motion on Time for Appeal.** If any party makes a timely motion of a type specified immediately below, the time for appeal for all parties runs from the entry of the order disposing of the last such motion outstanding. This provision applies to a timely motion:

(1) to amend or make additional findings of fact under Rule 7052, whether or not granting the motion would alter the judgment;

(2) to alter or amend the judgment under Rule 9023;

(3) for a new trial under Rule 9023; or

(4) for relief under Rule 9024 if the motion is filed no later than 10 days after the entry of judgment. A notice of appeal filed after announcement or entry of the judgment, order, or decree but before disposition of any of the above motions is ineffective to appeal from the judgment, order, or decree, or part thereof, specified in the notice of appeal, until the entry of the order disposing of the last such motion outstanding. Appellate review of an order disposing of any of the above motions requires the party, in compliance with Rule 8001,

to amend a previously filed notice of appeal. A party intending to challenge an alteration or amendment of the judgment, order, or decree shall file a notice, or an amended notice, of appeal within the time prescribed by this Rule 8002 measured from the entry of the order disposing of the last such motion outstanding. No additional fees will be required for filing an amended notice.

(c) **Extension of Time for Appeal.** The bankruptcy judge may extend the time for filing the notice of appeal by any party for a period not to exceed 20 days from the expiration of the time otherwise prescribed by this rule. A request to extend the time for filing a notice of appeal must be made before the time for filing a notice of appeal has expired, except that a request made no more than 20 days after the expiration of the time for filing a notice of appeal may be granted upon a showing of excusable neglect if the judgment or order appealed from does not authorize the sale of any property or the obtaining of credit or the incurring of debt under § 364 of the Code, or is not a judgment or order approving a disclosure statement, confirming a plan, dismissing a case, or converting the case to a case under another chapter of the Code.

Rule 8003

LEAVE TO APPEAL

(a) **Content of Motion; Answer.** A motion for leave to appeal under 28 U.S.C. § 158(a) shall contain; (1) a statement of the facts necessary to an understanding of the questions to be presented by the appeal; (2) a statement of those questions and of the relief sought; (3) a statement of the reasons why an appeal should be granted; and (4) a copy of the judgment, order, or decree complained of and of any opinion or memorandum relating thereto. Within 10 days after service of the motion, an adverse party may file with the clerk an answer in opposition.

(b) **Transmittal; Determination of Motion.** The clerk shall transmit the notice of appeal, the motion for leave to appeal and any answer thereto to the clerk of the district court or the clerk of the bankruptcy appellate panel as soon as all parties have filed answers or the time for filing an answer has expired. The motion and answer shall be submitted without oral argument unless otherwise ordered.

(c) **Appeal Improperly Taken Regarded as a Motion for Leave to Appeal.** If a required motion for leave to appeal is not filed, but a notice of appeal is timely filed, the district court or bankruptcy appellate panel may grant leave to appeal or direct that a motion for leave to appeal be filed. The district court or the bankruptcy appellate panel may also deny leave to appeal but in so doing shall consider the notice of appeal as a motion for leave to appeal. Unless an order directing that a motion for leave to appeal be filed

provides otherwise, the motion shall be filed within 10 days of entry of the order.

Rule 8004

SERVICE OF THE NOTICE OF APPEAL

The clerk shall serve notice of the filing of a notice of appeal by mailing a copy thereof to counsel of record of each party other than the appellant or, if a party is not represented by counsel, to the party's last known address. Failure to serve notice shall not affect the validity of the appeal. The clerk shall note on each copy served the date of the filing of the notice of appeal and shall note in the docket the names of the parties to whom copies are mailed and the date of the mailing. The clerk shall forthwith transmit to the United States trustee a copy of the notice of appeal, but failure to transmit such notice shall not affect the validity of the appeal.

Rule 8005

STAY PENDING APPEAL

A motion for a stay of the judgment, order, or decree of a bankruptcy judge, for approval of a supersedeas bond, or for other relief pending appeal must ordinarily be presented to the bankruptcy judge in the first instance. Notwithstanding Rule 7062 but subject to the power of the district court and the bankruptcy appellate panel reserved hereinafter, the bankruptcy judge may suspend or order the continuation of other proceedings in the case under the Code or make any other appropriate order during the pendency of an appeal on such terms as will protect the rights of all parties in interest. A motion for such relief, or for modification or termination of relief granted by a bankruptcy judge, may be made to the district court or the bankruptcy appellate panel, but the motion shall show why the relief, modification, or termination was not obtained from the bankruptcy judge. The district court or the bankruptcy appellate panel may condition the relief it grants under this rule on the filing of a bond or other appropriate security with the bankruptcy court. When an appeal is taken by a trustee, a bond or other appropriate security may be required, but when an appeal is taken by the United States or an officer or agency thereof or by direction of any department of the Government of the United States a bond or other security shall not be required.

Rule 8006

RECORD AND ISSUES ON APPEAL

Within 10 days after filing the notice of appeal as provided by Rule 8001(a), entry of an order granting leave to appeal, or entry of an order disposing of the last timely motion outstanding of a type specified in Rule 8002(b), whichever is later, the appellant shall file with the clerk and serve on the appellate a designation of the items to be included in the record on appeal and a statement of the issues to be presented. Within 10 days after the service of the appellant's statement the appellee may file and serve on the appellant a designation of additional items to be included in the record on appeal and, if the appellee has filed a cross appeal, the appellee as cross appellant shall file and serve a statement of the issues to be presented on the cross appeal and a designation of additional items to be included in the record. A cross appellee may, within 10 days of service of the cross appellant's statement, file and serve on the cross appellant a designation of additional items to be included in the record. The record on appeal shall include the items so designated by the parties, the notice of appeal, the judgment, order, or decree appealed from, and any opinion, findings of fact, and conclusions of law of the court. Any party filing a designation of the items to be included in the record shall provide to the clerk a copy of the items designated or, if the party fails to provide the copy, the clerk shall prepare the copy at the party's expense. If the record designated by any party includes a transcript of any proceeding or a part thereof, the party shall, immediately after filing the designation, deliver to the reporter and file with the clerk a written request for the transcript and make satisfactory arrangements for payment of its cost. All parties shall take any other action necessary to enable the clerk to assemble and transmit the record.

Rule 8007

COMPLETION AND TRANSMISSION OF THE RECORD; DOCKETING OF THE APPEAL

(a) Duty of Reporter to Prepare and File Transcript. On receipt of a request for a transcript, the reporter shall acknowledge on the request the date it was received and the date on which the reporter expects to have the transcript completed and shall transmit the request, so endorsed, to the clerk or the clerk of the bankruptcy appellate panel. On completion of the transcript the reporter shall file it with the clerk and, if appropriate, notify the clerk of the bankruptcy appellate panel. If the transcript cannot be completed within 30 days of receipt of the request the reporter shall seek an extension of time from the clerk or the clerk of the bankruptcy appellate panel and the action of the clerk shall be entered in the docket and the parties notified. If the reporter does not file the transcript within the time allowed, the clerk or the clerk of the bankruptcy appellate panel shall notify the bankruptcy judge.

(b) Duty of Clerk to Transmit Copy of Record; Docketing of Appeal. When the record is complete for purposes of appeal, the clerk shall transmit a copy thereof forthwith to the clerk of the district court or the clerk of the bankruptcy appellate panel. On receipt of the transmission the clerk of the district court or the clerk of the

bankruptcy appellate panel shall enter the appeal in the docket and give notice promptly to all parties to the judgment, order, or decree appealed from of the date on which the appeal was docketed. If the bankruptcy appellate panel directs that additional copies of the record be furnished, the clerk of the bankruptcy appellate panel shall notify the appellant and, if the appellant fails to provide the copies, the clerk shall prepare the copies at the expense of the appellant.

(c) Record for Preliminary Hearing. If prior to the time the record is transmitted a party moves in the district court or before the bankruptcy appellate panel for dismissal, for a stay pending appeal, for additional security on the bond on appeal or on a supersedeas bond, or for any intermediate order, the clerk at the request of any party to the appeal shall transmit to the clerk of the district court or the clerk of the bankruptcy appellate panel a copy of the parts of the record as any party to the appeal shall designate.

Rule 8008

FILING AND SERVICE

(a) Filing. Papers required or permitted to be filed with the clerk of the district court or the clerk of the bankruptcy appellate panel may be filed by mail addressed to the clerk, but filing shall not be timely unless the papers are received by the clerk within the time fixed for filing, except that briefs shall be deemed filed on the day of mailing. An original and one copy of all papers shall be filed when an appeal is to the district court; an original and three copies shall be filed when an appeal is to a bankruptcy appellate panel. The district court or bankruptcy appellate panel may require that additional copies be furnished.

(b) Service of All Papers Required. Copies of all papers filed by any party and not required by these rules to be served by the clerk of the district court or the clerk of the bankruptcy appellate panel shall, at or before the time of filing, be served by the party or a person acting for the party on all other parties to the appeal. Service on a party represented by counsel shall be made on counsel.

(c) Manner of Service. Service may be personal or by mail. Personal service includes delivery of the copy to a clerk or other responsible person at the office of counsel. Service by mail is complete on mailing.

(d) Proof of Service. Papers presented for filing shall contain an acknowledgment of service by the person served or proof of service in the form of a statement of the date and manner of service and of the names of the persons served, certified by the person who made service. The clerk of the district court or the clerk of the bankruptcy appellate panel may permit papers to be filed without acknowledgment or proof of service but shall require the acknowledgment or proof of service to be filed promptly thereafter.

Rule 8009

BRIEFS AND APPENDIX; FILING AND SERVICE

(a) Briefs. Unless the district court or the bankruptcy appellate panel by local rule or by order excuses the filing of briefs or specifies different time limits;

(1) The appellant shall serve and file a brief within 15 days after entry of the appeal on the docket pursuant to Rule 8007.

(2) The appellee shall serve and file a brief within 15 days after service of the brief of appellant. If the appellee has filed a cross appeal, the brief of the appellee shall contain the issues and argument pertinent to the cross appeal, denominated as such, and the response to the brief of the appellant.

(3) The appellant may serve and file a reply brief within 10 days after service of the brief of the appellee, and if the appellee has cross-appealed, the appellee may file and serve a reply brief to the response of the appellant to the issues presented in the cross appeal within 10 days after service of the reply brief of the appellant. No further briefs may be filed except with leave of the district court or the bankruptcy appellate panel.

(b) Appendix to Brief. If the appeal is to a bankruptcy appellate panel, the appellant shall serve and file with the appellant's brief excerpts of the record as an appendix, which shall include the following:

(1) The complaint and answer or other equivalent pleadings;

(2) Any pretrial order;

(3) The judgment, order, or decree from which the appeal is taken;

(4) Any other orders relevant to the appeal;

(5) The opinion, findings of fact, or conclusions of law filed or delivered orally by the court and citations of the opinion if published;

(6) Any motion and response on which the court rendered decision;

(7) The notice of appeal;

(8) The relevant entries in the bankruptcy docket; and

(9) The transcript or portion thereof, if so required by a rule of the bankruptcy appellate panel.

An appellee may also serve and file an appendix which contains material required to be included by the appellant but omitted by appellant.

Rule 8010

FORM OF BRIEFS; LENGTH

(a) Form of Briefs. Unless the district court or the bankruptcy appellate panel by local rule otherwise provides, the form of brief shall be as follows:

(1) *Brief of the Appellant.* The brief of the appellant

shall contain under appropriate headings and in the order here indicated:

(A) A table of contents, with page references, and a table of cases alphabetically arranged, statutes and other authorities cited, with references to the pages of the brief where they are cited.

(B) A statement of the basis of appellate jurisdiction.

(C) A statement of the issues presented and the applicable standard of appellate review.

(D) A statement of the case. The statement shall first indicate briefly the nature of the case, the course of the proceedings, and the disposition in the court below. There shall follow a statement of the facts relevant to the issues presented for review, with appropriate references to the record.

(E) An argument. The argument may be preceded by a summary. The argument shall contain the contentions of the appellant with respect to the issues presented, and the reasons therefor, with citations to the authorities, statutes and parts of the record relied on.

(F) A short conclusion stating the precise relief sought.

(2) *Brief of the Appellee.* The brief of the appellee shall conform to the requirements of paragraph (1) (A)–(E) of this subdivision, except that a statement of the basis of appellate jurisdiction, of the issues, or of the case need not be made unless the appellee is dissatisfied with the statement of the appellant.

(b) Reproduction of Statutes, Rules, Regulations, or Similar Material. If determination of the issues presented requires reference to the Code or other statutes, rules, regulations, or similar material, relevant parts thereof shall be reproduced in the brief or in an addendum or they may be supplied to the court in pamphlet form.

(c) Length of Briefs. Unless the district court or the bankruptcy appellate panel by local rule or order otherwise provides, principal briefs shall not exceed 50 pages, and reply briefs shall not exceed 25 pages, exclusive of pages containing the table of contents, tables of citations and any addendum containing statutes, rules, regulations, or similar material.

Rule 8011

MOTIONS

(a) Content of Motions; Response; Reply. A request for an order or other relief shall be made by filing with the clerk of the district court or the clerk of the bankruptcy appellate panel a motion for such order or relief with proof of service on all other parties to the appeal. The motion shall contain or be accompanied by any matter required by a specific provision of these rules governing such a motion, shall state with particularity the grounds on which it is based, and shall set forth the order or relief sought. If a

motion is supported by briefs, affidavits or other papers, they shall be served and filed with the motion. Any party may file a response in opposition to a motion other than one for a procedural order within seven days after service of the motion, but the district court or the bankruptcy appellate panel may shorten or extend the time for responding to any motion.

(b) Determination of Motions for Procedural Orders. Notwithstanding subdivision (a) of this rule, motions for procedural orders, including any motion under Rule 9006, may be acted on at any time, without awaiting a response thereto and without hearing. Any party adversely affected by such action may move for reconsideration, vacation, or modification of the action.

(c) Determination of All Motions. All motions will be decided without oral argument unless the court orders otherwise. A motion for a stay, or for other emergency relief may be denied if not presented promptly.

(d) Emergency Motions. Whenever a movant requests expedited action on a motion on the ground that, to avoid irreparable harm, relief is needed in less time than would normally be required for the district court or bankruptcy appellate panel to receive and consider a response, the word "Emergency" shall precede the title of the motion. The motion shall be accompanied by an affidavit setting forth the nature of the emergency. The motion shall state whether all grounds advanced in support thereof were submitted to the bankruptcy judge and, if any grounds relied on were not submitted, why the motion should not be remanded to the bankruptcy judge for reconsideration. The motion shall include the office addresses and telephone numbers of moving and opposing counsel and shall be served pursuant to Rule 8008. Prior to filing the motion, the movant shall make every practicable effort to notify opposing counsel in time for counsel to respond to the motion. The affidavit accompanying the motion shall also state when and how opposing counsel was notified or if opposing counsel was not notified why it was not practicable to do so.

(e) Power of a Single Judge to Entertain Motions. A single judge of a bankruptcy appellate panel may grant or deny any request for relief which under these rules may properly be sought by motion, except that a single judge may not dismiss or otherwise decide an appeal or a motion for leave to appeal. The action of a single judge may be reviewed by the panel.

Rule 8012

ORAL ARGUMENT

Oral argument shall be allowed in all cases unless the district judge or the judges of the bankruptcy appellate panel unanimously determine after examination of the

briefs and record, or appendix to the brief, that oral argument is not needed. Any party shall have an opportunity to file a statement setting forth the reason why oral argument should be allowed.

Oral argument will not be allowed if (1) the appeal is frivolous; (2) the dispositive issue or set of issues has been recently authoritatively decided; or (3) the facts and legal arguments are adequately presented in the briefs and record and the decisional process would not be significantly aided by oral argument.

Rule 8013

DISPOSITION OF APPEAL; WEIGHT ACCORDED BANKRUPTCY JUDGE'S FINDINGS OF FACT

On an appeal the district court or bankruptcy appellate panel may affirm, modify, or reverse a bankruptcy judge's judgment, order, or decree or remand with instructions for further proceedings. Findings of fact, whether based on oral or documentary evidence, shall not be set aside unless clearly erroneous, and due regard shall be given to the opportunity of the bankruptcy court to judge the credibility of the witnesses.

Rule 8014

COSTS

Except as otherwise provided by law, agreed to by the parties, or ordered by the district court or the bankruptcy appellate panel, costs shall be taxed against the losing party on an appeal. If a judgment is affirmed or reversed in part, or is vacated, costs shall be allowed only as ordered by the court. Costs incurred in the production of copies of briefs, the appendices, and the record and in the preparation and transmission of the record, the cost of the reporter's transcript, if necessary for the determination of the appeal, the premiums paid for cost of supersedeas bonds or other bonds to preserve rights pending appeal and the fee for filing the notice of appeal shall be taxed by the clerk as costs of the appeal in favor of the party entitled to costs under this rule.

Rule 8015

MOTION FOR REHEARING

Unless the district court or the bankruptcy appellate panel by local rule or by court order otherwise provides, a motion for rehearing may be filed within 10 days after entry of the judgment of the district court or the bankruptcy appellate panel. If a timely motion for rehearing is filed, the time for appeal to the court of appeals for all parties shall run from the entry of the order denying rehearing or the entry of a subsequent judgment.

Rule 8016

DUTIES OF CLERK OF DISTRICT COURT AND BANKRUPTCY APPELLATE PANEL

(a) **Entry of Judgment.** The clerk of the district court or the clerk of the bankruptcy appellate panel shall prepare, sign and enter the judgment following receipt of the opinion of the court or the appellate panel or, if there is no opinion, following the instruction of the court or the appellate panel. The notation of a judgment in a docket constitutes entry of judgment.

(b) **Notice of Orders or Judgments; Return of Record.** Immediately on the entry of a judgment or order the clerk of the district court or the clerk of the bankruptcy appellate panel shall transmit a notice of the entry to each party to the appeal, to the United States trustee, and to the clerk, together with a copy of any opinion respecting the judgment or order, and shall make a note of the transmission in the docket. Original papers transmitted as the record on appeal shall be returned to the clerk on disposition of the appeal.

Rule 8017

STAY OF JUDGMENT OF DISTRICT COURT OR BANKRUPTCY APPELLATE PANEL

(a) **Automatic Stay of Judgment on Appeal.** Judgments of the district court or the bankruptcy appellate panel are stayed until the expiration of 10 days after entry, unless otherwise ordered by the district court or the bankruptcy appellate panel.

(b) **Stay Pending Appeal to the Court of Appeals.** On motion and notice to the parties to the appeal, the district court or the bankruptcy appellate panel may stay its judgment pending an appeal to the court of appeals. The stay shall not extend beyond 30 days after the entry of the judgment of the district court or the bankruptcy appellate panel unless the period is extended for cause shown. If before the expiration of a stay entered pursuant to this subdivision there is an appeal to the court of appeals by the party who obtained the stay, the stay shall continue until final disposition by the court of appeals. A bond or other security may be required as a condition to the grant or continuation of a stay of the judgment. A bond or other security may be required if a trustee obtains a stay but a bond or security shall not be required if a stay is obtained by the United States or an officer or agency thereof or at the direction of any department of the Government of the United States.

(c) **Power of Court of Appeals Not Limited.** This rule does not limit the power of a court of appeals or any judge thereof to stay proceedings during the pendency of an appeal or to suspend, modify, restore, or grant an injunction during the pendency of an appeal or to make any order appropriate to preserve the status quo or the effectiveness of the judgment subsequently to be entered.

Rule 8018

RULES BY CIRCUIT COUNCILS AND DISTRICT COURTS

Circuit councils which have authorized bankruptcy appellate panels pursuant to 28 U.S.C. § 158(b) and the district courts may by action of a majority of the judges of the council or district court make and amend rules governing practice and procedure for appeals from orders or judgments of bankruptcy judges to the respective bankruptcy appellate panel or district court, not inconsistent with the rules of this Part VIII. Rule 83 F.R.Civ.P. governs the procedure for making and amending rules to govern appeals. In all cases not provided for by rule, the district court or the bankruptcy appellate panel may regulate its practice in any manner not inconsistent with these rules.

Rule 8019

SUSPENSION OF RULES IN PART VIII

In the interest of expediting decision or for other cause, the district court or the bankruptcy appellate panel may suspend the requirements or provisions of the rules in Part VIII, except Rules 8001, 8002, and 8013, and may order proceedings in accordance with the direction.

PART IX
GENERAL PROVISIONS

Rule 9001

GENERAL DEFINITIONS

The definitions of words and phrases in § 101, § 902 and § 1101 and the rules of construction in § 102 of the Code govern their use in these rules. In addition, the following words and phrases used in these rules have the meanings indicated:

(1) "Bankruptcy clerk" means a clerk appointed pursuant to 28 U.S.C. § 156(b).

(2) "Bankruptcy Code" or "Code" means title 11 of the United States Code.

(3) "Clerk" means bankruptcy clerk, if one has been appointed, otherwise clerk of the district court.

(4) "Court" or "judge" means the judicial officer before whom a case or proceeding is pending.

(5) "Debtor." When any act is required by these rules to be performed by a debtor or when it is necessary to compel attendance of a debtor for examination and the debtor is not a natural person: (A) if the debtor is a corporation, "debtor" includes, if designated by the court, any or all of its officers, members of its board of directors or trustees or of a similar controlling body, a controlling stockholder or member, or any other person in control; (B) if the debtor is a partnership, "debtor" includes any or all of its general partners or, if designated by the court, any other person in control.

(6) "Firm" includes a partnership or professional corporation of attorneys or accountants.

(7) "Judgment" means any appealable order.

(8) "Mail" means first class, postage prepaid.

(9) "Regular associate" means any attorney regularly employed by, associated with, or counsel to an individual or firm.

(10) "Trustee" includes a debtor in possession in a chapter 11 case.

(11) "United States trustee" includes an assistant United States trustee and any designee of the United States trustee.

Rule 9002

MEANINGS OF WORDS IN THE FEDERAL RULES OF CIVIL PROCEDURE WHEN APPLICABLE TO CASES UNDER THE CODE

The following words and phrases used in the Federal Rules of Civil Procedure made applicable to cases under the Code by these rules have the meanings indicated unless they are inconsistent with the context:

(1) "Action" or "civil action" means an adversary proceeding or, when appropriate, a contested petition, or proceedings to vacate an order for relief or to determine any other contested matter.

(2) "Appeal" means an appeal as provided by 28 U.S.C. § 158.

(3) "Clerk" or "clerk of the district court" means the court officer responsible for the bankruptcy records in the district.

(4) "District court," "trial court," "court," "district judge," or "judge" means bankruptcy judge if the case or proceeding is pending before a bankruptcy judge.

(5) "Judgment" includes any order appealable to an appellate court.

Rule 9003

PROHIBITION OF EX PARTE CONTACTS

(a) General Prohibition. Except as otherwise permitted by applicable law, any examiner, any party in interest, and any attorney, accountant, or employee of a party in interest shall refrain from ex parte meetings and communications with the court concerning matters affecting a particular case or proceeding.

(b) United States Trustee. Except as otherwise permitted by applicable law, the United States trustee and assistants to and employees or agents of the United States trustee shall refrain from ex parte meetings and communications with the court concerning matters affecting a particular case or proceeding. This rule does not preclude communications with the court to discuss general problems of administration and improvement of bankruptcy administration, including the operation of the United States trustee system.

Rule 9004

GENERAL REQUIREMENTS OF FORM

(a) Legibility; Abbreviations. All petitions, pleadings, schedules and other papers shall be clearly legible. Abbreviations in common use in the English language may be used.

(b) Caption. Each paper filed shall contain a caption setting forth the name of the court, the title of the case, the bankruptcy docket number, and a brief designation of the character of the paper.

Rule 9005

HARMLESS ERROR

Rule 61 F.R.Civ.P. applies in cases under the Code. When appropriate, the court may order the correction of any error or defect or the cure of any omission which does not affect substantial rights.

Rule 9006

TIME

(a) Computation. In computing any period of time prescribed or allowed by these rules or by the Federal Rules of Civil Procedure made applicable by these rules, by the local rules, by order of court, or by any applicable statute, the day of the act, event, or default from which the designated period of time begins to run shall not be included. The last day of the period so computed shall be included, unless it is a Saturday, a Sunday, or a legal holiday, or, when the act to be done is the filing of a paper in court, a day on which weather or other conditions have made the clerk's office inaccessible, in which event the period runs until the end of the next day which is not one of the aforementioned days. When the period of time prescribed or allowed is less than 8 days, intermediate Saturdays, Sundays, and legal holidays shall be excluded in the computation. As used in this rule and in Rule 5001(c), "legal holiday" includes New Year's Day, Birthday of Martin Luther King, Jr., Washington's Birthday, Memorial Day, Independence Day, Labor Day, Columbus Day, Veterans Day, Thanksgiving Day, Christmas Day, and any other day appointed as a holiday by the President or the Congress of the United States, or by the state in which the court is held.

(b) Enlargement.

(1) *In General.* Except as provided in paragraphs (2) and (3) of this subdivision, when an act is required or allowed to be done at or within a specified period by these rules or by a notice given thereunder or by order of court, the court for cause shown may at any time in its discretion (1) with or without motion or notice order the period enlarged if the request therefor is made before the expiration of the period originally prescribed or as extended by a previous order or (2) on motion made after the expiration of

the specified period permit the act to be done where the failure to act was the result of excusable neglect.

(2) *Enlargement Not Permitted.* The court may not enlarge the time for taking action under Rules 1007(d), 1017(b)(3), 2003(a) and (d), 7052, 9023, and 9024.

(3) *Enlargement Limited.* The court may enlarge the time for taking action under Rules 1006(b)(2), 1017(e), 3002(c), 4003(b), 4004(a), 4007(c), 8002, and 9033, only to the extent and under the conditions stated in those rules.

(c) Reduction.

(1) *In General.* Except as provided in paragraph (2) of this subdivision, when an act is required or allowed to be done at or within a specified time by these rules or by a notice given thereunder or by order of court, the court for cause shown may in its discretion with or without motion or notice order the period reduced.

(2) *Reduction Not Permitted.* The court may not reduce the time for taking action under Rules 2002(a)(4) and (a)(8), 2003(a), 3002(c), 3014, 3015, 4001(b)(2), (c)(2), 4003(a), 4004(a), 4007(c), 8002, and 9033(b).

(d) For Motions—Affidavits. A written motion, other than one which may be heard ex parte, and notice of any hearing shall be served not later than five days before the time specified for such hearing, unless a different period is fixed by these rules or by order of the court. Such an order may for cause shown be made on ex parte application. When a motion is supported by affidavit, the affidavit shall be served with the motion; and, except as otherwise provided in Rule 9023, opposing affidavits may be served not later than one day before the hearing, unless the court permits them to be served at some other time.

(e) Time of Service. Service of process and service of any paper other than process or of notice by mail is complete on mailing.

(f) Additional Time After Service by Mail. When there is a right or requirement to do some act or undertake some proceedings within a prescribed period after service of a notice or other paper and the notice or paper other than process is served by mail, three days shall be added to the prescribed period.

(g) Grain Storage Facility Cases. This rule shall not limit the court's authority under § 557 of the Code to enter orders governing procedures in cases in which the debtor is an owner or operator of a grain storage facility.

Rule 9007

GENERAL AUTHORITY TO REGULATE NOTICES

When notice is to be given under these rules, the court shall designate, if not otherwise specified herein, the time within which, the entities to whom, and the form and manner in which the notice shall be given. When feasible, the court may order any notices under these rules to be combined.

Rule 9008

SERVICE OR NOTICE BY PUBLICATION

Whenever these rules require or authorize service or notice by publication, the court shall, to the extent not otherwise specified in these rules, determine the form and manner thereof, including the newspaper or other medium to be used and the number of publications.

Rule 9009

FORMS

The Official Forms prescribed by the Judicial Conference of the United States shall be observed and used with alterations as may be appropriate. Forms may be combined and their contents rearranged to permit economies in their use. The Director of the Administrative Office of the United States Courts may issue additional forms for use under the Code. The forms shall be construed to be consistent with these rules and the Code.

Rule 9010

REPRESENTATION AND APPEARANCES; POWERS OF ATTORNEY

(a) Authority to Act Personally or by Attorney. A debtor, creditor, equity security holder, indenture trustee, committee or other party may (1) appear in a case under the Code and act either in the entity's own behalf or by an attorney authorized to practice in the court, and (2) perform any act not constituting the practice of law, by an authorized agent, attorney in fact, or proxy.

(b) Notice of Appearance. An attorney appearing for a party in a case under the Code shall file a notice of appearance with the attorney's name, office address and telephone number, unless the attorney's appearance is otherwise noted in the record.

(c) Power of Attorney. The authority of any agent, attorney in fact, or proxy to represent a creditor for any purpose other than the execution and filing of a proof of claim or the acceptance or rejection of a plan shall be evidenced by a power of attorney conforming substantially to the appropriate Official Form. The execution of any such power of attorney shall be acknowledged before one of the officers enumerated in 28 U.S.C. § 459, § 953, Rule 9012, or a person authorized to administer oaths under the laws of the state where the oath is administered.

Rule 9011

SIGNING AND VERIFICATION OF PAPERS

(a) Signature. Every petition, pleading, motion and other paper served or filed in a case under the Code on behalf of a party represented by an attorney, except a list, schedule, or statement, or amendments thereto, shall be

signed by at least one attorney of record in the attorney's individual name, whose office address and telephone number shall be stated. A party who is not represented by an attorney shall sign all papers and state the party's address and telephone number. The signature of an attorney or a party constitutes a certificate that the attorney or party has read the document; that to the best of the attorney's or party's knowledge, information, and belief formed after reasonable inquiry it is well grounded in fact and is warranted by existing law or a good faith argument for the extension, modification, or reversal of existing law; and that it is not interposed for any improper purpose, such as to harass or to cause unnecessary delay or needless increase in the cost of litigation or administration of the case. If a document is not signed, it shall be stricken unless it is signed promptly after the omission is called to the attention of the person whose signature is required. If a document is signed in violation of this rule, the court on motion or on its own initiative, shall impose on the person who signed it, the represented party, or both, an appropriate sanction, which may include an order to pay to the other party or parties the amount of the reasonable expenses incurred because of the filing of the document, including a reasonable attorney's fee.

(b) Verification. Except as otherwise specifically provided by these rules, papers filed in a case under the Code need not be verified. Whenever verification is required by these rules, an unsworn declaration as provided in 28 U.S.C. § 1746 satisfies the requirement of verification.

(b) Copies of Signed or Verified Papers. When these rules require copies of a signed or verified paper, it shall suffice if the original is signed or verified and the copies are conformed to the original.

Rule 9012

OATHS AND AFFIRMATIONS

(a) Persons Authorized to Administer Oaths. The following persons may administer oaths and affirmations and take acknowledgments: a bankruptcy judge, clerk, deputy clerk, United States trustee, officer authorized to administer oaths in proceedings before the courts of the United States or under the laws of the state where the oath is to be taken, or a diplomatic or consular officer of the United States in any foreign country.

(b) Affirmation in Lieu of Oath. When in a case under the Code an oath is required to be taken, a solemn affirmation may be accepted in lieu thereof.

Rule 9013

MOTIONS: FORM AND SERVICE

A request for an order, except when an application is authorized by these rules, shall be by written motion, unless made during a hearing. The motion shall state with particularity the grounds therefor, and shall set forth the relief

or order sought. Every written motion other than one which may be considered ex parte shall be served by the moving party on the trustee or debtor in possession and on those entities specified by these rules or, if service is not required or the entities to be served are not specified by these rules, the moving party shall serve the entities the court directs.

Rule 9014

CONTESTED MATTERS

In a contested matter in a case under the Code not otherwise governed by these rules, relief shall be requested by motion, and reasonable notice and opportunity for hearing shall be afforded the party against whom relief is sought. No response is required under this rule unless the court orders an answer to a motion. The motion shall be served in the manner provided for service of a summons and complaint by Rule 7004, and, unless the court otherwise directs, the following rules shall apply: 7021, 7025, 7026, 7028–7037, 7041, 7042, 7052, 7054–7056, 7062, 7064, 7069, and 7071. The court may at any stage in a particular matter direct that one or more of the other rules in Part VII shall apply. An entity that desires to perpetuate testimony may proceed in the same manner as provided in Rule 7027 for the taking of a deposition before an adversary proceeding. The clerk shall give notice to the parties of the entry of any order directing that additional rules of Part VII are applicable or that certain of the rules in Part VII are not applicable. The notice shall be given within such time as is necessary to afford the parties a reasonable opportunity to comply with the procedures made applicable by the order.

Rule 9015

[ABROGATED]

Rule 9016

SUBPOENA

Rule 45 F.R.Civ.P. applies in cases under the Code.

Rule 9017

EVIDENCE

The Federal Rules of Evidence and rules 43, 44 and 44.1 F.R.Civ.P. apply in cases under the Code.

Rule 9018

SECRET, CONFIDENTIAL, SCANDALOUS, OR DEFAMATORY MATTER

On motion or on its own initiative, with or without notice, the court may make any order which justice re-

quires (1) to protect the estate or any entity in respect of a trade secret or other confidential research, development, or commercial information, (2) to protect any entity against scandalous or defamatory matter contained in any paper filed in a case under the Code, or (3) to protect governmental matters that are made confidential by statute or regulation. If an order is entered under this rule without notice, any entity affected thereby may move to vacate or modify the order, and after a hearing on notice the court shall determine the motion.

Rule 9019

COMPROMISE AND ARBITRATION

(a) **Compromise.** On motion by the trustee and after notice and a hearing, the court may approve a compromise or settlement. Notice shall be given to creditors, the United States trustee, the debtor, and indenture trustees as provided in Rule 2002 and to any other entity as the court may direct.

(b) **Authority to Compromise or Settle Controversies Within Classes.** After a hearing on such notice as the court may direct, the court may fix a class or classes or controversies and authorize the trustee to compromise or settle controversies within such class or classes without further hearing or notice.

(c) **Arbitration.** On stipulation of the parties to any controversy affecting the estate the court may authorize the matter to be submitted to final and binding arbitration.

Rule 9020

CONTEMPT PROCEEDINGS

(a) **Contempt Committed in Presence of Bankruptcy Judge.** Contempt committed in the presence of a bankruptcy judge may be determined summarily by a bankruptcy judge. The order of contempt shall recite the facts and shall be signed by the bankruptcy judge and entered of record.

(b) **Other Contempt.** Contempt committed in a case or proceeding pending before a bankruptcy judge, except when determined as provided in subdivision (a) of this rule, may be determined by the bankruptcy judge only after a hearing on notice. The notice shall be in writing, shall state the essential facts constituting the contempt charged and describe the contempt as criminal or civil and shall state the time and place of hearing, allowing a reasonable time for the preparation of the defense. The notice may be given on the court's own initiative or on application of the United States attorney or by an attorney appointed by the court for that purpose. If the contempt charged involves disrespect to or criticism of a bankruptcy judge, that judge is disqualified from presiding at the hearing except with the consent of the person charged.

(c) **Service and Effective Date of Order; Review.** The clerk shall serve forthwith a copy of the order of contempt on the entity named therein. The order shall be effective 10 days after service of the order and shall have the same force and effect as an order or contempt entered by the district court unless, within the 10 day period, the entity named therein serves and files objections prepared in the manner provided in Rule 9033(b). If timely objections are filed, the order shall be reviewed as provided in Rule 9033.

(d) **Right to Jury Trial.** Nothing in this rule shall be construed to impair the right to jury trial whenever it otherwise exists.

Rule 9021

ENTRY OF JUDGMENT

Except as otherwise provided herein, Rule 58 F.R.Civ.P. applies in cases under the Code. Every judgment entered in an adversary proceeding or contested matter shall be set forth on a separate document. A judgment is effective when entered as provided in Rule 5003. The reference in Rule 58 F.R.Civ.P. to Rule 79(a) F.R.Civ.P. shall be read as a reference to Rule 5003 of these rules.

Rule 9022

NOTICE OF JUDGMENT OR ORDER

(a) **Judgment or Order of Bankruptcy Judge.** Immediately on the entry of a judgment or order the clerk shall serve a notice of the entry by mail in the manner provided by Rule 7005 on the contesting parties and on other entities as the court directs. Unless the case is a chapter 9 municipality case, the clerk shall forthwith transmit to the United States trustee a copy of the judgment or order. Service of the notice shall be noted in the docket. Lack of notice of the entry does not affect the time to appeal or relieve or authorize the court to relieve a party for failure to appeal within the time allowed, except as permitted in Rule 8002.

(b) **Judgment or Order of District Judge.** Notice of a judgment or order entered by a district judge is governed by Rule 77(d) F.R.Civ.P. Unless the case is a chapter 9 municipality case, the clerk shall forthwith transmit to the United States trustee a copy of a judgment or order entered by a district judge.

Rule 9023

NEW TRIALS; AMENDMENT OF JUDGMENTS

Rule 59 F.R.Civ.P. applies in cases under the Code, except as provided in Rule 3008.

Rule 9024

RELIEF FROM JUDGMENT OR ORDER

Rule 60 F.R.Civ.P. applies in cases under the Code except that (1) a motion to reopen a case under the Code or for the reconsideration of an order allowing or disallowing a claim against the estate entered without a contest is not

subject to the one year limitation prescribed in Rule 60(b), (2) a complaint to revoke a discharge in a chapter 7 liquidation case may be filed only within the time allowed by § 727(e) of the Code, and (3) a complaint to revoke an order confirming a plan may be filed only within the time allowed by § 1144, § 1230, or § 1330.

Rule 9025

SECURITY: PROCEEDINGS AGAINST SURETIES

Whenever the Code or these rules require or permit the giving of security by a party, and security is given in the form of a bond or stipulation or other undertaking with one or more sureties, each surety submits to the jurisdiction of the court, and liability may be determined in an adversary proceeding governed by the rules in Part VII.

Rule 9026

EXCEPTIONS UNNECESSARY

Rule 46 F.R.Civ.P. applies in cases under the Code.

Rule 9027

REMOVAL

(a) Notice of Removal.

(1) *Where Filed; Form and Content.* A notice of removal shall be filed with the clerk for the district and division within which is located the state or federal court where the civil action is pending. The notice shall be signed pursuant to Rule 9011 and contain a short and plain statement of the facts which entitle the party filing the notice to remove, contain a statement that upon removal of the claim or cause of action the proceeding is core or non-core and, if non-core, that the party filing the notice does or does not consent to entry of final orders or judgment by the bankruptcy judge, and be accompanied by a copy of all process and pleadings.

(2) *Time for Filing; Civil Action Initiated Before Commencement of the Case Under the Code.* If the claim or cause of action in a civil action is pending when a case under the Code is commenced, a notice of removal may be filed only within the longest of (A) 90 days after the order for relief in the case under the Code, (B) 30 days after entry of an order terminating a stay, if the claim or cause of action in a civil action has been stayed under § 362 of the Code, or (C) 30 days after a trustee qualifies in a chapter 11 reorganization case but not later than 180 days after the order for relief.

(3) *Time for Filing; Civil Action Initiated After Commencement of the Case Under the Code.* If a case under the Code is pending when a claim or cause of action is asserted in another court, a notice of removal may be filed with the clerk only within the shorter of (A) 30 days after receipt, through service or otherwise, of a copy of the initial plead-

ing setting forth the claim or cause of action sought to be removed or (B) 30 days after receipt of the summons if the initial pleading has been filed with the court but not served with the summons.

(b) Notice. Promptly after filing the notice of removal, the party filing the notice shall serve a copy of it on all parties to the removed claim or cause of action.

(c) Filing in Non-bankruptcy Court. Promptly after filing the notice of removal, the party filing the notice shall file a copy of it with the clerk of the court from which the claim or cause of action is removed. Removal of the claim or cause of action is effected on such filing of a copy of the notice of removal. The parties shall proceed no further in that court unless and until the claim or cause of action is remanded.

(d) Remand. A motion for remand of the removed claim or cause of action shall be governed by Rule 9014 and served on the parties to the removed claim or cause of action.

(e) Procedure After Removal.

(1) After removal of a claim or cause of action to a district court the district court or, if the case under the Code has been referred to a bankruptcy judge of the district, the bankruptcy judge, may issue all necessary orders and process to bring before it all proper parties whether served by process issued by the court from which the claim or cause of action was removed or otherwise.

(2) The district court or, if the case under the Code has been referred to a bankruptcy judge of the district, the bankruptcy judge, may require the party filing the notice of removal to file with the clerk copies of all records and proceedings relating to the claim or cause of action in the court from which the claim or cause of action was removed.

(3) Any party who has filed a pleading in connection with the removed claim or cause of action, other than the party filing the notice of removal, shall file a statement admitting or denying any allegation in the notice of removal that upon removal of the claim or cause of action the proceeding is core or non-core. If the statement alleges that the proceeding is non-core, it shall state that the party does or does not consent to entry of final orders or judgment by the bankruptcy judge. A statement required by this paragraph shall be signed pursuant to Rule 9011 and shall be filed not later than 10 days after the filing of the notice of removal. Any party who files a statement pursuant to this paragraph shall mail a copy to every other party to the removed claim or cause of action.

(f) Process After Removal. If one or more of the defendants has not been served with process, the service has not been perfected prior to removal, or the process served proves to be defective, such process or service may be completed or new process issued pursuant to Part VII of these rules. This subdivision shall not deprive any defendant on whom process is served after removal of the defendant's right to move to remand the case.

(g) Applicability of Part VII. The rules of Part VII apply to a claim or cause of action removed to a district court from a federal or state court and govern procedure after removal. Repleading is not necessary unless the court so orders. In a removed action in which the defendant has not answered, the defendant shall answer or present the other defenses or objections available under the rules of Part VII within 20 days following the receipt through service or otherwise of a copy of the initial pleading setting forth the claim for relief on which the action or proceeding is based, or within 20 days following the service of summons on such initial pleading, or within five days following the filing of the notice of removal, whichever period is longest.

(h) Record Supplied. When a party is entitled to copies of the records and proceedings in any civil action or proceeding in a federal or a state court, to be used in the removed civil action or proceeding, and the clerk of the federal or state court, on demand accompanied by payment or tender of the lawful fees, fails to deliver certified copies, the court may, on affidavit reciting the facts, direct such record to be supplied by affidavit or otherwise. Thereupon the proceedings, trial and judgment may be had in the court, and all process awarded, as if certified copies had been filed.

(i) Attachment of Sequestration; Securities. When a claim or cause of action is removed to a district court, any attachment or sequestration of property in the court from which the claim or cause of action was removed shall hold the property to answer the final judgment or decree in the same manner as the property would have been held to answer final judgment or decree had it been rendered by the court from which the claim or cause of action was removed. All bonds, undertakings, or security given by either party to the claim or cause of action prior to its removal shall remain valid and effectual notwithstanding such removal. All injunctions issued, orders entered and other proceedings had prior to removal shall remain in full force and effect until dissolved or modified by the court.

Rule 9028

DISABILITY OF A JUDGE

Rule 63 F.R.Civ.P. applies in cases under the Code.

Rule 9029

LOCAL BANKRUPTCY RULES

Each district court by action of a majority of the judges thereof may make and amend rules governing practice and procedure in all cases and proceedings within the district court's bankruptcy jurisdiction which are not inconsistent with these rules and which do not prohibit or limit the use of the Official Forms. Rule 83 F.R.Civ.P. governs the procedure for making local rules. A district court may autho-

rize the bankruptcy judges of the district, subject to any limitation or condition it may prescribe and the requirements of 83 F.R.Civ.P., to make rules of practice and procedure which are not inconsistent with these rules and which do not prohibit or limit the use of the Official Forms. In all cases not provided for by rule, the court may regulate its practice in any manner not inconsistent with the Official Forms or with these rules or those of the district in which the court acts.

Rule 9030

JURISDICTION AND VENUE UNAFFECTED

These rules shall not be construed to extend or limit the jurisdiction of the courts or the venue of any matters therein.

Rule 9031

MASTERS NOT AUTHORIZED

Rule 53 F.R.Civ.P. does not apply in cases under the Code.

Rule 9032

EFFECT OF AMENDMENT OF FEDERAL RULES OF CIVIL PROCEDURE

The Federal Rules of Civil Procedure which are incorporated by reference and made applicable by these rules shall be the Federal Rules of Civil Procedure in effect on the effective date of these rules and as thereafter amended, unless otherwise provided by such amendment or by these rules.

Rule 9033

REVIEW OF PROPOSED FINDINGS OF FACT AND CONCLUSIONS OF LAW IN NON-CORE PROCEEDINGS

(a) Service. In non-core proceedings heard pursuant to 28 U.S.C. § 157(c)(1), the bankruptcy judge shall file proposed findings of fact and conclusions of law. The clerk shall serve forthwith copies on all parties by mail and note the date of mailing on the docket.

(b) Objections: Time for Filing. Within 10 days after being served with a copy of the proposed findings of fact and conclusions of law a party may serve and file with the clerk written objections which identify the specific proposed findings or conclusions objected to and state the grounds for such objection. A party may respond to another party's objections within 10 days after being served with a copy thereof. A party objecting to the bankruptcy judge's proposed findings or conclusions shall arrange promptly for the transcription of the record, or such portions of it as all

parties may agree upon or the bankruptcy judge deems sufficient, unless the district judge otherwise directs.

(c) Extension of Time. The bankruptcy judge may for cause extend the time for filing objections by any party for a period not to exceed 20 days from the expiration of the time otherwise prescribed by this rule. A request to extend the time for filing objections must be made before the time for filing objections has expired, except that a request made no more than 20 days after the expiration of the time for filing objections may be granted upon a showing of excusable neglect.

(d) Standard of Review. The district judge shall make a de novo review upon the record or, after additional evidence, or any portion of the bankruptcy judge's findings of fact or conclusions of law to which specific written objection has been made in accordance with this rule. The district judge may accept, reject, or modify the proposed findings of fact or conclusions of law, receive further evidence, or recommit the matter to the bankruptcy judge with instructions.

Adopted Mar. 30, 1987, eff. Aug. 1, 1987.

Rule 9034

TRANSMITTAL OF PLEADINGS, MOTION PAPERS, OBJECTIONS, AND OTHER PAPERS TO THE UNITED STATES TRUSTEE

Unless the United States trustee requests otherwise or the case is a chapter 9 municipality case, any entity that files a pleading, motion, objection, or similar paper relating to any of the following matters shall transmit a copy thereof to the United States trustee within the time required by these rules for service of the paper:

(a) a proposed use, sale, or lease of property of the estate other than in the ordinary course of business;

(b) the approval of a compromise or settlement of a controversy;

(c) the dismissal or conversion of a case to another chapter;

(d) the employment of professional persons;

(e) an application for compensation or reimbursement of expenses;

(f) a motion for, or approval of an agreement relating to, the use of cash collateral or authority to obtain credit;

(g) the appointment of a trustee or examiner in a chapter 11 reorganization case;

(h) the approval of a disclosure statement;

(i) the confirmation of a plan;

(j) an objection to, or waiver or revocation of, the debtor's discharge;

(k) any other matter in which the United States trustee requests copies of filed papers or the court orders copies transmitted to the United States trustee.

Rule 9035

APPLICABILITY OF RULES IN JUDICIAL DISTRICTS IN ALABAMA AND NORTH CAROLINA

In any case under the Code that is filed in or transferred to a district in the State of Alabama or the State of North Carolina and in which a United States trustee is not authorized to act, these rules apply to the extent that they are not inconsistent with the provisions of title 11 and title 28 of the United States Code effective in the case.

Rule 9036

NOTICE BY ELECTRONIC TRANSMISSION

Whenever the clerk or some other person as directed by the court is required to send notice by mail and the entity entitled to receive the notice requests in writing that, instead of notice by mail, all or part of the information required to be contained in the notice be sent by a specified type of electronic transmission, the court may direct the clerk or other person to send the information by such electronic transmission. Notice by electronic transmission is complete, and the sender shall have fully complied with the requirement to send notice, when the sender obtains electronic confirmation that the transmission has been received.

GLOSSARY

Abandonment The release by the bankruptcy trustee or debtor in possession of the estate's rights in property.

Abstention The refusal of a court to hear and rule with respect to a particular case or proceeding despite the fact that it has jurisdiction to do so.

Adequate Information Information in sufficient detail that would enable to hypothetical reasonable investor to make an informed decision whether to vote for or against a plan of reorganization.

Adequate Protection Property, lien, conduct, or other asset or act that is sufficient to ensure that a creditor with an interest in property to be used, sold or leased by the estate will not be disadvantaged.

Administrative Claim A claim incurred after the commencement of the bankruptcy case that is a reasonable and necessary expense of the estate.

Adversary Proceeding Litigation in the bankruptcy court that is commenced by the filing of a complaint.

Affiliate An entity that owns twenty percent or more of the debtor's stock, a corporation twenty percent or more of whose stock is owned by the debtor, a person whose business or property is operated by the debtor, or an entity that operates the debtor's business or property.

Affirmative Defenses Procedural or substantive claims that a defendant may use to defeat the claims made by the plaintiff in a complaint.

Answer The pleading filed by a defendant that admits or denies the allegations in a complaint and asserts any affirmative defenses.

Antideficiency Laws Legislation that prevents a se-

Assignee for the Benefit of Creditors The person who acts like a bankruptcy trustee in an assignment for the benefit of creditors.

Assignment for the Benefit of Creditor A nonbankruptcy proceeding that is similar to a Chapter 7 case, in which the debtor turns over all of its nonexempt property to a third party for liquidation and distribution of the proceeds to creditors.

Assignment of Rents An agreement between a lender and a borrower that provides that the rental proceeds from property will be paid to the lender.

Assumption The means for the estate to bind itself to an executory contract or unexpired lease of the debtor.

Attachment Making a security interest enforceable. Unless explicit agreement postpones the time of attachment, it occurs when: (a) secured party pursuant to agreement possesses collateral, or debtor has signed a security agreement describing collateral; (b) value has been given; (c) debtor has rights in the collateral.

Automatic Stay The injunction that becomes effective upon the filing of a bankruptcy petition (whether voluntarily or involuntarily) and that prevents virtually all actions by creditors to collect their claims, enforce their liens, or exercise control over the debtor's property.

Balance Sheet Insolvency When the amount of liabilities on an entities' balance sheet exceeds the value of the assets on the balance sheet.

Ballot The document submitted by holders of impaired claims or interests accepting or rejecting a Chapter 11 plan of reorganization.

Bankruptcy An organized system for creditor payment from a debtor's nonexempt assets.

Bankruptcy Act The bankruptcy law enacted by Congress in 1898 that was substantially amended in 1938 and repealed in 1978.

Bankruptcy Code The bankruptcy law enacted by Congress that became effective on October 1, 1978, as it has been subsequently amended, and that is found in Title 11 of the United States Code.

Bankruptcy Courts The branch of the federal judicial system that presides over bankruptcy cases and proceedings. Bankruptcy Courts are units of the district court.

Bankruptcy Rules The rules of practice and procedure governing bankruptcy cases and proceedings drafted by the Judicial Conference of the United States and adopted by the Supreme Court.

Bluebook The common name for A *Uniform System of Citation*, the standard most often used for proper citation format.

Book Value The value of an asset as carried in the owner's books and records. Typically, cost less accumulated depreciation.

Cash Collateral Property of the estate that is cash, negotiable instruments, deposit accounts, and other cash equivalents in which a creditor has an interest.

Chain of Title   A list of successive transfers of real property arranged consecutively, from the government or original source of title down to the present holder.

Cite Checking   The process of reviewing legal writing to ensure that all cases have not been reversed or modified, are correctly cited, and that all quotations are accurate.

Claim   A right to payment from the debtor, whether or not such right is liquidated contingent, disputed, or secured.

Claims Register   A list prepared by the clerk of the bankruptcy court of all proofs of claim filed in the bankruptcy case.

Collateral   Property subject to a security interest.

Commercial Transaction   A phrase used to designate dealings of persons engaged in business.

Consequential Damages   Damages that do not flow directly and immediately from the wrongful act of the party but only from the consequences or results of such act.

Contested Matter   An action in the bankruptcy court seeking relief that is commenced by the filing of a motion.

Contingent Claim   A debt for which liability is dependent on a future event that may or may not occur.

Conversion   The voluntary or involuntary transfer of a bankruptcy case from one chapter of the Bankruptcy Code to a different chapter.

Core Matters   Those matters directly tied to a bankruptcy case and arising under the Bankruptcy Code.

Core Proceeding   Those matters directly concerning the bankruptcy case and arising under the Bankruptcy Code.

Cram Down   The approval of a plan of reorganization over the objection or negative votes of creditors.

Creditors' Committee   A committee comprised of two or more of the debtor's creditors appointed in a Chapter 11 case by the United States trustee for the purpose of representing the creditors' interests in the case.

Cross Collateralization   The securing of prepetition claims with assets acquired postpetition or the securing of postpetition claims with prepetition assets.

Debtor in Possession   A debtor in a case under Chapter 13, a debtor in a case under Chapter 11 in which no trustee has been appointed, and a debtor in a case under Chapter 12 unless the standing trustee has been directed to take control of the debtor's farming operations.

Deed   A document conveying an interest in real property other than a leasehold estate.

Deed of Trust   A document used in many states that takes the place of a mortgage and by which legal title is placed in a trustee to secure repayment of a loan or performance of an obligation.

Discharge   The release given to an individual debtor of the difference between the amount of creditor's unsecured claims and the assets distributed to creditors in a bankruptcy case.

Disclosure Statement   The document containing adequate information that is distributed with a Chapter 11 plan of reorganization.

Disposable Income   A debtor's income that is not necessary for the payment of the reasonable living expenses of the debtor and his or her dependents, or if the debtor is engaged in business, the income that is not necessary for the payment of the expenses necessary for the continuation, preservation, and operation of the business.

Disputed Claim   A debt of which the debtor objects to the amount or allowability.

Domicile   The principal place of residence in which the debtor intends to remain.

Earn-out   A plan of reorganization that provides for distributions to creditors to be made from the debtor's future income.

Enabling Loans   A loan made for the purpose of paying the purchase price of property.

Entity   A person, estate, trust, governmental unit, and the United States trustee.

Equity Committee   A committee of equity security holders (e.g., stock holders, warrant holders, general or limited partnership interests) appointed in a Chapter 11 case by the United States trustee.

Equity Cushion   The excess of the value of property over the claims secured by that property.

Examiner   A court appointed investigator authorized to delve into the financial and business affairs of a debtor in possession in a Chapter 11 case.

Excise Tax   A tax on a transaction, event, or occurrence.

Exclusivity Period   In a Chapter 11 case, the period of time in which only the debtor may propose a plan of reorganization.

Executory Contract   An agreement between two parties in which sufficient performance remains on each side such that failure of one party to perform will excuse performance by the other.

Exempt Property   The property that a debtor is allowed to keep and not make subject to creditors' claims.

Exemptions   Those interests in property that a debtor is allowed to keep and not make subject to creditors' claims.

Ex parte A latin term used to describe an act done without notice to other parties.

Face sheet filings The commencement of a bankruptcy case by filing only the minimal amount of papers required, usually just the petition.

Family Farmer An individual receiving more than fifty percent of income, and incurring debts not exceeding $1,500,000 from farming. Or a corporation or partnership where the majority of stock is held by one family and more than eighty percent of the corporation's assets relate to farming, and debts, arising from farming, do not exceed $1,500,000.

Family Farmer with Regular Income A family farmer whose annual income is sufficiently stable and regular to allow it to make payments under a Chapter 12 plan.

Fee Simple Absolute An estate in property held by a person and his or her heirs and assigns forever and without limitation.

Final Report and Account The document filed by the trustee at the end of a Chapter 7 case that sets out the receipts, distributions, and allowed claims of the estate as well as any other relevant information.

Financing Statement The document typically filed with the secretary of state that contains the name of the debtor, the name of the secured creditor, and a description of the collateral and that is used to perfect a secured interest for most types of collateral.

Fixtures Goods that are so related to a particular parcel of real estate that an interest in them arises under real estate law.

Foreclosure The enforcement of a security interest, mortgage or deed of trust in which the secured creditor takes the collateral in partial or full satisfaction of the debt.

Fraudulent Conveyances The transfer of the debtor's property with an actual intent to defraud creditors or for less than reasonably equivalent value while the debtor was insolvent or became insolvent as a result.

Goods All things that are movable or are fixtures, but not money, documents, instruments, accounts, chattel paper, general intangibles or minerals or the like before extraction.

Hardship Discharge The discharge granted to a Chapter 12 or 13 debtor who did not complete all plan payments but whose failure to do so was due to circumstances for which the debtor should not justly be held accountable.

Headnotes Summaries of points of law made in a judicial opinion. They generally precede the text of the opinion.

In propria persona A latin term used to describe a person acting without an attorney. Usually shortened to "pro per."

Incidental Damages Damages incurred in connection with the principal damages.

Income Tax Any tax on or measured by gross receipts.

Indenture Trustee A trustee appointed under a mortgage, deed or trust or other document under which there is a debt against or interest in the debtor.

Insider For individual debtors, a relative, partnership in which the debtor is the general partner, or corporation in which the debtor is an officer, director or otherwise in control. For partnership debtors, a general partner or its relative or person in control. For corporate debtors, a director, officer, or person in control, or a relative of an insider.

Intangibles Assets that are owned by an going business such as goodwill, trade marks, copyrights, franchises and the like.

Interim Compensation Postpetition payments made to professionals employed at the expense of the estate prior to the end of the bankruptcy case.

Interim Fee Application The document filed with the court by which professionals seek interim compensation.

Involuntary Case A bankruptcy case commenced by one or more creditors against a debtor.

Ipso Facto Clauses A provision in a contract or lease that provides that the contract or lease is breached or terminated if one of the parties become insolvent or the subject of a bankruptcy case.

Joint Administration or Administrative Consolidation The merger of two or more bankruptcy cases for the limited purpose of making their administration more convenient.

Judicial Foreclosure An action to obtain a court order requiring the sheriff to hold an auction sale of collateral.

Judicial Lien A lien obtained by judgment, levy or other legal or equitable process or proceeding.

Jurisdiction The power of a court to preside over and decide a dispute between people or property.

Land Sale Contract An agreement whereby the seller of real property retains title to the property until the full purchase price is paid by the buyer.

Leasehold An estate in real property held under a lease; an estate for a fixed term.

Levy The physical or constructive seizure of property in order to enforce a judgment.

Life Estate An estate whose duration is limited to the life of the person or of some other person.

Liquidating or Pot Plan   A plan of reorganization that provides for the sale or other disposition of all of the assets of the estate or distributes the proceeds of a previous sale or other disposition in the plan.

Liquidation   A form of bankruptcy in which the debtor's nonexempt property is sold or otherwise disposed of and the proceeds are distributed to creditors.

Mortgage   An agreement that creates or provides for a security interest in real property.

Municipality   A political subdivision, public agency, or instrumentality of a state.

Nondischargeable Claims   Claims that will be enforceable against the debtor despite the discharge.

No Asset Case   A bankruptcy case in which there are no assets to sell by the trustee. As a result, creditors do not receive a distribution.

No Asset Report   A report filed by a Chapter 7 trustee upon determining that there are no assets to be administered by the trustee and no likelihood of a distribution to creditors.

Opting Out   An option granted to the states allowing them to require their residents to use the state statutory exemptions rather than those in the Bankruptcy Code.

Ordinary Course of Business   Transactions made by a business in its day to day operations.

Perfection   The steps necessary under the Uniform Commercial Code or other law to make a lien effective against a third party and a bankruptcy trustee.

Person   An individual, partnership or corporation, but not a governmental unit unless it is acting as a receiver or liquidating agent of a person.

Personal Property   Property that consists of temporary or moveable things.

Petition   The paper filed with the bankruptcy court that commences a bankruptcy case.

Petitioner   Another name for the debtor in a voluntary case.

Plan Exclusivity   The fact that for a period of time only the debtor may propose a plan of reorganization.

Plan of Reorganization   A document filed in a reorganization case that divides the claims of creditors into classes and provides for their payment or other treatment.

Plan Proponent   The entity that proposes a plan of reorganization.

Pocket Parts   The method of updating bound compilations of decisions, statutes or digests that consist of periodically issued paperback editions that are usually attached to the inside back cover of a bound volume.

Postpetition Transfers   A transfer made after the commencement of a bankruptcy case that may be avoidable.

Precedent   A case or decision considered as authority for an identical or similar case or question of law arising later.

Preferences   A transfer of the debtor's property to a creditor in satisfaction of an existing debt made during the ninety days (or one year if the transfer was made to an insider) before the bankruptcy case was commenced and which enable the creditor to receive more than other creditors.

Priming Lien   A new lien that is made senior in priority to existing liens.

Priority Claim   A type of claim that Congress has decided should receive special treatment. Priority claims must be paid in full before general unsecured creditors receive a distribution.

Proof of Claim   The form completed and filed by a creditor in order to protect its right to payment or performance in a bankruptcy case.

Property Tax   Tax imposed on the ownership or real or personal property based on the property's value, number, weight or size.

Purchase Money Security Interest   A security interest to the extent that it is taken or retained by the seller of the collateral to secure all or part of its price, or taken by a person who gives value in order to enable the debtor to acquire the collateral if such value is in fact so used.

Reaffirm   The act of agreeing to remain liable on a claim despite a discharge.

Receiver   A person usually appointed by a state court whose duties are similar to those of a bankruptcy trustee.

Reclamation   The right of a person to seek to obtain possession of its property in the hands of the estate.

Redemption   The payment to a secured party of the value of its collateral in exchange for the release of the security interest.

Regular Income   A source of income that is fairly stable whether earnings, pension or other retirement benefits, public assistance benefits, or dividends.

Rejection   The means for the estate to rid itself of any ongoing obligations under an executory contract or unexpired lease of the debtor.

Related Matters Disputes that would have existed between parties even if one of them was not in a bankruptcy case.

Related Proceeding Those matters concerning a bankruptcy case only because one of the parties to the dispute is a debtor in a bankruptcy case.

Remand The return of a removed proceeding to the court in which it was originally commenced.

Removal The transfer of an adversary proceeding from the court in which it was commenced to a different type of court.

Reorganization A form of bankruptcy in which the debtor's business is preserved and its creditors are paid from the business' earnings.

Revested Debtor A debtor after confirmation of a plan of reorganization if the plan provides that title to the estate's assets will be vested in the debtor upon confirmation.

Right of Redemption The right to free property from a foreclosure or other judicial sale or recover the title that passed in a foreclosure by paying what is due.

Rights Evidenced by a Writing Instruments, documents of title, and chattel paper.

Schedules The document filed by a debtor that discloses all of its property and debts and other pertinent information.

Secret Liens A lien, usually created by statute, the existence of which cannot be discovered through a search of the applicable public records.

Secured Party A lender, seller or other person in whose favor there is a security interest.

Secured Transactions A phrase used to describe dealings involving the granting or taking of a security interest.

Security Agreement An agreement that creates or provides for a security interest.

Security Interest A lien created by an agreement.

Setoff The application of a debt owed to a person against a debt owed from that same person.

Shepardizing Determining the subsequent history of a case by use of *Shepard's Citations*.

Stare Decisis The policy of courts to abide by or adhere to precedent.

Statement of Financial Affairs The document filed by a debtor that discloses all information not found in the schedules that a trustee would need to effectively administer the estate.

Statutory Liens A lien arising under a state or federal statute solely due to specified circumstances or conditions.

Substantial Abuse A Chapter 7 bankruptcy case of a debtor with primarily consumer debts that offends notions of the proper use of bankruptcy. Typically used to refer to a case in which the debtor could fund a Chapter 13 plan.

Substantially Contemporaneous Exchange for New Value A preference defense that destroys the creditor's liability if the antecedent debt was intentionally created at or about the same time as the otherwise preferential transfer was made.

Substantive Consolidation The merger of two or more entities, at least one of which is a debtor, into a single entity under a plan of reorganization or by motion.

Summons A document issued by the clerk of the court when a complaint is filed that informs the defendant when it must answer or otherwise respond to the complaint.

Surcharge The payment of administrative expenses from the proceeds of collateral because the expenses benefited the secured party.

Trustee A person appointed to administer the bankruptcy estate. The nature and extent of a trustee's duties differs among Chapters 7, 11, 12, and 13 of the Bankruptcy Code.

Turnover The act of delivering possession or control of property of the estate to the trustee.

Unexpired Lease A lease whose term has not been reached prior to its rejection or assumption.

Uniform Commercial Code The law enacted in every state that governs commercial transactions.

United States Code A compilation of the laws enacted by Congress and organized into fifty titles.

Unliquidated Claim A debt that has not been fixed as to amount.

Venue Where, either geographically or among different types of courts, a case or proceeding is or may be pending.

Wage Earner Reorganization Chapter 13 cases so designated under the misconception that only employed persons qualify for relief. The statute requires only a regular income that may come from a variety of sources.

☐ TABLE OF STATUTES

☐ TABLE OF RULES AND FORMS

□ INDEX